Congratulations

You have just purchased a book that was developed by hospitality industry experts.

Keep this book — you will use it throughout your career.

SANITATION MANAGEMENT

Educational Institute Books

MAINTENANCE AND ENGINEERING FOR LODGING AND
FOOD SERVICE FACILITIES
Frank D. Borsenik

CONVENTION MANAGEMENT & SERVICE
Frank W. Berkman/David C. Dorf/Leonard R. Oakes

HOSPITALITY FOR SALE
C. DeWitt Coffman

UNIFORM SYSTEM OF ACCOUNTS AND EXPENSE DICTIONARY
FOR SMALL HOTELS AND MOTELS
Revised Edition

RESORT DEVELOPMENT AND MANAGEMENT
Chuck Y. Gee

BASIC FINANCIAL ACCOUNTING FOR THE HOSPITALITY INDUSTRY
Clifford T. Fay, Jr./Raymond S. Schmidgall/Stanley B. Tarr

PLANNING AND CONTROL FOR FOOD AND BEVERAGE OPERATIONS
Jack D. Ninemeier

STRATEGIC MARKETING PLANNING IN THE HOSPITALITY INDUSTRY:
A BOOK OF READINGS
Edited by Robert L. Blomstrom

TRAINING FOR THE HOSPITALITY INDUSTRY
Lewis C. Forrest, Jr.

UNDERSTANDING HOTEL/MOTEL LAW
Jack P. Jefferies

SUPERVISION IN THE HOSPITALITY INDUSTRY
John P. Daschler/Jack D. Ninemeier

SANITATION MANAGEMENT: STRATEGIES FOR SUCCESS
Ronald F. Cichy

ENERGY MANAGEMENT
Robert E. Aulbach

PRINCIPLES OF FOOD AND BEVERAGE OPERATIONS
Jack D. Ninemeier

MANAGING FRONT OFFICE OPERATIONS
Charles E. Steadmon

MANAGING SERVICE IN FOOD AND BEVERAGE OPERATIONS
Anthony M. Rey/Ferdinand Wieland

THE LODGING AND FOOD SERVICE INDUSTRY
Gerald W. Lattin

SECURITY AND LOSS PREVENTION MANAGEMENT
Raymond C. Ellis, Jr. & the Security Committee of AH&MA

HOSPITALITY INDUSTRY MANAGERIAL ACCOUNTING
Raymond S. Schmidgall

STRATEGIC HOTEL/MOTEL MARKETING
Christopher W.L. Hart/David A. Troy

PURCHASING FOR HOSPITALITY OPERATIONS
William B. Virts

SANITATION MANAGEMENT

Strategies for Success

Ronald F. Cichy, Ph.D., CHA, CFBE

the EDUCATIONAL INSTITUTE
OF THE AMERICAN HOTEL & MOTEL ASSOCIATION

Disclaimer

The author, Ronald F. Cichy, is solely responsible for the contents of this publication. All views expressed herein are solely those of the author and do not necessarily reflect the views of the Educational Institute of the American Hotel & Motel Association (the Institute) or the American Hotel & Motel Association (AH&MA). Nothing contained in this publication shall constitute an endorsement by the Institute or AH&MA of any information, opinion, procedure, or product mentioned, and the Institute and AH&MA disclaim any liability with respect to the use of any such information, procedure, or product, or reliance thereon.

Neither AH&MA nor the Institute make or recommend industry standards. Nothing in this publication shall be construed as a recommendation by the Institute or AH&MA to be adopted by, or binding upon, any member of the hospitality industry.

Accredited by the Accrediting
Commission of the National
Home Study Council

Library of Congress Cataloging in Publication Data

Cichy, Ronald F.
    Sanitation management.
    Includes index.
    1. Food service — Sanitation — Handbooks, manuals, etc.
    2. Hotels, taverns, etc. — Sanitation — Handbooks, manuals, etc. 3. Restaurants, lunch rooms, etc. — Sanitation — Handbooks, manuals, etc. 4. Food service management — United States — Handbooks, manuals, etc. I. Title.

TX911.3.S3C53   1984   647'.95   84-4092

ISBN 0-86612-018-1

Editor: Margo Bogart

Contents

Preface

Sanitation Management: Strategies For Success has been published with several target markets in mind. Food service industry supervisors, managers, employees, and owners will find this book to be a valuable reference source for the systems design of the operation's sanitation program. Lodging industry groups may use this information in the same manner. The advantage of this book over others on the same topic is its business and bottom-line management orientation. It incorporates the Food and Drug Administration's 1976 Model Ordinance for food service operations and stresses the importance of a uniform nationwide code.

Students majoring in hotel, restaurant, and institutional management curricula in two- and four-year college and university programs will realize that this book is a source of detailed information on sanitation management. After entering the field as supervisors and managers, they can use the material to train employees. It is hoped that the voluntary training and certification of food service professionals in the area of sanitation management will reduce the need for mandatory certification programs.

This book views a food service operation as a system with definable subsystems or control points. It integrates these control points with the four resources (personnel, inventory, equipment, and facilities) under a manager's influence. For each control point, standards for quality control, cost control, and sanitation management are presented.

It is certain that the one thing hospitality operators will need to know in the next decade is how to be a better competitor. The comprehensive systems approach used in this book will help them meet or exceed customer expectations and, thus, survive and prosper. Becoming a better competitor should result in increased business and revenue.

The underlying theme of this book is excellence. Success is a direct result of an establishment's quest for excellence. There is only one thing more important than attaining excellence—maintaining it. The step-by-step approach used in this book will help readers build a winning hospitality operation.

Part One of the book begins with an introduction to the management of success. Food service systems and management are presented next. Information on food contamination, food spoilage, and food preservation provides the underpinning for the sanitation program to be introduced later. A discussion of regulatory and professional organizations concludes the material in Part One.

Part Two is an in-depth treatment of each of the ten food service control points as they relate to the four resources. From menu planning to cleaning and maintenance, each control point is analyzed. Recommendations are based on the provisions of the FDA's Model Ordinance. In fact, we have quoted directly from appropriate sections of the model ordinance throughout the book. Within these quotations specific references to other sections of the model ordinance have been eliminated for ease of reading.

Part Three begins with a discussion of the sanitation management of lodging properties, including specific recommendations for the cleaning and maintenance of lodging facilities. Next, safety management is presented in relation to the operation's sanitation management program. Part Three concludes with a chapter on programming for success. This final chapter integrates the various topics and tips into a workable system.

The objectives of this text are (1) to develop an awareness of the opportunities and challenges presented by hospitality facilities, personnel, inventory, and equipment; (2) to help managers establish proactive sanitation and safety programs; and (3) to reduce the risks to the public while improving the operation's bottom line. Sanitation management in any hospitality operation must be a partnership among management, employees, public health officials, and suppliers.

The author wishes to acknowledge the contributions of many commercial and noncommercial operations in the preparation of this manuscript. Several food service and lodging owners, managers, chefs, and employees provided necessary information and critiqued the manuscript as it was being developed. It is virtually impossible to individually recognize the significant contributions made by each person.

The author would also like to acknowledge several industry professionals who reviewed the proposed outline and the completed manuscript: R. C. Hann, RPS, Denver Department of Health and Hospitals; D. L. Lancaster, National Sanitation Foundation; D. J. Inman, Food and Drug Administration; Dr. M. Skelton, School of Hotel and Restaurant Management, University of Denver; J. Wagner, Hilton Harvest House Hotel; Alain Piallat, Marriot Hotel at City Center; and Troy Campbell, Mr. Steak Restaurants, Inc. These individuals provided a "reality focus" for the book. In addition, the author would like to thank all of the industry professionals whose philosophies of success and quality are included in this book.

The author also wishes to thank George R. Conrade, Director of Educational Programs at the Educational Institute of the American Hotel & Motel Association, for his commitment to excellence.

Sanitation Management: Strategies for Success is dedicated to Dr. Lewis J. Minor, founder of the L.J. Minor Corporation, Cleveland, Ohio, and Distinguished Visiting Professor in the School of Hotel, Restaurant and Institutional Management, Michigan State University. Dr. Minor has been my role model, teacher, mentor, and coach.

Ronald F. Cichy
Denver, Colorado

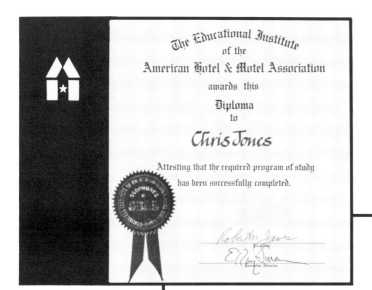

This text, used in conjunction with the corresponding student manual, is one in a series of courses available through the Educational Institute of the American Hotel & Motel Association leading to completion of a certification program. To date, nearly half a million individuals have benefited from Educational Institute programs, distinguishing the Institute as the world's largest educational center for the hospitality industry. For information regarding the available programs, please contact:

> The Educational Institute of AH&MA
> 1407 South Harrison Road
> P.O. Box 1240
> East Lansing, Michigan 48823
> (517) 353-5500

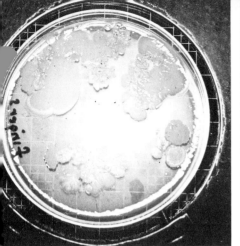

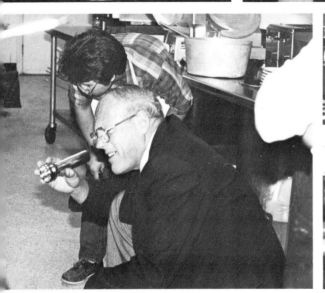

Part One

To succeed, the manager of a hospitality operation must achieve a delicate balance between profitability (in commercial operations) or cost containment (in noncommercial operations) and customer satisfaction. The challenge of the hospitality manager's position is heightened by the fact that today's food service and lodging customers are demanding more than ever before. Customers expect food to be properly prepared, attractively presented, and efficiently served with friendliness and courtesy. They also expect a clean and comfortable environment in which to enjoy their dining and/or lodging experience. Finally, customers are careful consumers who expect to get their money's worth.

In light of these demands, is it unreasonable to think that a manager can satisfy customers and still achieve profitability or cost containment? Not at all. However, a certain amount of technical knowledge, a systematic approach, and a commitment to excellence are prerequisites to achieving success.

In Chapter 1, the characteristics of a successful hospitality business are discussed in more detail. Industry trends and the importance of quality are also emphasized. These management concerns provide the backdrop for the discussion of sanitation throughout the rest of this book.

Chapter 2 emphasizes the importance of a systematic approach to food service management. Many lodging properties have food service outlets with separate identities, intended to attract local customers as well as guests. In fact, many people identify a "great hotel" by its food service excellence. Today, managers of lodging operations are finding that food service outlets can be profit centers instead of cost centers if they are properly controlled. By looking at the basic operating activities in a food service system and understanding the resources available to the manager, the control of the entire food service facility becomes more systematic. Thus, management can achieve its cost control objectives, ensure quality, and maintain sanitation standards. Finally, the Food and Drug Administration's Model Food Service Sanitation Ordinance is introduced. While local sanitation codes may vary, the FDA's Model Ordinance is the source of almost all the sanitation guidelines in the chapters which follow.

In Chapter 3, important information on food contamination is presented. The manager who is armed with a knowledge of microbial, chemical, and physical contaminants is better prepared to prevent these agents of food intoxication, food infection, foodborne disease, and physical injury from entering the food service system.

Chapter 4 covers the topic of food spoilage and how to prevent it. Methods of commercial food preservation are explained, and recommendations are given for the proper preservation of foods within the hospitality operation.

In Chapter 5, food regulations and government inspections are discussed. In particular, procedures for obtaining a license to operate a food service establishment and guidelines for handling a suspected outbreak of foodborne illness are explained in detail. In addition, descriptions of various industry and trade associations which may be useful to food service and lodging managers are provided.

ONE

The Management
of Success

Strategies for Success at the Aspen Hotel

Paul James just finished talking on the telephone with his supervisor at company headquarters. The supervisor informed Paul that he received a very favorable performance review for the past quarter. Paul's supervisor summarized the review by telling him that he was impressed with Paul's commitment to excellence, quality, and service. As the general manager of a 150-room metropolitan hotel, Paul was known in the company as a builder, a possibility thinker, and an action-oriented person. Paul's career with the Mountain States Hotel Management Company had progressed rapidly as a result of his attitude toward the company, his employees, and his customers. Paul's supervisor reminded him that there are three kinds of people in the hospitality industry: those who make things happen, those who watch things happen, and those who wonder what has happened.

The supervisor had reaffirmed what Paul already knew. Paul's success was directly related to the fact that he was one of those people who make things happen. He was never satisfied with mediocrity or the status quo. Since graduating from college ten years ago with a business degree in hotel and restaurant management, Paul was always developing higher standards with which to critique his own performance.

Paul James constantly reminded himself, his departmental supervisors, and his employees that the customer was the main reason for being in business. He encouraged everyone in the hotel to work on developing a customer awareness. "Put yourself in the customer's shoes and look at our hotel through the customer's eyes. Successful people are successful because they *want* to be successful. If we are successful in meeting or exceeding customer expectations, we will all be winners. And our property will be more profitable." This was Paul's challenge to every one of the hotel's employees at every staff meeting. He realized that it was his responsibility, as the general manager, to set the pace. The GM creates the enthusiasm that the supervisors and employees need. The GM's level of enthusiasm affects everyone in the hotel.

Paul's supervisor informed him that he would be flying into town tomorrow morning to meet with Paul. The supervisor said that a very important career move could be in Paul's immediate future. Paul was anxious to know the details but his supervisor said that he would rather discuss them in person the next day. As Paul left his office for the weekly meeting of department heads, he was already looking forward to next morning's meeting with his supervisor.

For those who want a responsible position in a dynamic field, the management of a hospitality facility can be a rewarding career choice. Of course, food service and lodging businesses face many challenges to their survival, not the least of which is continual change. Current challenges include finding qualified personnel, training employees to provide quality products and services, increasing productivity, and developing new markets. Other challenges are providing a total dining or lodging experience to satisfy increasingly sophisticated customers, expanding menu offerings and hours of operation to increase revenues, while offering special promotions to maximize the customers' perceived value (quality versus cost). Many examples of strategies for meeting these challenges will be presented later in this chapter. Generally, however, if a food service or lodging operation is going to survive in the 1980s, its managers, supervisors, and workers need to understand success, social trends affecting the industry, quality, and how sanitation relates to these concepts.

What Is Success?

Before writing their best-selling book *In Search of Excellence*, authors Thomas J. Peters and Robert H. Waterman, Jr., studied scores of innovative corporations in the United States. The firms they studied were considered innovative because they respond to change continually as their environments change. From these corporations, the authors selected the most successful firms for further research. They proceeded to discover that the excellent companies are both flexible and adaptive. They achieve their financial objectives while satisfying the needs and wants of customers and employees alike. As a result, they are winners.

Characteristics of Successful Firms   After completing their research and analysis, the authors of *In Search of Excellence* identified eight attributes or characteristics which the most successful companies have in common. These eight characteristics are:

1.   A bias for action

2.   Close to the customer

3.   Autonomy and entrepreneurship

4.   Productivity through people

5.   Hands-on, value driven

6.   Stick to the knitting

7.   Simple form, lean staff

8.   Simultaneous loose-tight properties[1]

These eight attributes form the core and framework of the winning companies. Each of these characteristics can be discussed in relation to

---

[1] Thomas J. Peters and Robert H. Waterman, Jr., *In Search of Excellence* (New York: Harper & Row, 1982), pp. 13-15.

food service and lodging businesses because every one of them is crucial to the success of hospitality operations.

A Bias for Action. This first attribute of excellent companies is clearly applicable to food service and lodging operations. The successful hospitality companies are action-oriented. The winners are not content just to analyze each situation; they follow through by taking the necessary action. Without losing sight of their mission, the successful operations are willing to try new and different approaches—whatever gets the job done. They continually try new concepts and upgrade or modify existing concepts. Some of the fast-food chains exemplify this attribute. They constantly experiment with new menu items, decor packages, and pricing strategies. The unsuccessful properties are generally those that have not adapted to changes in their markets, their customers' desires, and/or their employees' needs. At the very least, the inflexible food service and lodging companies have experienced a decrease in customer counts, market share, and revenues. In many cases, they have closed their doors and gone out of business.

Close to the Customer. The excellent companies believe that the customer is extremely important. Without the customer, the firm cannot prosper or even survive. The objective of winning firms is to provide the level of service, product quality, and overall satisfaction desired by the customer. Because they view the customer as a partner in the success of the firm, they are not afraid to ask for suggestions on how to improve. When new ideas are being tested, customer comments are welcomed. In fact, the winning companies constantly seek customer feedback at all stages of production and service. Rather than considering the customer's opinion worthless and ignoring it, winning companies use this market intelligence to their advantage. Successful firms regard customer satisfaction as the hinge upon which their flow of business (and profitability) swings.

Also, successful firms emphasize customer service. Everyone in the organization becomes a public relations agent. The strategy of the winners is to meet or exceed the customer's expectations. They view customer service as crucial to the long-term survival of the company. Rather than viewing the serving of customers as a bother or an interruption of their business, they recognize that customer service *is* their business.

Food service and lodging operations are classified in the service sector of the American business community. Yet, it probably isn't hard for you to remember the last time you were disappointed or treated rudely in a hotel or restaurant. Have you ever walked into a restaurant five or ten minutes before it was scheduled to close? How were you treated by the host and the server? Was the food quality and presentation as good as it would have been earlier in the meal period? Did the busperson or server begin sweeping the floor, blowing out the candles on the tables, and blinking the lights before you were finished with your dining experience? For years this service nightmare has been a reality in hundreds of restaurants and hotels across the United States. Establishments that permit such poor treatment of their customers have forgotten that it is the customer who ultimately determines their success (or failure). It is time for some food service and lodging managers to wake up, reevaluate their approach, and upgrade their service to the customer. The excellent companies schedule such evaluations on a regular basis.

Autonomy and Entrepreneurship. Excellent companies realize the importance of their middle managers and employees being able to make or influence the decisions that affect them. The winners encourage their people to innovate. They provide incentives for their staff to think of new ideas for improving the firm and its customer service.

A champion is someone who comes up with new ideas and is allowed to act as an entrepreneur in developing them. Of course, not all ideas will turn out to be feasible or profitable. In some cases, the champion fails. However, in excellent companies this failure is not seen as the downfall of the champion. The successful companies realize that champions are original thinkers and dedicated workers. They need freedom to develop into innovators. If some ideas don't work, at least the champions can learn important lessons from their mistakes and failures. In other words, most innovators whose ideas have been worth millions to their companies have made many mistakes and experienced failure before they became successful. Because innovative companies are willing to give their champions room to experiment, their people frequently come up with new ideas, many of which pay off. And because excellent companies support their champions—even if a mistake was made—their employees continue to try new ideas, secure in the knowledge that they will not be personally destroyed if their experiments fail. Innovators will emerge in a company only if they are supported by management, employees, and their peers.

With the trend toward chain and multi-unit businesses in the food service and lodging industries, autonomy and entrepreneurship within individual operations may seem to be impossible. However, the excellent operations and their managers overcome the limits of standardization. The winning corporations foster a spirit of competition among their unit managers. Then, within each unit, the manager creates a spirit of competition and a desire to be the best among the employees. Such competition is healthy because it results in better service to the customer.

Productivity Through People. In a service industry like food service or lodging, a people orientation is critical. The excellent companies have a simple but very effective management style. Basically, they treat everyone from top management to the hourly line worker with respect and dignity. Winning companies see all of their employees as partners in the business. They have respect for their staff because they realize that people are the most important resource any company has. Because employees can either make or break a business, successful companies take a positive approach toward their managers and bring out the best in them. In turn, these managers communicate their positive mental attitude and enthusiasm to everyone in the company through frequent informal conversations as well as through the traditional, formal channels. Employees can feel their openness and naturally respond to their genuine interest.

Training also plays a major role in people-oriented companies. The excellent companies recognize that training is an investment in their employees' success. They help their employees grow, develop, and improve. Consequently, employees feel more important to the company and may overcome negative feelings about themselves and their work. Effective training results in a commitment to quality as well as pride in the company, its management, and its products. Of course, a feeling of pride cannot be taught; it must be caught. When employees take pride in their work, the overall productivity of the company naturally improves. Excellent companies emphasize the importance of their employees and, as a result, achieve more and better results with fewer people.

Many restaurants and hotel managers talk quite convincingly about their interest in people but, unfortunately, not all of them follow through with open communication and evidence of a genuine interest in their staff. Unsuccessful managers view their employees as a necessary evil and treat them in a shabby, unproductive, and unprofessional manner. Not surprisingly, this often results in the employees treating customers the same way.

The unsuccessful companies haven't the time or money for training. The average hotel or restaurant probably spends more money annually in maintaining and repairing the equipment and facilities than in developing and training its supervisors and employees. They fail to see that a well-trained staff is the key to the loyal patronage and better-than-average revenue enjoyed by successful operations.

Hands-On, Value Driven. The successful companies in the United States and around the world have an identifiable value system which is linked to a clearly stated purpose. Successful companies take their company philosophy seriously and work at achieving objectives that are compatible with the philosophy. The policies and procedures of the winning companies spring from the value system and reflect what the companies consider to be most important.

In the excellent companies, the value system has a quality focus more than a quantitative or "numbers" orientation. Naturally, the winners have financial or quantitative goals; without these the companies would not stay in business. But the *primary* values are nonnumerical. Successful companies see a reasonable profit as the result, not the cause, of a well-planned value system.

The winners value excellence and actively attempt to rid themselves of mediocrity and negativism. Managers and supervisors in the successful companies are enthusiastic about the company values, so they make excellent role models for employees. They realize that an environment of positiveness and fun can improve the bottom line on their income statements. But they are always aware that profitability (or cost containment) is not the major goal. Financial success is actually a by-product of creating a value system that is shared by everyone in the organization.

Food service and lodging operations should consider their value system because it filters down through managers to employees and eventually to customers. Are employees less than enthusiastic when serving customers? If so, it is probably because the manager and department heads have not shown by their own actions how important customers are to the business. Perhaps top management values its employees but has failed to emphasize this to its middle managers. Thus, middle managers give the impression that they do not care about employees. Whether they like it or not, managers and supervisors are role models for their employees. If a company's managers or supervisors are positive and enthusiastic, so are the employees; if the managers or supervisors are depressed or down, so are the employees. Employees look to management to set the tone of the workplace. If management is committed to efficiency, quality, and cleanliness, the employees are also. However, when top management does not take the time to consider its values, or fails to share these values with managers, supervisors, and workers, customer satisfaction is bound to be adversely affected.

Stick to the Knitting. Successful companies concentrate on doing what they do better than anyone else. Some firms rapidly diversify in an attempt to attract new business. The result is often the loss of their original customers and financial failure. Although some companies have succeeded in expanding their offerings, generally they have planned well for their diversification.

Like an individual, each company has a definable, yet limited, group of skills. These skills permit the company to perform well within its area of expertise. However, to diversify outside the realm of expertise can be very dangerous to the company as a whole. Excellent companies do not tamper to any great extent with the components that made them winners in the first place.

The successful companies focus on the fundamentals. They constantly improve their delivery of a tried and tested product, never jeopardizing it by doing a mediocre job with dozens of other products. They minimize long-shots and stick with a sure thing. These winners capitalize on their achievements within a particular field and wisely use their well-developed expertise to gradually increase their market share.

Food service and lodging businesses frequently violate the principle of "stick to the knitting." Think about the fast-food operation that adds new items to its menu each year, without considering the limitations of the unit's equipment, the skill levels of employees, or the desires of its target markets. How about the specialty restaurant that adds Tex-Mex food to its menu and does a poor job of preparation and delivery? Consider the hotel that adds a full room service menu without thinking about the distance between the kitchen and the guestrooms, timing, or the potential loss of food quality during transportation. Poorly conceived diversification can actually harm rather than help the operation's long-term survival.

Simple Form, Lean Staff. Excellent companies keep things simple. This simplicity minimizes the growth of an uncontrollable and unwieldy bureaucracy. A lean organizational form permits rational, yet rapid, responses to changing conditions. Top managers in the excellent companies are personally in touch with operations on a day-to-day basis. As a result, these corporate leaders are tuned into the needs and expectations of the firm's customers and its employees.

In the winning companies, most staff functions and assignments are made on a temporary basis. This prevents complacency and territorialism among managers. The people in successful companies seek new challenges. They do not wish to and are not permitted to stagnate.

Food service and lodging operations can learn from the "simple form, lean staff" attribute of the excellent companies. Many hospitality businesses suffer from "too many chiefs and not enough Indians." For example, a busperson in a restaurant is often expected to work for and take orders from eight or more food servers. Complexity and overlapping breed confusion, wasted time, and productivity losses.

Some hotel and restaurant managers prefer to escape from daily interaction with employees and customers. As a result, they often hide in their offices and delegate this duty to subordinates. The more layers they add to the organizational structure to protect them, the farther out of touch they become with the desires of the people who work in and patronize their establishments. A company that is top-heavy or neglects to streamline its operations is probably headed for failure.

Simultaneous Loose-Tight Properties. The winning companies have a well-defined combination of operating strategies. They provide the individual units with direction from the corporate office, while permitting unit autonomy and decision-making. The successful companies achieve a delicate balance between rules and regulations and the needs of their people. They encourage innovation on the part of their employees without sacrificing systematic management.

Successful companies never abandon their system of shared values. When employees fail to act in accordance with it, the value system provides the framework for discipline. But generally they do things right because they concentrate on the details that made the company great. Thus, the winners hold internal and external objectives as equally important, and they achieve both.

Internal objectives often focus on communication, competition, and quality control. The excellent companies emphasize communication. Top management and department heads regularly solicit comments from both employees and customers. People are important, and their suggestions and input are critical to the success of the firm. Also, the winners refuse to compromise their standards in order to edge out the competition in the short-run. The long-term well-being of the firm and its people takes precedence over all other goals or objectives.

External goals involve giving the customer quality products and service. Lodging and food service operations that are winners realize that the customer is their reason for being in business. The excellent hospitality businesses meet or exceed their customers' expectations, and this results in financial success. Companies that compromise their standards by giving bad service or selling inferior products are certainly losers. But, unfortunately, they also cause their customers, employees, managers, suppliers, and the economy as a whole to suffer from their lost business and lost revenue.

Exhibit 1.1 The Success Equation

S +	**U** +	**C** +	**C** +	**E** +	**S** +	**S**
—Safety	—Uniformity	—Customers	—Change	—Enthusiasm	—Sanitation	—Service
—Satisfaction	—Uniqueness	—Controls	—Champions	—Education	—Support	—Self-Improvement
—Standards	—Unbeatability	—Consistency	—Competence	—Economics	—Self-Confidence	—Systems
—Striving	—Ultimate	—Certainty	—Caring	—Ethics	—Stability	—Sensibleness
—Survival	—Understanding	—Compliance	—Communicating	—Employees	—Significance	—Strength

The Success Equation

The concept of success can be presented in a number of ways. As we have already seen, success is closely associated with excellence. What else is important in achieving success? Exhibit 1.1 summarizes many other components of the success equation which are important to the success of food service and lodging establishments.

A number of successful food service and lodging managers were asked how they define success in their own properties. These winners described success in the following ways:

''When everything is said and done, in spite of all the marketing studies, success in business comes about when you have a product that the customer wants. We focus on delivering a product, concept, and service level that is satisfying to the customer. We are successful as a company because we do not get lost in grand concepts. We use common sense and attention to detail to provide a nice, clean product. Our hotel spends tremendous amounts of time making sure everything is in top condition. We have a commitment to excellence. The most frequent comment that we receive from customers is their impression with the positive attitude of our employees and the overall cleanliness.''

Alain Piallat, General Manager
Marriott Hotel at the City Center

''Success is learning from your mistakes and the mistakes of others. You should improve on your errors by finding a better way to do something. Adding new ideas to your field is important. Success is helping others through your contribution. Success is how others perceive you. It is a way of looking at life.''

James Kosec, CEC, CCE, Corporate Chef Advisor
L.J. Minor Corporation

''Success in the restaurant business is continued guest count growth. Our goal is to serve at least one more guest this Saturday night than we did the same night last year. Excellence is deciding on a workable concept and determining objectives. These objectives must be achieved based on what the consumer wants. Once the objective is determined and customers accept your concept, success is the result."

Troy Campbell, Vice President of
Franchise Operations and Management Development
Mr. Steak, Inc.

"You never really achieve *ultimate* success. Show me a totally satisfied person and I will show you a fool. You have to keep trying. Appoint yourself as your greatest critic. Success can either be an end in itself or a trip. Success has plateaus that allow you to reset and modify your goals. Once you reach your goals, you can either reset and revise new goals or sit on your old accomplishments. You don't want to live on your reputation instead of up to it."

Robert Krump, President, Food Service Marketing,
Board of Directors, Colorado-Wyoming Restaurant Association

"Extremes make you a success or failure. The general manager and department heads create the atmosphere for excellence. Success from a financial viewpoint is beating the budget and growing and constantly improving. Keep changing and upgrading. Concentrate on property performance to reduce employee and guest complaints. Success is seeing your management people grow. Company recognition and reduced employee turnover add to success."

John Wagner, General Manager
Hilton Harvest House—an AIRCOA Property

"Success helps satisfy you and the people that are important in your life. You should try to accomplish what you set out to do at a given point in time. Then it is time to reset your goals. Success comes from the team of people in your organization. The owner, manager, chef, and all employees provide the support for success. When preparation meets opportunity, the result is success."

Peggy Salzer, CWC, Chef Consultant and Seafood Specialist
Seattle Fish Company

These six managers echo one common thought—success *is* possible in food service and lodging operations. From these many views of success, we can conclude that excellent companies encourage both management and employees to develop an acute customer awareness. They look at their operations through their customers' eyes and judge their performance according to their customers' needs and expectations. By taking the customer's perspective, they see new ways of improving the operation. They show genuine care and concern for their customers. With all this in their favor, it is not surprising that the excellent food service and lodging businesses are also financially successful.

The Future of Food Service and Lodging

In his book *Megatrends*, author John Naisbitt presents ten indicators of new directions in which American society is moving.[2] Already these major trends are transforming our lives. Naisbitt suggests that we can better anticipate the future if we understand the megatrends of the present. According to Naisbitt, we are moving:

1. From an industrial society to an information society

2. From forced technology to high tech/high touch

3. From a national economy to a world economy

4. From short term to long term

5. From centralization to decentralization

6. From institutional help to self-help

7. From representative democracy to participatory democracy

8. From hierarchies to networking

9. From north to south

10. From either/or to multiple option

These ten trends could have a major effect on American businesses. Each trend will be presented and discussed in relation to its potential impact on food service and lodging operations.

From an Industrial Society to an Information Society

The main growth area for employment today is in the information field. Whereas capital was once the strategic resource in the industrialized United States, today information takes precedence in our "technocracy." Rapid increases in technology are responsible for the emergence and growth of this trend.

The "information explosion" has made knowledge more accessible to the masses. Also, the flow of information in today's society is faster than ever before. We can now use this information to anticipate future conditions. Better sources of information enable managers to be better predictors and, thus, better decision makers.

To take a specific example from the food service industry, electronic

---

[2] This discussion is based on John Naisbitt, *Megatrends* (New York: Warner Books, 1982).

point-of-sale registers were only used by a handful of food service businesses ten years ago. Today, they are commonplace. These electronic tools provide managers with accurate data on their food cost, labor cost, menu item popularity, and inventory value each day. Consequently, food service managers can make decisions or take corrective action much more rapidly. The computerization of guest registration, billing, and check-out procedures has provided similar advantages to lodging properties.

From Forced Technology to High Tech/ High Touch

In the past 25 years, Americans have moved away from the regimentation and uniformity associated with a highly industrialized society preoccupied with efficiency and automation. While most managers realize that today's computerized information systems can help them be efficient and effective and make more timely decisions, they are finding that "high tech" requires a balancing dose of "high touch" if it is to be accepted by others. High tech appeals to the need for information, while high touch appeals to human needs and desires.

Because people are increasingly involved with high tech in the workplace, they will pursue high touch activities in their spare time. Witness the astounding growth in recent years of physical fitness and sports-related activities. Cooking and entertaining at home is also on the rise. Evidence of the increasing interest in the culinary arts includes the expansion of areas devoted to cookbooks in bookstores, kitchen gadgets in department stores, and specialty or gourmet foods in supermarkets.

Home entertainment centers make it possible to watch current movies, "attend" plays and concerts, and be a spectator at distant sporting events without ever leaving home. Home computers are making trips to the department store, library, and video arcade unnecessary. High tech/high touch activities centered at home may emerge as direct competitors to food service and lodging operations in the not too distant future.

From a National Economy to a World Economy

In the past, the United States was considered to be the top manufacturer of industrial equipment and products. Today, America's role as an industrial superpower is being seriously challenged. Foreign manufacturers have gained strong toeholds in the world market and even in the United States. The nation's largest industry, automobile manufacturing, has been severely buffeted by the American consumers' increasing acceptance of foreign automobiles in recent years.

Third-world nations, with their rapidly growing populations, have provided a new source of industrial labor. Modern scientific research in biology and genetic engineering is creating tremendous opportunities for the United States to take a leadership role in these fields. The worldwide demand for American technology remains very high, so America's business links to the international community are likely to remain strong.

This megatrend has already begun to influence both menu options and facilities design in lodging and food service establishments. Commercial and noncommercial operations are adding Mexican, Oriental, and Italian items to their menus. These choices are popular because customers perceive these ethnic foods as nutritious, filling, and a good value. By incorporating an ethnic influence into their decor, traditionally designed restaurants and hotels have developed a more interesting ambience or international atmosphere to attract today's more cosmopolitan customers.

From Short Term to Long Term

In the past, some American companies compromised long-term considerations for short-term profits. They concentrated on short-term profits at the expense of the long-term survival or growth of the company. A short-term outlook often involves resistance to change. Flexibility and openness to change are necessary if the firm is going to survive in a changing environment.

Companies, labor unions, universities, and each of us as individuals must rethink our goals and roles periodically. Companies are realizing that a long-term outlook is necessary if they are to survive in the short run. Labor unions are modifying their approaches with an eye to the future. Colleges and universities are implementing continuing and lifelong education programs to serve the ever-increasing numbers of middle-aged and senior citizens.

Food service and lodging businesses are going to be increasingly scrutinized by consumer groups. Food safety laws will continue to be reevaluated and rewritten. Hospitality industry employees and managers will expect their operations to contribute to their personal growth and career development. The need for continual retraining will emerge as an issue of importance to employees and employers alike.

From Centralization to Decentralization

In the past, centralization of power in the United States and in companies was prevalent. Today this trend has begun to reverse itself, and in the future, decentralization will continue. State and local governments are already pushing for more autonomy and less central direction by the federal government. States within a region are banding together to speak with a united voice on common issues. Companies are demanding a reduction of red tape and a streamlining of bureaucracy, both in their own organizations and in the government. Decentralization in government and in companies will stimulate change, since change is more likely to occur where power is distributed throughout an organization, instead of tightly held by a few key offices.

In lodging and food service facilities, unit managers and department heads will demand more freedom and autonomy. Nationwide restaurant and hotel chains will abandon the "cookie cutter" standardized design concept and will allow each unit to have a decor and interior design that reflects the region in which the unit is located. Menu offerings will also vary according to regional preferences and availability of raw ingredients within the region.

From Institutional Help to Self-Help

Institutions like the government of the United States have historically provided public assistance for basic needs such as food, housing, and health care to those who could not provide for themselves. Today, with government cutbacks in social welfare programs, the trend is toward more self-reliance and self-help.

This megatrend has extended into the areas of diet, medicine, and business. People are more health-conscious than in the past. They are exercising on a regular basis and reducing their intake of calories. There appears to be a stronger interest in preventive health care. Also, many Americans are becoming entrepreneurs instead of relying upon established companies to supply their incomes.

Food service and lodging establishments have already begun to respond to the self-help trend. Several restaurants now offer low-calorie, multiple portion size menu items. A number of hotels have exercise and health facilities available for in-house guests. Capitalizing on America's changing eating and living patterns may be highly profitable for lodging and food service operations.

From Representative Democracy to Participatory Democracy

Americans are more interested today in being involved with decisions that will directly affect their lives. People are demanding a voice in both government and corporations. They want to have a say in the policies and procedures that influence their ability to function in society. The ever-growing consumer movement in the United States is a direct outgrowth of this new activism. For food service businesses, truth-in-menu regulations will continue to multiply. Customers will demand to know more about the sanitary condition of restaurants that they choose to patronize.

Furthermore, today's customers want to participate, or at least have a voice in, decisions that directly affect them. Some businesses are resisting this trend. They are likely to find that customers will exercise their freedom of choice and decide to patronize businesses that permit customers to be heard. Hotels and motels can only benefit from customer input and comments about operations. One lodging chain which is aware of this possibility is now advertising that it will do everything possible to guarantee that customers are satisfied with their rooms; if they aren't satisfied, their rooms are free.

From Hierarchies to Networking

This megatrend relates to those already discussed. In general, large organizational hierarchies and bureaucracies have not effectively dealt with the problems of people. As a result, people within large organizations have formed networks. A network is simply a group of individuals with a common interest who exchange information on an informal basis. The advantage of networking is that it permits a free flow of information throughout the organization. The movement for equal rights for women and all human beings was stimulated by networks. As people in the "baby boom" generation take over key management positions in increasing numbers, networks will grow in popularity.

Several food service and lodging operations are using the networking concept to their advantage. Some hotels and restaurants have assigned responsibility for quality control to groups of people from a variety of departments. More attention is being paid to the ideas of individual department heads and people within those departments. Managers are realizing that often the best solution to a problem can be found by listening to the individual who is directly involved and confronts the problem on a daily basis.

From North to South

According to U.S. Census Bureau figures for 1980, dramatic shifts in the American population have taken place. For the first time, the southern and western states now have more people than the northern and eastern states. This trend will continue for the foreseeable future. Also, most of the new job openings in the last ten years have occurred in southern and western states. With the shift in population, some companies are finding a glut of job applicants while other firms are searching desperately for workers.

Because young adults are highly mobile, lodging and food service operations in areas with diminishing populations are being forced to find new ways to hire adequate numbers of employees. For example, more senior citizens and part-time workers are being utilized. In such cases, the responsibilities of various positions may need redefining.

Furthermore, whereas the infrastructure (highways, powerlines, water and sewage systems, etc.) in the North and East is now overbuilt, the infrastructure in the West and South is generally under capacity. Therefore, the hospitality industry may find it costly to expand in places where the population is growing rapidly.

From Either/Or to Multiple Option

More product choices are available than ever before in modern American society. More important, people can choose from a variety of lifestyles which were once considered socially unacceptable. Women are entering the work force in record numbers, and couples are choosing to have fewer children later in life.

Cultural diversity is the watchword today. Schools are debating bilingual teaching methods. The United States has over 15 million Spanish-speaking people constituting 6.4% of the nation's population. This ethnic group is growing, as is the number of Asian-Americans. The increasing numbers of Spanish-speaking workers in hotels and restaurants require managers, supervisors, and other employees to become more sensitive to cultural and language differences.

Hospitality establishments are appealing to customers in two-career families by offering convenience and an escape from the pressures of time. The wide range of dining and lodging options is constantly being extended. For example, gourmet carry-out food is now available from a select group of restaurants catering to working couples. Also, vacation condominiums are springing up to meet the popular demand for lifestyle variety.

The megatrends just presented reflect significant changes taking place in the world around us. Some short-sighted companies continue to resist these changes at all costs. The excellent companies realize that changes are always taking place and they have to anticipate them. The successful companies view change as healthy and fearlessly respond to it. Responding to change makes the successful companies more prosperous because it enables them to meet their customers' and employees' evolving needs, desires, and expectations.

What Is Quality?

Although the meaning of **quality** may be diluted due to overuse in advertising, it is an important term for hospitality industry people at all levels to understand. Basically, quality is consistent delivery of a product at a level which satisfies the company's customers. Since food service and lodging operations are in the service sector of the economy, their "product" is frequently a service. Specifics vary with the nature of the business, but almost every component of a dining-out or lodging experience is an indicator of quality. Customers judge a restaurant or hotel by components such as menu variety, prompt service, food preparation techniques, cleanliness, comfort, and decor. To provide quality, management must first determine what level of quality is required by customers and then establish standards for the personnel, raw materials, and equipment utilized throughout the operation.

Determining the level of quality desired by customers can be a challenge for several reasons. First, it may vary from person to person because each individual has a unique background. When asked to define quality, customers may express subjective personal preferences, according to what they like or consider excellent, superior, great, or good. To gather this valuable market intelligence, managers must listen to customers. This presents another challenge. Feeling the pressure of day-to-day operations, unit managers are sometimes tempted to "tune out" additional problems or complaints. But ignoring customers' input is no solution. The customers' opinions must be heard if the business is to survive.

Once the necessary customer input is gathered, it must be translated into specific standards, because the only way to ensure consistent delivery of a certain level of product quality is to enforce specific standards in all areas of the operation. Such systematic enforcement of product standards is called **quality control.**

To enforce quality control standards, the operation must sample and evaluate its products using the appropriate sensory, chemical, and physical methods. Employee training should include the development of quality judgment so they can monitor their own production. Clear concepts of quality are best learned through firsthand experience. For example, if the product being judged is a food item, flavor, texture, appearance, consistency, palatability, nutritional value, safety, ease of handling, convenience, storage stability, and packaging are the essential characteristics to be evaluated to ensure its acceptability to customers. Management may additionally judge a new product based on certain economic factors, such as the cost of the new item, projected sales within the intended price range, and the profit it is expected to generate. These characteristics influence whether or not the item will be added to the menu.

Quality cannot be the responsibility of the quality control or quality assurance department alone. Rather, the entire food service or lodging establishment must strive for quality. Management must be certain that an understanding of and commitment to quality permeates the entire business, because it is a major organizational goal and requirement. The development of a quality product and positive organizational image, together with a consistent marketing effort, can enhance a company's market share and improve its bottom line.

A number of food service and lodging managers were asked to define quality in their own words. The following comments represent their responses.

"Quality is simple consistency in all products produced and served. One must look at the overall package, the total experience. Quality should embrace both products and personnel. You need clearly defined goals and objectives. They help you decide specifically what you are going to do. The general manager sets the overall tone. The department heads follow through for each department."

John Wagner, General Manager
Hilton Harvest House—an AIRCOA Property

"Quality is doing whatever you are doing better the next time. Quality is value in relation to price. It is a professional use of standards to achieve consistency. Quality is affected by eye-appeal, flavor, texture, and atmosphere."

James Kosec, CEC, CCE, Corporate Chef Advisor
L.J. Minor Corporation

" If guests buy your product consistently, you have achieved a sufficient level of quality. The quality has to be correct based on the utilization of the product. For example, prime beef is not the best quality for ground beef products. Quality should be based on what your customers want. Once you are to the point where you assume that the quality is right for your customers, it may be time to reevaluate what you are doing. You may want to upgrade or change slightly."

Troy Campbell, Vice President of
Franchise Operations and Management Development
Mr. Steak, Inc.

"Quality is doing what you tell the customer you are going to do. You are going to make mistakes occasionally because everyone is human. It is important that you repair the mistakes as soon as possible. In this way, you will keep your customers satisfied and coming back."

Alain Piallat, General Manager
Marriott Hotel at the City Center

"Quality levels depend on the markets being served. The best products are those that are chosen based on the end-use. Quality is a safe product served in a clean environment. This leads to the customer's satisfaction and enjoyment."

Robert Krump, President, Food Service Marketing,
Board of Directors, Colorado-Wyoming Restaurant Association

"Quality is consistency. Consistency in presentation, size, and portions is most important. Consistency in the entire dining experience is our objective. We want to give the customer a good dollar value."

Richard Weil, Vice President—Operations
Westman Commission Company

"Quality is uniqueness. It is the timing of your production and delivery systems to yield a class performance. You have to look at the total experience. Quality is artistry that is used to strengthen the bottom line."

Peggy Salzer, CWC, Chef Consultant and Seafood Specialist
Seattle Fish Company

We can summarize the foregoing discussion of quality by saying that quality is delivering your product—whether it is a meal, a drink, or a hotel room—in a uniform or consistent way. The quality level offered in your lodging or food service operation must satisfy the needs and desires of your target markets. Of course, the introduction of new products and the identification of new markets tend to complicate things. Therefore, it is increasingly important for managers to regularly ask themselves, "What business is our establishment in? Who are our customers?" Only then can they begin to define quality for their operation. This is a "back to the basics" approach. Knowing who you are (as a business) and who your customers are will help your operation to be a success.

How Does Sanitation Relate to Success, Industry Trends, and Quality?

When you started to read this book you may have asked yourself, "Why do I need to read a book on sanitation?" If so, you are not alone. Some managers consider the topic of sanitation boring and uninteresting. Others question the practicability of the subject, commenting that the concepts are good on paper but don't work in the "real world"—an actual restaurant or hotel. Both of these objections are overcome when we look at sanitation in terms of something any manager can relate to: dollars and cents.

Economic Impact of Sanitation Management

Let us consider for a moment the financial risk taken by a food service facility that lacked an adequate sanitation program. The management learned the hard way that the economic effects of a foodborne disease outbreak can be disastrous. In 1974, an outbreak of human salmonellosis was traced to the food service operation.[3] The following figures indicate the cost in 1984 dollars of that incident:

Costs of the Outbreak	1984 Dollars
Lost Salaries and Productivity of Wage-earner Victims	$31,302
Medical and Hospital Expenses	5,041
Economic Losses for the Restaurant Owner	8,500
Cost of the Investigation	4,021
Total Cost of the Outbreak	**$48,864**

In this case, 125 people became ill after eating contaminated food. Fifty of the victims consulted a physician, and 11 were subsequently hospitalized. The salmonellosis lasted an average of five days and ranged from moderate to severe.

Putting the costs of the outbreak in terms of today's dollars, over $31,000 was lost in wages and productivity. Medical and hospital expenses for the victims exceeded $5,000. The restaurant lost $8,500 in business due to negative publicity. Additionally, the investigation cost more than $4,000. The total cost of the outbreak was well over $48,000.

Contrast this staggering sum to the current costs of prevention shown here:

Costs of Prevention	
Training Course for Food Service Personnel	$850
Regular Quality Control Inspection (twice a year)	36
Total Cost of Prevention	**$886**

The owner could have spent $850 for a sanitation training course for the operation's personnel. An in-house inspection by the facility's management could have been scheduled every six months for an additional cost of only $36. Thus, the total cost of prevention would be just $886. When the cost of prevention is compared to the total cost of the outbreak, it is clear that the expenditure of a few hundred dollars and a little time is a small price to pay to prevent outbreaks before they occur. This cost-versus-benefit approach clearly and dramatically illustrates the potential impact of a foodborne disease outbreak on a food service or lodging establishment's bottom line. It should serve as a warning to operators who run dirty establishments because they think, "sanitation management

---

[3] The data for the original outbreak were initially reported in 1974. All dollar values have been expressed in 1984 dollars by factoring in the annual rates of inflation since 1974.

costs too much." They are playing a game of chance with the operation's life as well as the public's.

It is difficult to determine the exact costs of a sanitation program for your operation. However, it is relatively easy to identify the potential effects of food contamination and spoilage on the bottom line if your business is implicated in a foodborne disease outbreak.

First, when the news media learns of the outbreak, they will spread the word. Since you have endangered the public, the news media must inform the public that the illness they may be experiencing might be a result of eating in your establishment. This news will damage your hard-earned reputation and that of your business. The deterioration of public confidence in your operation may be devastating to your business. The loss of customers which is sure to follow an outbreak of foodborne disease may force your business to close its doors forever.

Even if your operation remains in business, however, the results of the outbreak will only compound your problems. Employees may ask themselves, "Who wants to work for a company that has been implicated in a foodborne disease outbreak?" As employee morale dips to new lows, absenteeism rates may skyrocket. Being short of staff will make it even more difficult to rebuild your operation's reputation. Those employees who do report to work will require training to bring their food handling practices up to a safe level.

The objective, of course, of any sanitation program is to avoid these embarrassing situations and crippling costs *before* they occur. The dollars spent to establish and maintain your problem-preventing sanitation management program is money well spent. The costs associated with your sanitation program are simply fixed costs—a type of preventive medicine—which help you and your establishment stay in business.

Cleanliness— The Customer Expects It and Deserves It

Several years ago, the National Restaurant Association conducted an attitude survey among customers in three types of restaurants: quick service, moderate service, and full service. These customers were asked to rank various characteristics according to their importance in selecting a restaurant. The results of the study are shown in Exhibit 1.2. In all three types of restaurants, the same two factors were considered most important: cleanliness and food quality/preparation. Any business that wants to succeed has to meet or exceed the expectations of its customers. Clearly, sanitation management is an essential part of the operation's marketing strategy.

Naturally, customers expect all the meals served in restaurants and hotels to be safe and sanitary. But even more important, they have a *right* to expect food which is fit for human consumption. The customer also assumes that hospitality operations are regularly inspected by health officials and that these establishments are in compliance with local, state, and federal ordinances. If deficiencies are discovered during inspections, the customer has the right to believe that corrective action has been taken by management. Sanitation management is important to preserving the public trust in food service and lodging establishments. An effective sanitation management program helps keep customers satisfied. Thus, it

**Exhibit 1.2 Consumer Reactions Toward Restaurant Practices/
Responsibilities: Characteristics Important in
Choosing a Restaurant**

Rank Order	Type of Restaurant		
	Quick Service	Moderate Service	Full Service
1	Cleanliness	Cleanliness	Food quality/ preparation
2	Food quality/ preparation	Food quality/ preparation	Cleanliness
3	Price	Menu variety	Menu variety
4	Location	Price	Courtesy/ friendliness
5	Courtesy/ friendliness	Courtesy/ friendliness	Type of atmosphere
6	Speed of service	Speed of service	Price
7	Menu variety	Location	Nutrition of meals
8	Nutrition of meals	Nutrition of meals	Location
9	Type of atmosphere	Type of atmosphere	Speed of service
10	Choice of portion sizes	Choice of portion sizes	Individual preparation of meals
11	Individual preparation of meals	Individual preparation of meals	Choice of portion sizes
12	No-smoking section	No-smoking section	Reservations
13	Reservations	Reservations	Liquor
14	Liquor	Liquor	No-smoking

Source: Sanitation Operations Manual. *Chicago, Ill.: National Restaurant Association, 1979.*

has the potential to build business, enhance the operation's competitive position, and strengthen its market share.

Sanitation— The Competitive Edge

Competition in food service and lodging markets is severe these days. Every property wants a competitive edge. In many cases, having the necessary information and using it effectively can give the manager the desired advantage. With added knowledge, the resources under the control of the manager can be used more efficiently and effectively.

The more you know about the industry, the better you will be able to surpass your competition. More knowledge will permit you to better satisfy your customers' needs and desires. The more satisfied your customers are, the more money both you (as a manager, supervisor, or employee) and your business will make. And you will have the satisfaction of making this money in an honorable and professional manner.

The information in this book will permit you to be a better competitor. It will provide you with an advantage by showing you how to run a cleaner and safer establishment. By operating your establishment according to the principles in this book, you will save money, increase your customers' satisfaction, and increase the likelihood of your operation's success.

Summary

Success is the reward of those companies which achieve excellence. Basically, the excellent companies are committed to key values but are flexible and adaptable to change in other areas. The success equation spells out factors which produce excellence in food service and lodging businesses.

Megatrends help predict the directions in which society is moving. Food service and lodging operations that are aware of current trends can use them to their advantage now and in the future.

Quality can mean many things to many people. Quality must be judged according to the standards for a product. Within the context of food service and lodging, the excellent operations are those that provide a consistent quality level based on the needs and desires of their target markets.

Sanitation management is an essential cost of doing business in the hospitality industry. The economic effects of a foodborne disease outbreak can be devastating on a food service operation. Although it may be difficult to state the value of a sanitation program in dollars and cents, it is relatively easy to see the effects of spoilage and contamination on the bottom line of any business that lacks such a program. It is management's responsibility to establish and monitor the sanitation program. The public has a right to expect safe, sanitary food whenever they dine in a food service or lodging establishment.

References

Busta, F. F. "Food Protection for the 80's." *Journal of Food Protection*, July 1979. 42(7):596-598.

Cichy, Ronald F. "Lifestyle Trends Affect Foodservice." *The Concessionaire*, July 1982. 23(7):1.

Food and Drug Administration, Public Health Service, U.S. Department of Health, Education, and Welfare. *Food Service Sanitation Manual*. Washington, D.C.: U.S. Government Printing Office, 1976.

The Future: A Guide to Information Sources. Washington, D.C.: World Future Society, 1982.

Kolb, P. M. "Focus on Sanitation." *Restaurant Business*. 1 December 1978. 77(13):100.

Minor, Lewis J., and Cichy, Ronald F. *Foodservice Systems Management*. Westport, Conn.: AVI, 1984.

Naisbitt, John. *Megatrends*. New York: Warner Books, Inc., 1982.

National Restaurant Association. *NRA News*, December 1982. 2(11):9-20.

Peters, Thomas J., and Waterman, Robert H., Jr. *In Search of Excellence*. New York: Harper & Row, 1982.

Roy, C. A. "Milk and Foodservice Programs: Taking Stock as We Enter the 80's." *Dairy and Food Sanitation*, May 1981. 1(5):184-187.

Sanitation Operations Manual. Chicago, Ill.: Public Health and Safety Department, National Restaurant Association, 1979.

"Sanitation and Safety Update." *Restaurant Business*, 1 December 1979. 78(15):125.

"Sanitation — What It Is and Isn't." *Food Service Marketing*, September 1976. 38(9):66.

Strategies for Success at the Aspen Hotel

"Paul," the supervisor began, "we in the corporate office have been impressed with your track record since you joined our company almost five years ago. We believe that you are committed to excellence and look to tomorrow, not yesterday. Your property's operating results and your performance reviews have consistently been above average."

Paul nodded and said, "I enjoy the freedom I have to make decisions as a GM with this hotel management company."

The supervisor continued, "We appreciate your take-action attitude, Paul. That component of your personality will be even more important in your next assignment with our company."

"Next assignment!" Paul thought. "So that's why he's here in person."

After a momentary pause, Paul's supervisor began to describe what the position would entail. "The Mountain States Hotel Management Company has recently acquired a majority interest in a 225-room suburban hotel. We are taking over as the managing partners. The Aspen Hotel was built and expanded over the last 20 years. Most of the rooms business comes from transient guests. There doesn't appear to be a major problem with room sales; the hotel was running a 72% occupancy before we purchased it.

"The main dining room seats 200, the coffee shop seats 72, and the lounge has 50 seats. The property has four meeting rooms and a medium-sized banquet facility. The hotel's outdoor pool area has doubled as a banquet area for special functions, and there is a barbecue area outdoors near the pool. Many of the department supervisors and key employees have been with the hotel over ten years.

"We believe that you are the best person for the GM's job at this property, Paul. Our company believes that a guest can quickly identify a great hotel through an outstanding food and beverage experience. As you know, the complexity of food and beverage is so great today that it takes a GM who understands its dimensions to make it work. Your extensive food and beverage background will be one of the keys to your success. What do you think, Paul? Are you ready for this new challenge?"

Paul thought about the offer for a moment. It would mean relocating and starting to build all over again to make the property a success. "I accept," said Paul. "When does this new assignment begin?"

The supervisor replied, "The hotel is scheduled to reopen in ten weeks. We would like to have you on-site in three weeks. That should give you enough time to tie up any loose ends here." Paul's supervisor stood up, shook hands with Paul, and then left for the airport.

"What a challenge!" Paul thought. "A 20-year-old hotel with complete food and beverage facilities." Paul thought of the complexities of a GM's responsibilities in a hotel. "There are millions of details to attend to, and all of these details affect each other. If one detail is off-balance or substandard, the guest's experience can be ruined. But this will be a good learning experience and a wise career move."

TWO

Food Service Systems and Management Resources

Strategies for Success at the Aspen Hotel

Paul James, the new general manager, arrived at the Aspen Hotel without fanfare. When Paul spotted the hotel from the main highway, he thought to himself, "A building is just a building. It takes a staff and a plan to make the building a successful hotel."

The first person that Paul met on his way into the Aspen Hotel was Terri Martin, his executive secretary. Terri told Paul that a number of important telephone messages and letters were waiting for him on the desk in his office. She directed Paul to his office and said that she would check back with him after she returned from lunch. Paul promptly began looking through the letters and telephone messages. One note, marked **"urgent,"** caught his attention immediately. The message simply said, "Call your supervisor as soon as possible."

Upon telephoning his supervisor, Paul was informed that the local health department had refused to transfer the license to operate his hotel's food and beverage facilities to the Mountain States Hotel Management Company. The health department said it would issue the license to operate only if major deficiencies were first corrected. Paul's supervisor asked him to contact the local health department and request a meeting.

The GM called the health department and set up a meeting for the following morning. Paul left his office and took a tour of the property. He noticed that the kitchen facilities were in terrible shape. The lounge and dining room facilities were not much better. Paul knew that the property had been gradually expanded, piece-by-piece, over the 20 years since it was first built. He had also learned that the person who owned the hotel for the last five years had his own construction company. Paul suddenly realized why the hotel was in such bad shape: the former owner had made numerous property additions and renovations without health department approval.

As he made his tour of the facility, Paul tried to look at the property from the standpoint of the customer. He thought, "Customers look for cleanliness and sanitation when they eat out. They expect it. If their first impression of our hotel is bad, we will be fighting an uphill battle to gain the customers' confidence from then on. Right now it looks like this hotel is at the bottom of the hill. And it's going to be a real challenge to reach the top of the hill."

In addition to understanding success, future trends, quality, and the role of sanitation, hospitality industry managers must understand the food service system. In this chapter, four types of food service systems and the ten components of a typical system will be briefly described. Examples of different approaches to the ten control points will be given. Next, four resources under the influence of managers will be presented and discussed in relation to the ten control points. Then the responsibilities of managers will be reviewed. Finally, the Food and Drug Adminis-

Exhibit 2.1   A Classification of Food Service Systems

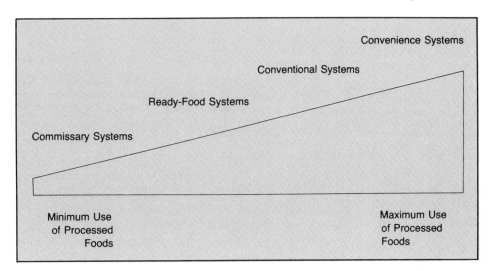

tration's (FDA's) food service sanitation ordinance for facilities in the United States will be introduced.

Food Service Systems

Food service systems may be classified according to a number of variables including food product flow, personnel requirements, management control areas, and the number of menu items.[1] One such classification places the four food service systems on a continuum according to the degree to which they use processed foods. Although this arrangement of the four systems (illustrated in Exhibit 2.1) tends to oversimplify reality in that it fails to suggest that more than one system can be used in the same establishment, it is, nevertheless, a useful generalization.

Commissary Systems   A commissary is a central production facility where food products are purchased, received, stored, initially processed, and stored again for later distribution to restaurants. Commissary systems attempt to gain economies of scale by concentrating most of the production activities in one location. This saves times, money, and space. The individual restaurant spends less time on basic food preparation. Centralized production facilities can purchase raw ingredients in large quantities and, thus, achieve a lower per-unit price. Expensive specialized equipment can be used efficiently in a commissary system, so production equipment and space required at the individual restaurant is reduced.

The other resources of the business (personnel, inventory, and facilities) are also more efficiently used. However, proper food distribution to

---

[1] Details regarding food service systems are beyond the scope of this book. Interested readers should refer to Lewis J. Minor, and Ronald F. Cichy, *Foodservice Systems Management*, Westport, Conn.: (AVI, 1984).

individual units is crucial to the success of this system. Timing is important, and food temperatures must be carefully monitored. Today several large food service and lodging operations with multiple units are utilizing commissary systems successfully.

Ready-Food Systems

Ready-food systems use more processed foods than commissary systems. Cook-chill and cook-freeze systems are examples of ready-food concepts. Food production takes place in the individual food service operation, frequently in large batches. However, it is often necessary to modify the recipes of some food products, such as sauces, meats, and baked products, so they will withstand the freezing and thawing cycles. Finished food products are packaged in containers and either frozen or chilled. Immediately prior to service, the menu items are reheated in their containers.

Ready-food systems can be thought of as an on-premises convenience food system. As with commissary systems, economies of scale are achieved because the establishment's resources can be effectively utilized. Large hospitals and health care institutions can offer a wide selection of menu items to customers by using ready-food systems.

Conventional Systems

Conventional systems most closely approximate the traditional approach to food service in that many items are prepared individually to the customer's order. However, today, finished menu items are prepared on the premises from a combination of convenience foods and raw ingredients. Kitchen production areas are filled with traditional equipment, for example ranges, ovens, griddles, and deep-fat fryers. Highly skilled employees may be needed to produce the operation's menu selection. However, the use of processed foods can reduce the number and skill level of employees required in restaurants using conventional systems.

Because all food preparation steps take place on the premises, management time is largely spent in the control of these activities. High quality menu items can be prepared and safely held for serving if holding times and temperatures are regularly monitored. The proper holding of finished food products, either by chilling or heating, is crucial to the success of conventional systems. These systems are used by most large hotels and restaurants.

Convenience Systems

Convenience systems have proliferated due to the acute shortage of highly skilled labor and the high cost of equipment, space, and energy. Processed foods are used wherever possible in this system, so food preparation is greatly simplified. Employees need not be highly skilled since processed foods have "built-in labor." Of course, the initial cost-per-unit (the as-purchased price) is higher because much of the preparation has already been done by the food processing company.

Usually convenience products simply require reheating prior to service. As a result, convenience systems are termed minimal cooking or assembly-serve systems. Currently, processed foods are available in pre-plated, preportioned, and bulk market forms. Hundreds of high-quality convenience products are available today from food distributors. Future technological advances will continue to raise quality levels while providing the food service industry with a greater selection of convenience food products. Fast-food and limited-menu restaurants effectively utilize this type of food service system.

Increasingly, food service operations are utilizing a combination of these four systems to reduce costs and provide the customer with the best value. A systems approach can also be used in managing each of the basic operating activities which constitute a food service system. Overall efficiency and control are improved when the operation is seen as a series of interrelated activities.

Food Service Subsystems

Whether the operation is a freestanding restaurant, an institutional food service operation, or a food service located within a hotel, the basic components of the operation are the same. These subsystem components are called **control points**. The **basic operating activities** or control points which must be addressed by any food service establishment are illustrated in Exhibit 2.2.

At first, these ten components may seem obvious to anyone with experience in food service. However, a closer examination will reveal that each control point is a miniature system with its own recognizable structure and functions. For each subsystem there are specific objectives, guidelines, and internal processes which contribute to the overall success of the operation.

More specifically, when a food service business is seen as a system made up of control point subsystems, the otherwise overwhelming task of sanitation management is kept in perspective. When management views the establishment as a series of control points, the sanitation requirements associated with each function are easier to identify and carry out on a daily basis. This systems approach enables a manager to be proactive instead of reactive. It helps improve coordination between the departments and increases worker productivity. In short, an understanding of food service subsystems points the way to success for food service operations.

The Ten Control Points

The basic operating activities begin with menu planning and end with cleaning and maintenance. Because future chapters will describe each of the ten food service control points in detail, the definitions which follow are intentionally brief.

Menu Planning. Menu planning is the initial control point that demands management's attention. Items selected for inclusion in the menu should be based on the needs and desires of the operation's target markets. The format should reflect the ambience and image of the establishment. A menu is best developed when the nine other control points are understood, because the menu exerts an influence over all of the other control points.

Exhibit 2.2 A Flow Chart of Basic Operating Activities or Control Points in a Food Service System

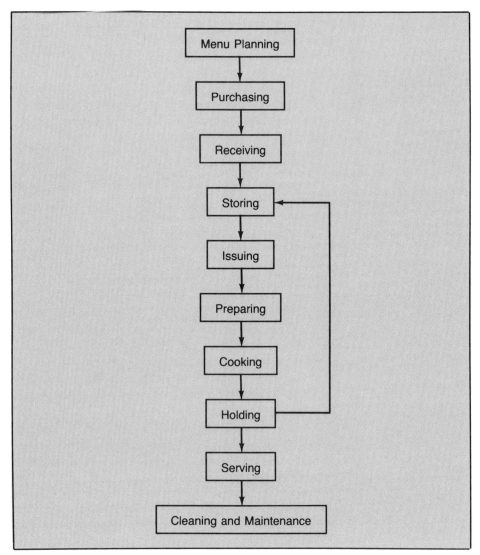

For example, to kitchen employees, the menu provides guidelines on how to purchase, receive, store, issue, prepare, and cook food products. To dining room employees, the menu dictates proper methods for presenting and serving the menu items. The menu also affects, and in some cases, may be affected by, the facility's design and layout, equipment requirements, and labor needs. A properly designed sanitation program must consider the menu as the starting point.

Purchasing. Purchasing is important because a correctly designed purchasing system will maintain value and quality, minimize the investment in inventory, and strengthen the operation's competitive position. As price increases are experienced in key commodities, sound purchasing techniques can protect profits (or contain costs). A viable purchasing subsystem makes the operation's sanitation program easier to manage.

Receiving. Receiving is a critical control point because ownership of the products is transferred from the supplier to the operation. Skillful purchasing, coupled with correct receiving practices, can maximize the benefits of a carefully planned menu. The receiving function involves checking quality, quantity, and price. The result is an accept or reject decision. Once receiving is completed, prompt storage of the food is important.

Storing. Storing is the function of preventing deterioration and theft of valuable food products before they are used by the operation. Food products are assets that must be protected. Contamination, spoilage, theft, and pilferage must be prevented if costs are to be minimized and profits maximized. Standards for storage control are part of the operation's sanitation management program. Different standards apply to the three types of storage areas: dry, refrigerated, and frozen. Most food products do not improve in quality while in storage. Therefore, it is important to know how products should be stored and to use the proper facilities and equipment to keep ingredients and finished menu items in optimal condition.

Issuing. Issuing is the control point where food products are released from storage. The objective of issuing is to ensure that products are only released to the production department with proper authorization. A poorly designed issuing system can adversely affect the facility's sanitation status and jeopardize profits.

Preparing. Preparing is the series of activities that take place before the food product is cooked. Vegetable cleaning and peeling, meat trimming, and assembly of raw ingredients are examples of preparation functions. Some establishments minimize the time spent on preparing by purchasing convenience food products with "built-in labor." Without an adequate sanitation program, food can be exposed to sanitation hazards during preparation.

Cooking. Cooking is the control point where heat is applied to food products. Cooking can significantly alter the color, odor, texture, taste, appearance, and nutrient content of the raw ingredients. Batch cooking in small quantities helps maintain food quality. Food products can be exposed to sanitation hazards during cooking. Implementing a sanitation program can reduce the risks associated with this control point before problems surface.

Holding. Holding is a critical control point, particularly in food service operations where products are prepared well in advance of service. The menu items may be held hot or chilled prior to service. To maintain product quality and reduce sanitation hazards, holding times should be as short as possible. Holding temperatures must also be monitored. As Exhibit 2.2 shows, unused products may be returned to storage for service at some future time.

Serving. Serving involves physically transferring finished menu items from the production department to the consumer. This control point should be designed to deliver quality products to the customer with speed and efficiency. A comprehensive sanitation program is necessary to reduce sanitation risks associated with serving and to maximize customer satisfaction.

Cleaning and Maintenance. Although cleaning and maintenance is the last control point listed on the flow chart, it is far from being the least important function. In fact, cleanliness is intimately related to every other basic operating activity. Focusing on sanitation in every subsystem enhances the operation's cost control system, long-term survival, and success. Today's customer demands cleanliness, so an effective program of sanitation management makes good business sense.

The ten control points or basic operating activities are the foundation of any food service establishment. Each point must be addressed in all food service operations and in all segments of the industry (commercial, institutional, and military). Of course, the particular standards and operating procedures will be different for various types of food service establishments.

Approaches May Vary

Consider how the control points might be addressed in a college dormitory versus a hotel food service. The examples presented here do not represent a norm or standard for *all* colleges and hotels.

The manager of the food service unit in Columbine Hall plans the menus on a cyclical or rotational basis, so that items are repeated only once every six to eight weeks. Purchasing simply involves placing an order with the university's central food stores and commissary. Receiving takes place at precisely defined times. Product quality standards have been established already by the director of all campus food service outlets.

Raw ingredient storage in this dormitory food service unit is minimal since deliveries can be arranged on a daily basis. Issuing is only permitted with a preauthorized requisition. Preparation of most fruits and vegetables takes place in the central commissary. Peeled and cut fruits and vegetables are purchased directly from food stores. All meat is cut into portions, placed in plastic bags, vacuum-sealed, and stored in the central processing plant.

Large batch cooking is necessary for Columbine Hall to serve 1,800 meals each day. Hot food items are held in mobile hot-holding carts and steam tables. Cold items are held prior to service in a number of reach-in and walk-in refrigerators. Service is largely cafeteria style (self-service). Students may return for as many portions as they desire. Cleaning and maintenance are routinely performed as part of a detailed sanitation program. Columbine Hall's food service unit is inspected once each week by the university's sanitarians.

By contrast, the Arbor Hotel belongs to a small regional chain of nine hotels. This hotel operates several food service outlets, each with its own unique identity. Menu planning is extensive and challenging, due to the number of food service outlets in the hotel. Food and beverage merchandising is necessary to appeal to local target markets as well as in-house guests. Daily specials, room service, banquets, and special functions add to the complexity of the menu-planning function.

The Arbor Hotel's food service has a number of suppliers for each of the key commodities. The frequency of raw ingredient purchases is governed by the hotel's level of business. Receiving is complex because many suppliers are making deliveries. A large share of the physical facility is allocated to storage of raw ingredients because suppliers only deliver twice each week. Issuing is extremely complex because the hotel has a coffee/snack shop, main dining room, meeting rooms, and banquet facilities with a separate banquet kitchen.

The Arbor Hotel has no commissary or centralized food processing facility to prepare raw ingredients. Most preparation is done on the premises; for example, wholesale cuts of meat are purchased and cut in-house to meet the firm's specifications. Cooking takes place in a variety of locations. Standards for preparation and cooking are complex. Many menu items are held for later service. They cannot be cooked to order during intense rush periods or for banquets and special functions.

Standards of service vary according to the identity and image of the food service outlet. Cleaning and maintenance are not standardized because the outlets are so different. Public health department sanitarians inspect the Arbor Hotel's food service outlets every three to six months.

As these two examples illustrate, food service establishments deal with the same control points, but they do so according to their individual needs. Control of each function results in consistency, and consistency is the key to quality in any food service or lodging operation. By controlling the operation's resources, managers can achieve success.

Resources Under a Manager's Control

Managers in lodging and food service businesses have four basic resources under their control. As Exhibit 2.3 shows, these resources are personnel, inventory, facilities, and equipment. The control of these resources permits managers to make the most of their expenditures in these four areas. An effective sanitation program must address all four of these resources.

Personnel   Because the hospitality industry is labor intensive—that is, reliant on large numbers of employees—**personnel** is a key resource. It is management's responsibility to hire sanitation-conscious employees. Otherwise, the effectiveness of the establishment's entire sanitation program can be jeopardized. Some managers of food service businesses are unwilling to train their employees in proper sanitation practices. They believe that training is an unnecessary expense, particularly when they hire employees with "experience." By failing to control the operation's most important resource—people—they are endangering the public and compromising the establishment's bottom line.

Actually, a food service operation cannot afford *not* to train. Em-

Exhibit 2.3 The Resources Under a Manager's Control

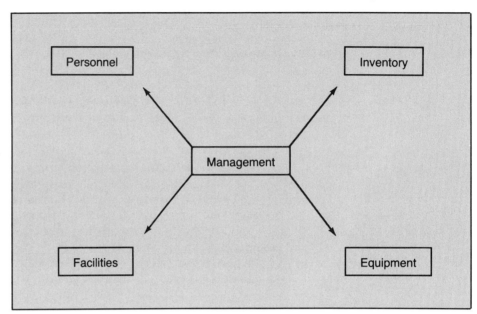

ployees trained in proper sanitation practices can increase customer satisfaction levels. Employee morale and productivity levels may also improve as they become more sanitation-conscious. Teaching employees to carry out the operation's sanitation program improves their personal hygiene practices and tends to decrease employee sick days. A well-designed sanitation program may even reduce the operation's insurance premiums.

Training employees to be sanitation-conscious pays off in other ways, too. Teaching employees how to keep equipment and facilities clean increases the useful life of equipment and slows the deterioration of walls, ceilings, and floors. Their knowledge and use of proper food handling and storage techniques can decrease the operation's food cost because spoilage organisms will be under control. In addition, sanitation training decreases the probability of bad publicity and lost business from a foodborne illness outbreak.

Obviously, the cost of sanitation training is far outweighed by its advantages. However, just training once when a new employee is hired is not enough. Management must train and retrain all food service and maintenance employees to ensure that the proper techniques remain fresh in their minds. Thorough initial training (followed by frequent reminders) results in consistent sanitation excellence. Such consistency enhances the establishment's image and increases customer satisfaction.

Inventory

Inventory is an essential management resource because it is converted into revenue and, ultimately, into profits. Inventory in a food service operation normally consists of food products, beverage products, and nonfood items (linens, cleaning and sanitizing chemicals, etc.). Inventory in a lodging property with one or more food service outlets includes these same items plus guestroom linens and supplies.

Inventory control is a vital link in the facility's total cost control system. Inventory items are assets and these assets must be protected from spoilage, contamination, pilferage, and waste. Inventory is an investment which does not appreciate. In fact, most food products, including frozen items, decrease in volume and quality if stored too long. If storage areas are inadequate to handle a large inventory, the percentage of food lost to spoilage increases. Also, excessive stockpiling of food encourages contamination.

The potential for pilferage increases in direct proportion to the dollar amount of products in stock. When employees see a large inventory, they may rationalize petty thefts on the basis that one less item will not be noticed. Furthermore, a large inventory invites waste. Production employees who know that there is a huge supply to work with are likely to be more careless when using the food products in recipe preparation.

Amassing huge inventories in inadequate storage areas requires more payroll dollars since employees are forced to handle and rehandle the products. Moreover, inventory is more difficult to record in overstocked freezers, refrigerators, and dry storage areas. Excessive inventories can tie up the operation's money for unnecessarily long periods of time.

Inventory control and storage will be discussed in more detail in Chapter 7, which focuses on the receiving, storing, and issuing control points. At this point, however, it is clear that inventory is an important resource which must be protected by the establishment's sanitation program.

Facilities   The third resource under a manager's control is the **facilities** of the business. Often these capital assets require a greater investment than any other resource of the business. However, the facilities can help to attract customers and build the business. To guarantee that safe food is delivered to customers, preventive sanitation features must be carefully designed into the operation's physical facilities. The objective is to design an environment that can be kept both safe and sanitary. With the proper facilities design, food products can be received, stored, prepared, and served in a sanitary manner. Facilities which lack proper sanitation features can be redesigned to make them easier to clean and maintain.

Floor, wall, and ceiling construction affects the establishment's ability to maintain a clean and safe environment. Fundamentally, floors, walls, and ceilings must be nontoxic and able to withstand normal abuse. Lighting levels have an impact on both safety and sanitation. Specific ventilation requirements are dictated by building codes. Both the interior and the exterior of the facilities help develop an impression and expectation level in the minds of its customers.

The water supply, plumbing, and sewage facilities influence the sanitary operation of the business. Garbage and refuse removal is essential. Insect and rodent control is important because these disease-carrying pests can contaminate food, equipment, and utensils.

The facilities resource often represents a major investment for the establishment but, because the physical structure and layout have an impact on the success of the operation's sanitation program, proper design and construction are worthwhile investments. Designing facilities for better sanitation and safety is a protection to employees and customers alike.

Equipment   The food service establishment's equipment represents another substantial investment in capital assets. Like the operation's facilities, its equipment is used to produce income. Food service equipment may be classified into four general categories: equipment that adds heat, equipment that removes heat, equipment that changes the form of food, and equipment that cleans and sanitizes. Fundamentally, a food service facility's equipment needs are governed by its menu. Basing equipment needs on the menu prevents the business from purchasing equipment that will never be used or will be used only infrequently. It also helps to ensure that the capacity of the equipment selected will be sufficient to produce all the menu items.

Most food service operations select equipment which provides flexibility and versatility. This reduces the operation's costs for additional equipment when the menu is expanded or modified. Flexible food service equipment is adaptable to the establishment's changing needs. If menu items are modified, flexible equipment can be adjusted to accommodate the modifications. An example of flexible equipment is a high-pressure steamer. Versatile equipment adds to the operation's flexibility because it can be used to prepare a variety of menu items. An example of versatile equipment is a tilting braising skillet.

In addition to menu and cost considerations, capacity, maintenance, compatibility, durability, safety, and cleanability must be considered. The capacity of the equipment is important in terms of both initial costs and operating costs. The establishment may decide to buy equipment with a larger capacity than immediate needs dictate in order to allow for growth. Alternatively, a smaller capacity may be specified at first with additional equipment being purchased as demand increases.

The availability of repair services affects the choice of equipment. If the service is available locally, the purchase is more desirable, since most food service operations do not have qualified equipment maintenance people on their full-time staff.

Management must also determine if the planned purchase is compatible with other equipment in the kitchen in terms of utility requirements, size, and appearance. Generally, the establishment need only specify the desired characteristics to sales representatives in order to be presented with a range of alternatives to choose from. Properly selected equipment will also blend with the skill level of the facility's personnel. Employees must be able to use the equipment correctly if it is to increase the productivity of the operation's staff.

Because equipment is a major investment, it should be durable. While commercial equipment is more expensive than corresponding home appliances, it is designed to withstand the rigors and potential abuses of a quantity food production kitchen.

In addition, the equipment should not add any safety hazards. Managers who are considering a purchase of equipment should ask about possible risks of using the equipment and how to avoid them. Built-in safety features should also be known, since these can prevent injuries and insurance claims.

Finally, equipment must be selected based on how easy it is to clean and maintain. Careful consideration of the materials and design of equipment is an important part of the operation's sanitation management program. The manufacturer's recommendations for the cleaning and maintenance of the equipment should be considered during the selection process. These concerns are equally valid for utensils used in a food service business. Therefore, references to equipment should be understood to include utensils. Cleaning and maintaining the equipment protects the establishment's assets and contributes to a sanitary food service environment.

The FDA's Food Service Sanitation Ordinance states:

Equipment means stoves, ovens, ranges, hoods, slicers, mixers, meatblocks, tables, counters, refrigerators, sinks, dishwashing machines, steam tables, and similar items other than utensils, used in the operation of a food service establishment.

Utensil means any implement used in the storage, preparation, transportation, or service of food.

Source: Food and Drug Administration, Public Health Service, U.S. Department of Health, Education, and Welfare, Food Service Sanitation Manual, *1976, pp. 21-22.*

A Model for Success

By now it is clear that the management of a food service or lodging business can be made easier: (1) by viewing the food service system as a series of interrelated control points and (2) by organizing the resources under the manager's control. Managers who can see the basic operating activities underlying the complexities of day-to-day operations are on the road to success. Managers who know how to control and direct resources for maximum results are also likely to succeed. And those who grasp the interrelationship of their control points and resources have a model for success. The model for success in Exhibit 2.4 shows the resources under a manager's influence in combination with the basic operating activities in a food service operation.

Notice that the menu-planning control point is listed at the base of the model because it is fundamental; all of the other control points build on and relate to menu planning. Also, the control points and resources are interrelated. That is, each control point affects and is affected by each of the resources.

Finally, the shape of the model for success indicates the results of

Exhibit 2.4   A Model for Success

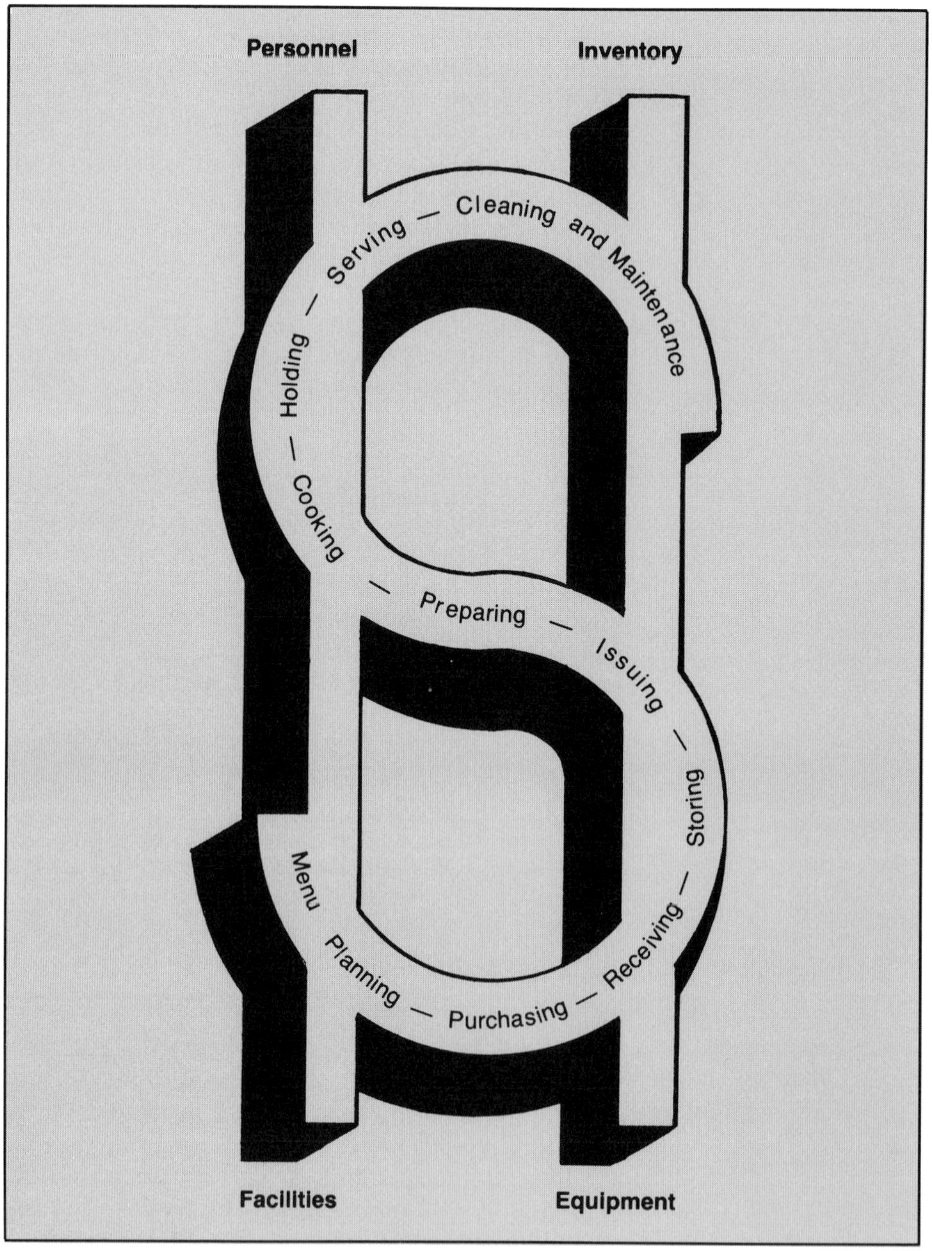

using the model. It is shaped like a dollar sign because the elements that form it all contribute to the operation's financial well-being. Successful food service and lodging establishments naturally generate more revenue and profits for employees, managers, and investors because these operations emphasize cost control, quality control, sanitation, and safety.

To achieve success managers must perform many functions, each of which can be related to the operation's sanitation program.

Management Responsibilities

Ultimately, the responsibility for the success of a sanitation program rests with the management and employees of the business. As more consumers eat out more frequently and the food service industry's annual sales figures continue to grow, the responsibilities of the industry as a whole and of its managers, in particular, continue to expand. Sanitation-related responsibilities enter into a manager's performance of the traditional management functions: planning, organizing, staffing, directing, controlling, evaluating, and leading and motivating.

Planning. Planning is essential to minimize crises and keep things running smoothly. Both short-range and long-range objectives are established during planning. From the standpoint of sanitation management, the goals should include preventing a foodborne disease outbreak. In case an outbreak should occur, the operation should have a plan—a series of procedures—for handling the outbreak. Additionally, management must reduce the risks of food spoilage.

Organizing. Organizing aligns the operation's resources to achieve the planned objectives. Personnel, facilities, equipment, and inventory resources are arranged so as to maximize effectiveness, efficiency, and productivity. Any sanitation program should take into account all of the relevant resources of the business.

Staffing. Staffing is the next component of the management cycle. Job descriptions help all employees—new and old—to know their responsibilities and to perform their duties satisfactorily. Each employee's job description should clearly define the sanitation responsibilities of his or her position.

Directing. Directing, the assigning of specific tasks to individuals, occurs once plans are formalized, the system is organized, and the staff is hired. Policies, procedures, schedules, and standards are the tools which aid managers in directing employees. Training, an essential ingredient of any sanitation program, is part of the directing function. It is management's responsibility to train every person in the food service operation to be a sanitation-conscious employee.

Controlling. Controlling is enforcing the work performance standards established for each job. The control function of management is achieved through follow-up checks. Once a sanitation program is in place, management uses follow-up checks to ensure that the necessary tasks related to sanitation are being properly performed. Disciplinary actions are associated with the control function because poor performance must be corrected.

Evaluating. Evaluating is comparing overall results with objectives. It involves the identification of system strengths and deficiencies. The evaluation task is likely to result in an altered set of plans with which management can begin again. This management cycle must be an ongoing process in a dynamic food service business. If the sanitation program is evaluated and it is determined that the operation is not meeting its objectives, management must take action. No unsanitary practices should be allowed to prevent the operation from achieving its sanitation program objectives.

Leading and Motivating. Leading and motivating are the traits that separate excellent managers from the others. Successful managers are leaders. They search for people to help them accomplish the goals and objectives of the organization. Leaders have an overriding commitment to a goal which they want to share with the entire organization. They have the ability to take their employees to heights that have never been achieved before. Their leadership is reflected in the way they perform all the traditional management functions. That is, instead of pushing their staff to excel, they excel themselves so that their employees naturally want to follow in their footsteps. Leaders act as role models for their employees, inspiring and motivating them. They give positive reinforcement and praise when they see a supervisor or line worker doing something right. This stimulates the individual's desire to continue doing the job properly.

Leaders also handle discipline in a professional way. When they notice the need for corrective action, they tell the employee specifically what is wrong. They criticize the person's behavior, but never the person. This approach generally effects a change in the employee's behavior; thus, the overall effectiveness of the organization is increased. Leaders are comfortable giving praise and constructive criticism to their employees because leaders are secure in their role.

Leaders have a great desire to see everyone in the company succeed. Winners want to be associated with other winners—with success. Leaders do everything possible to help their people succeed. Leaders realize that their individual success is directly related to the success of their people. They recognize that employees need to excel and be rewarded.

Finally, leaders know how to turn an aggregation of isolated individuals into a unified group. Leaders create a company-wide feeling of "togetherness." Employees of the business feel that they are part of something special—a winning team. Leaders earn the cooperation, involvement, and commitment of everyone in the operation. Naturally, leaders accomplish far more than ordinary managers. Some people believe that a small percentage of us are "born leaders" or are natural leaders, while the rest of us lack this advantage. Actually, everyone has leadership potential; every manager can develop into a leader, given a desire to improve and consistent effort.

You can become more effective in your present position and realize your potential if you remember that you can demonstrate leadership when you perform all the traditional management functions.

1. You can set organizational goals and show by your actions that you are committed to achieving them.

2. You can organize all the resources under your control to achieve the stated objectives.

3. You can select positive, hard-working employees who understand the goals of your company and how they are expected to help achieve them.

4. You can clearly define performance standards for each task required of your employees.

5. You can give positive reinforcement for proper performance and constructive criticism where improvements are needed.

6. You can use a systematic checklist approach to verify that the organization is meeting its goals.

7. You can continually strive to improve the performance of all team members including yourself.

The requirements for success may at first appear overwhelming to aspiring hospitality managers. It is helpful, however, to remember that success is a team effort. Therefore, managers can continually improve their operational results by working with their "partners in success."

Partners in Success

Basically, a lodging or food service operation must keep its customers happy and keep them coming back. Word-of-mouth is the best advertising, but it is the most expensive to obtain and retain. It has been said that the best possible atmosphere for a restaurant is simply "satisfied customers on chairs." Just by their presence they contribute to the reputation of the establishment. Thus, we can say your *satisfied customers are partners in the success of your business.*

Of course, winning managers realize that they cannot please their customers singlehandedly. Therefore, they delegate appropriate levels of authority and responsibility to others in the business. To avoid getting in a rut, these managers constantly experiment with various management styles and select the style that is best for each situation. They set aside enough time to deal with employee problems by counseling their team members and showing they care. Excellent managers realize that they can be sucessful only to the degree that their employees are motivated and productive. Therefore, we can say that your *motivated and productive employees are partners in the success of your business.*

Like partners in any endeavor, customers and employees make certain demands on managers. Sometimes these demands may conflict. For example, servers want more tables and a larger station to increase their tips. Customers want more and better service from the servers. Although it is often difficult, successful managers find ways of balancing employees' wants with customers' expectations. Besides these partners, you have another associate whose help is valuable—the sanitarian.

Winning managers look to the health department sanitarian as an ally, not an adversary. Excellent managers maintain a spotless establishment not simply because the sanitarian expects it, but because it makes good business sense. In the long run, cleanliness will cut food and labor costs and make the operation more prosperous and productive. Finally, the sanitarian can give professional assistance and advice on how to improve the operation's level of sanitation or safety. For these reasons, we can say that *professional sanitarians are partners in the success of your business.*

A Professional Standard

In 1940, the Public Health Service of the United States (which oversees the Food and Drug Administration [FDA] in the Department of Health and Human Services) [2] began publishing an official ordinance and code for the sanitary control of food prepared and served to the public. The ordinance and code were designed to guide state and local health authorities in the performance of their duty to protect the public food supply. These guidelines were developed with the assistance of experts in the public health field and the food service industry.

Since 1940, the ordinance and code have been revised three times to keep them abreast of advances in food technology and changes in the eating habits of the American public, both of which have substantially altered the nature of the food service industry. While the current **Model Food Service Sanitation Ordinance** is not mandatory but rather a recommended set of standards, state and local jurisdictions are encouraged to adopt and implement the ordinance. By incorporating the 1976 recommendations into their regulations and enforcing them, states, counties, municipalities, and health districts are contributing to a higher level of public health throughout the United States.

Of course, food service operators need not wait for health department officials to inspect their operation and recommend improvements. Rather than hurrying to "put out fires" after the sanitarian has discovered problems, a proactive manager wisely prevents fires—that is, recognizes potentially troublesome sanitation practices and corrects them before they threaten the customers' health. The FDA's *Food Service Sanitation Manual* (1976) is designed to inform all food service managers and their employees of what they must do to protect the food they prepare and serve to the public.

Because the FDA's Model Ordinance can help food service businesses be more successful, most of the chapters which follow will include direct references to its contents. To provide an idea of the scope of the FDA's Model Ordinance, a general outline is presented in Exhibit 2.5.

By becoming familiar with the contents of the Model Ordinance, hospitality managers are better able to develop a food service sanitation program tailored to their operation's individual needs. Generally, any

---

[2] Formerly the Department of Health, Education, and Welfare.

Exhibit 2.5 Outline of FDA's Food Service Sanitation Ordinance (1976 Recommendations)

CHAPTER	TOPIC
1	General Provisions
2	Food Care —Food Supplies —Food Protection —Food Storage —Food Preparation —Food Display and Service —Food Transportation
3	Personnel —Employee Health —Personal Cleanliness —Clothing —Employee Practices
4	Equipment and Utensils —Materials —Design and Fabrication —Equipment Installation and Location
5	Cleaning, Sanitization, and Storage of Equipment and Utensils —Equipment and Utensil Cleaning and Sanitization —Equipment and Utensil Storage
6	Sanitary Facilities and Controls —Water Supply —Sewage —Plumbing —Toilet Facilities —Lavatory Facilities —Garbage and Refuse —Insect and Rodent Control
7	Construction and Maintenance of Physical Facilities —Floors —Walls and Ceilings —Cleaning Physical Facilities —Lighting —Ventilation —Dressing Rooms and Locker Areas —Poisonous or Toxic Materials —Premises
8	Mobile Food Units or Pushcarts —Mobile Food Service —Commissary —Servicing Area and Operations
9	Temporary Food Service —Temporary Food Service Establishments
10	Compliance Procedures —Permits, Licenses, and Certificates —Inspections —Examination and Condemnation of Food —Review of Plans —Procedure When Infection is Suspected —Remedies

Source: Food and Drug Administration, Public Health Service, U.S. Department of Health, Education, and Welfare, Food Service Sanitation Manual, *1976, pp. ix-xiv.*

such program is established to protect the health of the customer. Specifically, a food service sanitation program should accomplish the following objectives:

- Protect the food against contamination

- Ensure the soundness of food

- Meet consumer expectations [3]

Any sanitation program which accomplishes these three objectives is likely to strengthen the operation's bottom line. Managers who maintain an effective sanitation program recognize its relationship to their success as well as the potentially disastrous effects of not having such a program. Excellent managers realize that a sanitation program is not a luxury but rather a necessity if they are to remain successful.

Summary

There are four basic food service systems: commissary, ready-food, conventional, and convenience systems. Today, many operations combine two or more of these systems.

A food service operation can be described as a system of ten interrelated control points. The basic operating activities are menu planning, purchasing, receiving, storing, issuing, preparing, cooking, holding, serving, and cleaning and maintenance.

The resources under a manager's control are personnel, facilities, inventory, and equipment. The four resources and ten control points can be integrated into a $-shaped model for success. The dollar sign indicates that the businesses which use the model generate more revenue and profits to benefit investors, employees, and managers.

Managers of food service businesses have the usual management responsibilities: planning, organizing, staffing, directing, controlling, and evaluating. They also have a special responsibility to protect the public health by adhering to the food service sanitation regulations governing their business. Excellent managers are leaders. They join forces with their partners in success: customers, employees, and health department officials. The successful food service operations are those which precisely define the expectations of their target markets and aim to meet or exceed those expectations.

The current FDA Model Food Service Sanitation Ordinance (1976) provides guidelines for the operation of a safe and clean food service establishment by means of an ongoing sanitation program. This model ordinance helps hospitality managers achieve success.

---

[3] Food and Drug Administration, Public Health Service, U.S. Department of Health, Education, and Welfare, *Food Service Sanitation Manual* (Washington, D.C.: U.S. Government Printing Office, 1976), p. 3. (Note: It is even better to exceed customer expectations.)

References

Cichy, Ronald F. "Productivity Pointers to Promote a Profitable Performance." *The Consultant,* Winter 1983. 16(1):35-36.

——."The Ten Commandments of Successful Foodservice Management." *Rocky Mountain Chefs Magazine,* June 1983. 5.

—— "Why Foodservice Firms Fail." *Rocky Mountain Chefs Magazine,* February 1983. 8.

Food and Drug Administration, Public Health Service, U.S. Department of Health, Education, and Welfare. *Food Service Sanitation Manual.* Washington, D.C.: U.S. Government Printing Office, 1976.

Minor, Lewis J. and Cichy, Ronald F. *Foodservice Systems Management.* Westport, Conn.: AVI, 1984.

Strategies for Success at the Aspen Hotel

The GM's meeting with the local health department took place on Tuesday as scheduled. Paul told the health inspector that it was his management company's policy to comply with all local, state, and federal requirements. After reviewing the major sanitation problems at the Aspen Hotel, the health inspector reiterated the health department's position that all major deficiencies would have to be corrected before the license to operate the hotel's food and beverage facilities could be transferred. Paul told the inspector that the health department's cooperation was essential, if the hotel was to reopen on schedule. Before leaving, the inspector gave the GM a copy of the local health code.

Paul thought about the challenge facing him as the new GM. As he mentally reviewed the condition of the basic control points in each food service outlet within the hotel, Paul jotted down the deficiencies identified by the health department at each control point. Next, he thought about the resources under his control: people, inventory, facilities, and equipment. Paul had recently attended a seminar where the speaker had integrated the food service system control points and the manager's resources into a model for success. Paul realized that the hotel invests in its resources, and it is the GM's responsibility to maximize the return on this investment. Paul was a builder at heart. His new challenge was clear: to use his resources to build and strengthen the hotel's competitive position. It was up to Paul James to bring it all together, and he knew just where to start.

He returned to his desk to jot down a few ideas in preparation for his first meeting with the department heads. He wrote: "A hotel's success is enhanced through its sanitation program. A well-designed program results in more money for the property and its employees, greater customer satisfaction, and higher staff motivation and productivity levels. In short, the program gives the hotel a competitive edge."

In light of the poor sanitation conditions, Paul had a hunch the staff was demoralized. He would have to get his people thinking more positively. He would also have to convince them that he was a builder and that he wanted every person in the hotel to be a part of a winning team. Of course, they would believe his actions more than his words. So the process of building morale, as well as building his organization, would take place step-by-step, one day at a time.

Terri Martin returned from lunch and checked with the GM. Paul told his secretary to schedule a department head meeting for 9:00 a.m. on Thursday. Paul had two days to prepare. He wanted to use this meeting to acquaint key staff members with his company's philosophy and his own personal philosophy. He also planned to solicit their suggestions for and commitment to the successful operation of the Aspen Hotel.

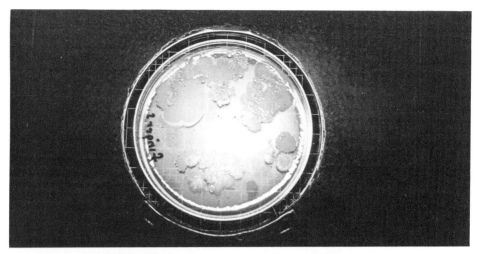

THREE

Food Contamination

Strategies for Success at the Aspen Hotel

To prepare for the department head meeting the next day, Paul James decided to look over some of his college course notes to get some ideas. He mentally reviewed the various subjects he had studied. One class in particular seemed to relate directly to the hotel's noncompliance with local health code requirements. Paul went to his bookshelf and pulled out the notebook on which a younger and far less experienced Paul James had printed "Sanitation Management."

Paul realized that he had not reviewed these notes since college. As he leafed through the pages, some of the material was vaguely familiar. He saw the names of microorganisms that can cause foodborne diseases and food spoilage. He reviewed biological, chemical, and physical sources of food contamination.

One statement concerning the importance of sanitation management stood out from his course notes. It said, "A knowledge of microorganisms is the basis for designing, implementing, and evaluating a food service operation's control system." Paul had underlined that statement in red ink. Paul remembered how the professor who taught this course always emphasized the relationship of sanitation management to cost and quality controls.

Paul was impressed with the way the professor approached the topic of sanitation management from the viewpoint of the customer. The professor had told Paul over ten years ago that, in the hospitality business, the customer's expectations must be met. Paul had never forgotten that the operation's sanitation program has a major impact on customer opinion formation, repeat business, and the public's trust in the establishment and its products.

Food service businesses are responsible for serving safe food to the public. Customers expect food service establishments to provide safe, wholesome food.

The FDA's Food Service Sanitation Ordinance states:

Food means any raw, cooked, or processed edible substance, ice, beverage or ingredient used or intended for use or for sale in whole or in part for human consumption.

*   *   *

Food service establishment means any place where food is prepared and intended for individual portion service, and includes the site at which individual portions are provided. The term includes any such place regardless of whether consumption is on or off the premises and regardless of whether there is a charge for the food. The term also includes delicatessen-type operations that prepare sandwiches intended for individual portion service. The term does not include private homes where food is prepared or served for individual family consumption, retail food stores, the location of food vending machines, and supply vehicles.

Source: Food and Drug Administration, Public Health Service, U.S. Department of Health, Education, and Welfare, Food Service Sanitation Manual, *1976, p. 21.*

Managers of food service businesses can protect the public health, as well as the establishment's reputation and profits, by making sure that all personnel understand the fundamentals of food contamination and how to prevent it. Since much of this chapter concerns microbial contamination, a classification of microorganisms will be presented first. (See Appendix A for a summary of pathogenic microorganisms and their pronunciations.)

Classification of Microorganisms by Effects

A **microorganism** is a small living organism. Other organisms (humans, plants, and animals) are made up of many specialized cells, while microorganisms, for the most part, consist of one cell. Microorganisms are ubiquitous—that is, widely distributed in the environment. They are found on plants, humans, animals, and in the air and soil. In general, microorganisms are flora (plants). Their primary role in nature is self-perpetuation by producing others like themselves. This reproduction requires organic matter which, in many cases, comes from our food supply. **Organic matter** contains the element carbon. Some microorganisms can undergo complex chemical reactions in order to obtain food. Microorganisms can be harmful, beneficial, or inert.

Harmful microorganisms fall into two broad categories: pathogens and spoilage organisms. **Pathogens** are associated with foodborne and waterborne diseases that affect humans, plants, and animals. Pathogens are the source of many types of foodborne diseases described later in this chapter. **Spoilage organisms** do not cause disease but they make food products unusable. These microbes render food products unfit for human consumption by altering their color, odor, texture, taste, and appearance. (The topics of food spoilage and food preservation are covered in Chapter 4.)

Fortunately, not all microorganisms are harmful to other living things. In fact, the majority of microorganisms fall into the beneficial category. **Beneficial microorganisms** offer several advantages to humans and animals. They are used as food for humans or feed for animals, in the production of special nutrients (e.g., vitamins, organic acids), for food fermentations, and as a source of enzymes. Other beneficial microbes are used in the decay of organic matter. Simple, inorganic compounds are produced from complex, organic compounds present in dead animals and plants. The inorganic compounds are then made available for new plant growth. This recycling of inorganic nutrients is called the

Exhibit 3.1 Beneficial Effects of Microorganisms

Dairy Product Production	Vinegar Production
Sausage Production	Fermented Vegetables
Bread Production	Coffee and Tea Production
Cheese Production and Ripening	Soy Sauce Production
Bakery Product Production	Animal Feed Production
Alcoholic Beverage Production	Vitamin Production
Leavening	Antibiotic Production
Enzyme Production	Decay of Organic Matter

nitrogen cycle. A summary of the beneficial effects of microorganisms is presented in Exhibit 3.1.

Inert microorganisms are neither harmful nor beneficial. They have no effect on humans, animals, or plants. Since sanitation management is largely concerned with protecting the public from harmful microorganisms, this classification is explained in much more detail in the next section.

Harmful Microorganisms

Within the broad classification of harmful microorganisms, there are four subcategories: bacteria, parasites, fungi, and viruses. The characteristics, factors affecting reproduction, common food sources, incubation period, resulting symptoms, and techniques for prevention and control of each type of harmful microorganism should be understood by food service managers. In describing these microorganisms, special emphasis will be placed on the largest group: bacteria.

Bacteria

Bacteria are single-celled plants which do not contain the green pigment **chlorophyll**. A single bacterium is extremely small. For example, if 60 *Escherichia coli* cells could be lined up, end-to-end, their length would be approximately the same as the diameter of a human hair. Most bacterial cells are about 1/25,400th of an inch (one micrometer) in size. They can only be individually detected using a microscope with a power of magnification of 1000x or more.

If a large number of bacterial cells are present, the mass or **colony** can be seen with the naked eye. A colony usually numbers more than 10 million cells. Bacteria possess rigid cell walls which give them their characteristic shape. They take in nutrients and expel waste products across

Exhibit 3.2 Microscopic Appearance of Bacterial Cells

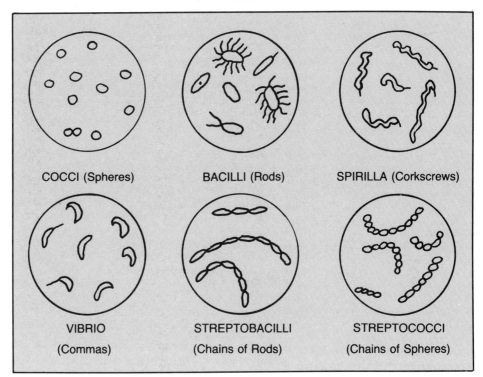

COCCI (Spheres)   BACILLI (Rods)   SPIRILLA (Corkscrews)

VIBRIO   STREPTOBACILLI   STREPTOCOCCI

(Commas)   (Chains of Rods)   (Chains of Spheres)

the cell wall. Various bacterial shapes as seen under a microscope are illustrated in Exhibit 3.2.

Bacteria reproduce asexually. That is, all necessary genetic material for reproduction is present in each growing cell. Only **vegetative** (actively growing) bacterial cells reproduce. Their reproductive process is called **binary fission**, which means splitting in two. The bacterial nucleus splits and the cell divides into two similar vegetative cells. Bacterial growth, therefore, is correctly termed reproduction since the two cells are the same size as the parent cell. The time it takes for one reproductive cycle is called the **generation time**.

Some bacterial cells can assume dormant (inactive) forms called **spores.** Spores are formed only by some bacilli (rod-shaped bacteria). They are produced by vegetative cells subjected to environmental conditions which are adverse or not favorable to the formation of more vegetative cells. However, once conditions again become favorable, the spore can germinate to form a vegetative cell. Bacterial spores are more resistant than vegetative cells to low humidity, high heat, cold temperatures, and chemicals.

Bacterial growth refers to an increase in the number, not the size, of bacterial cells. A theoretical bacterial growth curve is illustrated in Exhibit 3.3. The **lag phase** is the initial growth period. Bacterial activity takes place during the lag phase, but there is no increase in the number of

Exhibit 3.3 Theoretical Bacterial Growth Curve

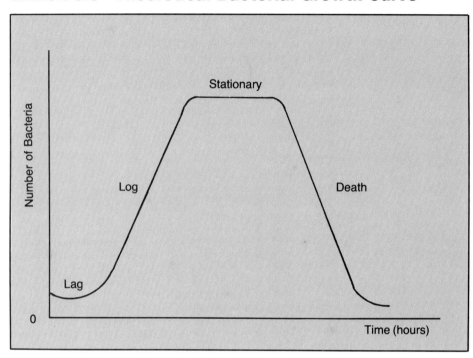

cells. In fact, a decline in total numbers is possible during the lag phase if some organisms fail to adjust to the new environment. The lag phase can be as short as a few minutes or as long as several days, weeks, or months. The objective of low temperature food preservation (e.g., refrigeration and freezing) is to lengthen the lag phase. Also, when food products are canned, frozen, chilled, dried, or irradiated, or preservatives are added, the length of the lag phase is extended.

Once the lag phase has been completed, the bacterial cells have adjusted to their new environment and rapid growth takes place. The **log phase** is the second stage of bacterial growth. Bacterial generation time is shortest during this stage. The number of cells increases geometrically. If the number of cells is plotted against time, a straight line progression results. That is, the bacterial population grows at an increasing rate. Most new cell reproduction takes place during the log phase, which may last 15 to 40 minutes. Some bacteria have a generation time of even less than 15 minutes. Time periods vary with the size of the initial colony, the age of the cells, and the general environmental conditions.

The third stage of bacterial growth is called the **stationary phase**. In this stage, the number of new bacterial cells equals the number of dying cells so there is no *net* increase in the bacterial population. Therefore, the total number of cells remains constant. The length of the stationary phase depends on the reduction in nutrients available to the microbes, the amount of accumulated waste products, and the specific type of microorganisms present.

Once bacterial growth in food products reaches the stationary phase, the food products are generally unacceptable in terms of appearance, odor, taste, texture, and color. An exception to this is fermented foods, such as olives and pickles. Also, during slow roasting at relatively low temperatures, bacterial growth follows a normal curve but the food is not unpalatable at any time.

The **death phase** is signaled by a reduction in the total number of bacteria present. When the number of cells is plotted against time, the result is again a straight line. That is, during this stage, the population declines at a rapid rate. However, when no effort is made to completely destroy the bacteria, the death rate eventually levels off and a number of organisms survive to begin the cycle again.

The bacterial growth curve presented in Exhibit 3.3 is a theoretical illustration. Under actual conditions, the curve may look slightly different. (Some factors affecting bacterial reproduction are presented in the next section.) Nevertheless, the theoretical growth curve illustrates the basic principles of bacterial growth. It helps us understand events which we are unable to directly observe. By understanding how bacterial reproduction occurs in theory, we can apply these principles to the construction of a program for controlling bacteria. It is important to remember that any method used to destroy bacteria will not accomplish the destruction instantaneously. Just as it takes time for bacteria to reproduce, it also takes time to kill bacteria or effectively reduce their numbers.

To illustrate what can happen when bacteria are not properly destroyed, let's assume a bacterial cell has a generation time of 30 minutes under ideal conditions. Starting with one cell at time zero, over 280 trillion cells would be present at the end of 24 hours. Exhibit 3.4 illustrates this phenomenal growth. Of course, in reality, it would be unusual to find one cell existing alone; therefore, increases would normally occur at a much faster rate. To put it another way, assume you could work for an employer at the rate of $1.00 for the first day, $2.00 for the second, $4.00 for the third, $8.00 for the fourth, and so on. You might be amazed to find that on the twentieth working day, you would have accumulated earnings of $1,048,575!

Factors Affecting Bacterial Reproduction. Environmental conditions influence the rate of bacterial reproduction. Different types of bacteria can vary in their required environmental conditions from simple to complex. Food products also vary in the degree to which they provide favorable conditions for bacterial growth. The most important conditions involve moisture, oxygen, the level of acidity, time, and temperature.

Moisture. Moisture must be present in a form usable by bacteria. The amount of available water in an environment is expressed as its **water activity** value or a_w. The water activity value is simply the ratio of the water vapor pressure in the food to the vapor pressure of pure water at the same temperature. The a_w of pure water is 1.0. In general, bacteria prefer an a_w greater than 0.85.

The amount of available water in a food product can be reduced in several ways. First, water may be physically removed by drying. Food products which have been dried generally last longer than they would in their original moist state because they have a reduced a_w. Second, when

Exhibit 3.4   Growth Rate of Bacteria Under Ideal Conditions

Number of Organisms	Time	
	in Minutes	in Hours
1	0	0
2	30	0.5
4	60	1
8	90	1.5
16	120	2
64	180	3
256	240	4
1,024	300	5
4,096	360	6
65,536	480	8
1,048,576	600	10
1,073,700,000	900	15
1,099,500,000,000	1,200	20
281,470,000,000,000	1,440	24

food is frozen, water is unavailable to bacteria because the water has changed to a solid form. Bacteria cannot use water unless it is liquid. Finally, adding sugar or salt to food also binds water and reduces the a_w.

Oxygen. Oxygen requirements vary based on the species of bacterium. **Aerobic** organisms require free oxygen. **Anaerobic** microbes grow best in the absence of oxygen. **Facultative** organisms reproduce either with or without free oxygen. Bacteria can be either aerobic, anaerobic, or facultative.

Acidity or alkalinity. The degree of acidity or alkalinity of a food is important to bacterial activity. The standard measure of acidity or alkalinity is **pH**. As Exhibit 3.5 illustrates, the pH scale has values from 0 to 14. Values less than 7 are acidic, while values greater than 7 are basic or alkaline. A pH of 7 is considered neutral.

In general, bacteria reproduce best in food products with a pH above 4.6. These products are termed **potentially hazardous foods**. Natural food products (e.g., fresh fruits) and fermented foods (e.g., pickles, cheese, fermented sausages) have a pH low enough to halt the activity of most pathogenic bacteria. Exhibit 3.6 shows the pH values of several common foods.

The FDA's Food Service Sanitation Ordinance states:

Potentially hazardous food means any food that consists in whole or in part of milk or milk products, eggs, meat, poultry, fish, shellfish, edible crustacea, or other ingredients, including synthetic ingredients, in a form capable of supporting rapid and progressive

Exhibit 3.5 The pH Scale and Some Representative Foods

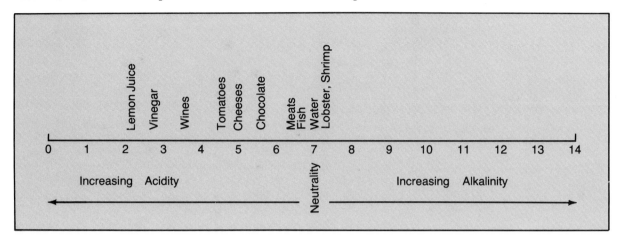

growth of infectious or toxigenic microorganisms. The term does not include clean, whole, uncracked, odor-free shell eggs or foods which have a pH level of 4.6 or below or a water activity (a_w) value of 0.85 or less.

Source: Food and Drug Administration, Public Health Service, U.S. Department of Health, Education, and Welfare, Food Service Sanitation Manual, *1976, pp. 21- 22.*

Time and temperature. Time and temperature requirements are interrelated. Fluctuating temperatures are hazardous to food products because they may favor food spoilage and/or the proliferation of foodborne illness microbes. Microorganisms may be classified by the temperature conditions in which they thrive. **Psychrophiles** are the cold-loving microorganisms. They survive at temperatures as low as -19° F (-28° C) and can reproduce at temperatures as high as 68°F (20°C). **Mesophiles** are microbes which prefer intermediate temperatures, generally from 68°F (20°C) to 113°F (45°C). **Thermophiles** are the heat-loving organisms which prefer temperatures in the range of 113°F (45°C) to 140°F (60°C) and sometimes higher. Most pathogenic bacteria are mesophiles, so they thrive at normal room temperatures.

The temperature at which raw ingredients are stored influences later bacterial activity. Since most pathogens prefer intermediate temperatures, contact with such temperatures must be kept to a minimum. The U.S. Public Health Service has defined the temperature range of 45°F (7°C) to 140°F (60°C) as the **temperature danger zone (TDZ)**. Most pathogenic activity takes place in this range of temperatures. When storing, preparing, or serving food products, care should be taken to minimize the amount of time the food spends in the TDZ.

Besides the factors already mentioned, bacterial growth is affected by the characteristics of the species, the initial population size, and competition from other organisms in the environment. In any case, sanitiza-

Exhibit 3.6 Approximate pH of Some Common Foods

Food	pH Range
Apples	2.9-3.3
Bananas	5.0-5.3
Beers	4.0-5.0
Bread	5.3-5.7
Cheese, Cheddar and American	4.9-5.0
Chocolate	5.2-6.0
Cocoa, Dutch Process	6.0-8.8
Eggs	
Whole	7.5-8.2
White	8.6-9.0
Yolk	6.4-6.9
Fish, Cooked	6.0-6.9
Grapes	2.8-3.8
Lemon Juice	2.2-2.4
Lobster or Shrimp, Cooked	7.1-7.3
Meat, Cooked	5.6-7.0
Milk	6.3-6.8
Oranges	3.6-4.3
Pickles, Dill	3.2-3.5
Sauerkraut, Cooked	3.3-3.5
Strawberries	3.1-3.5
Tomatoes	4.0-4.5
Vinegar	2.4-3.4
Water, Distilled	6.8-7.0
Wines	2.8-3.8

tion of equipment and utensils is an effective method of controlling bacterial growth.

The FDA's Food Service Sanitation Ordinance states:

Sanitization means effective bactericidal treatment by a process that provides enough accumulative heat or concentration of chemicals for enough time to reduce the bacterial count, including pathogens, to a safe level on utensils and equipment.

Source: FDA, p. 22.

Other Bacterial Characteristics. Bacterial cells of the genera *Bacillus* have the ability to form a dense, slime-like protective coating around their cell wall. The effect of this **encapsulation** is to protect the organism from chemicals and heat. Encapsulation also increases the bacterial cell's resistance to death by normal methods.

Other types of bacteria form long chains or groups of cells called **cell aggregates**. Examples of bacteria in this category are *Staphylococcus au-*

reus and *Streptococcus pyogenes.*[1] The formation of cell aggregates also increases their resistance to death.

Most foodborne pathogens move from place to place in the environment by "hitchhiking" on humans, dust, air, food, clothing, or sneezes and coughs. Other cells have their own methods of moving short distances within their environment. These cells move with the aid of tiny whip-like structures called **flagella**. Flagella move the cells around so they can find the food they need to survive. In general, none of the cocci (spheres) have flagella, some of the bacilli (rods) and vibrio (commas) have flagella, and all of the spirilla (corkscrews) have flagella (refer to Exhibit 3.2).

Foodborne Parasites

Foodborne **parasites** are intestinal nematodes (worms) that affect animals. Trichinosis is a disease that takes place in three stages: invasion, muscle penetration, and tissue repair. Symptoms surface in an average of 9 days but may occur from 4 to 28 days. It is caused by a parasite known as *Trichinella spiralis* found in infected hogs and the flesh of some wild animals such as bear and walrus. This delicate thread-like roundworm can be destroyed by heating pork to an internal temperature of 150°F (66°C) or above. It can also be destroyed by freezing.

The incidence of trichinosis is on the decline in the United States. Farmers who feed hogs garbage are required to cook the garbage to 212°F (100°C) for 30 minutes before it is fed to the hogs. However, most hog farmers are now feeding their animals selected grains instead of cooked garbage to maximize the amount of lean on the carcass.

Foodborne Fungi

Microscopic **fungi** can be either molds or yeasts. Although foodborne fungi are generally beneficial, some are harmful microorganisms. Most yeast and molds are aerobic mesophiles—that is, they prefer oxygen and medium temperatures. Yeasts and molds grow best in foods with a pH low enough to stop or slow the growth of bacteria, their natural competitors.

Yeasts are generally not responsible for outbreaks of foodborne illness, but they may cause food spoilage. These single-celled organisms are abundant in nature. Those that prefer oxygen are found in orchards and on fruits. They prefer a relatively low pH and reproduce by a process called **budding**, as illustrated in Exhibit 3.7.

The economic importance of yeasts lies in their ability to ferment carbohydrates. Yeasts are used in the production of wines, beers, alcoholic spirits, bread, cheese, baked products, and enzymes. Yeasts contain a collection of enzymes called **zymase** which brings about the breakdown

---

[1] Just as human beings are scientifically named in Latin by their genus and species (*Homo sapiens*, literally, "knowing man"), so are microorganisms. The first letter of the genus is always capitalized; the first letter of the species is not capitalized. The species name given to a microorganism and the genus in which it is placed describe the microorganism and may give a clue as to its shape, the foods it prefers, what it ferments, or the person who has researched the microorganism.

Exhibit 3.7   Reproduction by Budding—Yeast Cells

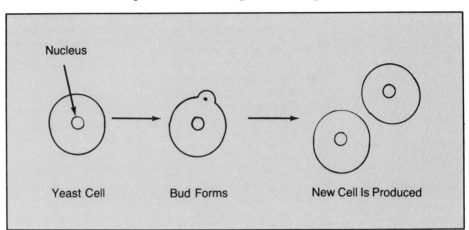

of glucose to form ethanol and carbon dioxide. The basic reaction is illustrated as follows:

$$\text{Glucose} \xrightarrow[\text{Zymase}]{\text{Yeast}} \text{Ethyl Alcohol} + \text{Carbon Dioxide Gas}$$
$$\qquad\qquad\qquad\qquad\qquad\text{(Ethanol)}$$

Ethanol is what produces the light-headedness associated with drinking alcoholic beverages. In baked products, the ethyl alcohol is driven off by the heat of the oven. The carbon dioxide gas provides leavening action during baking. It also gives beer and some sparkling wines their effervescence (bubbly appearance).

Molds are multicellular organisms. The beneficial and harmful effects of molds are presented in Exhibit 3.8. All molds use spores as means to reproduce. The thread-like structures on molds are called **hyphae**. Molds are often a good indication that food spoilage is taking place.

Mycotoxins are poisonous substances produced by molds. **Aflatoxin** is a mycotoxin that is produced by a mold called *Aspergillus flavus*. This mold is found worldwide and grows on nuts, corn, wheat, maize, and in other cereals and animal feed. Aflatoxin cannot be destroyed by heat or effectively removed. As a result, it may be found in finished products like bread and peanut butter. Fortunately, aflatoxin usually only causes low grade fever in humans, but it can produce cancer in trout, rats, and ducks. Aflatoxin has been linked to liver cancer in some humans.

Penicillium molds are used in the production of antibiotics and cheese. *Penicillium roqueforti* is used to make a blue-veined cheese. If produced in the designated caves in France, the cheese is called

Exhibit 3.8   Effects of Molds on Foods

Beneficial	Harmful
Enzyme production	Spoilage
Industrial fermentations	Undesirable pigments
Acid fermentations	Off-flavors
Cheese ripening	Mycotoxins
Soy sauce production	

Exhibit 3.9   Viral Reproduction

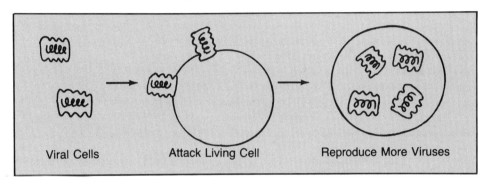

Viral Cells   Attack Living Cell   Reproduce More Viruses

Roquefort. *Fusarium*, on the other hand, is not so desirable. It is a genus of molds responsible for fruit and vegetable spoilage.

In general, molds require a lower a_w value (less moisture) than bacteria or yeasts. Most molds require oxygen, medium temperatures, and foods with a pH of 4 to 6. Some are extremely salt tolerant. They are destroyed by carefully controlling moisture and by properly applying fungicides (substances that kill molds). Most molds are not stable to heat and can be killed by heating food to 140°F (60°C) for ten minutes or longer.

Foodborne Viruses

Viruses are microorganisms that are even smaller than bacteria. If you could design a filter fine enough to trap individual bacterial cells, it would still permit viruses to pass through. Viruses use food as a vehicle of transmission, but they do not reproduce in food products. Viruses are constructed of genetic material surrounded by a protein coating. They are always parasites of other living cells since they cannot grow, feed, or reproduce in isolation. The method of viral reproduction is illustrated in Exhibit 3.9. Once the virus attacks a living cell, it forces the cell to produce or clone other viruses. The cell bursts and the new viral cells are free to attack other healthy living cells. Some examples of pathogenic viruses are those responsible for poliomyelitis and influenza.

Exhibit 3.10   A Classification Scheme for Foodborne Diseases

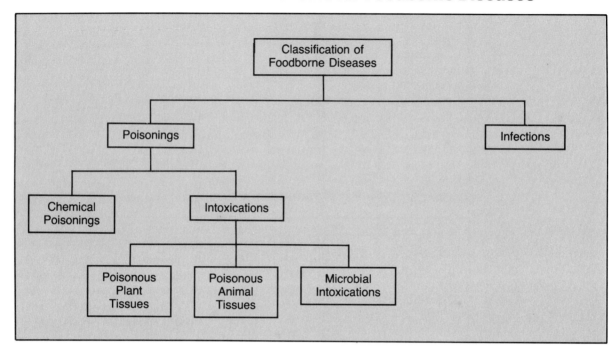

Excerpted from: Centers for Disease Control, Public Health Service, U.S. Department of Health and Human Services, Foodborne Diseases and Their Control, *1980.*

Causes of Foodborne Diseases

A **foodborne disease** results when food containing either infectious, toxic, or toxigenic agents is eaten. As Exhibit 3.10 shows, foodborne diseases are of two general types: infections and poisonings. **Infections** are caused by bacteria and viruses that are transmitted in food and later reproduce inside the body. These agents of food infection invade the gastrointestinal system of humans and may affect other organs. **Poisonings** result: (1) when harmful chemicals are ingested, (2) when poisonous plants or animals are eaten, or (3) when bacteria produce **toxins** or poisons in food and the food is eaten. Illnesses of the third type are caused by poisonous waste products of the toxigenic bacteria, since the bacterial cells themselves may already have been destroyed by the time the poisoned food is eaten. Except for chemical poisonings, these types of poisonings are called **intoxications**.

Both infections and microbial intoxications have similar symptoms: nausea, diarrhea, intestinal cramps, and vomiting. In general, the symptoms of microbial intoxications appear much sooner than those of infections. This is because the agents of infection require time to reproduce in the human body. The amount of time it takes from eating the contaminated food until the first symptoms surface is called the **incuba-**

tion time. Thus, the incubation time for microbial intoxications is generally shorter than that of infections.

Agents of Food Infection

Foodborne infections result when relatively large numbers of infectious microorganisms are eaten. These contaminants of the food supply use food as a vehicle to enter the human body. Once inside the body, the infectious microorganisms multiply in the intestines. They can also move to other tissues in the body and reproduce.

Salmonella spp.[2] comprise over 1,600 species. The pathogens in the genus *Salmonella* are the number one cause of foodborne infection in the United States. These organisms can survive in oxygen-rich or oxygen-poor environments. Some species are mobile rods. In general, *Salmonella* organisms do not form spores and prefer medium temperatures.

Salmonella spp. are most often found in the intestinal tract of animals and humans. These pathogens have been isolated from turkeys, chickens, hogs, cattle, dogs, cats, frogs, turtles, and birds. The incubation time ranges from 5 to 72 hours, although in most cases symptoms appear in 12 to 48 hours. Symptoms are abdominal pain, diarrhea, fever, chills, vomiting, dehydration, headache, and prostration. Symptoms may last several days or longer.

Typical food sources of *Salmonella spp.* are meat, poultry, and egg products. Other foods which have been implicated in outbreaks are coconut, yeast, chocolate candy, smoked fish, raw salads, fish, and shellfish. Humans can become carriers of *Salmonella* pathogens after an illness; a carrier does not exhibit the symptoms of the bacterial disease, but can still transfer the microorganisms to humans or food products. Some species are responsible for two forms of salmonellosis (*Salmonella choleraesuis* and *Salmonella enteritidis*), while others are the cause of typhoid fever (*Salmonella typhi*).

Salmonellosis can be prevented if food products are cooked thoroughly and then rapidly chilled. This microorganism is not heat stable so it can be destroyed by normal cooking procedures. Human carriers are a major cause of food being contaminated with *Salmonella typhi*. Therefore, food handlers should adhere to rules of good personal hygiene. *Salmonella spp.* can be transferred to food in two other ways. Whenever a food product comes into contact with a contaminated nonfood source (knives, cutting boards, equipment, etc.), it is **cross-contaminated**. Cross-contamination can also occur between raw and cooked food. The prevention of *Salmonella spp.* reproduction is critical to the success of any food service sanitation program.

Shigella spp. constitute a genus of microorganisms responsible for shigellosis (bacillary dysentery). Their nonmobile rod-like cells tolerate conditions of oxygen or no oxygen. More than ten *Shigella* species have been identified as causes of illness in humans. Most of these pathogens are transmitted to food from the feces of infected humans, by direct contact, and in water. *Shigella spp.* have been discovered in moist, mixed

---

[2] Spp. is an abbreviation for species. In cases where it is used, the species is not known or specified.

foods, for example, tuna, shrimp, turkey, macaroni, and potato salads. Other food sources are milk, beans, apple cider, and contaminated produce.

The incubation period for *Shigella* pathogens ranges from one to seven days, but it is usually less than four days. Symptoms include abdominal pain, diarrhea, fever, chills, headache, blood in the feces, nausea, dehydration, and prostration. The symptoms are extremely variable, from mild to severe, based on the number and species of *Shigella* microorganisms ingested.

These organisms are controlled by chilling and heating food products rapidly, practicing good personal hygiene, controlling flies, and preparing food products in a sanitary manner.

Vibrio parahaemolyticus cells are mobile, straight or slightly curved rods. This pathogen generally prefers environments with no oxygen. *Vibrio parahaemolyticus* is frequently found in marine life and sea water. Most diseases associated with this organism have been observed in Japan, although the number of outbreaks in the United States has risen with the increased popularity of sushi bars, where raw fish is consumed.

Incubation times vary from 2 to 48 hours, but symptoms usually surface 10 to 20 hours after eating the contaminated food. Symptoms are abdominal cramps, diarrhea, nausea, vomiting, mild fever, chills, headache, and prostration. Recovery occurs within two to five days.

Typical food sources of *Vibrio parahaemolyticus* are raw foods of marine origin, saltwater fish, shellfish, and fish products. Salty foods and cucumbers have also been identified as sources. This organism can be controlled by proper cooking and chilling procedures. Raw foods should always be kept separate from cooked foods. Proper icing or refrigeration of seafood may minimize the spread of *Vibrio parahaemolyticus* if it is present. Sea water should never be used for rinsing food that is to be eaten raw.

Escherichia coli is a mobile rod. It survives in environments with or without free oxygen. Many strains of this microorganism are harmless, but some others are responsible for food infections. This microbe is found in the feces of infected humans and is transmitted to food by direct contact with carriers. *Escherichia coli* can also be airborne or waterborne. Infants and young people are most susceptible to this microorganism.

The incubation time for this pathogen ranges from 8 to 24 hours with an average of 11 hours. Symptoms are similar to shigellosis. *Escherichia coli* has been isolated from cheese, shellfish, and watercress. Any food exposed to sewage-contaminated water may carry *Escherichia coli*. This organism should be controlled in the same way as *Shigella spp.*

Clostridium perfringens is classified as a nonmobile, spore-forming, encapsulated rod. It proliferates when no oxygen is present. This organism is more likely to form spores in the human body than in food. *Clostridium perfringens* is widely distributed in nature. It has been found in animal manure, human feces, dust, and soil.

The incubation time for this pathogen ranges from 6 to 24 hours with the majority of symptoms surfacing in 8 to 12 hours. Symptoms are acute abdominal cramps and diarrhea. Occasionally, dehydration and prostration occur, but nausea, vomiting, chills, and fever are rare. The symptoms clear up in one day or less.

Typical food sources of *Clostridium perfringens* are products that are cooked and then cooled slowly or in large quantities at room temperatures. Examples are cooked meat and poultry, meat pies, gravies, and stew. Insufficient holding or reheating temperatures can also foster growth of this microorganism. Also, soil-grown vegetables that have not been cleaned properly have been implicated in *Clostridium perfringens* outbreaks. Thorough cleaning, cooking, and adequate holding temperatures will reduce problems. Good personal hygiene coupled with proper chilling and reheating of leftovers will also minimize the risks.

Other bacteria are less frequently identified in outbreaks of foodborne illness. *Streptococcus pyogenes* has been found in food containing milk or eggs. *Yersinia enterocolitica* is rare, but it has been discovered in pork and other meats, raw milk, and contaminated leftover food. *Vibrio cholerae* has been discovered in raw vegetables and mixed, moist foods. These bacteria are generally controlled by the same sanitary practices which control the more common agents of foodborne infection already described. Finally, in the past *Brucella spp.* have been found in raw goat cheese and raw milk. Milk pasteurization has kept *Brucella spp.* organisms in check.

Viruses have been found in a limited number of foods, particularly those consumed raw. The virus of infectious hepatitis takes 10 to 50 days to surface in humans, although the incubation time averages 30 days. It is found in the blood, urine, and feces of human and animal carriers. It is transmitted either person-to-person by direct contact or in water. Rodents and insects can also carry the virus of infectious hepatitis and other viruses.

The virus of infectious hepatitis causes fever, nausea, abdominal pain, and a tired feeling. It is often accompanied by jaundice which lasts a few weeks to several months. This pathogen has been detected in shellfish, milk, potato salad, cold cuts, frozen strawberries, orange juice, whipped cream cakes, glazed doughnuts, and sandwiches. The virus is controllable by buying foods only from approved sources, practicing good personal hygiene, and cooking foods thoroughly.

Agents of Food Poisoning

Foodborne poisonings are caused: (1) by bacteria that produce toxic waste products in food, (2) by naturally toxic plants and animals which are mistakenly eaten for food, and (3) by poisonous chemicals in the food supply. Each of these types of poisoning is explained in more detail in the following sections.

Bacterial Intoxications. There are three sources of bacterial intoxications: *Staphylococcus aureus, Clostridium botulinum,* and *Bacillus cereus.*

Staphylococcus aureus is a spherical, nonmobile, nonspore-forming organism. It has the ability to clump together in clusters like bunches of grapes. This makes the organism more difficult to destroy. *Staphylococcus aureus* can survive with or without oxygen. The name *aureus* is taken from the Latin word for gold because this pathogen often produces a yellow or gold-colored pigment on laboratory media. Although the organism itself is not very heat resistant, the toxin produced by *Staphylococcus aureus* is extremely heat stable. This poisonous waste is not destroyed by normal cooking procedures. The toxin is a protein which does not alter the texture, color, appearance, odor, or taste of food products.

Staphylococcus aureus is widespread in the environment, which accounts for the fact that it is the number one agent of bacterial intoxication in the United States. In general, this pathogen prefers medium temperature conditions. It is mostly found in and on human beings. It has been detected in nose and throat discharges, on hands and skin, in infected wounds and burns, and on pimples and acne. *Staphylococcus aureus* has also been found in feces and hair. It is estimated that this organism is present on 20% of the population that appears healthy. Food products may become contaminated with *Staphylococcus aureus* after cooking as a result of contact with infected food handlers.

This pathogen has an incubation time of one to eight hours, although symptoms usually surface in two to four hours. The incubation period depends upon the amount of toxin present in the food. As the toxin levels increase, the incubation time decreases. Symptoms include vomiting, abdominal cramps, diarrhea, nausea, dehydration, sweating, weakness, and prostration. These unpleasant conditions usually last one to two days.

Several foods have been identified as common sources of *Staphylococcus aureus* intoxications. They are cooked ham, poultry and poultry dressings, meat products, gravies and sauces, cream-filled pastries, milk, cheese, hollandaise sauce, bread pudding, and fish, potato, ham, poultry, and egg salads. High-protein leftover foods are frequently involved in outbreaks.

Control of *Staphylococcus aureus* may initially appear to be impossible since it is found virtually everywhere, but a two-sided strategy is effective. First, ill humans are potential carriers and must be eliminated from the operation's food production and handling system. Employees suffering from colds, diarrhea, skin eruptions, or infected cuts should not be handling food. Second, even employees who are apparently healthy should concentrate on proper personal hygiene. In addition, food products must be handled with the utmost care. Thorough cooking and reheating along with rapid chilling and proper refrigeration will minimize the risks.

Clostridium botulinum is the pathogen responsible for botulism. This type of bacterium is a spore-forming rod. The spore is extremely heat stable, so it can survive and begin to reproduce later as a vegetative cell. This pathogen is characterized by a preference for medium temperatures. It reproduces best in environments with no air, for example, in canned foods. The toxin it produces is very potent. For example, 1 teaspoon (4 grams) of pure *Clostridium botulinum* toxin is a lethal dose for 400,000 to 500,000 people; 1 gram (20 drops) could kill 100,000 people; and 1 drop is potentially fatal for 5,000 people. Fortunately, the occurrence of botulism in the United States is relatively rare.

Clostridium botulinum is found in the soil, contaminated water, and dust. It has been detected in fruits, vegetables, feed, manure, honey, and sewage. The incubation time for botulism is 2 hours to 14 days, although it usually surfaces in 12 to 36 hours. Since the toxin affects the body's neurological systems, signs of botulism include high fever, dizziness, dry mouth, respiratory difficulties including paralysis, and loss of reflexes. If the victim lives, the paralysis may last an additional six to eight months. Unless the correct antitoxin is administered rapidly, death occurs in three to ten days as a result of respiratory failure. Although the fatality rate in the past 60 years has been between 50% and 65%, in the past 5 years the mortality rate has been less than 15% of those poisoned with botulism.

Inadequately processed or heated canned foods are responsible for outbreaks of botulism more often than any other category of food. **Home-canned foods must not be served in a food service establishment** for this reason. Low-acid foods (e.g., peas, beans, beets, corn, asparagus, mushrooms, chili peppers, figs, tuna, olives) have been implicated in past outbreaks of botulism. These foods are potentially hazardous; they have a pH in excess of 4.6. Other outbreaks have been linked to inadequately processed smoked fish and fermented foods (such as salmon eggs).

Since *Clostridium botulinum* toxins can be destroyed by heating with correct time-temperature combinations, this is the most effective method of control. Other control measures are the addition of acids, storing foods under refrigeration, and curing food products in sufficient concentrations of salt. Since the pathogen produces a gas under airtight conditions, all bulging cans with off-odors and gas bubbles must be thrown out. **Never taste any product exhibiting these characteristics.** And remember: never serve home-canned foods in your establishment.

Bacillus cereus is classified as an agent of food intoxication because some strains produce poisonous waste products in food. The organism is a spore-forming rod. This organism is capable of reproducing in the presence or absence of free oxygen. It has a tendency to form chains and possesses flagella.

Bacillus cereus is found in the soil, on dust, and on grains and vegetables. The incubation period varies from 15 minutes to 16 hours, although the symptoms frequently surface 1 to 5 hours after eating the contaminated food. Symptoms are nausea, abdominal pain, vomiting, and diarrhea. Symptoms usually clear up in one day or less and are rarely fatal.

This pathogen has been isolated from a wide variety of food products, including cereal products, puddings and custards, sauces and soups, meat loaf and meat products, vegetables, and boiled or fried rice. The spores of *Bacillus cereus* can survive ordinary cooking procedures. Thus, susceptible food products should be cooked, served, and eaten immediately. Foods held hot must have internal temperatures of 140°F (60°C) or greater. Hot foods, especially cooked rice, must be chilled rapidly to less than 45°F (7°C) in small quantities. All leftovers must be reheated to a minimum internal temperature of 160°F (71°C) prior to service.

Poisonous Plants and Animals. A wide variety of plants and animals are toxic if consumed. Most people have read about the fatal hemlock "cocktail" that Socrates was forced to drink. Poisonous plants have long been the cause of accidental (and intentional) deaths.

Toxic plants implicated in food poisoning are usually poisonous mushrooms of the genus *Amanita*. Some toxic varieties of mushrooms look like edible varieties. These poisonous varieties are toxic whether they are raw or cooked. Refuse to serve wild mushrooms and never prepare or purchase home-canned mushrooms.

A variety of other plants have been identified as poisonous. The practice of foraging for edible plants freely available in nature should be left to experts—it is an extremely risky way to obtain food.

Scombroid poisoning is characterized by intense headache, diarrhea, nausea, dizziness, vomiting, difficulty in swallowing, and itching of the skin. It usually surfaces in a few minutes to 1 hour after eating the infected scombroid fish (tuna, bonito, and mackerel). However, the symptoms clear up in about 12 hours. These fish should be cooked and either cooled or eaten soon after they are caught.

Puffer fish poisoning causes a paralysis of the central nervous system and is followed by death in 50 to 60% of the cases. Toxic species of puffer fish (e.g., fugu, blowfish, balloonfish) are to be avoided. In Japan, the sale of puffers is closely regulated by the government. In that country, puffer restaurants and cooks are licensed and must operate under a strict set of controls.

Ciguatera poisoning is carried by many marine fish as well as clams and oysters. The ciguatoxin affects the central nervous system of the victim; recovery usually occurs within 24 hours. No reliable method for detecting the presence of this heat-stable neurotoxin is currently known. Therefore, it is best to avoid eating the liver, intestines, and roe (eggs) of tropical fish. Other toxic animals responsible for ciguatera poisoning are moray eels and contaminated tilefish and mussels.

To minimize the risks of poisonous plants and animals, only purchase and serve food products from approved sources.

Chemical Poisonings and Other Illnesses. The adulteration of food with undesirable chemicals can occur at any point throughout the channels of distribution or production. In food service establishments, it is important that all equipment and utensils be made of corrosion-resistant materials.

The FDA's Food Service Sanitation Ordinance states:

Corrosion-resistant materials means those materials that maintain their original surface characteristics under prolonged influence of the food to be contacted, the normal use of cleaning compounds and bactericidal solutions, and other conditions-of-use environment.

Source: FDA, p. 20.

Zinc poisoning occurred in one case where high-acid lemonade was stored in a galvanized container overnight. The acid in the drink leached zinc off the walls of the container and into the liquid. Other cases of zinc poisoning have been traced to cooked apples, spinach, mashed potatoes, chicken, tomatoes, and fruit punch. Galvanized containers must not be used for cooking or storing food or beverage products. **Cadmium poisoning** occurs and is controlled in the same way.

Antimony poisoning takes place when antimony-glazed enamel containers are used to store or cook acidic foods. These containers do not meet the requirements of the FDA's Model Ordinance and have no place in a food service or lodging establishment. Lemonade, punch, fruit gelatin, sauerkraut, and frozen fruit pops have been implicated in cases of antimony poisoning. Do not use antimony-glazed enamel containers under any circumstances.

Copper is a heavy metal that can enter the food supply from copper pipes, containers, and cake decorators. When carbonated beverages and acidic foods come into contact with copper, they can carry **copper poisoning.** **Lead poisoning** comes from lead pipes, sprays, and utensils. Common vehicles are lead-contaminated acidic drinks and foods. To minimize the risks, wash all fruits and vegetables to be used fresh, and protect foods in storage.

Intentional additives are incorporated into the food supply for specific reasons. Some intentional additives, when added to food products in excessive amounts, cause food poisoning. Some examples of additives that are toxic in excessive amounts are nitrites, niacin, and cobalt. Other additives cause an allergic reaction in some humans. Excessive use of monosodium glutamate (MSG), a flavor intensifier, is responsible for Oriental (Chinese) Restaurant Syndrome in some sensitive humans.

Chemicals called **sulfiting agents** are commonly known as potato whiteners or vegetable fresheners. They retard **oxidation** (browning reactions) and generally help maintain the fresh appearance of foods such as apples, avocados, lettuce, and potatoes. These foods are usually dipped or soaked in sulfite solutions while raw. If these foods are served raw, sulfiting chemicals can remain on or in them, despite additional rinsing before service.

Recent medical findings have linked the ingestion of sulfiting agents to severe adverse reactions among sensitive individuals, particularly asthmatics. Some people reportedly suffered from shock, respiratory distress, and even coma. For that reason, foods that are treated with sulfiting agents and then served raw are only considered safe if the potential consumer is notified. The notification can take the form of a conspicuous and easily readable sign, placard, or menu statement.

Incidental and accidental additives are those which enter the food supply unintentionally. Most of these chemical toxins are insecticides, soil fumigants, roach and rat poisons, and weed killers. Others are present in a food service operation in the form of cleaning and sanitizing compounds. These necessary chemicals are potentially toxic if added to food. Cleaners and sanitizers should be stored in a physically separate, locked area away from storage areas used for equipment, utensils, or food products. They are to be used only according to the manufacturer's recommendations.

Several undesirable accidental food additives have been discovered in the food supply of the United States. In the early 1970s, **polybrominated biphenyl** (PBB) was detected in high concentrations in farm animals in the state of Michigan. The PBB entered the food chain when a worker at a farm-supply center mistakenly added a poisonous fire retardant (Firemaster) instead of an animal-feed nutrient (Nutrimaster) to a livestock-feed formula. Customers of the supplier unknowingly fed this mixture to their animals. Over the next few years, the fire retardant entered tons of meat, milk, and other food eaten by millions of the state's residents. At least 23,000 cattle, 1.5 million chickens, and thousands of pigs, sheep, and other animals died or were intentionally slaughtered due to contamination. The Michigan Department of Agriculture has spent more than $21 million on the PBB incident.

Polychlorinated biphenyl (PCB) is a fire retardant used as an insulator in electrical transformers. This toxic chemical is present in some of the Great Lakes. It enters the human system if fatty fish (e.g., lake trout and salmon) from the affected lakes are consumed. Both PBB and PCB are stored in fat cells in the human body. Toxic concentrations of mercury and the pesticide Mirex have also contaminated parts of Lake Ontario.

Incidence of Foodborne Diseases in the United States

Reports of foodborne and waterborne diseases are periodically published in the United States. The number of outbreaks reported are thought to be fewer than the number of outbreaks which have actually occurred. Since many of the foodborne disease symptoms resemble symptoms of the 24-hour flu, the actual number of outbreaks occurring in the United States is probably far greater than the number being reported. Some experts estimate that for salmonellosis, only about 10% of the total outbreaks are reported. In any case, foodborne disease outbreaks in the United States are preventable. Exhibit 3.11 summarizes significant foodborne disease outbreaks in the United States between 1972 and 1976.

By reviewing the data in Exhibit 3.11, one realizes immediately that the largest category of outbreaks and cases falls into the unknown or unconfirmed classification. During the same period of 1972-1976, the Centers for Disease Control in Atlanta, Georgia, tracked where these outbreaks occurred. Based on the known cases, food mishandled in food service establishments was responsible for 67.3% of the outbreaks. Mishandling also occurred in known outbreaks in homes (27.2%) and food processing plants (5.5%).

Several key events are necessary for a foodborne disease outbreak. These events are illustrated in the form of a flow diagram in Exhibit 3.12. Initially, disease agents must be present in humans, animals, food, or the

Exhibit 3.11   A Summary of Significant Foodborne Disease Outbreaks in the United States (1972-1976)

Disease	Number of Outbreaks	Number of Cases
Bacterial Intoxications		
Staphyloenterotoxicosis	168	9,782
Botulism	68	146
Bacillus cereus gastroenteritis	7	121
Scombroid/histamine poisoning[a]	37	411[b]
Toxicoinfections (Bacterial)		
Clostridium perfringens gastroenteritis	55	4,188
Cholera	1	6
Bacterial Infections		
Salmonellosis	170	12,583
Shigellosis	23	2,373
Vibrio parahaemolyticus gastroenteritis	9	925
Enterococcal gastroenteritis	4	138
Streptococcal pharyngitis	3	610
Yersinia enterocolitica gastroenteritis	1	286
Escherichia coli gastroenteritis[c]	1	39
Viral Infections		
Hepatitis A	21	1,007
Parasitic Infections		
Trichinosis	60	357
Fish tapeworm *(D. latum)* infection	1	1
Poisonings by Plants		
Mushroom poisonings	30	77[c]
Other poisonings by plants	5	12
Poisonings by Animal Tissue		
Ciguatera poisonings	52	237[c]
Paralytic shellfish poisonings	10	23[c]
Puffer fish poisonings	1	2[c]
Chemical Poisonings		
Heavy metal poisonings	17	86
Monosodium glutamate poisonings	10	27
Other chemical poisonings	22	133[c]
Unknown or Unconfirmed Diseases	1,213	39,428
TOTAL	1,989	72,999

Source: Centers for Disease Control, Foodborne Diseases and Their Control, *1980.*

[a] Often classified as toxic animal (fish) poisoning.

[b] Cases not differentiated for these agents in summary report for 1972.

[c] Toxigenic or invasive strains not determined.

Exhibit 3.12   Events Necessary for a Foodborne Illness Outbreak

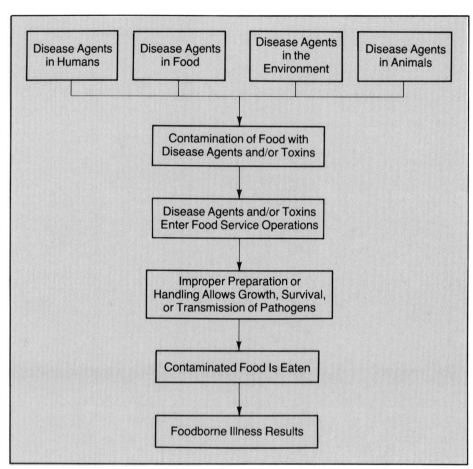

environment. These pathogenic agents can enter the food prior to receipt of the products by the food service establishment. Alternatively, the agents can enter food products once they are in the establishment. The critical factor is the contamination of food with the disease agents and/or their toxins. Once in the food service operation, the pathogens may reproduce in food. Some simply increase in numbers while others produce toxic waste products in the food. The contaminated food is then eaten, and foodborne illness results. Any sanitation program must be designed to eliminate the risks all along this chain of disease.

Several factors are responsible for outbreaks of foodborne illnesses. A summary of a study of causes of outbreaks during 1972-1976 is presented in Exhibit 3.13. "Factors affecting growth" enhance the reproduction of pathogens. "Factors affecting survival" permit both vegetative cells and spores to live through the variety of processes that take place in a food service operation. "Factors affecting contamination" are responsible for unnecessarily large numbers of pathogenic agents being introduced into the food supply.

Exhibit 3.13   Percent[a] of Factors That Contributed to Outbreaks of Selected Foodborne Diseases in the United States (1972-1976)

	Salmonellosis (238)[b]	Staphylococcal Intoxication (214)	Clostridium perfringens Gastroenteritis (93)	Botulism (85)	Shigellosis (27)	Typhoid Fever (14)	Vibrio parahaemolyticus Gastroenteritis (12)	Viral Diseases (44)	Parasitic Diseases (72)	Total[c] (1,152)
Factors Affecting Growth										
Improper cooling	48	78	76	13	56	7	67			46
Improper hot-holding	14	18	46	2		7				16
Lapse of day or more between preparing and serving	17	44	51		22				1	21
Use of leftovers	4	3	12		4				1	4
Faulty fermentations	1			9						
Factors Affecting Survival										
Inadequate cooking, heat processing, and canning	21	3	(9)[d]	80		7		2	59	16
Inadequate reheating	13	(7)[d]	45	2	7					12
Factors Affecting Contamination										
Infected person	13	53			89	79		66	1	20
Contaminated raw ingredients	32						42	36	64	11
Cross-contamination	21	3	2				33		8	7
Inadequate cleaning of equipment	15	9	1						8	7
Unsafe source	1					14	17			5
Contaminated water	1						8			

Source: Centers for Disease Control, *Foodborne Diseases and Their Control,* 1980.

[a] Percentages tabulated for each group of diseases separately. More than 100% shows in percentage figures because multiple factors are usually necessary for outbreaks of foodborne disease to occur. Factors occurring in less than 1% of outbreaks were omitted.

[b] Number of outbreaks on which data are based.

[c] Includes foodborne illness from toxic plants and chemical poisonings.

[d] Poor practices reported but probably would not have altered outcome of outbreak.

Above all other factors, neglecting to properly refrigerate food products was the most serious failing of food handlers. Improper cooling of food products contributed to more outbreaks of foodborne disease than any other single factor. In descending order of importance, the second major cause of outbreaks was a lapse of a day or more between the preparation and service of food products. The third most important factor affecting contamination was the contact of infected people with the food supply. The sanitation program in a food service operation should guard against growth, survival, and contamination factors. These statistics illustrating actual outbreaks should provide sufficient incentive for food service operations to establish a control program. Successful sanitation programs follow the requirements of the FDA's Model Ordinance.

Foodborne Physical Hazards

Physical hazards present in food service businesses should never be allowed to endanger the safety of customers. The possible hazards are numerous.

Metal fragments can end up in foods if can openers are not cleaned frequently. Pieces of metal in foods may also be caused by the careless use and cleaning of knives, forks, spoons, and pots and pans. When a cook opens a container with a knife blade, the risk of contaminating food with metal slivers increases. This practice should be forbidden.

Glass is a material frequently used for food and beverage containers. When handled or stacked carelessly, glass fragments can find their way into food products. Broken glass chips have been discovered on salad bars and in glasses containing beverages. Ice should be transferred with a metal or plastic scoop designed for that purpose. Never scoop ice with a glass container.

Cigarette butts and **matches** are nauseating and unsightly. Never permit food personnel to smoke in production, storage, or service areas.

Unrestricted hair on food handlers may be the greatest dissatisfier of many restaurant patrons. Hair in food is distasteful. All staff members should wear approved hats or hair nets and keep their hair short.

Physical hazards can be minimized if personnel are made aware of the hazards and take steps to reduce the risks. As with the other forms of food contamination, specific controls must be built into the operation's sanitation program.

Summary

There are many potential sources of food contamination. Agents of food poisoning and agents of food infection produce foodborne diseases. The characteristics, factors affecting reproduction, common food sources, incubation times, symptoms produced, and techniques for prevention and control of microbial contaminants were described. Pathogenic organisms were broadly categorized as bacteria, parasites, fungi, and viruses. Other sources of food contamination included poisonous plants and animals, heavy metals, intentional food additives, and accidental food additives. Foodborne physical hazards were also discussed.

An insight into the incidence of foodborne diseases in the United States was provided. The events which cause outbreaks to occur are controllable. Of all factors affecting the introduction, survival, and reproduction of pathogens in food, the factor most often responsible is the failure to properly refrigerate food. Negligence in this regard is probably responsible for more foodborne disease outbreaks than any other single failure. Natural contamination and additional contamination through improper handling also contribute to outbreaks.

AIDS and Herpes Transmission: The Scientific Consensus

Much sensationalism has surrounded the transmission of the Acquired Immune Deficiency Syndrome (AIDS) virus. Questions have been raised about the transmission of herpes simplex virus (HSV) from an infected individual to a non-infected individual via food or food-contact surfaces. The consensus of the scientific community remains the guiding light for food service operators.

AIDS is a virus that is spread by sharing needles, sexual contact, or through blood (least commonly). The Centers for Disease Control (CDC) in Atlanta has stated that AIDS is found in body fluids. However, there is no scientific evidence that AIDS is transmitted by casual contact (e.g., a kiss or a handshake) or through food, water, or air.

HSV, like other viruses, cannot survive very long away from the human body. Recent scientific data suggest that HSV may survive in warm, moist areas, such as wet towels, even though there is no good evidence that the virus is actually spread this way. HSV is not known to be spread by food or drinking water, through the air, by water in hot tubs and swimming pools, or on toilet seats. The Food and Drug Administration (in a recent *Interpretation*) stated that HSV is not transmitted via food-contact surfaces or food.

Therefore, based on present scientific information, it appears that there are no special steps that must be taken by the operator beyond those for all personnel in the areas of personal cleanliness, employee practices, and handwashing lavatory supplies. However, the FDA cautions that if an employee appears to be ill, that infected person—as a precaution—should be assigned to work in an area where there is no contact with food.

References

Berlinski, P. "Special Report on Sanitation and Safety." *Restaurant Business*, December 1975. 74(12):34.

Beuchat, L. R. "Yersinia Enterocolitica: Recovery from Foods and Virulence Characterization." *Food Technology*, March 1982. 36(3):84-88.

Bryan, F. L. "Current Trends in Foodborne Salmonellosis in the United States and Canada." *Journal of Food Protection*, May 1981. 43(11):859-876.

——."Epidemiology of Foodborne Diseases Transmitted by Fish, Shellfish, and Marine Crustaceans in the United States, 1970-1978." *Journal of Food Protection*, November 1980. 43(11):859-876.

Centers for Disease Control. *Diseases Transmitted By Food*. Atlanta, Ga.: Public Health Service, U.S. Department of Health, Education, and Welfare, 1979.

Centers for Disease Control. *Foodborne Diseases and Their Control*. Atlanta, Ga.: Public Health Service, U.S. Department of Health and Human Services, 1980.

Childers, A. B., and Vanderzant, C. "Yersinia enterocolitica: A New Problem in Foodborne Illness." *Dairy and Food Sanitation*, September 1981. 1(9):364-366.

Corwin, E. "A Food Poisoning Whodunit." *Dairy and Food Sanitation*, April 1981. 1(4):144-147.

Cummings, G. "Foodborne Illnesses are Rare, Precautions Are Mandatory." *Restaurant Business*, December 1981. 80(15):130.

"Food Poisoning: Everybody's Problem." *Cooking for Profit*, July 1978. (331):17-18.

Frazier, W. C., and Westhoff, D. C. *Food Microbiology*. 3rd ed. New York: McGraw-Hill, 1978.

Hauschild, A. H. W., and Bryan, F. L. "Estimate of Food- and Waterborne Illness in Canada and the United States." *Journal of Food Protection*, June 1980. 43(6):435-440.

Hopkins, H. "Danger Lurks Among the Molds." *Dairy and Food Sanitation*, June 1981. 1(6):246-247.

Jay, J. M. *Modern Food Microbiology*. 2nd ed. New York: Van Nostrand, 1978.

Kaufmann, O. W. "Public Enemy Number One." *Dairy and Food Sanitation*, July 1981. 1(7):280-284.

Larkin, E. P. "Food Contaminants — Viruses." *Journal of Food Protection*, April 1981. 44(4):320-325.

"Life in the Kitchen." *Food Management*, July 1982. 17(7):34.

Longree, Karla. *Quantity Food Sanitation*. 2nd ed. New York: Wiley-Interscience, 1972.

Ockerman, H. W. *Source Book for Food Scientists*. Westport, Conn.: AVI, 1978.

"Sanitation: The Dirty Word in Foodservice." *Food Management*, April 1976. 11(4):32.

Schaffner, R. M. "Government's Role in Preventing Foodborne Botulism." *Food Technology*, December 1982. 36(12):87-89.

Silliker, J. H. "Status of Salmonella — Ten Years Later." *Journal of Food Protection*, April 1980. 43(4):307-313.

Smith, J. L., and Palumbo, S. A. "Microorganisms as Food Additives." *Journal of Food Protection,* December 1981. 44(12):936-955.

Zottola, E. A. *Botulism.* St. Paul, Minn.: Agricultural Extension Service, University of Minnesota, 1976.

——.*Clostridium Perfringens Food Poisoning.* St. Paul, Minn.: Agricultural Extension Service, University of Minnesota, 1979.

——.*Staphylococcus Food Poisoning.* St. Paul, Minn.: Agricultural Extension Service, University of Minnesota, 1968.

Strategies for Success at the Aspen Hotel

After spending a few hours Wednesday evening reviewing his sanitation management course notes, Paul tried to develop a strategy for the department head meeting. Gradually, an agenda for the meeting began to take shape in his mind, so he decided to make some notes:

1. Briefly review my past educational and industry experiences.

2. Ask each supervisor to summarize his or her own experiences.

3. Present the corporate philosophy of the Mountain States Hotel Management Company.

4. Explain my own personal management philosophy (the key to success is a strong customer awareness).

5. Present the model for success, and explain how the control points and resources are interrelated.

The agenda for Paul's first meeting with the staff was shaping up nicely. The next few items on the agenda were the most important to Paul:

6. Discuss current noncompliance with health department code requirements.

7.   Briefly review the fundamentals of food microbiology.

8.   Challenge department heads: "We have six weeks till we're due to reopen."

9.   Solicit commitment of department heads to reopening on schedule by asking for recommendations on how to bring the property into compliance.

The following case studies are designed to enhance your understanding of the material in this chapter. If you are a Home Study student, use these case studies to stimulate questions about this chapter. If you are a Group or Institutional Study student, you may be asked to discuss these case studies as part of a regular classroom assignment.

CASE STUDY 3.1

On Tuesday at 5:00 p.m., Susan went to a family-style table service restaurant and ordered broccoli quiche, salad with blue cheese dressing, biscuits, and a cola beverage. When Susan had eaten about half of the quiche, she noticed that the middle of the quiche was cold, so she did not finish the rest. Then, she taught her graduate finance class from 6:30 to 9:30 p.m. By 9:30 p.m. Susan was experiencing nausea and an upset stomach, which made her wonder if she had influenza. By 10:00 p.m. she was at home with an attack of diarrhea.

At 3:00 a.m. on Wednesday, Susan had a 102°F (39°C) fever and was in the bathroom every three hours with diarrhea. As soon as she ate anything, she would have another attack. By 8:00 p.m. on Wednesday, Susan was completely bedridden with cramps, diarrhea, nausea, and abdominal swelling. She was in pain and could not lie comfortably on either side of her body.

Thursday morning found Susan suffering with increased abdominal swelling, excruciatingly painful cramps, and a 102°F (39°C) fever. The regular trips to the bathroom every three hours persisted. An appointment was made with the family physician for 3:30 that afternoon. By then her fever had dropped to 101°F (38°C). The doctor asked Susan if she had been out of the country, and she said no. He checked her blood for the electrolyte balance and prescribed Bactrin (similar to penicillin antibiotics). The doctor also told her to drink a beverage made from salt water, sugar, and orange juice to prevent dehydration. He told her to eat nothing. She agreed to follow his advice. However, by Thursday night, the symptoms were worse. The abdominal cramps were so bad that she couldn't lie down. The rate of bathroom visits accelerated to one every hour.

On Friday morning, Susan's fever dropped to 99°F (37°C). She began to feel better, although the abdominal swelling persisted. The doctor called and asked her to submit a fecal sample for analysis. The cramps were still painful but the bathroom visits dropped back to one every three hours. On Saturday, three days after the initial onset of symptoms, Susan could move from the bed to the couch. On Sunday, the fever was gone and she started to eat lightly and irregularly. When she weighed herself on the bathroom scale, she noticed that she had lost over ten pounds since Wednesday.

On Monday, Susan took her dog for a walk around the block. To recuperate from this physical exercise, Susan required a 2-hour nap. As soon as she ate anything, she had to go to the bathroom. The doctor called on Tuesday to inform Susan that the fecal sample had been tested and the results were positive for *Salmonella spp.* Later that day, a representative of the health department visited Susan and asked her, and all members of her family living with her, to submit two fecal samples within 24 hours. The health department official said that a person can become a carrier for up to one year after experiencing human salmonellosis. (In fact, if Susan had been a food handler, she would have needed a special clearance to return to work.) Susan and her family agreed to cooperate with the health department.

On Wednesday afternoon, Susan returned to the doctor's office for another blood test. Although the abdominal pain had lessened, the doctor told her that she should not eat dairy products, spicy food, or drink any alcoholic beverages for the next three weeks. Also, she was not allowed to work for two more weeks. On her way out, the doctor told Susan, "You were lucky that yours was a mild case of salmonellosis."

Test Your Understanding

1. How could this foodborne disease have been avoided?

2. Is human salmonellosis really a "mild" form of foodborne disease?

3. What would you recommend to the operator of the restaurant where Susan dined?

CASE STUDY 3.2

In a school district, the same lunch meal was served to elementary school children in schools throughout the city. Each day the meals were prepared in a central commissary kitchen and distributed to 16 satellite kitchens in the elementary schools. On a certain day, a total of 1,364 of the 5,824 children who had eaten the school lunch became ill. The menu consisted of chicken salad, lettuce and tomato, french fries, hot rolls, cupcakes, and milk. Upon questioning all the elementary school children, it was learned that over 90% of those who had eaten the chicken salad were ill afterwards. An investigation into the preparation of the suspected source of the illness was called for.

The preparation of the chicken salad started during the afternoon shift on the day before the lunch was served. The frozen chickens were boiled for three hours and cooled. Once cooled, the poultry was deboned and cooled with a fan to room temperature. Then the chicken was ground into small pieces, placed in 12-inch (30.48 cm) deep aluminum pans, and refrigerated overnight in a walk-in refrigerator registering temperatures of 42-45°F (6-7°C). The next morning, the chicken was combined with the other ingredients with the aid of an electrical mixer. The chicken salad was placed in cold food containers and transported to the schools. Because none of the schools had refrigerators, the chicken salad was exposed to room termperatures until service. However, on this particular day, the weather was relatively cold so the heating systems in the schools were operating at full capacity. The classrooms where the chicken salad was stored were described as "stuffy" and the food was warm when it was eaten.

Test Your Understanding

1. What microorganism was probably responsible for the outbreak of foodborne illness among the school children?

2. What factors contributed to this outbreak?

3. What would you recommend to the food service director of this school system to prevent further outbreaks from occurring?

CASE STUDY 3.3

A family of seven was involved in an outbreak of foodborne disease. The family ate a home-cooked dinner and, about 36 hours later, five of the seven family members were ill. One member of the family died from the illness three days later.

Prior to the foodborne illness outbreak, the family had made its own chili sauce using onions, carrots, garlic, and a jar of green and red chili peppers that had been home-canned six weeks earlier. When the batch of five jars of peppers were home-canned, no acid ingredients (e.g., vinegar) were added. Also, the jars of peppers were not canned under pressure, but simply boiled in the jars.

One jar had been consumed a few weeks earlier with no problems. Another bottle was discarded without being tasted because it looked spoiled. When the family opened the third jar to use in the chili sauce six weeks later, it was foamy and had a foul smell but they used it anyway.

Test Your Understanding

1. What microorganism was probably responsible for this outbreak of foodborne illness?

2. What factors contributed to this outbreak?

3. What would you recommend to prevent further outbreaks from occurring?

CASE STUDY 3.4

A banquet was served in a metropolitan hotel to 1,800 people. The menu entree was roast beef. Between 2 and 26 hours after the meal was eaten, approximately half of the 1,800 banquet guests complained of headaches, diarrhea, abdominal cramps, and nausea. The symptoms were relatively mild and cleared up in 12 to 24 hours.

Samples of the leftover roast beef which had been sliced for serving were found to be loaded with pathogenic bacteria. Kitchen equipment that was used to prepare and slice the roasts had not been cleaned or sanitized before, during, or after use. Once sliced, the beef was stored in holding carts with temperatures below 140°F (60°C). Samples of whole cooked beef roasts were also examined but these were not contaminated.

Test Your Understanding

1. What microorganism was probably responsible for this outbreak of foodborne illness?

2. What factors contributed to this outbreak?

3. What would you recommend to the food and beverage director of this hotel to prevent further outbreaks from occurring?

CASE STUDY 3.5

A catering company served a wedding dinner for 175 guests. Approximately 125 persons who attended the dinner became ill. About three and a half months later, the same company catered four different events, serving a total of 900 people on the same day. Three of the four parties complained of headaches, nausea, diarrhea, and abdominal cramps after consuming the catered meals. In total, over 100 people reported similar symptoms of illness. Most of the people who were ill had eaten chicken prepared and served by the catering company.

The health department was called in, and sanitarians investigated the outbreaks. After interviewing the catering company's production personnel, it was determined that the chicken had been baked in the kitchen's oven. After baking, the pans of chicken had been stacked on a shelf and held at room temperature. Then the chicken had been loaded into the firm's trucks and delivered to the four parties. Sanitarians found unsanitary conditions in the kitchen. The inside of the trucks had a build-up of decayed food particles and dirt. Cockroaches were also discovered in the trucks. Not surprisingly, skin swabs of employees and a laboratory analysis of leftover chicken revealed the presence of pathogens.

Test Your Understanding

1.   What microorganism was probably responsible for this outbreak of foodborne illness?

2.   What factors contributed to the outbreak?

3.   What would you recommend to the food service manager of this catering business to prevent further outbreaks?

CASE STUDY 3.6

The manager of a hotel food and beverage operation was expecting a large party for breakfast the next morning. He instructed production personnel to prepare several gallons of frozen orange juice in a clean, galvanized iron container. The frozen orange juice was reconstituted according to the manager's instructions, covered, and stored overnight in a walk-in refrigerator.

The next morning, the breakfast party servers ladled the orange juice into individual glasses and served it to the breakfast group. Customers became ill after drinking the juice, and many complained to the hotel's management. Further investigation revealed that the acid in the orange juice had dissolved the metal of the container in which it had been stored.

Test Your Understanding

1.   What was responsible for this outbreak of foodborne illness?

2.   What factors contributed to the outbreak?

3.   What would you recommend to the food and beverage manager of this hotel to prevent further outbreaks?

FOUR

Food Spoilage and Preservation

Strategies for Success at the Aspen Hotel

8:30...8:30. The electronic L.E.D. clock given to Paul James by the staff at his former property reminded him that he had only 30 minutes until his meeting with the Aspen Hotel's department heads was scheduled to begin. As Paul reviewed his written agenda, he remembered what he had learned the day before about foodborne illnesses and injuries and about food spoilage. He was pleased that he had taken the time to review his sanitation management class notes because they reminded him of the economic importance of controlling microorganisms.

Paul was keenly aware that a foodborne disease outbreak could bankrupt his hotel and put it out of business. He thought about how his reputation would be destroyed and his department heads would be discredited by an outbreak at the Aspen. Such a calamity had to be avoided. While uncontrolled food spoilage might be less obvious to the public, it would raise his food cost percentage and reduce the hotel's bottom line. Worst of all, Paul thought, contamination and spoilage would certainly lower customer satisfaction. Paul would not tolerate that in his hotel.

Paul thought about how customers are becoming more and more sophisticated in today's highly competitive market. Quality is important to customers now more than ever. As the new GM, Paul intended to share a simple definition of quality with the members of his staff: "Quality is nothing more than consistently prepared and delivered products and services. Quality relates to the total experience we provide with our personnel, products, equipment, and facilities. It is the overall package presented to the customer."

Paul firmly believed that quality is achieved only when goals and objectives are clearly defined and executed. He knew that as the GM he must set the tone for the entire hotel. By the same token, he would expect department heads to set the levels of quality in each of their departments. He would also expect good results from the hotel's workers, because employees want to work in a quality hotel. Naturally, customers want to be associated with a quality property.

Paul liked to think of quality and price as the components of value, something every customer is seeking. Paul's basic philosophy was, "If the value expected by the customer is the value given by our hotel, then we are sure to have a successful property. Every employee should strive to provide the value our customers desire. They deserve to get their money's worth."

Paul suddenly recalled a time, early in his career, when he worked as a front desk manager. One morning, as a guest was checking out, Paul overheard the guest tell the cashier, "This is the friendliest hotel I have ever stayed in." The guest summed up his lodging experience by saying, "I didn't expect that level of service!" That's it, Paul thought. That's the value I want all of our customers to perceive. On the way to his 9:00 a.m. meeting, Paul contemplated how he would instill in his department heads the importance of quality and value.

A discussion of food service sanitation would be incomplete if it failed to cover food spoilage and food preservation. Microorganisms are responsible for much of the food spoilage that occurs both in the channels of distribution and in food service operations. This chapter focuses on how food products spoil and the short-term and long-term methods used to minimize this spoilage.

Food Spoilage

Almost all food products are largely composed of organic material—that is, they contain the element carbon. Once the food is harvested or slaughtered, the organic material begins to break down chemically. Two distinct processes take place during food breakdown: autolysis and spoilage.

Autolysis is a breakdown of food products caused by substances (largely enzymes) within the food. **Enzymes** are proteins that catalyze this chemical reaction; that is, they speed up the rate of autolysis. In living cells, enzymes are held in check. Once the cell dies, the enzymes take over and cause a breakdown of tissue. The enzymatic autolysis of some foods is desirable. The tenderization of meat and the ripening of fruits and vegetables are examples of desirable autolysis. Autolysis destroys the cell walls of food products. Once the cells have been violated, food spoilage is easier to achieve.

Food spoilage primarily occurs through the action of bacteria, molds, and yeasts. These organisms turn the complex organic substances in foods back into their simple, inorganic components. This activity of spoilage organisms is responsible for changing the odor, color, texture, appearance, and taste of food products. These changes result in what we identify as food spoilage.

Spoiled food is unfit for human consumption. Judgments regarding what is fit to eat are individual but are heavily influenced by cultural factors. Some societies cherish as delicacies food products that Americans would refuse to eat. Also, under extreme conditions of hunger, humans have been known to survive by eating what would otherwise be unthinkable: human flesh. Under normal conditions, we would probably all agree on certain criteria for substances to be used as food products. These criteria would probably include:

1. The absence of undesirable changes caused by microorganisms or enzymes

2. The absence of objectionable adulteration or contamination

3. The desired state of maturity or ripeness

The absence of undesirable changes caused by microorganisms or enzymes is important in the fitness decision. This indicates that the food is not spoiled. Contamination of the food supply may occur at any stage of production or processing. The likelihood of the food being a vehicle for pathogens is greatly increased whenever food products are exposed to contaminants. The desired state of maturity affects the acceptability of food products to the consumer. Foods which are acceptable in taste are said to be **palatable**.

Food spoilage results in unusable food products. Many factors contribute to food spoilage. Often a variety of microorganisms are involved in the reversion of the organic substances in food to their inorganic components. Enzymatic autolysis accelerates the rate of spoilage. Insects and rodents damage food products and make them unfit for human consumption. Physical changes (when products are exposed to extremely low temperatures, high heat, or excessive pressure) and careless handling of foods cause bruising. Chemical reactions, not caused by enzymes, can also be responsible for food spoilage. This chapter deals exclusively with food spoilage caused by microorganisms.[1]

The spoilage of food products in a food service establishment is often linked to one or more of the following causes:

1. Improper storage temperatures

2. Incorrect or excessive storage times

3. Unacceptable levels of ventilation in storage areas

4. Failure to segregate foods in storage

5. Excessive delays between receipt and storage of food products

6. Inadequate or unacceptable sanitation standards resulting in exposure to unnecessary contamination

As this list suggests, most food spoilage occurs when foods are in the storing control point.[2] Storage area standards must be designed to minimize the risks of food spoilage. Furthermore, inadequate or unacceptable sanitation standards also contribute to food spoilage and expose food products to pathogenic organisms that can result in a foodborne disease outbreak.

In general, raw food products can be placed in one of three broad categories based on their susceptibility to microbial spoilage. **Perishable food products** require special processing or preservation techniques to prolong their shelf life. Without such added treatments, perishable products readily spoil. This category includes most products used on a daily basis in a food service facility: meats, poultry, fish, shellfish, eggs, dairy products, fruits, and vegetables. **Semiperishable food products** have a longer shelf life than perishable foods. These products have a slower spoilage rate when stored under recommended time-temperature combinations. Included in this category are nuts, apples, potatoes, and waxed

---

[1] Food spoilage caused by insects and rodents will be discussed in Chapter 10.

[2] A detailed discussion of storing may be found in Chapter 7.

vegetables (e.g., cucumbers). **Nonperishable food products** are the most resistant to spoilage unless they are handled and stored improperly. This category includes most dry grocery items, such as sugar, flour, spices, and dry beans.

Food Preservation

Food preservation methods are designed to increase the shelf life and maintain the desirable physical and chemical properties of food. Food preservation methods have been known since ancient times, but the technology remained somewhat primitive during most of the intervening centuries. Until a few generations ago, the United States was an agriculture-based society. Most people lived and worked on or close to farms, so a wide variety of fresh food products were available on a daily basis. With the Industrial Revolution, this pattern of rural living changed. Americans began moving from the farms to the industrialized cities. This migration radically altered the food supply needs of the population. Americans no longer had easy access to a supply of fresh food products because, as cities absorbed more of what was once farmland, the sources of fresh foods were farther and farther away.

Food processing establishments responded to this challenge by developing improved methods of food preservation. It was discovered that one of the best ways to preserve food was to practice strict microbiological control. Along with controlling the pathogenic organisms in food, food processors and manufacturers also learned to control organisms responsible for food spoilage. They succeeded in increasing the shelf life and availability of food products for the growing number of city dwellers. In time, processed food products even became popular with farm families. Today, food processing establishments use a variety of methods to provide wholesome food products to industrialized America.

The FDA's Food Service Sanitation Manual states:

Food processing establishment means a commercial establishment in which food is manufactured or packaged for human consumption. The term does not include a food service establishment, retail food store, or commissary operation.

Source: Food and Drug Administration, Public Health Service, U.S. Department of Health, Education, and Welfare, Food Service Sanitation Manual, 1976, p. 21.

In recent years, several self-proclaimed "food experts" have tried to persuade the American public that the food supply is loaded with unnecessary levels of food additives. Actually, these food additives perform several necessary functions related to the control of undesirable microbes and the increased availability of food. To condemn food additives without acknowledging their benefits does a disservice to the uninformed consumer. Without such additives, we would be buying food products like those in the turn-of-the-century general stores. Few of us would be willing to trade the convenience of modern supermarkets for such an archaic method of shopping, just to avoid additives.

The objectives of food preservation are many. As noted in Chapter 3, some preservation methods are designed to lengthen the lag phase of bacterial growth. If the lag phase can be increased from 20 or 30 minutes under uncontrolled conditions to days, weeks, or months under controlled conditions, food preservation will have been achieved. This objective is largely accomplished in one or more of these ways:

1. destroying the organisms,

2. removing the microbes,

3. preventing a microbial attack, and

4. slowing down or stopping the reproduction of the undesirable organisms.

Another objective of food preservation is to delay undesirable autolysis. This is achieved by the inactivation or destruction of enzymes. However, the prevention of microbiological breakdown of the food is probably the most important goal of food preservation. A fourth goal is to minimize the damage caused by insects, rodents, and mechanical causes. All methods of food preservation are designed to achieve one or more of these objectives.

Low Temperature Food Preservation

Low temperatures are used to preserve food products during their flow through the control points of a food service operation. They are effective because they slow the growth of spoilage organisms and decrease the rate of chemical reactions and enzyme activity. The reproduction rate of microbes decreases as the temperature drops. Eventually the growth stops altogether as the organism is inactivated. However, the organism may survive the low temperatures by forming spores. When temperatures again become favorable, the spore can germinate to form a vegetative cell and then reproduce.

Chapter 3 introduced the classification of microorganisms by their temperature preferences. Recall that psychrophiles are organisms that prefer cool temperatures. Some psychrophiles remain active at refrigerator temperatures, and some spores can even survive freezer temperatures.

Thus, low temperature preservation cannot be expected to thoroughly destroy spoilage or pathogenic microorganisms in food. However, a reduction in the rate of microbial reproduction (along with a decrease in the number of cells) can be expected if correct time-temperature combinations are followed. The numbers of microorganisms killed, inactivated, or unaffected by low temperature food preservation methods depend on the type and numbers of microbes present, the rate of cooling, the time-temperature combinations, the characteristics of the food, and other variables. However, low temperature food preservation is effective in many applications, particularly in controlling thermophiles and mesophiles.

Three general ranges of low temperature food preservation are recognized: chilled storage, refrigerated storage, and freezer storage.

Chilled Storage. These temperatures are lower than room temperature but higher than refrigerated temperatures. A typical range for chilled storage is between 50°F (10°C) and 59°F (15°C). It is recommended that some fruits and vegetables (e.g., potatoes and cucumbers) be stored in this range.

Refrigerated Storage. These temperatures range from 32°F (0°C) to 45°F (7°C). Most food products that are classified as perishable are best stored at refrigerator temperatures. Storage at refrigerator temperatures effectively slows the rate of growth of spoilage organisms. In addition, the growth of most pathogenic bacteria, with the exception of some strains of *Clostridium botulinum*, is slowed in this way. Enzymatic and chemical reactions are also significantly reduced at refrigerator temperatures.

Other factors affect the ability of refrigerator temperatures to control spoilage organisms. The **relative humidity** is defined as the ratio of the water vapor present in the air to the quantity of water vapor that would be present if the air were saturated at that same temperature. In other words, the relative humidity reports the amount of moisture in the air as a percentage. The relative humidity of a storage area affects microbial growth and, therefore, storage times. If the relative humidity is too high, excessive moisture is present in the environment and the growth of microorganisms is encouraged. If the relative humidity is too low, moisture is lost to the environment from the food in storage. Water loss in fresh fruits and vegetables is characterized by wilting, softening, shrinkage, and reduced weight.

A uniform level of relative humidity is maintained in storage areas by ventilation or air flow. Ventilation in storage areas also helps maintain an optimum storage environment by removing undesirable odors. In some cases, it is desirable to alter the storage area atmosphere. Some storage areas have carbon dioxide gas or nitrogen gas added to permit the use of higher storage temperatures, higher relative humidities, and to prolong the shelf life of food products. **Controlled atmosphere storage** of food products maintains the desirable qualities of fresh fruits and vegetables.

Freezer Storage. These temperatures are generally 0°F (-18°C) or below. As one would expect, these very low temperatures reduce the growth rate of microorganisms even further. However, some spores can even survive freezer storage temperatures. One advantage that freezing has over refrigerating is that freezing also reduces the water activity (a_w) of food products. When water is converted from a liquid to a solid form, it is no longer usable by microbes.

Only high quality food products should be selected for freezer storage because most food products do not improve in quality after freezing. Prior to freezing, fruits and vegetables are selected, sorted, and washed. Any physical evidence of food spoilage or damage should be removed before food products are frozen. All inedible parts of the food must be removed prior to freezing.

Fruit and vegetable products are blanched before freezing. **Blanching** may be accomplished by exposing the product to either steam or hot water. Blanching sets the color of green vegetables and renders enzymes inactive. The blanching process also destroys some microorganisms, forces trapped air out of the plant cells, and causes leafy vegetables to wilt, making them easier to pack. Chemicals may be added to food products prior to freezing. **Antioxidants** are incorporated into some bakery products to prevent their fat and oil components from becoming rancid. **Rancidity** is a chemical change or decomposition which produces a disagreeable taste or odor in fatty foods. **Ascorbic acid** (vitamin C) is added to some fruits and vegetables to minimize browning reactions during frozen storage.

Many people are surprised to learn that frozen fruits and vegetables may have a *higher* nutritive value than similar "fresh" products. Consider, for example, fresh grapefruits harvested in Florida and shipped to Michigan. The citrus fruits may take one or two days to reach the northern state. Once they are received by the food distributor in Michigan, they may be stored under refrigeration for a couple of weeks until a food service operation places an order for the grapefruits. Upon delivery, they may be stored for as long as a week before they are actually used. Throughout this storage, the fruit continues to lose vitamin C (ascorbic acid). On the other hand, grapefruit to be commercially frozen is processed immediately, sometimes the same day as it was harvested. Therefore, the vitamin C content of frozen grapefruit is often higher than that of "fresh" grapefruit.

A variety of quick freezing methods are used for food products, depending on the individual characteristics of the product type. **Immersion freezing** requires the dipping of food products such as fish fillets directly into a low temperature coolant. Liquid nitrogen, brine, or sugar solutions are used in this technique. **Plate freezing** is utilized for boxes and packages of food, such as 2 or 2 1/2 pound (0.91 or 1.14 kg) boxes of frozen vegetables. Each package is placed between two plates that have a low-temperature coolant passing through them. **Blast freezing** requires exposure of food to temperatures as low as 0°F (-18°C) to -30°F (-34°C). This technique is used for freezing meats, fish, poultry, fruits, and vegetables.

Quick freezing reduces the temperatures of the product to -4°F (-20°C) in 30 minutes or less, while **slow freezing** takes 3 to 72 hours. Quick freezing is more desirable than slow freezing for a number of reasons. First, quick freezing better preserves the products' quality. Quick freezing causes small ice crystals to form within the food. This minimizes damage to the food's cell structure and preserves its flavor and texture. Second, when thawed, products that have been quick frozen exhibit less drip loss than similar products that have been slow frozen. (Drip loss is the moisture eliminated from frozen foods when they are thawed.) Third, quick freezing more promptly slows both enzymatic and microbial activity. Nevertheless, the specialized equipment needed for quick freezing is seldom available within a food service establishment, so slow freezing methods are often used. In fact, most food service freezers are *storage* freezers designed to hold frozen products, not to quick freeze them.

Even though a food product is frozen and stored at freezer temperatures, several changes which adversely affect quality can still take place. **Freezer burn** is a dehydration that occurs when frozen products are not wrapped or packaged properly. This loss of moisture takes place on the surface of fruits, vegetables, meats, fish, and poultry. Unfortunately, it is irreversible. Freezer burn is a form of food spoilage because it renders food products unusable. Furthermore, the texture, color, odor, appearance, and taste of foods is slowly altered under freezer storage conditions. Maximum storage times for various types of food are discussed later in this chapter.

The FDA's Food Service Sanitation Ordinance states:

Packaged means bottled, canned, cartoned, or securely wrapped.

Source: FDA, p. 21.

Thawing. Frozen food products may be cooked directly from the frozen state or thawed prior to cooking. But frozen food thawing is potentially hazardous if food products are exposed to the temperature danger zone (TDZ). Recall that the TDZ is the range of temperatures from 45°F (7°C) to 140°F (60°C). The method of food defrosting selected should minimize contact with the TDZ.

Thawing under refrigeration at temperatures of 45°F (7°C) or less is recommended since it minimizes contact with the TDZ. This technique also minimizes product quality loss and exposure to contamination. This method works well for frozen fruit, poultry, fish, shellfish, and large cuts of meats. There is an added advantage to thawing under refrigeration. Refrigerators don't actually chill food; they remove heat from the products. So if frozen food is placed in refrigerators to thaw, it will draw heat from the other refrigerated products. This heat exchange saves energy by reducing the amount of time the refrigerator's cooling equipment has to run. Today's food service establishments are often designed with back-to-back walk-in freezer and refrigerator combinations. These allow the (outer) refrigerator to serve as a buffer zone between the heat of the kitchen and the freezer, thus reducing the amount of cold air lost from the freezer.

Thawing under cold running water (50°F [10°C] or less) is also acceptable. However, items thawed in this manner must be protected from water damage by being tightly wrapped or placed in watertight containers. This method works well with frozen fruit and small cuts of meat and poultry.

With some food products, **defrosting as part of a conventional cooking process** can save time and still be safe. Small cuts of meat, poultry, fish, and frozen vegetables are usually defrosted and cooked simultaneously. Breaded vegetables, fish, and shellfish are actually better when they are cooked directly from the frozen state.

Microwave oven thawing may be used for some food products although limitations exist. Microwave thawing is acceptable only when it is part of the cooking process or when it is followed immediately by cooking. Also, bread and rolls are toughened when heated in a microwave oven, and large pieces of meat may not fit into the chamber.

It is important to remember that since foods are not pure water, they are not frozen at 32°F (0°C) as water is. In fact, foods both freeze and thaw at temperatures between 25°F (-4°C) and 32°F (0°C). Frozen foods have several opportunities to defrost during handling, transportation, and storing. If the food is thawed and then refrozen, large ice crystals will form and will negatively affect the product's quality characteristics. **Never thaw frozen foods at room temperature.** The risks are too great.

High Temperature Food Preservation

High temperatures are effective in food preservation because they control the growth of microorganisms. When most microbial cells are heated, they are either injured and inactivated or destroyed. The exceptions are thermophiles, which prefer relatively high temperatures, and other microorganisms which have the ability to form heat resistant spores. The heat stability of vegetative cells and spores varies considerably among the types of microorganisms.

Several variables affect the survival rate of cells and spores exposed to high temperatures. First, the time-temperature relationship is critical to controlling the growth of microorganisms. Given sufficiently high temperatures, as the temperature is increased, the amount of time required for microbial inactivation or destruction is reduced. Second, the initial colony size influences the rate of inactivation or destruction. Everything else being equal, as the number of cells or spores initially present increases, the amount of heat needed to accomplish inactivation or destruction also rises.

Finally, the composition of a food product also determines the effectiveness of high temperature food preservation. In general, carbohydrates, proteins, and fats in food exert a protective influence over organisms which helps them resist destruction by heat. When the water activity (a_w) is reduced, some microbes present in food become more heat resistant. Also, a pH near 7.0 (neutral) provides an increased heat resistance to microorganisms. To overcome the resistance of microbes to destruction by heat, some food products may require added chemicals such as nitrites or preservatives.

High temperature food preservation can be achieved through pasteurization or sterilization. **Pasteurization** temperatures are used: (a) to extend the shelf life of food by reducing spoilage organisms, or (b) to destroy all pathogenic microorganisms present in the food. Pasteurization may be accomplished in either of two ways. The **holder process** of pasteurization involves heating the food product to 145°F (63°C) for 30 minutes. In the **high temperature-short time (HTST) method** of pasteurization, the product is heated to 161°F (72°C) for 15 seconds. Both techniques require the heated food to be immediately cooled to 50°F (10°C) or less.

Perhaps the best example of pasteurized food is fluid milk. Both pasteurization methods are used for milk and milk products, although the HTST process is preferred since it is so rapid. In both cases, the time-temperature combinations are sufficient to eliminate the possible presence of two pathogens: *Mycobacterium tuberculosis* and *Coxiella burnetti*. These nonspore-forming pathogens cannot survive either pasteurization method. The importance of the pasteurization process is readily apparent when one considers that more than 17 billion gallons of milk are produced annually in the United States.

In addition to milk, the government requires that ice cream mixes (used to manufacture ice cream) and liquid egg products (e.g., shelled whole eggs) be pasteurized. This process minimizes the risks of *Salmonella spp.* microorganisms. Finally, canned hams are also pasteurized. Pasteurization eliminates pathogens, but since pasteurization does not destroy *all* microorganisms present in the food products, pasteurized foods must still be stored under refrigeration for the consumer's protection.

Sterilization, the other high temperature food preservation method, destroys virtually all microorganisms and their spores. Once the food is batch sterilized, or before it is individually sterilized, it must be stored in a hermetically sealed container. These containers typically include cans, glass bottles, and jars. With advances in food technology, flexible plastic containers can now be used for sterilized food products also. Because the food inside is sterilized, the containers do not need to be refrigerated until they are opened.

The FDA's Food Service Sanitation Ordinance states:

Hermetically sealed container means a container designed and intended to be secure against the entry of microorganisms and to maintain the commercial sterility of its content after processing.

Source: FDA, p. 21.

The **canning process** is designed to achieve **commercial sterilization** of food products. Techniques have improved greatly since Nicolas Appert did his pioneer work in canning in the late 1700s and early 1800s. The modern canning process begins with the arrival of the freshly harvested or slaughtered food. The food is **cleaned** and all inedible parts are removed. Some vegetables are **blanched** prior to being placed in the can.

Next, the washed, opened cans are **filled** with food products during the filling step of the canning process. Brine (salt water) is added to vegetables during this step.[3] The trend today in canned vegetables is toward a lower concentration of salt in the brine resulting in low salt or salt-free canned vegetables. Fish products such as tuna may be packed in either

---

[3] The exception is pickled vegetables, which are preserved by the acetic acid formed during fermentation.

brine or oil. People who are reducing their intake of calories usually prefer the water pack. A sugar-water solution is usually added to fruits during filling, although fruits packed in their own juices have gained popularity among consumers in recent years.

Once they are filled, the containers are **evacuated**. This means a partial vacuum is created in the container. During the sealing stage, the lids are added and **sealed** to the body of the containers. The objective is to form an airtight or hermetic seal. After a batch of containers are sealed, they are **heated** to sterilization temperatures for carefully controlled time periods.

A number of variables affect the amount of heat required for sterilization. First, the size, shape, and material of the container affect the heat transfer rate. Smaller cans permit a faster heat transfer than larger cans or glass bottles. Second, the contents of the container have a tremendous effect on the heat transfer rate. Extremely viscous food products (for example, tomato paste) have a slower heat transfer rate than food products that are largely liquid (tomato puree). The pH of the food also influences the amount of heat necessary for sterilization. In general, food products can be placed in one of three categories based on their pH:

1. **Low-acid foods** (pH above 4.5) include: meats, fish, poultry, milk, spinach, asparagus, pumpkin, corn, and lima beans. Because of their low acid content, these products require a relatively severe heat treatment to guard against the growth of *Clostridium botulinum*. The sterilization process is frequently used to achieve a desirable level of microbial destruction, while minimizing the negative effects on the product's texture, taste, odor, color, and appearance.

2. **Medium-acid foods** (pH of 3.7 to 4.5) include: tomatoes, pineapples, and pears. The acidity in this group of food products inhibits the growth of *Clostridium botulinum*. However, spoilage organisms can grow at this level of acidity, so the heat treatment must be severe enough to destroy these undesirable microbes.

3. **High-acid foods** (pH below 3.7) include: sauerkraut and berries. Few pathogenic or spoilage organisms can survive in such high acidity. A relatively mild heat treatment is required for this group.

Heating for sterilization usually takes place in a large container which is pressurized according to the food product and its ability to withstand heat. Food products that are particularly sensitive to heat are processed using a variation of the normal canning process. **Aseptic canning** is a procedure involving the separate sterilization of containers and contents. Once sterilized, the contents are placed into the containers and packed in a sterile environment. This process conserves nutrients, color, taste, odor, and texture but it is relatively expensive.

After the heating process is completed, the containers are **cooled**.

The cooling process must be gradual to prevent cans from bending and bottles from cracking. Once they have cooled, the containers are labeled and placed in boxes or cases for later shipment. Due to modern technology, commercial canning is a highly automated continuous process.

Food Preservation by Dehydration

Food has probably been preserved by drying since prehistoric times. The process of dehydrating food was probably discovered by early humans when leftover food was accidentally left in the sun to dry. **Dehydration** is an effective method of preservation because it reduces the a_w of the food and, thus, inhibits microbial activity. Food drying takes a variety of forms, namely, sun drying, mechanical drying, freeze-drying, and drying during smoking.

Sun Drying. This is effective in areas with low humidity and high temperatures. Fruits and vegetables have been dehydrated outdoors for centuries. Today, grapes, plums, currants, and apricots are dried this way.

Mechanical Drying. This is the main drying method of commercial importance. Prior to mechanical drying, food products are prepared by trimming, washing, and removing the inedible parts. Then heat is applied, usually in combination with moving air. The three mechanical drying methods are spray drying, tunnel drying, and drum drying.

Spray drying is a mechanical form of dehydration used for liquid foods. The liquid is sprayed continuously into the top of a drying chamber that may be several stories in height. Hot air mixes with the falling food and evaporates the moisture. The result is a fine powder of dried food which exits at the bottom of the chamber. Milk, tea, eggs, coffee, and fruit purees are spray dried.

Tunnel drying uses a conveyor belt to move the food products into and out of a drying chamber. Like spray drying, tunnel drying is a continuous process. Once in the chamber, the food is exposed to blasts of hot air that evaporate moisture. Tunnel drying is effectively used for vegetables, fruits, nuts, confectionery products, and breakfast cereals.

Drum drying utilizes a large rotating drum that is heated from within by steam. The liquid food is applied to the drum in a thin film as it rotates. A scraper is used to remove the dried food from the drum in this continuous process. Potatoes, breakfast cereals, infant foods, soups, and sauces are dried using this mechanical technique.

Freeze-Drying. This technique uses a process known as **sublimation**—the direct conversion of solid water (ice) to gaseous water (water vapor) without the usual intermediate step of melting into a liquid. To freeze-dry a food product, the product must first be frozen. Sublimation takes place in a drying chamber where a vacuum and a small amount of heat are applied. This process results in a dried product that is porous and easy to rehydrate. Also, minimal damage is done to the food product because only a small amount of heat is required for this process. However, freeze-drying is relatively expensive. Freeze-drying has been used for meat, fish, shellfish, poultry, vegetables, fruits, and coffee.

Drying During Smoking. This method is quite slow compared to other means of drying but its results are unique. Smoking alters the odor, color, appearance, texture, and taste of food products. It also has a tenderizing effect on proteins. Since colonial times, Americans have enjoyed the taste of foods hung up to dry in closed sheds where the smoke of hardwoods, especially hickory, fills the air. This method of drying is used for meats, fish, and cheese.

Drying is an effective preservation method because it reduces the a_w of foods and destroys some, but not all, of the organisms present. To achieve the desired results, strict time-temperature combinations must be adhered to during drying. In addition, the relative humidity and the air speed must be carefully controlled.

Once a food product is dried, its storage stability varies according to the natural components of the food. Dried foods that contain a relatively high percentage of fats or oils (e.g., meats) are more susceptible to rancidity reactions. Also, some food products such as apricots undergo a browning reaction when dried. However, chemical additives can be incorporated into the food prior to drying to prevent this undesirable oxidation. Regardless of their ingredients, dried food products must be stored in airtight containers to prevent them from absorbing moisture from the environment. Most dried foods must be reconstituted before they can be served. Once it is reconstituted, the food should be handled carefully.

The FDA's Food Service Sanitation Ordinance states:

Reconstituted means dehydrated food products recombined with water or other liquids.

Source: FDA, p. 22.

Chemical Food Preservation

In the United States, several chemical food additives have been approved by the Food and Drug Administration for food preservation applications. These chemical preservatives inhibit the activity of selected pathogens and spoilage organisms. The FDA strictly monitors the use of chemical preservatives. The categories of chemical preservatives are nitrites and nitrates, sugar and salt, sulfur dioxides and sulfites, ethylene and propylene oxides, alcohol, organic acids and their salts, and spices and other condiments.

Nitrites and nitrates and their salts are used in the preservation of meat products. They inhibit the activity of *Clostridium botulinum*, give cured meats their typical color, and contribute to flavor. Nitrites and nitrates are added to bacon, lunch meats, ham, and other cured meats.

Sugar and salt bind water and lower a food product's a_w. Salt is used in brines in which canned fish, meats, and vegetables are packed, and enhances their flavor. Sugar is found in the syrups in which canned fruits are packed; it also contributes to their flavor. Salt and sugar are added to a wide variety of foods to function as preservatives.

Sulfur dioxides and sulfites have several uses. Their sanitizing action is effective on equipment used to make wine. Sulfur dioxides and sulfites are also added to carbonated beverages, fruit juices, beer, dried fruits and vegetables, and pickled vegetables as antioxidants (to help prevent browning).

Ethylene and propylene oxides are used to sterilize containers in which food is packaged. For example, wine bottles and juice packages are sterilized with these oxides before the beverage is added.

Ethanol (ethyl alcohol) is the main carrier of flavors in extracts used for cooking (for example, almond extract and vanilla extract). Alcohol is developed in wines, spirits, and beers during fermentation. The natural flavorings are dissolved in the ethanol.

Organic acids and their salts are sometimes added to food products as preservatives. Salts are formed when organic acids and metals (e.g., sodium, calcium, potassium) are combined. However, in some foods, these acids and salts are formed naturally during normal fermentation. **Benzoates** are salts derived from benzoic acid. Benzoates are added to carbonated beverages, pickled vegetables, fruit jams and jellies, and margarine. **Propionates** are salts made from propionic acid. They control mold growth in baked products and cheeses. **Sorbates** are salts derived from sorbic acid. They inhibit mold and yeast activity. Sorbates are added to cheeses, beverages, fruits, margarine, pickled vegetables, and jams and jellies. **Acetates** are derivatives of acetic acid, better known as vinegar. Acetates are used in pickled vegetables, condiments, pickled sausages, and mayonnaise.

Spices and other condiments constitute the last class of chemical preservatives. Not all spices and condiments have the effect of inhibiting bacterial activity in food products, but some have been valued for centuries as flavor enhancers and preservatives. Cinnamon and cloves have antimicrobial properties. Condiments that contain vinegar discourage the growth of pathogens and spoilage organisms. Mayonnaise is germicidal to *Staphylococcus aureus*, *Escherichia coli*, and *Salmonella spp*. Mayonnaise is often wrongly blamed for foodborne illness outbreaks traced to salads. When high protein foods (e.g., meat, poultry, fish, eggs) are added to mayonnaise, they raise the product's pH and increase the likelihood of microbial growth. Holding such salads in the temperature danger zone (45-140°F[7-60°C]) compounds the dangers.

Food Preservation by Radiation

The use of radiation in food preservation is presently limited, although further research may reveal new applications. This method of preservation involves exposing food to ultraviolet light, gamma rays, or X rays to destroy harmful organisms. **Ultraviolet light** only acts on the surface of food products. In the past, it has been used in the aging (tenderization) of meats at relatively high temperatures. Ultraviolet light is now effectively used in reducing bacterial activity on the surface of fruit cakes before they are wrapped.

Gamma rays are produced by radioactive elements such as cobalt. They can be used to sterilize or pasteurize food products such as meats and poultry. They are also used, in some instances, to reduce insect infestation in newly harvested grains. Nevertheless, gamma radiation has a limited application in food preservation due to its adverse effects on foods from animal sources. High doses of gamma rays negatively alter the color, odor, taste, and appearance of these foods. In discussing the unacceptability of food from animal sources which was exposed to high doses of gamma rays, one food scientist said, "The food tastes like a wet dog smells." Current research and development of low dosage gamma radiation may result in a preservation technique that will not significantly alter either the appearance or taste of food. Fruits, vegetables, fish, and poultry are some of the products which may be preserved by low dosage gamma radiation in the future. **X rays** are essentially the same as gamma rays.

Having explored the causes of food spoilage and the methods used for commercial preservation, we can now consider specific recommendations for preserving foods of various types. The recommendations which follow should be valuable to food service and lodging operations due to the large sums of money they spend on food products.

Preservation Methods for Various Types of Foods

The characteristics of each category of food provide an insight into the potential spoilage problems food service companies may encounter. In this section, each group of food products is discussed in terms of its characteristics, spoilage potential, and preservation methods. (Since most of the food preservation methods have already been described in the previous section, the details are not repeated here.) The two main categories are foods from animal sources and foods from plant sources, although fats and oils will be seen as overlapping these categories somewhat. Within each main category, subcategories may have their own unique preservation methods.

Preservation of Foods from Animal Sources

Foods from animal sources include meats, poultry, fish and shellfish, eggs, dairy products, and fats. These foods represent a large portion of the food dollar spent by the average food service operation, so their preservation is important.

Meat. Meat is generally defined as the flesh of any animal used for food. For purposes of this discussion, meat includes beef, lamb, veal, and pork. The U.S. Department of Agriculture (USDA) classifies all edible parts of skeletal muscles, variety meats (tongue, diaphragm, esophagus, heart) and glandular meats (liver, kidney, brain, spleen, pancreas, thymus, and stomach linings) in the meat category. However, lean muscle is what most Americans call meat. The components of lean muscle tissue are listed in Exhibit 4.1. In light of the fact that lean muscle is mostly moisture, it is not surprising that meat is capable of supporting rapid bacterial growth. Recall that microbes need a certain level of water activity to survive and reproduce. Because meat and meat products have a relatively high a_w and are not highly acidic, they are considered potentially hazardous foods.

Several pathogenic bacteria have been detected in fresh meat products. Among the most prominent are *Staphylococcus aureus*, *Salmonella spp.*, and *Clostridium perfringens*. Spoilage organisms have also been

Exhibit 4.1 The Composition of Meat

Component	Percentage Range
Moisture	65 — 80
Proteins	16 — 22
Fats and Lipids*	1.5 — 42
Cartilage and Bone	0 — 26
Carbohydrates	1 — 2
Minerals	0.5 — 1
Vitamins	trace

*"Lipids" is a term for fats and oils and other substances that do not dissolve in water.

detected in fresh meat products. (These organisms are discussed in detail later in this section.)

Generally, the normal muscle tissue of healthy living animals does not harbor pathogenic microorganisms. However, spoilage organisms and pathogens can invade the muscle tissue from the animal's intestinal tract at the time it is slaughtered. The extent of the invasion is governed by the following:

1.　The microbial content in the animal's intestines

2.　The physiological condition of the animal before slaughter

3.　The method of slaughter

4.　The method of carcass cooling

The microbial content in the animal's intestines probably exerts the greatest influence over the potential contamination. For this reason, meat animals are usually starved for 24 hours before they are slaughtered.

The animal's physiological condition determines its internal body chemistry to some extent. Normally, after an animal is slaughtered, its muscles become stiff—a condition known as **rigor mortis**. Rigor mortis takes place in meat animals about 6 to 12 hours after slaughter depending on the carcass size. As rigor mortis sets in, a chemical reaction called **anaerobic glycolysis** takes place. During anaerobic glycolysis, **glycogen** (a chemical form of energy stored in muscle tissue) is converted to lactic acid. Calm, rested animals have more glycogen to be converted. Thus, the production of lactic acid in their carcasses causes a dramatic pH drop (from 7.0 to 5.6). An animal that is excited or fatigued prior to slaughtering will have used up its stored energy. Having less glycogen left in its tissue at the time of slaughter, less lactic acid will be produced. Thus, the pH drop will not be as dramatic. The result is **dark cutting meat**, which is less tender and more susceptible to microbial attack.

The method of slaughter should be quick and efficient. Besides being more humane, quick slaughtering can accomplish the objective of rapid bleeding in a relatively sanitary environment. The method of carcass cooling is important to meat preservation. Carcasses must be cooled quickly to reduce contact with the temperature danger zone (TDZ).

Additional microorganisms are introduced after the animals are slaughtered. For example, contaminants may enter the meat tissue from the animal's hide when it is skinned. When meat products are cut up or boned, further contamination may be introduced through knives and cutting surfaces. Ground (comminuted) meats and finely chopped meats are most susceptible to contamination because of their large surface areas and the additional handling they receive. Nevertheless, the majority of meat contamination comes from the penetration of pathogens from the intestinal tract of the animal. The survival and growth of microorganisms in meat are influenced by the kinds of organisms present, the physical and chemical characteristics of the meat, the storage temperature, and the amount of available oxygen. Besides contamination with pathogens, which has already been discussed, meats are susceptible to two broad types of spoilage: anaerobic and aerobic.

Anaerobic (without oxygen) spoilage of meat tissue takes place under conditions of a limited amount of oxygen. **Putrefaction** is a bacterial splitting of meat proteins, resulting in the formation of foul odors. *Pseudomonas spp.* are the bacteria responsible for this type of spoilage. **Souring** is a form of anaerobic spoilage caused by the production of acids. This process results in a sour odor and taste in meats.

Aerobic (with oxygen) spoilage of meat tissue is more likely to occur since fresh meat is rarely stored in an oxygen-free environment (a vacuum). Bacteria are responsible for the greatest amount of aerobic meat spoilage. Some bacteria form slimy capsules and surface slime on meat. Other bacteria change the color of meat to gray, green, and shades of brown. Still others frequently cause fat rancidity in meats. Finally, surface colors on meats can be changed to red, green, blue, or yellow by bacteria that produce pigments.

Molds are aerobic organisms that cause fuzziness or stickiness on meats. Color changes in the form of green, black, and white pigments are caused by molds. Other molds can decompose fats and proteins in meats because they have enzymes that accelerate the breakdown. This results in an unacceptable odor, color, taste, texture, and appearance. The genus of molds called *Penicillium* is often responsible for meat spoilage.

Food preservation methods for meat products are designed to prevent the activity of pathogenic and spoilage microorganisms. Meat products may be rendered commercially sterile by the canning process and, thus, do not usually have to be refrigerated. Also, meat products may be pasteurized, and then are stored under refrigeration. Low temperature preservation is the most common method of preserving fresh meats. Freezing and refrigerating are preferable to canning, in that they do not significantly alter the taste and texture of the meat. However, some psychrophilic spoilage organisms (*Pseudomonas spp.*) can grow on meats stored at refrigerator temperatures. Whenever meat products are chilled or frozen, they should be carefully wrapped to minimize contamination and dehydration. Recommended temperatures, times, and relative

Exhibit 4.2   Recommended Storage Temperatures, Times, and Relative Humidities for Fresh and Frozen Meats

PRODUCT	STORAGE TEMPERATURES	RELATIVE HUMIDITY (Percent)	STORAGE TIMES
Refrigerated Storage			
Beef			
Wholesale Cuts	34—36°F (1—2°C)	85	1-2 weeks
Portion Cuts	34—36°F (1—2°C)	85	4-6 days
Ground Beef	34—36°F (1—2°C)	85	1-2 days
Pork			
Wholesale Cuts	34—36°F (1—2°C)	85	5 days
Portion Cuts	34—36°F (1—2°C)	85	3 days
Ground Pork	34—36°F (1—2°C)	85	1-2 days
Lamb			
Wholesale Cuts	34—36°F (1—2°C)	85	1 week
Portion Cuts	34—36°F (1—2°C)	85	3-4 days
Veal			
Wholesale Cuts	34—36°F (1—2°C)	90	5 days
Portion Cuts	34—36°F (1—2°C)	90	3 days
Cured Meats	34—36°F (1—2°C)	75	2 weeks
Variety Meats	34—36°F (1—2°C)	85	3-5 days
Freezer Storage			
Beef			
Wholesale Cuts	−10—0°F (−23—−18°C)	—	6-10 months
Portion Cuts	−10—0°F (−23—−18°C)	—	4-8 months
Ground Beef	−10—0°F (−23—−18°C)	—	4-6 months
Pork			
Wholesale Cuts	−10—0°F (−23—−18°C)	—	4-8 months
Portion Cuts	−10—0°F (−23—−18°C)	—	2-6 months
Cured/Smoked	−10—0°F (−23—−18°C)	—	1-2 months
Lamb			
Wholesale Cuts	−10—0°F (−23—−18°C)	—	6-10 months
Portion Cuts	−10—0°F (−23—−18°C)	—	4-8 months
Veal			
Wholesale Cuts	−10—0°F (−23—−18°C)	—	4-8 months
Portion Cuts	−10—0°F (−23—−18°C)	—	2-6 months

humidities for storage of fresh and frozen meats are presented in Exhibit 4.2.

Some meat products are preserved by drying. This was a common practice among the pioneers who settled the western part of the United States. They made jerky by cutting meat into strips and drying it in the sun. Modern-day adventurers who backpack in the wilderness often take foil-packaged freeze-dried meat products which are easy to carry and prepare. Freeze-dried meat products are shelf stable as long as they are stored properly and their packages are not opened. Other dried meat products are often cured and/or smoked. Curing is the addition of common table salt, sugar, nitrites, or nitrates to meats. Smoking provides additional flavor to cured meats. Furthermore, the smoking process helps to tenderize beef and pork products. Meats can also be dried by smoking, apart from the curing process.

Poultry Products. This category includes chickens, turkeys, ducks, geese, and game birds. Like meats, poultry products are classified as potentially hazardous foods. Pathogenic and spoilage organisms prefer poultry products because they have a favorable pH, high moisture content, and high nitrogen content. The intestinal tract and skin of poultry may contain a variety of pathogenic bacteria, including *Staphylococcus aureus*, *Salmonella spp.*, and *Escherichia coli*. The frequent identification of poultry products with cases of human salmonellosis makes it especially important to properly preserve poultry products.

Spoilage is apparent when the poultry is sticky, slimy, and possesses an objectionable odor. Generally, two types of spoilage affect poultry products. Enzymes, present within the poultry cells, can cause chemical changes and deterioration. Fortunately, enzymatic changes are rapidly slowed down when poultry products are refrigerated or frozen. Bacteria are even more responsible for spoilage in poultry. Bacterial spoilage is usually traceable to the *Pseudomonas* and *Flavobacterium* genera. As with meat, most spoilage bacteria come from the live animal's skin and intestinal tract. Bacteria reproduce on the skin of slaughtered birds, in the cavity of whole carcasses, and on any cut tissue. Slowly, these spoilage organisms penetrate into the poultry tissue. Molds also accelerate the spoilage of poultry products.

Many precautionary measures are taken to properly process poultry products. After the animals are slaughtered, the carcasses are washed with chlorinated water to kill germs. Then the carcasses are immediately chilled by cold air, ice, or iced water. The cold air method is preferred because it rapidly brings the temperature down to 32°F (0°C) and does not add extra moisture to the carcass. If the poultry is cut up, additional steps must be taken to ensure that contamination is not added.

Low temperature preservation is frequently used for poultry products. Poultry products can be refrigerated or frozen successfully if they are carefully wrapped to minimize dehydration, contamination, and quality deterioration. Rapid freezing is desirable for the reasons previously discussed. Recommended temperatures, times, and relative humidities for storage of fresh and frozen poultry are presented in Exhibit 4.3.

Poultry products may also be preserved with the addition of heat. Poultry may be canned whole, in pieces, or completely boned. Some canned poultry products have a chemical preservative added. Organic acids, such as acetic acid, lengthen the shelf life of poultry products by lowering the pH. Some turkey products are cured; others are cured and then smoked.

Seafood. Consumption of seafood is on the rise in the United States. Seafood products may be subdivided into a number of categories, the most

Exhibit 4.3 Recommended Storage Temperatures, Times, and Relative Humidities for Fresh and Frozen Poultry

PRODUCT	STORAGE TEMPERATURES	RELATIVE HUMIDITY (Percent)	STORAGE TIMES
Refrigerated Storage			
Chickens			
Whole	30—34°F (−1—1°C)	85	2-4 days
Pieces	30—34°F (−1—1°C)	85	1-2 days
Turkeys			
Whole	30—34°F (−1—1°C)	85	2-4 days
Pieces	30—34°F (−1—1°C)	85	1-2 days
Ducks	30—34°F (−1—1°C)	85	2-4 days
Geese	30—34°F (−1—1°C)	85	2-4 days
Freezer Storage			
Chickens			
Whole	−10—0°F (−23—−18°C)	—	4-10 months
Pieces	−10—0°F (−23—−18°C)	—	3-6 months
Turkeys	−10—0°F (−23—−18°C)	—	4-10 months
Ducks	−10—0°F (−23—−18°C)	—	4-10 months
Geese	−10—0°F (−23—−18°C)	—	4-10 months

common being finfish and shellfish. **Finfish** come either from freshwater lakes and rivers or from the ocean.

Finfish can be classified as either fatty or lean. **Fatty finfish** have a relatively high natural fat content. Included in this category are bass, bluefish, bonito, grouper, halibut, herring, mackerel, pompano, salmon, sardines, shark, smelt, snapper, swordfish, tuna, and whitefish. Generally, other species of finfish are classified as **lean**. Catfish, cod, flounder, haddock, sole, perch, pike, pollock, scrod, and whiting fall into this category. (Shellfish are also considered lean.)

Shellfish are classified as crustaceans (shrimp, lobsters, crabs) or mollusks (oysters, clams, snails). Fish and shellfish have less connective tissue and a relatively high moisture content compared to meat and poultry. Therefore, fish and shellfish are more susceptible than meats and poultry to enzymatic autolysis and microbial spoilage.

Of all the types of products used in a food service operation, seafood is potentially the most hazardous. First, contamination can come from the natural slime present on the skin of fish. Most of this natural coating is harmless, but if the fish are taken from contaminated waters, their slime covering may be expected to contain contaminants. Typical pathogens on the skin of fish are *Vibrio parahaemolyticus*, *Clostridium botulinum*, *Salmonella spp.*, and the virus of infectious hepatitis. Further contamination can be introduced during processing and handling. The intestinal tract of fish may contain pathogens of the genera *Escherichia*, *Clostridium*, and *Bacillus*.

Quality levels in fish and shellfish are measured by smell and appearance. Fresh finfish has a mild agreeable odor. The skin should be bright and shiny with scales (if present) tightly attached. If the head is left on the fish, the eyes should be bright, clear, and protruding. The flesh of fresh fish is firm and elastic to the touch. Frozen fish should be solid with no discoloration on the firm flesh. Prior to freezing, the fish should be tightly wrapped or carefully packaged to withstand the low temperatures.

Many food service businesses in coastal areas have access to live shellfish; others must settle for frozen shellfish or fresh shellfish meat. (Some outstanding inland restaurants overcome this limitation by having a fresh catch flown in daily from coastal cities.) Fresh clams and oysters in the shell should be alive. This is indicated by a closed shell or one that closes tightly when tapped. If taken out of the shell, the meat of shellfish should be plump and free from off-odors. Live lobsters show movement in their claws and tails. The shell color of live lobsters is a bluish-green. Live crabs possess a sweet odor and show movement in their legs. Fresh shrimp have a firm texture with a mild sea odor. All frozen shellfish are undesirable if they have slimy or sticky flesh and a sour ammonia odor.

Finfish and shellfish may be preserved by canning. In most cases, a brine solution or oil is added to finfish and shellfish during the canning process. However, low temperature preservation is most frequently used for fish and shellfish. At all temperatures above freezing, the enzymatic autolysis (breakdown) of finfish and shellfish continues. However, at refrigerator temperatures this process is slower than it would be at room temperatures.

Today's freezing techniques permit the quick freezing of finfish and shellfish immediately after they are caught. Many modern fishing ships are actually floating processing plants where fresh fish can be efficiently cleaned, packaged, and refrigerated or frozen. Freezing prevents autolysis but it does not prevent fat oxidation from occurring, especially in fatty finfish. Recommended temperatures, times, and relative humidities for storage of fresh and frozen finfish and shellfish are illustrated in Exhibit 4.4.

Some fish products are preserved by drying, often with the addition of salt and/or smoke. Besides contributing flavor, salt added during drying may also act as a chemical preservative. Other chemical preservatives used with fish are nitrites, nitrates, and sorbic acid. The acetic acid in sauces made of wine, vinegar, or sour cream is used to pickle fish such as herring. Antioxidants are frequently added to fatty fish to prevent their natural fats and oils from becoming rancid.

Eggs. Eggs, the fourth category of foods from animal sources, are an excellent source of high quality protein, both for humans and microorganisms. The inside of eggs is protected by the shell, a porous and often contaminated covering. If the laying flock is contaminated, the pathogens will be present on the shell and can penetrate to the inside. Pathogens which have been known to contaminate eggs are *Salmonella spp.*, *Bacillus spp.*, *Escherichia coli*, and *Staphylococcus aureus. Salmonella spp.* are the pathogens most frequently found on fresh eggs. These microbes can come from the hen's intestinal tract or feathers, from the

Exhibit 4.4 Recommended Storage Temperatures, Times, and Relative Humidities for Fresh and Frozen Fish and Shellfish

PRODUCT	STORAGE TEMPERATURES	RELATIVE HUMIDITY (Percent)	STORAGE TIMES
Refrigerated Storage			
Finfish			
Fatty	28—32°F (−2—0°C)	95	1-2 days
Lean	28—32°F (−2—0°C)	95	1-3 days
Shellfish			
Mollusks	34—36°F (1—2°C)	85	1-7 days
Crustaceans	30—34°F (−1—1°C)	90	1-3 days
Freezer Storage			
Finfish			
Fatty	−10—0°F (−23—−18°C)	—	2-6 months
Lean	−10—0°F (−23—−18°C)	—	2-6 months
Shellfish			
Mollusks	−10—0°F (−23—−18°C)	—	2-6 months
Crustaceans	−10—0°F (−23—−18°C)	—	2-6 months

hands of humans, and from pests such as mice and rats.

Two types of spoilage take place during the storage of shell eggs. The first type is due to nonmicrobial penetration of the porous shell in two directions. Since the shell of an egg is porous, moisture gradually passes out of the egg. This moisture is displaced by oxygen entering the egg through the shell. Thus, as an egg ages, the size of the airspace increases. Also, the white albumin of the egg thins and the egg yolk membrane weakens, producing a "watery" egg. Furthermore, the pH increases from 7.6 to 9.5 as the egg gets older. This type of deterioration is not caused by microorganisms, but it is clearly undesirable.

The second type of spoilage affecting shell eggs is due to microorganisms. A high level of moisture in the air enhances the rate of microbial penetration from the shell to the interior of the egg. Thus, spoilage rates of fresh eggs are increased as the relative humidity rises. Several forms of microbial spoilage have been identified in eggs. **Green rot** in egg whites, **colorless rot**, **black rot**, and some mold spoilage may occur in eggs and egg products.

Egg products may be preserved in a number of ways. Heat preservation is somewhat limited due to the fact that the egg white has a tendency to coagulate. Nevertheless, the United States Department of Agriculture requires that liquid whole eggs and egg whites be pasteurized to control the proliferation of *Salmonella spp.* Eggs may also be successfully dried, usually by means of the spray drying technique. Prior to drying, egg whites must be treated with an enzyme to prevent the appearance of undesirable brown colors. Dried eggs must be stored carefully due to their tendency to absorb excess moisture and contaminants.

Exhibit 4.5 Recommended Storage Temperatures, Times, and Relative Humidities for Fresh and Frozen Eggs

PRODUCT	STORAGE TEMPERATURES	RELATIVE HUMIDITY (Percent)	STORAGE TIMES
Refrigerated Storage			
Shell Eggs	29—35°F (−2—2°C)	80-85	2-4 weeks
Dried Eggs	35°F (2°C)	minimum	6-12 months
Reconstituted Eggs	29—35°F (−2—2°C)	80-85	2-4 weeks
Freezer Storage			
Whole Eggs	−10—0°F (−23—−18°C)	—	6-8 months

Low temperature preservation techniques are effective for eggs. To lengthen the shelf life of refrigerated shell eggs, some egg producing companies coat the shells with a colorless, odorless, tasteless mineral oil. On the other hand, whole eggs and egg whites can be successfully frozen without any such coatings. To freeze egg yolks, sugar or salt must first be added. Without the addition of sugar or salt, frozen yolks form a gel which persists even after thawing. Because their ease of handling and long shelf life make them practical, frozen eggs are frequently purchased in 30- to 50-pound (13.62 to 22.70 kg) containers. A summary of temperatures, times, and relative humidities for storage of various forms of eggs is presented in Exhibit 4.5.

Dairy Products. These products constitute the fifth category of foods from animal sources. This large category encompasses milk, cream, butter, cheese, frozen desserts, and fermented milk products. All of these products begin with the milking of cows. The milk of healthy cows contains few pathogens or spoilage organisms. However, contamination has been traced to equipment and handlers. Equipment may harbor *Staphylococcus aureus* and *Salmonella spp.* organisms. Because milk and milk products are highly perishable, they are classified as potentially hazardous foods.

Dairy products may spoil in a variety of ways. Fresh milk may sour by the action of either *Streptococcus lactis, Lactobacillus bulgaricus,* or *Lactobacillus thermophilus,* depending on its temperature. While this souring is undesirable in milk and most other dairy products, it adds to the characteristic flavor of yogurt. When *Bacillus, Clostridium,* and *Pseudomonas* organisms are present in milk, a protein breakdown results. Other organisms are responsible for the rancidity of milk fat, flavor changes, and color changes in milk.

Dairy products are primarily preserved by pasteurization, because the fresh milk used to make them is pasteurized. The United States Department of Agriculture also requires that ice cream mixes be pasteurized.

A comparison of the components of the four basic types of milk—fresh whole, evaporated, condensed, and dried—is given in Exhibit 4.6.

Exhibit 4.6   Approximate Compositions of Fresh Whole, Evaporated, Condensed, and Dried Milk

Component	Type of Milk			
	Fresh Whole	Evaporated	Condensed	Dried
Water	88%	74%	30%	3%
Fat	3.5	8	8	27
Nonfat Solids	8.5	18	20	70
Sugar	—	—	42	—

Fresh milk is potentially hazardous and must be stored under exact time-temperature combinations. In the United States, **fresh whole milk** is usually homogenized, although this does not contribute to its preservation. **Homogenization** is a process that uses pressure to force milk through tiny openings. This breaks up the fat globules present in whole milk so that they are permanently suspended in the whey (liquid portion of the milk). Thus, the fat globules cannot recombine and rise to the top as cream. Before the process of homogenization became widely used, consumers had to vigorously shake bottles of unhomogenized milk to distribute the milk fat but soon after it would recombine. Many dieters prefer to drink low fat milk or skimmed milk. These products have some of the fat already skimmed off.

In addition to being pasteurized, **condensed milk** and **evaporated milk** are also canned, so they last much longer than fresh milk. Few spoilage problems arise as long as their containers have been properly sealed and heat processed. The high sugar content of condensed milk also helps to preserve it.

Dried milk is made by preheating milk and then spray drying it. Usually the combination of heat and drying results in low bacterial counts. Dried milk is relatively safe as long as it is properly stored to prevent the addition of moisture. **Ice cream** is generally free of bacteria. It benefits from the combination of pasteurization and freezer temperatures which kill most organisms and prevent the reproduction of survivors.

Butter is made from pasteurized cream. Once the butter is produced, it is held at freezer temperatures. Butter containing salt is more inhibiting to bacteria than salt-free butter. The low moisture content of butter provides favorable conditions for mold growth.

Cheese is manufactured from pasteurized milk. Some cheeses such as Romano and Parmesan are so low in moisture that they will not support the normal growth of bacteria. However, molds frequently attack cheeses. Cheese may be salted or smoked during processing. Selected temperatures, times, and relative humidities for storage of various dairy products are illustrated in Exhibit 4.7.

Fats and Oils. Fats and oils constitute an important food category because they are a part of a wide variety of food products, including cookies, crackers, butter, cheese, breakfast cereals, salad dressings, milk, nuts, snack foods, meats, poultry, some fish, and some fruits and veget-

Exhibit 4.7 Recommended Storage Temperatures, Times, and Relative Humidities for Dairy Products

PRODUCT	STORAGE TEMPERATURES	RELATIVE HUMIDITY (Percent)	STORAGE TIMES
Refrigerated Storage			
Butter	32—36°F (0—2°C)	85	2-4 weeks
Cheese, Hard	38—40°F (3—4°C)	75	4-6 months
Cheese, Soft	38—40°F (3—4°C)	75	3-14 days
Fluid Milk	36—38°F (2—3°C)	85	6-14 days
Reconstituted Dried Milk	36—38°F (2—3°C)	85	5-8 days
Freezer Storage			
Ice Cream and Frozen Desserts	0—10°F (−18—−12°C)	—	2-4 months
Dry Storage			
Condensed Milk	50—70°F (10—21°C)	50—60	2-4 months
Evaporated Milk	50—70°F (10—21°C)	50—60	8-10 months
Dried Milk	50—70°F (10—21°C)	50—60	8-10 months

ables. Fats and oils in their pure form may be contrasted in three ways. Fats come from animal sources, are solid at room temperature, and are usually saturated. Oils are generally from plant sources, are liquid at room temperature, and are unsaturated. **Saturated fats** contain the maximum amount of hydrogen in the molecule and, therefore, are less susceptible to breakdown than unsaturated oils.

Foods containing fats and oils can undergo three types of breakdown reactions: autoxidation, hydrolytic rancidity, and flavor reversion. **Autoxidation** is a form of oxidative rancidity caused by the exposure of the fat or oil to oxygen. The reaction is increased in the presence of heat, metals (e.g., iron, copper), salt, and light. **Unsaturated oils** are more susceptible to autoxidation than saturated fats. Oxidative rancidity gives off-odors and flavors to food products. It is controlled by the addition of antioxidants such as BHA (butylated hydroxyanisole) and BHT (butylated hydroxytoluene). BHA and BHT are added to many bakery products to control autoxidation.

Hydrolytic rancidity is responsible for flavor, odor, and taste changes in butter and products containing milk fat. It is caused by an enzyme called **lipase**. Lipase breaks down milk fat (triglyceride) into its components. Since the fatty acids in milk fat are saturated, they possess a noticeable odor at room temperature. This reaction is controlled by heating the milk fat to destroy the lipase enzyme.

Flavor reversion is another form of oxidative rancidity. It occurs in vegetable oils that are highly unsaturated and contain linolenic acid, a polyunsaturated fatty acid. The result of flavor reversion is an unacceptable beany, fishy, or paint-like odor. Flavor reversion is controlled by a process known as **partial hydrogenation**. Hydrogen gas is added so that the polyunsaturated linolenic fatty acid becomes saturated and the problem is eliminated. Soybean oils used in the manufacture of salad dressings are partially hydrogenated to control flavor reversion.

The reasons for the proper preservation of foods from animal sources are obvious. First, proper preservation controls pathogenic microorganisms which could cause a foodborne disease outbreak. Thus, it contributes to the operation's sanitation program. Second, effective control of spoilage reduces food waste. Because foods from animal sources constitute the majority of all purchases made by most food service establishments, proper preservation of these products is essential to any operation's cost control program. Finally, proper storage of foods preserves their desirable qualities and, thus, contributes to customer satisfaction.

Preservation of Foods from Plant Sources

Foods from plant sources have increased in popularity in recent years. In keeping with the trends toward physical fitness and weight-consciousness, food service customers are demanding more fruits, vegetables, grains, cereals, and nuts.

Fresh Fruits and Vegetables. These products generally continue respiring (living) after they are harvested. As they pass through the channels of distribution, their respiration is counteracted by autolysis and microbial spoilage. The rate of enzymatic autolysis in fruits and vegetables varies directly with the temperature. That is, autolysis is substantially reduced when temperatures are decreased in the product.

A number of microorganisms may be present on the exteriors of fresh fruits and vegetables. The microbes include *Pseudomonas spp.*, *Bacillus spp.*, *Streptococcus faecalis*, *Staphylococcus aureus*, *Clostridium botulinum*, and a variety of molds. Most of these are spoilage organisms although a few are pathogenic to humans.

Bacteria are responsible for several types of vegetable spoilage. *Pseudomonas spp.* cause a mushy, soft, odorous spoilage called *soft rot*. Other bacteria cause vegetables to rot and develop sour off-odors. *Botrytis cinerea* is a mold which causes gray rot on vegetables. Other molds can cause soft rot, black rot, and sour rot to develop on vegetables.

Most fruit spoilage is the result of mold growth. Molds may produce gray, green, blue, and white pigments on fruit. For example, *Botrytis cinerea* causes a gray rot, while *Penicillium spp.* are responsible for a blue-colored rot. The activity of molds can also cause softening, souring, and the development of bitter flavors in fresh fruits.

Fresh fruits and vegetables acquire their microbial populations from the water and the soil as they grow. Since plants consist largely of moisture and carbohydrates, organisms that prefer these nutrient sources are most frequently found on fruits and vegetables. Washing the surfaces of fresh fruits and vegetables reduces the population of microorganisms on their exteriors.

Fresh fruits and vegetables are preserved by the use of low tempera-

Exhibit 4.8   Recommended Storage Temperatures, Times, and Relative Humidities for Fruits

PRODUCT	STORAGE TEMPERATURES	RELATIVE HUMIDITY (Percent)	STORAGE TIMES
Fresh Fruits			
Apples	30—32°F (−1—0°C)	85	2-6 months
Grapefruits	32—45°F (0—7°C)	85	1-2 months
Lemons	46—50°F (8—10°C)	85	1-4 months
Limes	46—50°F (8—10°C)	85	1-2 months
Melons	40—45°F (4—7°C)	85	2-4 weeks
Oranges	32—36°F (0—2°C)	85	2-3 months
Peaches	30—32°F (−1—0°C)	85	2-4 weeks
Berries	30—32°F (−1—0°C)	85	1-2 weeks
Grapes	30—32°F (−1—0°C)	85	1-2 months
Strawberries	30—32°F (−1—0°C)	85	4-8 days
Canned Fruits	50—72°F (10—21°C)	50-60	8-12 months
Frozen Fruits	−10—0°F (−23—−18°C)	−	6-12 months

tures. When they are harvested, their temperature is immediately dropped for preservation purposes. Many fruits and vegetables can be frozen, as described earlier in this chapter. Others are refrigerated as they move to fresh produce markets. However, some fruits (e.g., bananas) are susceptible to chill shock and must be stored at higher temperatures. Some recommended temperatures, times, and relative humidities for storage of fresh, canned, and frozen fruits and vegetables are presented in Exhibits 4.8 and 4.9, respectively.

The year-round availability of fruits and vegetables throughout the United States is largely due to freezing and canning. Of course, some canned foods still spoil due to can corrosion, leakage, or insufficient heating during the canning process. Three types of canned food spoilage are flat sour spoilage, thermophilic gas spoilage, and carbon dioxide gas spoilage.

Flat sour spoilage of canned foods is caused by the anaerobic growth of heat resistant bacteria that form spores. *Bacillus coagulans* is responsible for this kind of spoilage in tomatoes and tomato juice. These organisms change the flavor but not the appearance of canned foods.

Thermophilic gas spoilage is also caused by heat resistant microbes that form spores. However, when these microorganisms survive the heating process (due to insufficient time-temperature combinations), they produce gas. Examples are *Clostridium sporogenes*, *Clostridium putrefaciens*, and *Clostridium thermosaccharolyticum*. These organisms cause food cans to swell and become distorted. In general, if the top and

Exhibit 4.9 Recommended Storage Temperatures, Times, and Relative Humidities for Vegetables

PRODUCT	STORAGE TEMPERATURES	RELATIVE HUMIDITY (Percent)	STORAGE TIMES
Fresh Vegetables			
Asparagus	32—34°F (0—1°C)	90	2-4 weeks
Beans	40—45°F (4—7°C)	85	7-10 days
Cabbage	32—34°F (0—1°C)	90	2-3 months
Carrots	32—34°F (0—1°C)	90	1-3 weeks
Cauliflower	32—34°F (0—1°C)	85	2-3 weeks
Corn	31—32°F (−1—0°C)	85	4-7 days
Cucumbers	45—48°F (7—9°C)	90	1-2 weeks
Lettuce	32—34°F (0—1°C)	90	2-4 weeks
Onions	32—34°F (0—1°C)	75	5-8 months
Potatoes	50—55°F (10—13°C)	85	2-4 months
Spinach	32—34°F (0—1°C)	90	1-2 weeks
Squash, Zucchini	32—36°F (0—2°C)	85	1-2 weeks
Tomatoes, Ripe	32—34°F (0—1°C)	85	7-10 days
Canned Vegetables	50—70°F (10—21°C)	50-60	8-12 months
Frozen Vegetables	−10—0°F (−23—−18°C)	—	6-10 months

bottom of a can are flat, it is a safe product. A **flipper** is a can with flat ends that bulge when the can is warm. A **springer** is a can with moderate bulges on both top and bottom. A **soft swell** is similar to a springer, however, the bulges can be pushed back with finger pressure. A **hard swell** has both ends bulged, and they cannot be pushed back with finger pressure.

Carbon dioxide gas spoilage occurs when nonspore-forming bacteria enter the product after processing. These spoilage organisms get into the can because of a faulty seal or a leak. For example, *Micrococcus spp.* and *Streptococcus thermophilus* can make the contents of a can frothy and slimy. Flippers, springers, soft swells, and hard swells result from carbon dioxide gas spoilage.

Of course, there is always the possibility that the deadly toxin of the pathogen *Clostridium botulinum* may be present in a swollen can. If you ever observe *any* abnormal conditions in canned products, *throw them out.* Don't take a chance with your own life or the lives of your customers and employees.

In addition to freezing and canning, drying is used to preserve some fruits and vegetables. This process destroys molds and yeasts along with nonspore-forming bacteria. Freeze-drying is very effective with fruits and vegetables. Regardless of how fruits and vegetables are preserved, care must be taken to avoid introducing pathogenic and spoilage organisms during processing and handling.

Cereals, Grains, and Flours. These products are various forms of wheat, oats, rice, barley, corn, rye, and chicory plants. They can be grouped together because they have similar contamination problems. The exterior of these products can be contaminated by soil, insects, and equipment. *Bacillus cereus* is an organism frequently found on cereal grains. Most microbial contamination is removed from grains during milling. Flours are relatively free of pathogens and spoilage organisms. However, if the moisture content of flour is raised, certain bacteria can cause a fermentation which results in spoilage. Also, molds frequently attack baked products made from flours.

Among the most familiar spoiled food products are bakery products which frequently exhibit *Rhizopus nigricans* (a black mold) or *Penicillium expansum* (a green mold). Mold growth can be controlled in baked products by fast cooling followed by prompt wrapping. Also, the addition of chemicals (e.g., calcium propionate, sodium propionate) to doughs and batters prior to baking inhibits mold activity.

The formation of **rope** in bakery products is characterized by an odor of ripe melons, yellow crumb color, sticky crumbs, and a slimy, stringy threadlike material when the product is sliced. Rope is caused by a spore-forming group of *Bacillus* organisms. It is controlled by the addition of acid prior to baking, fast cooling, and freezing.

Spices. Spices are normally not prone to spoilage although they may have molds present. Some spices exhibit bacterial spoilage if their water content is excessively increased.

Nuts. Nuts do not normally spoil by the action of bacteria because their moisture content is too low and their fat content too high. They are susceptible to rancidity reactions, however. Molds may also cause some slight problems if the water content of the nuts is raised.

Carbonated beverages. These products generally do not spoil if stored properly. The trapped carbon dioxide gas lowers the pH, and added acids (e.g., citric, benzoic) inhibit microbial activity. Because yeasts can spoil carbonated beverages containing sugar, beverage canners and bottlers carefully control the yeast content of their products.

Beer is generally not susceptible to spoilage because it contains alcohol and carbon dioxide. Most bottled and canned beer is pasteurized and, if stored below 70°F (21°C), will not spoil. Keg beer is more delicate since it is usually not pasteurized. Table wine may be attacked by yeasts and bacteria. The result is the formation of acetic acid (vinegar). Alcoholic spirits and liqueurs contain so much alcohol they are virtually free of all forms of spoilage.

Summary

Food spoilage and food contamination are intimately related in that they are both largely caused by the action of bacteria and molds. One startling difference separates the pathogens from the spoilage organisms. Pathogens, which cause foodborne disease, are often undetectable until after the food products are eaten, whereas spoilage organisms, which are not responsible for foodborne outbreaks, are usually readily detectable by sight and smell.

Many food preservation techniques are designed to lengthen the lag phase of bacterial growth. Food products are preserved by techniques in five categories: high temperatures, low temperatures, dehydration, chemical preservatives, and irradiation. Each preservation technique has its own advantages in food processing.

Foods from animal sources readily spoil through the action of spoilage bacteria and molds. These potentially hazardous foods also harbor a variety of pathogenic microorganisms. Foods from plant sources may also be attacked by spoilage bacteria, though mold spoilage is more frequent.

Recommended storage temperatures, times, and relative humidities for various food types were presented to show how food service operations can minimize food contamination and spoilage. A reduction in food waste alone can have a positive impact on a hospitality operation's bottom line.

References

Dawson, L. E.; Chipley, J. R.; Cunningham, F. E.; and Kraft, A. A. "Incidence and Control of Microorganisms on Poultry Products." *North Central Regional Research Publication No. 260*, November 1979. pp. 3-36.

Denny, C. B. "Thermophilic Organisms Involved in Food Spoilage: Introduction." *Journal of Food Protection*, February 1981. 44(2):144-145.

Fennema, O. R., ed. *Principles of Food Science. Part II. Physical Principles of Food Preservation*. New York: Dekker, 1975.

Frazier, W. C., and Westhoff, D. C. *Food Microbiology*. 3rd ed. New York: McGraw-Hill, 1978.

"The Gamma Ray Gourmet." *INC.*, August 1983. 5(8)23.

Jay, J. M. *Modern Food Microbiology*. 2nd ed. New York: Van Nostrand, 1978.

Kaufman, O. W. "Microbiology in Food Processing." *Dairy and Food Sanitation*, January 1982. 2(1):18-19.

Longree, Karla. *Quantity Food Sanitation*. 2nd ed. New York: Wiley- Interscience, 1978.

Mutkoski, S. A., and Schurer, M. L. *Meat and Fish Management*. North Scituate, Mass.: Breton, 1981.

Ockerman, H. W. *Source Book for Food Scientists*. Westport, Conn.: AVI, 1978.

Richter, R. "Microbiological Problems in Dairy Foods in the 1980's." *Journal of Food Protection*, June 1981. 44(6):471-475.

Smith, J. L., and Palumbo, S. A. "Microorganisms as Food Additives." *Journal of Food Protection*, December 1981. 44(12):936-955.

Sofos, J. N.; Busta, F. F.; and Allen, C. E. "Botulism Control by Nitrite and Sorbate in Cured Meats: A Review." *Journal of Food Protection*, September 1979. 42(9):739-770.

Tiwari, N. P., and Kadis, V. W. "Microbiological Quality of Some Delicatessen Meat Products." *Journal of Food Protection*, November 1981. 44(11):821-827.

Strategies for Success at the Aspen Hotel

Paul James entered the conference room with a feeling of confidence. He introduced himself to the seven department heads in the room. Terri Martin, the GM's executive secretary, was also present. Paul acknowledged that Terri's efficiency and organization had already proved to be helpful. She had been very instrumental in coordinating the schedules of all the department heads and in setting up the meeting. Terri was also responsible for much of the paperwork at the Aspen Hotel, where she had been working for the past eight years.

George Allen introduced himself as the front office manager. George had six years of service with the hotel. His staff consisted of an assistant front office manager and a number of desk clerks and cashiers. George explained that his department was critical to the success of the hotel because it was the first department to welcome guests and the last department to serve them during their lodging experience.

The executive housekeeper was seated to George's left. She introduced herself as Angie Jack and said that she had 15 years of service with the hotel. Angie explained that she had seen a great deal of change at the hotel during her tenure in the housekeeping department. Her department was responsible for cleaning guestrooms and public areas, as well as operating the in-house laundry.

Harry Gregor introduced himself as the hotel's chief engineer. Harry was the only department head who had been with the hotel since the day it opened. The engineering department consisted of Harry and one other man who were responsible for the physical facilities, including equipment repair and maintenance. Paul James had heard reports that Harry's department had run on a shoestring budget for years.

Elisabeth Mueller said she was the hotel's food and beverage director. She was directly responsible for all food and beverage service at the Aspen Hotel, including coffee shop operations, dining room service, room service, special functions, and beverage operations. Elisabeth had been the F&B director at the hotel for 12 years. Her main assistants were the kitchen manager, two dining room managers, and a bar manager.

Paul James realized that Elisabeth's position was a very important one from the standpoint of customer satisfaction and the overall image of the hotel.

Mike Beers, the director of sales and catering, introduced himself next. Mike explained that it was his responsibility to handle group bookings, advertising, public relations, and convention services. Mike admitted that, of all the department heads, he had the least amount of service with the Aspen Hotel. He had been the property's director of sales and catering for less than six months.

Finally, the Aspen Hotel's controller, Bob Campbell, was introduced. Bob's department was responsible for all accounting functions in the entire hotel. Also, the Aspen's two purchasing agents reported directly to the controller. One purchasing agent was in charge of buying all food and beverage supplies. The other purchasing agent handled all nonfood supplies.

As Paul James listened, he detected varying levels of enthusiasm and commitment to excellence among the department heads. These people were his key personnel resources. They could either help him become a winner or contribute to his failure. Paul knew he had to generate a commitment to excellence in each of these key people. If he could do that, the department heads would work to achieve success in their own areas. Paul sensed that he had his work cut out for him; it wasn't going to be easy.

Nevertheless, the rest of the meeting went well. The GM obtained a verbal promise from all of the department heads that they would submit their ideas, suggestions, and goals by next Tuesday. Paul ended the meeting on a positive note. He told his key staff members that he was a builder. He said that his position obligated him to encourage growth in both the professional knowledge and the personal objectives of each person in the hotel. He emphasized that he wanted and needed each one of the department heads to be a member of his building team. The GM challenged each department head to help make the Aspen Hotel a great property. Paul knew that was the only route to excellence.

The following case studies are designed to enhance your understanding of the material in this chapter. If you are a Home Study student, use these case studies to stimulate questions about this chapter. If you are a Group or Institutional Study student, you may be asked to discuss these case studies as part of a regular classroom assignment.

CASE STUDY 4.1

A restaurant called Two's Company is located in the Rocky Mountains. Chef Cheech Anderson is responsible for all food purchasing, receiving, storing, and production. The restaurant was built in the early 1970s and has a reputation for serving high quality fish and meat products.

Two days ago, Chef Anderson placed an order with the Clover Leaf Food Distribution Company for frozen shrimp in the shell. The chef uses the shrimp for appetizers and as a component of his famous "shrimp rocky mountain" entree.

The driver from Clover Leaf is now in the process of unloading the chef's weekly order. Chef Anderson is personally checking each item on the invoice. As he starts his inspection of the frozen shrimp, the chef notices that the box has been opened and resealed. Upon opening the box, Chef Anderson discovers that the shrimp have a large deposit of ice crystals on them.

Test Your Understanding

1.   What factors are likely to be responsible for the shrimp's appearance?

2.   Should the chef accept the shrimp?

3.   What are your recommendations to Chef Anderson?

CASE STUDY 4.2

The Buccaneer Inn is an ocean-front resort hotel. The annual food and beverage volume at the Buccaneer Inn exceeds $1 million. In addition to its high quality seafood, the inn also offers a wide variety of beef, pork, lamb, and veal entrees. The food and beverage manager of the inn, Louie Carpinelli, is in the process of taking a month-end inventory of meat in the walk-in refrigerator.

As Louie enters the walk-in, he notices an off-odor in the meat storage area. Further inspection reveals that some oven-prepared beef ribs feel sticky and have a green appearance and an unpleasant odor. Also, a round of beef stored near the back of the walk-in refrigerator has a slimy coating all over its surface.

Test Your Understanding

1.   What organisms are likely to be responsible for this meat spoilage?

2.   How should the products be handled?

3.   What are your recommendations to Louie Carpinelli?

CASE STUDY 4.3

As Louie Carpinelli continues his month-end inventory of all food products, he enters the freezer. As usual, the freezer is in a state of disarray. Food products are stacked on shelves, in aisles, and directly on the floor. (The chef of the Buccaneer Inn has often complained that he never seems to have enough frozen food storage space.) Upon checking his inventory records, Carpinelli realizes that some of the frozen food products have been in storage for over a year. In the meat section of the walk-in freezer, Carpinelli notices several beef loins wrapped in freezer paper. Some of the wrappings are loose, and the meat is partially exposed. Carpinelli spots a brown dried area on three of the beef loins.

Test Your Understanding

1. What is the cause of the surface discoloration on the beef loins?

2. How could this situation have been avoided?

3. What are your recommendations to food and beverage manager Carpinelli?

CASE STUDY 4.4

The Portentous Palace is an extremely expensive supper club in a major city. Food and beverage checks average $43 per person. All menu items are prepared to order at the Palace. Diners usually spend three hours and sometimes the entire evening consuming a seven-course meal at the Palace.

The manager of the Portentous Palace, Mary Harrison, believes that "fresh is best." Only fresh fruits and vegetables are used in the preparation of menu items. The chef has just informed Ms. Harrison that the fresh zucchini squash that was to be served as the vegetable tonight is spoiled. According to the chef, the zucchini is mushy and soft with an unacceptable odor. Mary Harrison tries to find out how the zucchini spoiled. When she asks the chef, he replies, "I don't know. It was stored in the vegetable walk-in for one week and should still be servable." Mary Harrison looks at the thermometer hanging from the shelf in the vegetable walk-in and, to her surprise, the reading is 45°F (7°C).

Test Your Understanding

1. What microorganisms are likely to be responsible for spoilage of the zucchini?

2. How could the spoilage have been avoided?

3. What are your recommendations to Ms. Harrison?

CASE STUDY 4.5

Dennis Star is the new owner of the Cul-de-Sac Restaurant, an existing business. He has just closed the deal on the restaurant, and he feels he got a real bargain. Included in the sale price was the building, furniture and fixtures, and food inventory. Before he bought the restaurant, Dennis took a quick tour of the Cul-de-Sac with its former owner. Rather than looking over the actual food inventory, Dennis looked at the physical inventory records kept by the former owner.

Now Dennis takes a closer look around his restaurant. In the basement, Dennis notices a small storage area located directly under the stairway to the main floor. Upon entering the storage area, Dennis notices that the room is unusually warm so he removes his sport coat. Several steam pipes are located on the ceiling of the storage area.

Various canned fruits and vegetables are stored in this dry storage area. Some cans have bulging ends, and one can has exploded and splattered its contents on the shelf and floor.

Test Your Understanding

1. What microorganisms are likely to be responsible for the bulging cans and exploded food container?

2. What should be done with the canned fruits and vegetables in the storage area?

3. What are your recommendations to Dennis Star?

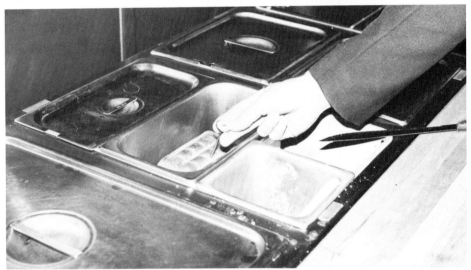

FIVE

Regulatory and Professional Organizations

Strategies for Success at the Aspen Hotel

Paul James, the new GM of the Aspen Hotel, felt good after the first department head meeting. He asked Angie Jack, Harry Gregor, and Elisabeth Mueller to meet with him during lunch to discuss the hotel's noncompliance with the local health department's code. Since none of the hotel food service outlets were operable, Paul suggested that the department heads meet him in the main dining room of their nearest competitor, the Twin Towers Hotel. Paul opened the meeting by asking each of the three department heads to talk about the nature of the Aspen's noncompliance.

Chief Engineer Harry Gregor spoke first. "During the past ten years, most of the hotel construction and renovation was done without the health department reviewing our plans. They never asked us to submit plans for construction or renovation, and we never volunteered the information. I don't understand why they're enforcing codes now that they never cared about in the past."

"I agree," said Angie Jack, the Aspen Hotel's executive housekeeper. "As far as I can tell, the local health department is understaffed and overworked. Most inspections are routine and perfunctory. Even if they do identify violations, the local inspectors don't have much time to follow up with us and make sure our mistakes have been corrected. Still, I can't think of any major violations resulting from inadequacies in my department."

"It's true," said Paul James, "most violations are in the food and beverage department. That is the one area of the hotel that health inspectors usually focus on. What are your thoughts, Elisabeth?"

Elisabeth contemplated the question for a moment and responded. "I usually accompany the sanitarian on his inspection. Of course, I can't drop everything if the health inspector arrives immediately before or right in the middle of a busy meal period," said the food and beverage director. "But when I do have time to accompany the inspector," she continued, "I usually try to dance him around quickly and get him out of the hotel with a minimum of problems. In my opinion, health department inspections are a pain. A lot of their regulations are impractical from an operational standpoint. One time the health inspector wrote us up because we didn't have sneeze-guards on an outdoor buffet. I think that's absurd, because the food is set up, served, and gone within two hours."

As Paul James listened intently to his department heads, he began to understand some of the problems unique to the Aspen Hotel. He could see that some of their concerns were legitimate. "I understand your position," said the GM, "because I've had similar experiences in other hotels. But the situation we are facing now is an emergency. We will not be able to reopen our food and beverage outlets without a license. And the health department won't grant us the license until we're in compliance with their local code. Getting this situation resolved has to be our top priority.

"In the past whenever I've taken a new assignment," the GM continued, "I have asked the local health department to come in and tell me exactly what's wrong. This started our relationship off on the right foot. It also prevented us from spending thousands of dollars on upgrading only to find that we didn't do it right. As I see it, the health department is good as long as they don't nitpick. They keep you on your toes. In this case, we have to cooperate with them or we won't have a hotel to open."

The department heads all agreed with the GM. The only answer was to cooperate with the local health department.

"I need your help," said Paul. "I would like each of you to prepare a list of what has to be accomplished on a week-to-week basis to bring our hotel into compliance before we reopen. The list for each area can be developed from the health department's summary of violations. We will use these lists as both a timetable and a countdown checklist. Do I have your commitment?"

Each department head consented to the idea and agreed to have the lists ready next Monday. Paul James felt positive about the commitment from the department heads as they left the dining room of the Twin Towers Hotel.

The food industry is one of the most regulated industries in the United States. A number of laws cover the land on which food is grown and the oceans from which it is harvested. Pesticides and chemicals used during the growing and raising of agricultural products are regulated by law. Once processing of raw ingredients begins, other governmental agencies enter the picture. Finally, the preparation and service of food in food service establishments is further regulated. The objective of all of this control is to protect the consumer's health and safety.

Food Laws in the United States: A Brief History

The first food law in the United States was enacted in 1646 in Massachusetts Bay Colony. The governor of the colony specified how much a loaf of bread should weigh to be sold for a penny. In 1785 in Massachusetts, the state's first general food law was passed. It was titled An Act Against Selling Unwholesome Provisions. The Food and Drugs Act of 1906 was the first federal food and drug law in the United States. This act was the forerunner of the 1938 Food, Drug, and Cosmetic Act.

The 1938 Food, Drug, and Cosmetic Act provided increased consumer protection. The 1938 Act covered labeling requirements, standards of identity and fill, sanitary manufacturing techniques, and misbranding and mislabeling of food products. The Pesticide Chemicals Amendment (1954), the Food Additives Amendment (1958), and the Color Additives Amendment (1960) altered the 1938 Act and brought it up to date with technological advances in food production. This Act (and its amendments) continues to be the most all-encompassing law related to the food industry in the United States.

A few other food laws are historically significant to the food service industry. The 1906 Meat Inspection Act made the inspection of meat and meat products shipped across state lines mandatory. The licensing of dealers, commission agents, and brokers of fresh fruits and vegetables was required in the 1930 Perishable Agricultural Commodities Act. The functions of the United States Department of Agriculture (USDA) were defined by the 1946 Agricultural Marketing Act.

The Poultry Products Inspection Act was passed in 1957. It covered wholesomeness and package labeling. The 1967 Wholesome Meat Act amended the 1906 Federal Meat Inspection Act. It extended the inspection program to meat shipped within a state. The Egg Products Inspection Act (1970) improved the safety and wholesomeness of eggs and egg products.

These federal food laws continue to be enforced by the United States government. Several states, counties, and cities have additional food laws that are more rigorous than the federal requirements. Government regulations at all levels are designed to protect the individual consumer and the food processing and food service industries.

Of course, people argue that too much government involvement is undesirable and unnecessary. Critics say some government regulations are too broad and, thus, require interpretation by the individual regulatory official or inspector. On the other hand, they say other regulations are too specific and leave no room for the official to take into consideration certain variables or unique conditions. Worst of all, some regulations are said to contradict or overlap with others; so compliance with one necessitates noncompliance with another. Some companies complain that careful compliance with government regulations puts a strain on productivity. Regulations are often complex and confusing. Some laws require a great deal of paperwork and recordkeeping.

Opponents of more regulation often argue that it costs taxpayers too much to enforce some food laws. Other critics point out that some regulations are outdated and impractical because of rapid technological advances in recent years. Perhaps the largest problem with some federal regulations in the United States is that they are written by one group (lawmakers) and enforced by another group (administrators).

Although each individual must make up his or her own mind about these charges, certain procedural recommendations can be made for lawmakers. First, an in-depth examination of the issue under consideration should be undertaken before a new regulation is written. Second, the cost/benefit ratio and possible implications for operators and consumers should be determined before a proposal becomes law. Finally, a balance between the needs of the industry, consumer protection, and governmental organizations should be sought.

It would be wrong to infer from the criticisms already cited that most people are opposed to current food regulations. In fact, many Americans feel fortunate to live in a country with so many laws pertaining to food safety. Those who have visited countries where there is little or no gov-

Exhibit 5.1   Reasons for Customers' Return Visits to Food Service Establishments

Reason for Return Visit	Percent of Customers
High Quality	82
Good Service	77
Cleanliness	39

Source: L. Reedy, "Safety and Health—No Betting Matter," Food Service Marketing, *December, 1980, p. 44.*

ernment regulation of food safety often comment about the difficulty of adjusting to the relatively low level of sanitation.

Advocates of food regulations point to the fact that the United States has relatively few food-related health problems on a per capita basis. Also, they argue that written standards in the form of federal, state, and local food laws make the immense job of running a food service business more manageable. Finally, the defenders of food regulations argue that customers demand that operators maintain high safety and sanitation levels anyway.

This last argument is supported by some recently reported data on cleanliness in food service establishments. A major manufacturer and supplier of food service cleaning products polled a number of food service customers and asked their *primary reason* for making a return visit to a food service establishment. The major findings are presented in Exhibit 5.1. Of these survey respondents, 57% said they notice the general level of cleanliness in fast-food operations. Of this 57%, 30% said they do not return to that restaurant location or to any other restaurant in the chain when they observe unacceptable levels of sanitation. According to the survey, "These patrons appeared to notice cleaning problems in restrooms most frequently, followed by floors and tables."[1] Therefore, while governmental regulations stimulate food service establishments to run clean operations, customer preferences provide a financial incentive to maintain a sanitary environment.

Federal Regulatory Agencies

The government of the United States is organized into three branches: legislative, executive, and judicial. Most agencies that regulate the food supply are in the executive branch of the federal government. The executive branch is divided into a number of departments. Of these, the Department of Agriculture, the Department of Health and Human Ser-

---

[1] L. Reedy, "Safety and Health—No Betting Matter," *Food Service Marketing,* December 1980, p. 44.

Exhibit 5.2   The Government of the United States

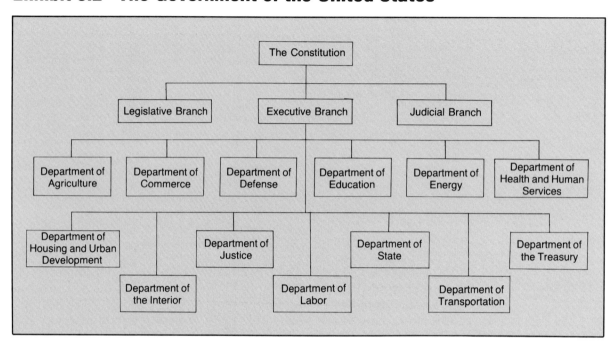

vices, the Department of the Treasury, and the Department of Commerce are most important to the food service industry. Exhibit 5.2 illustrates the general organization of the executive branch.

The **Food and Drug Administration (FDA)** is a division of the Public Health Service within the Department of Health and Human Services (formerly the Department of Health, Education, and Welfare). The main responsibility of the FDA is to enforce the Federal Food, Drug, and Cosmetic Act and to protect the public health of the nation. The many ways in which the FDA improves food service sanitation are presented in Exhibits 5.3 and 5.4.

Among other duties, the FDA develops and interprets surveillance and compliance programs, model ordinances, codes and regulations, and good manufacturing practices. The FDA administers the Bureau of Foods and seven other bureaus. The **Bureau of Foods** generates policies covering the safety, composition, quality, and labeling of foods and food additives.

The FDA's Bureau of Foods also assists other federal, local, and state agencies in ensuring a safe and wholesome food supply for the consuming public. This assistance is provided through the Bureau's **Retail Food Protection Branch**. Traditionally, FDA conducts its activities at the wholesale level, while retailers are regulated through state and local public health agencies. The organization and functions of the Bureau of Foods, its Retail Food Protection Branch, and one of its regions are shown in conjunction with state and local agencies in Exhibit 5.5.

The **U.S. Centers for Disease Control (CDC)** are another part of the Public Health Service in the U.S. Department of Health and Human Ser-

Exhibit 5.3 Two Roles of the FDA in Improving Food Sanitation

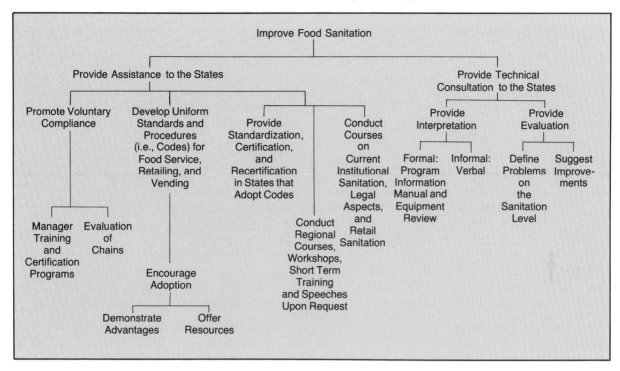

Exhibit 5.4 Two Roles of the FDA in Improving Food Sanitation

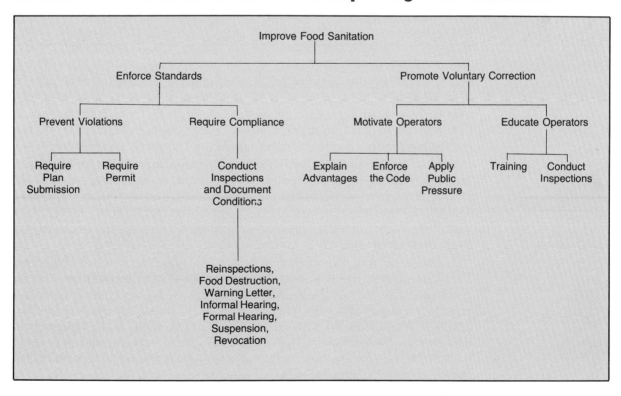

Exhibit 5.5   Organization and Function of Federal, State, and Local Food Service Sanitation Regulatory Agencies

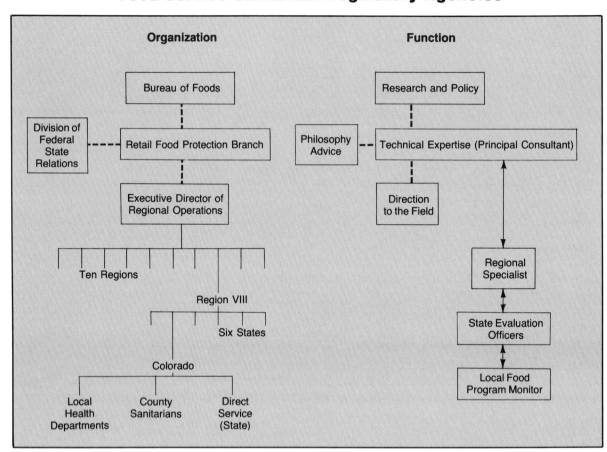

vices. The CDC investigate foodborne disease outbreaks, analyze surveillance data, and publish the results of their data analyses. The CDC also provide training materials and services on the topic of food service sanitation. The CDC perform a variety of valuable field services such as compiling foodborne illness statistics for the Public Health Service.

The **United States Department of Agriculture (USDA)** is another major department in the federal government's executive branch. The USDA consists of four broad divisions: Food and Consumer Services, Marketing Services, Economic Policy Analysis and Budget, and Conservation Research and Education. The first two divisions are of interest to the food service industry.

The **Food and Consumer Services** division contains two agencies. The first agency, the **Food Safety and Quality Service (FSQS)**, provides continuous in-plant inspection of all manufacturers processing meat and poultry products and eggs and egg products. The FSQS also reviews inspection procedures in foreign plants shipping meat and poultry products to the United States. The FSQS establishes and maintains uniform quality standards for food commodities and provides inspection and grading services (see Exhibit 5.6).

Exhibit 5.6 Sample USDA Quality and Yield Grade Stamps

Sample Stamp	Use	Sample Stamp	Use
USDA QUALITY APPROVED / USDA AA	Dairy Products Quality Grades	USDA PRIME / USDA CHOICE / USDA GOOD / USDA STNDRD / USDA COMRCL / USDA UTILITY	Meat and Meat Products Quality Grades
USDA A / USDA U.S. EXTRA GRADE		USDA YIELD 1 GRADE	Meat and Meat Products Yield Grade
USDA AA GRADE / USDA A GRADE / INSPECTED EGG PRODUCTS	Eggs and Egg Products Quality Grades	USDA A GRADE	Poultry and Poultry Products Quality Grades
U.S. GRADE A	Fish Quality Grade	U.S. GRADE B / PACKED UNDER CONTINUOUS INSPECTION	
U.S. GRADE NO.1	Fresh Fruits and Vegetables Quality Grade	U.S. GRADE A FANCY	Processed Produce and Other Grocery Items Quality Grade

Exhibit 5.7   Sample USDA Wholesomeness Inspection Stamps

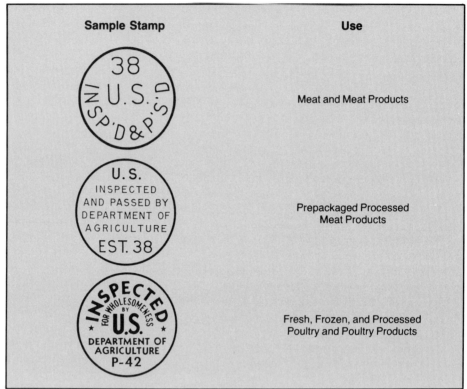

The FSQS inspects all meat, poultry, and egg products shipped interstate for wholesomeness and sanitation. The USDA mark of wholesomeness (see Exhibit 5.7) means that the food is fit for human consumption. The FSQS also provides commodity purchase services which remove surplus quantities of food from market channels.

The other agency of the USDA's Food and Consumer Services division is the **Food and Nutrition Service (FNS)**. The FNS administers the food stamp program, the national school lunch program, and the child nutrition program.

The **Marketing Services** division of the USDA comprises the **Agricultural Marketing Service (AMS)**, the **Animal and Plant Health Inspection Service (APHIS)**, and the **Federal Grain Inspection Service (FGIS)**. AMS provides market news, guidelines for fair business practices, and freight rate services. APHIS prevents the introduction of animal and plant diseases and pests at ports-of-entry into the United States. FGIS monitors the marketing of grains for animal, human, and industrial uses.

The **United States Department of the Treasury** is important to food service businesses in that it includes the **Bureau of Alcohol, Tobacco, and Firearms**. This bureau enforces laws and regulations pertaining to

Exhibit 5.8   Sample Inspection Stamp for Fish and Shellfish

Sample Stamp	Use
	Fish and Shellfish

the production and sale of distilled spirits, beers, and wines.

The **United States Department of Commerce** includes the **National Marine Fisheries Service (NMFS)**. This service monitors the product quality, safety, and identity of fish and shellfish. NMFS provides a voluntary inspection and grading service for the fishing industry. The inspected products are permitted to bear the stamp "Packed Under Federal Inspection—Department of Commerce—United States of America" (see Exhibit 5.8). The stamp is used on the packer's products, packages, and in advertising to indicate that the products are clean, safe, and wholesome.

Besides major departments, the executive branch contains independent agencies. Three of these are of interest to managers of hospitality operations.

The **Environmental Protection Agency (EPA)** is an independent agency in the executive branch of the United States government. The major mission of the EPA is to control and minimize pollution of water, air, and the environment in general. The EPA monitors and enforces regulations related to toxic substances (pesticides, sanitizers, germicides, and other chemicals), waste management, noise control, radiation, and environmental pollution.

The **Federal Trade Commission (FTC)** is another independent agency in the executive branch. The FTC monitors and eliminates unfair methods of competition and deceptive trade practices. The FTC also enforces the Clayton Act which outlaws monopolies in commerce.

The **Occupational Safety and Health Administration (OSHA)** was developed as a result of the 1970 Occupational Safety and Health Act. OSHA is charged with developing and monitoring regulations and standards related to occupational safety and health. OSHA also conducts inspections and investigations and may issue citations for noncompliance.[2]

---

[2] The topic of safety management is discussed in detail in Chapter 12.

State and Local Regulatory Agencies

State, county, and municipal regulatory agencies play an important role in guaranteeing food safety and correct food handling across the United States. For example, the government of the state of Colorado includes a health department. The Colorado State Department of Health enforces Rules and Regulations Governing the Sanitation of Food Service Establishments. These rules and regulations, which generally follow the FDA's Model Ordinance, were effective July 1, 1978.

Some states have launched food service sanitation management certification programs. Ohio's program, initiated in 1973, was the first comprehensive program at the state level. Managers must attend a minimum of four all-day sessions on various aspects of food service sanitation. Recertification of managers is required every two years. Other states have adopted Ohio's certification program.

Within the states, local regulations may differ but usually the FDA's Ordinance is adopted statewide. Some county and municipal health departments have adopted the ordinance even though their states have not adopted it yet.

For an example of local regulation, consider the city and county of Denver. The Denver Department of Health and Hospitals—Environmental Health Service adopted Rules and Regulations Governing Restaurants in the City and County of Denver in June 1980. This regulation closely parallels the state and federal ordinances. Obviously, the FDA's Model Ordinance is adaptable to the needs of local agencies.

Besides the assistance available through regional FDA offices, state and local regulatory agencies can be very helpful in sanitation training for the food service industry. State and local agencies can be invited to monitor training programs to ensure that they are satisfactory and complete. Whenever possible, sanitation training programs should be jointly sponsored by industry associations and regulatory agencies. Certification of managers and employees is a desirable and attainable goal of interest to both groups.

In the past, however, mobility and turnover in the food service industry have made it difficult for previously certified individuals to be recognized as such in a new jurisdiction. Therefore, it is desirable to have reciprocal recognition for state-approved training programs. These reciprocal agreements are beneficial for regulatory agencies because uniformity may reduce enforcement costs. Uniformity in the enforcement of rules and regulations covering food service is to everyone's benefit, especially the industry's. First, when a manager moves from one state to another, regulations are similar. Second, multi-unit chains operating in more than one state can function under similar regulations.

Industry and Trade Organizations and Associations

A number of industry and trade organizations and associations, including the following, exert an influence over the food service industry.

These professional organizations complement regulatory agencies by furnishing valuable information to hospitality businesses. The major push for uniformity in nationwide regulations for the food service and lodging industries has, in large part, emerged from industry and trade organizations. These organizations can be a valuable source of training ideas and materials.

The **American Hotel & Motel Association (AH&MA)** is an organization of over 9,000 hotels and motels all over the world. The Educational Institute, a nonprofit educational foundation of AH&MA, is in the forefront in providing educational materials for hotel, motel, restaurant, and institutional managers and employees. The Educational Institute of AH&MA has developed textbooks, such as this one, and certification courses leading to its highest designation: Certified Hotel Administrator (CHA). Of particular interest to food service managers is the new Certified Food and Beverage Executive (CFBE) program.

The **American Public Health Association (APHA)** is one of this nation's oldest professional societies for doctors, nurses, and sanitarians. APHA's Food Protection Committee focuses on public health and periodically recommends standards and policies pertaining to food protection.

The **Food Research Institute (FRI)** generates research data in the areas of food contamination and the prevention of foodborne diseases. FRI works closely with food processing establishments and the food service industry.

The **International Association of Milk, Food, and Environmental Sanitarians (IAMFES)** is a professional organization for people in the fields of food research and technology and food protection. IAMFES publishes two journals featuring articles on the topic of food protection.

The **International Food Service Executives Association (IFSEA)** is a professional organization dedicated to raising food service industry standards, educating members and future industry leaders, and recognizing members' achievements. Active members include personnel in all aspects of food service: executive chefs; operators; dietitians; consultants; and managers and owners of catering firms, restaurants, hotels, clubs, institutions, armed forces dining facilities, and other organizations having food service operations.

The **National Environmental Health Association (NEHA)** is a society for environmental health officials at various levels of government. NEHA provides educational services, publishes a journal, and conducts research and programs in the field of environmental health.

The **National Institute for the Foodservice Industry (NIFI)** provides a number of certification courses for food service industry professionals. NIFI is involved with the training of food service managers and employees. Perhaps NIFI's best-known course is *Applied Foodservice Sanitation*, the second edition of which was published in 1978.

The **National Restaurant Association (NRA)** is a trade organization for food service industry professionals in the United States. The NRA adopts policies and publishes position statements on issues of concern to commercial and noncommercial food service owners and managers. The NRA's Health and Safety Committee addresses issues of public health as they relate to the food service industry. NRA also maintains a strong lobbying force in the nation's capital.

The **National Sanitation Foundation (NSF)** is a not-for-profit organization that tests equipment and utensils and evaluates them according to NSF's standards. These standards are agreed upon by public health officials and industry representatives alike. The purpose of these standards is to assist manufacturers in the production of equipment that meets minimum health code requirements.

If NSF determines that equipment and utensils meet its minimum acceptance levels, the manufacturer can display the NSF seal on the tested equipment. This seal indicates that the equipment or utensil will normally meet regulatory requirements as they relate to public health. (In some areas, the NSF standards *are* the regulatory requirements.) Thus, NSF standards also make it easier for equipment buyers and regulatory agencies to determine if equipment meets the code requirements.

Several of these trade, industry, and professional organizations also operate at the state and local levels. Both AH&MA and NRA have state groups that are affiliated with the national organizations. Food service owners, managers, and employees are encouraged to join and become active in local and national associations and professional organizations. Aside from the usual advantages of informal contacts with other professionals, these groups offer two clear benefits to their members: (1) these groups are valuable sources of training materials and (2) industry-sponsored educational programs help reduce the need for governmental regulations and mandatory inspections.

Obtaining a Permit, License, or Certificate to Operate a Food Service Establishment

The FDA's Model Ordinance sets forth minimum requirements for the operation of a food service establishment. As mentioned earlier, most states and localities have used the FDA's Model Ordinance in formulating their regulations. Some have adopted the ordinance verbatim; others have made minor changes to fit local conditions. Since it would be impossible to cover all of these variations and adaptations, this book focuses on the original federal compliance procedures. However, after you are familiar with the FDA's Model Ordinance, you should obtain a copy of the regulations used by your state and county or city. Ask the appropriate health authorities if these codes are based on the FDA's 1976 Ordinance and, if so, what changes (if any) have been made. In this way, you will know how closely the recommendations given here match with those in effect in your area.

The FDA's Food Service Sanitation Ordinance states:

COMPLIANCE PROCEDURES

Permits, Licenses, or Certificates

General.

No person shall operate a food service establishment who does not have a valid permit, license, or certificate issued to him by the regulatory authority. Only a person who complies with the requirements of this ordinance shall be entitled to receive or retain such a permit, license, or certificate. Permits, licenses, or certificates are not transferable. A valid permit, license, or certificate shall be posted in every food service establishment.

Issuance of permit, license, or certificate.

(a) Any person desiring to operate a food service establishment shall make written application for a permit, license, or certificate on forms provided by the regulatory authority. Such application shall include the name and address of each applicant, the location and type of the proposed food service establishment, and the signature of each applicant.

(b) Prior to approval of an application for a permit, license, or certificate, the regulatory authority shall inspect the proposed food service establishment to determine compliance with the requirements of this ordinance.

(c) The regulatory authority shall issue a permit, license, or certificate to the applicant if its inspection reveals that the proposed food service establishment complies with the requirements of this ordinance.

Suspension of permit, license, or certificate.

(a) The regulatory authority may, without warning, notice, or hearing suspend any permit, license, or certificate to operate a food service establishment if the holder of the permit, license, or certificate does not comply with the requirements of this ordinance, or if the operation of the establishment does not comply with the requirements of this ordinance, or if the operation of the food service establishment otherwise constitutes a substantial hazard to public health. Suspension is effective upon service of the notice required by . . . this ordinance. When a permit, license, or certificate is suspended, food service operations shall immediately cease. Whenever a permit, license, or certificate is suspended, the holder of the permit, license, or certificate shall be afforded an opportunity for hearing within 20 days of receipt of a request for hearing.

(b) Whenever a permit, license, or certificate is suspended, the holder of the permit, license, or certificate, or the person in charge shall be notified in writing that the permit, license, or certificate is, upon service of the notice, immediately suspended and that an opportunity for hearing will be provided if a written request for hearing is filed with the regulatory authority by the holder of the permit, license, or certificate within 10 days. If no written request for hearing is filed within 10 days, the suspension is sustained. The regulatory authority may end the suspension at any time if reasons for suspension no longer exist.

Revocation of permit, license, or certificate.

(a) The regulatory authority may, after providing opportunity for hearing, revoke a permit, license, or certificate for serious or repeated violations of any of the requirements of this ordinance or for interference with the regulatory authority in the performance of duty.

(b) Prior to revocation, the regulatory authority shall notify, in writing, the holder of the permit, license, or certificate, or the person in charge, of the specific reason(s) for which the permit, license, or certificate is to be revoked and that the permit, license, or certificate shall be revoked at the end of the 10 days following service of such notice unless a written request for hearing is filed with the regulatory authority by the holder of the permit, license, or certificate within such 10-day period. If no request for hearing is filed within the 10-day period, the revocation of the permit, license, or certificate becomes final.

Service of notices.

A notice provided for in this ordinance is properly served when it is delivered to the holder of the permit, license, or certificate, or the person in charge, or when it is sent by registered or certified mail, return receipt requested, to the last known address of the holder of the permit, license, or certificate. A copy of the notice shall be filed in the records of the regulatory authority.

Hearings.

The hearings provided for in this ordinance shall be conducted by the regulatory authority at a time and place designated by it. Any oral testimony given at a hearing shall be reported verbatim, and the presiding officer shall make provision for sufficient copies of the transcript. The regulatory authority shall make a final finding based upon the complete hearing record and shall sustain, modify or rescind any notice or order considered in the hearing. A written report of the hearing decision shall be furnished to the holder of the permit, license, or certificate by the regulatory authority.

Exhibit 5.9 Sample License Form for a Food Service Establishment

Source: Colorado State Department of Public Health.

Application after revocation.

Whenever a revocation of a permit, license, or certificate has become final, the holder of the revoked permit, license, or certificate may make written application for a new permit, license, or certificate.

Source: Food and Drug Administration, Public Health Service, U.S. Department of Health, Education, and Welfare, Food Service Sanitation Manual, 1976, pp. 72-73.

In the United States, a food service establishment cannot be operated without the required certificates, permits, or licenses (see Exhibit 5.9). Usually these documents are issued by local or state regulatory authorities, and they are generally nontransferable. The valid documents must be posted in the food service facility. Permits, licenses, or certificates can only be issued to businesses that comply with the requirements of the FDA's Model Ordinance. For establishments serving beer, wine, and alcoholic spirits, additional documents must be obtained from the state liquor control commission.

The FDA's Food Service Sanitation Ordinance states:

Regulatory authority means the State and/or local enforcement authority or authorities having jurisdiction over the food service establishment.

Source: FDA, p. 22.

At first, the process for obtaining a valid permit, license, or certificate may appear to be long and drawn out. However, the objective of the paperwork is to make it possible for the government to protect the public health. Application must be made in writing to the appropriate regulatory agency. Required information includes the name and address of each applicant, the signature of each applicant, and the type and location of the proposed food service business.

Approval is also required whenever any of the following activities takes place:

1.   Construction of a new food service establishment

2.   Extensive remodeling of an existing food service establishment

3.   Conversion of an existing building into a food service establishment

All of these situations require a submission of plans and a review of the plans by the appropriate regulatory authority. Plans and specifications must contain the proposed layout, arrangement, mechanical plans, and construction materials of work areas and the type and model of proposed fixed equipment and facilities. Approval is based on whether the new, remodeled, or converted facility meets the minimum specifications of the Model Ordinance. After plan approval and prior to the opening of the establishment, the regulatory authority must inspect the completed construction to ensure that it was built according to the approved plans.

The FDA's Food Service Sanitation Ordinance states:

Review of Plans

Submission of plans.

Whenever a food service establishment is constructed or extensively remodeled and whenever an existing structure is converted to use as a food service establishment, properly prepared plans and specifications for such construction, remodeling, or conversion shall be submitted to the regulatory authority for review and approval before construction, remodeling or conversion is begun. The plans and specifications shall indicate the proposed layout, arrangement, mechanical plans, and construction materials of work areas, and the type and model of proposed fixed equipment and facilities. The regulatory authority shall approve the plans and specifications if they meet the requirements of this ordinance. No food service establishment shall be constructed, extensively remodeled, or converted except in accordance with plans and specifications approved by the regulatory authority.

Pre-operational inspection.

Whenever plans and specifications are required by . . . this ordinance to be submitted to the regulatory authority, the regulatory authority shall inspect the food service establishment prior to the start of operations, to determine compliance with the approved plans and specifications and with the requirements of this ordinance.

Source: FDA, p. 76.

On the other hand, when an existing food service facility is purchased, the procedures vary. Some jurisdictions do not automatically issue a permit, license, or certificate to the new owner simply because the previous owner was once granted permission to operate. The jurisdiction may reserve the right to inspect the premises. If any problems are discovered, the new owner may be required to bring the operation into substantial compliance with the jurisdiction's code. Anyone who plans to purchase an existing food service business should: (a) check the inspection history with the local health department; (b) try to obtain a commitment (preferably in writing) from the health department stating that the existing operation has no problems requiring correction to achieve compliance; (c) consider hiring a facility consultant; and (d) make the purchase contingent upon the seller's correction of all health code violations.

Regardless of how the food service facilities are acquired or remodeled, regulatory officials must inspect them prior to issuing a permit, license, or certificate. The inspectors determine whether the facilities comply with the jurisdiction's sanitation requirements. If the application has been properly filed and the facilities pass the inspection, the agency's approval will be forthcoming. According to the FDA, most agencies use FDA Form 2420 (see Exhibit 5.10, Food Service Establishment Inspection Report) for the pre-opening inspection, concentrating on the structural aspects.

A permit, license, or certificate of operation for a food service establishment may be suspended if either the operator or the holder of the permit does not comply with relevant food service regulations or if there is a substantial hazard to public health. The regulatory agency may suspend the permit, license, or certificate without notice or warning. Once the suspension takes place, all food service operations must stop. The holder of the certificate, license, or permit is entitled to a hearing by the regulatory agency within 20 days of the agency's receipt of a request for a hearing.

Permits, licenses, or certificates may be revoked if the operation has a number of serious or repeated violations. Revocation can also take place if the manager or employees interfere with the regulatory agent's performance of duties. However, prior to revocation, the regulatory agency must notify the holder of the permit, license, or certificate in writing. Notices are usually sent by certified or registered mail. If a permit, license, or certificate is revoked, a written application for new documents must be filed. Obviously, the regulatory authorities will not approve the new application until previous deficiencies have been corrected.

Inspections by Regulatory Agencies

The Model Ordinance states that food service establishment inspections should be performed at least once every six months. State and local jurisdictions may perform more or less frequent inspections depending on budgets, available personnel, and philosophy. Generally, facilities which regularly receive low sanitation scores are more frequently inspected.

The FDA's Food Service Sanitation Ordinance states:

Inspections

Inspection frequency.

An inspection of a food service establishment shall be performed at least once every 6 months. Additional inspections of the food service establishment shall be performed as often as necessary for the enforcement of this ordinance.

Access.

Representatives of the regulatory authority, after proper identification, shall be permitted to enter any food service establishment at any reasonable time for the purpose of making inspections to determine compliance with this ordinance. The representatives shall be permitted to examine the records of the establishment to obtain information pertaining to food and supplies purchased, received, or used.

Report of inspections.

Whenever an inspection of a food service establishment or commissary is made, the findings shall be recorded on the inspection report form set out in . . . this ordinance. The inspection report form shall summarize the requirements of this ordinance and shall set forth a weighted point value for each requirement. Inspectional remarks shall be written to reference, by section number, the section violated and shall state the correction to be made. The rating score of the establishment shall be the total of the weighted point values for all violations, subtracted from 100. A copy of the completed inspection report form shall be furnished to the person in charge of the establishment at the conclusion of the inspection. The completed inspection report form is a public document that shall be made available for public disclosure to any person who requests it according to law.

Correction of violations.

(a) The completed inspection report form shall specify a reasonable period of time for the correction of the violations found; and correction of the violations shall be accomplished within the period specified, in accordance with the following provisions:

(1) If an imminent health hazard exists, such as complete lack of refrigeration or sewage backup into the establishment, the establishment shall immediately cease food service operations. Operations shall not be resumed until authorized by the regulatory authority.

(2) All violations of 4- or 5-point weighted items shall be corrected as soon as possible, but in any event, within 10 days following inspection. Within 15 days after the inspection, the holder of the permit, license or certificate shall submit a written report to the regulatory authority stating that the 4- or 5-point weighted violations have been corrected. A followup inspection shall be conducted to confirm correction.

(3) All 1- or 2-point weighted items shall be corrected as soon as possible, but in any event, by the time of the next routine inspection.

(4) When the rating score of the establishment is less than 60, the establishment shall initiate corrective action on all identified violations within 48 hours. One or more reinspections will be conducted at reasonable time intervals to assure correction.

(5) In the case of temporary food service establishments, all violations shall be corrected within 24 hours. If violations are not corrected within 24 hours, the establishment shall immediately cease food service operations until authorized to resume by the regulatory authority.

(b) The inspection report shall state that failure to comply with any time limits for corrections may result in cessation of food service operations. An opportunity for hearing on the inspection findings or the time limitations or both will be provided if a written request is filed with the regulatory authority within 10 days following cessation of operations. If a request for hearing is received, a hearing shall be held within 20 days of receipt of the request.

(c) Whenever a food service establishment is required . . . to cease operations, it shall not resume operations until it is shown on reinspection that conditions responsible for the order to cease operations no longer exist. Opportunity for reinspection shall be offered within a reasonable time.

Source: FDA, pp. 74-75.

Exhibit 5.10   Food Service Establishment Inspection Report Form

DEPARTMENT OF HEALTH AND HUMAN SERVICES
PUBLIC HEALTH SERVICE — FOOD AND DRUG ADMINISTRATION

PURPOSE		
Regular 29-1		
Follow-up 2		
Complaint....... 3		
Investigation 4		
Other 5		

Food Service Establishment Inspection Report

Based on an inspection this day, the items circled below identify the violations in operations or facilities which must be corrected by the next routine inspection or such shorter period of time as may be specified in writing by the regulatory authority. Failure to comply with any time limits for corrections specified in this notice may result in cessation of your Food Service operations.

OWNER NAME

ESTABLISHMENT NAME

ADDRESS

TIME ON LOCATION

ZIP CODE

EST. I.D. (1-7)	REC		ESTAB. NO.	SANIT. CODE 8-10		11-16	YR.	MO.	DAY	TRAVEL TIME 17-19	INSPEC. TIME 20-22	STATE CODE 23-24	INSP. PROCESS 25-27

ITEM NO.   WT. COL.

ITEM NO.   WT. COL.

FOOD

*01	Source; sound condition, no spoilage	5	30
02	Original container, properly labeled	1	31

FOOD PROTECTION

*03	Potentially hazardous food meets temperature requirements during storage, preparation, display, service, transportation	5	32
*04	Facilities to maintain product temperature	4	33
05	Thermometers provided and conspicuous	1	34
06	Potentially hazardous food properly thawed	2	35
*07	Unwrapped and potentially hazardous food not re-served	4	36
08	Food protection during storage, preparation, display, service, transportation	2	37
09	Handling of food (ice) minimized	2	38
10	In use, food (ice) dispensing utensils properly stored	1	39

PERSONNEL

*11	Personnel with infections restricted	5	40
*12	Hands washed and clean, good hygienic practices	5	41
13	Clean clothes, hair restraints	1	42

FOOD EQUIPMENT & UTENSILS

14	Food (ice) contact surfaces: designed, constructed, maintained, installed, located	2	43
15	Non-food contact surfaces: designed, constructed, maintained, installed, located	1	44
16	Dishwashing facilities: designed, constructed, maintained, installed, located, operated	2	45
17	Accurate thermometers, chemical test kits provided, gauge cock (1/4'' IPS valve)	1	46
18	Pre-flushed, scraped, soaked	1	47
19	Wash, rinse water; clean, proper temperature	2	48
*20	Sanitization rinse: clean, temperature, concentration, exposure time; equipment, utensils sanitized	4	49
21	Wiping cloths; clean, use restricted	1	50
22	Food-Contact surfaces of equipment and utensils clean, free of abrasives, detergents	2	51
23	Non-food contact surfaces of equipment and utensils clean	1	52
24	Storage, handling of clean equipment/utensils	1	53
25	Single-service articles, storage, dispensing	1	54
26	No re-use of single service articles	2	55

WATER

*27	Water source, safe: hot & cold under pressure	5	56

SEWAGE

*28	Sewage and waste water disposal	4	57

PLUMBING

29	Installed, maintained	1	58
*30	Cross connection, back siphonage, backflow	5	59

TOILET & HANDWASHING FACILITIES

*31	Number, convenient, accessible, designed, installed	4	60
32	Toilet rooms enclosed, self-closing doors; fixtures, good repair, clean: hand cleanser, sanitary towels/hand-drying devices provided, proper waste receptacles	2	61

GARBAGE & REFUSE DISPOSAL

33	Containers or receptacles, covered: adequate number insect/rodent proof, frequency, clean	2	62
34	Outside storage area enclosures properly constructed, clean; controlled incineration	1	63

INSECT, RODENT, ANIMAL CONTROL

*35	Presence of insects/rodents -outer openings protected, no birds, turtles, other animals	4	64

FLOORS, WALLS & CEILINGS

36	Floors, constructed, drained, clean, good repair, covering installation, dustless cleaning methods	1	65
37	Walls, ceiling, attached equipment: constructed, good repair, clean, surfaces, dustless cleaning methods	1	66

LIGHTING

38	Lighting provided as required, fixtures shielded	1	67

VENTILATION

39	Rooms and equipment—vented as required	1	68

DRESSING ROOMS

40	Rooms, area, lockers provided, located, used	1	69

OTHER OPERATIONS

*41	Toxic items properly stored, labeled, used	8	70
42	Premises maintained free of litter, unnecessary articles, cleaning maintenance equipment properly stored. Authorized personnel	1	71
43	Complete separation from living/sleeping quarters-Laundry	1	72
44	Clean, soiled linen properly stored	1	73

Received by: name _____

title _____

Inspected by: name _____

FOLLOW-UP	RATING SCORE 75-77	ACTION
Yes 74-1	100 less weight of	Change 78-C
No 2	Items violated➡	Delete.........D

*Critical Items Requiring Immediate Attention.   Remarks on back (80-1)

Source: Food and Drug Administration, Public Health Service, U.S. Department of Health and Human Services.

When the health inspector enters a food service establishment, the sanitarian, the management, and the employees have a number of responsibilities to ensure a professional approach to the inspection.

First, let us pinpoint the *inspector's or sanitarian's responsibilities.* As a representative of the regulatory agency, the sanitarian has the responsibility to carry out his or her duties in a professional manner. The sanitarian may inspect all areas of the facility and may even examine the records of the business to obtain information on the purchase, receipt, and use of food supplies. The sanitarian must record all inspection findings on an inspection report form. Generally, jurisdictions which have adopted the Model Ordinance use the FDA's Form 2420 **Food Service Establishment Inspection Report**. (The newest edition is dated January 1983.) The front of this form is shown in Exhibit 5.10.

A number of the items in the inspection report are weighted more heavily than the others. The following 4- or 5-point weighted items are the *most* important factors:

> Item #01—Food source must be in sound condition with no spoilage.

> Item #03—Potentially hazardous food must meet temperature requirements during storage, preparation, display, service, and transportation.

> Item #04—Facilities must be designed to maintain food product temperatures.

> Item #07—Unwrapped and potentially hazardous food must not be re-served.

> Item #11—Personnel with infections must be restricted.

> Item #12—Acceptable handwashing procedures and good hygiene practices must be followed.

> Item #20—Sanitization rinse water for utensils and equipment must be clean and at or above the minimum temperature for the correct time at the proper concentration.

> Item #27—Water must be from a safe water source and must run hot and cold under pressure.

> Item #28—Waste water and sewage must be disposed of properly.

> Item #30—Plumbing cross-connections, back siphonage, and backflow must be prevented.

> Item #31—Handwashing and toilet facilities must be adequate in regard to their number, convenience, accessibility, design, and installation.

Item #35—Insects, animals, and rodents must be properly controlled to prevent them from entering the premises.

Item #41—Toxic items must be correctly stored, labeled, and used.[3]

These 13 inspection points make up 59 of the total 100 points on the inspection report. If any of these critical items are in violation, the sanitarian will require immediate action to correct them within ten days. The sanitarian will expect other violations to be corrected as soon as possible, certainly by the time of the next inspection.[4] If an imminent health hazard is discovered, the sanitarian may require food operations to cease immediately. Imminent health hazards include a sewage backup, a complete lack of refrigeration, or evidence of a communicable disease outbreak such as hepatitis.

The FDA's Food Service Sanitation Ordinance states:

Examination and Condemnation of Food

General.

Food may be examined or sampled by the regulatory authority as often as necessary for enforcement of this ordinance. The regulatory authority may, upon written notice to the owner or person in charge, specifying with particularity the reasons therefor, place a hold order on any food which it believes is in violation of . . . this ordinance. The regulatory authority shall tag, label, or otherwise identify any food subject to the hold order. No food subject to a hold order shall be used, served, or moved from the establishment. The regulatory authority shall permit storage of the food under conditions specified in the hold order, unless storage is not possible without risk to the public health, in which case immediate destruction shall be ordered and accomplished. The hold order shall state that a request for hearing may be filed within 10 days and that if no hearing is requested the food shall be destroyed. If a request for hearing is received, the hearing shall be held within 20 days after receipt of the request. On the basis of evidence produced at that hearing, the hold order may be vacated, or the owner or person in charge of the food may be directed by written order to denature or destroy such food or to bring it into compliance with the provisions of this ordinance.

Source: FDA, pp. 75-76.

---

[3] FDA, p. 88.

[4] These time periods may or may not coincide with those in your jurisdiction.

The inspector may examine or sample food products. Using a written notice to the owner or person in charge, the sanitarian may place a hold order on food products that, for reasons specified in the notice, cannot be served. In extreme cases, immediate destruction of the food may be ordered. The manager should voluntarily destroy food of questionable quality or safety.

The FDA's Food Service Sanitation Ordinance states:

Person in charge means the individual present in a food service establishment who is the apparent supervisor of the food service establishment at the time of inspection. If no individual is the apparent supervisor, then any employee present is the person in charge.

Source: FDA, p. 21.

At the conclusion of any inspection, the sanitarian is required to present the written final report. Often inspectors are willing to discuss the findings.

In the course of regular in-house inspections, areas for improvement are identified. Sanitarians respond to requests for assistance from food service owners and managers who would like professional advice on how to correct sanitation problems. Sanitarians may also provide training upon request. However, the primary responsibilities of a sanitarian are determining the compliance of food service establishments and requiring corrections of deficiencies.

Food service managers and employees also have a set of responsibilities when it comes to inspections. Fundamentally, the manager and employees must act in a professional manner. If an adversary relationship has been established between the operation and the regulatory officials, it was probably initiated by an overly defensive or unreasonable manager or employee. Professionals recognize the defined roles of inspector and manager and strive for a spirit of cooperation. The responsibilities of the manager or licensee are to be in substantial compliance at all times and to correct any deficiencies as required by the health authority. No one gains by noncompliance or by perpetuating an adversary relationship.

Managers should instruct employees to allow properly identified sanitarians to enter the food service operation at any reasonable time for the purpose of making an inspection. Managers are obligated to furnish any relevant records the sanitarian may require. The manager or a designated employee of the food service establishment should accompany the sanitarian on the inspection. This allows the establishment's representative to observe any violations first-hand, to answer any questions, and to correct problems immediately, if possible. When the sanitarian presents the inspection report, the manager should review it for accuracy. Corrections, additions, or deletions to the report may be requested. Any deficiencies corrected at the time of the inspection should be so noted.

Since the completed inspection form is a public document, it may be made available for public disclosure to people who legally request the completed form. In addition, most courts have ruled that inspection records are subject to access by the public. Reporters and other news media personnel may review health department records. Some newspapers publish inspection scores along with the names of businesses on a regular basis. Food service managers can protect the reputation of their establishments by improving their sanitation scores. In cases where the overall sanitation score is less than 60, corrective action on all violations must be initiated within 48 hours. All violations must be corrected within 24 hours in a temporary food service unit. In other cases, the completed inspection report form must specify a reasonable period of time for the correction of unresolved deficiencies. The manager may ask to see the section of the code covering any deficiency. If there is any question about the justification for marking any serious or expensive deficiency, the manager may tactfully request that the sanitarian's supervisor resolve the problem.

If an imminent health hazard is discovered, the manager is obligated to cease operations. Otherwise, the establishment is liable to be fined and/or the owner and operator jailed, for continued operation under an imminent health hazard. Again, local jurisdictions may vary, but it is always the manager's responsibility to follow through and see that violations are corrected. The burden is on management to take the necessary action. Food service managers should feel free to ask questions of the health inspector. The objective is to set up a two-way communication flow between the sanitarian and the operation's management. Such cooperation has an added benefit: the operation's history of compliance could be important if complaints or allegations of injuries or foodborne illness outbreaks are made.

The FDA's Food Service Sanitation Ordinance states:

Remedies

Penalties.

Any person (or responsible officer of that person) who violates a provision of this ordinance and any person (or responsible officer of that person) who is the holder of a permit, license, or certificate or who otherwise operates a food service establishment that does not comply with the requirements of this ordinance, shall be imprisoned for not more than 6 months or fined not more than $3,000 or both.

Injunctions.

The regulatory authority may seek to enjoin violations of this ordinance.

Source: FDA, p. 77.

Regulatory officials and food service managers work together because they are professionals. They share responsibility for achieving a common goal—the safe and sanitary operation of a food service business.

What If a Foodborne Illness Outbreak Is Suspected?

Assume you are a food service manager and a customer calls to inform you that she and her husband became ill after eating in your establishment. What will you say, and what action will you take? How will you handle the customer's accusation that your facility may be a source of foodborne illness? What steps will you take to close this complaint with the customer? The answers to these questions might depend on whether or not your operation has an established procedure for dealing with suspected outbreaks of foodborne illness.

If you have a written procedure detailing what to do and when, you will probably respond to this potential crisis in a logical, proactive way. If no set of procedures exists, your response is likely to be reactive and disorganized. Having a detailed procedure can save you time when you need it most. In such an emergency situation, prompt action will prevent further problems and will minimize the likelihood of other outbreaks. With your reputation, your customer's health, and the image of your operation at stake, you cannot afford to be unprepared.

Granted, the regulations and recommendations discussed throughout this book are aimed at preventing the situation just described from occurring. But with so many potential sources of food contamination (see Chapter 3), it is only sensible to be ready to deal with a foodborne disease outbreak. Such readiness is not a sign that the operation is negligent; rather, it shows that management is realistic.

The following 11-step procedure for handling customer foodborne illness complaints may prove valuable to food service and lodging managers.

The FDA's Food Service Sanitation Ordinance states:

Procedure When Infection is Suspected

General.

When the regulatory authority has reasonable cause to suspect possible disease transmission by an employee of a food service establishment, it may secure a morbidity history of the suspected employee or make any other investigation as indicated and shall take appropriate action. The regulatory authority may require any or all of the following measures:

(a) The immediate exclusion of the employee from employment in food service establishments;

(b) The immediate closing of the food service establishment concerned until, in the opinion of the regulatory authority, no further danger of disease outbreak exists;

(c) Restriction of the employee's services to some area of the establishment where there would be no danger of transmitting disease;

(d) Adequate medical and laboratory examination of the employee and of other employees and of his and their body discharges.

Source: FDA, p. 76.

Step 1   **Just one person in the operation, usually the manager, should be responsible for the investigation.** It is important that this person keep detailed records. The health department and/or legal counsel may request these records, so it is important that they be accurate.

If statements to the public are necessary, the responsible person should also act as the authoritative spokesperson for the establishment. Only this person should handle communications to and from the media and other individuals who need information. If more than one spokesperson is used to explain the same circumstances, there may be a loss of credibility. All relevant information should be made public unless it involves security or a confidential issue. When in doubt, the person in charge should check with legal counsel. If the outbreak is prolonged, the responsible person must provide regular updates to the media and others. The less people know about what is going on, the more they fear possible consequences.

Step 2   **Listen to the complaint.** The interviewer should be courteous and should avoid arguing with the complainant. The responsible person should not talk about other similar problems which have occurred in the past. Also, no mention of insurance or claim settlements should be made at this point.[5]

---

[5] In cases where insurance claims or lawsuits are filed against the establishment, other strategies may be necessary. The person being served should say nothing to the process server and should get a lawyer as soon as possible. Fundamentally, food service businesses must exercise "reasonable care." If the situation that caused the outbreak can be shown to be an isolated incident, the liability may not be as severe as when the facility has persisted in unsanitary practices against health department recommendations. If the facility has practiced "reasonable care" and has corrected health violations previously reported by the health department, the liability may not be as severe. The insurance company, lawyers, and/or health department may wish to subpoena past inspection reports. Managers subject themselves to the possibility of punitive damages if an illness or injury occurs from a practice or condition about which prior warnings have been received from the health department.

Step 3   **Obtain the facts.** The person designated as the complaint investigator should keep a supply of complaint recording forms on hand. By using a standard form such as the one shown in Exhibit 5.11, the investigator is sure to get all of the essential information. The **complaint record form** should include the menu item eaten, meal period, time, date, and the names, addresses, and telephone numbers of others who ate with the complainant.

The person in charge should also conduct an in-house investigation by interviewing both production and service personnel who were on duty when the complainant was served. A good source for a standard complaint record form is the publication "Procedures to Investigate Foodborne Illness." This booklet may be obtained from:

> International Association of Milk, Food, and Environmental
> Sanitarians, Inc.
> P.O. Box 701
> Ames, IA 50010

In addition to the complaint record form, this source provides a review of foodborne diseases and a form for detailing the food history and common sources of any questionable foods served.

Step 4   **Promptly and properly evaluate the customer complaint.** Now the investigator should contact the people who dined with the complainant to determine whether these patrons have experienced similar symptoms. If so, the investigator should sort through the guest checks from other customers and identify those who consumed the same food. By matching credit card receipts to guest checks, the person in charge can gather the information necessary to contact these other diners. Detailed records should be made on every conversation related to the suspected outbreak. In the event that the complaint is totally unfounded, the manager may choose to handle it in-house. In most cases, however, it is recommended that management call in the health department to assist in the investigation of the complaint.

Step 5   **The health department should be promptly notified if the complaint appears to be valid.** It is the obligation of the health department to investigate foodborne illness outbreaks. An outbreak is a situation in which two or more people become ill from eating the same food.

Step 6   **Isolate the suspected food products, if samples are still available.** By this time, the responsible person should have a reasonably good idea of what food may have caused the outbreak. The person in charge should promptly take ingredients or batches of finished menu items that might be contaminated out of circulation. These samples should be placed in clean, sanitized containers and then covered, dated, and labeled "DO NOT USE—SUSPECTED SOURCE OF FOODBORNE ILLNESS." All suspected food should be refrigerated and all staff members informed that the containers are not to be tampered with until further notice.

Step 7   **Cooperate with the health department.** Cooperation with the health department is essential. Tell them everything, accurately and quickly. If the operation helps them do their job, the sanitarians will be saving time and effort. They will be able to determine if any other similar complaints have been filed with the health department office by people the food service establishment could not identify or locate.

In cases of foodborne illness outbreaks, the health department conducts detailed interviews with complainants to determine symptoms and the food history. The health department may be able to draw a preliminary conclusion regarding the organisms responsible for the symptoms, based on these interviews. By knowing the foods in which the suspected organisms usually proliferate, the health department can identify which one of the complainants' meals is most likely to have caused the problem. This input from the health department helps to determine whether the complaint against the operation is valid or not. The health department may uncover other causes for the complainants' symptoms. This is helpful in cases involving infections, which are slow to surface. People naturally associate illness with the last meal consumed away from home, but if the illness can be traced to a much earlier meal eaten elsewhere, the operation may be cleared of the accusation.

The health department may conduct interviews of employees and managers. Swabs of equipment, surfaces, and personnel may be required. Food samples may be sent to a lab for analyses. Fecal samples may be requested from employees. Naturally, the health department checks the sanitary condition of the operation in question. The authorities may immediately close the operation if an imminent health hazard is discovered. If a problem is traced to the establishment's personnel, the health department may immediately exclude one or more employees from employment in the facility. Or, if the employee presents a potential risk, his or her services may be restricted to an area of the operation where no possibility of foodborne disease transmission exists.

Step 8   **Take corrective action to reduce future risks.** The manager of a business implicated in an outbreak of foodborne disease has a powerful incentive to evaluate the operation's employee training, its system of food handling, and its overall sanitation program. The result of this evaluation should be improvements which will minimize the risk of another outbreak. Corrective action should address the four resources under the manager's control and the problems associated with them—that is, human hazards, product hazards, equipment hazards, and facilities hazards.

The health department is usually very willing to suggest procedures for corrective action. Following these recommendations helps the operation avoid future incidents similar to the one under investigation.

Step 9   **Close the complaint with the customer.** When the investigation is completed, it is time to contact the complainant, apologize, and offer to present a token of management's sincerity. The token may be a gift, a free meal, a coupon, or a small check.

Exhibit 5.11   Sample Food-Related Complaint Record

Name of Complainant

| Address |

| Telephone Number |

| Summary of the Complaint |

| Number Affected | Date of Meal | Time Eaten |

| Foods and Beverages Consumed |

Symptoms _____ Nausea   _____ Vomiting
              _____ Diarrhea   _____ Abdominal Cramps
              _____ Fever   _____ Other (specify) _____

| Did others consume the same food and beverage? |

| Names and Address of Other Consumers |

| Management Action to Resolve the Complaint |

Date _____   Signature _____

Step 10   **Index all complaints.** The person responsible for the investigation should maintain a file of complaint record forms. This file should contain all relevant information obtained as a result of the investigation. Complaints from customers which were validated should be "red-flagged" for future reference. This file is helpful in planning the corrective action phase (Step 8) and the follow-up phase (Step 11).

Exhibit 5.12   Suggested Procedures for Handling Foodborne Illness Complaints from Customers

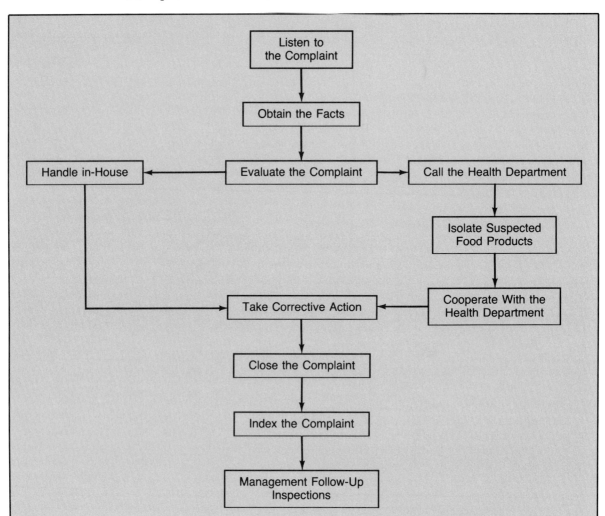

Step 11   **Follow up to determine that corrective action has been taken.** Regardless of who handles the in-house investigation of a suspected foodborne illness outbreak, management is ultimately responsible for preventing a recurrence. Thus, the operation's manager should conduct an in-house follow-up inspection. This inspection should be documented in the complaint file. After that, the manager should periodically spot-check the critical areas associated with past problems to make sure they are under control.

The 11-step procedure for handling customer complaints of foodborne illness is summarized in Exhibit 5.12. The basic procedure suggested here applies to both independent and chain food service and lodging operations. However, the chain's single-unit manager is advised to contact the corporate office as soon as it is determined that the unit may be involved in an outbreak. The corporate office may have its own written procedures that must be followed.

Without a doubt, the best time to counteract foodborne illness is before it starts. An outbreak could cost your business thousands of dollars. Weighed against the costs of proper training, correct sanitation and maintenance of equipment and facilities, and proper inventory control, the outbreak is certainly costlier.

Furthermore, a foodborne disease outbreak can disrupt or close your business. Finally, the damage done to your establishment's image lasts long after the outbreak has been handled. The remaining chapters of this book outline specific preventive measures you can take to protect your customers' health and your operation's future.

How Does Your Food Service Establishment Rate?

In a 1978 FDA field study, the Food Service Establishment Inspection Report (FDA Form 2420) was used to record inspections of 140 food service establishments in a major midwestern city. Seven different segments of the food service industry were inspected and classified, namely full menu restaurants, luncheonettes, fast-food units, cafeterias, chicken restaurants, steakhouses, and pizza establishments. A score of 80 to 100 was considered good to excellent, and 31% of the total earned this rating. Scores ranging from 60 to 79 were considered marginal to acceptable, and 60.7% of the businesses were classified in this middle range. The range of 0 to 59 was considered inadequate, and 7.9% of the total fell into this category. Exhibit 5.13 presents a summary of the data. The average score for all 140 companies was 74.9% (in the marginal to acceptable range).[6]

There is no evidence to suggest that the results of this study are representative of the levels of sanitation in food service operations across the United States. On the other hand, it is certainly possible that operations in other cities would fare no better on average.

If you want to see how your establishment compares, make a note to compare your next inspection score with the figures in your industry segment. You may also want to track your inspection scores over time to determine the efficiency and effectiveness of your in-house sanitation program. Strive to obtain and maintain inspection scores in the good to excellent range. Of course, if you are an operator, you should regularly do your own inspections to ascertain your operation's sanitation level. After all, why wait for an official inspection when you can start improving your operation's performance today?

---

[6] P.M. Kolb, "Focus on Sanitation." *Restaurant Business*, December 1, 1978, pp. 100-104, 107-108.

Exhibit 5.13 Range of Sanitation Inspection Scores by Type of Food Service Establishment

Inspection Scores	Type of Food Service Establishment							
	Full Menu	Luncheon-ettes	Fast Food	Cafe-terias	Chicken	Steak Houses	Pizza	Total
95–100				1			1	2
90–94		1	4		1		1	7
85–89	4		5	3	2	1	2	17
80–84	6	1	5	1	1	1	3	18
75–79	8	7	10	1	4	2	1	33
70–74	5	5	6	2	3	2	1	24
65–69	5	4				3	1	13
60–64	8	2	2			1	2	15
55–59	3	1	2			1		7
50–54				1				1
45–49	2		1					3
Total	41	21	35	9	11	11	12	140

Source: P.M. Kolb, "Focus on Sanitation," Restaurant Business, December 1, 1978, p. 104.

Summary

As the population of the United States has grown, so have the food laws which are designed to protect the public health. Several federal regulatory agencies oversee a considerable number of food handlers to ensure the safety of products as they move through the channels of production, processing, and distribution. State and local regulatory agencies promote food safety in retail food service establishments.

Industry and trade organizations and associations exert a positive influence on the food service industry through the voluntary cooperation of their members. A number of educational materials and a variety of training programs are available at both the national and the state level from these organizations and associations. These groups work with regulatory agencies to improve the level of food safety in this country.

Regulatory agencies are empowered to enforce current requirements for the operation of a food service establishment. Permits, licenses, or certificates are issued if the operation complies with relevant rules, regulations, and ordinances. Management, employees, and regulatory officials all have responsibilities during sanitation inspections. An 11-step procedure was presented as a proactive approach to handling suspected outbreaks of foodborne disease.

It is important that a food service establishment operate in compliance with the sanitation rules and regulations governing its jurisdiction for several reasons. First, customer satisfaction will be increased, and so will repeat business. Second, the reputation of the business and the manager will be enhanced. Third, employees will feel proud to work in an operation that takes a professional approach to sanitation. And last (but not least), the business will enjoy a stronger financial position.

References

Baker, K. J. "Foodservice Sanitation Training and Reciprocity in the 80s." *Journal of Food Protection*, October 1980. 43(10):805-807.

Bryan, F. L. "Foodborne Disease Risk Assessment of Foodservice Establishments in a Community." *Journal of Food Protection*, January 1982. 45(1):93-100.

Centers for Disease Control. *Guide for Investigating Foodborne Disease Outbreaks and Analyzing Surveillance Data*. Atlanta, Ga.: Public Health Service, U.S. Department of Health, Education, and Welfare, 1973.

Cichy, Ronald F. "What to Do When a Customer Complains of Foodborne Illness?" *Restaurants and Institutions*, 1 March 1983. 92(5):145.

Ebert, H. "Government Involvement in the Food Industry." *Dairy and Food Sanitation*, November 1981. 1(11):458-459.

Food and Drug Administration, Public Health Service, U.S. Department of Health, Education, and Welfare. *Food Service Sanitation Manual*. Washington, D.C.: U.S. Government Printing Office, 1976.

Kaplan, O. B., and El-Ahraf, A. "Relative Risk Ratios of Foodborne Illness in Foodservice Establishments: An Aid in Deployment of Environmental Health Manpower." *Journal of Food Protection*, May 1979. 42(5):446-447.

Kolb, P. M. "Focus on Sanitation." *Restaurant Business*, 1 December 1978. 77(13):100.

Mutkoski, S. A., and Schurer, M. L. *Meat and Fish Management*. North Scituate, Mass.: Breton, 1981.

National Institute for the Foodservice Industry. *Applied Foodservice Sanitation*. 2nd ed. Chicago, Ill.: D.C. Heath, 1978.

Procedures to Investigate Foodborne Illness. 3rd ed. Ames, Iowa: International Association of Milk, Food, and Environmental Sanitarians, 1976.

Reedy, L. "Safety and Health — No Betting Matter." *Food Service Marketing*, December 1980. 42(12):43-46.

Rules and Regulations Governing Restaurants in the City and County of Denver. Denver, Colo.: Denver Department of Health and Hospitals, Environmental Health Services, 1980.

Rules and Regulations Governing the Sanitation of Food Service Establishments in the State of Colorado. Denver, Colo.: Colorado State Department of Health, 1978.

Sanitation Operations Manual. Chicago, Ill.: Public Health and Safety Department, National Restaurant Association, 1979.

Schultz, H. W. *Food Law Handbook*. Westport, Conn.: AVI, 1981.

Semling, H. V. "Forecast for Food Safety Legislative Changes." *Food Processing*, July 1981. 42(7):8-9.

———."New Food Policy Lines Begin to Sharpen, Reinforce Industry's Hopeful Mood." *Food Processing*, August 1981. 42(9):10-12.

Stefanelli, J. M. *Purchasing: Selection and Procurement for the Hospitality Industry.* New York: Wiley, 1981.

Weckel, K. G. "Professionalism: What It Should Mean to You." *Journal of Food Protection*, March 1979. 42(3):273-276.

Whitmarsh, J. "Is Your Kitchen Clean Enough for Uncle Sam?" *Institutions/Volume Feeding*, 1 March 1976. 78(5):50-51.

Strategies for Success at the Aspen Hotel

Paul met again with the chief engineer, food and beverage director, and executive housekeeper the following Monday. The meeting was designed to review the lists each department head had prepared and to develop a strategy to bring the hotel into compliance with the health department's code. Paul James began the meeting by reviewing the following compliance procedures from the local code:

1.   Permits, Licenses, and Certificates—General

2.   Issuance of Permit, License, or Certificate

3.   Suspension of Permit, License, or Certificate

4.   Revocation of Permit, License, or Certificate

5.   New Construction Code Requirements

6.   Remodeling of an Existing Building

7.   Purchase of an Existing Food Service Establishment

8.   Submission of Plans

9.   Pre-Operational Inspection

Paul realized that a critical error was made before the Aspen Hotel was purchased. Someone should have reviewed the inspection history with the local health department. A sanitation consultant should have been hired to conduct the review. The purchase of the hotel could have been contingent upon correction of all health code violations. It was too late for these steps now. The only choice now was to work in close cooperation with the local health department. The goal was to reopen the hotel on schedule in six weeks.

The chief engineer was assigned the responsibility of coordinating plan submission and review. He would file a weekly report with the GM indicating the progress of the review. Both the food and beverage director and the executive housekeeper agreed to work closely with the chief engineer on the details affecting their respective departments. Paul felt confident about this strategy.

The GM asked the food and beverage director to review her copies of health department inspection reports for the last five years. Elisabeth agreed to furnish the GM with a summary of deficiencies and suggested strategies for correcting the violations. Paul also asked Elisabeth to prepare a list of responsibilities of the food and beverage department related to health department inspections. In addition, he asked Elisabeth to suggest a contingency program that could be rapidly implemented if a foodborne outbreak was suspected.

The following case studies are designed to enhance your understanding of the material in this chapter. If you are a Home Study student, use these case studies to stimulate questions about this chapter. If you are a Group or Institutional Study student, you may be asked to discuss these case studies as part of a regular classroom assignment.

CASE STUDY 5.1

At the peak of the dinner hour rush, the manager of a family-style table service restaurant receives a telephone call. As soon as he can get to it, the manager answers the telephone.

The caller says, "Our group of 150 association members had a banquet in your restaurant last night. We were served spinach salad, broccoli quiche, bran muffins, chocolate mousse, and a choice of beverage. You poisoned us! Over 100 of our members called me, as the executive director, to say they are experiencing nausea, diarrhea, stomach cramps, and dizziness. I have a fever of 102°F (39°C)! What are you going to do about it?"

Test Your Understanding

1. How should the manager handle this customer's accusation that his establishment caused a foodborne illness outbreak?

2. What should the manager do to close this complaint with the customer?

3. What are your recommendations for preventing similar incidents in the future?

CASE STUDY 5.2

Johnny Lee is the general manager of the Town and Country Restaurant. The operation features fresh fish and shellfish and a 100-item salad bar. The salad bar is so elaborate that the Town and Country Restaurant features it in all their advertising as "a fresh fruit and vegetable market."

It is Sunday afternoon, and Johnny is supervising the lunch rush. A server informs Johnny that a woman customer at table #32 wants to see the manager. As Johnny walks over to the table, he notices that the three women seated there have already started to eat their selections from the fresh fruit and vegetable bar.

"Look at this!" exclaims one of the women. "There is a piece of glass in my salad, and I demand you do something!" Johnny is shocked because he has never had a complaint like this before.

Test Your Understanding

1. How should Johnny handle this customer's complaint?

2. What should Johnny do to close this complaint with the customer?

3. What are your recommendations to Johnny Lee?

CASE STUDY 5.3

Johnny Lee has never joined a local or national trade association; he has no interest in being a member of such a group for several reasons. First, Johnny believes that such organizations overcharge their members, so he wouldn't get a good return on his investment of time and money. Second, Johnny is not willing to share any of his operational "secrets" with other members of an association. And finally, Johnny doesn't feel that he needs anyone's help to run his restaurant.

Test Your Understanding

1. What are the advantages of joining a trade association?

2. Comment on Johnny's philosophy of management.

3. What are your recommendations to Johnny Lee?

CASE STUDY 5.4

The Nelson Motor Hotel is located in a major metropolitan city. The food and beverage manager of the property, Marty Gormless, has been having a bad day. First, his Monday morning started with a department head meeting in the general manager's office. The GM told Marty that his food cost percentage for last month was 7% over budget. The GM asked for a report within 24 hours on how Marty plans to resolve the problem.

Then, as Marty left the meeting, the executive chef rushed up to Marty to tell him that the power was out on the large walk-in refrigerators and freezers in the main kitchen. These units have been virtually packed to capacity with food products in anticipation of a convention to be held from Tuesday through next Saturday.

Now, on his way to the kitchen, Marty is greeted by the sanitarian from the City Department of Health. "What do you want?" Marty snaps.

"I'm here to perform a routine inspection," states the sanitarian.

"Well, we are very busy around here, so make it quick," replies Marty.

Test Your Understanding

1. Did Marty interact with the health inspector in a professional manner?

2. What noticeable sanitation hazards exist at the Nelson Motor Hotel?

3. What are your recommendations to Marty Gormless?

CASE STUDY 5.5

The sanitarian from the City Department of Health has just completed his inspection of the Nelson Motor Hotel. The inspector calculates the sanitation score—68—and hands the form to Marty Gormless. When Marty glances at the form, he is outraged.

"What do you mean by this?" shouts Marty.

The sanitarian replies, "I would be happy to sit down with you and explain the deficiencies."

"I don't have time for that nonsense now," screams Marty. "If I ever see you in here again, I'll break your back and send you floating down the river!" Marty storms off, leaving the shocked health inspector behind.

Test Your Understanding

1. Was the health inspector treated in a professional manner?

2. What is the basic problem at the Nelson Motor Hotel?

3. What are your recommendations to Marty Gormless?

Part Two

It has been said that four out of five *chain* restaurants that open this year will still be open in three years. On the other hand, only one out of five *independent* restaurants that open today will still be viable businesses in three years. Why is there a relatively high success rate for chain restaurants compared to their independent counterparts? Perhaps the chain restaurants are better competitors and survivors because they have recognized the importance of systematic management. While some independent operators use this systematic approach and prosper, many more could benefit from following the example of the successful chains. Although there is no corporate headquarters to oversee the independent restaurateur's performance, the tasks are much the same. It is management's responsibility to establish and enforce the **standards** of the business. Employees may be (and should be) consulted but, ultimately, the manager must set the standards and see that they are maintained. Standards are, of course, based on the expectations of the target markets.

At first glance, the job of standardizing an entire food service operation may appear overwhelming. How can the task of standardization be made more rational and logical? A systems approach, which permits analysis and adjustment of substystem control points, provides a good starting point. In the following chapters, the ten basic operating activities or control points in a food service facility will be explained in more detail, particularly as they apply to sanitation and success.

The discussion of each control point will begin with a description of the activity and its purpose. Each basic operating activity may be said to have several purposes: maximizing profits or containing costs, contributing to quality, and ensuring satisfactory sanitation levels. To consistently achieve these goals, however, standards must be established for cost control, quality assurance, and sanitation management. Therefore, the discussion of each food service control point will include a number of relevant standards. These standards lead to consistency, predictability, and greater management control.

Each of the four resources under a manager's control (personnel, facilities, equipment, and inventory) will also be presented in relation to each basic operating activity. Then, some tips on how to respond to changes at the control point will be offered. Finally, the discussion of each control point will conclude with a brief review of how to succeed in controlling the activity. Since this book is intended to be shared by managers with employees who need to brush up on their own responsibilities, the fact that certain key points appear in more than one chapter should not concern the reader.

Also, in reading Chapters 6 through 10, if some topics seem only distantly related to sanitation, it will be helpful to remember that the systems approach involves seeing the interrelationship of all the elements in the system. Thus, the standards and operating procedures discussed in these chapters are not directed at sanitation to the exclusion of cost control and quality assurance; rather, they are intended to contribute to the overall success of the operation by addressing all three goals.

SIX

The Menu Planning and Purchasing Control Points

Strategies for Success at the Aspen Hotel

It was six weeks before the Aspen Hotel was scheduled to reopen. General manager Paul James had spent the last ten days reviewing the functions and responsibilities of the front office, the controller, and the sales and catering departments. Each department head in those three areas was now developing a written operating plan. Each department's operating plan would include a detailed description of every facet and responsibility of that department. The description would specify how the department should operate, explain how it interfaces with other areas of the hotel, and suggest a strategy for employee training. With these plans well under way, Paul now turned his attention to the food and beverage department.

"Once again my knowledge of F&B operations will pay off," Paul thought. In light of his extensive food and beverage background, Paul felt that he was in a position to make realistic recommendations and to help Elisabeth Mueller develop her operating plan. Paul enjoyed the challenge of hotel food and beverage operations; there were so many variables to consider. At other hotels, Paul had often told his staff, "Guests usually base their overall perception of a hotel on the quality of its food and beverage operations. If the hotel has a great food and beverage operation, guests are impressed and think it is a great hotel. The guest's first impression during the food and beverage experience is most critical. You only have one opportunity to make a favorable first impression."

Paul James systematically reviewed the hotel's food and beverage operations on a control point basis. He started with the menu planning and purchasing control points. Paul talked to a number of customers and guests at competing hotels and restaurants to develop his customer awareness. Paul felt it was critical to know the expectations of the hotel's target markets if their desires were to be satisfied.

He had already conducted an analysis of past sales in the hotel's food and beverage operations. He was surprised to discover that 60% of breakfast and lunch business and 75% of dinner business came from the local market area. Because local customers made up the majority of the hotel's food and beverage business, Paul realized that it was especially important to identify the expectations of the local target markets. Only then could the menus for the Aspen Hotel be designed to satisfy its primary target market.

Paul soon discovered that the last menu change in the hotel took place three years ago. Now, new menus had to be developed before the hotel could reopen its food and beverage operations. In looking over the old menus, Paul saw that there had been little cross-utilization of raw ingredients. For example, Paul discovered that the hotel had been buying five different hams for use on breakfast, lunch, and dinner menus. Most hot food products listed on the menus were traditional. A survey of the kitchen revealed that the equipment and facilities were outdated. Paul learned that hot food items were usually prepared in large batches and held on a steam table.

Food and beverage supplies were purchased by Walter Joslin, one of two purchasing agents at the Aspen Hotel. Walter did not use written specifications but did use written purchase orders. He called each supplier on a weekly basis to obtain verbal bids on high volume raw ingredient purchases. Walter had extensive food production experience but had never been formally trained for the position of purchasing agent. He reported directly to the hotel controller, Bob Campbell.

The Aspen Hotel did not have an executive chef. Kitchen manager Peggy Herbert was in charge of the operation of the hotel's two kitchens: the main kitchen and the banquet kitchen. Peggy had been formally trained in culinary skills, having completed a two-year program at a well-known culinary institute in the United States. Both the GM and the F&B director agreed that Peggy Herbert was a real asset to the hotel.

Paul James had heard that the hotel had had some problems with banquet menus chosen by the sales department. Apparently, Mike Beers and his staff had failed to think about the production and service departments when selling banquets and special functions. Paul recently heard that a month before the hotel was purchased by the Rocky Mountain Hotel Management Company, Mike's staff sold a banquet for 300 people. The menu included twice-baked potatoes and a choice of two vegetables. On top of that, Mike's staff sold the most expensive dessert on the menu and discounted the price. The results were disastrous.

Paul realized that the problem was due, in part, to the fact that Mike Beers, the director of sales and catering, had only been with the hotel for six months. Paul also realized that effective cooperation was needed between the director of sales and catering and the director of food and beverage operations. Paul decided to institute a policy that a representative of the F&B department must attend sales and catering department meetings to give recommendations and input.

The more Paul thought about the menu planning and purchasing control points, the more he wanted to change the image of the hotel. His goal was to make the F&B operations both different and better. The GM wanted to add a touch of class in the main dining room and more creativity in the coffee shop. He would provide input to the F&B director to help her establish standards for sanitation, cost, and quality control in these two areas.

In this chapter, our systematic approach to food service management is initiated. The first two basic operating activities are addressed in this chapter. As we shall see, the menu exerts an influence over all the other control points, so menu planning is a crucial function. The purchasing control point is intimately related to the establishment's cost control, quality assurance, and sanitation goals.

The Menu Planning Control Point

Menu planning is the first control point in the food service system.

If the menu is properly designed, it can stimulate sales and increase the customer check average, because whenever a menu is presented to a customer, a sales transaction begins. The food service operation's menu creates an image of the establishment. Therefore, the appearance of the menu should be in harmony with the image the food service establishment wants to project. The image may be elegant, business-like, fun, ethnic, or trendy, depending on what the target markets desire.

Customers are influenced by visual cues provided by the menu, such as readability, physical design, layout, artwork, and type styles. As with other communication tools, "It's not just what you say, it's how you say it that counts." For example, fast-food restaurants offer a limited number of menu items but they sell these items in large quantities. Since their customers are served at a common sales counter, separate menus are not needed. Customers are familiar with the standardized menu offerings, so long, elaborate descriptions are not needed. They would only slow down the customer's decision-making process. Fast-food restaurants simply post names and prices of their products near the sales counters. Enlarged color photographs of the menu items show their color and texture and, thus, may contribute to increased sales. (However, it is imperative that the items served look exactly like the pictures; otherwise decreased satisfaction may be the result.) The overall effect is to convey simplicity, speed, and a limited selection of products prepared the same way at every unit.

On the other hand, an independently owned specialty restaurant catering to wealthy, sophisticated diners would have an altogether different menu. First, the number of menu items would probably be much greater. To project an image of elegance, the traditional table service restaurant might have a menu as large as a book with detailed descriptions of its wide range of food products. Such a restaurant recognizes that its customers enjoy the feeling of "endless possibilities" afforded by an extensive menu. Also, since this establishment's customers are seeking a leisurely and pleasurable dining experience, the time it takes them to peruse the voluminous menu is no problem.

To draw attention to daily specials and highlight signature items of the operation, some restaurants have found it useful to box these items on the menu. Another way to increase sales of featured items is to write the menu items (possibly with prices) on a chalkboard near the entrance. One restaurateur whose establishment specializes in fresh seafood uses a chalkboard to list the flight arrival times of the jet-fresh catch of the day. While this approach sacrifices a degree of elegance, it offers convincing evidence of the freshness and variety of the operation's offerings.

Generally, dynamic menus are preferable to static menus. However, menu variability depends on the seasonal availability of raw ingredients, the number and kind of courses offered, the potential for using leftovers and local ingredients, the preferences of the community, the operation's image, and the desires of its target markets.

Another element distinguishes the menu of an elegant restaurant from that of a fast-food restaurant: prices. In some cases, prices are omitted from extensive menus due to seasonal fluctuations in the operation's food cost for these items. In such cases, the management assumes either that money is no object or that, if it is, the customer will inquire about current prices. When setting menu prices, it is important to remember that today's sophisticated diner is searching for the best price-value relationship. If an operation's prices far exceed the perceived value of its menu items, this can decrease customer satisfaction and negatively affect repeat business.

Besides showing customers the operation's plan for satisfying their expectations, a menu serves another purpose: it functions as a plan for the entire food service system. The success of the menu planning activity has a direct influence on the success of the other basic operating activities. When a menu is initially planned, the resources under the control of the food service manager must be carefully considered. Personnel, equipment, inventory, and facilities all have an impact on menu planning.

Menu Planning and Personnel

The operation's employees are important to the success of its menu. Before management begins menu planning, the skill levels of production and service personnel must be assessed. It may be helpful to consider the production staff and service staff separately, although their functions are intimately related in actual operations.

The **production staff** is challenged to produce the menu items. This production takes place within the confines of the kitchen or "heart of the house." In planning the operation's menu, the objective is to avoid overloading any one person or work station. A well-planned menu features items that the operation's kitchen personnel can consistently produce while maintaining the operation's quality, cost, and sanitation standards.

Management should be realistic, not idealistic, in determining what can be accomplished with the existing staff. For example, consider a kitchen in a metropolitan hotel where every menu item is prepared from scratch. All meats are received in the wholesale cut form, which is less expensive than the retail- or portion-cut form. Therefore, the staff has to do the retail butchering. Unfortunately, the production staff has not been properly trained to butcher the wholesale cuts into retail cuts of meat. As a result, a lot of time and money is wasted and unnecessary sanitation hazards abound. Rather than saving the business money, this poorly conceived arrangement increases the food cost, adds to the labor cost, and destroys the quality control system. However, these problems can be avoided by organizing the menu planning function on the basis of personnel considerations.

The **service staff** transfers the menu items from the production staff to the customers. In order to properly serve customers, the server should be ready to answer their questions. For example, servers should know what items are on the menu, the portion sizes offered, how the items are prepared, and the prices. Even if the menu contains all of this information, the server can provide a personal touch by answering customers' questions directly. Servers should also know the meaning of all terms used on the menu so they can explain them to any customers who are puzzled. This is particularly true if the menu includes ethnic foods, since these items may be unfamiliar to the average customer.

Again, staff training is critical. In addition to thoroughly training new servers, some managers call a five- to ten-minute **line-up meeting** with service staff members before each meal period. These brief meetings are informal training sessions, in that (a) they give the chef and the manager an opportunity to explain daily specials, and (b) they give the servers an opportunity to sample portions of new menu items and ask questions.

Like the skill levels of production personnel, the skills of the service staff must be considered in menu planning. This is particularly true if management is considering menu items to be prepared in the "front of the house," such as tossed salads and flambeed desserts. Whether the operation uses tableside preparation or the more common plate-style service depends, in part, on the image it is seeking. However, once the decision is made, the service staff requires training in the serving skills dictated by the menu.

Suppliers are another personnel component to consider when planning a menu. Although suppliers are not, strictly speaking, under the manager's control, these people can contribute to the success of the business. Particularly at the menu planning control point, their input and suggestions can be used to make the business more profitable while enhancing the customer's satisfaction. For example, suppliers can offer preparation and merchandising suggestions for various menu items. The excellent food service companies utilize their suppliers as sources of creative ideas, market trend information, new promotion ideas, and informal competitive analyses as well as purveyors of food, beverage, and nonfood products.

Menu Planning and Equipment

Any food service establishment must make a sizeable investment in food service equipment before it can open for business. Naturally, the amount and type of production and service equipment owned by the business determines what items it can produce and, therefore, what it places on the menu. It is imperative to select equipment based on capacity, skill levels of employees, energy and maintenance costs, and initial purchase price. But above all, it is critical that equipment be easy to clean and sanitize.

The FDA's Food Service Sanitation Ordinance states:

Easily cleanable means that surfaces are readily accessible and made of such materials and finish and so fabricated that residue may be effectively removed by normal cleaning methods.

Source: Food and Drug Administration, Public Health Service, U.S. Department of Health, Education, and Welfare, Food Service Sanitation Manual, *1976, p. 20.*

The addition of a new menu item may require that the business purchase new production equipment. Such additions should not be made without an analysis of product flow and personnel movement. This analysis helps management to anticipate where cross-traffic may create safety and sanitation hazards. Many operations today use equipment on wheels or casters which permit rearrangement when necessary. Besides allowing for adjustments to the product flow and employee traffic patterns, this mobility facilitates cleaning. Before a new menu item is added, the proper equipment should be available to reduce sanitation hazards. For example, if the proposed menu change involves the addition of a soup bar to the dining room, the kitchen must have adequate steam table, steam-jacketed kettle, or range equipment to attain and maintain safe product temperatures during preparation.

A change in menu may also have implications for the operation's service equipment. Again, the sanitation hazards must be considered beforehand. Continuing with the soup bar example, the dining room should be equipped with suitable hot-holding equipment for the soup selections before these new items are added to the menu. Otherwise, dangerous product temperatures may cause problems for the operation and its customers.

A dramatically modified menu can have a devastating effect on the system if proper equipment is not available. Consider what could happen when the owner of a bar that serves a wide selection of drinks and cold snack foods decides to add hot barbecued meatballs to the snack food menu. She realizes from the start that equipment to produce and hold the product is necessary. However, she fails to realize the significance of the serving container to be used. She chooses reusable dishes, thinking that these will be less expensive in the long run than single-service disposable containers. Making a hasty decision on cost alone, she neglects to consider the fact that if the meatballs are served in reusable containers, proper provision must be made for washing, sanitizing, and storing the dishes. It is not acceptable to wash the sauce-laden meatball dishes in the bar's glass-washing equipment. In the end, she realizes that adding entirely new categories of product offerings can be very expensive.

The addition of banquet service to a traditional food service operation must be carefully weighed in light of the additional constraints banquets place on menu planning and equipment. For example, if a hotel is planning to serve a banquet for 800, all of the food items cannot be dished for all 800 guests immediately prior to service. Therefore, extra hot-holding and cold storage equipment is essential. Also, the hotel should limit its banquet menu to items which can safely withstand the extra handling and holding times involved.

Menu Planning and Inventory

A **menu** is a listing of the items the operation is offering for sale, whereas the **inventory** is the sum total of items the operation has purchased. The menu helps to create a demand for the finished food items produced from inventory. The customer's order is a purchase decision which results in a depletion of the goods on hand. Eventually, the operation must replenish the inventory, if it is to continue offering the items customers are buying. It is important to keep detailed records on the relative popularity of every menu item. This information is useful at the next step of the food service system: the purchasing control point (see page 172).

The menu directly affects the establishment's purchasing, receiving, and storing requirements. The size of storage areas needed for raw ingredients and finished menu items depends on the menu. One of the primary advantages of a limited menu is that it reduces storage area requirements.

In the past, food service managers attempted to achieve **diversification** of their menus. Often, this was accomplished by the addition of many new menu items. Since most items were made from scratch, the number and variety of raw ingredients was correspondingly increased.

Now there is a trend toward **rationalization** of menu items. That is, simplification is being sought for the sake of operational efficiency. This strategy frequently results in a limited menu. Alternatively, the operation can offer several menu items which use the same raw ingredients. The objective of this **cross-utilization** is to prepare and serve as many menu item selections as possible with a limited number of raw ingredients. When the menu is carefully planned to ensure a balance of menu selections in each category, the result of these new strategies can be a streamlining of purchasing, receiving, and storing functions.

Today, as in the past, food service managers are searching for new menu item alternatives. However, the proliferation of high quality convenience foods has made it easier for food service operations to offer new items without having to buy additional raw ingredients or elaborate equipment. High quality convenience products can be purchased in semiprepared or fully prepared forms. Because they have built-in labor, they also reduce in-house labor requirements. Of course, convenience food products usually have a higher **AP ("as purchased") price** than the raw ingredients from which they are made.

It is always best to base initial menu plans on the needs and desires of the target markets. However, several other factors may influence the menu selection. Among these factors are: the recommended storage conditions (time and temperature); personnel skill levels; the product's availability and seasonality; the stability of quality and price levels; and the operation's ability to purchase, prepare, and serve the menu item in a safe and sanitary way. (Other factors which cause menu modifications are discussed in a later section.)

Menu Planning and Facilities

The facilities, both indoor and outdoor, affect the image of a food service establishment. The layout and design of the facilities are also important considerations in menu planning, because they establish the physical limits within which food preparation and service take place. From the standpoint of menu planning, the kitchen and dining room facilities are a critical resource of the business. The facilities must be adequate for the purchasing, receiving, storing, issuing, preparing, cooking, holding, and serving of every item on the menu. Thus, a major change in menu may necessitate remodeling of the physical facilities. By the same token, a change in the facilities used by a food service business may force a revision of its menu. This mutual influence can be illustrated by the following examples.

First, consider a country club food service operation in which 80% of the space is allocated to the dining room and 20% to the kitchen. Since the kitchen generally prepares menu items from scratch, the production facilities are often pushed to their upper limit. The kitchen facilities are almost always overtaxed during the summer when the number of parties and special functions is greatly increased.

Now, suppose the manager of the country club decides to expand his dining and banquet facilities by adding a 90-seat outdoor patio service area with a clear glass roof. He is convinced that this area will appeal to customers planning parties and banquets because it has a breathtaking view of the golf course. However, the manager has not considered the effect of the expanded service facilities on the production capabilities of the kitchen. To increase the dining facilities without adding to the production area would be a critical error. Such a decision would be likely to result in lower productivity and morale levels among production personnel; a corresponding reduction in customer satisfaction levels could then be expected.

To take another example, a hotel may decide to add room service to its offerings to generate more revenue and profits. Again, the size and layout of the facility has an impact on the success of the effort. For example, the kitchen may produce a beautiful and tasty eggs Benedict entree for breakfast, but by the time room service delivers the order to the farthest wing of guestrooms, the product is cold and unappealing. Therefore, room service menus must be limited to those items that can be successfully and safely delivered to the customer.

Yet another problem is created when an overly ambitious hotel sales force convinces meeting planners that special entrees or desserts will add a touch of elegance and class to their banquets. These salespeople have not thought about the limitations of the hotel's production and service facilities. Again, an outdoor barbecue for 500 people in the hotel's gardens may sound like an exciting, fun affair; but if the kitchen or service staff cannot deliver the products, customer satisfaction will not be achieved.

In all of these examples, the unfortunate results could be prevented by structuring the operation's offerings around what the physical facilities can realistically handle. By now it should be clear that menu planning is a complex process, but menu planning is more successful when the establishment's resources are taken into consideration.

Menu Planning and Change

Because conditions change, a food service operation's menu must change also. Menu changes are modified by both external and internal factors.

External modifiers include consumer demands, economic factors, the competition, supply levels, and industry trends. Consumer demands are perhaps the most important factor to consider in changing a menu. Management should first decide which potential markets it wants to attract with the modified menu. Then the proposed menu change must be evaluated in light of the negative and/or positive effects it may have on the current clientele.

Economic factors include the cost of ingredients and the potential profitability of new menu items. Menu items offered by the competition may dictate choices to offer or not offer. For example, a hotel food service located next to a restaurant offering the "best Oriental food in town" may elect not to serve Oriental cuisine. Supply levels relate the price to the quality and quantity of the proposed menu items. Supply levels are highly variable for some seasonal raw ingredients such as fresh fruits and vegetables. Industry trends are general observations about how the industry is responding to new demands. At present, the overall trends relate to a more sophisticated average customer who is searching for the best price-value relationship.

Internal modifiers which may result in a proposed menu change are the facility's meal pattern, concept and theme, operational system, and menu mix. The typical meal pattern is breakfast, lunch, and dinner. Management must decide if existing meal periods should be continued or altered. The target markets' expectations have a direct influence on this decision. Any change must fit with the establishment's concept and theme. A restaurant that is known as the best steakhouse in the city may do itself a disservice by adding fresh fish and shellfish to the menu. An establishment's image may also rule out certain foods which do not blend with its theme and decor. For example, even though ethnic foods are growing in popularity, a hotel restaurant may find it difficult to fit ethnic foods into its projected image.

Menu changes are also modified by the establishment's operational system. For example, if extensive new equipment purchases are crucial to the successful production and service of the menu item, the change may be too costly. On the other hand, the change may raise both food and labor costs to unacceptable levels. Or, in some cases, the skill levels of production and service personnel may not be adequate to successfully produce and present the new menu item. The operation's existing menu has a certain overall combination or mix of items. This menu mix will be affected by any change in individual items. All of these modifiers should be evaluated before menu changes are finalized and implemented.

Finally, **truth-in-menu** is another menu planning consideration that is growing in importance. Above all, accurate descriptions of raw ingredients and finished menu items are essential. The correct quality or grade of food products must be stated. Care must be exercised when U.S. Department of Agriculture (USDA) grades are printed on the menu. "A choice top butt steak" listed on the menu implies that the meat is USDA Choice grade. A product billed as "fresh Lake Superior whitefish" should indeed be fresh from Lake Superior. Other representations of points of origin are presented in Exhibit 6.1.

The size, weight, or portion advertised on the menu also must be accurate. For meat items, it is generally accepted that the weight listed is the precooked weight. A bowl of soup should contain more than a cup of soup. Descriptions like "extra tall" drinks or "extra large" salads can open the door to possible complaints from customers. "All you can eat" implies that the customer is entitled to have exactly that. Fresh products are not frozen, canned, or preserved in any way. Canned green beans are not frozen, and frozen grapefruit juice is not fresh.

Exhibit 6.1 Typical Representations of Point of Origin

Dairy Products

Danish Bleu Cheese
Domestic Cheese
Imported Swiss Cheese
Roquefort Cheese
Wisconsin Cheese

Fish and Shellfish

Cod, Icelandic (North Atlantic)
Crab
    Alaskan King Crab
    Florida Stone Crab
    North Atlantic Crab
    Snow Crab
Frog Legs
    Domestic Frog Legs
    Imported Frog Legs
    Louisiana Frog Legs
Lobster
    Australian Lobster
    Brazilian Lobster
    Maine Lobster
    South African Lobster
Oysters
    Blue Point Oysters
    Chesapeake Bay Oysters
    Olympia Oysters
Salmon
    Nova Scotia Salmon
    Puget Sound Sockeye Salmon
    Salmon Lox
Scallops
    Bay Scallops
    Sea Scallops

Scrod, Boston
Shrimp
    Bay Shrimp
    Gulf Shrimp
Trout
    Colorado Brook Trout
    Idaho Brook Trout
Whitefish, Lake Superior

Meats

Beef, Colorado
Ham
    Country Ham
    Danish Ham
    Imported Ham
    Smithfield Ham
    Virginia Style Ham
Pork, Iowa

Poultry

Long Island Duckling
Maryland Milk-Fed Chicken

Vegetables and Fruits

Orange Juice, Florida
Pineapples
    Hawaiian Pineapples
    Mexican Pineapples
Potatoes
    Idaho Potatoes
    Maine Potatoes

Other truth-in-menu violations may occur. The preparation technique (e.g., sauteed in butter) must be accurate. If an additional charge will be assessed for extras (e.g., Roquefort dressing, substitutions, coffee refills), that must be clearly stated on the menu. Any pictures used to visually display a food product should be accurate. Dietary or nutritional claims must be precise, if used. "Low calorie" is vague because it implies that the product is lower in calories but it doesn't specify what the product is being compared to. It may be better to use terms like "slimline," "weight reduction plate," or "dieter's choice." Oral descriptions by servers are important merchandising aids. Their phrases should correctly describe the menu selections.

With rising consumerism in the United States, the trend toward truth-in-menu regulations will accelerate. As a result, stringent government regulations cannot be far behind. The New York State Restaurant Association has strongly supported truth-in-menu regulations. Their campaign is based on the slogan "We Believe in Accuracy." The association has established standards for restaurants related to truth-in-menu. In summary, the New York State Restaurant Association's standards state that all descriptions on menus must be accurate. If a substitution is necessary, the customer will be informed. When weight is stated on the menu, it means the precooked weight. All customer questions regarding menu items will be answered.

Truth-in-menu violations can be costly for a food service business. In 1978, a fast-food operation in California was investigated on two counts of truth-in-menu violations. The investigating unit, the Los Angeles County Health Department, confirmed the validity of the claims. The establishment advertised maple syrup and fresh orange juice on the breakfast menu. The syrup was not pure maple syrup, and the orange juice was frozen. The business was assessed a $2,500 fine for each violation and was forced to pay $5,500 in court costs. This $10,500 mistake could have been avoided by adhering to the basics of truth-in-menu.

Menu Planning and Success

Every aspect of the operation contributes to or detracts from its success. Dirty, worn, soiled, out-of-date, and unattractive menus indicate management's lack of concern for the establishment's image in the minds of its customers. Because they create a negative first impression, these menus should be eliminated from stock. Someone should be in charge of reviewing the condition of all menus before the meal period begins.

Sanitation management begins with menu planning, since the menu sets the stage for the remaining basic operating activities. Management must consider menu items in light of possible sanitation hazards at every control point. Once the potential hazards have been identified, the risks can be reduced. Several questions should be asked and answered before the menu planning process is completed. For example, can the facility procure the necessary raw ingredients from safe, approved sources? Can the raw ingredients be received and stored easily? Is the production staff able to prepare the menu items efficiently and in a sanitary manner? Can the finished products be served in a sanitary and safe way?

The Purchasing Control Point

Once menu planning is completed, the **purchasing control point** is the next logical step to be addressed. In fact, the menu determines the ingredients to be purchased, the variety of products needed, and the relative amounts. One of the major objectives of purchasing is to obtain the right quality and quantity of items at the right price from the right supplier. The goals are to maintain quality and value, strengthen the establishment's competitive position, and minimize the investment in inventory.

More than any other basic operating activity, purchasing relates to cost and quality controls. In fact, most food service businesses spend 30-

50% of their total sales revenue on product purchasing. Therefore, cost avoidance in purchasing has the potential to translate directly to the operation's bottom line. Conversely, the failure to properly control food costs can have a more devastating effect than overspending in most other cost categories. It is not surprising that the primary concern of many operators is their food cost. As costs increase, this concern grows. Rising food costs often force management to reexamine the operation's purchasing needs.

In addition to the menu, several other factors dictate purchasing needs. First, the forecasted sales volume is an estimate of how much business there will be in the facility on a given day. The operation's standardized recipes can be used to work backward from the number of servings to the amounts of ingredients needed. If there is a weight loss during processing (as when ribs of beef are roasted), the raw ingredient amounts must be increased accordingly.

Certain external factors also affect purchasing needs. The size and frequency of orders is affected by how much lead time the supplier requires before a delivery can be made. Also, the facility's location relative to the supplier may affect quantities purchased. For example, a steakhouse located high in the mountains or in a rural area probably receives less frequent deliveries than a steakhouse in a downtown metropolitan area. Since the steakhouse located downtown obtains more frequent deliveries, the quantities ordered at any given time tend to be smaller. Assuming the two steakhouses do the same amount of business, the steakhouse in the metropolitan area has less money tied up in inventory.

Of course, quantity (of food ordered or money spent) is not the only concern. Quality and sanitation standards must also be considered in purchasing. A poor quality or unsanitary product is never a bargain, no matter how inexpensive it is.

The factors affecting purchasing needs are directly related to the functions of the purchasing control point. The purchasing functions are:

1. Establishing and maintaining an adequate supply of food and nonfood products

2. Minimizing the operation's investment in inventory

3. Maintaining the operation's quality, sanitation, and cost standards

4. Maintaining the operation's competitive position

5. Buying the product, not the deal

Each of these objectives of purchasing will be discussed as they relate to the four resources: personnel, equipment, inventory, and facilities.

Purchasing and Personnel

A number of people have responsibilities related to the purchasing control point. However, purchasing itself is a management function. It must be done by the manager or delegated to a key subordinate (e.g., assistant manager, food and beverage director, executive chef, or steward). In any case, one person must be designated as the establishment's buyer.

The buyer is responsible for the operation's purchasing control point. Hotels often have a full-time purchasing agent. In large hotels, the purchasing department consists of more than one person and is responsible for all food and nonfood buying. Of course, not all operations can afford a full-time buyer. Smaller facilities and independent restaurants use the manager or a key assistant as a part-time buyer.

To be successful, the buyer must possess many skills. Broadly speaking, the skills of a buyer can be categorized as managerial, technical, and other. Managerial skills are necessary because the buyer is a part of the operation's management team. Therefore, the buyer must be able to plan, analyze, influence, control, and see the operation as a whole. A buyer must understand the establishment's present position and its short-term and long-term goals. This knowledge assists the buyer in carrying out purchasing activities according to management's overall plan.

Technical skills are necessary because they enable the buyer to do a more efficient job. New information is constantly becoming available on food marketing, packaging, distribution, and product yields. Besides textbooks, the operation's suppliers, trade journals, and industry associations are good sources of this technical information. The buyer's level of technical expertise also depends upon his or her knowledge of the operation's quality, sanitation, and cost standards and of which products meet these standards. A certain amount of purchasing experience may be necessary to develop technical skills.

Other characteristics the buyer should have are good interpersonal skills and high ethical standards. Interpersonal skills are critical because the buyer must be a communicator. This individual regularly interacts with other department heads, employees in the purchasing department, and management. The buyer's communication skills are also important when working with suppliers. Ethical standards may be difficult to specify, but certainly honesty and trustworthiness are two important considerations. A buyer frequently faces temptations in the form of personal rebates and "under-the-table" kickbacks. It is management's responsibility to spot-check how the business is handling the purchasing functions to keep its honest buyer honest. Unannounced checks provide a stimulus for the buyer to avoid compromising the establishment's sanitation, quality, and cost standards.

To perform well, buyers must accomplish the five functions of purchasing. Although the amount of time devoted to purchasing may vary with the facility's size, all five functions are addressed by a well-planned purchasing control point. First, buyers are responsible for maintaining adequate inventory levels. The objective is to reduce or eliminate stockouts which inconvenience production personnel and disappoint customers.

The buyer should also minimize the operation's dollar investment in inventory for two reasons. Excessive inventories promote spoilage and potential contamination of products. In addition, excessive inventories tie up dollars in an asset that does not earn interest. Thus, buyers must maintain an optimum level of food and nonfood supplies.

Buyers are additionally responsible for conducting negotiations with the operation's suppliers. The negotiations typically cover the AP (as purchased) price, quantities to be purchased, delivery schedules, and other supplier services. An intimate knowledge of the establishment's standards and its product needs is necessary if the buyer is to obtain acceptable products. The buyer must communicate quality, sanitation, and cost standards to suppliers. Also, buyers should keep suppliers informed of ways in which the suppliers can improve their services to the operation.

Furthermore, good relationships with suppliers guarantee that the buyer will get the best value each supplier can offer. To maintain the operation's competitive position, buyers should continually try to improve their performance. Of course, suppliers cannot always fill orders promptly. Some wise buyers have circumvented this problem by establishing a reciprocal relationship with competitors. Thus, when a competitor is temporarily out of a needed product, they lend the competitor the product from their own stock until the competitor's order is shipped in. The advantage to the lending business is that the next time it is out of a product, the buyer can call on the competitor and request a temporary loan.

Although they are not, strictly speaking, under the control of the operation's management, **suppliers** are another "human component" of the purchasing function. The role of suppliers has changed significantly in recent years. In the past, suppliers often had a specialty such as produce, meat, or coffee, and they sold a limited number of these products. Other supplier specialists were dairy, bakery, paper, sanitary and cleaning supplies, or ethnic food distributors. Each specialist was geared to buy, store, and sell a certain category of food products or supplies.

By the early 1970s, the supplier's role had evolved into the full-line or one-stop shopping distributor. Today, this trend in food service distribution continues and is called the **master distributor concept**. Now, many of the full-line distributors carry from 5,000 to 10,000 different products. One master distributor may be able to satisfy 90 to 100% of an operation's purchasing needs. Many businesses are currently purchasing most of their requirements from a small number of full-line distributors who sell meat, produce, fresh fish, groceries, canned foods, frozen foods, cleaning supplies, paper products, flowers for the table, utensils, and kitchen equipment. Larger operations may still buy a few specialty items (e.g., exotic fruits and vegetables, dairy products) from a specialist. However, a full-line distributor can probably satisfy all the purchasing needs of a small business.

This one-stop purchasing arrangement increases product consistency and provides purchasing leverage for the facility, while it builds the supplier's trust in the operation and gives management more time for planning, organizing, training, and public relations. Furthermore, master distributors often provide services that a specialist cannot give. These additional services include menu consulting, employee training programs and seminars, and new product presentations. These advantages make it likely that the master distributor concept will increase in popularity.

Regardless of a whether a specialist or full-line distributor is used, the establishment should periodically evaluate its supplier(s) based on the following criteria:

1. Sanitation policies

2. Size and services

3. Staff and labor relations

4. Purchasing power and financial position

5. Products and prices

6. Reputation

A supplier's sanitation policies can easily be spot-checked through periodic informal, unannounced visits to the distributor's warehouse or processing plant. A representative of the food service business making such a visit should check to see if the operation is clean and adequately maintained by taking a walking tour of the facility. Also, the person who receives deliveries can periodically inspect the supplier's delivery vehicles as food is unloaded. Refrigerated and frozen products must be delivered in vehicles equipped with refrigerated storage. Finally, the health department may be able to provide the food service establishment with a general, overall impression of the distributor's facilities, based on past inspections.

The size of the distributing company relates to its ability to meet the operation's needs. Supplier services include arranging delivery schedules according to the food service operation's preferences. This can eliminate overcrowding of the food service storage areas while simultaneously avoiding stockouts. Also, most suppliers are willing to carry unusual items as a special service to the operation if these items are needed on a regular basis. Other services such as menu planning assistance, employee training, and seminars have already been mentioned.

Management often forms an impression of a distributing company based on its sales and delivery personnel. Buyers prefer to work with knowledgeable salespeople who know their products and help the buyer become familiar with product alternatives that will meet the operation's needs. Also, the supplier's salesperson can provide valuable market information. The laws of supply and demand still govern the marketplace. For example, if the distributor learns that California is experiencing heavy rains, its sales representatives should inform the operation's buyer that the price of California lettuce will be higher in approximately six weeks. Similarly, as new produce items come into season, the supplier should keep the establishment abreast of changing market conditions. Also, the salesperson should keep the establishment informed of promotional discounts offered by processors and manufacturers.

Delivery personnel also represent the supplier. Their appearance, attitude, and courtesy contribute to the impression formed by the operation. In addition, labor relations factors, such as the supplier's ability to create a team spirit among the company's employees, should be considered.

The purchasing power and financial position of the supplier are important. High volume distributors buy in larger quantities, so the unit cost is much less. Thus, a portion of the savings can be passed on to the food service business. A supplier that is on sure financial grounds is more likely to give the operation a fair value for its food and nonfood product dollars.

Naturally, products and prices are a critical evaluation point for suppliers. Products should meet the establishment's stated specifications. Distributors offering greater product variety are able to serve more types of food service businesses. Suppliers are obligated to charge a competitive price. When buyers evaluate distributors on the basis of price, it is essential that they compare like items. In many cases, the **edible portion (EP)** price is more important than the as purchased (AP) price because the EP price takes into account the product's yield.

The reputation of a distributor relates to the supplier's reliability, consistency, and predictability. The food service operation should select suppliers who stand behind their products and services. It is a good idea to ask for references from the local health department and restaurant and hotel associations before deciding which supplier(s) will receive the operation's business. In one sense, suppliers are partners in the food service business because they have a stake in its success. Buyers and suppliers can work together to satisfy the desires of the operation's target markets.

Purchasing and Equipment	Food service businesses purchase a variety of utensils and equipment from suppliers. The material content, design, and fabrication of these items should be in accordance with the guidelines in the FDA's Model Food Service Sanitation Ordinance. Generally, the materials from which equipment and utensils are constructed must be safe (nontoxic) and easily cleanable.

The FDA's Food Service Sanitation Ordinance states:

EQUIPMENT AND UTENSILS

Materials

General.

Multi-use equipment and utensils shall be constructed and repaired with safe materials, including finishing materials; shall be corrosion resistant and nonabsorbent; and shall be smooth, easily cleanable, and durable under conditions of normal use. Single-service articles shall be made from clean, sanitary, safe materials. Equipment, utensils, and single-service articles shall not impart odors, color, or taste, nor contribute to the contamination of food.

Solder.

If solder is used, it shall be composed of safe materials and be corrosion resistant.

Wood.

Hard maple or equivalently nonabsorbent material that meets the general requirements set forth in . . . this ordinance may be used for cutting blocks, cutting boards, salad bowls, and baker's tables. Wood may be used for single-service articles, such as chop sticks, stirrers, or ice cream spoons. The use of wood as a food-contact surface under other circumstances is prohibited.

Plastics.

Safe plastic or safe rubber or safe rubber-like materials that are resistant under normal conditions of use to scratching, scoring, decomposition, crazing, chipping and distortion, that are of sufficient weight and thickness to permit cleaning and sanitizing by normal dishwashing methods, and which meet the general requirements set forth in . . . this ordinance, are permitted for repeated use.

Mollusk and crustacea shells.

Mollusk and crustacea shells may be used only once as a serving container. Further re-use of such shells for food service is prohibited.

Single service.

Re-use of single-service articles is prohibited.

Source: FDA, pp. 36-37.

Chapter 3 described the dangers of using equipment and utensils made of toxic materials. When they come into contact with acidic foods (e.g., fruit juices, tomato products), their surfaces can corrode. Thus, metal poisoning from zinc, cadmium, or lead can occur. To prevent this, the FDA's Model Ordinance only allows equipment and utensils which do not impart odors, colors, or tastes to food nor contaminate the food. For example, only food-grade plastic bags may be purchased for food storage; using utility (nonfood-grade) plastic bags can result in the addition of undesirable colors and odors to stored food products. Any unsafe equipment or utensils which do not meet these requirements should be eliminated from food service facilities. Single-service articles must meet similar standards to prevent undesirable additives from entering the food.

The Menu Planning and Purchasing Control Points

The FDA's Food Service Sanitation Ordinance states:

Single-service articles means cups, containers, lids, closures, plates, knives, forks, spoons, stirrers, paddles, straws, napkins, wrapping materials, toothpicks and similar articles intended for one-time, one-person use and then discarded.

Source: FDA, p. 22.

Single-service articles may not be reused. For example, plastic flatware used by customers at an outdoor buffet would be considered single-service articles. Therefore, these used items would be discarded after the buffet.

Equipment and utensils purchased by the operation must also be easy to clean. The FDA's Model Ordinance is quite specific regarding acceptable materials for multi-use equipment and utensils. They must be constructed and repaired with materials that are safe, corrosion resistant, and nonabsorbent. Multi-use equipment and utensils must also be smooth, durable, and easily cleanable. (Since single-service articles may not be reused, they need not be easy to clean.) Nonabsorbent hard wood such as hard maple may be used for baker's tables, salad bowls, and cutting blocks or boards. Wood is not permitted for any other food-contact surfaces.

The FDA's Food Service Sanitation Ordinance states:

Food-contact surface means those surfaces of equipment and utensils with which food normally comes in contact, and those surfaces from which food may drain, drip, or splash back onto surfaces normally in contact with food.

Source: FDA, p. 21.

Rubber or plastic materials are permitted if they are easily cleanable and resistant to scoring, decomposition, scratching, and chipping under normal conditions. (Rubber or plastic cutting boards are often preferred to wooden boards because they are easier to keep clean and maintain.)

The FDA's Model Ordinance also addresses the design and fabrication of equipment and utensils. The objectives of equipment and utensil design and fabrication are durability and cleanability. In particular, all food-contact surfaces must be designed and fabricated to be smooth and free from cracks, chips, breaks, and difficult-to-clean crevices and corners. Cast iron is permitted only on grills, griddles, skillets, and surfaces that are heated. Materials used as lubricants may not contaminate food or food-contact surfaces.

The FDA's Food Service Sanitation Ordinance states:

EQUIPMENT AND UTENSILS

Design and Fabrication

General.

All equipment and utensils, including plasticware, shall be designed and fabricated for durability under conditions of normal use and shall be resistant to denting, buckling, pitting, chipping, and crazing.

(a) Food-contact surfaces shall be easily cleanable, smooth, and free of breaks, open seams, cracks, chips, pits, and similar imperfections, and free of difficult-to-clean internal corners and crevices. Cast iron may be used as a food-contact surface only if the surface is heated, such as in grills, griddle tops, and skillets. Threads shall be designed to facilitate cleaning; ordinary "V" type threads are prohibited in food-contact surfaces, except that in equipment such as ice makers or hot oil cooking equipment and hot oil filtering systems, such threads shall be minimized.

(b) Equipment containing bearings and gears requiring unsafe lubricants shall be designed and constructed so that the lubricant cannot leak, drip, or be forced into food or onto food-contact surfaces. Only safe lubricants shall be used on equipment designed to receive lubrication of bearings and gears on or within food-contact surfaces.

(c) Tubing conveying beverages or beverage ingredients to dispensing heads may be in contact with stored ice: Provided, That such tubing is fabricated from safe materials, is grommeted at entry and exit points to preclude moisture (condensation) from entering the ice machine or the ice storage bin, and is kept clean. Drainage or drainage tubes from dispensing units shall not pass through the ice machine or the ice storage bin.

(d) Sinks and drain boards shall be self-draining.

Accessibility.

Unless designed for in-place cleaning, food-contact surfaces shall be accessible for cleaning and inspection:

(a) Without being disassembled; or

(b) By disassembling without the use of tools; or

(c) By easy disassembling with the use of only simple tools such as a mallet, a screwdriver, or an open-end wrench kept available near the equipment.

In-place cleaning.

Equipment intended for in-place cleaning shall be so designed and fabricated that:

(a) Cleaning and sanitizing solutions can be circulated throughout a fixed system using an effective cleaning and sanitizing regimen; and

(b) Cleaning and sanitizing solutions will contact all interior food-contact surfaces; and

(c) The system is self-draining or capable of being completely evacuated.

Pressure spray cleaning.

Fixed equipment designed and fabricated to be cleaned and sanitized by pressure spray methods shall have sealed electrical wiring, switches, and connections.

Thermometers.

Indicating thermometers required for immersion into food or cooking media shall be of metal stem type construction, numerically scaled, and accurate to $\pm 2°F$.

Non-food-contact surfaces.

Surfaces of equipment not intended for contact with food, but which are exposed to splash or food debris or which otherwise require frequent cleaning, shall be designed and fabricated to be smooth, washable, free of unnecessary ledges, projections, or crevices, and readily accessible for cleaning, and shall be of such material and in such repair as to be easily maintained in a clean and sanitary condition.

Ventilation hoods.

Ventilation hoods and devices shall be designed to prevent grease or condensation from collecting on walls and ceilings, and from dripping into food or onto food-contact surfaces. Filters or other grease extracting equipment shall be readily removable for cleaning and replacement if not designed to be cleaned in place.

Existing equipment.

Equipment that was installed in a food service establishment prior to the effective date of this ordinance, and that does not fully meet all of the design and fabrication requirements of this section, shall be deemed acceptable in that establishment if it is in good repair, capable of being maintained in a sanitary condition, and the food-contact surfaces are nontoxic. Replacement equipment and new equipment acquired after the effective date of this ordinance shall meet the requirements of this ordinance.

Source: FDA, pp. 37-39.

Equipment or utensils that do not meet these design and fabrication requirements are virtually impossible to keep clean. Violations of the FDA Ordinance (such as using dented or chipped equipment and utensils) invite sanitation problems. The common practice of lubricating a food mixer with a petroleum-based lubricant may result in the lubricant dripping into and contaminating food.

Glass stem thermometers may not be used to check food temperatures or the temperature of oil used in a deep-fat fryer. Soft wood is not permitted for nonfood-contact surfaces which are exposed to splash or food debris and, thus, require frequent cleaning. Improperly designed and fabricated ventilation hoods allow used, and possibly contaminated, grease to drip into food. All of these hazards can be eliminated by careful adherence to the FDA's Model Ordinance.

Sinks and drain boards should be designed and installed to be slanted so they can self-drain. If a piece of equipment must be taken apart for cleaning, the equipment should be designed to be easily disassembled.

In addition to the FDA's guidelines, help is provided by three independent organizations which test and evaluate food service equipment. Underwriters Laboratories (UL) evaluates electrically powered equipment, while the American Gas Association (AGA) performs similar testing on gas equipment. Knowing that a piece of equipment is tested and listed makes purchasing easier for food service managers. Where applicable, it is a good idea to specify UL-evaluated and AGA-tested equipment.

The National Sanitation Foundation (NSF) is a nonprofit organization that develops standards and criteria for equipment, products, and services in the interest of public health. The NSF seal on equipment and utensils indicates that these items meet most public health standards. The seal is only permitted on items that have passed a rigorous inspection. NSF's *Standard No. 2 for Food Service Equipment* and the FDA's Model Food Service Sanitation Ordinance are the basis for the recommendations NSF makes to manufacturers and others.

Equipment designed for home use (noncommercial equipment) may seem to be a bargain at first glance. However, this equipment is not designed for frequent, heavy-duty, large quantity use. In fact, warranties

Exhibit 6.2 Overview of Purchasing Activities

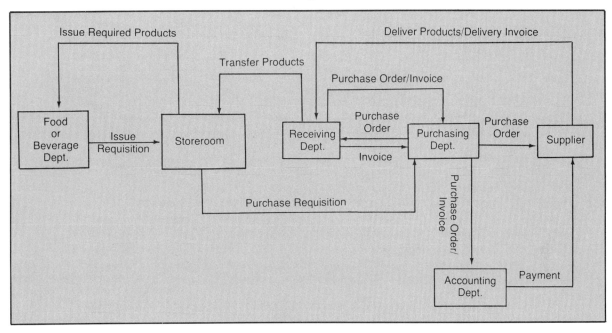

Source: Jack D. Ninemeier, Planning and Control for Food and Beverage Operations, *1982, p. 61.*

are usually voided when this equipment is used in a quantity food production setting.

**Purchasing
and Inventory**

Many functions of the food service operation can be delayed or stopped entirely if the necessary quantity and quality of inventory is not available. The purchasing department plays a major role in the flow of products through the food service facility. As Exhibit 6.2 illustrates, many areas of the operation interact with the purchasing department. Therefore, it is essential that the purchasing of inventory be properly handled. The overall goal of purchasing is to obtain the necessary food and nonfood items in the correct quality and quantity at a reasonable price. To reach this goal, buyers have many tools at their disposal. The first tool is a set of standard purchase specifications.

Standard purchase specifications precisely define the quality, quantity, and other relevant characteristics required in products purchased by the establishment. Standard purchase specifications are communication tools. They require management to define exactly what is needed. They eliminate confusion on the part of suppliers, and they facilitate the bidding process. A suggested standard purchase specification format is presented in Exhibit 6.3. Note the precise details required in a standard purchase specification. These specifications may be developed by a management team consisting of a food and beverage director, executive chef, buyer, and other end users. While it might take this team some time to develop standard purchase specifications for all the products normally

Exhibit 6.3 Purchase Specification Format

(name of food and beverage operation)

1. Product name: _____

2. Product used for:

> Clearly indicate product use (such as olive garnish for beverage, hamburger patty for grill frying for sandwich, etc.)

3. Product general description:

> Provide general quality information about desired product. For example, "iceberg lettuce; heads to be green, firm without spoilage, excessive,dirt or damage. No more than 10 outer leaves; packed 24 heads per case."

4. Detailed description:

> Purchaser should state other factors which help to clearly identify desired product. Examples of specific factors, which vary by product being described, include:
> - Geographic origin
> - Variety
> - Type
> - Style
> - Grade
> - Size
> - Portion size
> - Brand name
> - Density
> - Medium of pack
> - Specific gravity
> - Container size
> - Edible yield, trim

5. Product test procedures:

> Test procedures occur at time product is received and as/after product is prepared/used. Thus, for example, products to be at a refrigerated temperature upon delivery can be tested with a thermometer. Portion-cut meat patties can be randomly weighed. Lettuce packed 24 heads per case can be counted.

6. Special instructions and requirements:

> Any additional information needed to clearly indicate quality expectations can be included here. Examples include bidding procedures, if applicable, labeling and/or packaging requirements and delivery and service requirements.

Source: Jack D. Ninemeier, Planning and Control for Food and Beverage Operations, *1982, p. 63.*

Exhibit 6.4   Food Sample Data Sheet

1. Product: _____

2. Brand Name: _____

3. Presented By: _____ Date: _____

4. Varieties Available: _____

5. Shelf Life: (Frozen) _____ (Thawed, Refrigerated, Dry) _____

6. Preparation and Sanitation Considerations: _____

   _____

   _____

   _____

7. Menu Suggestions: _____

8. Merchandising Aids Available (Poster, Table Tents, etc.): _____

9. Case Size (Number of Portions): _____

10. Portion Size: _____

11. Distributed By: _____

12. Minimum Order: _____

13. Any Additional Ordering Information: _____

    _____

14. Lead Time: _____

15. Approximate Price Per Serving: _____

NOTE: Were the following information sheets received with products?

    a. Nutritional Analysis: Yes _____   No _____

    b. Specification Sheet: Yes _____   No _____

purchased by the operation, the results are well worth the investment of time. Once they are developed, the specifications can be used over and over again for new suppliers, for planning menu changes, and for quality control.

Quality is defined through the use of government grades or packer's brand names. For example, the "fancy" or "A" government grade indicates a certain quality level in fruits and vegetables. On the other hand, the quality of Heinz tomato ketchup, Swift's Premium ham, and Minor's beef base are implied by their packer's brand names. **Quantity** may be defined by the number of units per container, box, or case. Where container sizes are standardized, the size of the container may be specified (for example, #10 cans). Other descriptions contained in a standard purchase specification tell the supplier exactly what kind of product is desired. (See examples of other factors given in Exhibit 6.3.)

Standard purchase specifications are only useful if they accurately reflect the individual needs of the operation. Although several specification manuals such as *The Meat Buyer's Guide* and *NIFDA Canned Foods Manual* are available, the general specifications in these references should be tailored to the needs of the individual operation. In-house kitchen or performance tests can be used to alter general specifications to fit the establishment's needs. Also, market conditions which affect availability may modify the establishment's specifications. Ultimately, standard purchase specifications for each product must be based on the intended use of the product.

A second tool available to buyers is the **food sample data sheet** (see Exhibit 6.4). This sheet helps standardize the evaluation of a product. It can be used to record purchasing, storing, preparing, and serving information about products which the operation is sampling and considering purchasing. The food sample data sheet makes the selection of products more objective and less subject to the buyer's own personal preferences.

Once standard purchase specifications have been determined and suppliers have been selected, a third tool—the **purchase order**—assists in maintaining control. The purchase order contains the details of an order placed with a supplier. This standard form is filled in by the operation's buyer and is sent to the supplier. A copy of the purchase order is retained to facilitate in-house recordkeeping. A sample purchase order is displayed in Exhibit 6.5.

The FDA's Model Ordinance provides guidelines for food care related to food supplies. The objectives of these requirements are to prevent both food spoilage and contamination. Note that the Model Ordinance focuses on potentially hazardous foods, although all food intended for human consumption is covered.

The FDA's Food Service Sanitation Ordinance states:

FOOD CARE

Food Supplies

General.

Food shall be in sound condition, free from spoilage, filth, or other contamination and shall be safe for human consumption. Food shall be obtained from sources that comply with all laws relating to food and food labeling. The use of food in hermetically sealed containers that was not prepared in a food processing establishment is prohibited.

Special requirements.

(a) Fluid milk and fluid milk products used or served shall be pasteurized and shall meet the Grade A quality standards as established by law. Dry milk and dry milk products shall be made from pasteurized milk and milk products.

Exhibit 6.5 Purchase Order

Purchase Order Number:_____			Order Date: _____		
			Payment Terms_____		
To: _____ (supplier)			From/ Ship to: _____ (name of food service)		
_____ (address)			_____ (address)		
Please Ship:			Delivery Date: _____		

Quantity Ordered	Description	✓	Units Shipped	Unit Cost	Total Cost

Total Cost _____

IMPORTANT: This Purchase Order expressly limits acceptance to the terms and conditions stated above noted on the reverse side hereof, and any additional terms and conditions affixed hereto or otherwise referenced. Any additional terms and conditions proposed by seller are objected to and rejected.

_____
Authorized Signature

Source: Jack D. Ninemeier, Planning and Control for Food and Beverage Operations, *1982, p. 69.*

(b) Fresh and frozen shucked shellfish (oysters, clams, or mussels) shall be packed in nonreturnable packages identified with the name and address of the original shell stock processor, shucker-packer, or repacker, and the interstate certification number issued according to law. Shell stock and shucked shellfish shall be kept in the container in which they were received until they are used. Each container of unshucked shell stock (oysters, clams, or mussels) shall be identified by an attached tag that states the name and address of the original shell stock processor, the kind and quantity of shell stock, and an interstate certification number issued by the State or foreign shellfish control agency.

(c) Only clean whole eggs, with shell intact and without cracks or checks, or pasteurized liquid, frozen, or dry eggs or pasteurized dry egg products shall be used, except that hard-boiled, peeled eggs, commercially prepared and packaged, may be used.

Source: FDA, pp. 23-24.

Pointing out some typical violations may serve to reinforce this section of the ordinance. Home-canned products such as fruits, vegetables, and meats may not be served by a food service business because home-canned products are not prepared by processors licensed and inspected by governmental agencies. Nothing should be purchased after the expiration date printed on the product has passed. Suppliers are obligated to maintain the **first in-first out (FIFO) inventory system**, but once a food service operation buys, uses, and sells a bad product, it has the liability.

Unpasteurized (raw) milk cannot be served in a food service facility. Fish and shellfish cannot be purchased from sources that are not approved by the United States government. Egg products are expected to undergo preservation processing and handling under carefully controlled conditions. Rigorous requirements are imposed on all of these products because they are common food sources of pathogenic bacteria. The objectives of these requirements are obvious: to protect the public from potentially hazardous food products and to maintain high standards of public health.

Purchasing and Facilities

The facilities of a food service establishment affect its public image. In addition to cleanliness and decor, which are immediately apparent to customers, the size and location of the facilities contribute to the atmosphere. Consider the difference in ambience of a large hotel dining room and an intimate cafe. The size of the establishment's facilities also has implications for its operation. In terms of the purchasing control point, the limitations of the establishment's facilities affect the method of purchasing used. (Of course, the operation's personnel, inventory, and equipment also help to determine the method of purchasing.)

If the facilities are spacious and accommodate many customers, **formal purchasing methods** are more likely to apply. In the formal method of purchasing, relatively large orders are placed. Therefore, competitive buying is used to help control costs. In competitive buying, written specifications are prepared by the operation to communicate product needs to suppliers. Then, the suppliers submit written bids to the operation's buyer. These bids indicate the price they will charge for the desired products if their bid is accepted. Usually bids specify how long the quoted price will be in effect. Depending on the operation's needs, the buyer may use written negotiations during the formal purchasing process.

In smaller businesses, the amount purchased is minimal, so the method of purchasing is frequently less formal. Written specifications, bids, and negotiations are not utilized in the **informal method of purchasing**. Specifications are given, prices are quoted, and negotiations are conducted either in person or by telephone. While this method is less exact, it is simple and it saves time for the small operator.

Purchasing and Change

Perhaps more than any other control point, the purchasing activity is in a constant state of flux. Conditions change from season to season, from week to week, and in some cases, overnight. For example, the availability, seasonality, price trends, and supply levels of products purchased by a food service business often change. Successful managers realize that their purchasing specifications are not "cast in concrete." Purchasing patterns must be altered when conditions change. However, before a change is undertaken, it is important to systematically predict and evaluate its impact on the operation's sanitation, quality, and cost standards.

Purchasing and Success

Purchasing can be risky if menu planning is haphazard and the objectives of purchasing are not clearly understood. However, the risks can be reduced if the buyer arms himself with knowledge about the operation's:

1. Quality, sanitation, and cost standards

2. Food production methods

3. Purchasing procedures

4. Suppliers and competitors

Knowledge of quality, sanitation, and cost control standards is most important. Jeopardizing the operation's sanitation program in order to save a few dollars on the purchase price can prove to be a costly mistake. Similarly, to compromise the establishment's quality standards is to risk losing customers. The buyer must strike a balance between the three types of control, all of which are related to the expectations of the target markets.

Knowledge of food production methods is critical to the success of the purchasing control point. A buyer must know the yield of a raw ingredient in order to calculate its EP (edible portion) cost. The buyer should also know how to modify the AP (as purchased) cost based on how the product is prepared and served.

Knowledge of purchasing procedures must be a high priority if the buyer is to achieve success. A planned, organized system—complete with written product specifications, purchase orders, and product evaluation forms—increases the buyer's control. By carefully reviewing issuing records, the buyer can establish par stocks (minimum quantities) for each item the facility should have on hand. This helps to eliminate costly stockouts. The winning businesses know that they cannot negotiate either price or quality when they practice last-minute buying.

Knowledge of suppliers and competitors completes the purchasing success formula. Suppliers can be a valuable source of market information. They can assist the operation in the solution of yield, sanitation, quality, and cost problems. Winning food service businesses only deal with honest suppliers. Successful operations are not afraid to develop a reciprocal supply loan relationship with competitors because, in the end, it can be beneficial to them to do so.

In the final analysis, excellent businesses know the difference between control and controls. **Control** is the overall objective or goal management is striving to reach, whereas **controls** are the devices, tools, procedures, and policies used to reach the goal. Excellent managers are in control because they have set up a system to integrate sanitation, quality, and cost controls.

Summary

The menu, which details the operation's product offerings, is the blueprint for the success of a food service establishment. The menu influences the other control points in the food service system. Menu planning must be geared to the resources under a manager's control. The trend today is toward limited menus and cross-utilization of raw ingredients.

Purchasing needs are dictated by a careful analysis of the menu and its standard recipes. Purchasing patterns evolve as market trends, sources of supply, and customer needs change. Successful purchasing is the rule rather than the exception when the establishment's representatives arm themselves with knowledge. Control of the quality, sanitation, and cost of purchases is possible when a set of controls is systematically utilized.

References

Accuracy in Menu Guidelines. Denver, Colo.: Colorado-Wyoming Restaurant Association, 1981.

Albers, Carl. *Food and Beverage Cost Planning and Control Procedures*. Rev. ed. East Lansing, Mich.: Educational Institute of the American Hotel & Motel Association, 1976.

Cichy, Ronald F. "Inflation Fighting Through Profitable Purchasing, Rational Receiving, and Secure Storage." *Michigan Hospitality*, July/August 1980. 43(3):40.

——."The Magic of Menus." *Food Management,* June 1983. 18(6):52.

——."The Menu Is a Marketing Tool." *Rocky Mountain Chefs Magazine,* January 1983. 10.

Food and Drug Administration, Public Health Administration, U.S. Department of Health, Education, and Welfare. *Food Service Sanitation Manual.* Washington, D.C.: U.S. Government Printing Office, 1976.

McKennon, J. E. "How to Control Rising Food Costs, Part V: Purchasing, Receiving, Storing, Issuing," *Lodging*, October 1980. 6(2):77.

Ninemeier, Jack D. *Planning and Control for Food and Beverage Operations*. East Lansing, Mich.: Educational Institute of the American Hotel & Motel Association, 1982.

Strategies for Success at the Aspen Hotel

As Paul continued his evaluation of the menu planning and purchasing control points, he realized that these two activities would influence the success of the remaining control points. He worked closely with Elisabeth Mueller to develop checklists for the menu planning and purchasing control points. These checklists would be the basis for the operating plan in the food and beverage area. Paul discovered that Elisabeth had asked kitchen manager Peggy Herbert and controller Bob Campbell to participate in the formulation of the two checklists. The GM liked that kind of involvement.

Checklist for Menu Planning

Personnel

1. The menu communicates the strategy for meeting or exceeding customer expectations.

2. The image of the menu is evaluated based on appearance, readability, clarity, and pricing strategies.

3. The skill levels of production personnel are evaluated.

4. The skill levels of service personnel are evaluated.

5. Suppliers are asked for preparation and merchandising suggestions.

6. Sanitation, quality, and cost control standards are maintained.

7. Servers know the meaning of terms used to describe menu items and their preparation.

Equipment

1. Equipment is selected based on initial costs, capacity, availability of energy sources, operating costs, maintenance costs, and skill levels of employees.

2. Equipment is easy to clean and sanitize.

3. Equipment design, layout, and installation facilitate both product and people movement in the kitchen and service areas.

4. Special functions, banquets, and room service menus are planned realistically, based on the operation's equipment resources.

Inventory

1. The menu achieves the financial objectives of the establishment.

2. Records are maintained on the menu's sales mix and the popularity of every menu item.

3. The effect of the menu on the other control points is considered when the menu is planned.

4. Menu items are rationalized and ingredients are cross-utilized as much as possible.

5. High quality convenience foods are evaluated and used where appropriate.

6. Menu offerings are based on the expectations of the target markets.

Facilities

1. Traffic flow in the kitchen and dining room is evaluated, and the design and layout of the facilities are changed when necessary.

2. The ambience of the facilities is appropriate to the menu and the expectations of the target markets.

3. Special functions and banquets are booked with the limitations of the establishment's facilities in mind.

4. The facilities are maintained in a clean and sanitary manner.

Truth-in-Menu

1. Accurate descriptions are used for raw ingredients and finished menu items.

2. Quality or grade statements are factual.

3. Sizes, weights, or counts advertised on the menu are correct.

4. Frozen or canned items are never billed as fresh.

5. Preparation techniques are accurately stated.

6. Additional charges for extras are clearly stated on the menu.

7. Pictures used on the menu correctly illustrate the product to be served.

8. Oral descriptions by servers are factual.

9. Dietary or nutritional claims are precise.

10. Points of origin are accurate, not misleading.

Checklist for Purchasing

Personnel

1. Purchasing is done by a manager or a key subordinate.

2. The buyer establishes and maintains an adequate supply of food and nonfood products.

3. The buyer minimizes the investment in inventory.

4. The sanitation, quality, and cost standards are defined and maintained.

5. The operation's competitive position is maintained.

6. The buyer purchases the product, not the deal.

7. The buyer understands the operation's short- and long-term goals.

8. The buyer possesses managerial, technical, and interpersonal skills.

9. The buyer is ethical and loyal to the business.

10. The buyer has an intimate knowledge of the operation and its product needs.

11. The buyer establishes reciprocal supply loan relationships with the operation's competitors.

12. The buyer evaluates the master distributor versus the specialist supplier.

13. The buyer periodically checks the supplier's sanitation policies, size, services, staff and labor relations, purchasing power and financial position, products, quality, prices, and reputation.

14. The buyer uses the supplier as a source of market information.

15. The personnel in the purchasing department have a formal training program.

Equipment

1. The materials, design, and fabrication of equipment purchased by the facility meet local, state, and federal health codes.

2. The materials from which equipment is constructed are non-toxic.

3. Equipment purchased by the operation is easy to clean and maintain.

4. Single-service items are not washed and reused.

5. Food-contact surfaces are free from cracks, chips, breaks, and difficult-to-clean crevices and corners.

6. Materials used as lubricants do not contaminate food or food-contact surfaces.

7. Equipment has been tested and evaluated by NSF and AGA or UL where appropriate.

Inventory

1. Inventory and stock levels are based on the intended use of the product and the volume of business.

2. Written standard purchase specifications are used and periodically updated as conditions change.

3. Market conditions are evaluated regularly.

4. Food sample data sheets are used to select and evaluate products.

5. Written purchase orders are used to define the details of each order.

6. All inventory items are obtained from approved and safe sources of supply.

7. The FIFO inventory system is used by the facility and its suppliers.

Facilities

1. The formality or informality of the purchasing arrangement is based on the establishment's facilities.

2. Facilities are maintained in a clean and sanitary manner.

The following case studies are designed to enhance your understanding of the material in this chapter. If you are a Home Study student, use these case studies to stimulate questions about this chapter. If you are a Group or Institutional Study student, you may be asked to discuss these case studies as part of a regular classroom assignment.

CASE STUDY 6.1

Polly Thatcher is the food and beverage manager of the Suburban Restaurant. She is reevaluating her establishment's menu in order to increase customer satisfaction and profitability. Polly has noticed that several competing businesses in her area are offering *nouvelle cuisine*. Other competitors are featuring fresh pasta or mesquite charcoal-broiled fresh fish. Barbecued beef and pork menu items are being served by some operations as daily specials.

Because Polly wants her restaurant to stay competitive, she plans to experiment with some new food items similar to those of her competitors. She has asked her production and service staff to provide suggestions. Polly is in the process of reviewing food magazines and cookbooks for other possible menu ideas.

Test Your Understanding

1. What relevant factors, other than competition, does Polly need to consider in her menu planning?

2. What sanitation management considerations are important during menu planning?

3. What are your recommendations to Polly Thatcher?

CASE STUDY 6.2

Andy Amorphous has been challenged by the general manager of the Pacific View Hotel to revise and upgrade the hotel's menu. As food and beverage manager, Andy is responsible for all food and beverage production and service at the Pacific View. Andy has asked the hotel's executive chef to help with the development of a new menu.

In light of the increased consumption of fresh fish in this country, the chef has suggested adding a number of seafood entrees. The chef's menu recommendations include: fresh Colorado rainbow trout and Alaskan king salmon, Spanish shrimp, and fresh swordfish steaks. Andy has approved the menu ideas, but has questioned whether the hotel's suppliers can obtain all these food items. He has asked the chef to check with the best distributors in town.

The chef now brings the answer to Andy. "It looks like my menu ideas are going to work out. Our suppliers can get the 'Colorado rainbow trout' from Idaho, the 'Alaskan king salmon' from Seattle, Washington, and the 'Spanish shrimp' from Mexico. They can also get frozen swordfish steaks that taste very fresh."

"Good work," says Andy, "but what about the truth-in-menu violations?"

The chef replies, "The customers really can't tell the difference, can they?"

Test Your Understanding

1. What ethical and supply factors should Andy consider in regard to his new menu?

2. How do truth-in-menu considerations affect the success of a food service operation?

3. What are your recommendations to Andy Amorphous?

CASE STUDY 6.3

Sally Lively has a decision to make. She has recently been given responsibility for all food and nonfood purchasing at the Library Restaurant. The operation currently buys from over 15 suppliers. Most of the suppliers are specialists. Sally spends almost two full working days out of every week meeting with suppliers' representatives and giving them orders.

Sally has decided that there must be a more efficient way to accomplish her objectives as the new buyer. She is considering switching to a limited number of full-line distributors. Sally has started a list of the advantages and disadvantages of full-line distributors over specialist suppliers.

Test Your Understanding

1. Compare the advantages of a full-line distributor with those of a specialist supplier.

2. Compare the disadvantages of a full-line distributor with those of a specialist supplier.

3. What are your recommendations to Sally Lively?

CASE STUDY 6.4

The Cardinal Cafe features food and beverage service outdoors on the patio during summer months. The new manager of the cafe has decided to expand its self-service outdoor dining concept to include a salad and soup bar.

Also, on Friday afternoons, the cafe will offer Mexican food items, a make-your-own-sundae bar, and a sandwich bar with a weigh-and-pay concept. These foods will be displayed and served indoors. Finally, the Friday afternoon happy hour in the outside bar will feature a potato bar that permits customers to make unlimited trips to an area stocked with baked potatoes and toppings such as sour cream and chives, cheeses, guacamole, mushroom gravy, meats, chili, jalapenos, and whipped peanut butter.

Test Your Understanding

1. What are the possible sanitation and quality control implications of the Cardinal Cafe's planned menu expansion?

2. How will the new menu items affect personnel, inventory, equipment, and facilities resources?

3. What are your recommendations to the new manager?

CASE STUDY 6.5

The Uno Restaurant is famous for its fresh oysters. Oysters are a popular menu item during happy hour in the bar and as an appetizer in the restaurant. Presently, the restaurant buys its oysters live in the shell and shucks them to order.

However, the manager of the restaurant is planning to switch to shucked select oysters. He feels that the business can save labor costs with shucked products. And to maintain the fresh look, the shucked oysters will be served in oyster shells that have been washed and reused.

Test Your Understanding

1. What are the possible sanitation hazards inherent in this plan?

2. Is it acceptable to wash and reuse oyster shells for food service?

3. What are your recommendations to the manager of the Uno Restaurant?

SEVEN

The Receiving, Storing, and Issuing Control Points

Strategies for Success at the Aspen Hotel

Paul James proceeded to make mental notes of how the receiving, storing, and issuing control points were handled at the Aspen Hotel. The hotel was not currently receiving inventory items, but the GM evaluated the facilities, equipment, and personnel. Now he was ready to discuss the situation with Walter Joslin, the food and beverage purchasing agent, and Elisabeth Mueller, the food and beverage director.

Elisabeth told Paul that the last physical inventory taken at the Aspen showed a total for food and beverage products of $15,000. Based on past sales and inventory turnover calculations, the GM thought that this figure could be realistically reduced to $9,000 or $10,000. Paul had a hunch that the hotel was buying excessive quantities from too many suppliers.

Walter explained that, in addition to purchasing, he was in charge of receiving, storing, and issuing food and beverage products. "But sometimes I'm busy meeting with salespeople," said Walter, "and other times I'm not here when deliveries arrive."

"What happens in those situations, Walter?" asked the GM.

"Usually the breakfast cook receives the morning deliveries of bread and dairy products. The deliverymen put the inventory into stock and help us rotate the items. The kitchen manager is also authorized to receive products.

"We try to enforce the rule that no deliveries or salespeople can be received between 11:30 a.m. and 1:30 p.m., but a lot of the time they come anyway. The deliveryman says it's not his fault that the delivery route established by the supplier puts his truck at our back door at noon. If we want the merchandise, we have to accept the delivery at that time," Walter explained.

"Once the products are received, we try to get them into storage as soon as possible," Elisabeth added. "We can't really do a detailed check of all merchandise when there are two other suppliers waiting to deliver our orders."

"What about marking the date and unit price on the inventory?" asked Paul.

"We just don't have enough time," Elisabeth replied. "Sometimes Walter works overtime to complete all of his paperwork. The controller spot-checks our receiving reports and compares them to the invoices."

The comments made by Elisabeth and Walter increased Paul's suspicion that inventory procedures at the Aspen Hotel were really not as organized as they could be. Paul's thoughts flashed back to other problems he had noticed in the hotel's receiving, storing, and issuing control points. On a previous inspection, he had seen a number of dead stock items. Paul had discovered several dented cans which indicated to him that the inventory had been there for a long time. The diversity of the old menus and the sheer variety of menu items had probably contributed to the dead stock situation.

Paul had found even more abominable conditions in the walk-in refrigerators and walk-in freezers. The floor of the walk-in refrigerator was a chipped and unpainted, plain concrete surface. The GM had noticed that the compressor in the walk-in was leaking onto old and rusted shelving. There was no thermometer in any of the cold storage units except for the walk-in freezer, and there the temperature was too high. The freezer unit was operating at 10°F (-12°C). Most of the storage equipment and facilities were old and needed to be replaced. Paul had realized after that inspection that most of the F&B operating budget for the first two years would be spent on replacement or repair of equipment and facilities. After jotting some notes, Paul asked Walter to explain the issuing system for food and beverage inventory.

"We use key and lock control to limit access," Walter said. "Requisitions are mandatory for all high-cost inventory items. Low-cost items are simply placed in a storage area where everyone has access to them without a key. Our food cost percentage has remained between 43% and 45% during the past two years.

The GM felt that, with proper controls, the food cost percentage could be dropped to the range of 34-37%. Also, the dollar value of the hotel's food and beverage inventory needed to be reduced. This would lower the risks of contamination and spoilage, while raising the rate of inventory turnover. Paul challenged the F&B director to cross-utilize ingredients whenever possible on the new menus. Paul, Elisabeth, and Walter began working on checklists to bring the receiving, storing, and issuing functions under control.

The receiving, storing, and issuing control points are presented together in this chapter because these three activities are interrelated. They are essential to the success of the operation's sanitation, quality, and cost control systems. Therefore, an in-depth examination of receiving, storing, and issuing and how these activities are integrated with the operation's resources is important.

The Receiving Control Point

Receiving comes into focus after the menu has been planned and the products dictated by the menu have been purchased. The objectives of the receiving function include inspecting deliveries to evaluate the quality and determine the quantity of the products, checking prices, and arriving at an accept or reject decision. In reality, receiving practices range from carefully checking each item delivered to allowing the supplier's truck driver to put the order away. However, from a control standpoint, the former method is certainly preferable to the latter one.

The receiving function is critical because at this control point ownership of the products is transferred from the supplier to the operation. A carefully planned menu and skillful purchasing are useless if the operation accepts inferior products. Conversely, good receiving techniques can maximize the results of the other control points. Receiving success requires competent personnel, proper equipment, adequate receiving facilities, established receiving hours, and several types of receiving control forms.

Receiving and Personnel

The number of persons working at the receiving control point varies among food service operations. The major determining factor is the size of the operation and its annual sales volume. In a relatively small operation, the manager or the assistant manager is usually in charge of receiving. In a larger operation, one full-time or two part-time people typically handle the receiving function, and the person in charge of receiving may be called a receiving clerk, steward, or storeroom person. This individual usually reports either to the food controller, the assistant manager, or the food and beverage manager.

Regardless of how many individuals are assigned to the receiving function, the general requirements are the same:

1. Good health and personal cleanliness

2. Familiarity with the necessary forms, tools, and equipment

3. Literacy

4. Quality judgment

5. Product knowledge

6. Sanitation judgment

7. Personal integrity, precision, and accuracy

8. Willingness to protect the interests of the organization

9. Ability to coordinate the needs of the operation's departments with the supplies being delivered

Naturally, good health and personal cleanliness are essential in the receiver, as well as in all other personnel in the food service business. The FDA's Model Ordinance is specific on health and personal cleanliness requirements for food handlers and others who work in the food service environment. The goal is to prevent contamination of food and food-contact surfaces with diseases or pathogenic organisms. To protect the health of customers and employees alike, strict sanitation standards should permeate every aspect of food handling.

The person in charge of receiving should be able to effectively use all equipment, facilities, and forms required at this control point. (More will be said about these tools in later sections.)

Because of the volume of written information used at this control

The FDA's Food Service Sanitation Ordinance states:

PERSONNEL

Employee Health

General.

No person, while infected with a disease in a communicable form that can be transmitted by foods or who is a carrier of organisms that cause such a disease or while afflicted with a boil, an infected wound, or an acute respiratory infection, shall work in a food service establishment in any capacity in which there is a likelihood of such person contaminating food or food-contact surfaces with pathogenic organisms or transmitting disease to other persons.

Personal Cleanliness

General.

Employees shall thoroughly wash their hands and the exposed portions of their arms with soap and warm water before starting work, during work as often as is necessary to keep them clean, and after smoking, eating, drinking, or using the toilet. Employees shall keep their fingernails clean and trimmed.

Source: Food and Drug Administration, Public Health Service, U.S. Department of Health, Education, and Welfare, Food Service Sanitation Manual, 1976, pp. 33-34.

point, the operation's receiver must be able to read and write. Among other things, the receiver must be able to check the actual products delivered against the written purchase specifications and written purchase orders. A receiver who is illiterate would not see, for example, that the purchase order says "50 ten-ounce USDA Prime tenderloin steaks" and could mistakenly accept 40 twelve-ounce USDA Choice tenderloin steaks instead.

The receiver should know acceptable product quality characteristics based on the operation's standard purchase specifications. A knowledge of product grades, weight ranges, and fat trim factors is crucial to the success of receiving. In addition, the receiver should be able to assess packaging conditions. Furthermore, the receiver must be able to judge the sanitary condition of the products and the delivery vehicle.

The receiver should be a person who demonstrates honesty and attention to detail. The receiver's integrity ensures that the establishment's standards, policies, and procedures will not be compromised. The receiver must be someone who takes this important job seriously. Negligence or inaccuracy on the part of the receiver does financial damage to the business. Its reputation may be tainted if hazardous foods are carelessly accepted into the food service system.

Clearly, the receiver must be someone who is committed to protecting the interests of the operation. While food production experience is invaluable in the receiver, this does not imply that any kitchen worker in the operation is qualified to perform the receiving function. Only selected and trained employees should be permitted to receive food and nonfood products. A facility that allows the janitor, dishwasher, or busperson to do its receiving is opening the door for trouble. These individuals are not in a position to recognize product problems nor what to do about them.

A properly trained receiver, on the other hand, knows what to do when there is a problem with product deliveries. The receiver uses his or her clout with the supplier to point out problems to the delivery person and see that they are corrected. In this respect, the receiving function is even more important than the purchasing function because as soon as the receiver signs the invoice, the merchandise is legally accepted and is no longer the responsibility of the supplier. Thereafter, any problems with the products are the operation's problems.

Finally, the person in charge of receiving needs cooperation from other departments in the food service establishment or hotel. The receiver must coordinate supply requisitions from the departments with the delivery schedules of suppliers. Ideally, receiving should take place during slow periods in the operation's daily business cycle. This is particularly important when the receiver is also the chef, assistant manager, or manager. During rush periods, these individuals have other duties and responsibilities. By scheduling deliveries during slow periods, the receiver's undivided attention can be given to the receiving duties. The establishment's delivery hours should be posted on the back door as a guide for suppliers. Then, the receiver should be available during the times when deliveries are expected. Staggering food deliveries avoids overloading the storage area facilities. A smoothly run receiving control point is an indication of the receiver's competence and reliability as well as the supplier's service and performance.

Receiving and Equipment

As the previous section noted, the receiver must be able to use a number of pieces of equipment which are necessary for proper receiving. Some equipment is used to gain access to the food for the usual quality and quantity checks. The operation should keep such tools as hammers, pliers, and screwdrivers on hand for the receiver to use in opening crates and boxes.

Other equipment is used to verify product quality, quantity, and price. These tools include scales, thermometers, rulers, and calculators. An accurate scale is crucial to the success of the receiving control point because many products purchased by a food service facility are invoiced based on product weight. Any such product should be weighed by the receiver to be sure the weight on the invoice is correct.

Several types of scales are available for use during receiving. **Electronic read-out scales** are both easy to use and precise. Some of these scales are equipped with a device to stamp the recorded weight directly on the package. **Tabletop or counter scales** are suitable for checking the weight of lighter products. A large capacity **floor or platform scale** is used for products that are bulky and heavy. The products can often be rolled onto the floor scale with the aid of a handcart. To record the product's true net weight, the weight of the cart and packaging material must be subtracted.

Some operations attempt to save money by buying an inexpensive scale. However, inexpensive scales are often not accurate and, as a result, are not used. An accurate scale is a good investment because it will pay for itself in the long run. Scales should be checked for accuracy at least every three months by a qualified expert.

Thermometers are also indispensable for proper receiving. An accurate probe pocket thermometer is an invaluable tool in the hands of a knowledgeable receiver. The temperature of all perishable products (meats, fish, poultry, produce, frozen foods) should be monitored. The internal temperature of refrigerated products must be less than or equal to 45°F (7°C), while frozen foods must be 0°F (-18°C) or below. If products are delivered at higher temperatures, they must be further evaluated on the basis of appearance, odor, and perhaps taste.

Within the next two years, perishable product inspection during receiving may be made easier through the use of a time-temperature monitor currently under development. The device will be a relatively inexpensive monitor that can be attached to boxes or cartons of refrigerated and frozen products. It will measure the combined effects of heat and age by changing color in response to chemical and physical reactions which take place when a product's temperature exceeds a predefined level for an excessive length of time.

The use of these time-temperature monitors will benefit food service businesses by identifying weaknesses in the distribution system. This new technology will permit the operation's receiver to quickly see whether a product has been thawed and then refrozen. Thus, the accept/reject decision will be more objective and rapid. Widespread use of these monitors should also provide a stimulus for suppliers and distributors to maintain correct product temperatures and storage times.

A ruler is a useful tool to check the amount of fat covering and the size of steaks and roasts. A calculator permits the receiver to quickly verify the accuracy of the supplier's invoice.

After the delivery is accepted, other equipment is used to prepare the items for storage and to transport them. Marking pens, dollies, hand trucks, and other transportation equipment are included in this category. Marking pens are used to record the product's AP (as purchased) price directly on the product's package. This practice prompts other food handlers in the operation to think about the products as equivalent to money. This strategy also encourages proper food care to reduce contamination and spoilage losses. Marking pens are also used to record the date of delivery to ensure proper product rotation (the use of oldest items first). Other information may also be attached to products, as a later section explains. Dollies and other transportation equipment help the receiver to move marked products rapidly into storage, thereby retaining product safety and quality.

Receiving and Inventory

Before they become inventory items, all product deliveries must be verified. This verification is a two-step process. First, the supplier's invoice is checked against the establishment's purchase order and standard purchase specifications. The supplier's **invoice** is a document detailing all the products being delivered to the facility and the corresponding prices. (In some cases, it also shows products which are "back ordered" or not yet available for delivery.) Since the supplier uses the sum of invoices to calculate the bill, each invoice must be verified for accuracy. At the second step, when the order is delivered, the products themselves should be checked against the supplier's invoice. Any products invoiced on the basis of weight should be weighed using an accurate scale. To determine the net weight of the products, they should be removed from their packing containers or the weight of the containers should be subtracted from the gross weight. Different cuts of meat which are delivered together must be weighed separately because of varying per pound prices. Any products delivered on the basis of count should be counted before they are accepted. If more than one container of the same product is delivered, a spot-check of random containers to verify the count may be sufficient.

In some cases, the invoice may need to be modified because the products are spoiled, do not meet the establishment's specifications, or the wrong quantity has been delivered. A **request for a credit memo** is used by the operation to state the reasons why the products are unacceptable and to ask the supplier to credit the invoice. The supplier should then issue a **credit memo** to adjust the account. A sample request for a credit memo is illustrated in Exhibit 7.1. This form helps to ensure that the food service establishment is charged only for the products that conform to its standards.

If a thorough inspection of every product delivery seems to be unnecessarily complex or time-consuming, it isn't. The food service business can only gain from a policy of consistent inspection. It keeps honest suppliers honest and discourages dishonest suppliers from dealing with the operation.

Once the delivery check is completed and the products have been legally accepted, it is time to record the new inventory items and prepare them for storage. Tagging products when they are delivered aids in inventory control later. A sample **product storage tag** is presented in Exhibit 7.2. The date on the tag facilitates stock rotation, which is the goal of the FIFO (first in-first out) inventory system. Recording the cost of the product on its tag forces food service employees to think about the product as money and to avoid wasting it. Inventory tags with prices also speed up the physical inventory process.

In addition, the tagging system provides an audit trail for food products. Initially, one part of the tag is attached to the product, while the other portion is affixed to the invoice. Later, when the product is issued for use, the portion of the tag attached to the product is removed and sent to the operation's accounting office. By matching the product portion of the tag to the invoice portion, the accounting department maintains inventory control.

Of course, if certain products are to be used immediately, they are

Exhibit 7.1 Request for a Credit Memo

Request for a Credit Memo

(prepare in duplicate)   Number: _____

From: _____   To: _____
                                                        (supplier)

_____   _____

_____   _____

Credit should be given on the following:

Invoice Number: _____   Invoice Date: _____

Product	Unit	Number	Price/Unit	Total Price

Reason: Total: _____

_____   _____
(delivery person)   (authorizing signature)

Source: Jack D. Ninemeier, Planning and Control for Food and Beverage Operations, *1982, p. 75.*

Exhibit 7.2 Storage Tag

Tag Number ___1005___   Tag Number ___1005___

Date of Receipt ___8/1/00___   Date Received ___8/1/00___

Weight/Cost   Weight ___35#___

___35___ × ___2.85___ = ___99.75___   Price ___2.85___

No. of #s   Price   Cost   Cost ___99.75___

Name of Supplier: _____   Supplier ___Jacob___

___Jacob Meats___   Date Issued _____

Date of Issue: _____

Source: Jack D. Ninemeier, Planning and Control for Food and Beverage Operations, *1982, p. 76.*

sent directly to kitchen production areas without going through the usual storing and issuing control points. Nevertheless, everything that the facility receives must be recorded. A **receiving clerk's daily report** is the form used for this purpose. A sample receiving clerk's daily report is illustrated in Exhibit 7.3. It lists what was received, the date of the delivery, the name of the supplier, the quantity, the price, and any other relevant comments. The report also provides a record of the distribution of the delivery. The **Food Directs** column indicates the dollar value of products to be sent directly to kitchen production areas. The **Food Stores** column records the dollar value of products to be placed into storage. Generally, the food items placed in storage vastly outnumber the food items sent directly to production.

Storing new inventory items in the proper order can preserve product quality and food safety. The most perishable items (i.e., frozen products) should be placed in storage first. Next, refrigerated meats, fish, poultry, dairy products, and produce should be rapidly stored. Finally, the least perishable items (staple foods and nonfood supplies) should be stored. Adhering to this order minimizes product deterioration and loss of quality. At the moment the delivery is accepted, the safety of the food becomes the responsibility of the food service establishment. The receiver should strive to keep the time elapsed between acceptance and

---

The FDA's Food Service Sanitation Ordinance states:

Food Protection

General.

At all times, including while being stored, prepared, displayed, served, or transported, food shall be protected from potential contamination, including dust, insects, rodents, unclean equipment and utensils, unnecessary handling, coughs and sneezes, flooding, drainage, and overhead leakage or overhead drippage from condensation. The temperature of potentially hazardous food shall be 45° F or below or 140°F or above at all times, except as otherwise provided in this ordinance.

Emergency occurrences.

In the event of a fire, flood, power outage, or similar event that might result in the contamination of food, or that might prevent potentially hazardous food from being held at required temperatures, the person in charge shall immediately contact the regulatory authority. Upon receiving notice of this occurrence, the regulatory authority shall take whatever action that it deems necessary to protect the public health.

Source: FDA, pp. 24-25.

Exhibit 7.3 Receiving Clerk's Daily Report

							Distribution						
							Food		Beverages				Transfer to Storage
Supplier	Invoice No.	Item	Unit	No. of Units	Unit Price	Total Cost	Directs*	Stores	Liquor	Beer	Wine	Soda	
1	2	3	4	5	6	7	8	9	10	11	12	13	14
AJAX	10111	Gr. Beef	10#	6	28.50	171.00		171.00					Bill
ABC Liquor	6281	B. Scotch	CS(750)	2	71.80	143.60			143.60				Bill
		H. Chablis	gal	3	8.50	25.50					25.50		Bill
B/E Produce	70666	Lettuce	CS	2	21.00	42.00	42.00						
						Totals	351.00	475.00	683.50	—	102.00		

*The daily Food Directs dollar value can be added to the dollar value of food products issued from inventory to provide an accurate estimate of the daily food cost.

Source: Jack D. Ninemeier, Planning and Control for Food and Beverage Operations, *1982, p. 74.*

storage as short as possible, particularly for frozen and refrigerated food products because these require the most protection.

The FDA's Model Ordinance addresses the topic of food protection. The goal is to prevent contamination and proliferation of pathogens in the food supply. Food must be safe when it is accepted by the food service operation. Then the operation must protect the food as it passes through the system from storage to preparation, display, and service.

Receiving and Facilities

Proper receiving facilities are essential to the attainment of the establishment's sanitation, quality, and cost standards at the receiving control point. Receiving facilities include inside and outside areas surrounding the loading dock, the back door, and the receiving office.

The sanitary condition of the receiving area is critical. No buildup of debris or food particles is permitted on inside floors and walls or on the receiving dock because these unclean conditions could contaminate food or food containers prior to storage. After products are stored, empty shipping containers and packaging materials should be removed to disposal areas promptly. Some operations locate their refuse and trash areas near the receiving dock. This may create sanitation risks, the potential for thefts of inventory, and negative first impressions in the minds of customers. Whenever possible, trash containers should be located in an area which is physically separated from the receiving area.

The quality of a food service operation is also reflected in its outdoor receiving facilities. They give an impression of the establishment to customers, suppliers, and the competition. Ideally, receiving docks should be constructed so that deliveries from suppliers are easy to manage. Adequate ramps, platforms, and truck maneuvering space should be provided. For safety as well as security, the outdoor and indoor receiving areas should be well-lit. As another security precaution, the receiving door should be locked when not in use. Whenever possible, the receiving office should be located between the receiving dock and storage areas. This will minimize the effort and, more important, the time it takes to transport products to storage.

Costs are easier to control when the receiving facilities are equipped with the necessary tools and work surfaces. A work table or desk is essential for recordkeeping and administrative responsibilities. Additional table space should be available for opening product containers during inspection of deliveries. Adequate floor space is necessary so that orders do not pile up in the receiving area. Overcrowding in the delivery area results in safety and sanitation hazards.

Receiving and Change

Some establishments receive products in the same way they have done it for years. They never bother to reevaluate the function to identify areas for possible improvement. As a result, these operations are not maximizing their utilization of resources at the receiving control point. There is no room for negligence, waste, or error in receiving. Evidence of any of these problems may suggest the need for reevaluation of the receiving function.

Because the control points are all interrelated, receiving should also be reevaluated when menu planning or purchasing activities are changed. For example, if a small operation changes its menu, and business improves dramatically, perhaps the operation's increased sales volume would justify hiring a full-time receiving person. The operation's orders can only be checked in properly if the receiver has enough time and the correct tools.

Management should make periodic checks of the receiving function to evaluate how effectively the operation is handling this control point. Regardless of the size of the business, the more consistent and routine the receiving function becomes, the fewer problems there will be. As with all the other control points, an evaluation of the costs versus the benefits indicates the degree to which more sophisticated controls are required.

Receiving and Success

What takes place at the back door can make or break a business. Invoices are checked against the purchase order and specifications. The quality and condition of each delivered item is examined. A request for a credit memo is used for any damaged or spoiled products.

Perishable products are carefully checked by weight and/or count. Canned and staple items are also spot-checked. When the invoice is signed, the establishment is committed to payment. All of these procedures take time, but they increase the probability of success. The attitude of the receiver is important to the success of the business. If the receiver is thorough and honest, suppliers are much more likely to follow the operation's specifications. Receiving is an important part of the establishment's overall strategy for success.

The Storing Control Point

The **storing** control point has as its goal protecting the operation's food and nonfood purchases until they are put to work as income producers. To maximize income, profits, and customer satisfaction, spoilage and contamination must be minimized. Also, these assets must be protected from theft and pilferage. To maintain a high level of sanitation and quality while keeping down costs, a number of storage area controls are useful.

The key to proper food storage is knowing how items should be stored and having facilities and equipment to keep the products in optimal condition. Most food products do *not* improve in quality while in storage. (Recommended storage times, temperatures, and relative humidities for selected food products may be found in Chapter 4 on food spoilage and preservation.)

Storing and Personnel

The storing function is a weak link in the control system of some food service establishments. They experience large losses due to contamination, spoilage, and deterioration of their food products. These losses are usually due to the fact that no one is in charge of monitoring storage areas. Although a small business may not be able to justify hiring a storeroom person on a full-time basis, responsibility for the storage areas must be given to one dependable employee (e.g., chef or assistant manager). The establishment's investment in food and nonfood products is too large to be treated haphazardly.

The responsibilities of the storeroom person vary with the operation and the dollar value of its inventory. (Recall that inventory ties up money but does not earn interest for the business.) In smaller operations, the storeroom person often has other responsibilities such as receiving, issuing, and/or production. Splitting time between these responsibilities need not be a problem if the proper routines are being followed at each control point.

The functions of the storeroom person are:

1. To conduct frequent, careful inspections of product storage areas in the facility

2. To prevent waste in the form of spoilage and decreased product quality

3. To discard food which is contaminated or spoiled

4. To reduce financial losses due to theft and pilferage

5. To monitor rates of usage of each product

6. To record inventory dollar amounts using the perpetual inventory and/or physical inventory system

The purpose of the storeroom person's inspections is to ensure that the operation's quality and safety standards are being maintained. Proper care of inventory items contributes to the cost control program also.

Waste in the form of spoilage and decreased product quality increases the "cost of goods sold" expense and decreases profitability. By preserving food properly (see Chapter 4), the storeroom person makes a major contribution to the operation's bottom-line performance.

Obviously, contaminated food must be removed from inventory to protect the health of customers and the reputation of the establishment. (The proper procedure for disposing of food thought to be contaminated is described in Chapter 5.) When in doubt about the safety of an inventory item, it is better to throw it out than to risk an outbreak of foodborne disease.

Unfortunately, thefts and pilferage are not uncommon in the food service industry. However, the establishment of inventory controls (described later in this chapter) can make these losses easier to detect. Security precautions must be taken throughout the operation, and storage areas are no exception. Key and lock control and the establishment of an audit trail are examples of security measures at the storing control point.

There are several good reasons for monitoring product usage rates. First, the information gained in this process can help the purchasing agent to establish par stocks and automatic reorder points, thus minimizing stockouts. Second, surplus products which are not being used up fast enough can be brought to the attention of the production department. Then these "dead" inventory items can be worked into production before they spoil, causing the operation's food cost to increase.

Every food service business must keep proper inventory records for accounting and tax purposes. The specifics of the various methods for taking inventory will be presented in the section "Storing and Inventory."

Storing and Equipment

Equipment is an important consideration in each of the three areas of storage: dry, refrigerated, and frozen. Storage temperatures in all three of these areas must be monitored with thermometers that are accurate to $\pm 3^\circ$ F. A thermometer should be placed in the warmest part of each storage area in a location where it is easily readable. The warmest area in a refrigerator or freezer can usually be found near the door.

The FDA's Model Ordinance strictly defines proper storage of equipment and utensils. The goal is to avoid contamination from food, splash, and dust in the storage environment. It does not make sense to correctly clean and sanitize equipment and utensils only to store these items in an unsanitary way.

The FDA's Food Service Sanitation Ordinance states:

Equipment and Utensil Storage

Handling.

Cleaned and sanitized equipment and utensils shall be handled in a way that protects them from contamination. Spoons, knives, and forks shall be touched only by their handles. Cups, glasses, bowls, plates and similar items shall be handled without contact with inside surfaces or surfaces that contact the user's mouth.

Storage.

(a) Cleaned and sanitized utensils and equipment shall be stored at least 6 inches above the floor in a clean, dry location in a way that protects them from contamination by splash, dust, and other means. The food-contact surfaces of fixed equipment shall also be protected from contamination. Equipment and utensils shall not be placed under exposed sewer lines or water lines, except for automatic fire protection sprinkler heads that may be required by law.

(b) Utensils shall be air dried before being stored or shall be stored in a self-draining position.

(c) Glasses and cups shall be stored inverted. Other stored utensils shall be covered or inverted, wherever practical. Facilities for the storage of knives, forks, and spoons shall be designed and used to present the handle to the employee or consumer. Unless tableware is prewrapped, holders for knives, forks, and spoons at self-service locations shall protect these articles from contamination and present the handle of the utensil to the consumer.

Single-service articles.

(a) Single-service articles shall be stored at least 6 inches above the floor in closed cartons or containers which protect them from contamination and shall not be placed under exposed sewer lines or water lines, except for automatic fire protection sprinkler heads that may be required by law.

(b) Single-service articles shall be handled and dispensed in a manner that prevents contamination of surfaces which may come in contact with food or with the mouth of the user.

(c) Single-service knives, forks and spoons packaged in bulk shall be inserted into holders or be wrapped by an employee who has washed his hands immediately prior to sorting or wrapping the utensils. Unless single-service knives, forks and spoons are pre-wrapped or prepackaged, holders shall be provided to protect these items from contamination and present the handle of the utensil to the consumer.

Prohibited storage area.

The storage of food equipment, utensils or single-service articles in toilet rooms or vestibules is prohibited.

Source: FDA, pp. 47-48.

Storing and Inventory

Generally, the larger the inventory dollar value, the more difficult it is to achieve control of the storing function. While too small an inventory can lead to frequent stockouts, an excessively large inventory can cause a number of problems:

1. Most food products, including frozen items, experience a loss of volume and quality if stored too long.

2. Pilferage and spoilage losses tend to increase in direct proportion to the amount of inventory on hand. When employees see a large quantity of products in stock, they may be tempted to steal, figuring that one less will not be noticed.

3. Large inventory amounts encourage waste. Food preparation employees are not as likely to conserve food products that are obviously overstocked.

4. If storage areas are inadequate, excessive inventory can be costly in terms of the labor required to handle and rehandle the products.

5. It is more difficult to take inventory in overstocked freezers, refrigerators, and dry storage areas. Large errors in inventory dollar values can result in a significantly different bottom-line figure.

6. Excessive inventories can tie up the operation's money for long periods of time.

In light of these problems, managers may wonder how to achieve an optimum inventory level, thus avoiding shortages and overstocking. If sales are properly forecasted, purchasing is more accurate and inventory is easier to control. But suppose an establishment finds it necessary to maintain a large inventory, perhaps due to infrequent supplier deliveries and a high level of sales. Is a detailed security system necessary for every product in stock? Such a system might require a considerably larger storeroom staff, and might actually end up costing more than the losses from thefts, spoilage, and contamination.

Realistically, the dollar value of food products dictates the minimal amount of inventory control necessary to guarantee security. Foods can be compared by price per unit of weight or volume. On this basis, it is clear that relatively few food products have a high dollar value per unit of measure (pound, kilogram, quart, liter, etc.). On the average, less than 20% of the total items in a food service operation's inventory account for over 80% of the total dollar value of the food inventory. Therefore, the operation's inventory control measures should focus on these high cost items.

Several techniques for categorizing inventories have been developed. Perhaps the most useful one is the **A-B-C-D scheme**. This technique classifies inventory items according to perishability and cost per serving. (Both perishability and cost are determined on a relative basis.) The categories of the A-B-C-D scheme are presented in Exhibit 7.4.

Class A inventory items are high in both perishability and cost per serving. Examples of Class A items are fresh fish, fresh shellfish, and fresh meats. Class A items may account for up to 40% of a food service operation's total annual purchases.

Class B inventory items are relatively high in cost, but low in perishability. Frozen meats and seafood, canned meats and seafood, some canned and frozen fruits and vegetables, and preserved specialty items (e.g., caviar) are examples of Class B items. These may account for another 20% of a facility's total annual purchases.

Class C inventory items are relatively low in cost per serving, but relatively high in perishability. Fresh poultry products, fresh produce, and dairy products are in Class C.

Class D inventory items have both the lowest perishability and the lowest cost per serving. Examples of Class D items include spices and seasonings, condiments, some frozen and canned products, and staples such as flour and sugar.

The advantages of using the A-B-C-D classification scheme are numerous, particularly where the storeroom staff is limited. Analyzing the operation's inventory according to this scheme forces the inventory person to consider both relative perishability and cost per serving. The scheme is straightforward and easy to use. Very simply, inventory control should focus primarily on Class A and Class B items, since (a) these account for the greatest dollar volume of inventory, and (b) these comprise the products most likely to be stolen by employees. Of secondary importance are the Class C items, which should be monitored frequently for contamination and spoilage.

Like any other classification scheme, the A-B-C-D system is a simplification of reality. Since relative costs vary from operation to operation, some food items may not be categorized exactly as shown in Exhibit 7.4. However, the essence of the classification scheme remains the same: not all inventory items should be treated, or controlled, in the same way. The

Exhibit 7.4   The A-B-C-D Classification Scheme for Food Items in Inventory

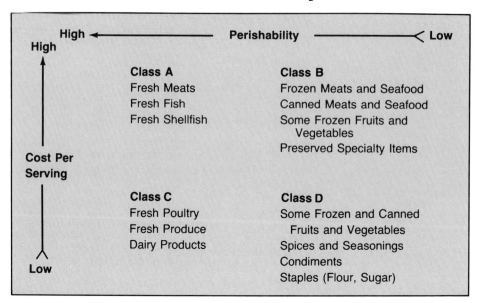

facility's control system should primarily focus on the high-cost-per-serving foods. Strict accounting for these items should, by definition, protect more than half of the total dollar value of all food products purchased by the business. Of course, to adapt the A-B-C-D classification scheme to an operation's own needs, management must know exactly what the operation's inventory consists of. There are two widely accepted methods of inventory control. One is taking a physical inventory; the other is the perpetual inventory system.

A **physical inventory** is an actual count of what is on the shelves. It must be taken each time an income statement is prepared. A sample **physical inventory form** is shown in Exhibit 7.5. The physical inventory must be precise and accurate since it is used to calculate the operation's cost of goods sold and food cost percentage. The relevant calculations are as follows:

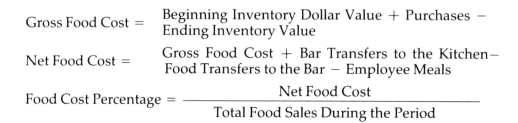

Gross Food Cost = Beginning Inventory Dollar Value + Purchases − Ending Inventory Value

Net Food Cost = Gross Food Cost + Bar Transfers to the Kitchen − Food Transfers to the Bar − Employee Meals

$$\text{Food Cost Percentage} = \frac{\text{Net Food Cost}}{\text{Total Food Sales During the Period}}$$

A physical inventory is also necessary in order to calculate inventory turnover. **Inventory turnover** is the rate at which inventory is converted

Exhibit 7.5   Physical Inventory Form

Type of Product: _____   Month: _____   Month: _____

Product	Unit	Amount in Storage	Purchase Price	Total Price	Amount in Storage	Purchase Price	Total Price
1	2	3	4	5	6	7	8
Applesauce	6 #10	4⅓	15.85	68.63			
Green Beans	6 #10	3⅚	18.95	72.58			
Flour	25# bag	3	4.85	14.55			
Rice	50# bag	1	12.50	12.50			
			Total	486.55			

Source: Jack D. Ninemeier, Planning and Control for Food and Beverage Operations, 1982, p. 84.

or turned into revenue during a given period. An excessively low inventory turnover is to be avoided because (a) spoilage rates may increase, and (b) the business may need the cash tied up in inventory. However, if turnover rates are too rapid, (a) the business may not be taking advantage of quantity discounts, and (b) production may be hampered by insufficient inventory. Ideal inventory turnover rates can only be established by tracking past rates and calculating averages. Inventory turnover is calculated as follows:

$$\text{Average Inventory} = \frac{\text{Beginning Inventory Dollar Value} + \text{Ending Inventory Dollar Value}}{2}$$

$$\text{Inventory Turnover} = \frac{\text{Net Food Cost}}{\text{Average Inventory}}$$

Combining the technique of inventory classification with the concept of inventory turnover, it is clear that inventory turnover for Class A and Class C items should be higher than for Class B and Class D items. Because of their perishable nature, fresh meats, seafood, poultry, produce, and dairy products should be turned over more frequently than any other products. To be sure that this is actually the case, the person in charge of inventory control can track turnover in each of the four classes of inventory items. It may be particularly useful from a sanitation standpoint to calculate turnover rates for all categories of potentially hazardous foods. Nevertheless, it must be remembered that the frequency of deliveries has an impact on turnover. To recall an earlier example, a steakhouse located in a downtown metropolitan area probably has a higher inventory turnover rate than a similar operation in the mountains or in a rural area because it receives deliveries more frequently.

A **perpetual inventory** continuously records what is in storage at any given time. As products are added to or removed from storage, the balance figure in the last column of the **perpetual inventory form** (see Exhibit 7.6) is adjusted. At all times, the amount on the shelves should agree exactly with the balance figure on the form.

Although the perpetual inventory system requires more recordkeeping, it offers several advantages. If filled out accurately, the perpetual inventory form provides tight control over food products. Also, unlike the physical inventory method, the perpetual inventory system is always up to date throughout the month. Furthermore, the close monitoring involved in this system prevents food spoilage from progressing uncontrolled in storage areas.

Since most operations have a shortage of personnel resources, the perpetual inventory system is mainly used for expensive (Class A and B) menu items such as meat, fish, shellfish, specialty foods, expensive spices. Using the perpetual inventory system for costly items tells employees that these items are being watched.

Another important inventory management technique for preventing spoilage is the rotation of food supplies on a first in-first out (FIFO) basis. Using the FIFO system of food rotation means that new stock is always placed behind old stock so that the older products will be used first. Any products in dry, refrigerated, or frozen storage areas that are damaged or have an abnormal color or odor should be discarded. Keeping records on all spoiled food products helps management identify areas for improvement and helps the accounting department maintain accurate values for inventory. During the physical inventory process, management can check each storage area to be sure that the FIFO system is being used. The food production supervisor (usually the chef or assistant manager) should also make a daily FIFO check.

Storing and Facilities

In this section, standards for the storing control point are presented in three parts corresponding to the three types of storage areas: dry, refrigerated, and frozen. **Dry storage** areas are designed to secure foods that do not require refrigeration and are shelf stable. A properly designed dry storage area is clean, orderly, and well-ventilated. Freedom from motors, compressors, machinery, water and heating pipes, and

Exhibit 7.6 Perpetual Inventory Form

Date	In Carried Forward	Out	Balance 15	Date	In Carried Forward	Out	Balance
1	2	3	4	1	2	3	4
5/16		3	12				
5/17		3	9				
5/18	6		15				
5/19		2	13				

Product Name: *Applesauce*   Purchase Unit Size: *Case (6#10)*

Source: Jack D. Ninemeier, Planning and Control for Food and Beverage Operations, *1982, p. 86.*

other undesirable structures is preferred in dry storage areas. The walls and floors are to be constructed of easy-to-clean materials. Protection from insects and rodents is essential. Locked doors coupled with proper key control add to the security system.

Good housekeeping in dry storage not only reduces contamination, it also reduces fire hazards. The light sources in storage areas should be sufficient to provide adequate illumination for reading product labels. A makeshift storage area located under a set of stairs is no solution; such areas are dark, dingy, and difficult to clean. No products should be stored closer than 18 inches (45.72 cm) to any light bulb or tube. Bulbs and tubes should be shielded so that, if they break, they won't shatter over food supplies.

All food stored in the dry storage area must be on shelves located at least two inches (5.08 cm) from walls and six inches (15.24 cm) off the floor. This not only facilitates inspection and cleaning but also aids in ventilation, prevents contamination, and eliminates pest harborage areas. Many operations use shelving on wheels to make it easier to move inventory when the area is to be cleaned. Shelves that are open on both sides and are built along the center of the room take advantage of floor space that otherwise would be wasted. This center aisle storeroom arrangement makes stock rotation easier. When products are stored on shelves, the bulkier and heavier items should be located on lower shelves. Frequently used items should be placed near the entrance. A specific location in the storeroom should be assigned for each type of product in inventory. Whenever a product is opened in storage, it must be kept away from containers that may be contaminated with dirt, wire, splinters, etc. The storeroom person must guard the food against physical contamination from glass fragments and metal chips at all times.

Storage time-temperature combinations are important because they keep food products high in nutrients, at peak flavor and texture, and safe to eat. All food in dry storage areas is to be covered, labeled, and dated. Ideal storage temperatures are 50 to 70°F (10 to 21°C) with a 50-60% relative humidity. A thermometer should be mounted in the dry storage area so that temperatures can be recorded by the storeroom person at least twice each day.

The FDA's Model Ordinance specifies dry food storage requirements. The objective is to minimize contamination and the proliferation of pathogens. By following the requirements of monitoring storage times and temperatures, food quality is enhanced and spoilage reduced.

The FDA's Food Service Sanitation Ordinance states:

Food Storage

General.

(a) Food, whether raw or prepared, if removed from the container or package in which it was obtained, shall be stored in a clean covered container except during necessary periods of preparation or service. Container covers shall be impervious and nonabsorbent, except that linens or napkins may be used for lining or covering bread or roll containers. Solid cuts of meat shall be protected by being covered in storage, except that quarters or sides of meat may be hung uncovered on clean sanitized hooks if no food product is stored beneath the meat.

(b) Containers of food shall be stored a minimum of 6 inches above the floor in a manner that protects the food from splash and other contamination, and that permits easy cleaning of the storage area, except that:

(1) Metal pressurized beverage containers, and cased food packaged in cans, glass or other waterproof containers need not be elevated when the food container is not exposed to floor moisture; and

(2) Containers may be stored on dollies, racks or pallets, provided such equipment is easily movable.

(c) Food and containers of food shall not be stored under exposed or unprotected sewer lines or water lines, except for automatic fire protection sprinkler heads that may be required by law. The storage of food in toilet rooms or vestibules is prohibited.

(d) Food not subject to further washing or cooking before serving shall be stored in a way that protects it against cross-contamination from food requiring washing or cooking.

(e) Packaged food shall not be stored in contact with water or undrained ice. Wrapped sandwiches shall not be stored in direct contact with ice.

(f) Unless its identity is unmistakable, bulk food such as cooking oil, syrup, salt, sugar or flour not stored in the product container or package in which it was obtained, shall be stored in a container identifying the food by common name.

Source: FDA, pp. 25-26.

Refrigerated storage areas are designed to maintain food products at temperatures of 45°F (7°C) or less. (The FDA's Model Ordinance combines specifications for refrigerated and frozen storage areas under the heading "Refrigerated Storage.") Refrigerators and freezers require visible thermometers so that temperatures can be checked at least four times per day. Most operators complain that they do not have adequate refrigerated and frozen storage space. In some cases this complaint is valid, and modification of the facilities and/or equipment may be in order.[1] However, limited refrigerated and frozen storage space may force the production supervisor to control food inventories more carefully, to organize the areas more efficiently, and to avoid spoilage. Also, use of a storage area temperature recording form can help control the storage function. A sample **storage area condition report** form is illustrated in Exhibit 7.7.

Refrigerated storage areas are used to prolong the shelf life of perishable foods so the FIFO system is indispensable. Foods must be stored at least six inches (15.24 cm) off the floor and two inches (5.08 cm) away from walls to allow for ventilation and air movement and reduce insect and rodent harborage areas. Doors on refrigeration units should only be opened for a short time and only when necessary. To avoid having to search, it is a good idea to post the contents of each cooling unit on its door. Placing frequently used foods near the door of the unit also reduces the amount of time the door is open. Food products on shelves must not be jammed against the doors of cooling units when the doors are closed. Refrigerators and freezers which have been jammed by food

---

[1] See Chapter 8 for a detailed discussion of refrigerators and freezers.

Exhibit 7.7 Storage Area Condition Report

AREA
☐ Dry
☐ Refrigerated
☐ Freezer   Date _____

Storage Area	Location	Temperature	Relative Humidity	Time Recorded	Signature of Recorder	Comments

inside often have damaged door gaskets that create leaks.

Once canned products are opened, they must be removed from their original containers and placed in clean, labeled, covered containers. Perishable or potentially hazardous foods should not be stored at room temperature, but stored in pans not more than four inches (10.16 cm) deep under refrigeration. Highly perishable foods (e.g., hollandaise sauce) are to be prepared not more than three hours before serving.

Leftover food products should be covered to prevent contamination during refrigeration. However, they should not be made airtight because this would encourage the development of anaerobic conditions during product cooling. Refrigerated leftovers should be dated with the day they were first stored; perishable leftovers should be used within 24 hours or thrown out. Any spoiled foods discovered in storage areas should be separated and discarded immediately. This problem occurs most frequently with fresh fruits and vegetables.

Leftover prepared food must be stored above raw ingredients to prevent cross-contamination. Warm foods stored above already refrigerated foods allow the heat to quickly dissipate. (Doing it the opposite way results in cold foods being heated.)

Sanitation management is often more critical in refrigerated areas than in dry storage areas. Coated wire shelving is usually a problem in high moisture areas. It has a tendency to rust and is difficult to keep clean. Any rusted shelving should be replaced with stainless steel shelving on wheels. The floors of walk-in refrigerators are easier to maintain if they are made of ceramic quarry tile. The floors in refrigerated storage areas are to be cleaned at least twice each day. The walls, ceiling, and shelves should be cleaned every two weeks. If more than one refrigeration unit is used to store ingredients, products requiring similar conditions should be stored together. For example, to prevent odor transfer from onions and fish to dairy products, the latter should be stored in a separate area.

The FDA's Food Service Sanitation Ordinance states:

Food Storage

Refrigerated storage.

(a) Enough conveniently located refrigeration facilities or effectively insulated facilities shall be provided to assure the maintenance of potentially hazardous food at required temperatures during storage. Each mechanically refrigerated facility storing potentially hazardous food shall be provided with a numerically scaled indicating thermometer, accurate to $\pm 3°$ F, located to measure the air temperature in the warmest part of the facility and located to be easily readable. Recording thermometers, accurate to $\pm 3°$ F, may be used in lieu of indicating thermometers.

(b) Potentially hazardous food requiring refrigeration after preparation shall be rapidly cooled to an internal temperature of 45° F or below. Potentially hazardous foods of large volume or prepared in large quantities shall be rapidly cooled, utilizing such methods as shallow pans, agitation, quick chilling or water circulation external to the food container so that the cooling period shall not exceed 4 hours. Potentially hazardous food to be transported shall be prechilled and held at a temperature of 45°F or below unless maintained in accordance with [the hot storage] section . . . of this ordinance.

(c) Frozen food shall be kept frozen and should be stored at a temperature of 0°F or below.

(d) Ice intended for human consumption shall not be used as a medium for cooling stored food, food containers or food utensils, except that such ice may be used for cooling tubes conveying beverages or beverage ingredients to a dispenser head. Ice used for cooling stored food and food containers shall not be used for human consumption.

Source: FDA, pp. 26-27.

Violations of the food storage section of the FDA's Model Ordinance occur regularly in food service operations. Products are stored uncovered in containers that are not labeled. Some operations use utility grade plastic bags instead of food grade bags for storage. In many establishments, refrigerated storage areas are not designed to keep products off the floor and away from walls. Toxic chemicals (cleaners, sanitizers, pesticides) are stored on the same shelf or in the same storage area as food supplies. Refrigerators, freezers, and dry storage areas are not equipped with accurate thermometers. Even if accurate thermometers are present, they are seldom monitored by an employee or a manager. All of these violations can and must be avoided if inventory is to be adequately protected.

Frozen storage areas are similar to refrigerated areas except the temperature maximum is 0°F (-18°C). Storage freezers require visible thermometers which should be checked four times each day. Unsafe temperatures or faulty thermometers are to be reported to the food production supervisor immediately. Chapter 4 mentioned that most food service operations do not have commercial freezing equipment. Instead most freezers in food service operations are designed to *keep* already frozen foods frozen. Storage freezers do not freeze foods rapidly but only relatively slowly. It is important to guard against freezer burn (dehydration) or quality deterioration during freezer storage. Careful wrapping of food products is a deterrent to dehydration and quality loss. The food production supervisor should personally inspect each storage area on a daily basis to be sure the operation's food and beverage assets are being protected and sanitation standards are being maintained.

Recommendations for properly thawing frozen foods were thoroughly discussed in Chapter 4. Basically, thawing is safer and more efficient if accomplished in a refrigerator because (a) food thaws under carefully controlled conditions and (b) the refrigerator's power demand is reduced.

Storing and Change

Management's role at the storing control point is twofold: (1) establish the standards and procedures to be followed, and (2) periodically perform a follow-up check to be certain that the standards are being upheld. It is difficult for some employees to break or change old habits which may be counterproductive. However, if they are expected to care about and uphold standards, it must be apparent to them that management cares about the standards enough to enforce them.

A change in storing procedures is necessary when any of the other three control points which precede it are altered. For example, storage area requirements may change drastically when the operation changes from an all-scratch preparation kitchen to the use of convenience foods. More refrigerated and frozen storage areas may be necessary, particularly in an older establishment where refrigerated and frozen storage space may already be inadequate. Product quality and costs are negatively affected if operational decisions are made without considering the resources of the storing control point.

Storing and Success

Success in storing means protecting assets while reducing spoilage losses, contamination, pilferage, and theft. The FIFO system helps achieve these objectives. Competent storage area personnel further enhance the success of the storing control point. Standards established by management should be designed to control costs, preserve quality, and maintain safe sanitation levels.

Control of the storage areas is possible if time and effort is directed toward success. Management must understand and impress upon employees that inventory is another form of money. A case of 50 steaks which cost $4 each represents $200 in total costs to the business. However, if they are sold for $10 each, the steaks will bring in $500 in revenue. No one would be careless about $500 in cash. In the same way, food and nonfood products must not be treated carelessly. Management's program for improving the storing function should emphasize that, at this control point, the success of the operation is on the line. The probability of the operation's success is significantly increased when its storing function is under control.

The Issuing Control Point

Issuing is critical from a cost control standpoint because the food products change departments. The objective of issuing is to ensure proper authorization for the transfer of food products to the production department(s) of the operation. The issuing function should be designed to guarantee that only authorized personnel order and receive products from the facility's storage areas. A properly designed issuing system also aids in the calculation of the daily food cost.

In small operations, formal issuing may be eliminated entirely. In such cases, all purchases are regarded as direct purchases. Supplies are charged directly to the department or unit in which they are used. This accounting transfer occurs even though the products are held in a central storage area. The direct purchase system eliminates the need for a formal requisition. Department personnel simply obtain supplies from a central area. Thus, the onus is placed on these individuals to inform the operation's purchasing agent of shortages or stockouts. Although this system is simple and less time-consuming, it does not provide as much control as the formal system described in the sections which follow.

Issuing and Personnel
The person in charge of the storeroom checks to determine that each order has been properly authorized, removes product storage tags, and proceeds to fill the order. The storeroom person then costs out each item ordered and totals the costs. A copy of the completed requisition is sent to the operation's accounting office along with any storage tags removed from the items. This system prevents personnel from helping themselves to whatever they want, whenever they want it.

While putting orders together, the storeroom person should note any items in short supply and direct this information to the operation's buyer so the items can be reordered. Careful inspection of written requests for inventory items and accuracy are important during product issuing. In some establishments, the storeroom person not only assembles the order for a department, but also delivers it to that area. Prearranged issuing times for each department can eliminate confusion and enable the storeroom person to work more efficiently.

Issuing and Equipment

Generally, the same kinds of equipment are used during the receiving and issuing of inventory. Products issued on the basis of weight should be weighed before they are released to the production department. Calculators are useful to determine the dollar amount of each department's order and the total of all issues for the day. Handcarts and dollies are used to transport the products from storage facilities to production areas.

Issuing and Inventory

Requisitions are the backbone of a successful issuing control point. A **requisition** is basically an internal communication and control tool that tells which items are needed and by which department. Written and authorized requisitions are required from a department before any products are released. The requisition forms may be sequentially numbered and/or color-coded by department for control purposes. Putting requisitions in writing provides documentation and, therefore, greater control. A sample food issue requisition sheet is shown in Exhibit 7.8. The need for documentation exists whenever a product is transferred from one area of responsibility to another. In this case, the products are transferred from storage to production. Usually a supply of products sufficient for one day or one meal period is issued to each department.

Issues should be properly costed. This facilitates the calculation of daily food cost and reminds employees to think of inventory as money. Requisitions must be subtracted from perpetual inventory records to maintain accuracy. Daily issues help establish usage rates and reorder points.

When products are issued, the FIFO system must be followed. Proper stock rotation minimizes spoilage, contamination, and loss of product quality. The order in which products are assembled for issuing is the reverse of the order in which they are stored. That is, the least perishable items are taken from storage first and the most perishable products last. This minimizes possible contamination and maintains product temperature control. The food production manager (chef or assistant manager) should be notified if perishable products are nearing the end of their shelf life.

Issuing and Facilities

Storeroom facilities cannot be left unattended if the issuing control system is to remain intact. For maximum security, storeroom facilities should be kept locked with access limited to the storeroom person and the manager. Restricting unauthorized access to storage areas helps to eliminate losses due to thefts and pilferage.

Issuing and Change

It is management's responsibility to establish policies and standards for issuing. Although some operations do not find it necessary to use a formalized issuing system, managers who view their inventory as a form of money realize the importance of carefully controlling the issuing function. It is management's job to follow up on the issuing control point to determine that standards are being maintained.

Issuing and Success

Excellent companies have carefully defined issuing procedures. They effectively use requisition forms for control. Only staff members

Exhibit 7.8 Food Issue Requisition Sheet

Storage Type (check one):   Date: _____

Refrigerated _____

Frozen _____   Work Unit: _____

Dry _____ ✓ _____

Item	Purchase Unit	No. of Units	Unit Price	Total Cost	Employee Initials	
					Approved By	Withdrawn By
1	2	3	4	5	6	7
Tomato Paste	CS-6#10	2½	28.50	71.25	JC	Ken
Green Beans	CS-6#10	1½	22.75	34.13	JC	Ken

Source: Jack D. Ninemeier, Planning and Control for Food and Beverage Operations, *1982, p. 90.*

who are properly authorized can request and receive issues from storage areas. Winning operations do not compromise their standards when the pace of business is faster (e.g., during rushes). Their success is evident in the sanitation, cost, and quality controls they achieve at this and every other control point.

Summary

The food service system concept was further developed in this chapter which focused on receiving, storing, and issuing activities. Each of these control points is affected by the resources under the manager's control. Receiving is an important control point because the ownership of food products is transferred from the supplier to the establishment. Mistakes which are not caught before the invoice is signed become the operation's errors. Only those products which meet the operation's sanitation, quality, and cost standards should be accepted.

The storing control point protects the establishment's inventory from spoilage, contamination, pilferage, and theft. A physical inventory is an actual count of what is on the shelves at a certain point in time. It is used to calculate inventory turnover and the food cost percentage. A perpetual inventory is a continuously adjusted (running) total of what is in inventory. It is used for the control of high-ticket and perishable raw ingredients. All stock should be rotated so the first items in are also the first items out.

Requisition forms are used to control the issuing function. Inventory items can only be issued to employees with properly authorized requisition forms. At this control point, products are changing departments, and documentation for cost control is critical.

References

Blynn, L. C. "Inventory Control." *Lodging*, September 1982. 8(1):75-77.

Bohan, G. T. "Food Receiving." *Lodging*, July 1982. 7(9):53-56.

Cichy, Ronald F. "The Role of the Executive Chef in Inventory Control." *Rocky Mountain Chefs Magazine*, March 1983. 8.

Ellis, Ray C. "How to Control Internal Theft." *Lodging*, November 1980. 6(3):21.

Food and Drug Administration, Public Health Service, U.S. Department of Health, Education, and Welfare. *Food Service Sanitation Manual*. Washington, D.C.: U.S. Government Printing Office, 1976.

Kornblum, K. "New Monitor May Keep Tabs on Perishables." *NRA News*, March 1983. 3(3):8-9.

McKennon, J. E. "How to Control Rising Food Costs, Part III: Daily and Semi-Monthly Food Cost Analysis." *Lodging*, July 1980. 5(10):36-39.

Ninemeier, Jack D. *Planning and Control for Food and Beverage Operations*. East Lansing, Mich.: Educational Institute of the American Hotel & Motel Association, 1982.

Pinkowski, C.G. *"Food Storing."* Lodging, August 1982. 7(10):69-73.

Preston, J. J. "Food Purchasing." *Lodging*, May 1982. 7(8):45-48.

Smith, D. "Food Issuing." *Lodging*, October 1982. 8(2):39-42.

Zaccarelli, Herman. "Receiving Check List." *Cooking for Profit*, 15 May 1983. (388):8.

Strategies for Success at the Aspen Hotel

As their meeting drew to a close, Paul thanked Elisabeth and Walter for taking an active part in developing the checklists for the receiving, storing, and issuing control points. All three of them agreed that the hotel's inventory turnover could be increased, while lowering the food cost percentage and the dollar value of inventory. More important, these goals could be achieved without compromising the customer's perceived value. Paul felt confident that these objectives would be reached if everyone maintained the standards that his management team was now developing.

Checklist for Receiving

Personnel

1. Receiving is done by a member of the management team or an employee selected and trained for the job.

2. The receiver possesses product knowledge, technical skills, and a commitment to the organization.

3. The receiver can judge the quality, quantity, and sanitary condition of products.

4. The receiver is in a good state of health and practices rules of personal hygiene.

5. The receiver understands how to accurately use all required equipment, facilities, and forms.

6. The receiver knows what to do when there is a problem with product deliveries.

7. The receiver is able to read and write.

8. The receiver knows the purchasing specifications for the items ordered.

9. Delivery hours, which do not include mealtime rush periods, are posted on the receiving door. Delivery times are staggered whenever possible.

10. Receivers are trained to perform their duties effectively and efficiently.

Equipment

1. An accurate scale is used during receiving to verify product weights.

2. The net weight of the products is recorded and checked against the supplier's invoice.

3. Thermometers are used during receiving to check the internal temperatures of refrigerated and frozen products.

4. Refrigerated products are 45°F (7°C) or less and frozen products are 0°F (-18°C) or less when delivered.

5. Tools needed to open containers and boxes are present.

6. Marking pens are used to record the date of the delivery and the product's as purchased (AP) price directly on the product's package.

7. Other tools (including rulers, calculators, transport trucks, dollies, and other equipment to move products) are readily available.

Inventory

1. Delivered products are checked against the operation's purchase specifications and purchase order.

2. The supplier's invoice is inspected for accuracy in quality descriptions, quantities, and prices.

3. All products billed on the basis of weight are weighed before signing the invoice.

4. Meat items are weighed separately.

5. All products billed on the basis of count are counted before signing the invoice.

6. Products are moved to storage in the following order:

   a. most perishable products (frozen foods)
   b. moderately perishable products (refrigerated foods)
   c. least perishable products (groceries and staples)

7. A request for a credit memo is used when products are spoiled, when they do not meet the operation's specifications, or when too many have been delivered.

8. Product storage tags are used where applicable.

9. The receiving clerk's daily report is used to verify all deliveries.

Facilities

1. The loading dock and receiving areas are cleaned daily and well-maintained.

2. The supplier's truck is periodically inspected for contamination.

3. Debris or food particles are not allowed to accumulate in receiving areas.

4. The garbage and trash areas are physically separated from the receiving area, if possible.

5. The receiving area is well-lit and equipped with the necessary tools and work tables.

Checklist for Storing

Personnel

1. Storage area personnel are aware of standards to reduce inventory contamination, spoilage, and quality losses.

2. Storage area personnel realize that inventory represents an investment that does not earn interest.

3. A specific person is in charge of accurate and careful inspections of storage areas on a daily basis.

4. Storage area personnel control the quality, sanitary condition, and costs of inventory.

5. Storage area personnel monitor the usage rates of inventory items.

6. Storage area personnel help establish par stocks and reorder points to minimize stockouts and spoilage.

7. Inventory dollar amounts are recorded by storage area personnel and the controller.

8. Storage area personnel are trained to maintain the operation's standards.

Equipment

1. All storage areas have thermometers accurate to $\pm 3°$F.

2. Storage area temperatures are monitored several times each day.

3. Cleaned and sanitized equipment and utensils are handled and stored in ways that prevent recontamination.

4. Cleaned and sanitized equipment and utensils are stored at least six inches (15.24 cm) off the floor and protected from splash and dust.

5. Equipment and utensils are not stored under exposed sewer or water lines.

6. No equipment, utensils, or single-service items are stored in toilet rooms or vestibules.

Inventory

1. Food stored in dry storage is on shelves at least six inches (15.24 cm) off the floor and two inches (5.08 cm) away from walls.

2. Storage temperatures and relative humidities are maintained as follows:

   a. Dry storage: 50-70°F (10°-21°C); 50-60% relative humidity
   b. Refrigerated storage: 45°F (7°C) or less; 80-90% relative humidity
   c. Freezer storage: 0°F (-18°C) or less

3. New inventory is placed behind old inventory as part of the FIFO system.

4. Bulky and heavy items are located on lower shelves.

5. High-use items are placed near the entrance.

6. A specific place is assigned for each type of item in inventory.

7. Storage time-temperature combinations are closely monitored.

8. Refrigerated leftovers are dated with the day they are first stored.

9. Perishable and potentially hazardous leftovers are stored under refrigeration in pans no more than four inches (10.16 cm) deep.

10. Inventory items are stored to prevent cross-contamination.

11. Packaged food is not stored in contact with water or undrained ice.

12. Toxic chemicals (cleaners, sanitizers, pesticides) are stored in physically separate, locked areas.

13. All damaged products and those possessing an off-odor or abnormal color are discarded.

14. A record of all spoiled food is maintained. Problem areas are identified and deficiencies are corrected.

15. The A-B-C-D inventory classification scheme is utilized where applicable.

16. Perpetual and/or physical inventory systems are used to control inventory.

17. Inventory turnover is calculated and monitored.

Facilities

1. The storage areas are clean, orderly, and well-ventilated.

2. Dry storage areas are free from motors, machinery, water and heating pipes, and other undesirable structures.

3. Walls and floors are constructed of easy-to-clean materials.

4. Insect and rodent controls are regularly checked in all storage areas.

5. Key and lock controls are used to maintain security in storage areas.

6. Adequate lighting is provided, and bulbs and tubes are shielded for protection.

7. The door of each refrigerator and freezer is marked with the contents of the unit.

8. Inventory in refrigerated and frozen areas does not overload the unit.

9. Stainless steel shelving on wheels is used in walk-in refrigerators and freezers.

10. A system of regular cleaning and maintenance is instituted.

11. A storage area temperature recording form is used.

Checklist for Issuing

Personnel

1. Products are only issued with a written requisition.

2. The issuer checks to see that the requisition is properly authorized.

3. The issuer costs the items and extends the figures on the requisition.

4. The issuer removes storage tags from products and attaches them to the requisition.

5. The issuer removes products from storage in the following order:

   a. least perishable products (groceries and staples)
   b. moderately perishable products (refrigerated foods)
   c. most perishable products (frozen foods)

6. The issuer has been trained to maintain the operation's standards.

Equipment

1. Products issued on the basis of weight are weighed before release to the production department.

2. Calculators, handcarts, and other tools are used when necessary.

Inventory

1. Requisition forms are sequentially numbered or color-coded to facilitate recordkeeping.

2. Sufficient product quantities are issued to each department to last for one meal period or one day.

3. Proper stock rotation (the FIFO system) is used to minimize contamination, spoilage, and product quality loss.

4. Issues are correctly costed, so that the total value of requisitions can be calculated on a daily basis.

Facilities

1. Storeroom facilities are locked when unattended.

2. Storeroom facilities are only accessible to authorized personnel.

The following case studies are designed to enhance your understanding of the material in this chapter. If you are a Home Study student, use these case studies to stimulate questions about this chapter. If you are a Group or Institutional Study student, you may be asked to discuss these case studies as part of a regular classroom assignment.

CASE STUDY 7.1

Bob Baldwin is responsible for monitoring the purchasing, receiving, storing, and issuing control points of the restaurant in the Aurora Hotel. Bob is presently buying food and nonfood products from 15 different suppliers. He feels that he is getting the best value for his purchasing dollar by shopping around. Salesmen call on Bob every day of the week from 8:00 a.m. to 1:00 p.m.

Bob has not developed specifications for products in writing. He has never had the time to prepare written purchasing standards. Besides, he doesn't believe in the value of standard purchase specifications because conditions change too frequently. If deliveries come while Bob is busy talking to a salesperson, a dishwasher checks in the food and nonfood products.

Usually that same dishwasher is responsible for putting the order in storage. If he doesn't finish by the end of his shift, the other dishwasher who comes in at 3:00 p.m. finishes storing the products. All products are stored in unlocked storage areas because the production personnel seem to run out of products at all times of the day.

Test Your Understanding

1. Are the purchasing, receiving, storing, and issuing activities under control in the Aurora Hotel's restaurant?

2. What sanitation risks are being taken in this food service operation?

3. What are your recommendations to Bob Baldwin?

CASE STUDY 7.2

The health inspector has arrived at the Royal Lodge to inspect the facilities. The lodge's food and beverage manager, Mark Perry, greets the inspector at the door and accompanies her on her inspection rounds. As they enter the walk-in refrigerator, the inspector notices that plastic trash can liners are being used for food storage. Sauces, soups, and prepared salads are stored on shelves in airtight, covered, labeled, and dated containers.

In the same walk-in refrigerator, the metal shelves have been covered with aluminum foil to conceal the rust. The evaporator motor fan is covered with a greasy buildup. The inspector can see no thermometer in the walk-in, and when she asks Mark Perry if he has one in his pocket, he admits that he does not. Large roasts are found stored in uncovered roasting pans. Several washed heads of lettuce are discovered in a cardboard box lined with a trash can liner.

Test Your Understanding

1. What sanitation risks exist in the Royal Lodge's refrigerated walk-in?

2. How can these problems contribute to food contamination and spoilage?

3. What are your recommendations to Mark Perry?

CASE STUDY 7.3

Joe Linguine's Italian Restaurant is known for its traditional northern Italian foods and beverages. This restaurant's offerings have a high perceived value in the minds of customers.

The manager of the restaurant has recently decided to install a pasta bar in the dining room. This self-service concept will offer five pastas (rigatoni, spaghetti, shells, springs, and fettucine), eight sauces (meat, white clam, marinara, mushroom, cacciatore, butter and garlic, sausage, and a sauce of the day), peppers, grated cheeses, and other toppings.

Test Your Understanding

1. What are the sanitation considerations in the operation's receiving control point?

2. What are the sanitation considerations in the operation's storing control point?

3. What are the sanitation considerations in the operation's issuing control point?

CASE STUDY 7.4

The Menage Hotel is a suburban facility with 600 guestrooms. The hotel has two restaurants. One is a breakfast and lunch room; the other is used mainly for the evening meal. Food and beverage business in the hotel has been growing at a steady rate.

The Menage Hotel's food service operations never have enough storage space. When equipment and utensils are cleaned and sanitized, they are stored on the floor in the pot and pan washing area. The pot and pan washer has to towel dry these items to keep excess water from collecting on the floor. Some food inventory items are stored in the receiving area because the dry storage area is always overcrowded.

Test Your Understanding

1. Identify violations of the FDA's Model Ordinance in the Menage Hotel.

2. What can be done to improve the control points at the Menage Hotel?

3. What are your recommendations to management?

CASE STUDY 7.5

The food and beverage manager at the Solstice Restaurant has watched her food cost percentage steadily increase for the last four months. She is purchasing competitively from a limited number of full-line distributors. After talking to other food and beverage managers at local restaurant association meetings, she feels that she is paying a fair price for food products.

Receiving takes place anytime deliveries arrive at the Solstice Restaurant. Sometimes the manager is too busy to check in the order, so the chef or his assistant checks it in. The operation does not have a full-time receiver because the restaurant cannot afford the added labor cost. Storage areas at the Solstice Restaurant are not the responsibility of any one person. They are never locked because they do not have doors to lock. Whenever employees need something from storage, they simply walk into the storeroom and help themselves.

Test Your Understanding

1. What are the quality, sanitation, and cost implications of this operation's control system?

2. What are the likely causes of the recent increases in the food cost percentage at the Solstice Restaurant?

3. What are your recommendations to the food and beverage manager?

EIGHT

The Preparing, Cooking, and Holding Control Points

Strategies for Success at the Aspen Hotel

As General Manager Paul James drove to work, he thought about how he had not actually observed the preparing, cooking, and holding control points at the Aspen Hotel. However, with his extensive food and beverage background, it was easy enough to picture some of the bottlenecks and problems simply by reviewing the menus. Paul was glad that he had started learning the intricacies of the kitchen while in high school. During the intervening 15 years, some of the products and production techniques had changed, but the fundamentals were still the same. Paul had learned from experience that the winning companies concentrate on the fundamentals. They make sure that the fundamentals are right, and then more complicated procedures usually fall into place.

Paul found Elisabeth Mueller and Peggy Herbert chatting over coffee in the executive conference room. Paul poured himself a cup of coffee, refilled their cups, and joined the conversation. Elisabeth continued, "I try to spend as much time in the kitchen as possible. Peggy, you're a talented kitchen manager, but don't forget that my help is always available."

The GM thought to himself, "Management people do not have to spend all of their time in the kitchen. When a control system is in place, management can devote its efforts to management functions."

Peggy said, "I see my position as somewhat similar to the conductor of an orchestra. Producing food is like a musical production. Timing is all-important. When you are cooking an order for a table of seven customers, everything should be ready at the same time."

The GM said, "I agree with you, Peggy. As you know, we have been reviewing our food service control points and developing checklists for each operating activity. Today we need to continue the process with the preparing, cooking, and holding control points. I'm interested in your view of these closely related activities, and I would like your suggestions for the checklists."

Peggy Herbert began, "Our old menus required little fresh preparation. We used a lot of canned and frozen items. But today's customer demands quality more than ever and freshness is one of the signs of quality customers are currently seeking. The new menus we're developing will feature more fresh ingredients. Of course, the change to more fresh ingredients will change the way we handle our basic operating activities, especially preparing, cooking, and holding."

"Good observation, Peggy," said the GM. "What are your thoughts, Elisabeth?"

The F&B director replied, "I think the most important activity to be controlled is preparation. We cannot afford to under- or over-prepare. In either case, the hotel and the customer both suffer. Our last GM never gave us forecasts of guestroom occupancy percentages. Maybe he didn't have the information himself. Having that information would help us develop better F&B sales forecasts and production schedules."

Paul interrupted, "You'll have that information if I have to give it to you myself, Elisabeth."

The F&B director continued, "We need some help in the kitchen. You may have noticed that our equipment is in a sad state of repair. Mixing bowls have rust in them and need to be resurfaced or thrown out. The ventilation hoods haven't been cleaned regularly by a contract service, and several hoods are missing filters. We store our utensils in pans because we don't have enough storage shelves. The crew's work knives are stuffed between equipment. There is no towel rack over the hand-washing sinks in the kitchen. I could go on and on. It's so frustrating! The previous GM absolutely refused to budget additional money to our department."

"I know," said Paul, "I've seen the kitchen facilities and reviewed the list of noncompliance items on the sanitarian's inspection report. I have been assured by our corporate office that we will have the financial support necessary to reopen the hotel, including the F&B outlets, on schedule. Now, let's talk about food quality for a moment. What is your definition of quality food, Peggy?"

"Quality food is my most important responsibility," said Peggy. "It is never an accident. Quality food is the result of all personnel cooperating to prepare a product that consistently satisfies the customer."

"Very good," said Paul. "And what about your concept of quality, Elisabeth?"

"Quality requires consistency in all of the control points. It means sticking to high standards from start to finish," said the F&B director. "We can only achieve quality food by identifying the expectations of our customers and then basing our standards on those needs and desires. We've had problems with the quality of products prepared way ahead of time and held hot. It seems that when business is slow, the cooks prepare products well in advance of the demand for them. Then they put these items on the steam table line for later use. Half the time the food is left uncovered, so it rapidly dries out and dies. I try to control food quality by tasting and testing products every day. Peggy also makes this a regular practice throughout the day."

"I consider it my responsibility as the GM to test food and beverage products regularly, too," said Paul. "Once the level of quality is established, we will need standards for preparing, cooking, and holding to consistently produce that level of quality. I need your suggestions for these standards. Please see what you two can come up with, OK?"

The integration of subsystems and management resources continues in this chapter with a discussion of the preparing, cooking, and holding control points. The emphasis on each of these three activities varies with the food service operation's menu. That is, certain menu items may not need to pass through all three control points. For example, when convenience products are used, a minimum of preparation takes place in the kitchen. When food is served raw and chilled, no cooking takes place.

And when menu items are cooked-to-order, they are seldom held for more than a few minutes before service.

The Preparing Control Point

Preparing covers all activities performed on food products before they are cooked, or cooked and held, or served raw. In terms of sanitation, preparation is a critical control point for several reasons. First, when food products are removed from storage and unwrapped, they are unavoidably exposed to many potential sources of contamination. Second, the preparation function takes place at room temperature, in the temperature danger zone (TDZ). Third, since food products are handled by humans, additional contamination can be introduced in the form of coughs, sneezes, and direct contact. Finally, some food products (e.g., salads, fresh fruits and vegetables, unbaked frozen desserts, some dairy products) move directly from preparation to service. Sanitary handling of these products is even more crucial because there is no opportunity to destroy harmful microorganisms. The enforcement of sanitation standards at the preparing control point enhances food safety and, thus, benefits both the operation and its customers.

The preparing function in a food service operation is also crucial to quality control. During preparation, products begin to be converted from their purchased state to the form in which they will be served to the customer. Mistakes made in food preparation may be irreversible. If poorly prepared items are served, they are likely to decrease the customer's satisfaction; if they are thrown out, this waste adds to the operation's food cost.

It is difficult to prescribe hard and fast rules for the preparing control point because there are so many different types of food service businesses, each with different procedures and objectives. Therefore, general principles which are applicable to most operations are presented in the sections which follow.

Preparing and Personnel

The skill levels of preparation personnel vary from operation to operation and from position to position. But regardless of their skills or their rank, the rules of personal cleanliness and proper hygiene practices must be followed by *all* employees involved in food preparation. The section of the FDA's Model Ordinance regarding personal cleanliness has already been presented (see p. 203). The ordinance is also very specific regarding employee clothing and practices. The standards for personnel in all food service establishments should conform to these important guidelines.

Unfortunately, violations of personnel provisions of the ordinance may be seen every day in food service establishments. When food preparation employees work in street clothes, unnecessary contamination is added to food, equipment, and utensils. When employees wear the establishment's uniforms on their way to work, they are also inviting trouble. A better approach is to require employees to change into their uniforms when they arrive for work.

The FDA's Food Service Sanitation Ordinance states:

PERSONNEL

Clothing

General.

(a) The outer clothing of all employees shall be clean.

(b) Employees shall use effective hair restraints to prevent the contamination of food or food-contact surfaces.

Employee Practices

General.

(a) Employees shall consume food only in designated dining areas. An employee dining area shall not be so designated if consuming food there may result in contamination of other food, equipment, utensils, or other items needing protection.

(b) Employees shall not use tobacco in any form while engaged in food preparation or service, nor while in areas used for equipment or utensil washing or for food preparation. Employees shall use tobacco only in designated areas. An employee tobacco-use area shall not be designated for that purpose if the use of tobacco there may result in contamination of food, equipment, utensils, or other items needing protection.

(c) Employees shall handle soiled tableware in a way that minimizes contamination of their hands.

(d) Employees shall maintain a high degree of personal cleanliness and shall conform to good hygienic practices during all working periods in the food service establishment.

Source: Food and Drug Administration, Public Health Service, U.S. Department of Health, Education, and Welfare, Food Service Sanitation Manual, *1976, pp. 34-35.*

Hair restraints include caps, chef's hats, and hair nets. It is important to keep hair out of food not just because it is very distasteful to customers but because it is a source of pathogenic organisms. When preparation personnel work without wearing proper hair restraints, they open the door for food contamination problems.

The consumption of food in food preparation or cooking areas is not allowed. Of course, every cook or chef periodically samples the operation's products, but this tasting must be done in a sanitary manner. It is not acceptable to taste products with a spoon or other utensil and then put that same utensil back into the food. Tasting products with the fingers is also prohibited.

Employees are not permitted to smoke in areas where food preparation, equipment and utensil cleaning, or food serving occurs. Tobacco products and ashes can contaminate food supplies. In addition, saliva passed from smokables to fingers to food results in contamination that is both unnecessary and unacceptable. Soiled tableware (plates, glasses, cups, and flatware) is to be handled carefully.

Besides being clean and properly dressed, it is important that food preparation employees be accurate. Accuracy reduces waste and losses resulting from improper ingredient handling, weighing, and measuring. The accuracy with which ingredients are prepared can also have a significant impact on the quality of the end product. Some operations have an ingredient room adjacent to the storeroom. Personnel in the ingredient room carefully measure and weigh raw ingredients before issuing them to the kitchen. The ingredient room concept reduces waste and helps ensure that the correct quantities are used in recipe preparation.

Mise en place is critical to the success of preparation and cooking. This French term, which means "put in place," suggests that before preparation begins, all ingredients should be assembled in the work area. Organizing in advance reduces errors and speeds up the actual preparation process. In addition, *mise en place* reduces the amount of time that food products are exposed to the TDZ. The preparation steps involved in getting raw materials ready to be cooked and served or directly served include washing, peeling, trimming, dicing, chopping, and cutting.

Some food service establishments still butcher their own meats, using wholesale cuts to prepare retail menu items. Others have decided that in-house meat cutting is no longer justified because it is too expensive. To achieve cost savings, these operations are buying precut and portioned meats. Where in-house meat cutting is still done, it is important that the meats be handled in a sanitary way since these products are potentially hazardous foods. The skill level of preparation personnel, the establishment's menu, and its facilities must be evaluated when deciding whether or not to butcher meats in-house.

Preparing may take place in any department in the kitchen. The salad or pantry department is usually responsible for bulk salad, appetizer, and seafood preparation. In a large hotel, this department may double as a *garde manger*. **Garde manger** is a cold food preparation department of a large kitchen where special dishes such as aspic, chaudfroid, pate, mousse, marinades, sauces, and dressings are prepared.[1] The *garde manger* department is also the source of show or display pieces, canapes, hors d'oeuvres, salads, galantines, and other cold food presentations.

The preparation function is easier to control in larger operations if a **master food production planning worksheet** is used. A sample master

---

[1] The term *garde manger* originally referred to the official in charge of the kitchen in a royal household. It is still used as a position title in some operations, but it now refers to a chef who specializes in the preparation of cold menu items.

Exhibit 8.1   Master Food Production Planning Worksheet

| | | Day Tuesday | | | | **THE EXAMPLE RESTAURANT** | | | Local Weather Forecast Cloudy & Mild | | |
| | | Date April 20, 19 | | | | **Master Food Production Planning Worksheet** | | | Special Considerations Party of 15 — Nine (9) Prime Ribs & 6 Steaks 8:30 p.m | | |

Items	Standard Portion Size	Forecasted Portions Customers	Officers	Total Forecast	Adjusted Forecast	Requisitioning Guide Data Raw Materials Requested	State of Preparation	Remarks	Number of Portions Left Over	Actual Number Served
APPETIZERS										
Shrimp Cocktail	5 ea.	48	X	48	51	12 lbs. of 21-25 count	R.T.C.		—	53
Fruit Cup	5 oz.	18	1	19	20	See Recipe for 20 Portions			—	19
Marinated Herring	2½ oz.	15	1	16	16	2½ lbs.	R.T.E.		—	14
Half Grapefruit	½ ea.	8	—	8	8	4 Grapefruit			—	9
Soup	6 oz.	30	3	33	36	Prepare 2 Gallons			5	32
ENTREES										
Sirloin Steak	14 oz.	28	X	28	29	29 Sirloin Steaks (Butcher)	R.T.E.		—	28
Prime Ribs	9 oz.	61	1	62	64	3 Ribs of Beef	R.T.C.	Use Re-heat if necessary	out at 10:45 p.m.	62
Lobster	1½ lb.	26	X	26	28	28 Lobsters (check stock)				26
Ragout of Lamb	4 oz.	24	2	26	26	12 lbs. lamb fore (¾" pieces)		Recipe No. E.402	1+	25
Half Chicken	½ ea.	34	2	36	38	38 halves (check stock)			—	39
VEGETABLES & SALADS										
Whipped Potatoes	3 oz.	55	1	56	58	13 lbs.	A.P.		2-3	56
Baked Potatoes	1 ea.	112	3	115	120	120 Idahos			out at 11:10 p.m.	120
Asparagus Spears	3 ea.	108	X	108	113	8 No. 2 cans			2	110
Half Tomato	½ ea.	48	4	52	54	27 Tomatoes			2	52
Tossed Salad	2½ oz.	105	3	108	112	See Recipe No. S.302			—	114
Hearts of Lettuce	¼ hd.	63	2	65	67	18 heads			—	69
DESSERTS										
Brownie w/ice cream	1 sq./1½ oz.	21	2	23	26	1 pan brownies			—	24
Fresh Fruits	3 oz.	10	—	10	11	See Recipe No. D.113			—	10
Ice Cream	2½ oz.	35	3	38	40	Check stock			—	43
Apple Pie	1/7 cut	21	—	21	21	3 Pies			out at 10:50 p.m.	21
Devils Food Cake	⅛ cut	8	—	8	8	1 cake			1	7
TOTAL NUMBER OF PERSONS		173	5	178	185					180

Source: Carl Albers, Food and Beverage Cost Planning and Control Procedures, *1976, p. 68.*

food production planning worksheet is presented in Exhibit 8.1. The worksheet provides a format for planning both personnel and product utilization for each meal or special function. First, the worksheet is used to inform production personnel exactly what menu items and quantities are to be produced. It lists each item to be prepared along with the standard portion size. It presents the forecasted portions, adjusted for special events and the weather. Then, the worksheet provides a guide to requisitioning and issuing of raw materials. It also has a place for both the number of portions served and the number of portions left over. Because the worksheet provides an overall plan for food production for a meal or special function, it can be used as a guide to the scheduling of production personnel.

Preparing and Equipment

Preparation equipment, if correctly installed and used, can raise the productivity and efficiency levels of personnel. The FDA's Model Ordinance specifies that equipment must be installed and located to prevent contamination of food-contact surfaces and food. In addition, it is critical that installation allow for easy cleaning of equipment and adjacent surfaces. Equipment, whether fixed or mobile, may not be installed under exposed or unprotected sewer lines or any other potential sources of contamination, such as stairs. This requirement may be extended to include water lines, if condensation is a problem.

The FDA's Food Service Sanitation Ordinance states:

Equipment Installation and Location

General.

Equipment, including ice makers and ice storage equipment, shall not be located under exposed or unprotected sewer lines or water lines, open stairwells, or other sources of contamination. This requirement does not apply to automatic fire protection sprinkler heads that may be required by law.

Table-mounted equipment.

(a) Equipment that is placed on tables or counters, unless portable, shall be sealed to the table or counter or elevated on legs to provide at least a 4-inch clearance between the table or counter and equipment and shall be installed to facilitate the cleaning of the equipment and adjacent areas.

(b) Equipment is portable within the meaning of . . . this ordinance if:

(1) It is small and light enough to be moved easily by one person; and

(2) It has no utility connection, or has a utility connection that disconnects quickly, or has a flexible utility connection line of sufficient length to permit the equipment to be moved for easy cleaning.

Floor-mounted equipment.

(a) Floor-mounted equipment, unless readily movable, shall be:

(1) Sealed to the floor; or

(2) Installed on a raised platform of concrete or other smooth masonry in a way that meets all the requirements for sealing or floor clearance; or

(3) Elevated on legs to provide at least a 6-inch clearance between the floor and equipment, except that vertically mounted floor mixers may be elevated to provide at least a 4-inch clearance

between the floor and equipment if no part of the floor under the mixer is more than 6 inches from cleaning access.

(b) Equipment is easily movable if:

(1) It is mounted on wheels or casters; and

(2) It has no utility connection or has a utility connection that disconnects quickly, or has a flexible utility line of sufficient length to permit the equipment to be moved for easy cleaning.

(c) Unless significant space is provided for easy cleaning between, behind and above each unit of fixed equipment, the space between it and adjoining equipment units and adjacent walls or ceilings shall be not more than 1/32 inch; or if exposed to seepage, the equipment shall be sealed to the adjoining equipment or adjacent walls or ceilings.

Aisles and working spaces.

Aisles and working spaces between units of equipment and walls shall be unobstructed and of sufficient width to permit employees to perform their duties readily without contamination of food or food-contact surfaces by clothing or personal contact. All easily movable storage equipment such as pallets, racks, and dollies shall be positioned to provide accessibility to working areas.

Source: FDA, pp. 39-41.

The equipment used in food preparation may be either mobile or fixed. **Mobile equipment** which is on wheels or casters is easier to clean and sanitize. Equipment placed on wheels can be moved to clean behind, under, and beside it. Utility connections should be flexible utility lines or should be fitted with quick-disconnects. Mobile equipment costs more and may require increased maintenance since wheels and casters are moving parts. Furthermore, even with wheels or casters, it would be difficult to move some larger pieces of equipment such as a 1500 lb. (681 kg) oven or refrigerator. Therefore, such equipment must be installed so that sufficient space is left for easy cleaning or should be sealed to the floor or wall.

The FDA's Food Service Sanitation Ordinance states:

Sealed means free of cracks or other openings that permit the entry or passage of moisture.

Source: FDA, p. 22.

Exhibit 8.2   Floor- and Pedestal-Mounted Equipment Installations

To be sealed around
entire perimeter

Seal pedestal
to floor

Floor-Mounted Equipment Installation—Side View

Pedestal–Mounted Kettle

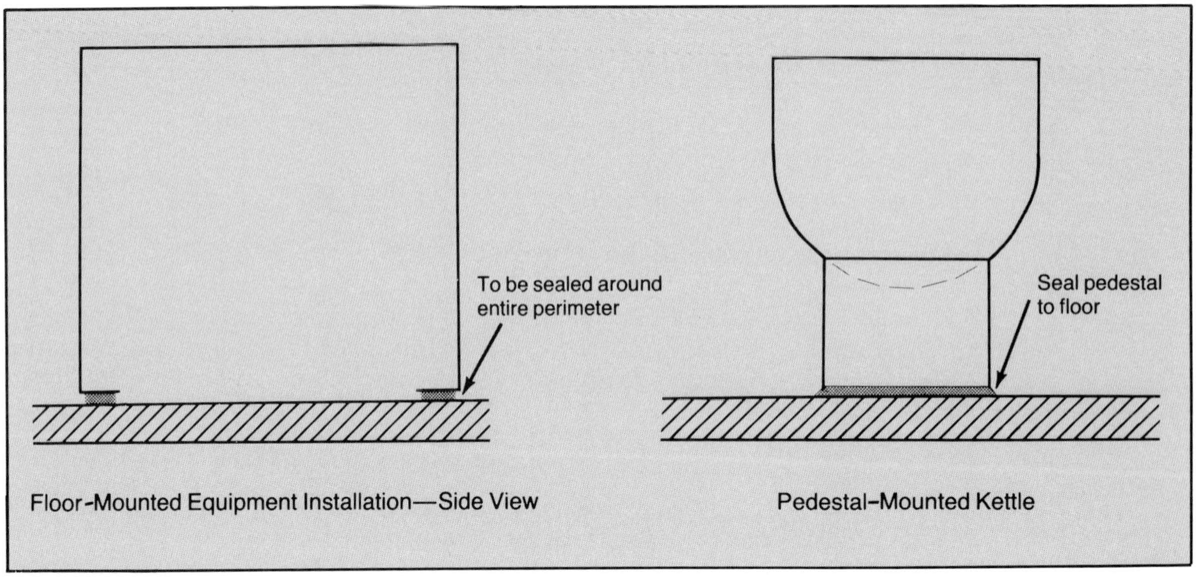

Source: National Sanitation Foundation, Sanitation Aspects of Food Service Facility Plan Preparation and Review, *1978, p. 73.*

Fixed equipment that is not provided with legs or casters is mounted and sealed to the floor. The installation around the base of the equipment must be sealed as illustrated in Exhibit 8.2. The platform on which the equipment rests must be constructed of concrete or smooth masonry material.

If the **floor-mounted equipment** has legs, the general requirement is a minimum clearance of six inches (15.24 cm) between the bottom of the equipment and the floor. If sufficient space is not provided for easy cleaning behind and between fixed equipment, a space of no more than 1/32 inch (0.79 mm) is permitted between fixed equipment and walls or ceilings.

Heavy equipment may be installed on a masonry base. This eliminates the necessity for cleaning below the equipment. Dirt and debris may collect in the space between the bottom of the equipment and the masonry. For that reason, the equipment must be installed as illustrated in Exhibit 8.3. All openings to hollow spaces beneath the equipment and between the masonry base and equipment must be sealed to prevent the entrance of insects or rodents. Once heavy equipment is sealed to a masonry base, it is extremely expensive to remove, so installations should be carefully considered in advance.

Some equipment is **cantilevered**—that is, wall-mounted with a horizontal support. For example, some models of steam-jacketed kettles are cantilevered. It is recommended that tilting steam-jacketed kettles be installed so that debris and liquid waste do not collect between the equipment and the wall or under the equipment. A proper installation of cantilevered equipment is illustrated in Exhibit 8.4.

Exhibit 8.3 Solid Masonry Base Installation — Side View

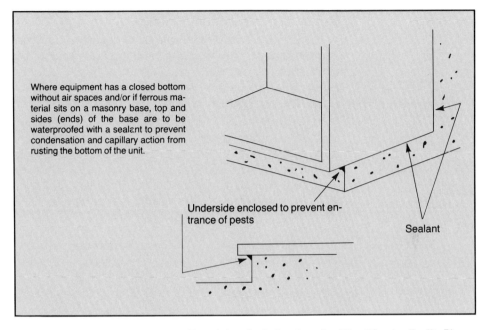

Where equipment has a closed bottom without air spaces and/or if ferrous material sits on a masonry base, top and sides (ends) of the base are to be waterproofed with a sealant to prevent condensation and capillary action from rusting the bottom of the unit.

Underside enclosed to prevent entrance of pests

Sealant

Adapted from National Sanitation Foundation, Sanitation Aspects of Food Service Facility Plan Preparation and Review, *1978, p. 74.*

Exhibit 8.4 Installation of Cantilevered Equipment

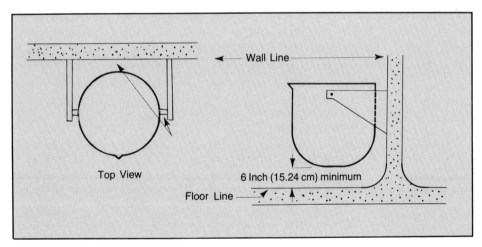

Top View

Wall Line

6 Inch (15.24 cm) minimum

Floor Line

Adapted from National Sanitation Foundation, Sanitation Aspects of Food Service Facility Plan Preparation and Review, *1978, p. 75.*

Table-mounted equipment fitted with legs must have a minimum clearance of four inches (10.16 cm) between the bottom of the equipment and the table. **Portable equipment** placed on a counter top must be easily movable by one person and must possess a quick-disconnect or flexible utility line. **Counter equipment** that is not portable and does not have legs must be sealed to the counter around the entire base.

All aisles and working spaces between equipment and walls must be unobstructed. They should be large enough to permit employees to perform their duties without contaminating food or food-contact surfaces. Equipment may be a source of contamination for food so, in all installations, the prevention of potential contamination is a high priority.

Equipment needed for preparation is based on the menu. If a menu change is anticipated, additional preparation or cooking equipment may have to be purchased. If a specialized piece of equipment is needed to prepare one new menu item, the cost of adding the equipment must be weighed against the profits it will generate. First, the gross profit projected for a new menu item can be calculated as follows:

$$\begin{matrix} \text{Gross Profit} \\ \text{(Per Month)} \\ \text{from New} \\ \text{Menu Item} \end{matrix} = \begin{matrix} \text{Monthly Revenues} \\ \text{from} \\ \text{New Menu Item} \end{matrix} - \begin{matrix} \text{Monthly Food and} \\ \text{Labor Costs} \\ \text{Associated with} \\ \text{New Menu Item} \end{matrix}$$

Then, the payback period for the new equipment can be determined with this formula:

$$\text{Payback (in Months)} = \frac{\text{Total Costs of Additional Equipment}}{\text{Gross Profit (Per Month) from New Menu Item}}$$

These two calculations permit management to quickly determine how many months it will take for the specialized equipment to generate enough profits to pay for itself. Some experts have suggested that a payback period of 18-24 months is good, while a 30-month payback period is marginal. Other factors such as operating skills required, monthly utility charges, and maintenance of the establishment's quality standards also must be considered, although some of these are difficult to quantify.

It is a good idea to submit an **equipment schedule** (Exhibit 8.5) and **equipment installation information** (Exhibit 8.6) to health officials prior to the purchase or installation of equipment. A review of these two documents will permit the health authorities to identify potential sanitation hazards. In the long run, this will prevent the operation from making unwise equipment purchases that add to the sanitation risks of running a food service establishment.

Preparing and Inventory

The fundamental question to be answered in relation to the preparing control point is: How much preparation should be done in-house? In other words, will the menu be prepared entirely from scratch, or use some convenience foods, or use all convenience foods? The answers to these questions can be found by evaluating: (1) the needs and desires of the operation's target markets, and (2) the equipment, facilities, and personnel resources of the operation.

Exhibit 8.5 Equipment Schedule

1 Item No.	Quantity	List of Equipment	2 3 4 Description & Model Nos.

Source: National Sanitation Foundation, Sanitation Aspects of Food Service Facility Plan Preparation and Review, *1978, p. 27.*

Footnotes:

[1]Key to Floor Plan.
[2]Indicate Custom Fabricated (C.F.).
[3]Indicate Listings (UL, NSF, AGA), etc.
[4]If narrative description is required, use back of this sheet.

Some food service managers are confused by the scratch versus convenience food decision. Convenience foods might be called "anti-inconvenience" foods because they do not eliminate personnel from the kitchen but they give them more time to plan and evaluate. For example, an executive chef who uses natural convenience food bases can devote more time to management responsibilities. These products are delivered to the facility in a ready-to-cook or ready-to-serve form. They have built-in labor that is added by the processor, manufacturer, or distributor. Consequently, they require less in-house labor to deliver the products to the customer.

Convenience food products offer several advantages. First, they provide a consistency that is often difficult to achieve in products the opera-

Exhibit 8.6 Equipment Installation Information

Item No.	Accessories	Plumbing									Remarks	Electrical								Installation Information
		Water[1]			Waste		Faucets													
		Cold	140° F	180° F	Size	Type	Height	Type	By											

Source: National Sanitation Foundation, Sanitation Aspects of Food Service Facility Plan Preparation and Review, *1978, p. 28.*

Footnote:

[1]If water at other temperatures is required, indicate as a remark and supply information separately.

tion prepares from scratch. The level of quality of a convenience product must be evaluated by management. A convenience product should never be purchased unless its quality is equal to or better than a similar product prepared in-house. Second, because convenience products offer a predetermined yield, they have an easy-to-calculate portion cost. Third, convenience products can reduce waste.

In some cases, convenience food products may reduce handling and storage costs. In other cases, storage costs increase because the products must be stored in a refrigerator or freezer. Therefore, each product must be evaluated individually. Finally, convenience food products facilitate menu expansion. These products can often be used in a variety of applications and menu items with little additional effort. The scratch versus convenience decision must be carefully evaluated before management decides to add or to rule out convenience food products.

Exhibit 8.7   Sample Standard Recipe Form

Standard Recipe No.: 696	**Yield** (No. of Servings): 32
Product Name: Cream of Lettuce Soup	**Portion Size:** 5 oz. (147.87 ml)
Pan Size: Saute Pan/Stock Pot	**Portion Utensil:** Ladle
Temperature: Simmer	**Special Directions:** Follow Chef Kosec's
Cooking Time: 20 minutes	garnish instructions.

Ingredients	Quantity	Method
L. J. Minor Supreme Sauce Mix Warm water	1-14 oz. (396.90 g) package 4 qts. (3.79 l)	1. Blend water and sauce mix. Heat slowly and stir to dissolve lumps. Simmer for 10 minutes and hold hot for the next step.
Butter or margarine Head lettuce, cut in julienne strips, 2 inches long (5.08 cm)	2 Tbsp. (28.35 g) 22 oz. (623.69 g)	2. Melt butter in the saute pan. Add lettuce and saute for 1 minute. Add to step one ingredients.
Half and half or milk, warm Cooked bacon strips	1 qt. (0.95 l) 4 oz. (113.4 g)	3. Add warm milk or half and half to other ingredients. Blend in the bacon strips. Keep hot for service.

Special Equipment Needed: None

Source: Lewis J. Minor and Ronald F. Cichy, Foodservice Systems Management, *1984.*

Food products are changed physically and/or chemically during preparation and cooking. The objective is to enhance the food quality while protecting the safety of the food and controlling waste. The yield of a raw product is influenced by the grade, weight, and quality of the ingredients. Preparing and cooking must be done correctly to provide safe products and maximum yields.

A **standard recipe** is a written procedure for the production of a given quantity of a food item. It lists the exact quantity of each ingredient to be used, the sequential order in which ingredients are put together, cooking times and temperatures, and the equipment necessary to produce the finished product. Using standard recipes is essential to achieving consistency in product quality, sanitation, and cost. Standard recipes permit the operator to precisely determine the cost per portion of finished menu items. A sample standard recipe form is illustrated in Exhibit 8.7.

Standard recipes should not be "cast in concrete." They should be changed if conditions in the environment or resource levels change. Standard recipes merely provide a minimum level of acceptance. They can be used to train preparation personnel. If the production manager or the employees can improve the results by changing the recipes, these changes should be documented by revising the standard recipes so the changes will be known to all who use them. New recipes copied from magazines or supplied by other establishments must be adapted to the needs of the operation, its personnel, and its customers.

Once a standard recipe has been developed for each menu item, the cost per portion or standard recipe cost can be calculated. Knowing the cost per portion is essential if the menu items are to be accurately priced. A **product cost analysis form** is used to calculate the cost per portion. A sample product cost analysis form is shown in Exhibit 8.8. The ingredients and amount used for a menu item can be entered directly from the standard recipe form. Costs are derived from invoices and should be updated whenever there is a significant change in the cost of any raw ingredient. The **standard recipe cost** is calculated by dividing the total product cost by the yield (number of servings).

$$\text{Standard Recipe Cost} \quad = \quad \frac{\text{Total Product Cost}}{\text{Yield}}$$

Preparing and Facilities

Preparation facilities vary in size and layout with the type of operation and its menu. However, every kitchen is divided into a series of work centers in which somewhat related products are produced. In some kitchens, certain work centers are in separate rooms (e.g., salad and dessert department, a la carte preparation). In smaller kitchens, all preparation may take place in one room without any obvious divisions between work areas. Nevertheless, the arrangement of equipment in the room provides a clue to the location of the various work centers.

Preparation facilities should be designed to efficiently move products from the issuing control point to the cooking control point. This avoids both congestion and delay. A minimum of handling and transfers is also desirable from a sanitation standpoint. Adequate equipment, work tables, lighting, and ventilation must be present in the preparation area to enable food preparation employees to work efficiently. It may be possible to concentrate food preparation in fewer areas to raise staff productivity levels.

To determine the layout of the preparation facilities, management must determine how much preparation will be done in each area. For example, suppose management is considering the preparation of fresh fruits and vegetables. Relevant questions might include these: Will all products be prepared in a single area or will preparation take place in a number of areas? Will the products be washed, peeled, chopped, or diced in the areas? Or will the fresh fruits and vegetables simply be cleaned and weighed? Who will be responsible for preparation in the areas?

All of these questions lead to answers regarding the type and extent of fruit and vegetable preparation facilities. The answers to these ques-

Exhibit 8.8 Sample Product Cost Analysis Form

Product Name: Cream of Lettuce Soup

Date Revised: 6/23/00

Standard Recipe No.: 696

Yield: 32 servings (5 qts. 4.73 l)

Ingredient	Unit Price	Amount Used	Ingredient Cost
Supreme Sauce	$2.43/14 oz. (396.90 g)	14 oz. (396.90 g)	$2.43
Water	–	4 qts. (3.79 l)	–
Margarine	.64/lb. (453.6 g)	2 Tbsp. (28.35 g)	.08
Head Lettuce	.45/lb. (453.6 g)	22 oz. (623.69 g)	.68
Half and Half	1.18/qt. (0.95 l)	1 qt. (0.95 l)	1.18
Bacon	1.20/lb (453.6 g)	4 oz. (113.4 g)	.30
Total Product Cost			**$4.67**

$$\text{Standard Recipe Cost} = \frac{\text{Total Product Cost}}{\text{Yield}} = \frac{\$4.67}{32 \text{ portions}} = 14.5\text{¢/serving}$$

Source: Lewis J. Minor and Ronald F. Cichy, Foodservice Systems Management, *1984.*

tions also influence equipment needs in the area. Perhaps in some work centers most of the products can be prepared with time-saving mechanical equipment rather than by hand. With careful planning, essential equipment for an area can be made available while unneeded equipment can be eliminated.

Preparing and Change

Changes in the preparing function occur daily in the food service industry. These changes are due to continually evolving customer demands and modifications in the food processing, manufacturing, and distribution systems. Many of these changes force food service managers to reevaluate their preparing control point.

Preparation activities that used to be essential in every food service business are no longer critical today. For example, in the past every operation cleaned, peeled, and trimmed fresh vegetables in-house. Today, many distributors sell already cleaned and trimmed produce.

Most food service establishments of yesteryear cut their own meat in-house and baked their own breads, cakes, and pastries. More often than not, today's operations buy preportioned meat products. Some are even purchasing fully cooked and ready-to-slice roasts for sandwiches and other menu items. The proliferation of high-quality frozen convenience doughs and bread products has minimized the need for a full-scale in-house bake shop in modern operations.

In the past, most food service establishments prepared their own stock from bones and vegetable products. Today, the simmering stockpot is considered a relic of the past in all but a few establishments. The availability of several high-quality natural food bases eliminates the need for the traditional stockpot. These convenience products reduce waste and spoilage while lowering the sanitation risks of the simmering stockpot.

Preparing and Success

Excellent operations maintain cost, quality, and sanitation standards at the food preparation control point. Managers of successful businesses realize that planning prevents poor performance. These individuals have developed standards for preparation because, at this control point, there are many variables to control.

Preparing requires a coordination of departments, product flow, and personnel flow. The objective is to not overburden or underutilize resources. Use of a master food production planning worksheet helps systematize the preparing control point. Standard recipes help to ensure that menu items will be prepared in a safe and sanitary manner. These written procedures also provide consistency for cost and quality control.

Successful operations use preparation equipment and facilities to maximize the productivity of production personnel. If equipment is designed and located correctly, the probability of success is increased. The winners continually reevaluate their preparation practices and standards. They are not afraid to try new products and procedures which are consistent with the establishment's standards.

The Cooking Control Point

The heat which is added to food during **cooking** can cause a number of physical and chemical changes in the products. The cooking control point should be designed to achieve three objectives: (1) to destroy harmful microorganisms, (2) to increase the digestibility of food, and (3) to alter the form, flavor, color, texture, and appearance of raw ingredients.

Cooking can destroy or inactivate some harmful microorganisms. The rate of inactivation or destruction depends on the temperature, time, cooking method, characteristics of the food product, and the type and quantity of organisms present. Recall that toxins and organisms that form spores are generally heat stable. For example, spores of *Clostridium perfringens* are not destroyed by normal cooking procedures. The toxin of *Staphylococcus aureus* is also stable at normal cooking temperatures.

Cooking is necessary to increase the digestibility of many food products. Proteins, fats, and carbohydrates in cooked foods are frequently easier to digest than the same nutrients in raw products. Unfortunately, cooking can also reduce the nutritional value of food products by destroying some of the vitamins they contain. In general, shorter cooking times help retain more vitamins.

Cooking alters the form, flavor, color, texture, and appearance of food products. These chemical and physical changes increase both the acceptability and palatability of food products. Strict time-temperature controls, combined with standardized production techniques, can enhance food quality and increase customer enjoyment of cooked menu items.

Cooking and Personnel

Many of the personnel considerations discussed under the preparing control point also apply to cooking. Personnel at the cooking control point are responsible for cooked-to-order appetizers, entrees, side dishes, and desserts. The number of people involved in the cooking control point depends on the extent of the menu and the volume of business done by the establishment.

Above all, accuracy is an important component of the cooking control point. Cooks and chefs are expected to follow the operation's standards for production. The master food production planning worksheet outlines what is to be requisitioned and cooked for each meal period. Standard recipes must be followed exactly, including ingredient amounts, cooking times, and cooking temperatures.

In many food service establishments, production and service personnel are frequently at odds with each other. At times it almost seems that these two departments deliberately create roadblocks for each other. The atmosphere of hostility which results is not conducive to achieving the goals of the operation. Management must care enough to take an active role in improving the situation by encouraging production and service personnel to work together and cooperate. Some managers have found that one way to reduce the chronic complaints of the kitchen staff is to have them trade jobs with servers one day each week or each month. In this way, each person begins to appreciate the complexities of the other person's job.

Cooking and Equipment

Equipment in a quantity food production kitchen varies based on the menu. In general, food service equipment can be divided into five categories:

1. Equipment used to add heat to food

2. Equipment used to remove heat from food

3. Equipment used to change the form of food

4. Equipment used to clean and sanitize

5. Miscellaneous equipment

The fourth category will be discussed in Chapter 10, which covers the cleaning and maintenance control point. The other categories will be discussed in this section, even though some of this equipment is used in one or more of the other control points. Food service equipment is an investment that must be regularly cleaned and maintained to prolong its useful life, to reduce repair and energy costs, to elicit proper care by employees, and to protect food products. For these reasons, the descriptions of equipment which follow include requirements for cleaning and sanitizing. However, manufacturers' instructions should be followed if they are available. Also, equipment cleaning procedures are available from several manufacturers of cleaning and sanitizing compounds.

Equipment Used to Add Heat to Food. Several types of equipment are used in a quantity production kitchen to add heat to food products. Included in this group are broilers, fryers, griddles and grills, ovens, ranges, steam-powered equipment, tilting braising pans, food warmers, coffee urns, and toasters.

Broilers heat food by dry heat generated from an intense heat source. In dry heat cooking methods, heat is introduced into foods without the use of moisture. A broiler provides flexibility, speed, and the ability to prepare many types of food products. A variety of broiler models and designs are available. An **overhead fired broiler** cooks food from the top. The rate of cooking is controlled by raising and lowering the grate on which the food is placed. A **salamander** is a small overhead fired broiler used to glaze or finish food products immediately before service. The **ceramic overhead broiler** uses a series of ceramic plates to evenly distribute the heat. An **infrared overhead broiler** offers the advantage of fast temperature recovery and is well-suited to high volume food service operations.

Char-broilers cook food on a grate with the heat source located below the food. Char-broilers may be gas, electric, or charcoal powered. This relatively slow broiler uses energy inefficiently and results in a great deal of product shrinkage. Nevertheless, a popular way of preparing fresh fish and seafood today is to use a char-broiler with mesquite or hardwood as the source of heat.

Conveyorized broilers are used by many fast-food chains (e.g., Burger King) due to their speed. **Rotisserie broilers** are used to cook food at the same time it is being displayed to customers. The food rotates on a shaft or skewer while cooking. The meat used in the popular Greek sandwich called a *gyro* is usually cooked on and then sliced from a rotisserie broiler.

In general, a broiler should be cleaned and sanitized according to the manufacturer's instructions. The grease drip pans should be emptied, washed, and dried on a daily basis. The grates and the drip shield must be washed and dried at least once each day or, better yet, at the end of each shift. The broiler chamber and the exterior of the broiler should be cleaned with hot water and detergent. After rinsing, they can be wiped dry with a clean cloth. Also, it is a good practice to degrease the broiler and clean the burners at least once a month. Finally, representatives of the local public utility should be called in periodically to recalibrate the controls on broilers and all cooking equipment.

Fryers cook food products in hot fat or oil by convection. Convection heat transfer is achieved by placing foods in moving gas or liquid. Fryers are classified as either gas-powered or electric. Most fryers are very energy efficient because their cooking temperature is controlled automatically. **Pressure fryers** decrease smoke and other vapors, while reducing the amount of oil absorbed by the food products. Pressure fryers are extremely energy efficient, fast, and cook more evenly than regular fryers.

The fat or oil selected for fryers should have a long useful life. Most frying oil is chemically modified to extend its useful life. Poor quality fat or oil can become unusable due to rancidity. (Rancidity reactions in fat and oil were discussed in Chapter 4.) Rancidity reactions occur at a faster rate in the presence of heavy metals, salt, moisture, and loose food particles. Therefore, foods to be fried should be as free as possible from moisture and crumbs, and they should never be salted directly over the frying oil. Filtering oil daily removes most of the food particles in the frying medium and, thus, slows the rate of breakdown. It is important to keep the fryer covered when it is not being used.

Regardless of the fryer design, certain recommended cleaning techniques should be followed. First, the outside of the fryer should be wiped every day with a clean, moist cloth. Also, it is usually recommended that fryers be emptied and cleaned at least once each week. If the operation does a great deal of frying, a thorough cleaning may be needed on a daily basis. The following procedure should be used to clean fryers:

1. The frying oil is removed and filtered or discarded, depending on its condition;

2. The frying chamber is filled with water and a cleaning compound, and this solution is boiled for 10-15 minutes;

3. The cleaning solution is drained from the fryer;

4. The inside of the fryer is cleaned with a specially designed fryer brush to remove any remaining food particles;

5. The fryer is rinsed with a vinegar-water solution followed by a clean water rinse;

6. The fryer is dried;

7. The clean fryer is filled either with the filtered frying oil which was in it before or with fresh oil; and

8. The fryer is covered until its next use.

Grease filters used to strain frying oil are single-service articles, and they should never be reused. Filtering equipment should be handled in the same way as food-contact equipment, and should not be stored uncovered.

A **griddle** cooks food on a metal surface that is heated from below by either gas or electricity. The temperature of the surface is automatically controlled by a thermostat. (The term "grill" is frequently used incorrectly to refer to a griddle. A **grill** is actually a broiler.) A **grooved griddle** is used to cook steaks and hamburgers. Its grooves or ribs create a pattern on the surface of food similar to markings from a broiler's grates. Griddles are not very energy efficient because of their large exposed heating surface, and dirty griddles are even less energy efficient than clean ones.

Griddles must be cleaned in two ways to prevent food from accumulating on them. Each time a food item is cooked on a griddle, a metal scraper should be used to scrape excess food off the surface. Then, a more thorough cleaning must be done at least once a day. First, the hot surface of the griddle should be rubbed with a liquid frying compound or unsalted shortening to soften burned-on food particles. This is followed by washing with a solution of detergent in hot water. Once it is clean, the surface of the griddle can be rinsed, dried, and rubbed with the liquid frying compound or shortening to protect the cooking surface.

Other parts of the griddle should be cleaned daily also. A small amount of water can be carefully poured on the back of the griddle's cooking surface to steam off cooked-on food. (Caution must be exercised to avoid burns from the steam generated by the hot griddle.) The drip pans should be removed, emptied, washed, and dried daily. Finally, the exterior of the griddle should be cleaned, rinsed, and dried on a daily basis.

An **oven** is simply a heated chamber used to cook food. A **conventional** or **deck oven** cooks food by a combination of conduction, convection, and radiation. Conduction is the transfer of heat when two items touch, while radiation is the transfer of heat by wave energy. Conventional ovens powered by gas or electricity are often used to bake and roast food products.

Convection ovens use a fan to force hot air into direct contact with the food. As a result, convection ovens cook food much faster at the same temperature. Products prepared in a convection oven exhibit less shrinkage, retain more moisture, and develop better crust color than foods prepared in a conventional oven, provided that both temperature and time are strictly controlled. It is best to follow the manufacturer's time and temperature recommendations.

Microwave ovens convert alternating electric current to electromagnetic energy. The microwaves are absorbed by the food and cause the water molecules in the food to vibrate rapidly. This vibration or friction generates heat which cooks the food. Metal dishes and utensils are generally not used in microwave ovens because they reflect the microwaves. It is a good practice to strictly follow the manufacturer's operating and cleaning instructions for microwave ovens.

All spills should be promptly wiped off and out of ovens. The daily cleaning of a conventional or convection oven can only take place once it cools. Baked-on spills inside the cooled oven chamber are removed with a scraper. The deck is brushed and the chamber is wiped with a cloth containing a detergent-water solution. Water should never be poured directly on the oven deck because water can warp a hot oven deck. Also, caustic (highly alkaline) solutions should not be used on the oven's interior or exterior because they will damage the finish. The burners of an oven should be cleaned monthly. Controls should be calibrated periodically by a public utility representative.

Racks on the inside of a convection oven can be removed, washed, rinsed, and dried. Each month, the fan in a convection oven should be disassembled, cleaned, and reassembled. The inside of a microwave oven usually only requires washing with a detergent-water solution. After the oven chamber is cleaned, the exterior of the oven can be washed with a hot water-detergent solution, rinsed, and dried.

Except for ovens, **ranges** are, without a doubt, the most frequently used type of cooking equipment. Ranges have heated surfaces for cooking food in pots and pans. In general, ranges use energy inefficiently because a large amount of the cooking surface is an exposed heating area. **Open top ranges** cook food directly on open burners. These ranges are well-suited to a la carte menus because the intensity of heat is reached instantly. **Hot top ranges** have a smooth surface made from a large metal plate or a series of concentric rings. The center ring is the hottest location on the surface. Placement of the pots and pans in relation to the center ring determines the amount of heat added to the food. Hot top ranges require more preheating time than open top ranges. Some ranges are designed with a combination of cooking surfaces.

All spills on ranges should be wiped off immediately. On an open top range, grates, burner bowls, and spillover trays should be cleaned daily. Each month, the gas burners must be unclogged with a stiff wire and the range should be degreased. The surface of a hot top range should be cleaned when slightly warm. A blunt scraper is used to remove stubborn food spills. After it has cooled, the top section can be removed, washed, and dried. All soil under rings and plates must be removed. The exterior surfaces of all ranges are to be washed, dried, and wiped with a soft cloth daily.

Steam-powered equipment is being installed in more quantity production kitchens because it is so energy efficient. A **steam-jacketed kettle** consists of a stainless steel kettle within a larger kettle. Steam is introduced into the enclosed space between the two kettles, and this steam cooks the food very rapidly. Steam-jacketed kettles are available with capacities ranging from 1 quart (0.95 l) to 200 gallons (757 l). They are powered by electricity, gas, or pressurized steam from another source.

Compartment steamers cook foods by exposing them directly to the steam. These devices are also rapid and energy efficient. They preserve much of the product's original nutrients, texture, taste, appearance, and color. They cook at a constant temperature, so time must be carefully controlled to avoid overcooking. Compartment steamers may operate with steam pressure ranging from 0 to 15 pounds per square inch (psi).

Steam-jacketed kettles must be cleaned after each use. If food has been crusted on the inside of the kettle, presoaking is necessary. The inside of the kettle is scrubbed using a clean brush with soft bristles that will not scratch the interior. Then the kettle is rinsed, and the drain valve (if any) is removed and cleaned. The draw-off line and the strainer are also cleaned at this point. Finally, the outside of the kettle should be washed with a hot water-detergent solution, rinsed, and wiped dry after each use. In addition, the steam trap should be checked weekly and scale (mineral buildup) must be removed from the boiler at least every six months. In areas with hard water (water with a high mineral content), the boiler may need to be descaled more frequently.

Compartment steamers are basically self-cleaning, except for their interior racks, which may be cleaned in a mechanical dishwasher. The interior of a compartment steamer should be wiped dry after each use. Any food debris should also be removed. In addition, the water line should be drained once each week and the boiler descaled once every six months, or more frequently if hard water conditions exist.

A **tilting braising pan** is a highly versatile unit, well-suited to quantity production kitchens. It can be used to fry, braise, simmer, or reheat a variety of food products. Food cooked in a tilting braising pan exhibits little shrinkage and retains its moisture. A tilting braising pan may be powered by gas or electricity. This equipment is also labor-efficient because, while it cooks a large volume of food, it only requires one person to operate it.

After a cooked food item is removed from the braising pan, a detergent-water solution is used to clean it. The cover of the unit is closed and the food debris is steamed off the pan. A clean brush with nonabrasive bristles is used to remove remaining food particles. Then, the pan is tilted to remove the detergent-water, rinsed, and dried. If grease is present on the outside surfaces, it can be easily removed with an ammonia-water solution. However, this solution should never be poured on hot surfaces because toxic ammonia gas will be released. The tilting mechanism of the braising pan should be lubricated at least once each month.

Food and plate warmers come in a variety of shapes and sizes. A **steam table** holds hot food near the service area. It is not designed to heat food to serving temperatures, but simply to hold food which has already been properly heated. For food safety, an internal product temperature of 140°F (60°C) or higher must be maintained during holding. Once the containers of food are removed and the water drained, the inside and outside of the steam table should be washed, rinsed, and dried. **Plate warmers** are electrically powered heaters for plates. Their interiors and exteriors should be washed, rinsed, and dried daily.

Coffee urns should be cleaned after each brew. Otherwise, the accumulated residue oils and deposits will spoil even the most expensive coffee. After each brew, the leftover coffee should be emptied out of the urn and the spent coffee grounds discarded. The basket which held the grounds should be rinsed with clean cold water only. Soap or detergent should never be added to a coffee urn. The inside of the urn should be rinsed with fresh water and then cleaned with an urn brush and a chemical specifically formulated for cleaning coffee makers. After cleaning, the cleaner should be thoroughly rinsed out by filling the urn with fresh water and emptying it twice. Then one or two gallons of fresh water should be left in the urn until it is used again. (At that time the stale water should be drained out.) The exterior of the urn, including gauges and faucets, should be wiped down daily.

Toasters must be cleaned daily. As with all electric appliances, for safety reasons toasters should be unplugged before they are cleaned. Crumbs on the moving parts and in the collection tray can be removed with a soft brush. (Trays and moving parts may be removable in some models.) The outside of a toaster can be cleaned with a mild detergent-hot water solution, rinsed, and wiped dry.

Equipment Used to Remove Heat from Food. Heat is generally removed from food products by refrigerators and storage freezers, though these cool foods more slowly than commercial freezers do. Refrigerators remove heat and hold products at temperatures of 32°F (0°C) to 45°F (7°C). Freezers operate at temperatures of 0°F (-18°C) and below. Refrigerators and freezers perform several functions in a food service operation. First, they slow down chemical, bacterial, and enzymatic activity. Second, they alter the form and texture of some food products. Finally, they remove moisture from food products. Generally, these functions are desirable but, for some products, the removal of moisture may result in dehydration of refrigerated foods and freezer burn on frozen foods.

Refrigerators for commercial kitchens are available in a variety of designs. **Walk-in refrigerators** are used to store large quantities of food in bulk. **Reach-in refrigerators** are short-term storage units, often placed near cooking stations. They are stocked with food products needed during the meal period. **Roll-in refrigerators** are specifically designed to accommodate carts. **Pass-through refrigerators** have doors on two opposing sides. The movement of food from production to service areas is made easier by placing a pass-through refrigerator between the two areas. **Counter-top refrigeration units** with glass doors may be utilized for food displays. **Refrigerated drawers** are an alternative to reach-in refrigerators located near the cook's station. **Mobile refrigeration units** are used to store food products near the point of service.

Some walk-in refrigerators are fitted with four-inch (10.16 cm) wide plastic strips which form a thermal curtain to conserve energy. The thermal curtain also prevents accidents because workers can easily enter and exit the cooler without having to open and close doors; they simply push the strips aside. Gravity forces the strips back together after they have passed through, so cold air loss is minimized. Unfortunately, the cleaning of these curtains is often neglected.

Refrigerators are relatively easy to clean and maintain if spills are wiped up promptly. A daily cleaning of the exterior of the refrigerator using a hot water-detergent solution is essential. Once it is cleaned, the unit should be rinsed and dried with a clean cloth. The floor of a walk-in refrigerator should be mopped daily.

On a weekly basis, or more frequently if necessary, the contents of each refrigerator should be transferred to another unit so the interior can be cleaned. All shelves should be removed and the inner walls of the compartment must be washed, rinsed, and dried. A mild sanitizing solution should be applied to the interior walls and interior floor to minimize mold and bacterial growth.

If the refrigerator has glass doors or plastic thermal curtains, these can be cleaned with glass cleaner. Refrigerator shelves are to be washed, rinsed, and dried. Once a month, the accumulation of dust and grease on the refrigerator's condensor and evaporator units should be cleaned away. Any water condensation should also be removed before the refrigerator is reassembled. The fans and motors inside and outside the refrigerator should be cleaned and checked every three months. Hinges and latches require oiling every six months. A thermometer is required in each unit and should be checked for accuracy periodically.

Freezers are available in many forms, including walk-in, reach-in, counter-top, and drawer models. To prevent a heavy frost buildup, freezers should be defrosted at least monthly. During defrosting, the frozen products which have been removed from the freezer must not be allowed to thaw. To prevent thawing, the contents of the freezer should be temporarily transferred to another freezer. It is much easier to transfer contents from one freezer to another if the freezer shelves are already on wheels.

Abrasive powdered cleaners and harsh soaps should be avoided when cleaning refrigerators and freezers. Condensers, evaporators, and other machinery should be checked monthly to determine whether maintenance is required. Keeping a running record of the internal temperatures of all refrigerators and freezers allows the manager to spot potential problems and have the needed maintenance performed before a major loss of food inventory occurs.

Ice machines operate by removing heat from water, thereby transforming it from a liquid to a solid. Even though ice is considered food, ice machines may not be used for chilled storage of other food products. It is important to store the scoop on a clean surface or in the ice with the handle extended out of the ice between uses. The scoop should be washed in a hot water-detergent solution, rinsed, and air-dried daily. The exterior of the ice machine should be similarly cleaned on a daily basis. Once a month, all ice should be removed from the ice machine, and the inside of the machine should be washed, rinsed, and dried. Evaporator and condenser motors can be checked and required maintenance performed at that time. The manufacturer's recommendations for cleaning and descaling the interior of the unit should be followed.

Equipment Used to Change the Form of Food. This category includes food mixers, food processors, slicers, and grinders. In general, these items are relatively easy to clean and maintain.

Food mixers are used to incorporate solids into liquids, liquids into solids, liquids into liquids, and gases into liquids and solids. Several attachments are available that grind, grate, whip, beat, knead, slice, emulsify, chop, and mix. Food mixers are highly versatile and are available in both counter-top and floor models. Since mixers are powered by electricity, the UL seal of approval should be sought on all equipment in this category. The capacity of mixers ranges from 5 quarts (4.73 l) to 100 gallons (378.5 l).

Food mixers are easy to clean. The bowl and beater can be cleaned, rinsed, and sanitized in the pot and pan station. The exterior of the mixer can be wiped after each use with a hot water-detergent solution, rinsed, and dried with a soft cloth. Lubricating movable parts once each month keeps the mixer in good working condition. In this case, a food-grade lubricant should be used since it may come into contact with unprotected food.

Food processors, slicers, and grinders can be true labor savers. They save time and reduce the number of monotonous kitchen tasks. A quantity kitchen food processor has heavy-duty construction that makes it highly versatile. This specialized equipment should be cleaned and maintained according to schedules and procedures recommended by the manufacturer. If it is not properly cleaned and maintained, it can spread contamination through countless batches of food, much of which will not be cooked or heated but served as is.

Miscellaneous Food Service Equipment. This section covers other frequently used equipment that does not fall into the other four categories. (Remember, cleaning and sanitizing equipment will be covered in Chapter 10.)

Can openers must be cleaned daily. It is important to scrub the blade to remove accumulations of food. Otherwise, a dull can opener blade can cause metal splinters to drop into food and, thus, lead to physical injuries. The outside of the can opener should also be washed, rinsed, and dried.

Exhaust hoods are designed to remove grease, heat, moisture, and odors from the kitchen. The outside of all hoods should be cleaned and polished weekly. Inside **filters** are to be removed for cleaning at least once a week. If the hoods are located near heavily used fryers, the filters should be cleaned more often. They should be steamed in-house or by a contract service to remove accumulated grease. Any gutters or pans used to catch grease can also be cleaned, rinsed, and dried at that time.

Work tables should be cleaned frequently, at the very least when a change in uses occurs. It is important to remove food and utensils from the surface before cleaning work tables with a hot water and detergent solution. After cleaning, stainless steel work tables can be polished with a stainless steel polish. Drawers under work tables are more useful and less crowded if they are cleaned out once a week.

Cutting boards and blocks, like work tables, must be cleaned after each changed use. Many public health departments do not permit wooden cutting boards because they are difficult to keep clean, particularly as they become more scored with use. These regulatory agencies specify cutting boards made of rubber or plastic materials that meet NSF standards. Rubber or plastic boards are not as easily scored by cutting as wooden boards are.

Cutting boards and blocks should be washed by hand in a hot water-detergent solution. Washing in a mechanical dishmachine may cause the boards to warp. Boards are sanitized by dipping them in a dilute chlorine bleach solution. Then, the boards should be rinsed and allowed to air dry. Because cutting boards are a potential source of cross-contamination in food products, they must be cleaned and sanitized after each use.

Cooking and Inventory

Cooking is combining appropriate weights and measures of ingredients according to a certain procedure and heating at the correct temperature for a designated period of time, as prescribed in a standard recipe. In many cases, raw ingredients bear little resemblance to the product resulting from the cooking process.

The FDA's Model Ordinance spells out food production techniques designed to protect food products. During the cooking process, food is exposed to many sources of contamination. Some products must be manipulated and formed by hand, which heightens the risks. The dangers inherent in the cooking control point can be reduced by following the FDA's Ordinance to the letter.

The FDA's Food Service Sanitation Ordinance states:

Food Preparation

General.

Food shall be prepared with the least possible manual contact, with suitable utensils, and on surfaces that prior to use have been cleaned, rinsed and sanitized to prevent cross-contamination.

Raw fruits and raw vegetables.

Raw fruits and raw vegetables shall be thoroughly washed with potable water before being cooked or served.

Cooking potentially hazardous foods.

Potentially hazardous foods requiring cooking shall be cooked to heat all parts of the food to a temperature of at least 140°F except that:

(a) Poultry, poultry stuffings, stuffed meats and stuffings containing meat shall be cooked to heat all parts of the food to at least 165°F with no interruption of the cooking process.

(b) Pork and any food containing pork shall be cooked to heat all parts of the food to at least 150°F.

(c) Rare roast beef shall be cooked to an internal temperature of at least 130°F, and rare beef steak shall be cooked to a temperature of 130°F unless otherwise ordered by the immediate consumer.

Dry milk and dry milk products.

Reconstituted dry milk and dry milk products may be used in instant desserts and whipped products, or for cooking and baking purposes.

Liquid, frozen, dry eggs and egg products.

Liquid, frozen, dry eggs and egg products shall be used only for cooking and baking purposes.

Reheating.

Potentially hazardous foods that have been cooked and then re-frigerated shall be reheated rapidly to 165°F or higher throughout before being served or before being placed in a hot food storage fa-cility. Steam tables, bainmaries [*sic*] , warmers, and similar hot food holding facilities are prohibited for the rapid reheating of potentially hazardous foods.

Nondairy products.

Nondairy creaming, whitening, or whipping agents may be re-constituted on the premises only when they will be stored in sanitized, covered containers not exceeding one gallon in capacity and cooled to 45°F or below within 4 hours after preparation.

Product thermometers.

Metal stem-type numerically scaled indicating thermometers, accurate to ±2°F, shall be provided and used to assure the attain-ment and maintenance of proper internal cooking, holding, or re-frigeration temperatures of all potentially hazardous foods.

Thawing potentially hazardous foods.

Potentially hazardous foods shall be thawed:

(a) In refrigerated units at a temperature not to exceed 45°F; or

(b) Under potable running water of a temperature of 70°F or below, with sufficient water velocity to agitate and float off loose food particles into the overflow; or

(c) In a microwave oven only when the food will be im-mediately transferred to conventional cooking facilities as part of a continuous cooking process or when the entire, uninterrupted cooking process takes place in the microwave oven; or

(d) As part of the conventional cooking process.

Source: FDA, pp. 28-30.

One of the primary objectives of the FDA's guidelines for food prep-aration is to prevent cross-contamination. Cross-contamination was de-fined in Chapter 3 as the contamination of food or equipment with a con-taminated raw food or nonfood item. Utensils, equipment (e.g., slicers), cutting boards, and tableware have been identified as nonfood sources of cross-contamination in food service establishments.

To prevent cross-contamination, equipment must be cleaned and sanitized before its use is changed. For example, if a food slicer is used to slice raw boneless beef loins to produce eight-ounce New York strip steaks, it must be cleaned and sanitized prior to slicing any item other than raw beef loins. Food-contact surfaces on equipment must also be cleaned and sanitized if an interruption in operations has occurred. For example, suppose a slicer was used to slice boneless prime rib for a banquet. After all of the prime rib was sliced and plated, it was placed in a food warmer and held at 140°F (60°C) or above. Forty minutes later, when the prime rib was served, the banquet servers discovered that they still needed 23 orders of prime rib. At this point, the slicer would have to be cleaned and sanitized before the additional prime rib could be portioned (unless, of course, another slicer were available and already clean).

Potentially hazardous foods which are cooked must be heated to a minimum internal temperature of 140°F (60°C). The exceptions to this rule are poultry and poultry products (165°F [74°C]), pork (150°F [66°C]), and rare roast beef (130°F [54°C]). Despite the long-standing tradition of doing so, poultry should not be cooked with a dressing stuffed into the cavity. Since dressing is a dense, moist, potentially hazardous product, the only way to guarantee that correct internal temperatures will be attained is to bake the dressing and roast the poultry *separately*. Because pork products may be contaminated with *Trichinella spiralis* organisms, higher internal temperatures are required.

Dry milk, dry eggs, and products made from these must be carefully handled after water is added. When rehydrated, these products are as hazardous as fresh milk and eggs. Also, eggs purchased in the frozen form must be properly thawed. Refrigeration is necessary for all of these products.

Reheating products on a steam table is unacceptable. Sufficient internal temperatures are rarely reached when reheating is done in this manner. (Product thermometers and temperature measures are discussed in detail later in this chapter.) Recommendations for thawing potentially hazardous food products must be followed if the amount of contact with the TDZ is to be controlled. Thawing at room temperatures is both unsafe and unacceptable.

Cooking and Facilities

Careful planning of production facilities reduces safety hazards and sanitation risks while creating a more efficient operation overall. Facilities planning begins with the menu, because its content determines what is to be cooked and, therefore, the types of facilities needed. The number of meals to be served also has an impact on facilities design. The allocation of work areas and storage space is directly affected by the food being prepared and cooked.

Distances between work stations are a critical consideration. The goal is to avoid traffic jams of people and products. On the other hand, having large distances between work areas may reduce traffic jams but it does not conserve space. A balance must be reached in order to maximize the return on the operation's investment in facilities. Management must review national, state, and local codes and ordinances before any decisions are made regarding facilities design. These codes cover lighting, ventilation, sanitation, and construction requirements.

Energy usage is another important consideration in facilities design. Well-planned facilities equipped with energy-efficient equipment can save the operation countless dollars in the form of lower energy bills. If a menu change is being contemplated, it is a good time to consider how the facilities and the equipment in those facilities can be made more efficient and cost effective.

Equipment and facilities do not last forever, but cleaning and preventive maintenance will prolong their useful life. Ease of cleaning and maintenance is an important consideration in the selection of wall, floor, and ceiling materials for the food production work centers.

Cooking and Change

Change affects the cooking control point in much the same way that it affects the other basic operating activities. That is, standards for cooking may need to be reevaluated if conditions change. For example, if the operation switches to the use of more convenience food products, this will change production requirements.

Another example of change is seen in some American establishments that are adding ethnic foods to their menus in response to customer demands. This change in menu has an impact on the operation's control points and resources. In terms of purchasing, Italian, Mexican, and Oriental menu items can be prepared using less expensive raw ingredients. However, these raw ingredients and the special spices used in ethnic foods may be decidedly different from any the operation's purchasing personnel are familiar with. Therefore, new guidelines for the purchase of these items may be needed. For example, over 100 varieties of chilies can be used in Mexican cuisine. In addition, these chilies are available in several different market forms (e.g., fresh, frozen, canned, dried, whole, sliced, diced, crushed, and ground). Similarly, some guidelines for preserving these new inventory items may be needed by storeroom personnel. And preparing and cooking techniques for ethnic foods often differ from some of the more traditional menu items. Therefore, production personnel may require special training.

Adding ethnic foods to the menu may affect other resource needs. For example, the operation needs the right equipment and facilities to make these menu items easy to produce. Without the right equipment and facilities, the production of ethnic foods can be time-consuming, tiring, and even dangerous. Steam equipment is often required for the production of ethnic foods. Specialty equipment (e.g., woks, Chinese barbecue ranges, taco ranges, and semiautomatic pasta cookers) may also be required. In light of all these implications, managers are advised to evaluate the effects of a change on the operation's resources and control points *before* the change is implemented.

Cooking and Success

Excellent businesses strive to achieve consistency and reduce risks at the cooking control point. From the standpoint of sanitation and quality control, the cooking function in winning operations conforms to five requirements: (1) all food production personnel are trained to strictly observe rules of personal hygiene and cleanliness; (2) safe and sanitary food handling techniques and procedures are used at all times; (3) by adhering to the recommended cooking and reheating temperatures and procedures, pathogens in cooked food products are destroyed; (4) all food consumed in the raw state is thoroughly washed to remove as much contamination as possible; and (5) food handling before, during, and after preparation is kept to a minimum. The excellent companies realize that, by following these guidelines, they can maintain safe food production standards and satisfy the customer at the same time.

The Holding Control Point

In many establishments, it is not feasible to cook all food products to order during intense rush periods. Out of necessity, some menu items are prepared in advance and held for later service. Thus, for many food service operations, **holding** is a critical control point. Menu items may be held hot or cold prior to service. To maintain product quality and minimize microbiological hazards, the holding time must be kept as short as possible and strict temperature controls must be observed. Holding is also critical for products which are removed from storage but not served; these should be promptly returned to the storage area for later service. However, food products rarely improve in quality during hot or cold holding, so extra portions which were not served should not be held too long. Of course, whenever possible, food should be served immediately after cooking, so it avoids the holding step altogether.

Holding and Personnel

Food production personnel should be aware of the potential for contamination and quality deterioration in menu items which are held for later service. Ideally, products would be prepared, cooked, and served almost simultaneously. However, limited resources (personnel, equipment, and facilities) make it difficult for food service operations to approximate this ideal flow.

Time-temperature control is essential to maintaining sanitary and culinary quality in food products. Food products held hot must be maintained at internal temperatures of 140°F (60°C) or higher. This temperature is not sufficient to cook foods; therefore, foods must be cooked or reheated at a higher temperature immediately before they are placed in hot food holding equipment. Internal temperatures can be frequently checked with the aid of a pocket probe thermometer. Hot food holding speeds up the deterioration of food but, if holding temperatures and moisture levels are carefully monitored, deterioration of food can be kept to a minimum. The **critical temperatures for food service** chart presented in Exhibit 8.9 can be used to train and remind food service personnel of the temperatures required for safe hot and cold food holding. This chart, which was developed by the National Restaurant Association (NRA), includes temperatures which are significant for some of the other control points also.

Exhibit 8.9 Critical Temperatures for Food Service

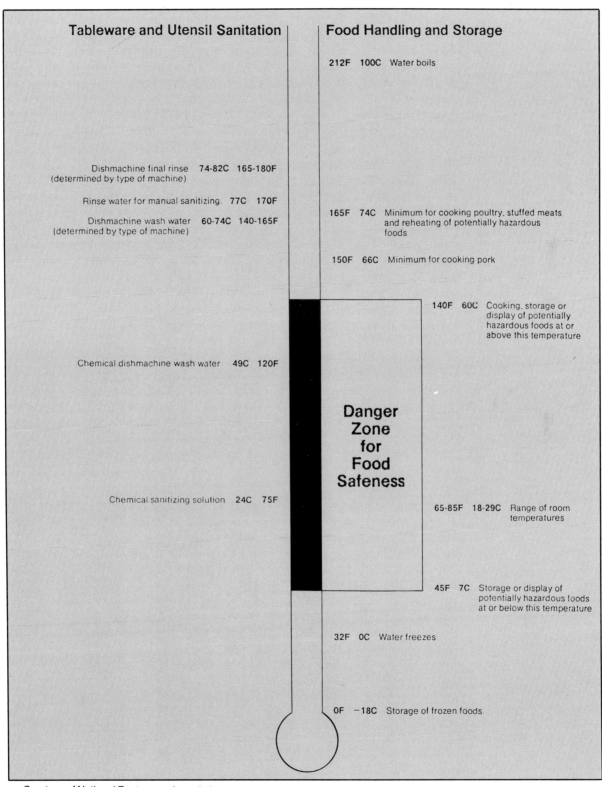

Tableware and Utensil Sanitation

Dishmachine final rinse   74-82C   165-180F
(determined by type of machine)

Rinse water for manual sanitizing.   77C   170F

Dishmachine wash water   60-74C   140-165F
(determined by type of machine)

Chemical dishmachine wash water   49C   120F

Chemical sanitizing solution   24C   75F

Food Handling and Storage

212F   100C   Water boils

165F   74C   Minimum for cooking poultry, stuffed meats
and reheating of potentially hazardous
foods

150F   66C   Minimum for cooking pork

140F   60C   Cooking, storage or
display of potentially
hazardous foods at or
above this temperature

**Danger
Zone
for
Food
Safeness**

65-85F   18-29C   Range of room
temperatures

45F   7C   Storage or display of
potentially hazardous foods
at or below this temperature

32F   0C   Water freezes

0F   −18C   Storage of frozen foods.

Courtesy of National Restaurant Association.

Holding and Equipment

The amount of hot-holding equipment needed by the operation depends on peak demand for the equipment. Generally, production personnel should replenish hot-holding equipment every 15 to 30 minutes so that product quality is not severely impaired. Small batch production methods help to control overproduction and excess holding. Any hot-holding equipment purchased by the operation should be able to withstand the rigors of intense rush periods. If mobile equipment is purchased, the necessary utility connections must be available. Mobile units should be loaded from the bottom up to prevent the carts from becoming top-heavy and possibly tipping.

Hot-holding equipment is designed to facilitate rapid service of hot foods with a minimum of effort. Food products near the service line in the kitchen are usually held hot on a steam table, a pass-through holding unit (located between preparation and service), in under-counter warming drawers, in bains-marie,[2] in heated cabinets, or in infrared warmers. This equipment is generally located in the hot food department and is considered the responsibility of the hot food department. Hot food holding equipment is designed to maintain product temperatures in ready-to-serve food. These food products are often called **wet foods** because they are ready to plate when the order is placed in the kitchen. Other food service equipment (e.g., broilers, griddles, fryers, etc.) is designed to cook **dry foods** to order. Here, the term "dry foods" is used to identify cook-to-order items.[3]

Cold food holding is designed to facilitate rapid pickup with a minimum amount of walking on the part of servers. Refrigerators, freezers, and mobile cold storage cabinets maintain cold food products at proper storage temperatures. It is essential that the temperature of refrigerated foods not exceed 45°F (7°C). Even lower temperatures may be preferred for some food items, such as frozen desserts. Frozen menu items should not exceed 0°F (-18°C). Cold food holding usually occurs in the salad or pantry department. It includes appetizers, salads, cold meats and seafood, and desserts.

Regardless of whether products are held cold or hot, the one piece of equipment that is absolutely necessary is a food thermometer, designed to measure a product's internal temperature rapidly and accurately. The thermometer preferred for monitoring internal temperatures in most products is the dial-face metal probe thermometer. It is accurate to $\pm 2°F$, has a range from 0° to 220°F (-18° to 104°C), and is easy to use correctly. First, the thermometer should be cleaned and sanitized after each use so that it does not become a source of food contamination. Then the clean, sanitized thermometer should be inserted into the geometric center of any food product being held. The thermometer may take time to stabilize, so the reading should only be taken when the indicated temperature is no longer changing. A review of the manufacturer's instructions for using the thermometer may provide other recommendations.

_____

[2] A bain-marie is a container of hot water used for keeping hot foods hot.

[3] Note that in this context, the terms wet and dry do *not* refer to the moisture content of a product.

Holding and Inventory
Product holding is designed to maintain the sanitary and culinary quality of food items until they are needed for service. When a customer orders a product which has not been preportioned, the product must be portioned and served. **Standard portion sizes** are required if consistency is to be maintained. It is management's responsibility to establish and monitor standard portion sizes. If actual portion sizes are smaller than the standard, the customer is being cheated. The perceived value of the establishment's offerings declines in the customer's mind. However, if portion sizes are larger than the standard, the food service establishment is being cheated. Since the operation's cost-per-serving calculations for each menu item are based on servings of a certain size, accurate cost estimates and pricing strategies are impossible without consistent portioning.

Portion size consistency can be maintained in a food service operation if a few common-sense suggestions are followed:

1. Standard recipes must be followed exactly to avoid excessive shrinkage.

2. Scales for measuring weight and other devices for measuring volume are essential. Scoops, spoons, and ladles can be used for salads, vegetables, soups, sauces, and gravies. Individual casseroles can be used for scalloped dishes, vegetables, and meat, poultry, and seafood pot pies.

3. Whenever possible, menu items should be portioned during preparation (e.g., steaks, orders of pasta). For example, solid sandwich filling portions can be presliced, weighed, and stored wrapped under refrigeration.

From the standpoint of food safety, hot foods must not be allowed to cool off between production and service. With the help of hot-holding equipment designed to operate at temperatures in excess of 140°F (60°C), hot food can be held safely.

Each hot food product category has its own holding temperature requirement. Entree and meat dishes are generally held at 140°F (60°C). Sauces, gravies, and thick soups are usually held between 140°F (60°C) and 180°F (82°C). Thin soups and hot beverages should be held in the range of 180° to 190°F (82° to 88°C).

Often part of a batch of hot food products is left in the hot-holding equipment and not served. If these leftovers have spent a considerable length of time in the TDZ (during the course of receiving, issuing, preparing, and cooking), they may be contaminated. Without a doubt, highly perishable leftovers like puddings, hollandaise sauce, and custards should be automatically thrown out. Other leftover foods should be quick-chilled to 45°F (7°C) or less in pans that are no more than four inches (10.16 cm) deep. The size of the pan is important because it has an impact on the rate at which heat is transferred out of the food being chilled.

The **heat transfer** out of (or into) a food product depends on both the nature of the item and its size and shape. As a general rule, heat is transferred more rapidly through liquid products than through solids. The size and shape of the product are important factors, because the heat transfer rate is proportional to the square of the greatest distance the heat must travel. This can be expressed by the following formula:

$$Htr \propto T^2$$

where:

Htr = Heat transfer rate

$\propto$ = is proportional to

T^2 = square of the greatest distance the heat must travel

For example, suppose some soup is leftover in a stockpot. The leftover soup is eight inches (20.32 cm) deep in the pot, so the greatest distance the heat must travel is four inches (10.16 cm). The square of this distance is 16. Now suppose that the greatest distance can be reduced to two inches (5.08 cm) by placing the soup in a shallow storage container. The square of this distance is only 4. By decreasing the square of the greatest distance from 16 to 4, the heat transfer time can be decreased by a factor of approximately four. In other words, the rate of heat transfer will be four times as fast in the container in which the heat only has to travel two inches (5.08 cm). The calculations are as follows:

For the stockpot:	For the shallow container:
$T = 4$	$T = 2$
$Htr \propto T^2$	$Htr \propto T^2$
4^2	2^2
16	4

This heat transfer rate formula illustrates an important point about the cooling of food. Large masses of foods (e.g., products in stockpots) cool very slowly, whereas smaller amounts cool much faster. This principle is illustrated in Exhibit 8.10. Slow cooling negatively affects the texture, quality, nutrient content, and safety of the food products.

It is imperative to cool leftovers to 70°F (21°C) or less within one hour and to 45°F (7°C) within three hours. Placing products in a freezer or in a refrigerator with a fan for 30 minutes will drop the temperature initially. Rapid chilling of large pieces of food (e.g., beef roasts) can be achieved by cutting them into smaller pieces before chilling. Liquid foods are quick-chilled by agitating them in containers exposed to ice or ice water. If the containers of leftovers can be completely enclosed, they can be submerged in ice water or exposed to cold running water for quick-chilling.

Before refrigerating leftovers, they should be covered, labeled, and dated. Storing leftovers in airtight containers may create favorable conditions for the growth of anaerobic microbes, so covers should be loose fitting or left slightly ajar. Leftover food products should never be refrozen.

Holding and Facilities

The FDA's Ordinance provides general requirements for the hot storage of potentially hazardous foods. These foods must be held at internal product temperatures of 140°F (60°C) or above. Thermometers

Exhibit 8.10 An Illustration of the Heat Transfer Rate Formula

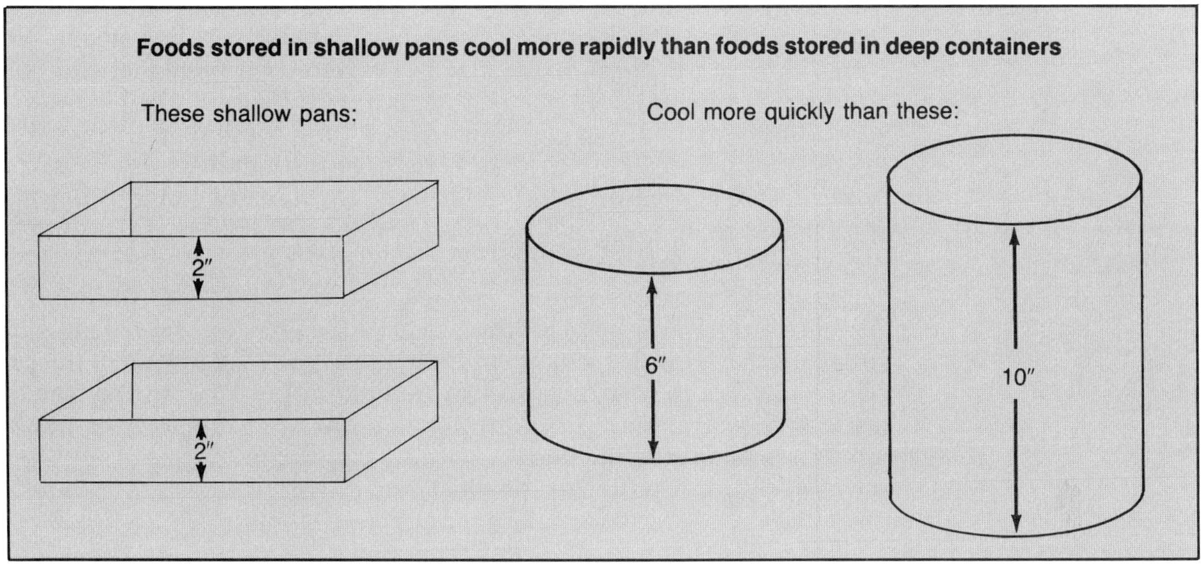

Foods stored in shallow pans cool more rapidly than foods stored in deep containers

These shallow pans: Cool more quickly than these:

2″   2″   6″   10″

may be installed or used manually to monitor internal temperatures during hot food holding.

The FDA's Food Service Sanitation Ordinance states:

Food Storage

Hot Storage.

(a) Enough conveniently located hot food storage facilities shall be provided to assure the maintenance of food at the required temperature during storage. Each hot food facility storing potentially hazardous food shall be provided with a numerically scaled indicating thermometer, accurate to ±3°F, located to measure the air temperature in the coolest part of the facility and located to be easily readable. Recording thermometers, accurate to ±3°F, may be used in lieu of indicating thermometers. Where it is impractical to install thermometers on equipment such as bainmaries, steam tables, steam kettles, heat lamps, cal-rod units, or insulated food transport carriers, a product thermometer must be available and used to check internal food temperature.

(b) The internal temperature of potentially hazardous foods requiring hot storage shall be 140°F or above except during necessary periods of preparation. Potentially hazardous food to be transported shall be held at a temperature of 140°F or above unless maintained in accordance with [the refrigerated storage section] of this ordinance.

Source: FDA, p. 27.

Holding and Change

Product holding requirements change with the menu and often with the meal period and day of the week. For example, a hotel with multiple food service outlets has a variety of hot- and cold-holding needs. In the coffee shop of the hotel, fruits may be prepared for breakfast and held in a refrigerator, while hot breakfast items are probably cooked to order and served immediately. Lunch in the main dining room may involve a combination of menu items held hot, held in refrigerators, and cooked to order. Dinner service in the hotel may require hot holding of sauces, soups, and prime rib, while other entrees are cooked to order. Most likely, salads and desserts are held at refrigerated temperatures.

Other forms of service in the hotel involve still other product holding needs. For a large banquet, all salads, entrees, side dishes, and desserts are held either hot or cold, depending on the nature of the product. Finally, room service products are held hot or cold during transportation to guestrooms. These examples show that managers must constantly reevaluate food product holding requirements based on the day of the week, the menu, and the meal period.

Holding and Success

Product holding, whether cold or hot, is influenced by a variety of factors. Success at this control point can be gauged by the operation's control of five crucial components of holding: containers, location, labeling, temperature, and cooling. Foods at the holding control point must be in containers that are covered. The location in which foods are held should be designed to reduce the risks of product contamination.

Labeling containers with their contents prevents costly mistakes in production. Putting dates on containers facilitates prompt use of leftovers. During holding, product temperatures should be frequently monitored with a probe thermometer. Food must be held outside the TDZ. Cooling of leftover cooked products must be achieved quickly so the safety and quality of the products are maintained.

Summary

Preparing, cooking, and holding standards vary from operation to operation. However, the standards presented in this chapter are generally applicable to any food service establishment. These standards integrate sanitation, quality, and cost controls with the resources under a manager's influence.

Standards for preparation include personnel practices, equipment installation and location, the master food production planning worksheet, and standard recipes. Guidelines for cooking cover personnel, equipment used to add heat, equipment used to remove heat, equipment used to change the form of food, miscellaneous equipment, inventory handling, and facilities design. Topics of significance for the holding control point include time-temperature control, hot- and cold-holding equipment, and heat transfer rates.

Avery, A.C. *A Modern Guide to Foodservice Equipment.* Boston, Mass.: CBI, 1980.

Caprione, C. "13 Tips for Planning an Efficient Kitchen." *NRA News,* April 1983. 3(4):23-26.

Cichy, Ronald F. "Control Waste and Increase Sales." *Michigan Hospitality Magazine,* July/August 1982. 47(4):21.

——. "Nutrient Retention in Foodservice Operations." *The Consultant,* January 1982. 15(1):43-48.

——. "The Role of the Professional Chef in a Foodservice Firm." *The National Culinary Review,* January 1983. 7(1):12-13.

"Cleaning Scheduled by Equipment." *Institutions/Volume Feeding,* 15 October 1974. 75(8):137.

Correll, J. D., and Wells, H. D. *Applied Cooking Technology for the Food Service Operator.* Fenton, Md.: Black Body Corporation, 1979.

DeRoin, N. R., and Strenck, T. H. "The Ethnic Cookbook." *Restaurants and Institutions,* 15 April 1983. 92(8).

Eaton, W. V. "What You Should Know About Hot Food Holding." *Food Service Marketing,* December 1979. 41(12):23.

Food and Drug Administration, Public Health Administration, U.S. Department of Health, Education, and Welfare. *Food Service Sanitation Manual.* Washington, D.C.: U.S. Government Printing Office, 1976.

Standard No. 2 for Food Service Equipment. Ann Arbor, Mich.: National Sanitation Foundation, 1976.

Kooser, R. "Sanitation and Facility Design." *Restaurant Hospitality,* December 1981. 65(12):74.

McKennon, J. E. "How to Control Rising Food Costs. Part IV: Recipes, Sales Records, and Portions." *Lodging,* September 1980. 6(1):62-64.

Minor, Lewis J., and Cichy, Ronald F. *Foodservice Systems Management.* Westport, Conn.: AVI, 1984.

Sanitation Aspects of Food Service Facility Plan Preparation and Review-Reference Guide. Ann Arbor, Mich.: National Sanitation Foundation, 1978.

"Sanitation Checklists for Management." *Cooking for Profit,* June 1978. (330):24-26.

"Sanitation Means More Than Looking Clean." *Institutions/Volume Feeding,* 1 August 1975. 77(3):33.

"Serving Hot Food Hot." *Institutions,* 1 July 1980. 87(1):37-40.

Swift, L. "Kitchen Cleaning Starts With Planning." *Cooking for Profit,* July-August 1980. 335:12.

Strategies for Success at the Aspen Hotel

The GM was again impressed by the commitment to excellence on the part of the F&B director and the kitchen manager. Together they developed three checklists for the preparing, cooking, and holding control points. These checklists would serve as the standards for each of these activities. Then it would be Elisabeth's responsibility in general, and Peggy's in particular, to implement, monitor, and evaluate the success of the standards. Without a commitment from both of these key people, the standards would be nothing more than words on paper; with their commitment, the standards could help the hotel gain and maintain control of its food service operations and exceed its customers' expectations. The GM knew that the saying "No pain, no gain" was true.

Checklist for Preparing

Personnel

1.   Rules of personal hygiene and cleanliness are strictly obeyed.

2.   Outer clothing of all food service employees is clean.

3.   Effective hair restraints are used to prevent contamination of food and food-contact surfaces.

4.   Employees consume food only in designated employee dining areas.

5.   Employees use tobacco only in designated areas.

6.   Employees handle soiled tableware in a way that minimizes contamination of their hands.

7.   Preparation employees are accurate in ingredient weighing and measuring.

8.   Employees gather the necessary ingredients and equipment before beginning preparation.

9.   A master food production planning worksheet is used.

10. Preparation employees are trained to maintain the establishment's standards.

Equipment

1.   Equipment is installed and operated to prevent contamination of food and food-contact surfaces.

2.   Whenever possible, equipment is mobile to facilitate cleaning.

3. Equipment is not installed under potential sources of contamination.

4. All openings to hollow spaces beneath equipment and between equipment are sealed.

5. Aisles and working spaces between equipment and walls are unobstructed.

6. The list of proposed equipment purchases and equipment installation plans are submitted to health department officials before equipment is purchased or installed.

Inventory

1. Products are protected from sanitation risks, quality deterioration, and needless waste.

2. Standard (written) recipes are used to maintain consistency in quality, sanitation, and cost.

3. A product cost analysis form is utilized and updated when market prices change.

4. The scratch versus convenience decision is regularly evaluated.

Facilities

1. Facilities are designed to efficiently and effectively move products from issuing to preparation areas.

2. Adequate equipment, work tables, lighting, and ventilation are available in preparation areas.

3. Essential equipment is added, while unnecessary equipment is removed.

Checklist for Cooking

Personnel

1. Personnel are accurate and precise in their work methods.

2. Standard recipes are used to maintain consistency in quality, sanitation, and costs.

3. Ingredient amounts, cooking times, and cooking temperatures are strictly followed.

4. Sampling of finished products is accomplished in a sanitary way.

5. Production personnel work closely and in cooperation with service personnel.

6. Production personnel are trained to maintain the operation's standards.

Equipment

1. Personnel treat equipment as an investment that must be regularly cleaned and maintained.

2. Manufacturers' instructions are followed for the cleaning, maintenance, and operation of equipment.

3. Supervisors inspect equipment daily to determine that the establishment's standards for cleaning, maintenance, and operation of the equipment are being followed.

4. Employees are trained to clean equipment as soon as they finish using it.

5. A cleaning schedule and instructions for cleaning and maintenance are developed for each piece of equipment and work area.

6. Equipment is selected on the basis of initial costs, availability of energy sources, operating costs, maintenance costs, and skill levels of employees.

Inventory

1. Food is cooked with as little manual contact as possible; the correct utensils are used to handle food.

2. Surfaces are cleaned and sanitized before use to avoid cross-contamination of food products.

3. Potentially hazardous foods are cooked to a minimum internal temperature of 140°F (60°C) *except*

    a. Poultry, poultry stuffings, stuffed meats, and stuffing containing meat are cooked to a minimum of 165°F (74°C).

    b. Pork and any food containing pork is cooked to a minimum of 150°F (66°C).

    c. Rare roast beef is cooked to a minimum of 130°F (54°C). Rare beef steak is always cooked to a temperature of 130°F (54°C), unless otherwise ordered by the customer.

4. Potentially hazardous foods are reheated to 165°F (74°C) internal temperature.

5. Product thermometers are accurate to $\pm 2°F$ and are used to monitor internal product temperatures.

6. Potentially hazardous foods are thawed safely.

Facilities

1. Facility requirements are based on the menu.

2. Distances between work stations are designed for efficient movement of people and products.

3. Cleaning and preventive maintenance are high priorities.

4. Walls, ceilings, floors, and equipment are easy to clean and maintain.

Checklist for Holding

Personnel

1. Personnel are aware of the potential for quality deterioration and sanitation risks during holding.

2. Personnel maintain strict time-temperature controls.

3. Personnel monitor internal temperatures of products and keep them at 140°F (60°C) or above, except for rare roast beef which is held at a minimum of 130°F (54°C).

4. Personnel are aware of the critical temperatures for food handling.

5. Personnel are trained to maintain the operation's standards.

Equipment

1. The quantity of hot-holding equipment available is based on peak demand estimates.

2. Small batch production is used whenever possible.

3. Food holding equipment is used correctly and carefully.

4. A pocket thermometer is available and used to monitor product temperatures.

Inventory

1. Standard portion sizes are used to maintain consistency.

2. Portioning utensils, tools, and scales are utilized to ensure accuracy and prevent contamination.

3. When leftovers remain after the meal period, they are cooled quickly and safely according to the principles of heat transfer, except that leftover egg- and cream-based potentially hazardous foods are thrown out immediately after the meal period.

4. Leftovers are cooled to 70°F (21°C) or less within one hour and to 45°F (7°C) or less within three hours.

5. Leftovers are covered, labeled, and dated before they are refrigerated.

6. Leftovers are not refrozen.

Facilities

1. Holding facilities are designed and operated to maintain correct internal product temperatures.

2. Thermometers are used to monitor temperatures during holding.

The following case studies are designed to enhance your understanding of the material in this chapter. If you are a Home Study student, use these case studies to stimulate questions about this chapter. If you are a Group or Institutional Study student, you may be asked to discuss these case studies as part of a regular classroom assignment.

CASE STUDY 8.1

Molly Andre is the food service manager at the Buffoonery Restaurant. To save on the operation's food cost percentage, Molly has the chef cut steaks in-house. Each Tuesday morning, the chef cuts meat for the week. He uses the trimmings to make beef stroganoff and beef tips with wine. The chef currently buys ten-pound (4.54 kg) top butts for $2.00 per pound (454 g). After a 10% trim loss, he cuts the butts into eight-ounce (226.8 g) club steaks. It takes 30 minutes to cut one trimmed butt into steaks and the chef is presently paid $6.00 per hour.

As another money-saving measure, the chef roasts raw bone-in turkey breasts for sandwiches on the lunch menu. The price of a ten-pound (4.54 kg) bone-in turkey breast is $1.20 per pound (454 g). The bone weighs two pounds (0.91 kg) and the shrinkage in cooking is 25%.

Test Your Understanding

1. What is the raw food cost for each steak cut in-house? How does the cost per steak change if you add in direct labor? Would you consider paying $2.60 per pound for portion-cut club steaks?

2. What is the raw food cost of a four-ounce (113.4 g) serving of cooked turkey breast at the Buffoonery Restaurant? Would you consider paying $2.08 per pound for boneless, oven-roasted, fully-cooked turkey breasts?

3. What are your recommendations to Molly Andre?

CASE STUDY 8.2

Bob Kissel is the executive chef at the Pines Restaurant. Chef Kissel does not believe in standard recipes because they limit his creativity. He wants to be able to constantly improve the products that he prepares for his customers.

Chef Kissel is in charge of training two assistant cooks. When one of his apprentices is watching him prepare a recipe, the chef often leaves out an ingredient or two so that the assistant will not know exactly how to prepare the menu item. Chef Kissel figures that this practice guarantees that he will always keep his job.

Also, the chef does not believe in measuring product temperatures when cooking. He does not feel he needs thermometers, because he was trained that the correct way to judge product doneness is by sight and touch. He portions products (e.g., hamburgers, fillings for sandwiches) by sight. Based on his years of experience, he feels he can judge how big a four-ounce portion of roast beef should be.

The chef has had an extremely busy day with a number of banquet functions. A few minutes before the restaurant is scheduled to close, the food and beverage manager, Mike Bauman, asks the chef if he will prepare dinner for a party of 12 that has just arrived.

The chef says, "No! Tell them to come back tomorrow. I'm leaving in five minutes." Five minutes later, Chef Kissel walks out of the restaurant. Mike Bauman is left with 12 hungry people in the dining room.

Test Your Understanding

1. How could this situation have been avoided?

2. Are the preparing and cooking functions under control at the Pines Restaurant?

3. What are your recommendations to Mike Bauman?

CASE STUDY 8.3

Susan Verbose is the food and beverage manager responsible for the operation of the Rainbow Room in the Suwanee River Hotel. The general manager of the hotel has asked Susan to submit her ideas for the new menu being developed. Susan wants to add mesquite-broiled fresh fish to the menu, but the hotel kitchen does not have a mesquite char-broiler at the present time.

Susan has checked with a local equipment supplier and has learned that the broiler sells for $1,700. Space and construction costs for installation of the broiler are estimated to be $1,300. Susan quickly calculates that the monthly revenues from the new menu item would be $4,200, while the monthly food and labor costs required for the new menu item would be $2,700.

Test Your Understanding

1. What is the estimated gross profit from the new menu item?

2. Based on the figures Susan has obtained plus your answer to the previous question, what would the payback period be (in months)?

3. What other factors must Susan Verbose consider in regard to the proposed new equipment purchase?

CASE STUDY 8.4

Susan Verbose has calculated the payback period (in months) for the new char-broiler. She considers the figures to be acceptable and, with her GM's approval, she has decided to purchase the equipment. When she calls the equipment supplier, he tells her about three options available with mesquite char-broilers. Susan can purchase the broiler with legs, without legs, or with heavy-duty rubber casters. Now Susan has to decide which option to specify.

Test Your Understanding

1. What are the advantages and disadvantages associated with each option?

2. Who should Susan consult before actually buying the char-broiler? Why?

3. What are your recommendations to Susan Verbose?

CASE STUDY 8.5

Robin Anderson is the executive chef and kitchen manager at the Carpe Diem Hotel. This week the hotel is hosting a convention of stamp collectors and has 100% occupancy in guestrooms. Room service breakfast business has been brisk this week because of the convention.

Tonight the hotel is hosting a banquet for 1,500 conventioneers in the outdoor gardens. Production for the banquet has already begun. Appetizer service begins at 6:00 p.m. It is now 4:00 p.m., and all of the appetizers have been cooked and are being held in hot-holding units at 130°F (54°C).

Dinner service is scheduled for 7:30 p.m. Dish-up for the main course will start at 6:30 p.m. The chef plans to plate 1,000 main courses and hold them in the same hot-holding units. Her crew will dish the other 500 entrees once dinner service has begun. Trays of salads and desserts for tonight's banquet are stored here and there throughout the hotel's production facilities, wherever there is room. Since the kitchen does not have enough refrigerated storage facilities, some of the salads and desserts are presently being held on the shelves in the dry storage area.

Test Your Understanding

1. What are the food quality implications of this case?

2. Identify the violations of the FDA's Model Food Service Sanitation Ordinance at the Carpe Diem Hotel.

3. What are your recommendations to Robin Anderson?

NINE

The Serving Control Point

Strategies for Success at the Aspen Hotel

The Aspen Hotel was scheduled to reopen in five weeks. Most of the noncompliance violations either were already corrected or were on their way to being corrected. An inspector from the local health department told General Manager Paul James that they were impressed with the progress being made. The health inspector assured the GM that the license to operate the hotel's food and beverage outlets would be issued in time for the grand opening, provided that the progress continued at the same rate. Paul James was pleased that he had solicited the help of the health department.

New menus were being printed and were to be delivered within the week. Standards had been developed in the purchasing, receiving, storing, issuing, preparing, cooking, and holding control points. The GM was satisfied with the improvement and the commitment to excellence on the part of his department heads. Of course, he expected nothing less from his team of professionals.

Paul knew that the next step was to discuss the serving control point and to develop service standards for the Aspen Hotel. This morning Paul James had invited the F&B director and her two dining room managers, Jack Raymond and Hilda Roben, to participate in a meeting focusing on the Aspen Hotel's service standards.

The GM set the tone for the meeting with his opening remarks. "We have taken action to develop standards for each food service control point. Elisabeth Mueller has been very helpful. Jack and Hilda, we have asked you to join us this morning to assist in our evaluation and standardization of the serving control point. Your input and commitment are critical if we are to successfully deliver the products produced in our kitchens to our customers. I'd like you to tell me your thoughts on quality food and beverage service, Jack."

"I have had over 20 years of experience in dining room service," Jack Raymond said. "My main responsibility, as a dining room manager, is to show care and concern. This has to be communicated to both employees and customers. No hotel will ever be perceived as a top-notch hotel unless its food service is top quality. Over the years I have worked in some second-rate hotels and restaurants. The reason I say that they were second-rate is that they didn't have standards for service."

"I agree," said Hilda Roben. "The biggest failure of the other operations I've seen is in their delivery system from the kitchen. I try to instill a sense of urgency in my dining room employees. When the customer's food is ready, it must be delivered immediately. Otherwise, it stays too long in the kitchen and dies. Hot food should be hot in front of the customer, not just in the kitchen."

"You and I think along the same lines," said Paul James. "Now, share your thoughts with us, Elisabeth."

Elisabeth began, "I can't argue with what Jack and Hilda have just said. Standards and speed are important. But I think we are forgetting a critical component of quality food and beverage service. I believe that the friendliness and courtesy of service personnel make the difference in the minds of customers. Servers have to be genuinely interested in satisfying their customers. Customers who enter our food and beverage outlets should be treated as the most important persons in the server's workday while they are being served. That approach really impresses the customers who choose to dine here."

"Excellent!" exclaimed the GM. "I can sense that all three of you have developed an acute customer awareness. However, I am aware of several problems in the serving control point at this hotel. First of all, the main dining room has a gloomy, heavy atmosphere which I find unappealing. With its dark decor and dim lighting, the dining room is difficult to keep clean because your employees can't see the dirt. We are renovating that room this week to make it brighter. The addition of natural lighting and plants will add a feeling of openness. A brighter, more comfortable atmosphere is sure to be more attractive to our customers, and it will be more appropriate for our new menus.

"By the way, I noticed that the server's sidestands were built with unfinished wood and covered with nonwashable paint; those will be replaced. The sink in each sidestand has been used for an ice bin. Also, glasses arc being stored improperly because of insufficient storage space. These deficiencies will be corrected before we open for business.

"We are also renovating the outdoor service area near the pool. The barbecue area has been fitted with automatic closures on the screen doors. The old carpet in that area collected and held food. It is being replaced. The health department has noted that no sneeze-guards have been used on buffets served outdoors. When food items sit in the sun, time-temperature control is impossible. In the future, we must concentrate on the timing of food served outdoors. The food should be brought out at the last minute. Buffets ought to be set up in shady areas. Also, we should have sufficient equipment available to maintain product temperatures."

The GM continued, "Effective planning is absolutely essential if our special functions and banquets are to be successful. For outdoor functions other than buffets, we might consider serving some prewrapped food. And when we do have buffets, indoors or outdoors, sneeze-guards must be used. Also, I never want to see customers having to use their hands to portion food. Proper portioning utensils must be provided for every item on the buffet tables.

"Room service has its unique problem," said the GM. "Timing is critical to avoid long delays. Room service always takes longer than other forms of service because of the distances traveled. We have to be honest with the customer about delivery times, especially at breakfast. Before we revised the room service menus, we researched how long it takes to transport a room service meal to various parts of the hotel. Based on the results of this simple study, our new room service menus only include items that can survive the trip from the kitchen to any of our guestrooms. We have eliminated items which take too long to prepare like French toast and eggs Benedict; these are three-and four-step items. Instead, our new breakfast menu is limited to egg dishes without sauces, fresh fruits and juices, pancakes, and cold cereals. We are featuring bagels, specialty pastries, and English muffins rather than toast. Our lunch and dinner room service menus are built around sandwiches, cold foods, and simple menu items. The new room service menu is much more realistic. Now we will only offer items that we can prepare and serve based on our personnel, equipment, and facilities resources. If guests want a full menu selection, they always have the option of coming to the main dining room."

Elisabeth Mueller complimented the GM on his extensive knowledge of potential problems with food service in a hotel. "Now, there is one other point that we need to agree on," said the F&B director. "We all know that the server is the last person to see the food before it is delivered to the customer. If the food doesn't meet the hotel's standards, I want the server to refuse to deliver the food to the customer. Then the server can go to the customer and tell him or her that we made a mistake. The customer should also be told that it will be 15 to 20 minutes before the kitchen can redo the order. I think the customer will appreciate the server's concern and honesty." The other three in the room agreed with Elisabeth's idea.

"Let's begin developing our hotel's standards for food and beverage service," said the GM. "Remember, we have to maintain a delicate balance between the expectations of our customers and the resources available to us. Let's keep that in mind as we work out our standards."

The **serving** function is critical from a cost control standpoint because menu items change departments. This activity may enhance or detract from the quality of food products. Many factors affect the quality of service in a food service operation. They include the communication and cooperation between kitchen and dining room personnel, the flow of products, the menu, the design and layout of the kitchen and dining room, and the style of service. Standards of service vary greatly with the type of establishment. Management is responsible for standardizing ordering procedures, abbreviations, serving procedures, sanitation practices, and personnel requirements. As with the other control points, the serving function requires sanitation, quality, and cost controls.

Food service assumes many forms today. Besides the traditional forms of table service found in lodging and food service operations, other types of service are becoming more popular in hospitality establishments. Each type of service requires slightly different standards. For example, special functions and banquets are served differently than cooked-to-order meals. Also, when food products are prepared and transported to a catered event off the premises, product holding becomes a critical control point. Similarly, hotel room service can be both profitable and safe if designed with sanitation considerations in mind. Temporary food service (e.g., outdoor functions) and mobile food service (e.g., pushcarts) also require standards for safe food service.

Traditional Table Service

This section focuses on traditional table service, as found in establishments other than fast-food restaurants. However, some of the standards presented in this section (e.g., standards of personal hygiene) are also applicable to other types of food service establishments.

Serving and Personnel

The term "server" may be used to refer to any person directly involved in the service of food or beverages. The **server** is responsible for serving the customers. Many operations use either **waiters** or **waitresses** exclusively. The image and size of the establishment generally determine whether other positions are included in the service function.

In most cases, the positions of host or maitre d' (sometimes assisted by a captain of service), busperson, and cashier are needed in addition to servers. The **host** or **hostess** greets and seats customers and supervises dining room personnel. In some large or formal dining rooms, a **maitre d'** supervises service and is assisted by a captain. The **busperson** assists the server in the functions of setting up clean tables and clearing soiled tableware. A **cashier** is frequently assigned the responsibility of handling all cash and noncash payments from customers.

The FDA's Food Service Sanitation Ordinance states:

Tableware means multi-use eating and drinking utensils.

Source: Food and Drug Administration, Public Health Service, U.S. Department of Health, Education, and Welfare, Food Service Sanitation Manual, *1976, p. 22.*

Of course, it is not always necessary to have different people assigned to each position. In some establishments, the duties of the positions are combined. For example, the person functioning as the cashier may also perform the duties of the host. Sometimes servers do not have buspersons to set up and clear tables, so they do these tasks themselves.

The number of employees at the serving control point is influenced by several variables. First, the size of the business affects personnel requirements. In general, establishments that are relatively large in size and sales volume require more people in the serving control point. Second, the hours of service have an influence on the number of servers needed. Third, the operation's menu affects personnel requirements, as well as the standards of service. For example, a menu with tableside preparation of salads, entrees, and desserts requires more servers than a menu with more self-service on the part of customers. Fourth, the skill level of servers influences the personnel requirements. All of these variables should be evaluated when determining the number of personnel needed at the serving control point.

Characteristics of Good Servers. Although the skill level and capability of servers vary according to the needs of the operation, several characteristics are desirable in all servers. The server is, first and foremost, a public relations agent for the establishment. The server spends more time with the customer than any other employee of the operation. Therefore, a genuine desire to please customers must be reflected in the server's work.

Second, the personality of the server is important to the serving function. A genial person is more likely to succeed than an argumentative individual. Third, it is critical that servers be dedicated to their work and interested in improving their work performance. When a server does not care, customers can sense this apathy.

Fourth, initiative on the part of servers is important. Most managers prefer to have employees that are self-starters and do not have to be told what to do every moment.

Fifth, servers must be honest to protect the operation's security and cost control systems. Honest servers charge correct prices for all food and beverage products served. They do not waste the establishment's resources because they recognize that these resources are alternative forms of money.

Sixth, servers must be dependable workers. Absenteeism puts a strain on those servers who do show up for work, so a good attendance record is important. Dependable servers come to work on time. Supervisors depend on servers to prepare themselves and their stations for service before service begins, to follow the supervisor's directions and suggestions, to restock stations near the end of the workshift, and to complete closing duties before leaving. Finally, loyalty in servers, as well as other personnel, is critical to the success of the business. Loyalty embraces pride, adherence to the establishment's standards and procedures, and a willingness to cooperate with other personnel.

All of these characteristics contribute to a person's aptitude for serving. Aptitude is simply the capacity to learn. It may be difficult to assess a person's aptitude for serving during an employment interview. A person's ability to learn might be indicated by the highest level of education the person has completed. Generally, applicants with a high school diploma or the equivalent are preferred. However, some managers judge the aptitude of newly hired employees by how well they respond to the demands of the job. These managers should not assume, however, that a new server who is not performing satisfactorily lacks aptitude. In many cases, service employees simply need to be properly trained in order to realize their potential.

Some managers try to escape the responsibility of training servers by hiring only those with prior training and service experience. While in some cases prior training and experience are desirable, the operation that avoids training its new employees is missing an opportunity to communicate its standards of service. The only way to ensure that servers know what is expected of them is to train them.

Besides traits such as confidence, calmness, and alertness, some professional skills are desirable in servers. Professional skills add to the efficiency of the staff and may increase customer satisfaction. These skills, which often improve with experience, include dexterity, speed, and carefulness. A server's dexterity, or ease in using his or her hands, improves with practice. Dexterity is related to manual work methods. In light of the tremendous number and variety of duties a server performs in the course of a single shift, it is clear that increased manual skills and improved work methods are crucial to the operation and its customers alike.

Speed is an essential professional skill in servers. Rapid service is probably more important during breakfast and lunch meal periods because a large percentage of customers may be on their way to work. After the workday is over, most customers eat dinner at a more leisurely pace. Time-saving techniques should be presented during the server's training program. However, these techniques should not compromise the operation's sanitation, quality, or cost standards.

While speed is essential, carefulness in the performance of service duties must never be sacrificed. Professional servers achieve a balance between speed and carefulness, while amateurs try to work rapidly and become careless. Carelessness in service raises the sanitation and safety risks. Carelessness may be evident in any service activity from writing orders to handling equipment to following directions from the supervisor.

Sanitation Standards for Service Employees. Naturally, servers must adhere to the operation's employee sanitation policies. Sanitation standards for serving personnel cover two broad areas: standards of personal hygiene and standards for cleanliness.[1] These standards should be adapted to the individual operation and presented to all production and service personnel during orientation and training.

Standards of personal hygiene cover a number of grooming essentials. Bodily cleanliness is a key component. Personnel should be reminded to bathe or shower daily and to use a deodorant. These practices reduce body odor which is objectionable to other employees and to customers.

Recall that several pathogenic organisms are present on and in the human body. The condition of a person's skin depends on their diet and exercise schedule. Women who choose to wear cosmetics should apply them lightly. Hair should be clean, odorless, and free from dandruff. Regular shampooing and hair care minimize potential personal hygiene problems. The required use of hair restraints by food production and service employees was discussed in Chapter 3. The goal is to keep hair out of food and beverage products.

Frequent handwashing is critical to the success of the operation's personal hygiene program. The area under the fingernails should be clean. The use of excessive nail polish is discouraged because it can chip and find its way into food. The proper care of teeth is necessary to maintain an appealing smile. Careful brushing at least twice a day and regular visits to the dentist help to prevent problems. Incidentally, the appearance and health of servers is an important consideration in the employment decision. Some employers require applicants for service positions

---

[1] Even though these standards are presented under the serving control point, they are generally applicable to all employees in a food service establishment.

to undergo and pass a physical examination by a medical doctor.

A person's posture gives others an indication of the person's attitude and outlook on life. Standing up straight reduces fatigue and permits the server to project a positive image to other people.

Other personal hygiene standards cover employee uniforms. Often a certain style of uniform is specified by management to reflect the image of the business. Also, when all service personnel are wearing matching uniforms, they can be easily identified. The style of uniform worn by service personnel should blend with and complement the decor and ambience of the establishment. It contributes to the general appearance and the customers' first impression. Thus, one style will not fit every company in every location. The uniform for a formal dining room might be quite elaborate, while a bar might only specify a golf shirt or t-shirt with the other components being chosen by the employee. In either case, regular cleaning and maintenance of employee uniforms is important because it keeps them in good condition.

Shoes which have been carefully selected and fitted make it easier for servers to be on their feet for hours at a time. Above all, shoes should be comfortable and should fit with the rest of the uniform. Closed-toe shoes are preferred for safety reasons. Shoes should be cleaned and polished frequently.

The amount of jewelry servers should be allowed to wear is often a point of controversy. Excessive jewelry (bracelets, necklaces, dangling earrings) can increase sanitation and safety risks. In general, only a wristwatch and one ring per hand is recommended while the employee is in uniform.

The concept of an employee line-up meeting immediately before the meal period was already discussed as an opportunity for the manager to review daily specials and important procedures. In addition, this meeting allows the dining room supervisor to conduct an inspection of servers and their uniforms immediately before service begins.

Standards of cleanliness are closely related to standards of personal hygiene. Standards of cleanliness not only reduce sanitation risks but also increase customer satisfaction. Familiarity with the following standards heightens sanitation awareness on the part of servers. Again, it is necessary to modify these standards to fit the individual needs of the operation.

1. Wash your hands before starting work and frequently throughout the meal period. It is important to wash your hands immediately after any of the following activities:

    a. Touching your hair or skin

    b. Sneezing or coughing

    c. Using a handkerchief or tissue

d. Smoking

e. Visiting the restroom

f. Handling soiled or used tableware

2. Avoid the practice of smoking, chewing gum, or eating while in the dining room or kitchen. These activities should be restricted to an area designated by management.

3. Never serve food that has left the plate or dropped to the floor.

4. Replace dropped flatware, napkins, and tableware with clean items.

5. Avoid touching food with your hands. Use recommended utensils, and store the utensils in a sanitary manner when not in use.

6. Minimize hand contact with parts of tableware that come into contact with food or with the customer's mouth. Specifically, the following practices should be strictly adhered to:

    a. Handle glasses and cups by the base or handles. Avoid touching the rims.

    b. Handle flatware by the handles. Avoid touching spoon bowls, knife blades, and fork tines.

    c. Handle all dishes, bowls, and plates carefully. Avoid touching the food or extending the fingers inside the rim of dishes, bowls, and plates.

7. Never carry a service towel or napkin over your shoulder or under your arm.

8. Be certain the bottom of tableware is clean before it is placed on the table. Remove all soiled tableware and return it to the dirty dish station to prevent its reuse before it is cleaned and sanitized.

9. Keep the tops, bottoms, and sides of serving trays clean. This will prevent unnecessary soiling of uniforms, tableware, and tablecloths.

10. Work carefully, keeping standards of cleanliness in mind. Remember that adhering to these standards of cleanliness and personal hygiene can increase customer satisfaction.

If servers violate the standards of personal hygiene or cleanliness with unsanitary practices, disease agents such as bacteria or viruses can be transmitted to the customer. In addition, physical foodborne contaminants (e.g., hair, glass fragments) can result in customer injuries or a distasteful dining experience.

Before Food Is Served. The server is responsible for several duties before the customer arrives. The tables, linens, and chairs in the dining area should be checked for cleanliness. The tabletop setup including flatware, dishes, and cups must be correct. Menus should be inspected daily to determine their condition. Any unacceptable menus should be discarded. If daily specials are offered, the servers should be made aware of the specials, their ingredients, preparation methods, and selling prices. If clip-ons are used to advertise daily specials, they should be on the menus.

Side work is the server's preparation before customers arrive and closing duties after customers leave. Side work is all of the other duties a server performs besides waiting on the customer. (More information about side work will be presented in the next section.)

Once the customer is seated, the server should approach the table promptly with a friendly smile, greeting, and introduction. It is important that the server have a genuine interest in customers. Some servers feel that customers are nothing more than an interruption in their day and treat them accordingly. Most of these customers never complain or tell management that they have been treated shabbily. However, these customers do express their dissatisfaction with the second-rate service. They simply never return to that establishment. The attitude and actions of a server are indications of that person's interest (or lack of interest) in the most important person in the establishment, the customer.

Prompt attention from the server is an essential component of good service. Customers expect their presence to be acknowledged soon after they are seated. If the server is busy at the moment, it is acceptable for the server to stop briefly at the table and explain that he or she will be back as soon as possible. When customers are seated and left waiting with no acknowledgment by the server for 5 minutes, this wasted time may seem more like 20 or 30 minutes to the customers. This is particularly true when the customer is sitting alone.

Courtesy is important when serving customers, both for personal and monetary reasons. Courteous personnel not only make the dining experience more enjoyable for customers, but they also make more money in tips.

Customers often ask servers to provide additional information about the operation, its menu, and its methods of food preparation. Most of the time, customer questions are triggered by the menu. For example, customers may ask how menu items are prepared. Are they fresh or frozen? What brand is used? Where does the operation buy these products, and what is their geographical point of origin? How long will it take the kitchen to prepare this entree? Servers are expected to answer the customers' questions or, if they are not sure, to obtain the answers from the food production department or the manager. It is important that customers be given correct answers to their questions; servers should not simply guess. Truth-in-menu requirements dictate that all information provided to customers be factual.

The server can help the customer decide what to order by suggesting menu items and daily specials. Selling by suggestion can boost customer check totals for the operation and thereby increase tips. Order taking is an information exchange. It is important that all of the details of the order be recorded at the time it is taken. At the very least, the server should record the customer's choices for each course, including the desired doneness of meats, the choice of dressing for salads, and the style of cooking for eggs. It is a good idea to repeat the order back to the customer to verify its accuracy.

The order is then placed with the kitchen using standard ordering procedures and abbreviations. The order may be placed orally, in writing, or by entering it into a computer terminal that simultaneously prints out the order in the kitchen. The kitchen processes orders in the sequence in which they are placed by servers.

In some operations, an **expeditor** acts as a communication link between the kitchen personnel and servers. All orders are given to the expeditor who calls the orders to the various stations in the kitchen, thus minimizing communication problems between the kitchen and the dining room. The expeditor also aids in quality control by checking finished food products before they are delivered to the customer.

Timing of orders is critical to the rapid flow of products from the kitchen to the dining room. If orders are placed at the correct time, they are plated and served almost simultaneously. Thus, product temperatures are maintained and sanitation risks are reduced. Once the order is prepared by production personnel, it must be served promptly to the customer. Otherwise, cooked food held hot under infrared heat lamps may lose some of its quality. In order to deliver cooked menu items to customers as soon as they are ready, some operations use the **flying food show** concept. Using this procedure, the first server to arrive at the pickup point delivers the menu items to the customers. This concept can only be implemented if the order ticket shows which table number and which customer is to receive each order.

When an order is assembled at the pickup point, the server's tray should be carefully loaded to reduce the likelihood of accidents. Time and money are wasted when food is dropped or otherwise rendered unservable; production personnel have to begin all over again. Some operations require servers to participate in part of the production and portioning of orders for their customers. For example, servers may be responsible for portioning beverages or soups, adding dressings to salads, cutting and/or portioning desserts, garnishing plates, and obtaining food accompaniments such as sauces. In these cases, servers must be taught to follow the establishment's sanitation and portioning standards at all times.

Styles of Table Service. As previously mentioned, each establishment has its own unique style of service. Most operations, with the exception of fast-food restaurants, practice one (or a combination) of the following forms of table service. **Plate service** is the service of fully cooked menu items which have been individually portioned, placed on plates in the kitchen, and carried to each customer directly. **Tableside service** is the style used for menu items prepared by the server beside the customer's table in the dining room. Menu items are cooked and/or flambeed in front of the customer. **Family-style service** is the presentation of fully cooked food on large platters or in large bowls. The food is passed around the table and customers serve themselves the amount they desire. **Platter service** also involves the placing of fully cooked food on platters. However, when this style is used, the platters of food are brought to the dining room, presented to the customer for approval, and then served by the server.

From a sanitation standpoint, several points can be made about each service style. In plate service, food products can be brought to proper serving temperatures in the kitchen. The key is to deliver these products to the customer fast enough that product temperatures and quality levels are maintained. The main advantage of the flying food show concept is that cooked food is delivered while it is still very hot.

Tableside service eliminates the transportation of fully cooked menu items from the kitchen to the dining room. However, servers must be certain that products cooked beside the customer's table are allowed to reach adequate internal temperatures. In addition, the ventilation system should be capable of removing heat, odors, and smoke from the dining room when tableside service is used. Finally, the safety of customers and servers must be ensured when flambeing items at tableside.

Family-style service is appropriate for banquets because it facilitates the delivery of menu items to large groups of people. However, product temperatures are often difficult to maintain as the food is passed around the table. Worse still, if a customer coughs or sneezes while passing a bowl or platter of food, the food becomes contaminated. Salad, soup, and dessert bars, three popular variations on family service, require sneeze-guards and shields to protect the products from contamination by customers.

Platter service, like plate service, aids sanitation because food products are cooked in the kitchen and are more likely to reach adequate internal temperatures. However, as with plate service, product temperatures are difficult to maintain as the items are carried from the kitchen to the dining room. The temperature of hot food items continues to drop as the server presents the platter for approval and transfers the food from the platter to the plates. Regardless of whether food is plated in the kitchen or the dining room, sanitary serving techniques (such as those already discussed) must be strictly followed.

After Food Is Served. Once the food is served, the server should check back with the table to see if the customers need any additional items. Prompt and proper removal of dirty dishes, refilling of water glasses, and emptying of ashtrays are essential for good service. When all the customers at a table have finished eating, a properly totaled guest check should be presented. If the server is required to take the customers' money and guest check to the cashier, this should be done promptly. Then, the server should thank the customers and invite them back.

After the customers leave, the table should be cleared and reset with clean tabletop items. This may be done by the server or a busperson. In either case, the person's hands must be washed after handling soiled tableware and before resetting the table with clean items. After the table is reset, the server should check to be sure that the chairs are clean and properly arranged for the next customer.

Occasionally a server may have to handle a customer complaint. The complaint may stem from customer dissatisfaction with the food, beverages, prices, or service. Chapter 5 explained how to handle accusations that the establishment is responsible for foodborne illness. But how should a complaint resulting from unmet customer expectations in other areas be handled?

Handling Customer Complaints. Whenever a customer complains, the complaint should be handled in a professional manner. The objective is to diffuse a potentially explosive situation. First, the server should listen carefully to the complaint. After the customer has finished airing the problem, the server should repeat the facts in summarized form. This helps to assure the customer that the complaint has been heard and understood. Then, regardless of who may seem to be at fault, the server should express sincere regret that the establishment did not meet the customer's expectations.

What happens next depends on the operation's policies regarding customer complaints. Generally, if a customer complains about an unacceptable food item, it should be replaced with an alternative menu item selected by the customer. If the customer does not choose to make an alternate selection, the price of the inferior product should be removed from the customer's check. In many operations, only the manager or dining room supervisor has the authority to waive the charges for an unsatisfactory item.

If a customer is dissatisfied with the entire dining experience, management often "comps" the entire meal. This means that the meal is "complimentary" (free). In addition to comping a meal, some operations have a policy of giving the dissatisfied customer a gift certificate for another meal.

It is a good policy to thank the customer for informing you about his or her dissatisfaction. When it is genuine, this expression of appreciation makes the customer feel better. With the problem resolved and negative feelings smoothed over, the customer may return on another day. It is critical to have written policies on how to handle customer complaints. These policies should be known to all personnel and enforced by management. More important is the identification and elimination of the sources of customer complaints. If servers are receiving complaints on food quality or temperatures, it is important that kitchen personnel be made aware of these causes of customer dissatisfaction so they can upgrade their purchasing specifications or their production methods or both.

Serving and Equipment   Servers work with a variety of equipment in the performance of their duties. Some mention has already been made in the previous section of equipment used in the service of food. This section will serve to reinforce some key points related to equipment and the serving function. Equipment used in the service of food must be cleaned and sanitized. Then, the cleaned and sanitized equipment should be stored and handled in a manner that prevents subsequent contamination.

To guard against contamination, dishes, cups, glasses, and flatware should only be handled in places that will not come into contact with food or with the customer's mouth. Dishes are to be held using four fingers on the bottom and the thumb on the edge, not touching the food. Cups and flatware should only be touched on the handles. Glasses are to be grasped at the base and placed on the table without touching the rim. Ice placed in glasses and bread and rolls placed in bread baskets should only be handled with scoops or tongs designed for these purposes. Sneeze-guards and proper serving utensils are required on self-service food bars located in the dining room.

Usually, each server is assigned to a **station** in the dining room. A station is a group of tables. Servers working in two or more stations frequently share a **sidestand**. Supplies of tableware, ice, condiments, dairy products, and some beverages are stored on the sidestand for easy access. One of the server's responsibilities is to stock the sidestand before a shift, restock it during the shift, and restock it once more at the end of the shift.

Two sanitation considerations are important at the sidestand. First, all equipment and food products must be stored to minimize contamination. No soiled napkins, tableware, or equipment should be placed on the sidestand. These items can contaminate clean food and utensils. Second, temperatures of food products stored on the sidestand must be kept out of the TDZ. This is particularly important for dairy products such as butter and coffee cream and any other potentially hazardous foods. These items must be refrigerated on the sidestand. It is helpful to stock the sidestand with enough cups, saucers, bread and butter plates, serving trays, tray stands, and other necessary items to last through a whole shift. Supplies should be stocked in a neat, orderly, and convenient way before customers arrive. If a busperson is on the payroll, he or she can assist with some of this side work and help to keep the station clean and neat.

Before opening each day, tables and chairs should be dusted or wiped to remove food debris. Floors should be checked for spilled food. If the dining room has windows, the ledges must be dusted at least once each day.

Equipment placed on the table must be kept clean. This is often a part of the server's side work. Sugar dispensers and salt and pepper shakers should be cleaned at least once a day. If glass dispensers or shakers are used, they must be emptied, washed, rinsed, dried, and refilled. The volume of business affects the amount of sugar, salt, and pepper used at each table and, therefore, the frequency of refilling. Some operations are now using disposable dispensers and shakers to reduce the labor costs associated with maintaining these table items.

If syrup or condiments such as catsup, mustard, and steak sauce are available on tables, the exterior of their containers should be cleaned regularly. They can be wiped with a damp cloth to remove fingerprints and any product drips on the outside. However, condiment bottles are not intended to be washed and refilled. Wide-mouth condiment or syrup bottles are not acceptable for customer self-service because they could easily become contaminated.

Napkins are usually folded before service begins. They should be stored so as to prevent soiling before they are used. Paper napkins are single-service articles which must be thrown away when a table is cleared, even if they look clean. Cloth napkins must be properly laundered after each use. They should never be used to wipe flatware, glasses, or cups. Ashtrays must be cleaned before placing them on the table. It is unacceptable to wipe ashtrays out with table linens. Besides being unsanitary, this practice can also stain the napkin or tablecover. For each ashtray, matches should be available.

Serving trays should be double-checked before service. The bottom, top, and sides of a tray must be free from grease, food, and other debris. One item frequently neglected during side work is the flatware. Soiled, spotted eating utensils are both unsightly and unsanitary. If this is an on-going problem, soiled flatware may require soaking before it is washed in the dishmachine. After washing, it should be checked to determine that soil and spots have been removed.

Care should be exercised in handling all equipment used for serving. Waste and breakage can harm the establishment's competitive position. If a server carelessly soils linen, wastes supplies unnecessarily, throws away flatware or dishes, or breaks cups, glasses, and tableware, the operation's costs are increased. If fragments of glass find their way into the customer's food or beverage products, the operation's revenues decrease. The net effect of such carelessness is generally poor bottom-line results.

In some operations, a busperson clears soiled tableware from the table and resets it with clean tableware. In other operations, these duties are handled by the server. In both cases, care must be taken when clean and sanitized tableware is handled after touching soiled tableware. Whenever soiled tableware or wiping cloths are handled, the person must wash his or her hands *before* touching cleaned and sanitized tableware. This minimizes the potential for cross-contamination.

Serving and Inventory

Inventory items prepared by the production department change departments during service. Generally, the food is picked up in the kitchen and served by dining room personnel. The FDA's Model Ordinance specifies requirements for safe food display and service. These guidelines can help the operation control its investment in the inventory resource at the serving control point.

The FDA's Food Service Sanitation Ordinance states:

Food Display and Service

Potentially hazardous food.

Potentially hazardous food shall be kept at an internal temperature of 45°F or below or at an internal temperature of 140°F or above during display and service, except that rare roast beef shall be held for service at a temperature of at least 130°F.

Milk and cream dispensing.

(a) Milk and milk products for drinking purposes shall be provided to the consumer in an unopened, commercially filled package not exceeding 1 pint in capacity, or drawn from a commercially filled container stored in a mechanically refrigerated bulk milk dispenser. Where a bulk dispenser for milk and milk products is not available and portions of less than 1/2 pint are required for mixed drinks, cereal, or dessert service, milk and milk products may be poured from a commercially filled container of not more than 1/2 gallon capacity.

(b) Cream or half and half shall be provided in an individual service container, protected pour-type pitcher, or drawn from a refrigerated dispenser designed for such service.

Nondairy product dispensing.

Nondairy creaming or whitening agents shall be provided in an individual service container, protected pour-type pitcher, or drawn from a refrigerated dispenser designed for such service.

Condiment dispensing.

(a) Condiments, seasonings and dressings for self-service use shall be provided in individual packages, from dispensers, or from containers protected in accordance with . . . this ordinance.

(b) Condiments provided for table or counter service shall be individually portioned, except that catsup and other sauces may be served in the original container or pour-type dispenser. Sugar for consumer use shall be provided in individual packages or in pour-type dispensers.

Ice dispensing.

Ice for consumer use shall be dispensed only by employees with scoops, tongs, or other ice-dispensing utensils or through automatic self-service, ice-dispensing equipment. Ice-dispensing utensils shall be stored on a clean surface or in the ice with the dispensing utensil's handle extended out of the ice. Between uses, ice transfer receptacles shall be stored in a way that protects them from contamination. Ice storage bins shall be drained through an air gap.

Dispensing utensils.

To avoid unnecessary manual contact with food, suitable dispensing utensils shall be used by employees or provided to consumers who serve themselves. Between uses during service, dispensing utensils shall be:

(a) Stored in the food with the dispensing utensil handle extended out of the food; or

(b) Stored clean and dry; or

(c) Stored in running water; or

(d) Stored either in a running water dipper well, or clean and dry in the case of dispensing utensils and malt collars used in preparing frozen desserts.

Re-service.

Once served to a consumer, portions of leftover food shall not be served again except that packaged food, other than potentially hazardous food, that is still packaged and is still in sound condition, may be re-served.

Display equipment.

Food on display shall be protected from consumer contamination by the use of packaging or by the use of easily cleanable counter, serving line or salad bar protector devices, display cases, or by other effective means. Enough hot or cold food facilities shall be available to maintain the required temperature of potentially hazardous food on display.

Re-use of tableware.

Re-use of soiled tableware by self-service consumers returning to the service area for additional food is prohibited. Beverage cups and glasses are exempt from this requirement.

Source: FDA, pp. 30-32.

Sanitation Considerations. Violations of the FDA's requirements for food display and service can be eliminated if the operation's serving function is under control. Potentially hazardous foods should be kept out of the TDZ for obvious reasons. The exception is rare roast beef, which can be held at temperatures of 130°F (54°C) or above. The FDA's Model Ordinance applies not only to foods served from the kitchen but also to items designed for customer self-service from salad bars, buffet tables, sandwich bars, soup displays, and dessert bars.

It is important that hot food be served on heated plates. Similarly, cold food items are better if served on chilled plates. This practice shows the operation's customers that management cares about product quality. It also helps to keep product temperatures outside the TDZ and enhances the customer's enjoyment of the dining experience.

Milk and milk products served as beverages are to be served in unopened, commercially filled packages of one pint (.473 l) or less. Alternatively, the milk can be drawn from a commerical milk dispenser into a glass that has been cleaned and sanitized. Milk served to customers from a one gallon (3.79 l) container is in violation of the FDA's Model Ordinance. Nondairy products such as coffee whiteners must be packaged individually, drawn from a refrigerated dispenser, or poured from a protected pitcher. If stored at the sidestand, milk or cream should be refrigerated during storage.

Dressings, condiments, and seasonings for self-service must be presented in protected containers, dispensers, or individual portion packages. Condiments for table service must be presented in a similar way. Catsup and other sauces can be served in their original serving containers or pour-type dispensers. Sugar used for table service must be either in individual packets or in pour-type dispensers.

Ice used for customer consumption must be handled with ice-dispensing utensils (scoops, tongs) or dispensed by automatic self-service machines. It is unacceptable to permit customers to obtain their own ice unless the automatic self-service machines are used. Utensils used by service personnel to handle ice must be stored in a sanitary manner between uses. Ice storage bins must be drained through an air gap.

Dispensing utensils are to be used for all food serving. Between uses, they can be stored in the food with the handle extended out of the food. Alternatively, they must be stored clean and dry, in running water, or in a dipper well (ice cream scoops) with cold running water. Food may not be dispensed without utensils or by permitting employees or customers to use their hands.

Generally, no portions of leftover food returned to the kitchen can be served again. For example, crocks of cheese and ramekins of butter can be served only once. The exception to this rule is food that is not potentially hazardous, is still packaged, and is still in sound condition. Self-service customers may not reuse tableware when they return to the service area for additional food. The exception is beverage glasses and cups. Food on display must be protected from customer contamination by using packaging or easily cleanable sneeze-guards for serving lines, food bars, and counters. Potentially hazardous food on display must be maintained at proper temperatures out of the TDZ.

These sanitation management tips for the service of food are designed to protect the establishment as well as the customer. However, sometimes the customer is the source of contamination. For example, customers have been known to finish their meal, wipe their mouth with their napkin, blow their nose in the napkin, and place it on the table. A sanitation program designed to reduce contamination hazards must consider the establishment's customers as well as its employees. The objective is to prevent thoughtless customers from contaminating both the food being served and the facilities.

Quality Considerations. Service and production personnel should be trained to recognize acceptable quality levels in food products. Servers often perform the final quality control check for finished menu items immediately before they are served to customers. The operation's quality standards should be maintained at all times. It is the manager's responsibility to set quality standards for all products. Without tasting food, its quality can be judged on the basis of appearance, texture and consistency, and temperature.

Appearance. Appearance components of quality vary with the product. The customer's overall impression is formed based on color, spacing, neatness, and garnishing of the food items being presented. Appearance is an important aspect of quality, because the old adage "customers eat first with their eyes" is still true today. For example, fruits and baked products that are served moist are more tempting than dried out products. The appearance of foods should always match the pictures of the items on the menu.

Color is a component of quality when judging soups, sauces, and beverages. A bright yellow, artificial-looking chicken gravy is unappealing to most customers. Golden brown bakery products have good eye-appeal. Casseroles are more appealing when they are evenly browned. Fruits, vegetables, seafoods, meats, and poultry products should possess a natural color.

The size and shape of food products contribute to their appearance. Broken, misshapen, or ragged vegetables destroy the appearance of the entire plate of food. Portion sizes should fit the plate so food items are not crowded on the plate or hanging over the edge.

The neatness of the food presentation makes a statement about the establishment's standards. Food in liquid form should not spill or run over the edges of tableware. If two foods with sauces are to be served at the same time, one should be served in a side dish. Similarly, if a food has a runny sauce, it should be served in a side dish. Garnishes are artistic touches which complete the picture "painted" with food on a plate. Some garnishes (e.g., parsley, spiced apple rings, orange wedges) are overused to the point of being ignored by customers. Several up-scale establishments use a variety of in-season fresh fruit garnishes that are relatively low in cost and are not labor-intensive. For example, melon wedges, strawberries, kiwi fruit and mango slices are interesting and edible garnish alternatives.

Texture and consistency. These are also important components of food quality. Dried out breads and rolls, broken breadsticks and crackers, wilted or discolored salads, lumpy gravies and puddings, and runny custards are examples of poor food quality. Several operations display photographs of standard food presentations in the pickup area in the kitchen. Servers and production personnel can easily refer to these photographs when questions arise.

Product temperature. Temperature contributes to the overall quality of food products. As previously noted, hot foods (e.g., cooked cereals, soups, appetizers, entrees, beverages, vegetables, desserts) should be served on heated tableware. Cold foods (e.g., appetizers, dry cereals, salads, entrees, beverages, desserts) should be served on chilled tableware. When assembling orders, the server should first gather room temperature products, then chilled foods, and finally hot foods.

Serving and Facilities

The cleaning, repair, and maintenance of the operation's facilities is indispensable at all control points. However, it is particularly important at the serving control point because the dining room environment directly affects customer satisfaction. Usually the customer's entire dining experience takes place in the dining room. The decor and cleanliness of the dining room contribute to the operation's image and a positive first impression in the minds of customers.

It is a good practice to have the dining room supervisor inspect the facilities with all the lights turned on before service begins. This daily inspection is part of the overall preparation for service. The supervisor should check floors, walls, and ceilings to see if maintenance or repairs are necessary. In addition, tables, chairs, and booths should be inspected for cleanliness. Sidestands, equipment, and inventory stock levels can be evaluated at the same time. Menus should be inspected to be certain that daily specials are attached and all dirty, spotted, or soiled menus are removed from circulation.

The inspection can also cover the salad bar and any other food displays in the dining room. Items held on these displays should be refrigerated or heated, depending on the nature of the product. A firm bed of ice on the salad bar maintains product temperatures. Foods on display should be arranged to achieve color contrasts and, thus, to create a pleasing array of selections.

After all the inspecting is done, the dining room supervisor should adjust the lighting levels to create the proper ambience. Also, the ventilation system in the dining room should be set so that the dining room does not become stuffy or smoky when customers are dining. Today, more customers than ever object to being exposed to tobacco smoke in public places.

Temporary Food Service Establishments

Temporary food service establishments are granted a license to serve food for a limited period of time. They are frequently found at fairs, sporting events, and concerts. Some food service and lodging establishments set up temporary service facilities for the outdoor service of luaus, barbecue buffets, and weddings. The rules presented in this section generally apply to these temporary arrangements.

The FDA's Food Service Sanitation Ordinance states:

Temporary food service establishment means a food service establishment that operates at a fixed location for a period of time of not more than 14 consecutive days in conjunction with a single event or celebration.

Source: FDA, p. 22.

The FDA's Model Ordinance clearly spells out the sanitation requirements for temporary food service establishments. Potentially hazardous foods may be prepared and served in temporary units, provided the food requires limited preparation (e.g., frankfurters, hamburgers). The preparation of other potentially hazardous foods is strictly prohibited. However, other potentially hazardous foods (e.g., ice cream, potato salad) may be served in individual servings, provided they have been prepared under sanitary conditions and are not stored in the TDZ before sale.

Ice may be cubed, crushed, or chipped and must be stored in single-use wet-strength paper or plastic bags sealed at the point of manufacture. Ice should be dispensed by employees using proper utensils. Equipment in a temporary unit must be installed so that it is easy to clean and so contamination is avoided. Only single-service articles can be used by the customer if there are no facilities for tableware cleaning and sanitizing. Potable (safe to drink) water in adequate quantities is necessary for food preparation, equipment and utensil cleaning, and handwashing. Food must not be stored in contact with water or undrained ice. All general food handling requirements discussed previously apply to temporary units. Waste and sewage must be disposed of according to law. It is not permissible to simply throw waste or sewage on the ground near the unit.

The FDA's Food Service Sanitation Ordinance states:

Law includes Federal, State, and local statutes, ordinances, and regulations.

Source: FDA, p. 21.

Handwashing facilities are required in a temporary food service unit. Floors are to be constructed of materials that are easy to clean. Ceilings may be constructed of canvas, wood, or other material that adequately protects food preparation areas. Walls, ceilings, and doors must prevent the entry of insects. Counter service areas are to be provided with tight-fitting windows or doors that are solid or screened and are kept closed except when actually in use. Temporary food service units can be safely operated if requirements in the FDA's Model Ordinance and local health codes are strictly observed.

The FDA's Food Service Sanitation Ordinance states:

Temporary Food Service Establishments

General.

A temporary food service establishment shall comply with the requirements of this ordinance, except as otherwise provided in this chapter. The regulatory authority may impose additional requirements to protect against health hazards related to the conduct of the temporary food service establishment, may prohibit the sale of some or all potentially hazardous foods, and when no health hazard will result, may waive or modify requirements of this ordinance.

Restricted operations.

(a) These provisions are applicable whenever a temporary food service establishment is permitted, under the provisions of . . . this ordinance, to operate without complying with all the requirements of this chapter.

(b) Only those potentially hazardous foods requiring limited preparation, such as hamburgers and frankfurters that only require seasoning and cooking, shall be prepared or served. The preparation or service of other potentially hazardous foods, including pastries filled with cream or synthetic cream, custards, and similar products, and salads or sandwiches containing meat, poultry, eggs or fish is prohibited. This prohibition does not apply to any potentially hazardous food that has been prepared and packaged under conditions meeting the requirements of this ordinance, is obtained in individual servings, is stored at a temperature of 45°F or below or at a temperature of 140°F or above in facilities meeting the requirements of this ordinance, and is served directly in the unopened container in which it was packaged.

Ice.

Ice that is consumed or that contacts food shall be made under conditions meeting the requirements of this ordinance. The ice shall be obtained only in chipped, crushed, or cubed form and in single-use safe plastic or wet-strength paper bags filled and sealed at the point of manufacture. The ice shall be held in these bags until it is dispensed in a way that protects it from contamination.

Equipment.

(a) Equipment shall be located and installed in a way that prevents food contamination and that also facilitates cleaning the establishment.

(b) Food-contact surfaces of equipment shall be protected from contamination by consumers and other contaminating agents. Effective shields for such equipment shall be provided, as necessary, to prevent contamination.

Single-service articles.

All temporary food service establishments without effective facilities for cleaning and sanitizing tableware shall provide only single-service articles for use by the consumer.

Water.

Enough potable water shall be available in the establishment for food preparation, for cleaning and sanitizing utensils and equipment, and for handwashing. A heating facility capable of producing enough hot water for these purposes shall be provided on the premises.

Wet storage.

Storage of packaged food in contact with water or undrained ice is prohibited. Wrapped sandwiches shall not be stored in direct contact with ice.

Waste.

All sewage, including liquid waste, shall be disposed of according to law.

Handwashing.

A convenient handwashing facility shall be available for employee handwashing. This facility shall consist of, at least, warm running water, soap, and individual paper towels.

Floors.

Floors shall be constructed of concrete, asphalt, tight wood, or other similar cleanable material kept in good repair. Dirt or gravel, when graded to drain, may be used as subflooring when covered with clean, removable platforms or duckboards, or covered with wood chips, shavings or other suitable materials effectively treated to control dust.

Walls and ceilings of food preparation areas.

(a) Ceilings shall be made of wood, canvas, or other material that protects the interior of the establishment from the weather. Walls and ceilings of food preparation areas shall be constructed in a way that prevents the entrance of insects. Doors to food preparation areas shall be solid or screened and shall be self-closing. Screening material used for walls, doors, or windows shall be at least 16 mesh to the inch.

(b) Counter-service openings shall not be larger than necessary for the particular operation conducted. These openings shall be provided with tight-fitting solid or screened doors or windows or shall be provided with fans installed and operated to restrict the entrance of flying insects. Counter-service openings shall be kept closed, except when in actual use.

Source: FDA, pp. 69-71.

Banquet and Buffet-Style Service

Most food service and lodging businesses provide some form of **banquet service.** The nature of the banquet function may vary from a simple coffee break with specialty pastries to a formal dinner with multiple courses. In any case, menu items should be chosen with ease and speed of service in mind, since all customers should be served at about the same time.

This segment of the business can be highly profitable if it is adequately planned. From a control standpoint, banquet service has two advantages: (1) the establishment knows how many people will be served, and (2) the menu is selected well in advance of service. Having this information makes the planning and allocation of the operation's resources more efficient in most cases. For example, many operations use a part-time staff to supplement their regular production and service staff during banquet service. On the other hand, the disadvantage of banquet service is that, if advance planning is not properly done, the banquet can be a disaster. The pressure is greater when large numbers of people must be served in a relatively short period of time. Under these circumstances, mistakes can happen in the process of serving. The problems are compounded when correct time-temperature controls are not in place.

Station setup is important because of the rapid speed at which banquets are served. Equipment requirements vary based on the type of banquet and the menu. General service standards apply, although they may be modified to facilitate the service of large numbers of people.

Buffet service is popular in many food service and lodging establishments. Some use buffet service in combination with banquet service. For example, at some special functions, appetizers may be served buffet-style during the cocktail hour; then the rest of the meal is served as a traditional banquet later. Other special functions use buffet service exclusively from appetizers to desserts. By attractively arranging a seemingly endless array of food products, establishments using this service style impress and excite customers, who enjoy being able to choose whatever they like in unlimited quantities. Buffet service also provides the opportunity to create food displays and show pieces such as decorated meat, fish, poultry, and shellfish platters.

Some buffets feature a carver, who slices meats or poultry at the buffet table in the dining room. Some buffets utilize servers to portion some of the food products and to assist customers. Most buffets use servers to deliver beverages, bread and butter, and perhaps desserts directly to the customers at their tables. However, some buffets are totally self-service affairs.

In banquet service, time-temperature control is critical. It is virtually impossible to prepare dozens, hundreds, and above all, thousands of individual plates as service progresses. Therefore, foods are usually pre-plated for large banquets and held hot or cold in food holding cabinets. Refrigerated mobile storage units must maintain internal product temperatures of 45°F (7°C) or lower. Hot mobile storage cabinets must achieve a minimum internal product temperature of 140°F (60°C).

Time-temperature control in buffet service is equally critical. Whenever large quantities of food are displayed, special equipment is necessary to maintain products at temperatures outside the TDZ. For cold products, ice is usually an acceptable means of maintaining refrigerator temperatures. However, the food products must not be directly exposed to the ice or melted water. Instead, bowls and containers must be used to hold food. Smaller containers, refilled more frequently, not only enhance the attractiveness of the buffet table but they also help to maintain correct temperatures.

Hot food can be kept above 140°F (60°C) on a buffet table in a number of ways. Chafing dishes powered by an electrical source or by canned heat are usually used to hold hot foods on a buffet table. Large roasts, hams, and turkeys to be carved in the dining room should be displayed under infrared heat lamps. Care should be taken to control time-temperature combinations, particularly when buffets are set up outdoors.

The main concern of health department officials regarding outdoor food service is that the food be free of dust and contamination when it is served. To accomplish this, the operation may need to use special coverings for food and beverage products from the time they leave the kitchen until they are served. Actual preparation of food outdoors may involve other special regulations enforced by local health department officials. It is a good idea to check with local authorities for information on local laws governing outdoor cooking and dining areas before planning any such functions.

Off-Premises Catering

In an effort to utilize resources more efficiently and to generate increased revenue, some food service and lodging businesses are catering functions off the premises. The FDA's Model Ordinance specifies how food products are to be transported.

The FDA's Food Service Sanitation Ordinance states:

Food Transportation

General.

During transportation, food and food utensils shall be kept in covered containers or completely wrapped or packaged so as to be protected from contamination. Foods in original individual packages do not need to be overwrapped or covered if the original package has not been torn or broken. During transportation, including transportation to another location for service or catering operations, food shall meet the requirements of this ordinance relating to food protection and food storage.

Source: FDA, p. 33.

Special equipment and transportation vehicles are necessary for off-premises catering. Today, some fast-food operations are offering a catering service to strengthen their bottom line. However, these operations have had to incur the expense of hot- and cold-holding equipment and delivery vans. This equipment is designed to consistently maintain specified product temperatures for safety and quality reasons. Because improper transportation of food products heightens the sanitation risks, special attention must be given to this aspect of off-premises catering in order to protect the health of customers.

Room Service

In many lodging properties, room service is evolving from a break-even or unprofitable business to a profit center. In the past, many room service menus were dull, service was minimal, and high prices were the norm. Today, managers of lodging properties are revamping room service with unique menu items, an emphasis on guest satisfaction, and realistic pricing strategies.

More and more business travelers are using room service as a dining option in lodging properties. Expectations of room service guests have become more sophisticated. Some properties are offering 24-hour room service. After the main kitchen is closed, menu items available through room service may include cold smoked fish (e.g., salmon) and vegetable platters. Some properties are offering "split service," which means the server brings dinner courses separately. Even though split service requires more trips to each room, the quality of the products is generally better when split service is used than when the entire order is delivered at one time.

The logistics of room service are closely tied to product quality and safety. Hot food should be hot; cold food should be cold. Both should be on time and tasty. Time and temperature are the critical elements, because as product holding times increase, the likelihood of contamination does, too. The training program for room service personnel should emphasize that, in the course of doing their job, they are invading the guest's privacy. Thus, the order should be delivered efficiently and with a minimum of interruption. Side work must be continuous, so that servers are ready when the order is called in and prepared. Dirty dishes should be removed promptly from guestrooms and hallways.

For almost all room service operations, breakfast is the easiest meal to sell and the most difficult to deliver properly. Many breakfast combinations featuring eggs simply do not maintain product temperatures during transportation. Also, it is virtually impossible to deliver toast to guestrooms at correct temperatures. A better approach is to offer a limited menu consisting of products that will survive the trip from the kitchen to the guestroom. Specialty pastries may be a suitable alternative to toast on room service menus. Also, scrambled eggs may be preferable to eggs Benedict because the hollandaise sauce required for the latter is highly perishable.

Most room service orders are called in to the room service operator, who relays the order to the kitchen and the room server. Today, lodging properties are training their room service operators to sell profitable add-ons by suggestion. Most operators are well versed in information about menu item ingredients and preparation techniques, so they can easily answer the guest's questions.

The specific procedure for room service varies from one lodging property to the next, but some general similarities exist. While the order is prepared by the kitchen, the server covers a rolling table with a clean cloth. An alternative to the rolling table is a service tray, which is frequently used for breakfast and relatively small orders. All tableware, cold beverages, condiments, and spices are assembled and placed on the table. Next, the other cold food items are gathered and placed on the table. Coffee or other hot beverages are added. When cooking is completed, the hot food is plated and covered. Then it is placed on a service tray, on the rolling table, or in a food warmer, and the order is delivered.

Upon arriving at the correct guestroom, the server should knock and announce "Room service." After greeting the guest, the server may need to ask where the order should be placed. If a table is used, it should be arranged for service by pouring beverages. Hot foods may be served from the warmer, if that is the guest's preference. Otherwise, the food should be left in the warmer for the guest's self-service. The server should then present the check to the guest for signature or payment. Before leaving, the server should ask the guest when the tray or table should be removed.

Although this general procedure is used for breakfast, lunch, and dinner room service, it may be modified slightly based on the needs of the guest, the menu, and/or the constraints of the property's resources. In any case, control of product temperatures is critical, and time is of the essence. A well-organized room service staff can turn room service into a profit center.

Mobile Food Service

Mobile food units are those that do not necessarily operate in a fixed location. Examples of mobile units are pushcarts, catering trucks designed to sell food in a number of locations, and ice cream and snack food trucks. Generally, all of the rules already discussed apply to mobile food service units. Some local health departments do not permit the sale of potentially hazardous foods from mobile units. It is a good idea to check with local regulatory authorities.

If a mobile food unit only sells prepared food packaged in individual servings, requirements for water and sewage systems do not apply. Cleaning and sanitizing equipment is not necessary in a mobile unit if the necessary equipment is provided and used at the unit's commissary. Frankfurters may be prepared in mobile units. Only single-service articles may be provided to the unit's customers. Single-service articles are, by definition, not reusable.

The FDA's Food Service Sanitation Ordinance states:

Mobile food unit means a vehicle-mounted food service establishment designed to be readily movable.

Pushcart means a non-self-propelled vehicle limited to serving nonpotentially hazardous foods or commissary-wrapped food maintained at proper temperatures, or limited to the preparation and serving of frankfurters.

Commissary means a catering establishment, restaurant, or any other place in which food, containers, or supplies are kept, handled, prepared, packaged or stored.

Source: FDA, pp. 20-22.

In mobile units other than those described in the preceding paragraph, a source of potable water must be provided. The water system has to be under pressure and of sufficient capacity to furnish enough cold and hot water for handwashing, equipment and utensil cleaning, and food preparation. Any liquid waste resulting from the operation of the mobile unit must be stored in a tank that is at least 15% larger in capacity than the water supply tank. Connections for servicing the water supply tank must be of a different size or type than the connections used for the waste tank.

Mobile units must operate from a commissary and report daily for cleaning, servicing, and resupply of food. The commissary must operate according to all requirements for food service operations. The commissary must have a servicing area for the mobile units. Servicing includes the emptying of liquid waste in a safe and sanitary manner. Overhead protection is required in the various areas where mobile units are supplied, cleaned, and serviced.

The FDA's Food Service Sanitation Ordinance states:

Mobile Food Service

General.

Mobile food units or pushcarts shall comply with the requirements . . . of this ordinance. The regulatory authority may impose additional requirements to protect against health hazards related to the conduct of the food service establishment as a mobile operation, may prohibit the sale of some or all potentially hazardous food, and when no health hazard will result, may waive or modify [certain] requirements of this chapter relating to physical facilities . . .

Restricted operation.

Mobile food units or pushcarts serving only food prepared, packaged in individual servings, transported and stored under conditions meeting the requirements of this ordinance, or beverages that are not potentially hazardous and are dispensed from covered urns or other protected equipment, need not comply with requirements of this ordinance pertaining to the necessity of water and sewage systems nor to those requirements pertaining to the cleaning and sanitization of equipment and utensils if the required equipment for cleaning and sanitization exists at the commissary. However, frankfurters may be prepared and served from these units or pushcarts.

Single-service articles.

Mobile food units or pushcarts shall provide only single-service articles for use by the consumer.

Water system.

A mobile food unit requiring a water system shall have a potable water system under pressure. The system shall be of sufficient capacity to furnish enough hot and cold water for food preparation, utensil cleaning and sanitizing, and handwashing, in accordance with the requirements of this ordinance. The water inlet shall be located so that it will not be contaminated by waste discharge, road dust, oil, or grease, and it shall be kept capped unless being filled. The water inlet shall be provided with a transition connection of a size or type that will prevent its use for any other service. All water distribution pipes or tubing shall be constructed and installed in accordance with the requirements of this ordinance.

Waste retention.

If liquid waste results from operation of a mobile food unit, the waste shall be stored in a permanently installed retention tank that is of at least 15 percent larger capacity than the water supply tank. Liquid waste shall not be discharged from the retention tank when the mobile food unit is in motion. All connections on the vehicle for servicing mobile food unit waste disposal facilities shall be of a different size or type than those used for supplying potable water to the mobile food unit. The waste connection shall be located lower than the water inlet connection to preclude contamination of the potable water system.

Commissary

Base of operations.

(a) Mobile food units or pushcarts shall operate from a commissary or other fixed food service establishment and shall report at least daily to such location for all supplies and for all cleaning and servicing operations.

(b) The commissary or other fixed food service establishment used as a base of operation for mobile food units or pushcarts shall be constructed and operated in compliance with the requirements of this ordinance.

Servicing Area and Operations

Servicing area.

(a) A mobile food unit servicing area shall be provided and shall include at least overhead protection for any supplying, cleaning, or servicing operation. Within this servicing area, there shall be a location provided for the flushing and drainage of liquid wastes separate from the location provided for water servicing and for the loading and unloading of food and related supplies. This servicing area will not be required where only packaged food is placed on the mobile food unit or pushcart or where mobile food units do not contain waste retention tanks.

(b) The surface of the servicing area shall be constructed of a smooth nonabsorbent material, such as concrete or machine-laid asphalt and shall be maintained in good repair, kept clean, and be graded to drain.

(c) The construction of the walls and ceilings of the servicing area is exempted from the provisions of [the walls and ceilings section] of this ordinance.

Servicing operations.

(a) Potable water servicing equipment shall be installed according to law and shall be stored and handled in a way that protects the water and equipment from contamination.

(b) The mobile food unit liquid waste retention tank, where used, shall be thoroughly flushed and drained during the servicing operation. All liquid waste shall be discharged to a sanitary sewerage disposal system in accordance with . . . this ordinance.

Source: FDA, pp. 65-68.

Serving and Change

Menu items change departments at the serving control point. The challenge of the serving function is to serve each customer in a way that meets or exceeds the person's expectations. This objective must be achieved without compromising the operation's sanitation, quality, or cost control standards.

A number of different food service outlets may be operating simultaneously in a hospitality property. Each function requires a slightly different approach to service. Consider a lodging property with a coffee shop, a restaurant, banquet facilities, and 600 guestrooms. In the evening, the coffee shop may be serving sandwiches, salads, and lighter foods for customers who are not interested in a large meal or formal dining. The coffee shop only uses plate service because it is rapid and efficient.

The formal dining room features tableside preparation of some appetizers, salads, entrees, and desserts. Service is stretched out over a longer time period in this restaurant because a slower customer turnover is more desirable.

At the same time, banquet service for 1,000 customers is taking place in the grand ballroom of this hotel. The food for the banquet has been prepared in the main kitchen but is being served from a separate banquet kitchen. Food items have been plated and held hot in mobile holding equipment. At the appropriate time, the equipment is rolled to locations just outside the doors of the grand ballroom and the items are served from the carts.

This hotel is also hosting an outdoor Hawaiian luau for 300 guests. Food has been prepared in the main kitchen and is being served outdoors buffet-style. Guests have been provided with disposable dishware. They are eating with single-service utensils and drinking from single-service cups and glasses. Meanwhile, the room service operator continues to relay orders to the kitchen from guests on various floors of the 600-room hotel. Obviously, the simultaneous occurrence of several different styles of service makes food service in a lodging property more complex. Although service styles also change in a food service property, these changes may not be as noticeable as those in a hotel. The key to successful service is to handle these changes with flexibility.

Serving and Success

Success in the serving control point depends on standards. Standards for each style of service used should be established and monitored by management. The standards for service vary greatly depending on the menu, the location (dining room versus room service), the skill level of personnel, and the expectations of customers.

Excellent food service and lodging operations realize the importance of timing at the serving control point. Winning managers continually reevaluate their service system. The system evolves as the operation's resources change and as customers become more sophisticated. Winning businesses design their service standards to meet or exceed customer expectations. Each time the service style changes, the techniques of service are reevaluated and upgraded.

Summary

The purpose of the serving control point is to deliver food products from the production department to the customer in a way that is safe and satisfying. Resource levels influence the success of service. Personnel skill levels dictate the style(s) of service an operation can use successfully. The equipment used during service depends on the style of service. Equipment should be cleaned, maintained, and stored so as to prevent contamination.

Control of the display and service of food inventory during service is critical. The last opportunity to assess product quality is immediately before the menu item is served to the customer. Facilities must be clean and maintained in good repair. A pleasant environment enhances the customer's enjoyment of the entire dining experience.

Several styles of service are used to deliver food to customers. The options for table service include plate service, tableside preparation, family-style, and platter service. Each style has its advantages and disadvantages from the standpoint of sanitation. Other types of service discussed were temporary food service establishments, banquets and buffets, off-premises catering, room service, and mobile food service. Regardless of the type of service used, two goals must be given priority: protection of the product and customer satisfaction.

References

Cichy, Ronald F. "The Role of the Professional Chef in a Foodservice Firm." *The National Culinary Review*, January 1983. 7(1):12-13.

——."Control Waste and Increase Sales." *Michigan Hospitality Magazine*, July/August 1982. 47(4):21.

Faulkner, E. "Room for Growth: Room Service Gains in Popularity, Elegance." *Restaurants and Institutions*, 1 June 1983. 92(11):123.

Finley, M. "Cashing In On the Sun—Prospering With a Patio." *Host Magazine*, June 1983. 19(6):16-17.

Food and Drug Administration. Public Health Service, U.S. Department of Health, Education, and Welfare. *Food Service Sanitation Manual*. Washington, D.C.: U.S. Government Printing Office, 1976.

Goodman, Raymond J. *The Management of Service for the Professional Restaurant Manager*. Dubuque, Iowa: Brown, 1979.

U.S. Department of Health, Education, and Welfare. *Training Food Service Personnel for the Hospitality Industry*. Washington, D.C.: U.S. Government Printing Office, 1969.

Strategies for Success at the Aspen Hotel

The standards for service at the Aspen Hotel were not developed without a thorough discussion of the hotel's resources and the expectations of its customers. The dining room managers initially pushed for full-scale tableside preparation in the main dining room during the evening meal. However, the group finally agreed on a combination of plate service with a few specialty appetizers, salads, entrees, and desserts prepared in the dining room. The GM felt that a spirit of cooperation and understanding was created during this meeting.

Checklist for Serving

Personnel

1. Servers understand the operation's standards for quality, cost, and sanitation.

2. Service standards are developed based on the menu, personnel skill levels, hours of service, the size of the operation, and its sales volume.

3. The servers see themselves as public relations agents for the establishment.

4. The appearance and health of servers is evaluated before each meal period.

5. Servers are friendly, calm, confident, alert, dependable, and honest. In addition to professional skills, they possess initiative and a willingness to adhere to the establishment's procedures and standards.

6. Prior to service, servers prepare themselves and their stations for service.

7. Servers restock their stations and complete closing duties before leaving.

8. Servers adhere to standards of personal hygiene covering:

    a. bodily cleanliness

    b. posture

    c. hair and hair restraints

    d. handwashing

e. uniforms

f. jewelry

9. Supervisors of service conduct an employee line-up meeting and inspection of the facilities immediately before the meal period begins.

10. Servers adhere to standards of cleanliness covering:

a. handwashing

b. gum chewing, smoking, and eating

c. food that has left the plate or dropped on the floor

d. replacing dropped tableware

e. touching food with the hands

f. hand contact with tableware

g. service towels or napkins

h. serving trays

11. Servers know the answers to questions about menu items, including preparation techniques and raw ingredients.

12. Servers place orders with the kitchen using standard ordering procedures.

13. Servers realize that the timing of orders is critical.

14. Servers load their trays carefully and safely.

15. Servers understand the different styles of service and only use the style(s) specified by management.

16. Servers check back with customers once their orders have been delivered to see if everything is satisfactory.

17. When the customers are leaving, the servers thank them and invite them back.

18. Servers know the operation's procedures for handling customer complaints.

19. Servers are trained to maintain the operation's standards.

Equipment

1. Personnel regularly clean and sanitize equipment and utensils used in the service of food and beverage products.

2. Cleaned and sanitized utensils and equipment are stored in a way that prevents recontamination.

3. Tableware is handled so as to prevent contamination.

4. Stations and sidestands are kept restocked with adequate supplies of tableware and other necessities.

5. Food products at stations and sidestands have minimum contact with the temperature danger zone (TDZ).

6. Tables, chairs, floors, and windows are regularly cleaned and maintained.

7. Condiment and spice containers are regularly cleaned.

8. Care is exercised in the handling of all equipment used in service.

Inventory

1. Potentially hazardous foods have minimum exposure to the TDZ during display and service.

2. Ice is dispensed by employees with ice-dispensing equipment or by customers if an automatic dispensing machine is available.

3. Condiments, seasonings, and dressings are available in single-service packages or approved self-service containers.

4. Dispensing utensils are stored in a safe and sanitary manner before and during service.

5. Reservice of food is limited to items that are not potentially hazardous and are still packaged and in sound condition.

6. Food on display is protected from contamination and has minimum contact with the TDZ.

7. Tableware (except beverage cups and glasses) is not reused by self-service customers.

8. Acceptable quality levels defined in terms of appearance, texture, color, odor, and temperature are known to servers and checked before an order is delivered to the customer.

Facilities

1. Facilities are routinely cleaned, maintained, and repaired.

2. Restrooms are regularly inspected and cleaned.

3. Facilities are clean, dry, and odor-free.

4. Adequate lighting levels are maintained.

5. The supervisor conducts a facility inspection immediately before the meal period.

6. Menus are inspected to remove all dirty, soiled, or spotted menus from circulation.

Temporary Food Service Establishments

1. Local health codes regarding potentially hazardous food are strictly observed.

2. Ice is stored in single-use wet strength paper or plastic bags and dispensed by employees using correct utensils.

3. Equipment is correctly installed, cleaned, and maintained.

4. Only single-service articles are used if no facilities are available for tableware cleaning and sanitizing.

5. Potable water is available for food preparation, handwashing, and equipment and utensil cleaning.

6. Food is not stored in contact with undrained ice or water.

7. Sewage and waste is disposed of according to law.

8. Handwashing facilities are available.

9. Insect entry is prevented through walls, ceilings, floors, and doors.

Banquet and Buffet Food Service

1. Correct time-temperature controls are practiced.

2. Station setup is checked before service begins.

3. Menu items are chosen for the ease, safety, and speed with which they can be served.

4. The necessary equipment and utensils are available to maintain product temperatures.

5. Food and beverage products are free of contamination.

Off-Premises Catering

1. Special equipment and transportation vehicles are available in sufficient quantity.

2. Product time-temperature controls are closely monitored.

3. Food is protected during storage and transportation.

Room Service

1. Room service standards are established based on guest satisfaction and the resources of the property.

2. Product quality and time-temperature controls are assessed.

3. Servers are trained to adhere to the property's standards.

4. Menus are limited to those items that the operation can successfully prepare and deliver to the guestrooms.

5. Soiled tableware, linen, and equipment is promptly removed from the guestrooms or hallways.

Mobile Food Units or Pushcarts

1. Local health department requirements are investigated and enforced.

2. Equipment is regularly cleaned, sanitized, and maintained.

3. Food products prepared and served in mobile units are limited to those permitted by the local health authority.

4. Only single-service articles are permitted for use by the customer.

5. The water and waste retention systems conform to local health codes.

6. Mobile food units report daily to the commissary for cleaning, servicing, and resupplying of food and beverage inventory.

7. The mobile food units' commissary is operated under the requirements of the local health authorities.

The following case studies are designed to enhance your understanding of the material in this chapter. If you are a Home Study student, use these case studies to stimulate questions about this chapter. If you are a Group or Institutional Study student, you may be asked to discuss these case studies as part of a regular classroom assignment.

CASE STUDY 9.1

Jimmy Sinning is a waiter at the D&B Restaurant in the Watertower Hotel. While setting up the dining room for the evening meal, Jimmy checks each table to be certain that all tabletop items are present. He notices that some flatware is missing from a table near the kitchen. Discovering that it fell on the floor, he picks up the flatware and places it on the table so the place setting will be complete.

Flatware on other tables appears spotted, so Jimmy wipes it off with the towel he just used to clean a soiled table. Once the tabletops are checked, Jimmy places dishes containing cream in individual portion packages on all of the tables. He has been trained to make sure the daily special is clipped on each menu. While putting the specials on the menu, he notices that several menus are torn and soiled. Since the restaurant doesn't have any new menus, Jimmy uses the soiled menus.

Test Your Understanding

1. Is the serving function under control at the D&B Restaurant?

2. What sanitation deficiencies need to be corrected?

3. What are your recommendations to Jimmy Sinning and the management of the D&B Restaurant?

CASE STUDY 9.2

The Ranch Restaurant serves breakfast, lunch, and dinner in addition to banquets. Later today, a luncheon banquet will be served to 240 conventioneers. The meal will consist of a fresh fruit appetizer, rolls and butter, swiss steak, oven-browned potatoes, green beans almondine, and rainbow sherbet. Plate-style service will be used for all menu items.

One hour before the conventioneers are due to arrive, the manager of the Ranch Restaurant decides to check on the table setup and the various menu items being held for service. He finds that the fruit appetizers are already on the table. In the kitchen, a few rolls chosen at random feel chilled, as if they were recently removed from the refrigerator. In the hot-holding equipment, the manager finds swiss steak, potatoes, and green beans crowded onto every plate. The meat and vegetables are swimming in sauce. The garnish is a parsley sprig. The sherbet has been dished into frozen dessert glasses.

Test Your Understanding

1. Comment on the Ranch Restaurant's quality standards for this banquet.

2. Will the conventioneers who attend this banquet face any sanitation risks?

3. What are your recommendations to the manager of the Ranch Restaurant?

CASE STUDY 9.3

The Eastside Restaurant features a 60-item salad bar. This salad bar is available in combination with the restaurant's evening buffet. The buffet offers customers a choice of roast beef, ham, or turkey, and several hot vegetables. The meat and poultry are carved in the dining room in front of the customers.

Meat and poultry for the buffet are placed on a wooden cutting board in the dining room. Although the food is hot when it leaves the kitchen, no attempt is made to maintain correct product temperatures in the dining room. The carver periodically wipes his carving knife and fork on a soiled kitchen towel. Customers have never complained about the food display or service, so the manager and chef have made no changes.

Test Your Understanding

1. What sanitation hazards exist at the Eastside Restaurant?

2. Which microorganisms would be likely to be responsible for a foodborne outbreak, if one were to surface among diners at the Eastside Restaurant?

3. What are your recommendations to the manager and chef of the Eastside Restaurant?

CASE STUDY 9.4

The general manager of the Lake View Hotel is developing a weekend promotion with his sales staff. The hotel's new "getaway package" will include a room for two for the weekend, plus breakfasts and dinners for two. The breakfasts will be served in the guests' room or the coffee shop; dinner must be eaten in the main dining room.

The breakfast menu for the special promotion includes main course choices like omelets, eggs Benedict, three-minute eggs, scrambled eggs, and pancakes. The hotel has 430 guestrooms and expects to run a 65% occupancy on the weekend. Over 150 rooms have already been sold for this weekend's "getaway package."

Test Your Understanding

1. What breakfast menu considerations have been overlooked by the Lake View Hotel's management in planning this package?

2. What sanitation and quality control problems could occur with the breakfasts?

3. What are your recommendations to the Lake View Hotel's management?

CASE STUDY 9.5

The chef from the Roundup Restaurant, Arnold Ambivalence, has been contracted to serve an outdoor banquet this weekend for 500 oil executives. The site of the banquet will be a ranch 60 miles from the restaurant. All food and equipment will be transported to the banquet site on a 24-foot (7.2 meter) refrigerated truck. Arnold has driven to the site and planned how his staff will prepare the banquet.

Hot food items will be cooked in a field stove powered by propane gas. Preparation of fresh fruits and vegetables will take place at the site. Once the platters of raw fruits and vegetables are assembled, they will be stored on the floor of the refrigerated truck. Beef will be cooked over an open fire and sliced on a table outdoors. Then, it will be held hot in chafing dishes on the buffet table.

The source of water for this event will be a garden hose. Since handwashing facilities are not available, the eight production and service workers will use moist towelettes to clean their hands. Utensils will be rinsed in cold water and wiped dry since there is no source of hot water.

* * *

On the day of the banquet, Arnold's staff had the food ready right on schedule at 5:00 p.m. Arnold was pleased that his plans had been carried out and seemed to work. Then, he received a message that the banquet would have to be delayed 1-1/2 hours because the oil executives were watching a horseshow.

Test Your Understanding

1. What sanitation violations occurred at this outdoor banquet?

2. How could Arnold have improved the service of this off-premises catered event?

3. What are your recommendations to Arnold Ambivalence?

TEN

The Cleaning and Maintenance Control Point

Strategies for Success at the Aspen Hotel

Paul James realized the importance of this morning's special department head meeting. The GM believed that it was his responsibility to "manage the managers." That is, it was his duty to create the atmosphere that would bring the various departments' activities under control.

The GM had asked three key department heads to be present this morning to discuss the cleaning and maintenance control point. Assembled in the room were Angie Jack, the executive housekeeper; Harry Gregor, the hotel's chief engineer; and Elisabeth Mueller, the food and beverage director.

The GM opened the meeting by asking a question. "What do you do when you first walk up to a hotel or restaurant?" No one answered the GM's question. "I'll tell you what I do," said the GM. "I immediately look at the parking lot and the outside of the building to determine if they are clean and properly maintained. If I have a feeling of disarray or disorganization, I get a negative first impression of the property. The hotel or restaurant has to fight an uphill battle from that point on to satisfy me — the customer."

"Our previous GM had a different philosophy," said the chief engineer. "He believed that we only needed to repair or perform maintenance on something when it was broken. As far as he was concerned, this hotel didn't need a formal program for cleaning and maintenance. That's why this facility and its equipment are in such a sad state. It makes my job as chief engineer more difficult because every day I am running from one crisis to another. Sometimes I think of myself as a 'jack of all trades and master of few' around here. I spend too much time with paperwork."

"That is going to change for the better," said the GM. "What are your thoughts, Angie?"

"Some people just can't see dirt," said the executive housekeeper. "Everyone is different. I inspect guestrooms on a daily basis. It would be a good idea if you would take an active interest in my department. I expect you, as the GM, to make some unannounced inspections of guestrooms and public areas. That helps keep our housekeepers motivated to do the job right. As I see it, written standards in the Rooms Department would help me enforce our hotel's policies. Also, we need to upgrade the position of housekeeper. A good start would be new uniforms."

"I think our budget can handle that expense, Angie," said Paul James. "What do you think, Elisabeth?"

"It's been my experience that people complain about cleanliness the most," said the F&B director. "In the past, we haven't had a formal program of pest control. When we had a problem, we went to the supermarket and bought something. A lot of the time it didn't even work. Most supervisors that I've worked with in the kitchen and dining room do not like to manage the cleaning and maintenance of their areas. Maybe our orientation and training program could be expanded to include how to clean and maintain those areas."

"That's an excellent idea, Elisabeth," said the GM. "You all know how important I feel customer awareness is in a hotel. The appearance of clean facilities and an organized maintenance program are critical to the success of any hotel. Don't misunderstand me. I don't expect you to do it all alone. You have my unconditional support for our cleaning and maintenance program. We will work together to establish and implement standards for cleaning and maintenance. It will be your responsibility to communicate these standards to all employees in your area and see that they are followed."

This chapter concerns the last control point in the food service system: cleaning and maintenance. Even though this function is presented last in the sequence of basic operating activities, it is definitely first in importance. In a recent *Restaurants and Institutions* magazine survey, 5,000 food service operators were asked what, in their opinion, was the quickest way to turn off a customer. A summary of the research findings is presented in Exhibit 10.1. With the exception of fast food restaurants, commercial and noncommercial industry subsegments across the board identified soiled dishware as the greatest cause of customer dissatisfaction. (Responses of fast-food restaurant operators deviate from the national averages because single-service articles are often used in place of multi-use dishware.) Food service managers in all industry segments are realizing that customers are more sanitation-conscious than ever before.

In keeping with other chapters in Part Two, this chapter focuses on the resources under a manager's control and how these affect the control point. Accordingly, the role of personnel in using equipment to clean and sanitize, and inventory resources in the form of cleaners and sanitizers, are both discussed. However, the majority of this chapter is devoted to the facilities resource. The maintenance of the establishment's physical facilities is discussed in detail. In addition to maintenance procedures, construction specifications for various parts of the facilities are also given, even though construction is not part of the daily operational flow in a food service establishment.

Cleaning and Maintenance and Personnel

The success or failure of the operation's sanitation program is influenced to a large extent by the personnel resource. The success of the cleaning and maintenance control point is particularly dependent upon the operation's systematic approach to this function.

In some cases, outside personnel resources are brought in to help with cleaning and maintenance. Outside contractors may be employed for monthly, quarterly, or semi-annual heavy cleaning and maintenance jobs. For example, these contractors may strip and reseal floors in public areas or clean ventilation exhaust hoods and ductwork in the kitchen. In

Exhibit 10.1   Causes of Customer Dissatisfaction Based on Surveys in Seven Industry Subsegments

Industry Subsegment	Customer Dissatisfiers			
	Soiled Dishware	Dirty Restrooms	Unclean Dining Areas	Other
College/University Food Service	64.0%	26.1%	36.9%	4.5%
Employee Feeding	77.2%	29.8%	42.1%	3.5%
Fast-Food Restaurants	33.5%	37.2%	48.9%	9.0%
Full Service Restaurants	58.1%	48.1%	38.8%	8.8%
Hospital Food Service	67.0%	32.2%	31.3%	4.3%
Hotel/Motel Food Service	57.9%	50.4%	37.6%	9.8%
School Food Service	67.8%	39.7%	38.8%	11.6%

Source: Restaurants and Institutions Magazine, *August 15, 1982, p. 32.*

Note: Totals for each industry subsegment are in excess of 100% because, in many cases, more than one dissatisfier was identified.

most establishments, an outside contractor regularly provides pest control services. However, daily and routine cleaning is usually the responsibility of in-house personnel. All employees should understand the correct procedures for cleaning and maintenance of equipment and facilities in their work areas. Each person in the operation is responsible, to some degree, for the cleaning and maintenance of the operation's resources.

Employees are more likely to follow cleaning and maintenance procedures if they understand the importance of these routine functions. The operation's philosophy of cleaning and maintenance should be put in writing and periodically brought to the attention of all employees. If production or service employees are not busy preparing and cooking food or serving food, they should be cleaning. Pride in the business and its sanitation program makes employees willing to do this important work. Cleaning requires effort from everyone but the effort pays off in the short run and the long run. Regular cleaning and maintenance can actually save time. If equipment and facilities resources are permitted to deteriorate, it will be more difficult to achieve the required sanitation and quality standards. The emphasis on cleaning and maintenance must continue beyond the employees' orientation and training programs.

Training of personnel in correct cleaning procedures must be systematic if it is to be effective.[1] Training should cover standards for cleanliness and recommended methods, products, and equipment to be used in cleaning and maintenance. Only after employees are properly trained in correct cleaning and maintenance procedures can they be assigned regular duties. For example, a preparation cook should not be responsible for the operation and cleaning of a meat slicer until that individual has been properly trained.

---

[1] Specific training techniques are discussed in Chapter 13.

Of course, a schedule of routine cleaning and maintenance duties must be based on a **survey of cleaning needs**. If a survey has never been done, managers, supervisors, and employees should participate in the initial identification of cleaning needs for each area in the food service operation. This would minimally include entrance, public, kitchen, dining, garbage storage, restroom, work, and exit areas. Lodging properties have additional areas requiring cleaning and maintenance (see Chapter 11).

Once the areas to be cleaned and maintained have been identified, a **cleaning and maintenance schedule** can be written for each piece of equipment and each area. The cleaning and maintenance schedule is developed by thoroughly answering a number of questions such as:

- What is to be cleaned or maintained?

- Who is responsible for the cleaning or maintenance?

- When is the area or equipment to be cleaned or maintained?

- How is the cleaning or maintenance to be accomplished?

- What are the safety and sanitation precautions associated with this cleaning or maintenance procedure?

- How should the cleaned item be stored to prevent recontamination?

- Who is responsible for supervising and checking the cleaning or maintenance effort?

Even if the establishment has surveyed its cleaning needs and developed schedules for the cleaning and maintenance of each area, managers, supervisors, and employees should periodically reevaluate their cleaning and maintenance schedules. This emphasizes the importance of the procedures and makes the program more acceptable to all employees.

Cleaning and Maintenance and Equipment

Kitchen equipment must be cleaned and sanitized to prevent cross-contamination of food during preparing, cooking, holding, and serving.[2] Utensils, equipment (e.g., slicers), cutting boards, and tableware have been identified as sources of cross-contamination in food service establishments. The requirements for cleaning, sanitizing, and storing other types of equipment and utensils are specified in the FDA's Model Food Service Sanitation Ordinance.

---

[2] Cross-contamination is defined and discussed in Chapter 3. Sanitization is also defined in Chapter 3.

The FDA's Food Service Sanitation Ordinance states:

Equipment and Utensil Cleaning and Sanitization

Cleaning frequency.

(a) Tableware shall be washed, rinsed, and sanitized after each use.

(b) To prevent cross-contamination, kitchenware and food-contact surfaces of equipment shall be washed, rinsed, and sanitized after each use and following any interruption of operations during which time contamination may have occurred.

(c) Where equipment and utensils are used for the preparation of potentially hazardous foods on a continuous or production-line basis, utensils and the food-contact surfaces of equipment shall be washed, rinsed, and sanitized at intervals throughout the day on a schedule based on food temperature, type of food, and amount of food particle accumulation.

(d) The food-contact surfaces of grills, griddles, and similar cooking devices and the cavities and door seals of microwave ovens shall be cleaned at least once a day; except that this shall not apply to hot oil cooking equipment and hot oil filtering systems. The food-contact surfaces of all cooking equipment shall be kept free of encrusted grease deposits and other accumulated soil.

(e) Non-food-contact surfaces of equipment shall be cleaned as often as is necessary to keep the equipment free of accumulation of dust, dirt, food particles, and other debris.

Wiping cloths.

(a) Cloths used for wiping food spills on tableware, such as plates or bowls being served to the consumer, shall be clean, dry and used for no other purpose.

(b) Moist cloths or sponges used for wiping food spills on kitchenware and food-contact surfaces of equipment shall be clean and rinsed frequently in one of the sanitizing solutions permitted in. . . this ordinance and used for no other purpose. These cloths and sponges shall be stored in the sanitizing solution between uses.

(c) Moist cloths or sponges used for cleaning non-food-contact surfaces of equipment such as counters, dining table tops and shelves shall be clean and rinsed as specified in . . . this ordinance, and used for no other purpose. These cloths and sponges shall be stored in the sanitizing solution between uses.

Source: Food and Drug Administration, Public Health Service, U.S. Department of Health, Education, and Welfare, Food Service Sanitation Manual, *1976, pp. 41- 42.*

Cleaning and sanitizing of kitchen equipment and utensils can be accomplished manually or mechanically. **Manual cleaning and sanitizing** is usually used for in-place cleaning of equipment and for the cleaning and sanitizing of some portable equipment or its components and utensils. For example, large ovens, broilers, griddles, and steam-powered equipment are cleaned and sanitized manually. (The cleaning of preparation and cooking equipment was already discussed in Chapter 8.)

Most food service businesses also use manual warewashing to clean and sanitize pots, pans, and utensils such as mixing bowls, wire whips, and knives. On the other hand, the washing of glassware, flatware, and dishware usually takes place in a mechanical dishwashing machine. The general procedural flow for warewashing is presented in Exhibit 10.2.

Manual cleaning and sanitizing requires a three-compartment sink. The area should have adequate space for the accumulation of soiled equipment and utensils during the **soiled holding** step. Of course, soiled equipment and utensils should not come into contact with sanitized equipment and utensils. Also, cross-contamination will occur if employees do not wash their hands after handling soiled items and before touching clean items. The **scrape and presoak** step is designed to remove larger food particles from the equipment.

Washing takes place in the first compartment of the sink. A hot detergent solution is essential for the washing step. Using the correct concentration of detergent prevents expensive chemicals from being wasted and protects the customer from excess detergent residues on food-contact surfaces. (More will be said about detergents and other chemicals in the next section.)

Rinsing occurs in the second compartment of the sink. Rinsing removes detergent and food particles. Rinsing is accomplished with clean water at proper temperatures.

Once the equipment is washed and rinsed, it is sanitized in the third compartment. **Sanitizing** may be done in several ways. The equipment or utensil can be placed in 170°F (77°C) water for at least 30 seconds. Alternatively, the rinsed item may be exposed to a 50 parts per million (ppm) chlorine solution in water at 75°F (24°C) or above for at least one minute. Exposing the surface of the item to an iodine solution of 12.5 ppm in water at least 75°F (24°C) for one minute or longer will achieve the same results.

It is a good practice to regularly change the water used for washing, rinsing, and sanitizing. Water temperatures must be frequently monitored with an accurate thermometer. A chart which can serve as a reminder of the correct procedure for dishwashing by hand is presented in Exhibit 10.3.

All equipment and utensils should be **air dried** prior to clean storage. Once dried, the equipment and utensils should only be handled in ways that prevent recontaminaton of the food-contact surfaces. Knives, forks, spoons, and cups should only be grasped by their handles. Bowls, dishes, and glasses should only be handled from the bottom in areas that will not come into contact with the customer's mouth. Flatware which is to be self-served, such as in cafeterias, should be inserted in holders so that customers can grasp it by the handles.

Exhibit 10.2   Procedural Flow for Manual and Mechanical Warewashing

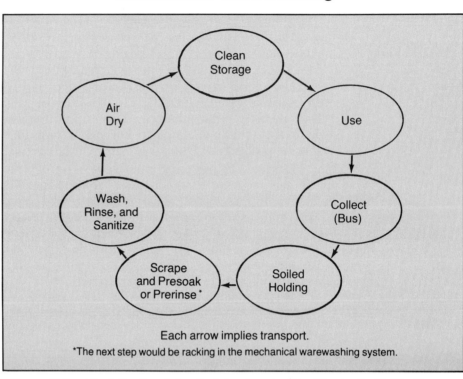

Each arrow implies transport.
*The next step would be racking in the mechanical warewashing system.

Source: National Sanitation Foundation, Sanitation Aspects of Food Service Facility Plan Preparation and Review, *1978, p. 20.*

Exhibit 10.3   Correct Dishwashing by Hand

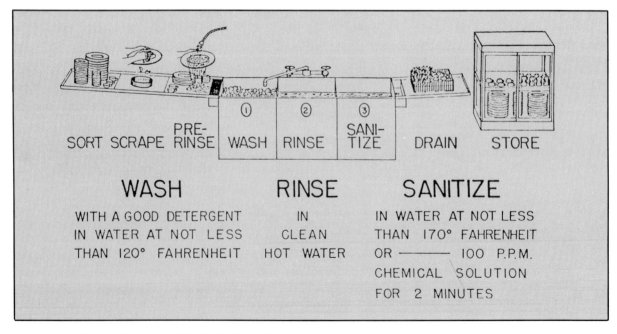

Courtesy of Denver Department of Public Health and Hospitals.

Exhibit 10.4 Recommended Daily Cleaning Procedures for Meat Slicers — English Version

Equipment Required:

Double compartment plastic pail
Cellulose sponges

Procedure:

1. Immediately after use, take all removable parts to pot-sink for washing and sanitizing according to manual pot-washing instructions.

2. Fill both compartments of pail with warm water. To the wash compartment, add ____ in the ratio of ____ per gallon of water. To the rinse side, add ____ in the ratio of ____ per gallon of water.
Use separate sponges for wash and rinse compartments.

3. Unplug slicer.
Besides the electrical hazard, serious injury could result if motor were to start while working near blade.

Product Recommendation:

_____

_____

4. Use wash solution and cellulose sponge to scrub all stationary parts of slicer. Pay particular attention to corners, handles, and hard to get at places.

5. Sanitize, using clean sponge dipped in rinse solution and squeezed nearly dry.
Dip and wring sponge frequently to be sure sanitizer contacts all surfaces.

6. Reassemble slicer.

7. Replace plug.

8. Return cleaning equipment to proper storage.

Source: DuBois Chemicals, Sanitation Procedures Manual, *(Undated), p. D-41.*

Exhibit 10.5 Recommended Daily Cleaning Procedures for Meat Slicers — Spanish Version

Equipo Necesario:

2 cubetas de plástico
esponjas de celulosa

Procedimiento:

1. Inmediatamente después de usar la rebanadora, lleve todas las partes removibles al fregadero para limpiar y sanitizar de acuerdo al manual de instrucciones de lavado de ollas.

2. Llene ambas cubetas con agua caliente. A cubeta (de lavar) agregue ____ a razón de ____ por lt. de agua. A otra cubeta (de enjuagar) agregue ____ a razón de ____ por lt. de agua. Use diferentes esponjas para cubeta de lavar y cubeta de enjuagar.

3. Desconecte la rebanadora.
Además del riesgo eléctrico, pueden resultar graves daños si el motor funciona mientras se está trabajando cerca de la cuchilla.

Producto Recomendado:

_____

_____

4. Use solucion de lavado y la esponja de celulosa para frotar todas las partes no removibles de la rebanadora. Ponga interés especial en las esquinas, rincones y lugares dificiles de lavar.

5. Sanitize, usando la esponja limpia sumergida con solución de enjuague y estrujada casi seca. Sumerja y exprima la esponja frecuentemente para asegurarse de que la solución hace contacto con todas las superficies.

6. Arme nuevamente la rebanadora.

7. Coloque el cordón en el enchufe eléctrico.

8. Regrese el equipo de limpieza a su lugar.

Adapted from: DuBois Chemicals, Sanitation Procedures Manual, *(Undated), p. D-41.*

Besides cleaning and sanitizing, safe **storage** is essential for utensils and equipment. If utensils and equipment are stored on shelves that are too deep, the items stored on the back of the shelf will be used infrequently. If the items are stored in drawers with items such as marking pen, pencils, paper, and invoices, they may be contaminated before they are used. Cleaned and sanitized equipment and utensils must be stored at least six inches (15.24 cm) off the floor. Wherever possible, they should be stored in a self-draining position (inverted). It is unacceptable to store clean and sanitized equipment and utensils in vestibules or toilet rooms. Following these requirements prevents recontamination of clean items.

Equipment cleaning procedures are frequently available from manufacturers of cleaning and sanitizing compounds. For example, one company's recommended procedures for cleaning a food slicer are presented in Exhibit 10.4. Exhibit 10.5 presents these same procedures for Spanish-speaking food service employees. Product recommendations are to be made by the manufacturer's field representative. Other manufacturers also make cleaning procedures available.

The FDA's Food Service Sanitation Ordinance states:

Equipment and Utensil Cleaning and Sanitization

Manual cleaning and sanitizing.

(a) For manual washing, rinsing and sanitizing of utensils and equipment, a sink with not fewer than three compartments shall be provided and used. Sink compartments shall be large enough to permit the accommodation of the equipment and utensils, and each compartment of the sink shall be supplied with hot and cold potable running water. Fixed equipment and utensils and equipment too large to be cleaned in sink compartments shall be washed manually or cleaned through pressure spray methods.

(b) Drain boards or easily movable dish tables of adequate size shall be provided for proper handling of soiled utensils prior to washing and for cleaned utensils following sanitizing and shall be located so as not to interfere with the proper use of the dishwashing facilities.

(c) Equipment and utensils shall be preflushed or prescraped and, when necessary, presoaked to remove gross food particles and soil.

(d) Except for fixed equipment and utensils too large to be cleaned in sink compartments, manual washing, rinsing and sanitizing shall be conducted in the following sequence:

(1) Sinks shall be cleaned prior to use.

(2) Equipment and utensils shall be thoroughly washed in the first compartment with a hot detergent solution that is kept clean.

(3) Equipment and utensils shall be rinsed free of detergent and abrasives with clean water in the second compartment.

(4) Equipment and utensils shall be sanitized in the third

compartment according to one of the methods included in . . . this ordinance.

(e) The food-contact surfaces of all equipment and utensils shall be sanitized by:

(1) Immersion for at least one-half (1/2) minute in clean, hot water at a temperature of at least 170°F; or

(2) Immersion for at least one minute in a clean solution containing at least 50 parts per million of available chlorine as a hypochlorite and at a temperature of at least 75°F; or

(3) Immersion for at least one minute in a clean solution containing at least 12.5 parts per million of available iodine and having a pH not higher than 5.0 and at a temperature of at least 75°F; or

(4) Immersion in a clean solution containing any other chemical sanitizing agent allowed . . . that will provide the equivalent bactericidal effect of a solution containing at least 50 parts per million of available chlorine as a hypochlorite at a temperature of at least 75°F for one minute or;

(5) Treatment with steam free from materials or additives other than those specified . . . in the case of equipment too large to sanitize by immersion, but in which steam can be confined; or

(6) Rinsing, spraying, or swabbing with a chemical sanitizing solution of at least twice the strength required for that particular sanitizing solution under . . . this ordinance in the case of equipment too large to sanitize by immersion.

(f) When hot water is used for sanitizing, the following facilities shall be provided and used:

(1) An integral heating device or fixture installed in, on, or under the sanitizing compartment of the sink capable of maintaining the water at a temperature of at least 170°F; and

(2) A numerically scaled indicating thermometer, accurate to ±3°F, convenient to the sink for frequent checks of water temperature; and

(3) Dish baskets of such size and design to permit complete immersion of the tableware, kitchenware, and equipment in the hot water.

(g) When chemicals are used for sanitization, they shall not have concentrations higher than the maximum permitted . . . and a test kit or other device that accurately measures the parts per million concentration of the solution shall be provided and used.

Source: FDA, pp. 42-44.

After manual cleaning and sanitizing, air drying is recommended. The other technique for warewashing is **mechanical**. As already pointed out, most glasses, dishes, and flatware are cleaned and sanitized using a dishwashing machine. Glasses used to serve juice or other beverages containing fruit pulp are very difficult to clean. A presoaking step may be required. Food products like eggs and cheese also have a tendency to stick to plates and dishes. If these food items are featured on an operation's menu, management should plan dishwashing resource requirements accordingly.

The general recommendations for mechanical cleaning and sanitizing given here are extracted from the FDA's Model Ordinance and NSF's *Standard No. 3 for Spray-Type Dishwashing Machines.* Mechanical warewashing machines are designed both to remove soil and to sanitize. It is important to operate dishmachines according to the manufacturer's instructions. After the owner's manual or service manual for the operation's dishmachine has been carefully read, a cleaning and maintenance schedule can be set up according to the manufacturer's recommendations. This will ensure optimal short-term performance and minimize time-consuming and costly repairs in the long run.

The basic mechanical warewashing procedure is a ten-step process. A summary of the multitank conveyor machine requirements follows:

1. Scrape soiled dishes and presoak flatware.

2. Prerinse to remove all visible soil.

3. Rack dishes and flatware so the water will spray evenly on all surfaces.

4. Wash dishes and flatware in a detergent-water solution at 150°F (66°C) to 160°F (71°C).

5. Rinse dishes and flatware in clean water at 160°F (71°C) to 180°F (82°C).

6. Final rinse dishes and flatware in a sanitizer-water solution at 180°F (82°C) to 195°F (91°C).

7. Air dry dishes and flatware.

8. Stack clean and sanitary items, being careful not to touch surfaces that will contact food or the customer's mouth.

9. Store clean and sanitary items in a clean, dry area.

10. Clean the machine, including the spray arms, trays, tanks, and tables.

Sufficient counter space must be provided for the accumulation of soiled glasses, dishes, and flatware. These soiled items must not contact clean and sanitary items. **Scraping** with a rubber scraper into a disposer

Exhibit 10.6   Required Minimum Dishmachine Wash and Rinse Temperatures

Type of Machine	Wash Temperature	Rinse Temperature
Single Tank, Stationary Rack, Single Temperature	165°F (74°C)	165°F (74°C)
Single Tank, Stationary Rack, Dual Temperature	150°F (66°C)	180°F (82°C)
Single Tank, Conveyor	160°F (71°C)	180°F (82°C)
Multitank, Conveyor	150°F (66°C)	160-180°F (71-82°C)
Chemical Sanitizing Machine	120°F (49°C)	120°F (49°C)
Single Tank, Pot, Pan, and Utensil Washer	140°F (60°C)	180°F (82°C)

Adapted from: *Food and Drug Administration,Public Health Service, U.S. Department of Health, Education, and Welfare,* Food Service Sanitation Manual, *1976, p. 46; and National Sanitation Foundation,* Food Service Recommended Field Evaluation Procedures for Spray-Type Dishwashing Machines, *1982.*

or garbage can and **presoaking** are required to remove larger food particles. Abrasive cleaning pads should not be used for scraping because they can scratch the surface of dishes and glasses. These scratches are not only unsightly; they also provide grooves where microbes can accumulate. Some operators do not presoak dishes in order to reduce handling and breakage. Instead, they only presoak flatware.

In any case, dishes, glasses, and flatware should be washed as soon as possible after soiling to prevent food particles from drying on surfaces. This is especially true of dishes that are soiled with sauces or eggs. **Prerinsing** further removes any remaining visible soil. A pressure sprayer located over a garbage disposal can simplify this step. Once items are prerinsed, they should be **racked** according to type (glassware, dishware, flatware). Glasses are racked bottom side up, and dishes are racked on edge; flatware is placed in baskets. All items should be arranged in the racks so that the water spray in the machine can fully contact all surfaces. Items should not be stacked on top of each other. Overcrowding increases breakage and prevents proper cleaning and sanitizing.

The temperature generally recommended for **machine wash** water is 150°F (66°C) to 160°F (71°C) for not less than 40 seconds. Requirements, which vary based on the type of machine, are listed in Exhibit 10.6. Some machines **rinse** the clean items at temperatures of 160°F (71°C) to 180°F (82°C). The **final rinse** is designed to sanitize at temperatures of 180°F (82°C) to 195°F (91°C) for not less than 10 seconds. Items are **air dried** for at least one minute to remove moisture. A drying agent can be used to minimize water spotting on dishes, glasses, and flatware. It is important to permit cleaned and sanitized dishes to thoroughly air dry. Moisture on dishes can cause damage through friction. Any chipped or cracked dishes must be thrown out, because they are unsanitary and unsafe.

Exhibit 10.7   Correct Dishwashing Procedure Using a Conveyor Machine

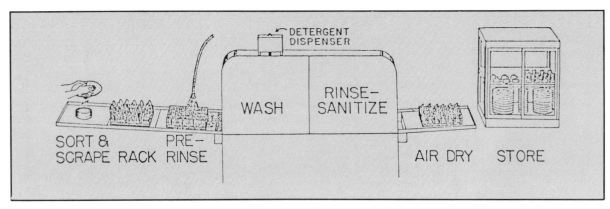

DETERGENT DISPENSER

WASH

RINSE-SANITIZE

SORT & SCRAPE   RACK   PRE-RINSE

AIR DRY   STORE

Courtesy of Denver Department of Public Health and Hospitals.

After air drying, the items should be sorted and **stacked** for storage. Employees who scrape, prerinse, and rack soiled tableware should not handle clean tableware without first washing their hands. Glasses, cups, and flatware may be left in their dishwashing racks as long as they are **stored** in a way that prevents contamination. A clean, dry storage area is desirable. At the end of the shift, or more frequently if necessary, the dishwashing machine should be disassembled and cleaned. Spray arms and scrap collection trays should be removed and cleaned. The next step is to drain the tanks and wipe off the tables and exterior surfaces of the machine. Finally, the detergent and sanitizer dispensers should be refilled as needed.

Any one of various types of dishwashing machines may be purchased by a food service operation. **Single tank, stationary rack machines** wash one rack of dishes at a time. They are operated by opening a door, inserting the rack of dishes, closing the door, and starting the machine. Single tank machines operate either at a single temperature or at dual temperatures for wash and rinse cycles. **Conveyor machines** are built with either single or multiple tanks. The racks move through the machine automatically. The operation of a two tank conveyor machine is illustrated in Exhibit 10.7.

Flight-type machines also have a conveyor belt. The dishes are placed not on racks but directly on the conveyor belt's plastic pegs or bars. (Flatware must be placed on racks.) This machine operates continuously with a person stationed at each end. This high capacity dishwasher is ideally suited to large volume operations. **Carousel-type machines** are set up with a circular conveyor belt. **Immersion dishwashers** clean dishes in racks with an arrangement similar to the manual dishwashing procedure already discussed.

Chemical sanitizing machines are an answer to rising energy costs. Many models of these low-temperature dishwashers have been evaluated by the NSF and local health officials. Normally, dishwashers operate at relatively high temperatures and low water pressures. By contrast, chemical sanitizing machines function at relatively low temperatures and high water pressures. Although the final rinse temperature is only 120°F (49°C) in low-temperature dishwashers, sanitization is still achieved because an acceptable sanitizer (e.g., chlorine) is added to the final rinse water. The energy savings of operations that have switched to low-temperature machines have been reported to be as high as 35 to 40% in the dishwashing department.

It is critical for food service managers to test the operation of their commercial dishwasher daily. The machine's data plate on the outside gives specific operating information. In addition, to prolong its useful life, a dishmachine must be serviced regularly.

Finally, the person hired to run the dishwashing machine should be well trained. Supervision of the warewashing function is important. A dishmachine is an expensive piece of equipment, both in terms of its initial cost and cost of operation. It uses chemicals, energy, and hot water almost continuously. Dishmachine manufacturers and/or chemical manufacturers usually provide free materials to help train and retrain dishwashing personnel.

Cleaning and Maintenance and Inventory

Cleaning and sanitizing agents are toxic or poisonous chemicals. They are, nevertheless, essential for the normal operation of a food service business. Cleaners and sanitizers are used to maintain safe facilities, equipment, and utensils by removing soil and killing bacteria and other harmful pathogens. However, before a discussion of cleaners and sanitizers can be thoroughly understood, several basic definitions must be given.

Soil is simply a substance which is in the wrong place. Fats and oils are necessary for the proper operation of a deep-fat fryer. However, if those same fats and oils are present in glasses and on plates, they are classified as soil. Fats, oils, and foods are **organic soil**. Soil may also be present in the form of **airborne dust** or **bonded dust**. Airborne dust is free floating, and bonded dust adheres to the surface of equipment or facilities. **Chemical deposits** caused by hard water conditions are sometimes seen on tableware, utensils, and equipment. These deposits, which include residues of detergents and mineral scale, are also considered soil.

Cleaning is the removal of soil or matter which is out of place. Cleaning operations in food service businesses are designed to prevent the accumulation of food residues, the growth of pathogens, and the production of their toxins. The cleaning process also has the potential to reduce spoilage. **Sanitizing** destroys pathogens which may remain on utensils and equipment, even after cleaning. It is virtually impossible, from a technical point of view, to sanitize an unclean utensil or piece of equipment. Items which look clean are not necessarily sanitary. Tableware which looks clean could be contaminated with pathogens from a person's respiratory tract, if they were scattered on the tableware by a sneeze.

Exhibit 10.8   The Four-Step Cleaning Process

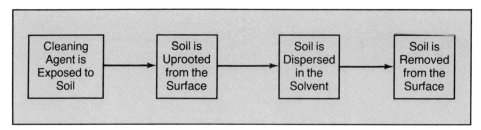

Cleaning is a four-step process, as illustrated in Exhibit 10.8. In the first step, the cleaning agent has to be exposed to the soil. Next, the soil must be uprooted from the surface. In the third step, the soil is dispersed in the solvent (usually water). Finally, the soil must be removed to prevent recontamination of the surface. If an effective cleaning agent is used under recommended conditions, the entire cleaning process can take place in a matter of seconds.

Cleaning agents include soaps and detergents. **Soaps** are sodium salts of organic acids. They are primarily used for handwashing because they do not irritate the skin.

Detergents are agents that clean by chemical and/or physical action. Detergents often contain chemicals not present in soap to enhance their cleaning action. Detergents perform a variety of useful functions:

1. They disperse or break up soil and suspend it in solution.

2. They dissolve solids and emulsify fats so they are easier to remove.

3. They suspend insoluble soil in solution and prevent it from becoming reattached to the surface.

4. Some detergents also soften water to make the water a more effective solvent.

Detergents should be selected according to the surface to be cleaned, the type of soil to be removed, the concentration of cleaning agents in them, the pressure which must be applied to get the desired results, and the combination of temperature and time they require. Ideal detergents are those that (a) soften water, (b) do not corrode metal surfaces, and (c) have a germicidal effect, all without being too expensive for frequent use.

An **all-purpose cleaner** can be used for a number of cleaning applications, so it eliminates the need for a large investment in a variety of specialized products. However, all-purpose cleaners are used in different concentrations for different surfaces, so employees must understand how to properly dilute and apply them for best results.

Cleansers are used to scour off rust, grease, and heavy soil. Because they contain abrasive substances, they will permanently scratch stainless steel and porcelain surfaces. Therefore, they should be used with caution.

Degreasers have a relatively high pH (i.e., they are highly alkaline). Although they saponify grease rapidly, they tend to irritate the skin. **Saponification** is the combination of fats and alkaline substances to form soap.

Deodorizers remove unpleasant, lingering odors but may leave a residue or film on surfaces, if used improperly. They are used in restrooms, but unfortunately, it is only to mask the odor of unclean facilities in many cases.

Dishwasher detergents clean tableware, equipment, and utensils, if used properly. If dishwasher detergents are not measured carefully, dishes may have a hazy look, spots, or a grease residue. In dishwashing machines, the measurement of the detergent is automatically controlled.

Drain cleaners provide an unclogging action for drains. They may irritate skin and contaminate foods if not used correctly.

Liquid dishwashing detergents, which are primarily used for manual warewashing, work well in both soft and hard water. Some highly alkaline detergents irritate skin, so waterproof gloves must be worn when using them.

Metal cleaners and polishes remove both soil and oxidation (discoloration) from pots and pans. After cleaning, they must be carefully rinsed off or they will leave a white film on the surface. This film can contaminate food and equipment.

Sanitizers are chemical compounds that destroy pathogens. The type of sanitizer selected by an operation depends on: (a) whether warewashing is done manually or mechanically, (b) the type of item being sanitized, and (c) specific characteristics which may be desired in the sanitizer. A table explaining the characteristics of several sanitizers and their effectiveness for various applications is shown in Exhibit 10.9. These sanitizers are classified based on their primary ingredient. Selection of a sanitizer is made more objective by learning the potential advantages and disadvantages of each type. The four types of sanitizers generally in use are chlorine compounds, iodine compounds, quaternary ammonium compounds, and acid-anionic surfactant germicides.

Chlorine-based sanitizers are inexpensive and, therefore, widely used. They are active against all microorganisms if used in a concentration of 50 parts per million (ppm) to 100 ppm. There is no advantage to using these sanitizers in excessive quantities. The concentration of chlorine sanitizers can be easily determined with a field test kit. Chlorine compounds are beneficial in that they are unaffected by hard water, are easily controlled and dispersed, and do not form a film. However, chlorine-based sanitizers possess a characteristic chlorine odor and have a relatively short shelf life. Other disadvantages include possible skin irritation, corrosion of some metals, and rapid dissipation from some solutions. Chlorine sanitizers are usually applied for one minute or more at temperatures of 75°F (24°C) or above.

Iodine-based sanitizers (iodophors) are stable, have a long shelf life, and will destroy most bacterial cells (but not spores). Advantages of iodophors are that they are unaffected by hard water, noncorrosive, easily controlled and dispersed, and nonirritating to the skin. Also, they do not form a film. Furthermore, iodine-based sanitizers have a brown or

Exhibit 10.9 Selecting a Sanitizer

TYPE OF SANITIZER E.P.A. Registered	BY APPLICATION — MECHANICAL: LOW TEMPERATURE DISHMACHINE	COLD WATER RINSE BAR GLASS WASHER	MANUAL: THIRD TANK MANUAL BAR GLASSES	UTENSILS, POTS, PANS	HARD SURFACE SANITATION (LIGHT SOIL)	HARD SURFACE CLEANING AND SANITIZATION	SOFT ICE CREAM MACHINES	BY CHARACTERISTICS: ODOR IN SOLUTION	FOAM – NONFOAM	WETTING ABILITY	HARD WATER LIME DEPOSITS	RESIDUAL BACTERIOSTATIC EFFECT	HEAT STABILITY	MILDNESS TO HANDS IN DILUTION	DEODORIZING ABILITY	COLOR INDICATION	CORROSIVENESS TO METALS	DILUTION FOR USE	TEST PAPERS AND KITS
CHLORINE (L)	Excellent (50 ppm)	Good	Good	Good	Fair	NR	Excellent	Chlorine	None	None	No	No	Moderate	No	Minimal	No	Yes	2 oz./5 gal (200 ppm) Low Temp (50 ppm)	Chlorine Test Paper
CHLORINE (P)	NR	NR	Excellent											Moderate	Minimal	No	Yes	½ oz./5 gal (100 ppm)	
IODINE L.F.	NR	Excellent	Good	Good	Very Good	NR	NR	Slight Odor of Iodine	Low Foam	Yes	Yes	No	Not Recommended for Use Over 120°F	Yes	Minimal	Yes Light Brown Color	Safe on Stainless Steel and Aluminum	1 oz./10 gal (12.5 ppm) / 1 oz./5 gal (25 ppm)	Iodine Test Kit
ACID	NR	NR	Excellent	Very Good	NR	NR	NR	None	Foam	Yes	Yes (Best)	No	Stable	Yes	Minimal	No	Safe on Stainless Steel and Aluminum	½ oz./1 gal (200 ppm) pH 4.5	Short Range pH Paper 3-5.5
QUATERNARY (Blue)	NR	NR	Very Good	Excellent	Excellent	NR	Good	None	Foam	Yes	Yes	Yes	Stable	Yes	Excellent	No	Safe on Stainless Steel and Aluminum	1 oz./2 gal (200 ppm)	QT-10 Paper
10% (Clear)			Good		Good						No							1 oz./4 gal (200 ppm)	
DETERGENT QUAT (Red)	NR	NR	NR	NR	Excellent	Excellent	NR	Spearmint	Foam	Yes	No	Yes	Stable	Moderate	Excellent	No	Safe on Stainless Steel and Aluminum	2 oz./2 gal (200 ppm)	QT-10 Paper
DETERGENT QUAT (Clear)					Excellent	Excellent		No									Yes	1 oz./3.5 gal (200 ppm)	
PHENOLIC	NR	NR	NR	NR	Sanitation Only	NR	NR	Pleasant and Fresh	None	None	None	Yes	Not Applicable	Not Applicable	Excellent	No	No	Spray	None Needed

(NR) Not Recommended

amber color, so their concentration is easily measured visually or with a field test kit. Disadvantages of iodophors include their slow action at a pH of 7.0 or above, their staining of some surfaces, and their cost. They cannot be used at temperatures of 120°F (49°C) or above. It is recommended that iodophors in a concentration of 12 to 25 ppm be applied for one minute or more at temperatures of 75 to 120°F (24-49°C).

Quaternary ammonium compounds (QUATS) are stable, have a long shelf life, and are active against most microorganisms. They form a film that controls bacterial growth. Also, QUATS are noncorrosive and nonirritating. Furthermore, they are easily controlled and dispersed, and they eliminate and prevent odors. The disadvantages of QUATS include their slow destruction of some microbes, their cost, and their residual effect. However, while the QUATS residue is undesirable on tableware, it is desirable on some surfaces (e.g., interiors of refrigerators) to control bacterial activity. QUATS are usually applied in concentrations of 180 to 220 ppm for one minute or longer at temperatures of 75°F (24°C) and above.

Acid-anionic surfactants possess a long shelf life, stability, and are active against most microorganisms. They are odorless, nonstaining, noncorrosive, effective in hard water, and easily controlled and dispersed. Acid-anionic surfactants are only effective at relatively low pHs. For example, they are used in the third compartment of a sink used for manual washing of bar glasses. They are corrosive to metal surfaces other than stainless steel and aluminum, do not perform well in hard water, and do not destroy most bacterial spores. Acid-anionic surfactants should be applied in concentrations of 100 to 200 ppm for at least one minute at temperatures of 75 to 110°F (24-43°C).

It is a dangerous practice to mix cleaning or sanitizing compounds in-house. The following case in point serves to illustrate the potential dangers. A food service manager decided to save money by mixing his own cleaning compounds. He realized that bleach is an effective sanitizer and that ammonia is an effective cleaner and deodorizer. He reasoned that a combination of bleach and ammonia would make an excellent cleaning compound. When the two chemicals were mixed, a deadly vapor was created that almost killed one of the amateur chemist's employees and completely evacuated his restaurant. If QUATS are mixed with chlorine compounds, a great deal of heat is released suddenly. Therefore, it is best for food service managers and employees to remember this safety rule: **Never mix your own cleaners or sanitizers.** The manufacturer's instructions for the proper application of these chemicals should always be carefully followed.

Thousands of dollars are wasted annually in the food service industry because cleaners and sanitizers are not applied in proper concentrations. Many managers have observed a pot and pan washer liberally pour a detergent or a sanitizer into a sink full of hot water without measuring. This senseless waste can be brought under control if management trains employees in the proper use of cleaners and sanitizers. Concentrations that are too low are ineffective, while concentrations that are too high are wasteful. The practice of using excessive quantities of cleaners and sanitizers can also be harmful to people and the items washed. Therefore, a second safety rule is: **Never use these chemicals in excess.**

An analysis of warewashing costs can point up areas where excessive amounts are being spent by the operation. On the average, the cost of the chemicals represents approximately 6% of the operation's total expenses for dishwashing. Another 11% is spent on energy. About 20% covers indirect equipment costs, such as maintenance, depreciation, and wear and tear on the machine. Dish breakage and theft amounts to 14% of total dishwashing costs. Finally, the cost of labor is a staggering 49%.[3] If these relative costs are tracked and analyzed in a food service operation, problem areas can be identified and corrective action taken.

Since cleaners and sanitizers are toxic or poisonous chemicals, all containers must be labeled and stored on the premises in a separate locked area that is used for no other purpose. The FDA's Model Ordinance addresses the topic of poisonous or toxic materials.

---

[3] This information is based on *Consultant's Handbook: Warewashing Cost Analysis* (St. Paul, Minn.: Economics Laboratory, Inc., 1978), p. 2.

The FDA's Food Service Sanitation Ordinance states:

Poisonous or Toxic Materials

Materials permitted.

There shall be present in food service establishments only those poisonous or toxic materials necessary for maintaining the establishment, cleaning and sanitizing equipment and utensils, and controlling insects and rodents.

Labeling of materials.

Containers of poisonous or toxic materials shall be prominently and distinctly labeled according to law for easy identification of contents.

Storage of materials.

(a) Poisonous or toxic materials consist of the following categories:

(1) Insecticides and rodenticides;

(2) Detergents, sanitizers, and related cleaning or drying agents;

(3) Caustics, acids, polishes, and other chemicals.

(b) Each of the three categories set forth in paragraph (a) of this section shall be stored and physically located separate from each other. All poisonous or toxic materials shall be stored in cabinets or in a similar physically separate place used for no other purpose. To preclude contamination, poisonous or toxic materials shall not be stored above food, food equipment, utensils or single-service articles, except that this requirement does not prohibit the convenient availability of detergents or sanitizers at utensil or dishwashing stations.

Use of materials.

(a) Bactericides, cleaning compounds or other compounds intended for use on food-contact surfaces shall not be used in a way that leaves a toxic residue on such surfaces or that constitutes a hazard to employees or other persons.

(b) Poisonous or toxic materials shall not be used in a way that contaminates food, equipment, or utensils, nor in a way that constitutes a hazard to employees or other persons, nor in a way other than in full compliance with the manufacturer's labeling.

Personal medications.

Personal medications shall not be stored in food storage, preparation or service areas.

First-aid supplies.

First-aid supplies shall be stored in a way that prevents them from contaminating food and food-contact surfaces.

Source: FDA, pp. 62-63.

Poisonous or toxic materials include cleaners, sanitizers, insecticides, rodenticides, and other materials not intended for human consumption. It is a good practice to leave chemicals in their original, clearly marked containers. Only those chemicals that are absolutely necessary for maintaining the operation's sanitary environment can be stored on the premises. Sanitizers and cleaners should not be stored with pesticides. The probability of a serious mistake is too great. For example, in one hotel, liquid chlorine bleach was purchased to use as a sanitizer at the cook's station. Some bleach was transferred from the original five-gallon (18.95 l) container into an empty one-gallon (3.79 l) vinegar container to make it easier to handle. The breakfast cook found the vinegar bottle the next morning as he started his shift. Not realizing what the vinegar container actually contained, he mixed up a solution in which to poach eggs. Due to the misleading label, the eggs were poached not in a vinegar-water solution but in a bleach-water solution. Therefore, a good rule is: **Never store cleaners and sanitizers or pesticides above or near food products**.

Employees must be trained to read directions and apply cleaners and sanitizers according to manufacturers' instructions. When necessary, employees must be provided with protective gloves, rubber aprons, boots, and safety glasses. Excessively high concentrations of these chemicals can leave an undesirable residue on surfaces which may be hazardous to customers. Poisonous compounds in powdered form should have a distinctive color so they will not be confused with sugar, salt, flour, or other powdered food. The importance of an obvious color difference between foods and poisons is illustrated in another actual incident. An institutional food service commissary typically made soup in a 50-gallon (189.5 l) stockpot using standard recipes. One day when the supervisor tasted the soup, it had a strange taste. To discover the source of the problem, the supervisor asked the cook about each item listed on the standard recipe for the soup. When they came to the recipe's salt content, the supervisor became suspicious and asked to see the "salt" used in the recipe. It turned out that the flakes, which had been placed in an unmarked container and used by the cook, were not *salt* but *soap* flakes.

If employees are required to take personal medications, they may not be stored in areas where food is prepared, stored, or served. A first aid kit is essential in a food service establishment. However, first aid supplies may not be stored in areas where they can contaminate food or food-contact surfaces. The objective of safe chemical storage is to prevent food and equipment contamination and to guard the safety both of employees and of customers.

Cleaning and Maintenance and Facilities

All floors, walls, and ceilings in the facility must be kept clean and in a state of good repair. Generally, these areas should be cleaned when the least amount of food is exposed. General cleanup is permitted during nonrush periods (e.g., between meals) and after closing. In some cases, emergency cleaning is necessary. For example, if a cook accidentally spills a gallon of beef stock on the kitchen floor, it must be cleaned up immediately to prevent further accidents.

The FDA's Food Service Sanitation Ordinance states:

Cleaning Physical Facilities

General.

Cleaning of floors and walls, except emergency cleaning of floors, shall be done during periods when the least amount of food is exposed, such as after closing or between meals. Floors, mats, duckboards, walls, ceilings, and attached equipment and decorative materials shall be kept clean. Only dustless methods of cleaning floors and walls shall be used, such as vacuum cleaning, wet cleaning, or the use of dust-arresting sweeping compounds with brooms.

Utility facility.

In new or extensively remodeled establishments at least one utility sink or curbed cleaning facility with a floor drain shall be provided and used for the cleaning of mops or similar wet floor cleaning tools and for the disposal of mopwater or similar liquid wastes. The use of lavatories, utensil-washing or equipment-washing, or food preparation sinks for this purpose is prohibited.

Source: FDA, p. 59.

Only dustless methods for cleaning floors are recommended. These include wet cleaning, vacuum cleaning, or sweeping with compounds that minimize dust. Wet floor cleaning tools (e.g., mops) must be cleaned and rinsed in a utility sink with a floor drain. Mopwater or similar liquid wastes are to be disposed of only in a utility sink. It is prohibited to use sinks in food preparation areas, utensil or equipment washing areas, or lavatories for the disposal of liquid cleaning wastes. It is also unsafe and unsightly to pour liquid cleaning waste on parking lot surfaces.

A number of factors affect a food service operation's ability to abide by these FDA guidelines. One major factor is the way the facility is built. Proper construction of the facility can make it easier to keep clean. For example, cramped work areas and traffic aisles are both difficult to clean and are unsafe. Therefore, in the remainder of this section, guidelines for the proper design and construction of a food service facility are presented. These recommendations also apply when a building is being converted into a food service business and when an existing operation is remodeled.

In general, local and state building codes dictate the construction and maintenance of physical facilities in a food service establishment. The FDA's Model Ordinance provides additional guidelines for construction and maintenance of physical facilities. These guidelines cover floors, walls, ceilings, lighting, ventilation, dressing rooms and locker areas, and the premises. Under the heading "Sanitary Facilities and Controls," the FDA's Model Ordinance also provides recommendations for the water supply, sewage, plumbing, toilets, lavatories, garbage and refuse, and insect and rodent control.

In 1978, the National Sanitation Foundation (NSF) in Ann Arbor, Michigan, published a reference guide titled, *Sanitation Aspects of Food Service Facility Plan Preparation and Review*. NSF's guide was designed for the food service industry and regulatory authorities to use as a primary reference to existing codes and standards. It integrated the FDA's *Food Service Sanitation Manual* (1976) containing "A Model Food Service Sanitation Ordinance" with existing state and local standards and codes written specifically for food service facilities.

The FDA's Food Service Sanitation Ordinance states:

CONSTRUCTION AND MAINTENANCE OF PHYSICAL FACILITIES

Floors

Floor construction.

Floors and floor coverings of all food preparation, food storage, and utensil-washing areas, and the floors of all walk-in refrigerating units, dressing rooms, locker rooms, toilet rooms and vestibules shall be constructed of smooth durable material such as sealed concrete, terrazzo, ceramic tile, durable grades of linoleum or plastic, or tight wood impregnated with plastic, and shall be maintained in good repair. Nothing in this section shall prohibit the use of antislip floor covering in areas where necessary for safety reasons.

Floor carpeting.

Carpeting, if used as a floor covering, shall be of closely woven construction, properly installed, easily cleanable, and maintained in good repair. Carpeting is prohibited in food preparation, equipment-washing and utensil-washing areas where it would be exposed to large amounts of grease and water, in food storage areas, and toilet room areas where urinals or toilet fixtures are located.

Prohibited floor covering.

The use of sawdust, wood shavings, peanut hulls, or similar materials as a floor covering is prohibited.

Floor drains.

Properly installed, trapped floor drains shall be provided in floors that are water-flushed for cleaning or that receive discharges of water or other fluid waste from equipment, or in areas where pressure spray methods for cleaning equipment are used. Such floors shall be constructed only of sealed concrete, terrazzo, ceramic tile or similar materials, and shall be graded to drain.

Mats and duckboards.

Mats and duckboards shall be of nonabsorbent, grease resistant materials and of such size, design, and construction as to facilitate their being easily cleaned. Duckboards shall not be used as storage racks.

Floor junctures.

In all new or extensively remodeled establishments utilizing concrete, terrazzo, ceramic tile or similar flooring materials, and where water-flush cleaning methods are used, the junctures between walls and floors shall be coved and sealed. In all other cases, the juncture between walls and floors shall not present an open seam of more than 1/32 inch.

Utility line installation.

Exposed utility service lines and pipes shall be installed in a way that does not obstruct or prevent cleaning of the floor. In all new or extensively remodeled establishments, installation of exposed horizontal utility lines and pipes on the floor is prohibited.

Source: FDA, pp. 56-57.

Floors   Generally, the FDA and NSF recommend that all floor coverings be nontoxic and able to withstand normal abuse. It is important that the

Exhibit 10.10 Recommended Floor Finishes

Food Service Area	Floor Finish			
	Commercial Grade Vinyl Asbestos Tile	Quarry Tile	Sealed Concrete	Poured Seamless
Kitchen		X		X
Dry Storage	X	X	X	X
Serving	X	X	X	X
Restroom	X	X		X
Bar	X	X		X
Janitor Closet		X	X	X

Source: National Sanitation Foundation, Sanitation Aspects of Food Service Facility Plan Preparation and Review, *1978, p. 9.*

floor surfaces be maintained in good repair. A smooth, durable floor material (e.g., sealed concrete, terrazzo, ceramic tile, a durable grade of plastic or linoleum, or tight wood impregnated with plastic) is essential in most food service areas. These areas include kitchen storage, preparation, equipment and utensil washing areas, along with locker rooms, dressing rooms, and vestibules. Anti-slip floor coverings are suggested for high traffic areas (e.g., behind the production line and in warewashing stations) for safety reasons. Recommended floor finishes are presented in Exhibit 10.10.

In most applications, red quarry tile with black hydroment acid-resistant grout is the best choice for flooring material. Slipperiness can be reduced by impregnating the tile with an abrasive material such as carborundum. Poured seamless floors are also highly acceptable. The quality of poured seamless floors is often a function of the installation crew rather than the products used.

The FDA's Model Ordinance prohibits the use of carpeting in areas where it would be exposed to large amounts of water or grease. Prohibited areas for carpeting are toilet rooms, dining room service stations, equipment and utensil washing areas, and food storage and preparation areas. If carpeting is used as a floor covering in the dining room or public areas, it must be closely woven and properly installed. Therefore, shag carpeting is not permitted because it is more difficult to vacuum. Also, servers carrying trays of food can trip on the carpet pile if it is not closely woven. Carpeting has to be easily cleanable and maintained in good repair. Sawdust, peanut shells, wood shavings, and other similar coverings are also prohibited. Obviously, it is impossible to clean floors covered with these materials.

When floors are cleaned with large amounts of water or if they are subjected to fluid waste from equipment, they must have properly in-

Exhibit 10.11   Characteristic Abuses of Areas in a Food Service Facility

Characteristic	Food Service Area						
	Kitchen Cooking	Kitchen Preparation	Dry Storage	Manual and Mechanical Warewashing	Serving	Restroom	Janitor Closet
Detergents/Chemicals				X		X	X
Dust			X				
Food Acid		X					
Food Splash		X			X		
Grease	X			X			
Heat	X			X			
Impact			X	X	X		X
Microbial Contamination		X					
Moisture				X		X	X
Rodents/Insects			X	X		X	X
Steam	X						

Source: National Sanitation Foundation, Sanitation Aspects of Food Service Facility Plan Preparation and Review, *1978, p. 10.*

stalled floor drains with traps. Proper grading of the floor ensures the required drainage. Such floors may only be constructed of terrazzo, ceramic tile, sealed concrete, or other similar materials.

Mats and duckboards may be placed on floors in areas where employees stand for long periods of time. For example, they may be used behind the production line, in the dishwashing area, behind the bar, around the pot and pan washing areas, and where there is a possibility of slipping on liquids. It is essential that these mats and duckboards be easily cleanable, grease resistant, and nonabsorbent. The use of duckboards as storage racks is prohibited. Soft wood is not permitted in the construction of duckboards.

The FDA's Model Ordinance also specifies that the junctures between walls and floors must be coved and sealed where water is likely to come into contact with the area. In dry areas, a closed seam no more than 1/32 of an inch (0.79 mm) is permitted at the juncture between floors and walls. Utility pipes and service lines must be installed so as to permit easy cleaning of the floor. Exposed pipes and sewer lines running horizontally on the floor are prohibited in all new and extensively remodeled food service operations. The objectives of the FDA's Model Ordinance are clear—to avoid the accumulation of soil and to permit easy cleaning and maintenance of all floors in food service facilities.

Walls and Ceilings   All wall coverings must be nontoxic and able to withstand normal abuse. Walls, doors, and windows should be designed so they can be easily maintained in good repair. Some characteristic problems of various wall areas in food service buildings are presented in Exhibit 10.11. Wall finishes for each area must be selected to withstand the abuses characteristic of that area.

The FDA's Food Service Sanitation Ordinance states:

CONSTRUCTION AND MAINTENANCE OF PHYSICAL FACILITIES

Walls and Ceilings

Maintenance.

Walls and ceilings, including doors, windows, skylights, and similar closures, shall be maintained in good repair.

Construction.

The walls, including nonsupporting partitions, wall coverings, and ceilings of walk-in refrigerating units, food preparation areas, equipment-washing and utensil-washing areas, toilet rooms and vestibules shall be light colored, smooth, nonabsorbent, and easily cleanable. Concrete or pumice blocks used for interior wall construction in these locations shall be finished and sealed to provide an easily cleanable surface.

Exposed construction.

Studs, joists, and rafters shall not be exposed in walk-in refrigerating units, food preparation areas, equipment-washing and utensil-washing areas, toilet rooms and vestibules. If exposed in other rooms or areas, they shall be finished to provide an easily cleanable surface.

Utility line installation.

Exposed utility service lines and pipes shall be installed in a way that does not obstruct or prevent cleaning of the walls and ceilings. Utility service lines and pipes shall not be unnecessarily exposed on walls or ceilings in walk-in refrigerating units, food preparation areas, equipment-washing and utensil-washing areas, toilet rooms and vestibules.

Attachments.

Light fixtures, vent covers, wall-mounted fans, decorative materials, and similar equipment attached to walls and ceilings shall be easily cleanable and shall be maintained in good repair.

Covering material installation.

Wall and ceiling covering materials shall be attached and sealed so as to be easily cleanable.

Source: FDA, p. 58.

Exhibit 10.12   Recommended Wall Finishes

Food Service Area		Wall Finish				
		Glazed Surface	Block Filled and Epoxy Paint	Drywall Taped Epoxy	Wall Panels	Stainless Steel or Aluminum
Kitchen	Cooking					X
	Food Prep.	X	X	X	X	X
Dry Storage		X	X	X	X	X
Warewashing	Manual	X	X			X
	Mechanical	X	X			X
Serving		X	X	X	X	X
Restroom		X	X	X	X	X
Janitor Closet		X	X	X	X	X

Source: *National Sanitation Foundation,* Sanitation Aspects of Food Service Facility Plan Preparation and Review, *1978, p. 10.*

The Model Ordinance suggests that easily cleanable, light-colored, smooth, nonabsorbent wall coverings be installed in food storage, food preparation, equipment washing, utensil washing, vestibule, and toilet room areas. Recommended wall finishes are presented in Exhibit 10.12. Walls in a food service facility are most frequently multicoated with epoxy-based paints applied to masonry walls. It is essential that all holes be filled in before the walls are painted to prevent splashed food and bonded dust from accumulating in crevices.

Drywall is usually less expensive than masonry, but in the long run it may require more repair. This is particularly true in high moisture areas. Corner and bumper guards are necessary to protect drywall construction. Modular, prefinished wall panels are easy to install and clean. They are usually constructed of fiberglass and are self-extinguishing when exposed to flames. It is important to check the requirements of the local fire code. Stainless steel and aluminum are ideal wall finishes but their high cost tends to limit their use. Ceramic tile and concrete or pumice blocks must be glazed. This provides an additional protection for walls and ceilings made of these materials.

No exposed wall construction (e.g., rafters, joists, studs) is permitted in walk-in refrigeration units, food preparation areas, equipment washing areas, utensil washing areas, vestibules, or toilet rooms. Exposed construction may be permitted on the walls of other food service areas, provided that it is surfaced or coated. Some food service establishments have a rustic Western decor, which is acceptable only if it is easy to clean. In some parts of the building, exposed utility service pipes and lines are permitted as long as the walls can be cleaned. However, in food preparation and refrigerated storage areas, utensil and equipment wash-

Exhibit 10.13   Recommended Ceiling Finishes

Food Service Area	Ceiling Finish				
	Fiber Board Plastic Coated	Metal Clad	Drywall Epoxy	Glazed Surface	Plastic Laminated Panels
All Areas	X	X	X	X	X

Source: National Sanitation Foundation, Sanitation Aspects of Food Service Facility Plan Preparation and Review, *1978, p. 11.*

ing areas, vestibules, and toilet rooms, unnecessary exposure of utility lines and pipes is not permitted. Wall attachments (e.g., light fixtures, decorations, fans) must be easily cleanable and well maintained.

Recommendations for ceiling construction also include skylights. Only nonporous, easily cleanable materials are permitted. No exposed construction is permitted on the ceilings of walk-in refrigeration units, food preparation areas, equipment and utensil washing areas, vestibules, and toilet rooms. If utility lines and pipes are exposed on the ceiling, it is imperative that the ceiling be easily cleanable. Light fixtures, fans, and other equipment or decorations attached to the ceiling must be in good repair and easily cleanable. Otherwise food could be contaminated by falling materials which are unclean. Recommended ceiling finishes are presented in Exhibit 10.13.

Noise control is important, especially in dishwashing areas. Some vinyl-clad fiberboard acoustical tile is acceptable for use in noisy areas. All ceiling coverings must be nontoxic and able to withstand normal abuse. Suitable materials are those which are easy to clean and meet the operation's acoustical needs.

To aid in the operation's plan preparation and review, the NSF has developed a room finish form that can be used to specify materials for construction or renovation of, or conversion to, a food service establishment. A **sample room finish schedule** is presented in Exhibit 10.14.

Lighting   Adequate lighting is essential in all areas of a food service establishment to guarantee that the facilities are kept clean. The intensity of light is measured in footcandles, the unit of illumination. One **footcandle** equals one lumen per square foot. A **lumen** is a measure of power equal to 0.001496 watt. The greater the number of footcandles, the more bright or intense the light source. Footcandles are measured with a light meter.

The FDA's Food Service Sanitation Ordinance states:

Lighting

General.

(a) Permanently fixed artificial light sources shall be installed to provide at least 20 foot candles of light on all food preparation surfaces and at equipment or utensil-washing work levels.

(b) Permanently fixed artificial light sources shall be installed to provide, at a distance of 30 inches from the floor:

(1) At least 20 foot candles of light in utensil and equipment storage areas and in lavatory and toilet areas; and

(2) At least 10 foot candles of light in walk-in refrigerating units, dry food storage areas, and in all other areas. This shall also include dining areas during cleaning operations.

Protective shielding.

(a) Shielding to protect against broken glass falling onto food shall be provided for all artificial lighting fixtures located over, by, or within food storage, preparation, service, and display facilities, and facilities where utensils and equipment are cleaned and stored.

(b) Infrared or other heat lamps shall be protected against breakage by a shield surrounding and extending beyond the bulb, leaving only the face of the bulb exposed.

Source: FDA, p. 60.

The FDA's Model Ordinance recommends a minimum of 20 footcandles of light in utensil and equipment washing areas and on food preparation surfaces. Measured 30 inches (76.2 cm) from the floor, at least 20 footcandles of light are required in equipment storage, utensil storage, lavatory, and toilet areas, and at least 10 footcandles are necessary in dry storage areas and walk-in refrigeration units. The minimum of 10 footcandles also applies to dining room areas during cleaning and to all other areas in the food service establishment. Most lighting engineers and occupational health and safety inspectors recommend 50-70 footcandles in work areas. The objective of these requirements is to provide adequate lighting for cleaning, food storage, food preparation, and the service of the food. A well-lit facility is more likely to be maintained in a clean condition. Some areas in the facility (e.g., exhaust hoods, walk-in refrigerators and freezers) usually require extra lighting.

In addition to lighting intensity, the FDA's Model Ordinance also addresses protective shielding for lighting fixtures. This protective shielding is required in all food preparation, food storage, food display, food service, and utensil and equipment cleaning and storage areas. Infrared and other heat lamps used in food pickup areas also must be protected with a shield that surrounds and extends beyond the bulb. The objective is to prevent broken glass from contaminating food products or raw ingredients. These precautions can actually be time savers, as the following actual incident illustrates. The chef in a restaurant was hurrying to keep up with a flurry of orders during a busy rush period. The chef had already put up five plates of food for a table of six. But as the chef placed the last plate of food under the infrared lamp, which was not

Exhibit 10.14   Room Finish Schedule

Room Number	Room Name	Floor Material	Base Material	Wall Finish Material				Ceiling		Remarks
				Top	Bottom	Top	Bottom	Material	Height	

Source: National Sanitation Foundation, Sanitation Aspects of Food Service Facility Plan Preparation and Review, *1978, p. 29.*

shielded, he accidently broke the lamp. Even though the waitress had already loaded the five plates of food and was just reaching for the sixth as the lamp broke and dropped glass on the plate, she could not serve any of the party of six until the entire order was complete. She had to keep all six people waiting while the chef prepared the sixth plate over again.

Ventilation   Various undesirable fumes and odors are created both in the kitchen and in the dining rooms of food service establishments. Ventilation equipment is designed to remove smoke, fumes, steam, condensation, excessive heat, vapors, and obnoxious odors. State and local building codes dictate specific ventilation requirements for food preparation areas, locker rooms, storage areas, and serving areas. The major ventilation problem food service businesses encounter is a transfer of obnoxious odors and gases from the kitchen to public areas such as dining, meeting, and banquet rooms. If the ventilation of kitchen areas is improperly linked to public areas, unwanted air current problems may be created. A separate source of make-up air is needed in the public areas to replace the air exhausted from these areas.

The FDA's Food Service Sanitation Ordinance states:

Ventilation

General.

All rooms shall have sufficient ventilation to keep them free of excessive heat, steam, condensation, vapors, obnoxious odors, smoke and fumes. Ventilation systems shall be installed and operated according to law and, when vented to the outside, shall not create an unsightly, harmful or unlawful discharge.

Special ventilation.

(a) Intake and exhaust air ducts shall be maintained to prevent the entrance of dust, dirt, and other contaminating materials.

(b) In new or extensively remodeled establishments, all rooms from which obnoxious odors, vapors or fumes originate shall be mechanically vented to the outside.

Source: FDA, p. 61.

Generally, air exhausted from a food service facility to the outside may not create an unlawful, harmful, or unsightly situation. Exhaust vents dripping with grease do not present an appealing sight to customers as they approach the building. All intake and exhaust air ducts must be well maintained. This prevents the entrance of dust, dirt, and other contaminants, and minimizes fire hazards. In new and extensively remodeled buildings, ventilation to the outside is required in all rooms where vapors, fumes, or obnoxious odors are likely to be created. Sufficient ventilation also helps to maintain comfortable temperatures and minimizes soil buildup on walls, ceilings, and floors in these areas.

Dressing Rooms and Locker Areas

Employees who wear their uniforms into the building may bring along several contaminants on their apparently clean uniforms. Therefore, it is desirable to have employees change into the required uniforms immediately before they begin their shift. If dressing rooms or areas are provided, they may not be used for food storage, preparation, service, or equipment and utensil washing or storage. The objective is to reduce the likelihood of contamination of food products by employees wearing street clothes.

Even if employees do not change into uniforms after arriving at work, management still has the responsibility to provide storage facilities for the employees' personal belongings (e.g., coats, shoes, personal medications, and purses). Locker storage areas must be sufficient, secure, and clean. It is important that the storage of employee belongings and clothing be neat and orderly. To avoid contamination, only completely packaged food and packaged single-service articles may be stored in locker areas.

The FDA's Food Service Sanitation Ordinance states:

Dressing rooms and areas.

If employees routinely change clothes within the establishment, rooms or areas shall be designated and used for that purpose. These designated rooms or areas shall not be used for food preparation, storage or service, or for utensil washing or storage.

Locker areas.

Enough lockers or other suitable facilities shall be provided and used for the orderly storage of employee clothing and other belongings. Lockers or other suitable facilities may be located only in the designated dressing rooms or in food storage rooms or areas containing only completely packaged food or packaged single-service articles.

Souroo: FDA, p. 61.

Premises   From a public health standpoint and from the standpoint of the customers' first impressions, the inside and outside of the facility must be free from litter. When the interior or exterior has accumulated litter, it shows customers that management does not care enough about the operation. It is important to control dust on walks and in parking areas. Only asphalt, concrete, treated gravel, or similar materials are permitted for surfaces in these areas. Exterior surfaces must be graded to prevent the pooling of water. Only items required for the normal operation of a food service business may be stored on the premises.

The FDA's Food Service Sanitation Ordinance states:

Premises

General.

(a) Food service establishments and all parts of property used in connection with their operations shall be kept free of litter.

(b) The walking and driving surfaces of all exterior areas of food service establishments shall be surfaced with concrete or asphalt, or with gravel or similar material effectively treated to facilitate maintenance and minimize dust. These surfaces shall be graded to prevent pooling and shall be kept free of litter.

(c) Only articles necessary for the operation and maintenance of the food service establishment shall be stored on the premises.

(d) The traffic of unnecessary persons through the food-preparation and utensil-washing areas is prohibited.

Living areas.

No operation of a food service establishment shall be conducted in any room used as living or sleeping quarters. Food service operations shall be separated from any living or sleeping quarters by complete partitioning and solid, self-closing doors.

Laundry facilities.

(a) Laundry facilities in a food service establishment shall be restricted to the washing and drying of linens, cloths, uniforms and aprons necessary to the operation. If such items are laundered on the premises, an electric or gas dryer shall be provided and used.

(b) Separate rooms shall be provided for laundry facilities except that such operations may be conducted in storage rooms containing only packaged foods or packaged single-service articles.

Linens and clothes storage.

(a) Clean clothes and linens shall be stored in a clean place and protected from contamination until used.

(b) Soiled clothes and linens shall be stored in nonabsorbent containers or washable laundry bags until removed for laundering.

Cleaning equipment storage.

Maintenance and cleaning tools such as brooms, mops, vacuum cleaners and similar equipment shall be maintained and stored in a way that does not contaminate food, utensils, equipment, or linens and shall be stored in an orderly manner for the cleaning of that storage location.

Animals.

Live animals, including birds and turtles, shall be excluded from within the food service operational premises and from adjacent areas under the control of the permit holder. This exclusion does not apply to edible fish, crustacea, shellfish, or to fish in aquariums. Patrol dogs accompanying security or police officers, or guide dogs accompanying blind persons, shall be permitted in dining areas.

Source: FDA, pp. 63-64.

Unauthorized people are not permitted in food storage, preparation, or utensil washing areas. Enforcing this rule minimizes additional contamination and reduces safety and security risks. Food service establishments may not have attached living areas unless these areas are separated by a complete partition and a self-closing door.

Laundry facilities may be installed if they are only used for the washing and drying of aprons, uniforms, cloths, and linens needed for normal operation. Ideally, an operation's laundry room should be located in a physically separate area. A washer and dryer may be placed in a storage area, provided that the room only contains completely packaged foods or packaged single-service articles. Clean linens and cloths must be protected from contamination before they are used. Washable laundry bags or nonabsorbent containers must be used for the storage of soiled linens and clothes.

A separate storage area is required for cleaning equipment. Mops, vacuum cleaners, brooms, and other cleaning equipment may not be stored in ways that permit the contamination of food, equipment, utensils, or linens. Live animals are not permitted in the food service operation because they can contaminate food, equipment, and facilities. (The exceptions are edible fish and shellfish, and fish in aquariums. Also, guide dogs for the blind and patrol dogs accompanying police or security officers are permitted in dining areas only.) This requirement reduces the likelihood of foodborne disease transmission through indirect or direct contact with food-contact surfaces or food products.

Water Supply

Food service personnel, management, and maintenance people must be made aware that faulty or careless water hook-ups can contaminate otherwise potable water. If the water is contaminated, it is likely to contaminate food, equipment, utensils, and humans. Hot and cold water of sufficient quantity and pressure is necessary for any food service operation. Plumbing codes govern the design and installation of the establishment's water supply. The water supply is used in food preparation, in cleaning and sanitizing operations, and in employee handwashing. Fundamentally, potable water must be obtained from a safe source of supply.

The FDA's Food Service Sanitation Ordinance states:

Sanitary Facilities and Controls

Water Supply

General.

Enough potable water for the needs of the food service establishment shall be provided from a source constructed and operated according to law.

Transportation.

All potable water not provided directly by pipe to the food service establishment from the source shall be transported in a bulk water transport system and shall be delivered to a closed-water system. Both of these systems shall be constructed and operated according to law.

Bottled water.

Bottled and packaged potable water shall be obtained from a source that complies with all laws and shall be handled and stored in a way that protects it from contamination. Bottled and packaged potable water shall be dispensed from the original container.

Water under pressure.

Water under pressure at the required temperatures shall be provided to all fixtures and equipment that use water.

Steam.

Steam used in contact with food or food-contact surfaces shall be free from any materials or additives other than those specified . . .

Source: FDA, p. 49.

In most localities, the public water supply is closely monitored. However, some food service operations may obtain their water supply from a private source. If water is supplied privately, it must be routinely monitored by the supplier in regard to testing (chemical and bacteriological), treatment, storage, and transport. Water may be transported in a bulk water system and delivered to the operation's closed-water system. Alternatively, packaged or bottled water, obtained from a licensed and approved source, can be used.

The types and sizes of equipment in the food service operation dictate hot and cold water requirements. Plumbing codes provide general requirements for water pressure and usage volume for fixtures and equipment. Water at the proper temperature and pressure must be provided to all of the necessary equipment. As a general rule of thumb, the volume of water supplied and its flow pressure must meet the anticipated *maximum* volume and pressure requirements. Required usage pressures and volumes can be obtained from equipment lists in catalogs.

If steam comes into contact with food or food-contact surfaces, it must be free from harmful additives or materials. Also, a source of potable water must be provided for ice-making equipment.

Sewage   Liquid waste and sewage must be removed from the premises promptly and properly. A public system may be used to transport the sewage. In some cases, pretreatment or conditioning of liquid waste is required. In some localities, an on-site private system for the elimination of sewage and liquid waste is permitted, although some localities limit the capacity of these systems. In all cases, the required permits must be obtained. Care in the disposal of sewage and liquid waste will prevent the contamination of potable water, equipment, utensils, and food.

The FDA's Food Service Sanitation Ordinance states:

Sewage

General.

All sewage, including liquid waste, shall be disposed of by a public sewerage system or by a sewage disposal system constructed and operated according to law. Non-water-carried sewage disposal facilities are prohibited, except as permitted by sections . . . of this ordinance (pertaining to temporary food service establishments) or as permitted by the regulatory authority in remote areas or because of special situations.

Source: FDA, p. 50.

Plumbing

The state or local plumbing code covers the installation requirements of the building's plumbing system. The basic objective is to guard against a cross-connection between potable water supplies and pollution. A **cross-connection** may be either indirect or direct. An **indirect cross-connection** occurs when potable water is contaminated by the action of pollutants being sucked into, blown across, or diverted into a safe water supply. For example, if a lavatory or washbasin has a faucet that is not sufficiently elevated above the rim of the basin, the potential for an indirect cross-connection exists. A **direct cross-connection** is a physical connection between potable water and nonpotable water. For example, if fixtures have a water supply connected directly to a sewer, a direct cross-connection exists. Both indirect and direct cross-connections are potentially very dangerous because they can be responsible for outbreaks of gastroenteritis, dysentery, and typhoid fever.

Backflow is a flow reversal due to a greater pressure in the system compared to the potable water supply. **Back siphonage** can occur when the supply pressure is less than the atmospheric pressure. This turns an outflow source into an intake source. A hose attached to a faucet with its tip submerged in contaminated water can create an indirect cross-connection subject to back siphonage. Harmful contaminants can be siphoned back into the potable water supply. Devices must be installed to prevent the possibility of backflow and back siphonage. Air gaps (see Exhibit 10.15) are often used for this purpose.

If grease traps are part of the plumbing system, they must be easily

Exhibit 10.15 An Air Gap Prevents Backflow and Back Siphonage

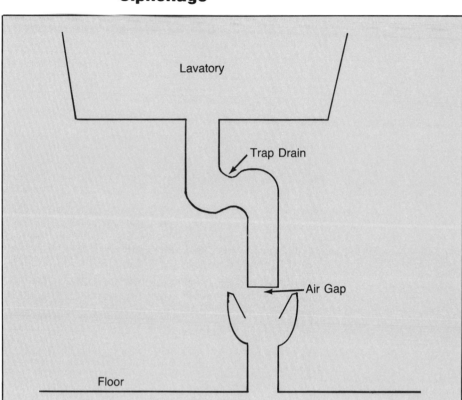

cleanable. Garbage grinders and disposers must be properly installed. Drains are an important component of the plumbing system. **Indirect drains** are essential to prevent the backup of sewage into sinks used to clean food, utensils, equipment, or tools. Strict observance of this part of the FDA's Model Ordinance serves to eliminate faulty plumbing installations and to provide a source of safe drinking water to the public.

The FDA's Food Service Sanitation Ordinance states:

Plumbing

General.

Plumbing shall be sized, installed, and maintained according to law. There shall be no cross-connection between the potable water supply and any nonpotable or questionable water supply nor any source of pollution through which the potable water supply might become contaminated.

Nonpotable water system.

A nonpotable water system is permitted only for purposes such as air-conditioning and fire protection and only if the system is installed according to law and the nonpotable water does not contact, directly or indirectly, food, potable water, equipment that contacts food, or utensils. The piping of any nonpotable water system shall be durably identified so that it is readily distinguishable from piping that carries potable water.

Backflow.

The potable water system shall be installed to preclude the possibility of backflow. Devices shall be installed to protect against backflow and back siphonage at all fixtures and equipment where an air gap at least twice the diameter of the water supply inlet is not provided between the water supply inlet and the fixture's flood level rim. A hose shall not be attached to a faucet unless a backflow prevention device is installed.

Grease traps.

If used, grease traps shall be located to be easily accessible for cleaning.

Garbage grinders.

If used, garbage grinders shall be installed and maintained according to law.

Drains.

Except for properly trapped open sinks, there shall be no direct connection between the sewerage system and any drains originating from equipment in which food, portable equipment, or utensils are placed. When a dishwashing machine is located within 5 feet of a trapped floor drain, the dishwasher waste outlet may be connected directly on the inlet side of a properly vented floor drain trap if permitted by law.

Source: FDA, pp. 50-51.

Toilet Facilities   The installation, number, convenience, and accessibility of toilet facilities is strictly defined in plumbing codes. Toilet facilities must be available for all employees and customers. Materials used in the construction of urinals and toilets must be dense, impervious, and easily cleanable. Toilet rooms should be enclosed completely and fitted with self-closing, solid doors. (To provide access for handicapped people, the self-closing door requirement may be waived.)

All fixtures in toilet areas must be clean and well maintained. An adequate supply of toilet tissue is essential. Receptacles in toilet rooms must be provided for waste materials. At least one covered waste receptacle is required in toilet rooms used by women. This portion of the code is designed to prevent the contamination of equipment, facilities, or food by human waste and disease-carrying insects.

The FDA's Food Service Sanitation Ordinance states:

Toilet Facilities

Toilet installation.

Toilet facilities shall be installed according to law, shall be the number required by law, shall be conveniently located, and shall be accessible to employees at all times.

Toilet design.

Toilets and urinals shall be designed to be easily cleanable.

Toilet rooms.

Toilet rooms shall be completely enclosed and shall have tight-fitting, self-closing, solid doors, which shall be closed except during cleaning or maintenance, except as provided by law.

Toilet fixtures.

Toilet fixtures shall be kept clean and in good repair. A supply of toilet tissue shall be provided at each toilet at all times. Easily cleanable receptacles shall be provided for waste materials. Toilet rooms used by women shall have at least one covered waste receptacle.

Source: FDA, pp. 51-52.

Lavatory Facilities

Lavatories (i.e., sinks) are used for handwashing. The installation, number, convenience, and accessibility of lavatory facilities is also governed by law. Lavatories may be located either in or immediately adjacent to toilet rooms. Handwashing sinks are *not* to be used for the preparation of food or the washing of equipment or utensils. Each lavatory must be provided with hot and cold running water. A 15-second minimum water flow is required on all metered, self-closing, or slow-closing faucets.

Hand cleaning soap or detergent is essential at each lavatory. Common towels are prohibited because they can spread contamination. Single-use sheet or roll paper towels are preferred. Heated air drying devices in lavatories probably provide the most sanitary method for hand drying. If disposable paper towels are used, a waste receptacle is necessary. All equipment in the lavatory must be easy to clean and maintain. The importance of adequate lavatory facilities is apparent when one realizes that human hands are continually coming into contact with food, equipment, utensils, and food-contact surfaces. Lavatories should be used often by food service employees to prevent their hands from becoming vehicles for contamination.

The FDA's Food Service Sanitation Ordinance states:

Lavatory Facilities

Lavatory installation.

(a) Lavatories shall be at least the number required by law, shall be installed according to law, and shall be located to permit convenient use by all employees in food preparation areas and utensil-washing areas.

(b) Lavatories shall be accessible to employees at all times.

(c) Lavatories shall also be located in or immediately adjacent to toilet rooms or vestibules. Sinks used for food preparation or for washing equipment or utensils shall not be used for handwashing.

Lavatory faucets.

Each lavatory shall be provided with hot and cold water tempered by means of a mixing valve or combination faucet. Any self-closing, slow-closing, or metering faucet used shall be designed to provide a flow of water for at least 15 seconds without the need to reactivate the faucet. Steam-mixing valves are prohibited.

Lavatory supplies.

A supply of hand-cleansing soap or detergent shall be available at each lavatory. A supply of sanitary towels or a hand-drying device providing heated air shall be conveniently located near each lavatory. Common towels are prohibited. If disposable towels are used, easily cleanable waste receptacles shall be conveniently located near the handwashing facilities.

Lavatory maintenance.

Lavatories, soap dispensers, hand-drying devices and all related fixtures shall be kept clean and in good repair.

Source: FDA, pp. 52-53.

Garbage and Refuse

Proper disposal and storage of garbage and refuse are essential if the contamination of food and the buildup of pests are to be avoided. Frequently, refuse and garbage are stored outdoors on the premises of food service operations. Containers used for that purpose must be insect- and rodent-proof, durable, and easily cleanable. It is recommended that wet-strength paper bags or plastic bags be used to line these containers. Plastic or wet-strength paper bags are not sufficient by themselves for the outside storage of garbage and refuse because they can be entered by insects and rodents.

The FDA's Food Service Sanitation Ordinance states:

Garbage and Refuse

Containers.

(a) Garbage and refuse shall be kept in durable, easily cleanable, insect-proof and rodent-proof containers that do not leak and do not absorb liquids. Plastic bags and wet-strength paper bags may be used to line these containers, and they may be used for storage inside the food service establishment.

(b) Containers used in food preparation and utensil washing areas shall be kept covered after they are filled.

(c) Containers stored outside the establishment, and dumpsters, compactors and compactor systems shall be easily cleanable, shall be provided with tight-fitting lids, doors or covers, and shall be kept covered when not in actual use. In containers designed with drains, drain plugs shall be in place at all times, except during cleaning.

(d) There shall be a sufficient number of containers to hold all the garbage and refuse that accumulates.

(e) Soiled containers shall be cleaned at a frequency to prevent insect and rodent attraction. Each container shall be thoroughly cleaned on the inside and outside in a way that does not contaminate food, equipment, utensils, or food preparation areas. Suitable facilities, including hot water and detergent or steam, shall be provided and used for washing containers. Liquid waste from compacting or cleaning operations shall be disposed of as sewage.

Storage.

(a) Garbage and refuse on the premises shall be stored in a manner to make them inaccessible to insects and rodents. Outside storage of unprotected plastic bags or wet-strength paper bags or baled units containing garbage or refuse is prohibited. Cardboard or other packaging material not containing garbage or food wastes need not be stored in covered containers.

(b) Garbage or refuse storage rooms, if used, shall be constructed of easily cleanable, nonabsorbent, washable materials, shall be kept clean, shall be insect-proof and rodent-proof and shall be large enough to store the garbage and refuse containers that accumulate.

(c) Outside storage areas or enclosures shall be large enough to store the garbage and refuse containers that accumulate and shall be kept clean. Garbage and refuse containers, dumpsters and compactor systems located outside shall be stored on or above a smooth surface of nonabsorbent material such as concrete or machine-laid asphalt that is kept clean and maintained in good repair.

Disposal.

(a) Garbage and refuse shall be disposed of often enough to prevent the development of odor and the attraction of insects and rodents.

(b) Where garbage or refuse is burned on the premises, it shall be done by controlled incineration that prevents the escape of particulate matter in accordance with law. Areas around incineration facilities shall be clean and orderly.

Source: FDA, pp. 53-55.

Refuse and garbage containers used in utensil washing or food preparation areas are to be kept covered. Containers stored outside of the building must have tight fitting lids. A sufficient number of containers must be provided. It is a good idea to store containers outside on a rack or in a storage box. In either case, they should be at least 18 inches (45.72 cm) off the ground. Soiled containers should be cleaned at regular intervals to prevent insect and/or rodent infestation. Containers can effectively be cleaned with a combination of detergents and hot water or steam.

It is essential that garbage and refuse be removed from the premises on a timely basis. This will prevent odor development and the attraction of rodents or insects. In some localities, garbage can be burned in an incinerator. Air pollution is an undesirable by-product of incineration. It is common for large food service operations to use waste compactors to compress refuse and garbage. Compactors can reduce solid waste bulk by at least 75% and make it easier to keep the premises clean. Any liquid waste generated by a compactor should be disposed of as sewage. Some compactors automatically deodorize and spray insecticides. Garbage and refuse storage areas must be designed to keep garbage and trash properly stored while preventing the breeding of insects and rodents on the premises. All outside garbage and refuse storage areas, dumpsters, and compactors must be located on a smooth, nonabsorbent surface (e.g., asphalt or concrete).

Insect and Rodent Control

Insects and rodents are disease-carrying pests. They not only contaminate food; they destroy it. Some insects and rodents spread disease through food, while others are classified as stored food insects because they damage and waste food products. The pests of public health significance are flies, cockroaches, rats, mice, small beetles, and moths. Both insects and rodents are potential carriers of pathogenic bacteria in and on their bodies. A common fly, for example, can carry over six million microbes on its body and many more internally.

The FDA's Food Service Sanitation Ordinance states:

Insect and Rodent Control

General.

Effective measures intended to minimize the presence of rodents, flies, cockroaches, and other insects on the premises shall be utilized. The premises shall be kept in such condition as to prevent the harborage or feeding of insects or rodents.

Openings.

Openings to the outside shall be effectively protected against the entrance of rodents. Outside openings shall be protected against the entrance of insects by tight-fitting, self-closing doors, closed windows, screening, controlled air currents, or other means. Screen doors shall be self-closing, and screens for windows, doors, skylights, transoms, intake and exhaust air ducts, and other openings to the outside shall be tight-fitting and free of breaks. Screening material shall not be less than 16 mesh to the inch.

Source: FDA, p. 55.

The **common housefly** (*Musca domestica*) is less than 3/8 of an inch (0.95 cm) in length. This germ-dispensing insect has been known to carry typhoid fever, leprosy, amoebic dysentery, tuberculosis, and bubonic plague. Flies do not hate humans; they simply enjoy eating the same food that humans eat. The female fly lays about 100 to 120 eggs in each batch. In warm, moist, decaying environments, the eggs hatch in as little as eight hours. In one or two weeks, the larvae are transformed into adult flies. As many as 14 generations may be produced in a single summer season.

A fly can only consume fluids. It draws liquid foods through its proboscis, a soft and fleshy sucking tube located at the bottom of its face.

Exhibit 10.16   Life Cycle of the Common Housefly

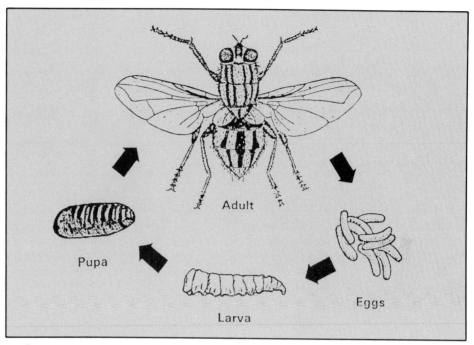

Source: H.D. Pratt et al., Flies of Public Health Importance and Their Control, *1975, p. 5.*

When a fly lands on solid food, it must dissolve the solids by regurgitating some of its stomach fluids. Once the fly has transformed some of the solid food into a liquid, it can consume the fluid. At this point the food is contaminated, because even if the fly is shooed away or killed, it has left behind thousands of invisible pathogens on the food.

A fly has six legs, each equipped with a claw and a sticky pad. The claws are used for clinging to rough surfaces, while the sticky pads are used to walk on smooth surfaces or upside down on the ceiling. Each foot pad is a germ-laden surface that can contaminate food. Fortunately for humans and other living things, spiders, wasps, toads, and lizards feed on flies whenever they can catch them. Exhibit 10.16 presents the life cycle of a common housefly.

Cockroaches are ubiquitous and troublesome pests. Cockroaches range in color from tan through chestnut brown to black. Four species of cockroaches account for the majority of cockroach problems in food service establishments. These four species are represented in Exhibit 10.17.

The **German cockroach** (*Blattella germanica*) is the most common type, recognizable by its approximate 3/4-inch (20 mm) length and its gray color. The German cockroach is most common in the northern United States. It has been found in areas that are warm and dry with ready access to water (e.g., kitchens, storerooms, bathrooms, and throughout buildings). At night, when the lights are turned on in a heavily infested area, the German cockroach can be observed scurrying from dishes, surfaces, utensils, and the floor.

Exhibit 10.17   The Four Most Common Species of Cockroaches in the United States

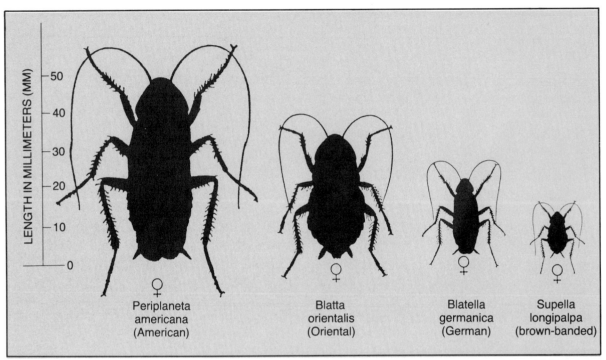

Source: H.D. Pratt et al., Household and Stored-Food Insects of Public Health Importance and Their Significance, *1975, pp. 7-8.*

The **brown-banded cockroach** (*Supella longipalpa*) is approximately 1/2 inch (10-15 mm) in length and has two brown to yellow bands on its wings. The brown-banded cockroach is found in most parts of the United States and in Canada. It prefers hiding in electric clocks, television sets, and radios which provide a dark, warm shelter.

The **Oriental cockroach** (*Blatta orientalis*) is black and roughly 3/4 to 1 1/2 inches (20-35 mm) in length. The Oriental cockroach lives under sinks and refrigerators and in sewers and cool, damp basements. It has a repulsive, strong odor.

The **American cockroach** (*Periplaneta americana*) is red to dark brown and about 1 1/2 to 2 inches (35-50 mm) in length. The American cockroach can be found in warm, humid environments, namely boiler rooms, basements, kitchens, and garbage areas. This species prefers sweets and beer, so it may be found in opened soft drink and beer bottles.

Beetles and moths are classified as **stored food insects** because they destroy food. Some species of beetles attack leather products, woolens, and food products such as hams, flour, spices, cookies, and dried fruits. Other beetles prefer the kernels of corn, rice, peas, beans, and wheat. Most people know that moths may be responsible for damage to wool carpets and holes in woolen clothes, but few people realize that other species of moths destroy wheat, corn, and other grains.

Exhibit 10.18   Field Identification of Domestic Rodents

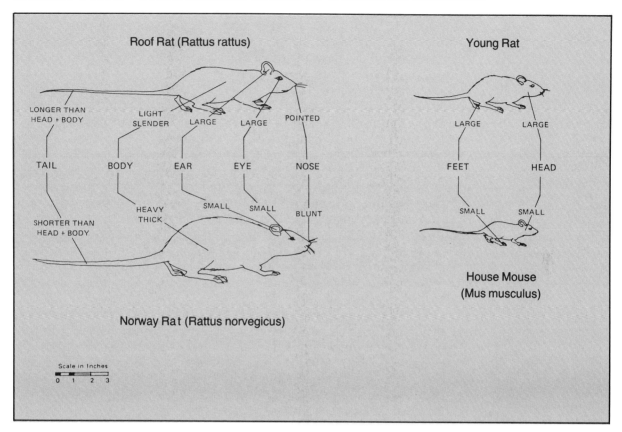

Source: H.D. Pratt and R.Z. Brown, Biological Factors in Domestic Rodent Control, *1976, p. 4.*

Rats and mice carry pathogenic microbes and destroy food products in storage. The three types of rodents which most frequently trouble food service facilities are the roof rat, the Norway rat, and the house mouse.

The **roof rat** (*Rattus rattus*) is either black or brown. It is found in the southeastern United States and in western states. The roof rat weighs from 4 to 12 ounces (113.4 - 340.2 g). It has a pointed nose and a slender body, measuring 14 to 18 inches (35.56 - 45.72 cm) in length.

The **Norway rat** (*Rattus norvegicus*) is red to gray-brown and weighs from 10 to 17 ounces (283.5 - 481.95 g). The Norway rat has a blunt nose and a heavy, thick body measuring 13 to 18 inches (33.02 - 45.72 cm) in length. The Norway rat can be found throughout most of North America.

The **house mouse** (*Mus musculus*) ranges in color from gray to brown. It weighs from 1/2 to 3/4 of an ounce (14.18 - 21.26 g) and measures 6 to 7 1/2 inches (15.24 - 19.05 cm) in length. It has a pointed nose and a small body. The house mouse is more widely distributed in the environment than the other two rodents. A field identification chart of domestic rodents is presented in Exhibit 10.18.

Rodents have a tendency to nest together in safe areas near water and food. They prefer quiet, out-of-the-way places like basements. All three rodents are exceptional swimmers, especially the rats. They can climb vertical walls and jump relatively large distances. Their front or incisor teeth are excellent for gnawing. Since these teeth continue to grow throughout their lives, rodents gnaw continually to keep their teeth short. Rodents have been known to gnaw wood, cinder blocks, aluminum, paperboard, cloth sacks, and lead pipes. All three rodents eat garbage, and if they are not controlled, they will consume a wide variety of foods. They have been known to eat grains, meats, eggs, potatoes, and even citrus fruits.

Rodents have been linked to a variety of human diseases. Salmonellosis is spread through food contaminated by rat or mouse droppings. Rat-bite fever is caused by a pathogenic *Streptobacillus* bacterium present in rats. Leptospirosis (Weil's disease) has been carried by all three rodents. Rats and mice can also spread trichinosis by contaminating hogfeed. Murine typhus fever is transmitted to humans by rats. Rickettsial pox is spread by the bite of house mice. The bubonic plague, or "Black Death," in 14th century Europe was caused by a bacterium (*Pasteurella pestis*) transmitted by rats.

At first glance, it may appear that the control of insects and rodents is almost impossible. Any successful control program has two parts: basic sanitation of the environment and effective chemical control. **Basic environmental sanitation** includes methods and procedures for keeping rodents and insects out of the facility. All materials that may provide food or shelter for pests should either be made rodent resistant or removed from the facility and the immediate vicinity.

Prompt refuse and garbage removal at least twice each week is critical. Storage areas for garbage and trash must be kept clean using the techniques already discussed. Prompt cleanup of spilled food in storage and preparation areas minimizes problems. All food service personnel must be trained to clean as they complete a job. Doors must be screened and fitted with self-closing devices. Windows must be screened and the screens maintained in a good state of repair. Flytraps, electrocution screens, and air curtains and screens usually have little effect on flying insects. A better approach is to keep toilet and lavatory facilities clean.

Shelves and floors in storage areas must be cleaned at least twice each week. Cool, dry storage areas inhibit insect and rodent breeding. All deliveries must be examined for signs of infestation. Stock rotation based on the FIFO inventory system reduces problems. All opened packages must be either used immediately or their contents stored in covered, dated, and labeled containers. Regular inspections will identify problems before they get out of hand and products become unusable.

Food products in storage areas should be at least two inches (5.08 cm) from walls and six inches (15.24 cm) off the floor. This reduces harborage areas and enhances ventilation. Minimum aisles of two feet (60.96 cm), provided along walls and through the center of storage areas, permit easy cleaning. Floor areas in food storage rooms are to be swept and mopped at least twice daily. This helps to eliminate one source of food for insects and rodents.

The physical facility itself can be made rodent resistant, if small openings are closed. A rat, for example, can crawl through a 1/2-inch (1.27 cm) opening, while a mouse can penetrate an opening of 1/4 inch (0.64 cm). Openings around fans, doors, windows, pipes, floor drains, and foundations can be effectively blocked with a combination of brick, mortar, concrete, and galvanized hardware cloth.

Rodent traps are preferred to toxic rodenticides. The snap trap kills mice and rats, while the "0" or live trap catches them alive. The cage trap also captures live rodents. Either trap can be an effective deterrent to expanding rodent populations. Traps should be checked frequently, at least once every 24 hours. Cockroach attractant traps are useful when the infestation is slight. They can help locate problem areas within the building.

In addition to basic environmental sanitation, food service operations can use **effective chemical control**. However, insecticides and rodenticides are poisonous and toxic chemicals. They are designed to destroy insects and rodents but, if improperly applied, they can also kill humans. Thus, it is easier and safer to keep insects and rodents out in the first place than to try to eliminate them after they have reproduced unchecked. These poisons can only be used safely in food service facilities when instructions are strictly followed.

Vapona strips, **fly paper**, and **insect vaporizers** are not permitted in areas where they might contaminate food. However, they can be used in garbage and refuse storage areas. Insecticide vaporizers that automatically spray pesticide at predetermined intervals should be installed according to label directions. All pesticides used in a food service operation must be labeled clearly. The label must also show the product has been registered with the Environmental Protection Agency. The manufacturer of the pesticide is responsible for this registration. The EPA only permits a pesticide to be used if, under normal application, it will not injure humans, plants, livestock, wildlife, or the environment. Pesticides may only be stored in locked areas separate from food storage rooms.

Only certified exterminators can use restricted pesticides. **General residual pesticides** may be applied to ceilings, floors, and walls. They are not permitted in food storage, preparation, or service areas. **Spot residual pesticides** are applied in an area not to exceed two square feet (0.19 m^2) to walls, ceilings, floors, and the undersides of equipment. They must not be used near food or on utensils and food-contact surfaces. Some pesticides are applied into cracks and crevices using a special fine pin stream nozzle. In all cases, the exterminator must guard against contaminating food, equipment, or utensils with the pesticide.

The management of a food service establishment, even on the best days, is a complex and demanding job. Why complicate matters by operating an in-house extermination operation? An in-house chemical control system requires properly trained employees. It is better to contract a commercial extermination service to handle the chemical control of pests. The professional exterminator can be scheduled for monthly visits or more frequent applications if there is evidence of infestation. This monthly service may cost about $50 to $100, depending on the number of inspections and the size of the facility. Of course, a pest control contractor cannot achieve the desired results if avenues of entry, harborage areas, or easily accessible food are still available for insects and rodents. Thus, food service establishments should concentrate their in-house efforts on basic environmental sanitation.

Pest control companies fall into one of two general categories: application companies and integrated pest management companies. Both companies must be licensed. The integrated pest management company makes a commitment to indirectly join the staff of the food service or lodging operation. Prevention of pest problems is the goal or objective of any pest control program. When selecting a pest control company, consider the following criteria:[4]

1. The pest control company conducts an audit of pest populations.

   a. The audit identifies why there are problems.

   b. The audit also pinpoints the factors that contribute to the existing problems or potential problems.

2. The pest control company establishes with management an outline of what is to be done and why it is necessary.

   a. An outline is presented in a management briefing session.

   b. Information presented includes the pesticides to be used, the application methods, and application times.

3. The pest control company presents a pest monitoring system.

   a. Nontoxic devices are used to identify the pest(s) present and their distribution and location within the facility.

   b. The system allows the pest control company to quantify the results and inform management whether or not the pest control program is actually working.

4. The pest control company applies the selected pesticides.

   a. Direct crack and crevice applications are preferred to general baseboard sprays.

   b. Capillary tubes can be used to place the pesticides in pest hiding places.

5. The pest control company periodically reports to management concerning the accomplishments of the program.

---

[4] This information is based on a discussion with Louis Keenan, RPE, President, Metro Pest Management Consultants, Denver, Colo.

a. These reports keep management informed of the effectiveness of the program.

b. They also permit management and the pest control company to decide if the program is working.

Cleaning and Maintenance and Change

The technology associated with cleaning and maintenance is evolving in the United States. Recent developments have permitted the use of low temperature dishwashing machines. New cleaners and sanitizers are on the market. New materials for building construction are being introduced as technology improves. This evolution in equipment and chemicals necessitates a periodic reevaluation of the cleaning and maintenance program in a food service business. Managers can keep abreast of changes in cleaning and maintenance technology by reading trade publications, attending trade shows and seminars, and communicating with supply company representatives.

Cleaning and Maintenance and Success

Winning food service businesses realize that cleaning, sanitizing, and maintenance programs depend on people. People can make or break an operation's cleaning and maintenance program. Successful companies train their personnel to follow required procedures. This training occurs at orientation, during regular on-the-job training, and in periodic refresher sessions.

The materials, design, and construction of food service facilities, equipment, and utensils also have a direct effect on the operation's performance at the final control point. Cleaning and sanitizing chemicals are important inventory resources because they help the operation's personnel to prolong the useful life of the other resources. Management can increase the probability of the establishment's success by following the FDA's Model Ordinance and NSF Standards.

Summary

Food service cleaning and maintenance management is a necessary link in the chain of food protection. Once the cleaning needs are determined, employees can be assigned regularly scheduled cleaning jobs. Cleaners and sanitizers are toxic chemicals that must be stored and used in a safe manner.

The construction and maintenance of physical facilities according to guidelines of the National Sanitation Foundation and the FDA's Model Ordinance can reduce risks. Floors, walls, and ceilings must be constructed and designed so they are easy to clean and maintain.

Lighting levels are important to maintain a clean and accident-free environment. Ventilation removes fumes, smoke, steam, condensation, heat, and obnoxious odors. Dining room and kitchen ventilation must be coordinated. Sanitary facilities are important from the standpoint of employee morale and public safety. A safe potable water supply must be provided in all food service establishments. Properly designed plumbing and sewage systems are essential components of sanitary facilities.

A variety of disease-carrying insects and rodents can invade a food service facility. Pest control requires both basic environmental sanitation and effective chemical control. It is easier to prevent the entry of pests than it is to destroy a population that has taken up residence in the building.

References

Caprione, C. "Sparkle! It's Top Priority." *NRA News*, February 1983. 3(2):26-29.

"Chemicals for Cleaning: Weigh the Advantages." *Institutions/Volume Feeding*, 15 February 1976. 78(4):55.

Consultant's Handbook: Warewashing Cost Analysis. St. Paul, Minn.: Economics Laboratory, Inc., 1978.

"Disposing of Waste Disposal Headaches." *Institutions/Volume Feeding*, 1 September 1974. 75(5):31-32.

"Don't Let Maintenance Bug You." *Institutions/Volume Feeding*, 15 April 1976. 78(8):57.

Dunsmore, D. G. "Bacteriological Control of Food Equipment Surfaces by Cleaning Systems, Part VI. Detergent Effects." *Journal of Food Protection*, January 1981. 44(1):15-20.

Eaton, W. V. "How Sanitary Conditions Affect Food Service Facility Design and Layout." *Food Service Marketing*, June 1981. 43(6):46.

Faulkner, E. "Ventilation: A Lot of Hot Air." *Restaurants and Institutions*, 15 November 1982. 91(10):137-139.

Finn, M. "Are Profits Going Out With the Garbage?" *Hospitality Food and Lodging*, January 1974. 13(1):69.

———."Light Up for Safety—and Savings." *Hospitality Food and Lodging*, October 1975. 14(10):L65-L67.

Food and Drug Administration, Public Health Administration, U.S. Department of Health, Education, and Welfare. *Food Service Sanitation Manual*. Washington, D.C.: U.S. Government Printing Office, 1976.

Food Service Recommended Field Evaluation Procedures for Spray-Type Dishwashing Machines. Ann Arbor, Mich.: National Sanitation Foundation, 1982.

Forwalter, J. "1980 Selection Guide—Cleaning and Sanitizing Compounds." *Food Processing*, February 1980. 41(2):40-43.

Giampietro, F. N. "Preventive Maintenance—The Best Cure for Trouble." *Restaurant Business*, December 1977. 79(12):101-102.

Gillespie, R. W. "Insect and Rodent Control in Food Establishments." *Dairy and Food Sanitation*, February 1981. 1(2):58-61.

— "Plumbing Hazards in the Food Industry." *Dairy and Food Sanitation*, January 1982. 2(1):14-17.

Haverland, H. "Cleaning and Sanitizing Operations." *Dairy and Food Sanitation*, August 1981. 1(8):331-335.

Kooser, R. "Sanitation and Facilities Design." *Restaurant Hospitality*, December 1981. 65(12):74.

"New Exhaust Systems Save $$$ and Btu's." *Cooking for Profit*, August 1977. (320):18-20.

Pratt, H. D., and Brown, R. Z. *Biological Factors in Domestic Rodent Control*. Atlanta, Ga.: Centers for Disease Control, Public Health Service, U.S. Department of Health, Education, and Welfare, 1977.

Pratt, H. D.; Littig, K. S.; and Scott, H. G. *Flies of Public Health Importance and Their Control*. Atlanta, Ga.: Centers for Disease Control, Public Health Service, U.S. Department of Health, Education, and Welfare, 1975.

—.*Household and Stored-Food Insects of Public Health Importance and Their Control*. Atlanta, Ga.: Centers for Disease Control, Public Health Service, U.S. Department of Health, Education, and Welfare, 1979.

Sanitation Aspects of Food Service Facility Plan Preparation and Review - Reference Guide. Ann Arbor, Mich.: National Sanitation Foundation, 1978.

Spray-Type Dishwashing Machines-Standard No. 3. Ann Arbor, Mich.: National Sanitation Foundation, 1976.

Swientek, R. J. "Insect Control Update." *Food Processing*, February 1982. 43(2):34-36.

Strategies for Success at the Aspen Hotel

After the morning meeting, Paul James had some time to think about the discussion of the hotel's standards for cleaning and maintenance. All three department heads had submitted their suggestions willingly. The GM decided there were several strategies that could improve the cleaning and maintenance control point.

First, Paul realized that the talents of his well-paid technicians in the Maintenance Department were being wasted on paperwork. Paul made the decision to hire a part-time secretary in the Maintenance Department. The secretary would be responsible for filling out reports, establishing schedules, and maintaining the work order program. This would maximize the output of his chief engineer and give Harry Gregor more time to keep the Maintenance Department under control. A regular repairs and maintenance schedule would be established for the various areas of the hotel and the equipment in them.

Second, Paul James took the executive housekeeper's suggestions for improving the Rooms Department. Standards for housekeeping would be put in writing and communicated to all employees in that department. He would occasionally supplement the housekeeper's daily inspections with his own surprise inspections. He planned to upgrade the position of housekeeper by purchasing new uniforms and establishing a formal training program.

Finally, from the standpoint of cleaning and maintenance, food and beverage would be the hotel's biggest challenge. Elisabeth had made an excellent suggestion for improvement in this area. She mentioned that housekeepers often avoid cleaning the dining room thoroughly because they feel that the servers make all of the money in tips in that room. Therefore, she suggested that food and beverage personnel be made responsible for cleanliness in their own areas, because they would be more sensitive than the housekeeping staff to sanitation concerns in those areas.

The GM planned to set up a training program for food production and service personnel. A contract service would be hired to do major cleaning jobs on a regularly scheduled basis. He would ask the cleaning supplies salesperson to put on training sessions for dishwashers and pot and pan washers. This would not only help train employees but would also cut down on the excessive use of costly cleaners and sanitizers.

The GM decided not to take risks with other chemicals either. The storage of pesticides in the hotel or the application of pesticides by employees were just too hazardous. Paul James decided that he would contract a licensed integrated pest management company. He knew from past experience that most contract services will come back during the month at no charge, if a problem surfaces.

Paul sat back in his office chair and reflected on the progress made during his first month at the Aspen Hotel. The date of the grand opening was less than a month away. And while there was still a lot to be accomplished, he had been able to develop a commitment to excellence in each of his department heads. Paul was proud of that accomplishment.

Checklist for Cleaning and Maintenance

Personnel

1. All food service employees understand their responsibilities in the areas of cleaning and maintenance.

2. All food service employees understand correct procedures for cleaning and maintenance.

3. Personnel understand the operation's policies regarding cleaning and maintenance.

4. Supervisors ask employees to help identify areas to be cleaned and maintained.

5. Personnel have input into the cleaning and maintenance schedules.

6. Personnel are trained initially and on an ongoing basis to enforce the operation's cleaning and maintenance standards.

Equipment

1. Equipment, utensils, and tableware are cleaned, sanitized, stored, and used so as to prevent cross-contamination.

2. Manual cleaning and sanitizing of equipment and utensils are achieved in a three-compartment sink.

3. Equipment used for manual warewashing is designed to hold, scrape and presoak, wash, rinse, and sanitize.

4. Equipment, utensils, and tableware are air dried before storage.

5. Equipment, utensils, and tableware are stored in self-draining positions at least six inches (15.24 cm) off the floor.

6. Cleaning procedures for equipment, utensils, and tableware are presented to employees in a language they can understand.

7. The basic ten-step process of machine warewashing is used.

8. Equipment for mechanical warewashing is regularly serviced by a qualified person.

9. Temperatures and times of washing, rinsing, and sanitizing operations are strictly followed.

10. Concentrations of cleaners and sanitizers are measured according to the manufacturers' recommendations.

Inventory

1. Cleaning and sanitizing personnel understand the basic definitions related to cleaning and sanitizing.

2. The four-step cleaning process is utilized.

3. The types of cleaners and sanitizers and differences between them are understood by all who need to use them.

4. No in-house mixing of cleaners or sanitizers is permitted.

5. Cleaning and sanitizing chemicals are always used in the concentrations recommended by the manufacturer.

6. Cleaning and sanitizing costs are tracked, analyzed, and minimized without compromising sanitation standards.

7. All containers of cleaners and sanitizers are labeled and stored in a separate locked area used for no other purpose.

8. Sanitizers and cleaners are not stored with pesticides or with food or beverage products.

9. Personal medications are stored away from areas where food is stored, prepared, or served.

10. First aid supplies are available and stored safely.

Facilities

1. State, local, and federal codes and ordinances are followed in the construction and maintenance of the physical facilities.

2. The menu is used as a guide to facilities design.

3. Floors, ceilings, and walls are selected, constructed, and maintained in good repair.

4. Anti-slip floor coverings are used, where permitted, for safety reasons.

5. A room finish schedule is submitted to local health officials when new facility construction or present facility renovation is planned.

6. Cleaning of facilities takes place when the least amount of food is exposed.

7. Dustless methods of floor cleaning are used.

8. Adequate lighting is provided in all areas of the facility.

9. Light bulbs and tubes are shielded in areas where food is stored, prepared, served, or displayed, and in equipment cleaning and storage areas.

10. Ventilation equipment is available and used to remove smoke, fumes, steam, condensation, excessive heat, vapors, and obnoxious odors.

11. Kitchen and service area ventilation requirements are coordinated.

12. Adequate amounts of make-up air are available.

13. Dressing and locker rooms are not used for food storage, preparation, or service, or equipment and utensil washing or storage.

14. The exterior of the facility is free from litter and debris.

15. Dust is controlled on outside walking and parking surfaces.

16. Unauthorized people are not permitted to enter storage, preparation, or equipment and utensil washing areas.

17. A separate storage area is maintained for cleaning equipment.

18. Water of the necessary quantity, quality, and temperature is available for normal operations.

19. Liquid waste and sewage are removed promptly and properly.

20. Plumbing codes are followed in the installation of the building's plumbing system.

21. The plumbing system is designed and maintained to prevent cross-connections, backflow, and back siphonage.

22. The operation follows plumbing codes when installing toilet and lavatory facilities.

23. Toilet facilities and lavatories are regularly inspected, cleaned, and maintained.

24. Containers used to store garbage and refuse are durable, easy to clean, insect-proof, and rodent-proof.

25. Garbage and refuse containers are kept covered.

26. Soiled containers are cleaned and maintained at regular intervals.

27. Basic environmental sanitation is used to keep insects and rodents out of the facility.

28. Effective chemical control is used to rid the facility of insects and rodents.

The following case studies are designed to enhance your understanding of the material in this chapter. If you are a Home Study student, use these case studies to stimulate questions about this chapter. If you are a Group or Institutional Study student, you may be asked to discuss these case studies as part of a regular classroom assignment.

CASE STUDY 10.1

Robert Dill is an extremely wealthy businessman interested in opening a restaurant in the Midwest. Mr. Dill has decided to name his restaurant The Peanut Shell. It will feature banjo and piano sing-along entertainment, pizzas, hamburgers, and hot dogs. Each customer in the dining room will be given a complimentary basket of peanuts in the shell. As the customers eat the peanuts, shells will undoubtedly end up on the floor. This doesn't bother Mr. Dill because it will contribute to the casual atmosphere he wants the restaurant to convey. Mr. Dill does not plan to have the dining room floor swept each day because, if it were, the atmosphere of The Peanut Shell would be lost.

Test Your Understanding

1. What do you think of Mr. Dill's concept?

2. Are there likely to be any sanitation problems in the dining room or kitchen of The Peanut Shell?

3. What are your recommendations to Robert Dill?

CASE STUDY 10.2

Robert Dill also plans to install drywall in the dishwashing area of the kitchen. It will be painted white. Mr. Dill has chosen this wall covering because it is relatively inexpensive. In addition, The Peanut Shell will have hundreds of antiques attached to the dining room walls and ceiling to create the desired atmosphere. Mr. Dill wants to leave the electrical and other utility lines exposed in the dining room because the restaurant has a rather low ceiling in public areas.

Test Your Understanding

1. Do you agree with Robert Dill's choice of a wall covering for the dishwashing area? Why or why not?

2. Identify additional sanitation problems which may occur in the dining room of The Peanut Shell.

3. What are your recommendations to Robert Dill?

CASE STUDY 10.3

The Congeries Cafe, located in the Southwest, has a dining room that seats 350, banquet facilities for 500, and a show bar with live entertainment. Joel Stephen is the food and beverage manager in charge of the operation of the Congeries.

The cafe's staff just served a large banquet to a group of people from the local Rotary Club. As the club treasurer is paying the bill, he comments that throughout the dinner and meeting, the group could smell fish frying in the kitchen. Also, the buildup of cigarette and cigar smoke in the room seemed to be unusually high that night. The club president informs Joel that his organization will not come back to the Congeries Cafe until the problem is resolved.

Test Your Understanding

1. What is likely to be the problem at the Congeries Cafe?

2. How can this problem be eliminated?

3. What are your recommendations to Joel Stephen?

CASE STUDY 10.4

The bartender at the main bar of the Satin Hotel is shaking a whiskey sour when a woman seated at the end of the bar suddenly jumps up. "Look at them!" she shouts. "This place is infested with cockroaches!" The bartender hurries down to the end of the bar and searches for the cause of the customer's anguish. The bartender doesn't see any insects and decides to ignore the complaint.

Test Your Understanding

1. Did the bartender make the right decision? Why?

2. If insects have invaded the hotel, what can be done to eliminate them?

3. What are your recommendations to the manager of the Satin Hotel?

CASE STUDY 10.5

Gary Gainsay is the pot and pan washer at the Fox Restaurant. Gary has never been trained because the manager of the restaurant believes it is a waste of money to train people for high turnover positions like Gary's. Ten minutes ago, the manager observed Gary freely pouring liquid detergent into a pot and pan sink filled with hot water. The manager immediately ran up to Gary and screamed, "Don't you know how much that stuff costs? I don't ever want to see you wasting detergent like that again!"

Gary felt so badly about the reprimand that he decided to wash all the rest of the dirty pots and pans in the same water for the remainder of his shift. Gary thought that by doing this he wouldn't have to worry about the manager screaming at him again.

Test Your Understanding

1. Who is at fault in this case?

2. What are the possible sanitation implications of Gary's decision?

3. What are your recommendations to the manager of the Fox Restaurant?

Part Three

Two topics remain to be covered before this discussion of sanitation strategies for success can be concluded; namely, sanitation management for lodging properties and safety management. Of course, the checklists for food service sanitation given in the chapter scenarios in Part Two are applicable to lodging properties with food service outlets. In fact, as previously mentioned, customers identify "great" hotels by the quality of the food, the efficiency and friendliness of the service staff, and the cleanliness of the hotel's food service operations. However, lodging properties are also judged on two other criteria: the cleanliness of the public areas and the condition of the guestrooms.

Therefore, Chapter 11 contains recommendations for the cleaning and maintenance of these important areas of lodging properties. However, this chapter may be equally useful to food service personnel because many of the surfaces, furnishings, and fixtures in their facilities are similar.

In Chapter 12, safety management is presented as a complement to sanitation management. Both subjects have as their goal the protection of the operation's customers, employees, and assets. Like sanitation management, safety management requires employee training and management follow-up to be effective.

Chapter 13 serves as a final summary of the strategies for success recommended in this book. It explains how to establish proactive programs of employee training, routine cleaning and maintenance, and periodic self-inspections.

The components of a successful sanitation program correspond to the chapters of this book:

1. A commitment to excellence and success (Chapter 1)

2. An understanding of the responsibilities of and resources available to the hospitality manager (Chapter 2)

3. A knowledge of food contamination including how to prevent it (Chapter 3)

4. An awareness of food spoilage processes and methods of food preservation (Chapter 4)

5. An appreciation for the importance of regular sanitation inspections in protecting the public health (Chapter 5)

6. An understanding of the sanitation hazards associated with every food service control point and how to minimize them (Chapters 6-10)

7. A knowledge of proper techniques for cleaning and maintaining the facilities and furnishings (Chapter 11)

8. An awareness on the part of all employees of safety hazards and how to eliminate them (Chapter 12)

9. Achieving and maintaining high standards (Chapter 13)

Naturally, the result of achieving and maintaining high standards is excellence. Therefore, while Chapter 13 is a conclusion, it is also, in some sense, a starting point for the reader's own quest for success.

ELEVEN

Sanitation Management of Lodging Properties

Strategies for Success at the Aspen Hotel

Paul James continued with his development of standards at the Aspen Hotel. He was taking a number of suggestions made by the hotel's executive housekeeper, chief engineer, and food and beverage director, and molding them into a workable set of standards for the cleaning and maintenance of public areas and guestrooms. This is what he called "guest awareness sanitation." During their meeting, he had again challenged these key supervisors to see the building through the guest's eyes. Paul had asked, "When a guest pulls up to the Aspen Hotel, what does the guest see? What is that person's first impression?"

Now Paul thought to himself, "A clean entrance and attractive live plants demonstrate that we at this hotel know how important cleaning and maintenance are to our guests. When the lodging or dining experience begins with a favorable first impression, the guest believes that this is the place to see and be seen. Guests come here to participate in an enjoyable experience. If it isn't enjoyable, they will go to one of our competitors or stay home." Paul knew his hotel could not afford to let that happen.

The GM had told his key people, "The customer or guest evaluates our hotel with all five senses. If we let our guests down in one area, their entire experience can be ruined. This evaluation begins with a visual inspection of the parking lot. As our guests drive up, they are consciously or unconsciously examining the building, the parking lot, and the outdoor plants. If the building shows signs of deterioration, if the parking lot is littered with beer cans or trash, or if the plants and shrubs are dead, we have lost our chance to make a favorable first impression.

"As our guests walk in the entrance of our hotel or dining room, they continue to evaluate the property with their eyes. Then their sense of smell adds to their overall impression. In some properties, the garbage areas and restrooms reek with unacceptable odors. I have been in motel rooms that overwhelm you with beer and cigar or cigarette odors. It's not surprising that more money is spent in hospitality businesses on odor control than anywhere else.

"Guests also evaluate our property with their sense of hearing. Loud music blasting out of the lounge into the dining room or guestrooms can interfere with the guest's dining or lodging experience. The noise of an unorganized front desk can also create a negative impression. Sound control is critical if guests are to enjoy their dining or lodging experience.

"The sense of touch is an important evaluation tool used by our guests. Bed linens and bathroom towels should feel and smell clean. The bathrooms in our guestrooms as well as our public area restrooms should feel clean. The same is true for carpeting, floors, and furniture in guestrooms and public areas.

"Customers constantly use their sense of taste to evaluate what we offer in our food and beverage outlets. They expect that if they order a bloody mary cocktail in the bar today, it will taste the same as the one they were served last week. Our food should be a blend of tastes, colors,

> and textures that appeal to our customers."
>
> After his remarks to the three department heads, the GM decided to test them with a question. "What is the key to quality?"
>
> They answered in unison, "Consistency."

The thrust of this chapter is the sanitation management of public areas and guestrooms in lodging properties, although much of the information presented here is also applicable to food service. We begin with a general overview of the housekeeping department of a lodging facility. This department is responsible for the cleanliness of public areas, which are always in the public eye, and guestrooms, where guests spend much of their stay. Their condition affects the image of the property formed in the minds of customers and guests.

Next, techniques for cleaning and maintaining carpeted and uncarpeted floors, walls, ceilings, upholstery, furniture, drapes, and curtains are presented. Also, restroom sanitation is discussed as an important indicator of the overall level of cleanliness in a hotel, motel, motor hotel, or food service operation. Other topics covered in this chapter are: waste collection and disposal, the care and maintenance of indoor plants, and exterior maintenance, all of which have an impact on the guest's or customer's first impression. Finally, preventive maintenance of public areas and a self-inspection checklist complete this chapter.

Cleaning and Housekeeping: General

The housekeeping department of a modern lodging property does more than just cleaning and maintenance. This department provides a pleasant, clean, and comfortable environment in which guests and customers can feel secure and satisfied. Thus, the housekeeping department makes a vital contribution to the property's overall image. In terms of its impact on guest satisfaction, housekeeping certainly ranks near the top of all departments in a lodging property. For these reasons, housekeeping personnel should be made aware of the fact that they are an important part of the property's public relations efforts.

The person in charge of the housekeeping department of a lodging property is the **executive housekeeper**. The executive housekeeper is a member of the lodging property's management team. Fundamentally, all duties and responsibilities of the executive housekeeper have an impact (positive or negative) on guest satisfaction and, therefore, on future revenues. By doing the job correctly, the housekeeping department encourages present guests and their acquaintances to return to the hotel, motel, or motor hotel for future business. In other words, the housekeeping function provides another opportunity to exceed the customer's expectations and to encourage both repeat business and word-of-mouth advertising.

Housekeeping department operations vary according to the size and uniqueness of the property. Housekeeping requires a 24-hour effort in most lodging properties. For example, consider a 400-room hotel that can accommodate 900 overnight guests. In addition to its guestrooms, the hotel has two restaurants, a large lobby area, four banquet/conference rooms, and an outdoor pool and courtyard area.

The equipment requirements of this 400-room hotel are staggering. The housekeeping department alone requires 30 vacuum cleaners, two wet vacuums, one extractor, three carpet shampooers, several portable "backpack" cleaning units for upholstery, and a floor machine. In addition, the property's housekeeping department requires a large inventory of cleaning chemicals, room supplies, and cleaning accessories.

The hotel also requires a sizeable housekeeping staff. The executive housekeeper is in charge of four supervisors; each supervisor oversees 100 guestrooms. The department also includes 70 room attendants, 20 laundry operators, and a complete in-house laundry operation.

Each month the laundry processes over 150,000 pounds (68,100 kg) of linens from the rooms department and the food and beverage department. That amounts to over 900 tons (816,000 kg) of linens in an average year. The cost of supplies (cleaning chemicals, equipment, room supplies) and labor for the housekeeping department is approximately half a million dollars annually. Obviously, the housekeeping department is a cost center which must be controlled.

In an average lodging property, a member of the guestroom cleaning staff cleans approximately 15 to 18 guestrooms in an eight-hour shift. The rooms are spot-checked by the person's supervisor. The supervisor is usually responsible for distributing supplies, training new staff members, and inspecting the cleaned rooms. The housekeeping staff may also assist the food and beverage department in the preparation of meeting and banquet rooms.

What makes an efficient and effective housekeeping department? Six basics of housekeeping have been identified in progressive and successful hotel, motel, and motor hotel properties. The following fundamentals form the core of a lodging property's housekeeping program.

1. Contact with top management on a regular basis

2. Development of supervisors' management skills

3. Training of supervisors and employees

4. Motivation of supervisors and employees

5. Providing the necessary equipment and supplies

6. Measuring the effectiveness and efficiency of the overall effort

The six basics of housekeeping management provide a realistic set of goals and objectives for any lodging property. They apply to the 14-room "mom and pop" resort motel as well as the 1400-room downtown convention hotel. The principles of housekeeping management are the same, regardless of the size of the lodging property.

Before general cleaning and maintenance recommendations for various areas of lodging properties are presented, some basic requirements must be made clear. First, in order to clean an area, housekeeping personnel must have access to the area. Therefore, cleaning and maintenance operations in every area of the property should take place when business is the slowest. For example, public areas in a lodging property are usually cleaned late at night. Chemicals used in public areas should work rapidly and, in the case of floor compounds, dry quickly. This will permit customers to safely use these areas as soon as possible after the cleaning and maintenance operation has been completed. Floor fans may be used to accelerate the drying of wet floors.

Guestrooms, on the other hand, are usually cleaned by mid-afternoon because they must be ready for assignment to guests, who generally arrive in the afternoon or early evening. All of the cleaning and maintenance tips given in this chapter apply to guestrooms as well as public areas.

Certain other fundamentals of all cleaning and maintenance jobs must be considered. Can the job be effectively accomplished with in-house personnel, or is a contract cleaning company needed? How much time is needed to complete the cleaning or maintenance job? Does the cleaning process require overtime or extra charges? The answers to all of these questions help to precisely define the property's cleaning and maintenance requirements. Once the property has answered these questions, realistic budgets for supplies and labor can be developed. Also, cleaning schedules and work schedules for housekeeping personnel can be coordinated.

Floor Cleaning and Maintenance

Of all the areas maintained daily by the houskeeping department, floors are probably the largest in terms of total surface area. Floor materials for each area are chosen based on how the area will be used.[1] Floor materials may be classified as hard or resilient. Exhibit 11.1 presents a breakdown of these two broad categories. This exhibit also presents recommendations (not strict rules) on how the various floor materials can be used.

Types of Hard Floors
Floors made of brick, slate, ceramic tile, quarry tile, concrete, granolithic, magnesite, marble, and terrazzo are classified as **hard floors**. After each hard floor material is described, some recommended procedures are presented for the care of these floor surfaces.

Brick is made from clay that has been heated to high temperatures. **Slate** is composed of quarried aluminum silicate. These two materials are seldom used for floors because of their dull appearance. **Ceramic tile** is a dense, hard material made from heating fine clay to extremely high

---

[1]Some basic recommendations on flooring materials for various areas of the facility were presented in Chapter 10.

Exhibit 11.1 A Classification of Floor Materials and Their Uses

	FLOOR MATERIAL	RECOMMENDED USES
HARD FLOORS	Brick and Slate	Stair Treads
	Ceramic Tile	Bathroom Kitchen Restroom Utility Room
	Concrete	Basement Garage Laundry Mechanical Room Service Room
	Granolithic	Hallway Lobby
	Magnesite	Hallway Office Workroom
	Marble	Bathroom Lobby Restroom Shower Room Stairs
	Terrazzo	Dressing Room Hallway Kitchen Lobby Utility Room Washroom
RESILIENT FLOORS	Asphalt Tile, Linoleum, Rubber Tile, Vinyl-Asbestos Tile	Lobby Elevator Hallway Office
	Carpet	Dining Room Elevator Guestroom Hallway Lobby Office
	Cork	Office Meeting Room
	Vinyl	Elevator Guestroom Hallway Lobby Office
	Wood	Dining Room Meeting Room

temperatures. It is durable, stain-repellent, easy to maintain, and expensive to install. **Quarry tile** is usually red or brown in color. It is porous and requires sealing with a water-dispersed polymer finish to protect the tile. It is often used in high traffic areas such as kitchens.

Concrete is a mixture of gravel, sand, cement, and water. It is relatively easy and inexpensive to install and maintain. It should be sealed and may be painted. **Granolithic** is a mixture of Portland cement and chips of granite. It resists abrasion more than concrete. **Magnesite** is a combination of asbestos, cork, leather, wood flour, and various talc fillers held together with magnesium oxychloride. Based on the fillers used, the appearance and durability of magnesite can vary. It should be sealed before use to protect the surface.

Marble is naturally crystallized limestone. Marble is very durable, but is also expensive, easily stained, and damaged by improper care. Acids should never be used on marble. **Terrazzo** is a mixture of cement or synthetic plastic combined with marble chips. It is expensive, durable, easy to clean and maintain, and must be sealed.

Care of Hard Floors. In general, hard floors are relatively easy to keep clean if they are maintained properly. Most sealed hard floors require daily sweeping with a dry mop or floor brush. These floors may be refinished after they have been swept clean.

All floor finishes provide three benefits: (1) they provide a glossy appearance that upgrades the environment of the property; (2) they protect the surface of the floor from abrasive traffic; and (3) they also facilitate daily cleaning of the surface of the floor without damaging the surface. The selection of a finish for a hard floor should be based on the manufacturer's recommendations. Over the years, some executive housekeepers have advocated floor stripping to remove the accumulated buildup of floor finishing materials such as waxes and polishes. Floor stripping may be done in one of two ways: dry stripping or wet stripping.

Dry stripping uses a small amount of moisture and mechanical agitation. The dry stripping medium is an abrasive scrubbing compound. A floor machine with a floor pad or brush is usually used to apply the dry stripping compound. As the floor machine agitates the abrasives on the floor, the floor's finish is turned into a powder which can be removed. Dry stripping is faster than wet stripping. However, some housekeepers believe that the surface of floors is damaged by the combination of agitation and abrasive compounds used in dry stripping.

Wet stripping of floors can be accomplished in two ways. The more common of the two procedures combines machine scrubbing with chemical emulsification. This procedure requires that a stripping solution be applied to the floor. After the chemical emulsifiers have dissolved the old finish, the floor is machine scrubbed. This scrubbing creates a thick gray slurry which is removed with a wet vacuum. Then the emulsifiers are neutralized and the floor is rinsed.

The other method of wet stripping involves total chemical emulsification of the old finish. This procedure eliminates the machine scrubbing step. First, the stripping chemical is mopped on the floor and allowed to completely emulsify the finish. After the finish has been dissolved, it is removed with a wet vacuum. Since no slurry is created, cleanup operations are faster and less expensive.

The trend in housekeeping today is away from the costly procedures of stripping, waxing, and polishing. As an alternative, the **no-wax spray buff system** saves time and money. When no-wax hard floors are manufactured, a water-dispersed, non-yellowing polymer compound is applied to the surface of the floor material at the factory. Once installed, the no-wax floor is initially buffed to achieve a mirror-like finish which resists scuffing and marking. Although waxes and stripping compounds are not needed in the no-wax spray buff system, daily damp mopping is required. A cleaner/polish is sprayed on the floor ahead of the machine. Then the floor is buffed while it is still wet. This repeated buffing maintains the floor's resistance to marking and scuffing. The labor and supply savings are potentially significant.

Some properties use **high-pressure cleaning** for their hard floors. This system is used for irregular surfaces such as refuse areas, loading docks, tile walls and floors, and kitchen areas. These surfaces are cleaned by the force of pressurized water sprayed on them. A chemical is added to the machine to break down and emulsify the dirt. Drainage is required in the area being cleaned to carry away the soil and water. The effectiveness of high-pressure cleaning depends on the size of the machine, its power source, its portability, and the water temperature it requires.

Types of Resilient Floors

Resilient floors are not necessarily springy, but they are relatively soft in comparison with the hard floors just described. This category includes floors made of asphalt tile, linoleum, rubber tile, cork, vinyl, wood, and carpeting. With the exception of carpeting, resilient floors require sealing.

Asphalt tile consists of asbestos fiber and pigments with a binder. It is inexpensive and resists moisture, but is easily dented and marked. **Linoleum** is a combination of ground cork, binders, mineral fillers, and oxidized linseed oil bonded to burlap or felt. Linoleum is available in sheet or tile form. It is moderately priced and is durable but it can be dented.

Rubber tile absorbs sound, is expensive, and is sold in sheets or tiles. It is easily damaged by oils, air, heat, and sunlight, and it may become dented.

Cork floors are made from ground cork and resins. This expensive material is difficult to maintain, dents easily, and is frequently damaged by oils or moisture. Cork floors must be sealed with solvent-based epoxy and urethane.

Vinyl floors are made from a combination of mineral fillers and acetylene, hydrochloric acid, and pigments. Vinyl is an expensive but highly resistant flooring material.

Wood floors may be constructed of hard or soft woods, although hardwood floors are expensive. Both types of wood floors are susceptible to warping if they are exposed to excessive moisture; however, they are durable if properly sealed. Wood floors are potential fire hazards and can be relatively difficult to maintain.

Carpeting is produced from natural or synthetic fibers. The type of carpeting selected is governed by the usage level in the area to be carpeted. Solid color carpeting shows traffic patterns, and crushed pile is more apparent in solid color than in patterned carpeting. Therefore, patterned carpeting is preferable in high-traffic areas. Carpeting helps to control noise and, when installed at entrances, reduces the amount of dirt tracked onto interior floors.

Modular carpeting may reduce a lodging property's overall carpet maintenance costs. Carpet modules or squares can be rotated from areas with less traffic to high traffic areas exhibiting premature wear. The rotation of modular carpeting results in a better overall appearance and extends the useful life of the carpet.

Care of Carpeting. Because carpeting is a widely used floor covering in lodging properties, proper carpet cleaning and maintenance concerns many operators. The time-consuming task of carpet cleaning is considered labor-intensive in that the cost of labor may be more than 80% of the total cost of carpet care. Special equipment such as wet vacuums, steam cleaning or extraction machines, or rotary floor machines may be needed. Carpet cleaning methods are broadly divided into two categories: dry and wet.

Dry carpet cleaning utilizes a cleaning compound or powder to suspend the dirt so it can be removed by a vacuum. However, this method can create problems. If some of the compound remains in the pile of the carpet, this residue will attract more soil and may cause the carpeting to require cleaning more frequently by a different method of carpet cleaning. The advantage is that it minimizes "down time" (the amount of time the carpet is not available for use).

Wet carpet cleaning methods require more labor and more down time. Overnight drying of the carpeting is usually necessary. Also, if wet methods are used carelessly, the carpeting can become oversoaked. Oversoaking leads to shrinkage, mildew, and a buildup of residue. All of these conditions have the potential to shorten the useful life of the carpeting.

The **steam cleaning or extraction method** of carpet cleaning requires specialized machinery that ranges in price from $1,500 to $10,000. Some extraction equipment is multifunctional and can be used to dry vacuum and clean hard floors as well. Because extraction cleaning is hard on carpeting, it should normally be done only once each year.

Some carpet cleaning procedures fall between the dry and wet categories. The **dry foam method** pushes carpet shampoo into the carpet pile with a dispensing machine. The rotating discs on the bottom of the machine are brushes which scrub the foam-covered carpet. After drying, heavy vacuuming is required to remove the shampoo residue. Again, if the residue is left in the carpet, resoiling will be more rapid.

The **rotary bonnet method** is closer to a wet method than a dry method. A rotary floor machine is fitted with a circular abrasive yarn pad. Then the machine scrubs shampoo into the carpet and, in the process, soaks up the dirt in the yarn pad. Unfortunately, this procedure does not effectively achieve deep cleaning. **Wet extraction** is required with all methods to remove all traces of dirt and shampoo residue. The frequency of carpet cleaning is dictated by the level of traffic in the area. However, the most important aspect of carpet care is vacuuming. **Vacuuming** at least once a day prolongs the life of a carpet by removing sand and other substances that can cut or shred carpet fibers. It has been said that the difference between a spot and a stain is about 12 hours. Spots should be removed daily to minimize the staining of carpeting.

Ceiling and Wall Cleaning and Maintenance

Wall and ceiling maintenance is important in relation to the overall image of the property. Some acceptable wall and ceiling finishes were presented in Chapter 10. The objective of removing dust and dirt can best be achieved through a regular cleaning and maintenance schedule. In general, walls and ceilings may be found unpainted, painted, papered, fabric-covered, vinyl-covered, tiled, constructed of marble or cement, or wood-paneled.

Unpainted walls and ceilings are generally unacceptable in a food service or lodging property. Such surfaces are difficult, at best, to clean and maintain. Dry dusting is the only method that can be used to clean unpainted ceilings and walls. Depending on the type of paint used, **painted ceilings and walls** can be dusted, washed, or cleaned with special chemicals formulated for this purpose.

Papered walls and ceilings may be either nonwashable or washable, depending on the composition of the paper. Nonwashable papered areas require dry dusting or cleaning with a specialized liquid or solid cleaner that will not damage the surface or loosen the paper. Washable papered areas can be dusted and washed. Care must be exercised to avoid damaging the paper.

Fabrics used to cover walls and ceilings are linen, burlap, damask, and canvas. These textured coverings may be dusted and then cleaned with specialized chemicals (solvents). Follow the manufacturer's recommendations and exercise caution. **Vinyl-covered areas** can be dusted and cleaned with a neutral washing solution.

The same care is required for **tile** and **marble walls**. Acids of any sort should never be used on marble, since a chemical reaction may occur and cause the marble to dissolve.

Cement walls and ceilings may be dusted and washed. A mildly acidic detergent applied with a stiff-bristle brush works well for the washing operation. After washing, rinsing with clean water is essential because the detergent residues must be removed.

Wood-paneled ceilings and walls are cleaned and maintained just like furniture. Frequent dusting to clean and an occasional waxing to protect the paneling are required.

Walls and ceilings may be washed by hand or with a machine specifically designed for this purpose. Using a proper concentration of washing solution is critical in either case. After the area is washed, the washing solution is removed from the surface, the surface is rinsed, and then it is final rinsed. Thorough rinsing removes the soil and chemical residues.

Curtains, Draperies, Upholstered Furniture, and Fixtures Cleaning and Maintenance

This category of decorative items adds to the image and comfort level of hospitality properties. The frequency of cleaning and maintenance depends on the furnishing.

Curtains and draperies can add to the ambience of a lodging property. In most cases, careful vacuuming will prolong the life of these items. Some fabrics may be hand washed when soiled, while other fabrics must be cleaned with a dry cleaning compound. Because of the variety of fabrics used for curtains and draperies, it is best to follow the manufacturer's recommendations specifically when removing soil from curtains and draperies.

Hot solvent cleaning is used by some properties for delicate fabrics and upholstery. This process can be used to clean silks, crushed velvet, and other fine fabrics. The hot solvent method minimizes color bleeding and shrinking problems which are frequently experienced with these fabrics. Portable equipment is used for on-location cleaning of curtains, draperies, and upholstered furniture. The equipment resembles a miniature version of a water extraction unit used for carpeting.

A **dry foam soil extractor** may be used to shampoo and remove spills from upholstery on furniture. The machine loosens dirt and spills, and the attached vacuum removes the soil. The equipment can also be used to clean carpeted stairs. Some upholstery fabrics can be made resistant to soil by applying a protective fluorocarbon coating to the item after it is cleaned.

Blinds and shades for windows should be vacuumed or dusted. Some metal and plastic surfaces can be washed with a mild detergent solution and rinsed with clean water. Cloth or fabric materials may require specialized cleaning chemicals and procedures. **Lamps and lamp shades** should be dusted or vacuumed daily. Most materials can be washed with a solution of mild detergent and rinsed.

Chandeliers and **glass fixtures** are difficult to clean because they are usually enormous and located high above the floor level. One lodging property uses a pressure sprayer to apply a special cleaning mixture. Prior to the application, a sheet of vinyl is draped over the floor directly below the chandelier. The housekeeping staff person gains access to the overhead chandelier with an airlift work platform. Once the chandelier is cleaned, another sprayer is used to rinse it with distilled water. Smaller glass fixtures are removed from the wall or ceiling and dipped in the cleaning solution. Then they are rinsed, dried, and rehung.

Glass and Window Cleaning and Maintenance

Glass is a common construction material in many modern buildings. Glass is relatively easy to clean and maintain if done properly and frequently. Also, the necessary equipment and supplies are relatively inexpensive. Squeegees range from 6 to 24 inches (15.24 - 60.96 cm) in width. For durability, brass construction and hardwood handles are preferred. Aluminum models are more likely to bend and become unusable.

Sponges, towels, or chamois cloths are used to wipe the squeegee between strokes. This eliminates dirt and prevents it from being reapplied to the glass surface. Window brushes are used to apply the cleaning compound (usually trisodium phosphate) for outdoor window cleaning. Lint-free cloths or sponges may be used to apply the cleaning compound for indoor window and glass cleaning.

An ammonia-water solution can be used to clean glass. However, some people find the odor disagreeable. Alcohol may be added to water as an antifreeze when windows are cleaned at temperatures below freezing. Commercial glass cleaners are effective also. They may be sprayed on the glass surface and wiped off. Periodic, scheduled cleaning of glass surfaces is necessary to prevent an excessive buildup of soil and to make cleaning easier. Some lodging properties contract their outside window cleaning to professional companies. This reduces the safety risks for the lodging property's personnel.

The cleaning and maintenance of food service and lodging facilities are very important to management and employees. Some suggested routine cleaning and maintenance procedures for various materials are presented in Exhibit 11.2. Management must demonstrate an interest in cleaning and maintenance procedures because they protect the property's investment in furniture, fixtures, and equipment. Employees must be a part of the cleaning and maintenance program. The property that is well cleaned and maintained fosters employee pride and can even raise productivity levels. Clean and well-maintained lodging and food service operations raise the overall level of customer satisfaction and promote repeat business and word-of-mouth advertising.

Interior Plant Care and Maintenance

Many food service and lodging establishments use a variety of live plants to create the desired ambience. The natural beauty of living plants enhances the interior of our manufactured environments. Their interesting shapes and colors complement the furnishings and decor of public areas. However, a plant care program is essential if the plants are to look their best. A typical plant care program encompasses weekly waterings, periodic trimming and grooming, fertilizing three times annually, insect and disease control, and replacement of unhealthy plants.

Interior plants should be selected and placed according to the individual plant's requirements. Each species may have slightly different needs for water, air, light, humidity, nutrients and soil, grooming, and transplanting. In most cases, light should be continuous for 12 to 14 hours daily. A minimum intensity of 50 footcandles is generally recommended. Ideal temperatures range from 70 to 75°F (21-24°C). Indoor plants usually come from tropical environments; therefore, they prefer humid, moist air.

Exhibit 11.2 How to Care for Materials in Your Building

MATERIAL	ROUTINE CLEANING AND MAINTENANCE
Acoustical Tile	Remove loose dirt or dust with a vacuum or soft brush. A gum eraser will remove most smudges. Soft chalk can cover many stains. More thorough cleaning can be accomplished with wallpaper cleaners or mild soap cleaners. Care must be taken to avoid excessive water and abrasive rubbing action; using a soft sponge is best.
Aluminum	Wash with a mild detergent solution; avoid common alkalies which dull the finish. A fine abrasive may be used periodically; rub in one direction, not in a circle.
Asphalt Tile	Wash with a mild detergent or soap solution; rinse with clean water and dry immediately either with mops or wet/dry vacuums.
Bamboo, Cane, Reed, Wicker, Rattan	Wash with a mild soap or detergent solution; rinse with clear water, dry. Periodic shellacking maintains a natural finish.
Brass	Acidic-type brass cleaners and polishes are used for unfinished brass. Wash lacquered brass with a mild detergent solution, rinse, and wipe dry.
Bronze	Clean with a metal cleaner or polish applied with a soft cloth; work with the grain, covering one small area at a time. Wash lacquered bronze with a mild detergent solution; rinse and wipe dry. Rub statuary finishes periodically with lemon oil on a soft cloth. Then rub briskly with a clean, soft cloth to remove excess oil.
Carpets	All types of carpeting—wool, polyester, nylon, polypropylene, etc.—must be vacuumed regularly to extend their useful life. (Abrasives which are allowed to accumulate in the carpet fibers will actually cut the fibers at the backing.) Also, a daily spotting program ensures prompt removal of spots. Overall cleaning can be accomplished with impregnated granular cleaners, shampoos, or extraction chemicals with a dry residue to prevent rapid resoiling.
Ceramic Tile	Use neutral soap or detergent applied with a sponge, mop, or brush, depending on the stain. Remove excess cleaning solution, rinse with clean water, and thoroughly dry the surface. Avoid alkalies, salts, acids, and abrasive cleaners. These tend to break down the surfaces of glazed and vitreous tiles, and cause problems with the porous cement grout. Some soap cleaners may result in a soap film buildup.
Chromium	Avoid harsh polishes and powders. A damp cloth is usually sufficient, or a mild detergent solution may be used. Then polish with a dry cloth.
Concrete	As soon as the floor can be used, it should be swept clean and a dust seal applied. Old concrete should be thoroughly cleaned and also sealed. Concrete floors can be swept with treated mops, damp mopped, or scrubbed with a neutral cleaner. Excess solution should be picked up with a squeegee or wet vacuum. Never use acids because concrete dissolves in acidic solutions.
Conductive Floors	These floors are found in hospitals, computer rooms, or anywhere that it is necessary to prevent the building of a static electrical charge on the floor. These floors must be kept *film-free*. This includes coatings, soap films or dust mop dressings, as they will build an insulating residue on the floors. In hospitals, clean with a disinfectant/detergent. In other areas, use a detergent recommended for conductive floors.
Copper	Wash with soap and water, rinse, and dry. Stains and corrosion may be removed with metal polishes. If acidic solutions are used, always rinse thoroughly to avoid excess tarnishing.
Cork Tile	Sweep with a treated mop and buff. Avoid excessive water. If wet cleaning is needed, a mild soap or detergent solution should be applied with a damp mop. Sealed cork floors are preferred as they protect the natural colors of the cork.
Glass	Wash with a special window cleaning concentrate dissolved in clean water; apply with a window washer's brush; use a squeegee or chamois to dry glass.
Granite	Polished granite may be washed with a detergent solution or applied poultices. Treat unpolished granite with water and sand cleaning at a pressure of 50 psi or less.

Iron	Wash with a soap or detergent solution, rinse, and dry. A phosphoric acid cleaner can also be used. Rinse and dry thoroughly. Rust can be removed with steel wool, soaked in mineral spirits. Surfaces which can withstand acid cleaning can be treated with a phosphoric-oxalic acid solution. Rinse thoroughly because oxalic acid is toxic.
Leather Furniture	Wash with a neutral soap or saddle soap. Leather trappings, etc., should be treated with neet's-foot oil to prevent drying and cracking.
Linoleum	Wash with a mild detergent solution; rinse with clear water. Remove water and dry as rapidly as possible. *Avoid* alkaline solutions.
Magnesite	Wash with a neutral detergent; do not use acids or alkaline cleaners. Remove solutions with a wet vacuum; avoid excess water.
Marble	Newly installed marble is best cleaned with a neutral cleaner and clean mops. Marble that has been soiled or stained through neglect has to be cleaned with the poultice method using a powdered abrasive cleaner and hot water. Only mildly alkaline detergent (never acids) should be used on seasoned marble; wash from the bottom up and rinse thoroughly. Then dry either with a chamois or soft cloth to prevent streaking.
Masonry	Steam cleaning with detergents or water and sand cleaning under low pressure may be required for brick, cement block, cinder block, stone and stucco. Interior masonry work may be vacuumed with heavy duty commercial-type machines.
Oil Paintings	Dust *lightly* with a soft dusting brush using extreme care. *Never use water or cleaners.* For badly soiled oil paintings, consult an expert.
Painted Surfaces	Immediately remove spots with a cloth wrung from a detergent solution. Washing should be performed under controlled conditions.
Pewter	Wash with a neutral detergent solution, rinse, and dry with a soft cloth. Apply a commercial silver polish to remove stains or browning.
Porcelain	Use an alkaline detergent; avoid acids, which can dissolve the surface and cause blemishes.
Rubber Tile	Use a mild detergent solution; rinse and remove water promptly.
Slate	Wash with a detergent solution; rinse and dry thoroughly. Chalkboards should *not* be washed on a regular basis; a thin film of chalk dust is best for vision and the care of the board.
Stainless Steel	Wash with a solution of soap or detergent. Rinse thoroughly; dry with a soft cloth. For heavier dirt, or deposits which require scrubbing, there are many specialty products; always rinse and dry, making sure to rub with the grain. Polish with a hydrocarbon-based stainless steel cleaner to prevent fingerprinting and resoiling.
Terra Cotta	Wash with a neutral detergent solution.
Terrazzo	Only neutral detergents should be used. Stains can be removed by the poultice method. Avoid alkaline cleaners as they cause powdering. Avoid using sweeping compounds which contain oil or wax. Acids dissolve the marble chips in terrazzo; soap tends to build up and leave a surface film; steel wool leaves splinters that rust.
Vinyl	Use a neutral detergent solution, rinse, and dry with a wet vacuum.
Wood	Wood floors must be sealed if they are to be maintained properly. Dust mopping and damp mopping sealed floors are usually all that is necessary if a regular maintenance program is followed. Polishing with a floor wax finish may be required. Some of the soft woods can be seriously damaged by strong solutions of soap or detergent and water; oils, grease, and strong alkalies are also harmful. Avoid excessive use of water and always remove water as rapidly as possible.
Hospitals	Where any of these surfaces are found in hospitals, nursing homes, or sanitary areas, a detergent solution may be used unless a disinfectant/detergent is required.
Vehicles	Trucks, buses, and forklifts should be cleaned with a concentrated alkaline cleaner/degreaser, using high pressure and hot water equipment, to effectively remove road soils, grease, soot, etc.

Source: Adapted from The Soap and Detergent Association, *Programmed Cleaning Guide,* 1983, p. 467.

Most plants prefer soil that is barely moist throughout at all times. Potting soil is a lightweight soil which drains quickly; it is cleaner and richer than ordinary soil found outdoors. Indoor plants should be fed lightly with fertilizer about three times annually. Many properties contract their plant care program to an expert service company. This ensures that the plants are always healthy, properly shaped, and attractive additions to the interior of the lodging or food service establishment.

Restroom Cleaning and Maintenance

Restroom cleaning and maintenance was covered from the standpoint of public health requirements in Chapter 10. A cleaned and well-maintained restroom contributes to a favorable image in the minds of the property's customers. Many people feel that the condition of the restroom reflects the general level of sanitation in a food service or lodging property. Thorough restroom cleaning and maintenance must be routine. Periodic monitoring of the facilities is crucial. Employees should be assigned to check restrooms according to a set schedule. A form for this purpose is presented in Exhibit 11.3. This system shows customers that the property cares.

Regular and thorough restroom cleaning with a germicidal cleaner usually eliminates the need for air fresheners and deodorant blocks. **Germicidal cleaners** are highly recommended for restroom areas. They effectively kill bacteria and their odors on walls, floors, urinals, toilets, partitions, and lavatories. A **bowl cleaner** is an acid compound used to remove hard water rings. **Scouring cream or powder** is only required when a harsh abrasive action is needed. Generally, bowl cleaners and scouring creams or powders are not necessary if the spray system is used.

The **spray system** keeps the cleaning solution free from contamination and maintains freshness better than mopping with a solution in a bucket. The bucket and mop system is ineffective because it continuously introduces bacteria and dirt into the washing solution. The germicidal cleaner may be applied with a sprayer. Ideally, germicidal cleaners should have a quaternary ammonium compound as their base with detergents added for cleaning power. These cleaners can be used on all restroom surfaces.

The following steps are recommended for cleaning restrooms:

1. Empty the trash and sweep the floor.

2. Spray the germicidal cleaner on and in urinals and toilets.

3. Scrub urinals and toilets with a bowl brush to clean them thoroughly, and then flush.

4. Spray the floor and partitions around toilets and urinals. (The cleaner is not wiped off these surfaces because the residue which remains after the cleaner dries inhibits bacterial growth.)

Exhibit 11.3   Restroom Inspection Report Form

Date	Time	Condition(s) Requiring Action	Time Action Taken	Employee's Initials	Supervisor's Initials

5. Spray the germicidal cleaner on mirrors and lavatories.

6. Wipe off mirrors with a chamois cloth or paper towel. (Again, a residue from the cleaner is left on sinks to inhibit further bacterial growth.)

7. Spray the germicidal cleaner on the walls and wipe off.

8. Spray the pipes and wall area under the lavatories.

9. Spray the floor and rinse with a clean mop dipped frequently in a bucket of clean water.

This spray system of restroom cleaning is effective, saves money, and reduces staff time spent on restroom housekeeping. Using this method regularly eliminates the need for bowl cleaners, scouring powders, and glass cleaners.

Restroom supplies are often a substantial part of the property's housekeeping budget. Costs can be controlled if the correct dispensers are selected and properly installed. Several alternative dispensing systems are available for restroom supplies such as towels, tissue, and soap. Economical dispensers discourage waste, provide easy refilling, and result in portion restriction of towels, tissue, and soap.

Dispensers should be constructed of durable materials to prevent vandalism. Toilet tissue dispensers with the capacity for a reserve roll are preferred. Paper hand towels can save as much as 50% of the cost of roll-type linen towel refills. Fully automatic paper towel dispensers control usage with a timed delay. Wall-mounted electric hand dryers eliminate paper costs and disposal problems; however, they do add to the property's energy costs. Also, purchase and installation costs are higher for electric hand dryers than for towel dispensers.

Lotion soap dispensers are widely used in public restrooms today. Typical liquid dispensers hold approximately 1 pint to 1 quart (500 ml - 1 liter) of soap. These can dispense enough soap to wash the hands of 1,000 to 3,000 people with each refill. Pump dispensers for lotion soap should be self-cleaning with no leakage or clogging. Powdered soap dispensers are also available. Bar soap is undesirable due to the potential for bacteria and disease transfer. Depending on their composition, bar soaps can become mushy or brittle, and they often appear dirty from prior use. In addition, caked-on bar soap on lavatories in restrooms looks unsightly.

Waste Collection and Disposal

One of the main functions of the housekeeping department is the collection and disposal of litter and waste. Urns and waste receptacles (including wastebaskets) are used to collect litter and waste discarded by the customer. In lodging properties, cigarette butts and other discarded smoking materials are generally collected either in water-quenching urns or in granular-filled urns.

Water-quenching urns may cause some odor problems. In addition, these urns are difficult to refill and may be corroded by nicotinic acid. **Granular-filled urns** contain stone chips or sand. If the sand is spilled on carpeted floors, it can damage the carpet and the floors. Self-closing urns are preferred because they minimize fire hazards and have a neater appearance. Regardless of the type selected, urns should be available near telephones, elevators, drinking fountains, restrooms, and on landings. To minimize fire hazards, they should only be emptied into metal containers.

Waste receptacles should be located near entrances, exits, and on terraces. Outside receptacles must be covered to protect them from the elements. In guestrooms, waste baskets should be conveniently located. Ideally, containers should be seamless to reduce odors and facilitate cleaning. Plastic film liners protect the interiors of waste receptacles and make them easier to empty.

Waste may be collected from urns and receptacles and placed on a custodial cart. Two alternatives to the custodial cart are a plastic drum on wheels and a litter vacuum which sucks up litter, shreds it, and stores it in a collection bag. Once collected, waste must be disposed of properly.

Some localities permit incineration of burnable waste. Where incineration is prohibited, waste is collected and placed in a dumpster for later removal. Most large properties contract their waste removal. Trash compactors reduce the volume of waste by applying pressure. Any waste collection and disposal system must be evaluated on the basis of cost, safety, pollution control, fire prevention, odor control, pest control, space utilization, appearance, noise, scheduling, and storing requirements. The best decision can only be achieved if all these relevant factors are addressed.

Exterior Cleaning and Maintenance

Some effective cleaning and maintenance procedures for **exterior areas** were already presented in Exhibit 11.2. Exterior masonry surfaces are typically brick, concrete, concrete block, stucco, stone, or a combination of these materials. As already pointed out, these surfaces are porous and attract water, dirt, and scale. The cleaning of masonry exterior surfaces is difficult but important. Cleaning methods vary according to the climate, the type and condition of the masonry, and the design of the building exterior.

Cleaners for masonry exteriors are frequently applied with spray guns and hoses. During cleaning operations, glass and aluminum exterior surfaces and plants and shrubs must be protected. Where damaged, masonry surfaces can be repaired and waterproofed with special chemical compounds. These applications not only enhance the exterior appearance of the building; they also prolong its life and increase its value.

Clean parking lots and sidewalks contribute to a positive first impression as the guest or customer approaches the facility. Outdoor cleaning equipment is selected based on the area to be cleaned, surface characteristics, the type of debris to be removed, the frequency of cleaning, and the financial resources available. A number of different types of sweeping machines are available for purchase. **Air-recycling machines** create an air blast with a fan to loosen debris. The debris is pulled up through a hose and deposited in a collection tank. **Broom-vacuum machines** loosen debris with a rotating broom. The debris is thrown into a hopper. **Push vacuum machines** are walk-behind units primarily used to clean large indoor surfaces. Manufacturers of these sweeping machines can provide detailed information on their features.

Where winters are snowy, **ice and snow melting compounds** play an important role in exterior building maintenance. Before these compounds are used, the bulk of the snow must be removed from sidewalk, entrance, stair, ramp, and parking lot surfaces. This effort can be expensive in terms of labor, but it is necessary for the sake of appearance and safety. The three major types of melting compounds are rock salt, calcium chloride, and preformulated chemicals. All ice and snow melting compounds should be used according to the manufacturer's directions.

Rock salt is relatively abundant and inexpensive. This compound lowers the freezing point of water; however, it is ineffective at temperatures below 0°F (-18°C). Rock salt leaves a powdered salt residue, which is frequently tracked into buildings and may soil carpeting near entranceways. Finally, rock salt can be corrosive to metal containing iron.

Calcium chloride compounds create an intense heat and absorb moisture. They are effective at temperatures below 0°F (-18°C). However, these compounds can destroy animal and plant life, concrete, carpeting, fabrics, and metal surfaces. Also, calcium chloride may irritate the skin through its burning action, so gloves should be worn when using this chemical. Finally, calcium chloride compounds are more expensive than rock salt.

The most expensive ice and snow removal compounds are the **preformulated chemicals**; they are also the safest. They melt snow and ice quickly and efficiently, are nontoxic to living things, and are noncorrosive to metals and fabrics. They effectively melt snow and ice at temperatures below 0°F (-18°C).

Ice and snow melting compounds should be selected based on the requirements of your individual property. They should be stored in low-moisture areas and applied with caution.

Cleaning Costs and Equipment Return on Investment

The costs of cleaning and maintenance can be a substantial portion of total expenses for a lodging or food service operation. A number of variables affect total cleaning and maintenance costs. The amount of employee time required and the rate of pay influence the costs. The square footage of the area to be cleaned not only affects total costs; it also has an impact on worker efficiency. The amount of work needed to clean the area must also be considered. More detail results in higher total cleaning costs.

Frequency of cleaning is important. More frequent cleaning raises total costs. Most methods for calculating cleaning costs arrive at a cost per day or cost per week figure after considering all of the variables just mentioned. The costs may be decreased by manipulating the variables. For example, labor time may be reduced by purchasing more efficient equipment or training workers to use more efficient procedures. It may be possible to clean a larger area once supplies and equipment are assembled and set up. This will reduce setup and breakdown time when moving to a new location. An analysis of the property's total cleaning costs is essential if deviations from budgeted amounts are to be identified and brought under control.

Besides supplies and labor, another component of total cleaning costs that contributes to the operating budget of the housekeeping department is equipment. The purchase prices and maintenance costs of equipment can be staggering. A calculation of equipment **return on investment (ROI)** provides the annual rate at which an equipment purchase generates savings for the property.[2] The objective is to purchase the equipment that will yield the greatest ROI while satisfying the cleaning and maintenance needs of the property. ROIs can be determined for various brands of each type of equipment. Then these ROI calculations

---

[2] The basic ROI calculation can be found in any elementary finance or accounting text.

Exhibit 11.4 Housekeeping Self-Inspection Checklist

AREA	CONDITION	ACTION REQUIRED	PERSON RESPONSIBLE
Building Exterior 1. Parking lot free from debris and litter 2. Sidewalks free from litter and debris 3. Garbage/refuse storage areas clean and orderly 4. Lawn, shrubs, plants maintained 5. Windows clean 6. Building free from soil buildup			
Entrances 1. Free from objectionable odors 2. Floor clean and maintained daily 3. Windows cleaned daily 4. Carpet walk mats cleaned and maintained daily 5. Ceilings and walls cleaned and maintained monthly			
Floor Care-Uncarpeted Areas 1. Dust mopping of resilient floors daily 2. Wet mopping of floor at least daily 3. Wax stripping of waxed floors monthly 4. Proper waxing and finishing of floors monthly 5. Safety signs used while wet mopping, stripping, and finishing floors			
Floor Care-Carpeted Areas 1. Vacuuming properly each day or more frequently 2. Spot-cleaning to remove soil buildup weekly 3. Shampooing or extraction done properly and regularly 4. Safety signs used while shampooing or extracting carpeting			
Hallways, Lobby, Elevators, Guestrooms 1. Vacuumed daily or more frequently 2. Spot-cleaning of soiled areas weekly 3. Shampooing of soiled areas monthly 4. Wet mopping of uncarpeted areas daily or more frequently 5. Safety signs used during shampooing, extraction, and wet mopping operations 6. Upholstery and furniture spot-cleaned monthly or more frequently 7. Draperies and curtains vacuumed weekly 8. Windows and glass cleaned daily 9. Lamps and shades dusted daily 10. Plants cared for regularly 11. Ceilings and walls cleaned and maintained monthly 12. Waste receptacles and urns regularly emptied			
Restroom Care 1. Urinals and toilet bowls checked and cleaned at least four times each day 2. Stalls and overhead areas checked and cleaned periodically 3. Waste receptacles and urns regularly emptied 4. Soap dispensers, tissue dispensers, and towel dispensers checked during cleaning operations and refilled when necessary 5. Free from obnoxious odors and the buildup of debris			

can help management to decide more objectively which equipment ought to be purchased.

ROI also points out the economic benefits of the equipment expenditure. It often highlights the benefits of mechanical systems over manual systems. ROI calculations can be used to illustrate why old equipment should be replaced with newer, more efficient systems. ROI can also be used to compare contract cleaning services with in-house purchases of equipment.

Preventive Maintenance

Preventive maintenance is an important component of any property's sanitation program. A certain amount of every employee's workday can be devoted to preventive maintenance, if proper training emphasizes its importance. Many problems can be minimized or eliminated entirely if preventive maintenance is performed regularly. This proactive approach ultimately reduces total cleaning and maintenance costs for the property. A self-inspection checklist is presented in Exhibit 11.4 for the housekeeping department of a food service or lodging operation.

The checklist in Exhibit 11.4 is not intended to be all-inclusive. It can be modified to fit the specific needs of the property. It is important to assign specific areas of responsibility to supervisors and employees alike. Once these responsibilities have been determined, the checklist helps the supervisor decide whether the employee is fulfilling the responsibilities. Management follow-up is an essential component of any self-inspection checklist.

Summary

This chapter highlighted sanitation management in hotels, motels, and motor hotels. Routine cleaning and housekeeping procedures in public areas and guestrooms contribute to the overall image of the hospitality property. The six basics of housekeeping management apply to any size property.

The cleaning and maintenance of floors represent a large amount of the housekeeping budget. Requirements vary with the flooring materials and the traffic patterns in different areas of the property. Ceilings, walls, furnishings, fixtures, glass, and windows were discussed, along with recommended routine cleaning and maintenance procedures.

Interior plant care and maintenance are important in today's lodging and food service operations. Correct restroom upkeep projects a desirable image to the property's customer. Waste collection and disposal are other functions of the housekeeping department. Exterior cleaning and maintenance are essential to positive first impressions of lodging or food service operations. Cleaning costs and the ROI on equipment are valid considerations in the housekeeping department. Preventive maintenance is a crucial component of any property's sanitation program.

References

Almond, J. "A Look at Applications for Truck Mounted Hot Water Extraction Equipment for Carpet Care and Pressure Washing." *Cleaning Management*, February 1982. 19(2):22.

Ames, A. "Checklists for Preventative Maintenance." *Cleaning Management*, November 1982. 19(11):13-14.

—."Hot Solvent Cleaning for Upholstery and Delicate Fabrics." *Cleaning Management*, July 1982. 19(7):28.

—."Planning for Preventive Maintenance." *Cleaning Management*, October 1981. 18(10):34.

—."Ultra High-Speed Cleaning and Polishing." *Cleaning Management*, April 1982. 19(4):24.

—."What's New in Floor Seals?" *Cleaning Management,* June 1982. 19(6):12.

Bondurant, J. "Caring for Interior Plants." *Cleaning Management*, December 1981. 18(12):6.

Borges, M. "Calculating Cleaning Costs." *Cleaning Management*, September 1982. 19(9):46.

"Electric Hand Dryers vs. Paper Towels." *Cleaning Management*, November 1982. 19(11):40.

Entzminger, B. "Improving Cleaning Accessibility." *Cleaning Management*, September 1982. 19(9):26.

Feldman, E. B. "Housekeeping's Role in Developing a Good Public Image." *Cleaning Management*, April 1982. 19(4):56-57.

—."Universal Factors of Effective Housekeeping." *Cleaning Management,* September 1982. 19(9):6.

—."Waste Collection and Disposal." *Cleaning Management,* October 1981. 18(10):24.

Fivecoat-Wilhelm, T. "A Look At Hotel Housekeeping Operations." *Cleaning Management*, November 1981. 18(11):6.

—."Dispensing With Restroom Servicing Problems." *Cleaning Management,* February 1982. 19(2):6.

—."Managing Your Window Washing Operation." *Cleaning Management,* May 1982. 19(5):6.

—."Selecting Ice and Snow Melting Compounds." *Cleaning Management,* November 1981. 18(11):32.

Green, A. S. "Cleaning Exterior Masonry Surfaces." *Cleaning Management*, May 1982. 19(5):30.

Heiland, R. "High-Pressure Cleaning Does the Tough Jobs." *Cleaning Management,* November 1981. 18(11):22.

Hillyard, S. "How A Chemical Manufacturer Views Carpet Care Methods." *Cleaning Management*, December 1981. 18(12):28.

Housekeeping Seminar, East Lansing, Mich.: Educational Institute of the American Hotel & Motel Association, 1982.

Koppi, J. "How to Calculate Your Return on Investment for Equipment Purchases." *Cleaning Management*, May 1982. 19(5):26.

—."Selecting Equipment for Grounds Sweeping." *Cleaning Management,* May 1982. 19(5):14.

"New Products Change Look — and Life — of Flooring." *Institutions/Volume Feeding*, April 1977. 80(7):65.

Programmed Cleaning Guide. New York: Soap and Detergent Association, 1983.

"Questions About Acoustical Ceiling Cleaning." *Cleaning Management*, July 1982. 19(7):24.

"There's More Than One Way to Strip a Floor." *Cleaning Management*, July 1982. 19(7):8.

Trainor, L. "How Modular Carpeting Saves on Maintenance." *Cleaning Management,* October 1982. 19(10):22.

"A Uniform Approach to Restroom Care." *Cleaning Management*, February 1982. 19(2):32-33.

"Upholstery Cleaning Made Easy at Disneyland Hotel." *Cleaning Management*, October 1982. 19(10):17-18.

Weeks, A. "Using a Spray System for Restroom and Shower Stall Cleaning." *Cleaning Management*, February 1982. 19(2):26-28.

Strategies for Success at the Aspen Hotel

Paul James thought about how customers evaluate a hotel or restaurant. A large part of developing the customer awareness of his staff was training them to perceive the property as customers do. Another important point he liked to emphasize was that the friendliness and enthusiasm of all employees affect customer satisfaction. Customers or guests patronize a hotel or restaurant to have a pleasant, enjoyable time. Therefore, it was his job as GM to instill customer awareness and courtesy in every employee and supervisor.

Checklist for Sanitation of Lodging Properties

Cleaning and Housekeeping – General

1. The housekeeping department provides a clean, pleasant, and comfortable environment.

2. Housekeeping personnel are aware that they are part of the property's public relations efforts.

3. Housekeeping personnel realize that their work performance affects repeat business.

4. The six basics of housekeeping management are used to evaluate the department's efficiency and effectiveness.

5. Cleaning and maintenance activities take place when business is slowest.

6. Chemicals used in public areas work safely and rapidly and dry quickly.

Floor Cleaning and Maintenance

1. Floor materials in various areas are selected according to the use planned for each area.

2. Recommendations are followed for selecting hard and resilient floor coverings.

3. Floor maintenance methods are chosen based on the characteristics of the materials.

4. High pressure cleaning is used for floors with irregular surfaces.

5. Chemicals selected and used on floors are based on manufacturer's recommendations.

6. Cleaning and maintenance are performed as part of a regular, ongoing program.

Ceiling and Wall Cleaning and Maintenance

1. A regular cleaning and maintenance program is established for walls and ceilings.

2. Proper concentrations of cleaning materials are used.

Curtains, Draperies, Furniture, and Upholstery Cleaning and Maintenance

1. Careful vacuuming is used to prolong the useful life of these items.

2. Fabrics are hand washed or dry cleaned based on manufacturer's recommendations.

Glass and Window Cleaning and Maintenance

1. Glass and windows are regularly cleaned.

2. A contract service is used for exterior window cleaning.

Interior Plant Care and Maintenance

1. The company utilizes a plant program which covers:

    a. weekly watering

    b. periodic trimming and grooming

    c. fertilizing three times annually

    d. insect and disease control

    e. replacement of unhealthy plants

Restroom Cleaning and Maintenance

1. Personnel realize that restroom cleaning and maintenance affects guest satisfaction and the property's image.

2. Effective restroom cleaning and maintenance are accomplished daily.

3. Employees are assigned to check the condition of restrooms frequently throughout the day.

4. Restroom supplies are checked regularly and replaced when necessary.

Waste Collection and Disposal

1. Urns, wastebaskets, and receptacles are used to collect waste and litter where it is discarded by the customer.

2. Waste receptacles are located near entrances and exits and on terraces.

3. Plastic film liners are used to protect the interiors of waste receptacles.

Exterior Cleaning and Maintenance

1. Cleaning methods for exterior building surfaces are selected based on the climate, the type and condition of the materials, and the design of the building exterior.

> 2. Parking lots and sidewalks are regularly cleaned and maintained.
>
> 3. Ice and snow melting compounds are used during the winter to maintain the attractiveness and safety of the property's sidewalks and entrance areas.
>
> **Preventive Maintenance**
>
> 1. A portion of each employee's workday is devoted to preventive maintenance.
>
> 2. A self-inspection checklist is used for preventive maintenance.

The following case studies are designed to enhance your understanding of the material in this chapter. If you are a Home Study student, use these case studies to stimulate questions about this chapter. If you are a Group or Institutional Study student, you may be asked to discuss these case studies as part of a regular classroom assignment.

CASE STUDY 11.1

Steve Wood is the general manager of the Pintail Drake Hotel. While walking through the hotel on his daily inspection, Steve notices that some of the facility's marble floors are very well maintained, while others appear dingy and unkempt.

The floor of the lobby is inlaid Italian marble. This area is currently swept and mopped once a day, during the early hours of the morning when traffic is light. The floor hasn't been stripped and refinished in the two years that Steve has been the general manager of the hotel.

Test Your Understanding

1. Is the floor maintenance program acceptable at the Pintail Drake Hotel?

2. What is the problem with the marble floor in the hotel lobby?

3. What are your recommendations to Steve Wood?

CASE STUDY 11.2

The grand ballroom of the Pintail Drake Hotel was recarpeted one year ago with a solid dark burgundy carpet. The carpet appeared very plush when it was first installed. Now the carpeting looks worn in traffic areas and has a crushed pile.

Carpeting in the grand ballroom is vacuumed before and after each function held in the room. Once each month, the carpet is cleaned by shampooing in high traffic areas. The executive housekeeper of the hotel requires her staff to clean the ballroom's carpeting by wet extraction every six months.

Test Your Understanding

1. Is the floor housekeeping program acceptable at the Pintail Drake?

2. What is the problem with the carpeting in the grand ballroom?

3. What are your recommendations to the executive housekeeper?

CASE STUDY 11.3

Janet Lion is the executive housekeeper at the Cardinal Motor Hotel. Janet has recently discovered that the brass fixtures in the lobby are cleaned each day by a housekeeper using a soap and water solution. Even though she has specifically instructed housekeeping employees in the proper cleaning methods, Janet has observed some of her staff members cleaning ceramic tile with an acid cleaner. The same compound was used last week to remove some grease stains from the concrete floor in the parking garage.

Test Your Understanding

1. Are the housekeeping employees at the Cardinal Motor Hotel using recommended cleaning procedures?

2. What should be used to clean brass, ceramic tile, and concrete?

3. What are your recommendations to Janet Lion?

CASE STUDY 11.4

Public restrooms at the Cardinal Motor Hotel are cleaned twice each day in the early morning and late afternoon. The housekeeper uses the old-fashioned mop and bucket procedure. Roll-type towel dispensers are installed in each restroom. The property utilizes slightly used bars of hand soap from guestrooms in the public restrooms.

Management at the Cardinal Motor Hotel requires housekeepers to place a guest survey form in each guestroom. In the past month, several guests have remarked about the unacceptable level of sanitation in the public restrooms in the lobby of the hotel. The GM has asked Janet Lion, the executive housekeeper, to take positive action to remedy the problem and to reduce the complaints.

Test Your Understanding

1. What are the sanitation implications of the public restroom housekeeping procedures at the Cardinal Motor Hotel?

2. How could housekeeping procedures in the public restrooms be improved?

3. What are your recommendations to Janet Lion?

CASE STUDY 11.5

Bill Thunder is the owner and operator of the J. B. Motel in northern Michigan. The motel is located on the shores of one of the Great Lakes and has 32 rooms for rent. The busy season for the hotel is from Memorial Day to Labor Day.

Because of the size of the facility, Bill does most of the repairs and maintenance himself. He hires two college students each summer to help him get through the busy season. Most cleaning operations are done by hand, because Bill believes that nothing beats muscle power or "elbow grease." It is February, and Bill is working on a self-inspection checklist for next summer.

Test Your Understanding

1. Comment on Bill's "elbow grease" philosophy.

2. What should be included on a housekeeping self-inspection checklist?

3. What are your recommendations to Bill Thunder?

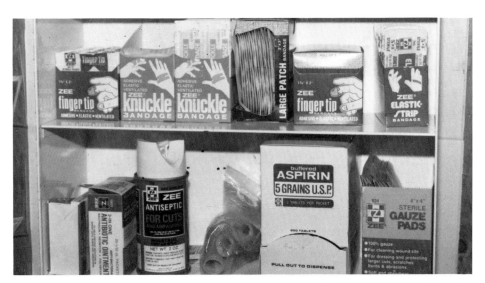

TWELVE

Safety
Management

Strategies for Success at the Aspen Hotel

Paul James decided that it was time to address the question of safety at the Aspen Hotel. The GM had assembled all his department heads at this morning's meeting to discuss and formulate a safety program for all areas of the hotel. Paul James opened the meeting by reading part of an article that had appeared in yesterday's daily newspaper.

The GM began, "Last week in a hotel in Colorado, over 100 guests were injured in the worst hotel fire in that state's history. Eighteen people died as a result of the fire. The cause of the fire is still under investigation. However, it appears as though the hotel did not have its primary life safety systems up-to-date."

Paul commented, "I believe that only a few of the employees knew what to do during this emergency. This tragedy could have been avoided if the hotel had prepared itself for emergencies and had trained the employees to respond rapidly and correctly."

Paul knew that his opening remarks had been effective in getting the attention of his key people when he saw the look of shock on their faces. Now they were interested in what he had to say. He knew that this group of professionals wanted to avoid a similar disaster at the Aspen Hotel.

"Fire safety is only one aspect of a safety program in a hotel," said the GM. "The prevention of injuries to employees and guests is another important component. In reviewing the Aspen Hotel's accident records, I discovered that this property is paying a premium for workers' compensation rates because of the relatively large number of accidents. Also, insurance rates are higher than they should be for a property of this size and volume of business. Worst of all, this hotel paid over $8,000 last year in out-of-court settlements to injured guests and employees.

"I'm not blaming any of you," continued the GM. "The answer lies in a detailed safety program. That will allow us to be proactive and solve these problems before it's too late. We need to develop emergency procedures in writing. Everyone must know what to do and who to call in an emergency. It will be your responsibility to train and retrain your employees. I have always believed that the best safety device in any hotel is a well-trained and careful employee.

"I realize that sanitation and safety can sometimes be in conflict. For example, a smooth finish on a floor is easier to keep clean while a rough surface is safer. We cannot afford to compromise either sanitation or safety. Both are critical to the success of our hotel.

"Part of our hotel's safety program will cover the primary life safety systems. These include exit lights, smoke detectors, sprinklers, and fire extinguisher systems. They must be regularly checked to be sure that they are working properly. The primary responsibility for these systems lies with the engineering and housekeeping departments. Of course, the insurance company and fire department will also conduct regularly scheduled inspections of the primary life safety systems.

"Our safety program must also include a procedure for following up on guest complaints. Yesterday, I reviewed the Aspen Hotel's guest complaint file. Two people broke their ankles sliding down the slide into our outdoor pool. Fortunately, that slide has since been removed. The dance floor in the banquet room is constructed of copper tiles attached to particle board. Somehow it became wet and warped, and now several tiles are coming up on the dance floor. Since someone could trip and cut their foot on that dance floor, it will be repaired or replaced before it is used again.

"Another letter from a guest last year said that there was no light in the hallway near her guestroom for two days during her visit. That is a dangerous situation which I consider completely unacceptable. Besides the fact that she felt insecure going in and out of her room in the dark, it could have resulted in a serious accident. Today, I would like each of you to contribute as many ideas as you can toward a safety program for the Aspen Hotel. We can improve our reputation with guests and maybe even save some money by planning to eliminate unsafe conditions. Now let's get started on our brainstorming session..."

This chapter focuses on safety management in food service establishments. However, many of the recommendations given also apply to lodging properties. Safety management is intimately related to the operation's sanitation management program. Sanitation and safety must both be planned programs. The well-being of the operation's employees and its customers are at stake. Both safety and sanitation techniques should be presented as a part of the operation's employee training program.

In general, **safety** can be defined as freedom from hurt, injury, or loss. In a food service or lodging operation, a safety management program must protect both the operation's customers and its employees to be successful. Safety covers two broad areas: accident prevention and security. Therefore, the first part of this chapter deals with accident prevention; the latter part covers security, including fire prevention.

Occupational Safety and Health Administration

The **Occupational Safety and Health Administration (OSHA)** was formed in 1970 to enforce the Occupational Safety and Health Act enacted that same year. OSHA is an independent regulatory agency in the executive branch of the United States government. Several states have established similar agencies at the state level.

OSHA develops and enforces mandatory standards and regulations related to the safety and health of workers throughout the United States. State and federal government safety inspectors periodically conduct inspections of businesses to determine their degree of compliance with the act. If the establishments are discovered to be violating OSHA regulations, the inspectors may cite the employers and propose penalties. Inspections generally focus on high-risk industries, claims of imminent danger, catastrophic or fatal accidents, and complaints from employees.

OSHA also provides training information for employers and educational materials for employees. OSHA inspectors consult with employers to assist them in detecting safety hazards and preventing accidents. OSHA publishes statistics annually on occupational illnesses, injuries, and fatalities in various industries. OSHA requires employers with 11 or more employees to maintain records of safety hazards, illnesses, injuries, and fatalities. OSHA inspectors may ask to review the records during their unannounced visits.

The National Restaurant Association (NRA) has developed a checklist of OSHA requirements customized for food service operations. The checklist was created to help reduce safety problems unique to the food service industry. Hospitality managers can also use the checklist to establish a safety self-inspection program that can be periodically conducted in-house. Copies of the checklist may be obtained by writing to: NRA, One IBM Plaza, Suite 2600, Chicago, IL 60611.

Food Service Accidents and Injuries

Injuries result when certain factors (unsafe features of the environment, unsafe practices, or negligence) cause accidents to occur in the establishment. Accidents and injuries are generally predictable and, therefore, are preventable.

Our discussion of food service accidents and injuries and how to prevent them begins with a description of typical accidents and injuries occurring in food and beverage establishments. Next, a form for reporting the types, causes, and costs of injuries and accidents is provided to help the manager put a dollar value on safety management. Accidents involving employees and customers are less likely to occur if a safety program is established. Therefore, this section contains recommendations for establishing a program for the prevention of accidents and injuries. Finally, employees must know how to deal with any accidents and injuries that may occur. Tips are given on how to treat a choking victim, and suggestions for first aid kits and special Red Cross training are offered.

Typical Accidents and Injuries

A major insurer of restaurants reviewed the 349 workers' compensation claims it received from restaurants during a one-year period (1977-1978) and analyzed these claims. Cuts, slips, burns, and falls led the list of 349 claims. The average cost per claim was $378.38. These 349 injuries, and the costs associated with them, could have been avoided through proper employee training and the removal of safety hazards in the food service environment.

The Texas Restaurant Association (TRA) kept track of insurance claims made by food service establishments in that state during 1974. TRA discovered that approximately one-third of the total claims came as a result of injuries from falls, another one-third were due to back injuries, and the rest resulted from cuts, burns, hernias, and miscellaneous causes. Employees 18 years old or younger filed 21% of the claims that resulted in settlements of $500 or over. Employees working in the establishments for 30 working days or less filed 24% of the claims. It seems reasonable to conclude that these new workers were not trained properly after they were hired by food service operations during the period covered by the study.

More often than not, accidents and injuries are caused by a lack of safety training. Untrained employees work carelessly unless someone takes the time to show them proper techniques and procedures. Safety training must be a part of every employee's job training. In food service operations, learning solely "by experience" may be dangerous.

Besides the lack of training, employee physical handicaps may be responsible for injuries or accidents on the job. Poor eyesight or defective hearing are classified as physical handicaps. Employees should be encouraged to have periodic medical checkups. Again, accidents and injuries also may be caused by unsafe equipment or conditions. It is management's responsibility to periodically conduct an in-house safety inspection to pinpoint and correct hazards.

A number of suggestions have been made by a variety of groups on how to establish safety programs. Based on the recommendations of the American Hospital Association and the National Safety Council, the following ten points should be included in a safety management program.

1. Review work procedures and inspect work areas for safety hazards.

2. Make department heads aware of the hazards.

3. Establish a safety committee.

4. Maintain accurate safety records.

5. Conduct periodic in-house safety self-inspections.

6. Train employees to be safety-conscious.

7. Motivate employees to be safety-conscious.

8. Investigate and analyze all accidents and injuries.

9. Practice management and committee follow-up.

10. Review the effectiveness and efficiency of the safety management program.

These ten points can serve as the basis for a safety management program. The overall objective is to eliminate hazards before they cause illness, injuries, or accidents. Therefore, the first step is to survey the operation in order to identify hazards. A team approach to self-inspections is desirable because it builds interest and involvement on the part of employees and supervisors. Teams made up of both employees and supervisors can be assigned to inspect various areas of the establishment and to jot down safety hazards to be eliminated. To ensure the thoroughness of each team's inspection, checklists for each area may be used.

The ten-point outline for safety management also recommends the establishment of a safety committee. While such a committee can help to maintain the operation's safety awareness, committee members should not be thought of as the only people responsible for safety. Actually, safety is the responsibility of everyone in the organization. Management must (a) motivate employees to work together to promote a safe environment and (b) train them to reduce the risks of daily operations.

Personnel Training: The Key to a Better Safety Record

Successful safety training is a combination of defining precise techniques and operating procedures, teaching employees these techniques and methods, assigning employees to specific jobs, carefully supervising the employees, and properly maintaining the facilities and equipment. Employees will show an interest in safety if management emphasizes its importance initially and then reminds employees about safety on a regular basis. A variety of posters, displays, and visual aids can be used to keep safety in the forefront of every person's mind.

Training Personnel to Prevent Accidents and Injuries. A number of safety rules must be followed by all employees and supervisors to prevent accidents and injuries. Supervisors should set a good example for employees, because employees will ignore the rules if they are not practiced by supervisors. Special care must be taken to work safely in food preparation and service areas. Production and service employees share in the responsibility to protect the safety and health of fellow workers and the establishment's customers. Employees should know safe and correct methods for operating equipment before they use it. All malfunctioning or broken equipment should be reported to the department supervisor. The supervisor should then contact the maintenance person so repairs can be completed as soon as possible.

Whenever employees are using potentially dangerous machinery or chemical solutions, they should protect their eyes. Floors are to be kept clean and dry; wet spots can be hazards. Employees must remember to wipe up spills immediately and pick up dropped items before they cause an accident.

Only dry cloths, mitts, pot holders, or towels are to be used when handling hot pans or utensils. Steam from boiling liquids is very dangerous and must be avoided whenever possible. Pot and pan washers should use long rubber gloves and exercise caution. If the tops of the gloves are submerged, hot water can run into the gloves and burn the person's hands and arms.

Food service employees work with many items made of glass. This glass is easily broken if handled carelessly. Broken glass should only be picked up with a broom and a dust pan, never with an employee's hands. Extreme caution must be exercised whenever glass is being handled, especially during dish and glass washing operations. Whenever trays or racks of glass items are moved, care must also be taken. It is not permissible to scoop ice with glass containers. Personal drinking glasses are not allowed in food preparation or service areas.

Sharp objects such as knives and saws should be handled with care.

Can openers with worn blades are dangerous, because they can add metal shavings to food. Several manufacturers are marketing cut-resistant, lightweight, seamless, knitted gloves for food service employees to use when cleaning slicers, electric saws, and knives.

Accidents can result from incorrect lifting or stacking. Containers can be safely lifted if the weight, size, and shape of the objects are assessed before lifting begins. After this assessment, if employees feel capable of lifting the containers, they should keep their backs straight and lift with their legs. Otherwise, they should use mechanical lifting devices to pick up heavy objects or get assistance before attempting to lift heavy objects alone. Heavy objects should be stored at least 12 inches (30.48 cm) off the floor to avoid strains.

Strains or falls occur when people stretch or overreach to obtain overhead objects. A ladder should be used to reach items on high shelves. Chairs, boxes, or containers are not safe substitutes for ladders. Awkward positions and twisting should be avoided when lifting. When boxes are being stacked, care should be taken to stack them squarely so they will not fall. In general, if the stack is higher than the eye, it is piled too high. Similarly, when employees carry stacks of items, they must be able to see where they are going. Caution should be exercised to avoid collisions when moving around corners and through congested areas. Running and sliding across floors should be forbidden. When carts or other equipment on wheels need to be moved, they should be pushed, not pulled.

For obvious reasons, employees and supervisors are forbidden to work under the influence of alcohol or illegal drugs. Such contraband should not be permitted on the premises. Employees and supervisors should be alerted at the time they are hired that any person working under the influence of alcohol or illicit drugs is subject to immediate termination.

Most injuries in food service and lodging operations are the result of employees and customers being burned, being cut, falling, or lifting improperly. Exhibit 12.1 presents some rules of safety management designed to prevent these four types of accidents.

If an accident occurs, employees are required to notify their supervisor immediately. It is then management's responsibility to immediately investigate the causes. Once the causes are identified, corrective action can eliminate the possibility of other similar accidents. An **accident reporting form** (see Exhibit 12.2) is used to record and analyze causes of accidents. If these causes are not identified and corrected, there is no guarantee that similar accidents will not continue to occur.

Training Personnel to Effectively Handle Accidents and Injuries. When an accident or injury affects a customer, someone on the establishment's staff must take action. Regardless of who might be at fault, the staff person must remember to avoid arguing with the customer and to practice courtesy. First aid may be undertaken by the supervisor or employee, if that person has been properly trained in first aid techniques. Immediate first aid treatment by a trained staff member can mean the difference between life and death to a severely injured person.

A **first aid kit** is invaluable in the initial treatment of many injuries.

Exhibit 12.1   Rules of Safety Management

BURN PREVENTION

1. Maintain traffic and work-flow patterns in production and service areas.
2. Maintain adequate working space around heating and cooking equipment.
3. Use a dry cloth when handling all hot dishes, pans, and equipment.
4. Have your hands free from grease when handling pots, pans, and knives.
5. Follow manufacturers' directions when operating all equipment.
6. Be careful when using coffee urns. Keep your attention undivided when making coffee.
7. Do not talk or turn while filling coffee pots or cups.
8. Put coffee servers on heating units only if they contain coffee. Empty coffee servers can quickly become overheated and explode.
9. When serving coffee, look first before turning with coffee in your hand.
10. Carry only as many cups of coffee at one time as you can manage conveniently.
11. Turn off all electrical equipment immediately after you are finished using it.
12. Safety and sanitation precautions should be maintained at all times.

CUT PREVENTION

1. Do not use any machinery without being instructed in how to operate it properly.
2. Be sure safety devices are all in place before using dangerous machinery (e.g., slicers and grinders).
3. Use the knife or cutting tool designed for each kitchen job. Do not use knives to open bottles or cans.
4. Keep knives and cutting tools sharp and in good condition. Dull knives are more dangerous than sharp knives when used carelessly.
5. Do not turn and talk to others while handling knives.
6. Do not pick up a knife by the blade. Never catch a falling knife.
7. Handle glass with care to avoid breaking it and cutting yourself.
8. Discard all chipped glasses and dishes with sharp edges promptly and safely.
9. Putting your hands in water where there are knives or broken dishes can be dangerous. Wear protective gloves and be careful.
10. Use a broom to pick up all broken china and glass. Do not use your hands.
11. When using steel wool, protect your hands with a cloth or gloves.
12. Remove or bend down nails and pieces of metal protruding from barrels and boxes.

FALL PREVENTION

1. Keep all floors dry around your work station.
2. Be sure spilled food, water, oil, or grease is wiped up immediately.
3. Keep all aisles and work areas clear and free of obstructions. Do not leave drawers or doors open.
4. Do not leave boxes (or debris) where fellow employees might fall over them.
5. Pick up all papers and foreign matter as soon as they are dropped.
6. When bending down, avoid blocking the passageway, and make sure no one is coming along with hot food.
7. Do not stand in a doorway or otherwise block the flow of traffic.
8. Do not run. When you walk, place your feet firmly on the floor.
9. Wear shoes with good soles and heels.
10. Load trays sensibly and distribute the weight evenly. Overloaded trays cause accidents.
11. Pass to the right of others when carrying trays.
12. Say, "Watch it, please," or "Allow for passing, please," in congested employee traffic areas.
13. Allow others the right of way when they are carrying trays.
14. Set trays, dishes, pots, and pans away from the edge of the work surface. Do not permit serving spoons or handles of pots to stick out into the aisle.
15. Do not use a chair or weak box to reach a high shelf; use a solid ladder.

LIFTING INJURY PREVENTION

1. Before lifting, get a firm grasp on the object.
2. When lifting, keep your back straight and bend only your knees.
3. Lift heavy objects with your legs, not your back.
4. Lift in a smooth action keeping the object close to your body. Never jerk the load.
5. If necessary, shift your footing, but do not twist your body while lifting.
6. Exercise caution to prevent fingers and hands from getting pinched.
7. Obtain help when lifting bulky or heavy objects. Never try to lift a load you know is too much for you. When in doubt, ask for assistance.
8. The probability of injury increases as the weight of the bulky object to be moved approaches 40 pounds (18.16 kg). Exercise caution before lifting.
9. Use available lifting and moving equipment (e.g., dollies, hand trucks).
10. Maintain clean, dry, and uncluttered floors in areas such as storerooms where lifting occurs.

Exhibit 12.2 Accident Reporting Form

Establishment: _____ Address: _____
Supervisor: _____ Name of Injured: _____
Department: _____ Position: _____
Date of accident: _____ Time of accident: _____
Place of accident: _____
Nature of injury: _____

☐ None   ☐ First aid   ☐ Medical doctor   ☐ Ambulance
☐ Hospital   ☐ Other (specify) _____

Medical attention necessary: _____
Action of injured at time of accident: _____
_____
_____
_____

Conditions in the environment contributing to the accident: _____
_____
_____

Corrective action necessary to prevent further accidents: _____
_____
_____

Date corrective action taken: _____
Employee's signature: _____ Supervisor's signature: _____
Date: _____ Date: _____

Every operation should have at least one kit in a convenient location. First aid kits are available in three basic types: unit, bulk, and combination. **Unit kits** are compact and contain compresses, splints, tourniquets, and triangular bandages. **Bulk kits** usually contain adhesive tape, bulk cotton, and elastic and plastic bandages. **Combination kits** contain a mixture of both unit kit and bulk kit supplies. In addition, combination kits usually contain antiseptic sprays, antacids, aspirin, burn sprays, cold treatments, eye solutions, and specialty bandages. A supervisor should be responsible for checking the first aid supplies each month and restocking the kit when necessary. Refills can be obtained from manufacturers, suppliers, or drug stores. At least one employee trained in first aid should always be available.

After an accident, employees and supervisors should remember to avoid discussing similar accidents with the injured customer. Also, the employee or supervisor should not discuss insurance or claim settlements with the injured person. When a customer is injured, an accident report must be filled out. The form shown in Exhibit 12.2 can be adapted to customer injury reporting. Employees and supervisors should notify top management of the injury as soon as possible. The supervisor should attempt to get all of the facts regarding how and why the accident occurred. It is a good idea to have emergency numbers (e.g., ambulance, doctor, hospital, fire department, police department) posted, so calls for assistance can be made quickly. The establishment should have a clearly stated policy on how to handle emergencies such as injuries to customers and employees. When in doubt about the injured person's condition, it is best to leave the treatment to a trained professional.

Training Personnel in Other Forms of First Aid. Another problem, which hospitality operations in particular must be prepared to handle, is choking. Choking is a leading cause of accidental death in the United States. Most deaths due to choking can be prevented. The key is to train the operation's personnel to recognize choking symptoms and to respond rapidly with acceptable techniques.

It is relatively easy to recognize the symptoms of a person who is choking. Often the person becomes quiet and has a look of alarm on his or her face. A person who is choking is unable to breathe or make a sound. The victim may attempt to stand up and may clutch at his or her throat in a desperate attempt to get air. A person with these symptoms is incapable of self-help. If the symptoms persist without any help from others, the person turns blue and becomes unconscious. Death may occur in a matter of minutes. Therefore, fast action is necessary to save a person who is choking.

There are two generally accepted techniques for saving a choking victim. Some rescuers attempt to remove the obstruction from the person's throat or esophagus directly. Usually a set of plastic tongs is used to capture and remove the object.

The other technique is called the **Heimlich maneuver,** an action which squeezes out the air trapped in the person's lungs. This burst of air forces the obstruction out. Regardless of which rescue method is used, treatment must begin immediately if the victim is to survive.

A brochure printed by the Fireman's Fund American Life Insurance Company of San Francisco, California, outlines an acceptable treatment for choking victims, including the Heimlich maneuver.

1. Send someone for help, but don't wait for it to arrive.

2. Ask the victim if he can talk. If he is conscious, but unable to make a sound, you can be reasonably sure he is choking.

3. Using a napkin to get a firm grip, pull the victim's tongue forward as far as possible. This should lift the obstruction to where it can be seen.

4. Using the index and middle fingers like tweezers, grasp the obstruction and pull it out. If first attempts fail, place the victim on his side and strike him several times between the shoulder blades with the heel of your hand. Try again to remove the object with your fingers.

5. If this fails, use the *Heimlich maneuver.* Stand behind the victim and wrap your arms around his waist, allowing his head and arms to hang forward.

6. Make a fist with one hand and clasp it with the other hand. Place the fist against the victim's abdomen just above the navel and below the rib cage.

7. Press in forcefully with a quick upward thrust. Repeat several times. This pushes the diaphragm up, compressing the lungs, and may force the object out of the windpipe.

    These measures may be used on children and adults. Infants and small children should be held upside down, over the arm of the rescuer, and then struck between the shoulder blades.

8. After the obstruction is removed, restore breathing by artificial respiration. Keep the patient warm and quiet. Seek medical attention.

Artificial respiration is used when a person's heart or lungs have stopped because of choking, a heart attack, or some other serious health threat. In most cases, a fatality can be avoided if prompt action is taken. **Cardiopulmonary resuscitation (CPR)** is a technique used to provide artificial circulation and breathing to the victim. The American Red Cross regularly conducts CPR courses consisting of lectures, demonstrations, and student practice. This valuable training usually takes only eight hours, and it could save a customer's or employee's life. It is a good idea to have someone who has received a certificate of completion in a CPR course on duty in the establishment during all hours of operation.

The Red Cross CPR course and other safety-related programs involve the operation's staff in another aspect of service to the dining public. Completion of these courses may raise the employee's pride in the establishment. The American Hotel & Motel Association awards safety certificates and plaques to members reporting no accidents or injuries for one year.

Some chains require an in-house safety chairperson to be appointed for each unit. This person holds monthly meetings to discuss safety hazards and how to minimize them. The chairperson may also be responsible for teaching other employees acceptable first aid procedures. Fundamentally, however, the manager of the operation has the sole responsibility for designing and implementing the safety program.

Safety problems are not resolved by in-house inspections alone. Employee training is another important component of successful safety management. Personnel motivation is a prerequisite if the establishment's safety management program is to have the desired results. Management must make safety a top priority and see that employees do, too.

Besides overseeing in-house safety inspections and motivating employees to work safely, managers must conduct employee training programs. Because high turnover is common in the hospitality industry, safety training has to be a component of every employee's job training and orientation program.

Food Service Security

A number of procedures to protect the establishment's assets were discussed in Chapters 6 through 10, covering the control points of a food service system. The most important asset of a business is its employees. The discussion of security which follows relates the protection of human life to safety management.

Prevention of Robberies

According to the Federal Bureau of Investigation (FBI), restaurant holdups in the United States increased 210% in the year between January 1, 1978, and January 1, 1979. This trend highlights the need for a security program to protect employees and customers of the operation.

The California Restaurant Association recently proclaimed that 70% of restaurant robberies occur between 6:00 p.m. and 2:00 a.m. It would appear that late-night operating hours make an establishment more susceptible to robbery. Alarms and safes with drop slots minimize financial losses during a robbery. Electronic surveillance equipment can provide a deterrent to would-be robbers.

The back door seems to be the entrance preferred by robbers. In some establishments, the back door is kept locked at all times. No one is permitted to open the back door in the evening without the manager's permission. Also, employee opening and closing teams consisting of two people provide an increased measure of safety. Finally, employees who leave work at night are encouraged to walk to the parking lot in groups.

Fire Protection

A fire can destroy the property of a food service or lodging operation and, more importantly, the lives of its employees and customers. The National Fire Data Center recorded 16,277 fires in eating and drinking establishments in the United States during 1980. These fires resulted in losses of $156 million in that year alone. The National Fire Protection Association (NFPA) estimates that there are thousands of unreported fires in hospitality establishments each year.

Exhibit 12.3 Causes of Fires in Food Service Establishments

Category/Item	Item Percent of Total	Category Percent of Total
Incendiary (Arson)		32.3%
Igniting flammable liquids	21.3%	
Igniting papers or trash	4.7%	
Igniting other or unknown materials	6.3%	
Electrical Causes		22.7%
Faulty wiring	13.4%	
Electrical appliances (except cooking and heating)	9.3%	
Cooking		15.8%
Igniting grease or fat not in fryers or ducts	6.3%	
Involving deep-fat fryers	5.5%	
Involving gas	2.4%	
Involving other factors	1.6%	
Smoking		14.2%
Igniting trash or paper	11.0%	
Igniting furnishings	3.2%	
Exhaust Ducts		7.1%
Ignition of grease in duct	6.3%	
Other factors	0.8%	
Heating Equipment	6.3%	6.3%
Other Causes	1.6%	1.6%
Total	100.0%	100.0%

Source: P. Berlinski, "Update: Sanitation and Safety," Restaurant Business, December 1976, p. 104.

More fires occur in the kitchen than in other areas of restaurants. Causes of fires in food service operations are presented in Exhibit 12.3. This exhibit is based on NFPA data compiled over a three-year period.

Causes of Fires. Arson is the leading cause of fires in food service operations. **Incendiary fires** are those which are set intentionally. Who would intentionally start a fire in a food service establishment? In the past, cases of restaurant arson have been traced to owners attempting to collect insurance money, angry employees, former employees who were recently terminated, vandals, customers with unsatisfied complaints, and persons who are mentally unbalanced. Good security will probably dampen an arsonist's attempts to start a fire. Locked doors, proper key control, bright outdoor lighting, and burglar alarms are recommended.

Faulty electrical wiring is the cause of the majority of fires in the kitchen. The wiring on electrical equipment should be periodically checked. Proper grounding is essential, as is strict adherence to all electrical codes. **Faulty electrical appliances** also cause fires. Manufacturers' recommendations should be followed to the letter when using equipment. A preventive maintenance program for equipment reduces the probability of an electrical fire.

Most **cooking fires** are caused by hot grease or fat on surfaces or in equipment. To prevent these fires, equipment and the exhaust hoods and filters must be kept free of grease. Appliances must be cleaned daily to prevent bonded dust (a film of grease and dust) from accumulating on the surface, because a flame can ignite the film. Grease drippings from broiler and griddle drip pans should be emptied daily. Spills of fats, oils, sugar sauces, and other flammable foods should be wiped up immediately.

Also, excessive reuse of deep-fat fryer oil should be prohibited. As fat in fryers gets old, the temperature at which it will spontaneously ignite is lowered. The oil level in deep-fat fryers should be at least three inches below the top of the fryer. Sudden immersion of frozen or wet food items may cause foaming, overflowing, or vaporization of the oil due to the release of water. All three of these conditions can cause the oil to be ignited by a nearby flame.

Smoking must be restricted to areas which are the least vulnerable to fires. Dry storage areas are particularly vulnerable to fires because of the dry foods they contain. In fact, powdery substances such as flour are susceptible to spontaneous combustion. Smokers should never discard smoking materials in receptacles containing paper trash. Signs to this effect should be posted in smoking areas.

Exhaust duct fires are preventable if regular maintenance is performed. The ducts should be cleaned at least quarterly (and more frequently, if necessary) by a qualified service contractor. An exhaust duct fire is very dangerous because it can smoulder unnoticed for hours and then rapidly burn out of control. These ducts should be checked regularly by a qualified person from a contract service or by in-house personnel who have been trained.

Heating and air conditioning equipment must be regularly checked and maintained. The inspection must include the chimney, flue, filters, and air ducts. Whenever parts must be replaced, the correct sizes and types should be installed. This is particularly important for fuses and circuit breakers.

Types of Fires and Extinguishers. Even if all of the these precautions have been taken, a fire may still occur. The NFPA uses three classes to categorize fires. **Class A fires** are caused by the burning of ordinary combustibles such as wood, paper, and cloth. Class A fires are extinguished by the cooling action of water-based or general purpose chemicals. **Class B fires** are those involving flammable liquids, such as grease, gasoline, paints, and oils. Class B fires are extinguished by eliminating the air supply and, thus, smothering the fire. **Class C fires** are electrical in nature and usually involve motors, switches, and wiring. Class C fires are extinguished using chemicals that do not conduct electricity.

Foam-type fire extinguishers contain a solution of bicarbonate of soda and aluminum sulfate. **Carbon dioxide extinguishers** contain pressurized carbon dioxide gas. A solution of sodium bicarbonate and sulfuric acid is found in a **soda acid fire extinguisher**. A **pump tank extinguisher** contains plain water, while a **gas cartridge extinguisher** contains water that is expelled by carbon dioxide gas. A **dry chemical extinguisher** uses sodium bicarbonate in a dry, powdered form.

Class A fires can be extinguished with foam, soda acid, pump tank, gas cartridge, or multipurpose dry chemical extinguishers. Foam, carbon dioxide, ordinary dry chemical, or multipurpose dry chemical extinguishers can be used to put out Class B fires. Class C fires are controlled with carbon dioxide, ordinary dry chemical, or multipurpose dry chemical extinguishers. A summary of fire classifications and the fire extinguishers approved for each of them is presented in Exhibit 12.4.

Never use water on a Class B or C fire. A grease fire may be smothered by simply covering it with a tight-fitting lid. Salt sprinkled on a grease fire may also put it out, if the fire is small enough. In the United States, all state fire codes require both hand-held portable fire extinguishers and fixed automatic fire suppression systems. These systems must be installed in exhaust hoods, duct work, and over char-broilers, upright broilers, fryers, and griddles. Both extinguishers and systems should be checked regularly by an expert. The fire department usually provides this service.

Employee training is the key to fire protection. The orientation and training of newly hired personnel should stress fire protection. Periodically, the topic must be reviewed at regular staff meetings. Fire departments, hotel/motel associations, and restaurant associations may offer in-house training sessions. In addition to fire prevention, training should cover specific employee duties in the event of a fire, such as fire-fighting techniques and evacuation procedures. Without proper training, employees are likely to panic if a fire breaks out.

If advance planning is a part of the operation's fire protection program, a fire emergency situation can be brought under control rapidly. Employees and supervisors should be taught what to do if a fire is discovered. First, they should call the fire department immediately and, second, calmly evacuate the customers. The establishment will generate goodwill by protecting its customers. Attempting to cover up a fire in the heart of the house may endanger everyone in the front of the house.

During an evacuation, each server is responsible for the customers in his or her station. The host or hostess should check restrooms, public areas, and the dining room to determine that everyone has been evacuated. Kitchen workers should be taught an evacuation plan. It is more important to protect human life than to stay and fight an overwhelming fire.

A fire safety self-inspection checklist can be used during the weekly or monthly facilities inspection. The team approach to fire safety inspections, involving both supervisors and employees, is again beneficial because it raises the fire safety consciousness of the entire staff. Fires are preventable if management and employees are aware of fire hazards, exercise caution, and use common sense.

Exhibit 12.4 Kinds of Fires and Approved Fire Extinguishers

KIND OF FIRE		APPROVED TYPE OF EXTINGUISHER							HOW TO OPERATE
DECIDE THE CLASS OF FIRE YOU ARE FIGHTING...	...THEN CHECK THE COLUMNS TO THE RIGHT OF THAT CLASS	MATCH UP PROPER EXTINGUISHER WITH CLASS OF FIRE SHOWN AT LEFT							FOAM: Don't Play Stream into the Burning Liquid. Allow Foam to Fall Lightly on Fire.
		FOAM Solution of Aluminum Sulphate and Bicarbonate of Soda	CARBON DIOXIDE Carbon Dioxide Gas Under Pressure	SODA ACID Bicarbonate of Soda Solution and Sulphuric Acid	PUMP TANK Plain Water	GAS CARTRIDGE Water Expelled by Carbon Dioxide Gas	MULTI-PURPOSE DRY CHEMICAL	ORDINARY DRY CHEMICAL	

Source: Centers for Disease Control, Public Health Service, U.S. Department of Health, Education, and Welfare, Health and Safety Guide for Hotels and Motels, 1975.

Summary

Sanitation and safety management are related in that they are both concerned with the health and well-being of customers and personnel. Safety includes injury and accident prevention and security. OSHA enforces a number of requirements that directly relate to safety in hospitality businesses in the United States.

Accidents and injuries can be prevented through safety training and the elimination of safety hazards. A self-inspection safety checklist permits a routine in-house survey of safety risks. Once hazards are identified, corrective action must be taken. The ten-point outline presented in this chapter can be used to design a safety management program. The establishment should concentrate its efforts on preventing those accidents and injuries that occur most frequently in the hospitality industry: burns, cuts, falls, and lifting injuries. Also, procedures for treating a choking victim can save a person's life. Someone who knows CPR techniques should be available in the establishment during operating hours.

Security is an important component of safety management. The objective is to protect the lives of customers and employees. Arson is the leading cause of fires in food service establishments. Proper fire-fighting and prevention techniques should be presented in every person's training program. After training, frequent reminders are necessary.

References

Berlinski, P. "Special Report on Sanitation and Safety." *Restaurant Business*, December 1975. 74(12):34.

——. "Update: Sanitation and Safety." *Restaurant Business,* December 1976. 75(12):98.

Buchanan, R. D. "How to Put Safety First." *Food Service Marketing*, June 1980. 42(6):67.

Centers for Disease Control, *Health and Safety Guide for Hotels and Motels.* Washington, D.C.: Public Health Service, U.S. Department of Health, Education, and Welfare, 1975.

"Checklist for Fire Safety." *Institutions/Volume Feeding*, 15 August 1975. 77(4):29-30.

Division of Housing and Food Services, Michigan State University. *Student Employee Handbook*. East Lansing, Mich.: MSU, 1981.

"Don't Get Burned by the Laziness Factor." *Restaurant Business*, 1 December 1982. 81(15):169-170.

"Don't Get Caught with Your Hands Up!" *Restaurant Business*, 1 December 1981. 80(15):134.

Eaton, W. V. "What You Can Do for Protection from Kitchen Fires." *Food Service Marketing*, September 1982. 44(9):72.

"Fire in the Kitchen." *Food Management*, February 1978. 13(2):43-44.

"Fire! The Tragedy of Unnecessary Loss." *Food Service Marketing*, January 1979. 41(1):94.

"Hospital Guards Employees Against Walk-In Injuries." *Institutions*, 15 November 1979. 85(10):144.

"How to Save Lives in a Restaurant Fire." *Restaurants and Institutions*, 1 April 1981. 88(7):135-136.

Kolb, P. M. "Focus on Sanitation." *Restaurant Business,* 1 December 1978. 77(13):100.

"Marriott Finds 'Real' Way to Stem Fire Threat." *Restaurants and Institutions*, 1 June 1982. 90(11):91.

Perkins, C. E. "What Every Supervisor Should Know About Hotel/Motel Safety." *The Cornell Hotel and Restaurant Administration Quarterly,* February 1965. 5(4):95- 113.

Reedy, L. "Safety and Health — No Betting Matter." *Food Service Marketing*, December 1980. 42(12):43.

Schultz, H. W. *Food Law Handbook*. Westport, Conn.: AVI, 1981.

"Seven Elements of an Effective Safety Program." *Food Service Marketing*, January 1979. 41(1):88.

Strategies for Success at the Aspen Hotel

Again, Paul James was impressed with the cooperation of the hotel's department heads. They had responded favorably to his challenge. The hotel was well on its way to developing a workable safety program to be integrated with the new sanitation program.

Checklist for Safety

General

1. OSHA regulations and standards are monitored and enforced.

2. OSHA, AH&MA, and NRA training materials are used for employee orientation, training, and retraining.

3. Records are maintained on safety hazards, illnesses, injuries, and fatalities associated with the operation.

Accidents and Injuries

1. The safety program is designed to protect both customers and employees.

2. Safety training is part of every person's job training.

3. Employees are encouraged to have periodic medical checkups.

4. Teams of managers and employees conduct in-house safety inspections to identify and correct hazards.

5. A food service safety checklist is used for self-inspection of the food service operation.

6. The ten-point outline for safety management is utilized in the design of a safety program.

7. Posters, displays, and visual aids are used to remind employees about safety.

8. Supervisors set a good example for employees.

9. All accidents and injuries are immediately investigated using an accident reporting form.

10. Corrective action is taken to prevent further accidents and injuries.

11. A well-stocked first aid kit is available and checked periodically.

12. Emergency numbers are posted near telephones.

13. Everyone practices the rules of safety management to prevent burns, cuts, falls, and lifting injuries.

14. Employees are trained in first aid procedures.

15. Personnel know the procedure for treating a choking victim, including the Heimlich maneuver.

16. Personnel are trained in cardiopulmonary resuscitation (CPR).

17. Personnel are motivated to maintain the operation's safety standards.

Security

1. Precautions to prevent robberies are known to all personnel.

2. Correct procedures to follow in the event of a robbery are a part of each employee's training.

3. Guidelines for security management are strictly practiced by all personnel.

Fire Protection

1. Security procedures are used to discourage a would-be arsonist from starting an incendiary fire.

2. Electrical appliances and electrical wiring are regularly checked for safety hazards.

3. Cooking fires are controlled by:

   a. keeping grease from building up on equipment and exhaust hoods and filters

   b. cleaning appliances daily

   c. emptying broiler and griddle drip pans daily

> d. avoiding excessive reuse of deep-fat fryer oil
>
> 4. Smoking is restricted to defined areas.
>
> 5. Heating, ventilating, and air conditioning (HVAC) equipment is regularly inspected and maintained.
>
> 6. Personnel know the classes of fires and the correct methods to use in extinguishing each class.
>
> 7. Personnel orientation and training programs emphasize fire safety.
>
> 8. Training covers procedures to follow if a fire is discovered on the premises.
>
> 9. A self-inspection fire protection checklist is utilized.

The following case studies are designed to enhance your understanding of the material in this chapter. If you are a Home Study student, use these case studies to stimulate questions about this chapter. If you are a Group or Institutional Study student, you may be asked to discuss these case studies as part of a regular classroom assignment.

CASE STUDY 12.1

Shelley West is the dining room manager at the British Red Restaurant. Recently, Shelley was supervising a luncheon banquet in the meeting/banquet room, located up two flights of stairs from the main dining room. Since there is no dumbwaiter or elevator in the restaurant, the servers Shelley was supervising were required to carry food up the 32 stairs to the meeting/banquet rooms. The steps were free from debris but were not well-illuminated.

A server named Molly was working that day. Shelley noticed that Molly was wearing high heels. Later, on her way down the steps with a load of soiled dishes, Molly slipped and fell down eight steps. The dishes came crashing down with her. Molly sprained her wrist and suffered severe bruises. She was off the job for 22 days. Shelley felt very badly, not only for Molly but also for the banquet customers whose luncheon was disturbed by the loud crash.

Test Your Understanding

1. How could this accident have been avoided?

2. Did any defects in the British Red's facilities contribute to the accident?

3.   What are your recommendations to Shelley West and Molly?

CASE STUDY 12.2

It is 8:00 p.m. on a Saturday night in the British Red Restaurant. The staff is in the middle of the second rush period of the evening. The dining room is packed, with a 45-minute waiting period for seating. A table of eight people has just returned from the salad bar with their selections.

Shelley West is walking past the table for eight as a server is serving them a third round of cocktails. A loud crash near this table draws Shelley's attention. Apparently, one customer in the party of eight abruptly stood up and bumped into the server holding the tray full of cocktails. The customer is clutching at his throat. Shelley asks him what is wrong, but the customer is unable to reply.

Test Your Understanding

1.   What is the problem with the customer?

2.   What action should Shelley West take?

3.   What are your recommendations for the staff of the British Red Restaurant?

CASE STUDY 12.3

Melanie Scott, the food and beverage manager at the Canon Hotel, is walking through the kitchen at 9:30 p.m. on a Wednesday night. Melanie notices that one of the cooks is changing the grease in the deep-fat fryer. Melanie mentally notes that there is an unusually large amount of food debris on the floor near the fryer.

As Melanie is leaving the kitchen, she hears a scream and rushes back to the production line. The cook who was changing the grease is lying on the floor. Apparently, he has slipped and dropped the pan of hot grease. He has severe burns on his left leg and left arm and is in excruciating pain.

Test Your Understanding

1.   What immediate action is required on the part of Melanie Scott?

2.   How could this accident have been avoided?

3.   What are your recommendations to Melanie Scott?

CASE STUDY 12.4

Melanie Scott has started an employee safety committee in the food and beverage department at the Canon Hotel. The committee performs a safety self-inspection twice each month and files a report. Melanie is reviewing the most recent report in which the employee inspectors have listed several hazards in the kitchen area.

The cooks in the saute station often leave the handles of their saute pans sticking out into the aisles. Also, when the cooks finish using knives and other sharp tools, they drop them into the pot and pan washing sink. During the last inspection, the salad preparation cook dropped a knife and caught it in mid-air. The employee inspectors also observed the cook in charge of banquet preparation improperly lifting a pan with three roasts in it.

Test Your Understanding

1.   What potential safety hazards exist at the Canon Hotel?

2.   What should the food and beverage manager do with the information in the safety report?

3.   What are your recommendations to Melanie Scott?

CASE STUDY 12.5

It is 7:00 p.m. on a Friday, and the dining room of the Canon Hotel is packed. Customers are crowded around the entrance of the hotel restaurant, waiting to take advantage of the Friday night all-you-can-eat batter-fried cod dinner. Suddenly, one of the cooks runs out of the kitchen yelling "Fire!"

At first, Melanie Scott thinks that the cook is playing a cruel joke. When she sees the look of panic in his eyes, she knows that he is serious. Melanie dashes back to the kitchen and observes that the deep-fat fryer is on fire and that the flames are shooting up through the exhaust system of the hood. The chef is frantically trying to put out the fire.

Test Your Understanding

1.   What immediate action is required?

2.   Outline a fire evacuation plan for this establishment.

3.   What are your recommendations to Melanie Scott?

THIRTEEN

Programming for Success

Strategies for Success at the Aspen Hotel

At last the day of the Aspen Hotel's grand reopening had arrived. On the way to his office, Paul realized that the problems he and his staff faced two months ago seemed insignificant now. In the past two weeks, the hotel had reawakened like a sleeping giant. Paul arrived at his office early because today would be a special day. He couldn't help reflecting on the achievements of his first two months at the Aspen Hotel.

He had been able to get his department heads to commit to excellence. They had reevaluated each control point of the food service system and set up standards to maintain consistency and predictability. The department heads had carried out the GM's idea of developing a detailed employee handbook for the Aspen Hotel. As Paul fanned the pages of the manual, he thought to himself that most employee handbooks he had seen mentioned very little about sanitation and safety. But the Aspen's new handbook integrated sanitation and safety with quality and cost controls. Unlike other manuals that simply listed rules and regulations, this one emphasized customer awareness.

The GM had carefully cultivated the cooperation and support of his department heads. He knew that they viewed the standards which they helped to develop as "their" standards, not just "his" standards. That was a step in the right direction. Paul intended to have all his people feel they were working with, not for, him. At this point, the department heads had already realized that the interest and commitment of their employees was directly related to how the department heads treated them. Paul knew all along that the employees would sense a commitment to excellence on the part of management and that this enthusiasm would be transferred to their interactions with the hotel's guests.

Paul James knew that, to the guest, the value of a hotel room or a meal experience was the value of the whole package of services. Customers evaluate the performance of the valet, room service, the concierge, the front desk person, food and beverage personnel, the housekeeping staff, and others employed by the hotel. Although pricing is an important factor, a hotel doesn't sell the guest on a room rate or a meal price alone. Rather, the hotel sells the guest on the *difference* between its offerings and those of the competition. Guests seek more quality for the money, so the hotel must sell them on more comfortable rooms, or tastier food, or more competent service. These comparative advantages make all the difference to today's sophisticated consumers.

Last week at a pre-opening staff meeting, Paul had told his entire staff that everyone is a potential customer at the Aspen Hotel. And once they become customers, the Aspen Hotel wants them all to return. Great hotels generate a good deal of repeat business. They do this because they have more customer awareness than their competitors. They exceed the guest's expectations. Therefore, they are not troubled with continual complaining on the part of their guests. If guests have total confidence in the hotel's handling of every detail, they will relax and concentrate on the vacation or the business that brought them to the hotel in the first place. The result is a happier, more harmonious experience for everyone—employees and guests.

In this chapter, all the aspects of sanitation and safety management presented in earlier chapters are combined into a workable system. The basics of programming for success cover personnel, equipment, inventory, and facilities resources. The operation's sanitation program must also address each of the ten basic operating activities of a food service system, as well as the cleaning and maintenance of guestrooms and public areas used by customers. Finally, the operation's sanitation program must be integrated with the cost control and quality control systems.

The Benefits of a Sanitation Program

Many objectives of a properly designed sanitation program have been presented already. In general, a formalized program ensures that the momentum of the operation's initial steps toward better sanitation is not lost. It provides a means of guaranteeing that important points are not overlooked or forgotten in the course of daily operations and personnel changes. Naturally, a comprehensive sanitation program costs money, but it provides an immediate payback to the business in the form of the following benefits:

1. Satisfaction of customer expectations upon which the establishment's success (and everyone's job) depends

2. Protection of customer and staff health

3. Decrease in employee absences (more healthy employees on the job each day)

4. Reduction of the operation's liability for accidents, injuries, or needless death due to falls, cuts, burns, toxic fumes, and fires

5. Increase in the useful life of the operation's facilities and equipment (less corrosion, breakage, and deterioration)

6. Reduction in the cost and increase in the effectiveness of cleaning and sanitizing procedures due to the use of appropriate levels of correct cleaners and sanitizers

7. Reduction in toxic chemical storing and application problems due to standardization of products and procedures

8. Simplification of supervision due to the use of checklists

9. Elimination of wasted products and simplification of employee work methods through the use of written cleaning procedures

10. Establishment of management objectives which can be used to measure the progress of the business

Obviously, a comprehensive sanitation program does not cost as much as it pays. The payback to the establishment is directly related to how well the operation's standards are communicated to employees and enforced by management. It is best to preface recommendations for the operation's sanitation program with a discussion of procedures for obtaining the personnel to implement the program.

Help Wanted—But What Kind?

Before a new employee can be hired, management must understand the requirements of the vacant position. It is important to determine why the position was vacated by the last employee. Is the job realistic? Is the job training adequate? Is the rate of pay competitive and fair? These questions can be answered by conducting an exit interview with the employee who is leaving.

If high turnover is experienced in a position, it may be time to restructure the position rather than hire another person. Rapid turnover of personnel is expensive. Unfortunately, it is a daily occurrence in the hospitality industry. However, if the operation can hire qualified people, train them, and keep them, it becomes a better competitor. A clear understanding of the job is essential before the position can be effectively filled. Fundamentally, management must answer the question, "What kind of person is needed to adequately perform the duties of this job?"

There are at least four ways to categorize employees according to the time they spend on the job. Regular full-time and regular part-time employees make up the majority of food service and lodging workers. Some operations use a number of "on call" and part-time employees on an intermittent basis. The category from which a new position is filled depends on the needs of the establishment. These needs are determined by preparing: (a) a job analysis, (b) a job specification, (c) a job description, and (d) job performance standards.

A **job analysis** investigates the duties, tasks, and responsibilities necessary to perform a job in an acceptable manner. A job analysis specifies the skills, abilities, and knowledge an employee needs to do the job properly. These factors must be identified in advance in order to communicate them to the employee. A job analysis focuses on what is expected of an employee performing a certain job. For example, an executive chef's job analysis would cover the management of all food preparation and production activities, cost percentages accountability, training and scheduling responsibilities, and other relevant control point activities.

A **job specification** is developed from the job analysis. It describes the type of individual needed for the job. For example, an executive chef should be calm, confident, alert, dependable, and honest. In addition to the required management skills, the chef should possess initiative and a willingness to help develop and adhere to the operation's procedures and standards. Job specifications are important in the recruitment and selection phases of the hiring process, which are discussed in the next section.

Exhibit 13.1 Sample Job Description for an Executive Chef

Date of Last Revision: 12/23/00
Department: Food and Beverage
Reports To: General Manager of the Hotel
Experience: Minimum of Ten Years in the
Culinary Profession

Job Title: Executive Chef
Section: Kitchen
Supervises: All Kitchen and Related Personnel
Education: High School Graduate or Equivalent

Major Accountabilities

1. Accountable to the General Manager of the hotel for all food preparation and production activities.
2. Involved with food purchasing, receiving, storing, preparing, serving, and cleaning and maintenance.
3. Accountable for the hotel's overall food and kitchen labor cost percentages.
4. Involved with training and scheduling food preparation and production employees.
5. Assists in the development of coffee shop, main dining room, and special banquet menus.

Duties and Responsibilities

1. Orders all food and nonfood supplies used in preparation, production, and service. Must purchase supplies from previously approved distributors.
2. Schedules food preparation and production on a daily basis, taking into account forecasted demand for all food and beverage outlets and special functions.
3. Is responsible for receiving all food and nonfood supplies used in preparation, production, and service. Must verify product quality, quantity, and price.
4. Secures all food and nonfood supplies in designated storage areas.
5. Schedules all kitchen personnel on a weekly basis based on the forecasted demand.
6. Is responsible for the training of all kitchen personnel in proper preparation and production methods, sanitation, and equipment use.
7. Supervises the cleaning and maintenance of all kitchen equipment and facilities along with the general level of sanitation in kitchen and storage areas.
8. May delegate duties and responsibilities to the sous chef and station cooks; however, the executive chef is responsible for the efficient and effective operation of the kitchen.

A **job description** summarizes the duties, responsibilities, and tasks of a particular job. It spells out the what, when, where, why, and how of a job. Job descriptions are useful in training and in conducting employee performance reviews. A sample job description for an executive chef is presented in Exhibit 13.1.

A number of forms are used for job descriptions; no one form is correct in every situation. However, at the very least, a job description should include the job title, the employee's supervisor's title, a job summary, a listing of duties and responsibilities, and the qualifications necessary for the job. The job description should be reevaluated at least once a year to be certain that it accurately reflects the job as it is presently structured. **Job performance standards** are developed from the job description. For example, it is realistic to expect the executive chef to be accountable for the hotel's overall food cost and kitchen labor cost percentages if that is specified in the chef's job description.

The Hiring Process

The hiring process is made up of three stages: recruitment, selection, and orientation. **Recruitment** takes place when a vacancy exists. Applicants can be recruited in a number of ways. Present employees may refer applicants to the business. Employment agencies can be a source of recruits. Some establishments advertise openings in newspapers, magazines, and trade journals. Others recruit employees at high schools, colleges, and universities. Industry associations (e.g., hotel/motel associations, restaurant associations, chefs' associations) may be excellent sources for referrals also. If the opening is made known to them, community, minority, and service organizations may also assist in employee recruitment.

The **selection step** follows recruitment. The objective of employee selection is to choose the best candidate for the job. Proper selection has the potential to raise employee productivity and lower employee turnover. The **selection interview** is used to screen potential employees. Usually an application form must be filled out by the candidate prior to the interview.

A selection interview should be conducted in a private area away from interruptions and distractions. Prior to the interview, the interviewer should review the completed application form. This gives the interviewer an opportunity to develop questions related to the information on the application form.

The employee interview is an essential communication tool used during selection. The objective of the interview is to establish two-way communication between the interviewer and the applicant. Open-ended interviewing questions are helpful because they require more than a simple yes or no answer. Sample open-ended interview questions are presented in Exhibit 13.2. Not all of these interview questions apply to all situations; they must be modified based on the needs of the business, the job vacancy, and the needs of the job applicant. Using a standard set of open-ended questions makes the interviewing process more objective and encourages an interchange of ideas.

The establishment's representative is responsible for clarifying the requirements of the vacant position and telling the recruit about the operation. During the interview, the interviewer should also assess the sanitation consciousness and practices of the applicant. Recruits who present themselves in a sloppy or disorganized way may not fit into the organization. Unhygienic personal habits should alert the interviewer that to hire the applicant would be to increase the operation's sanitation risks.

Once the interview is completed, the applicant should be told when the decision will be made and how the candidates will be informed of the decision. However, before any hiring decision is made, the applicant's previous employment history must be verified and references contacted.

The **orientation step** takes place after the hiring decision has been made and the new employee has reported for work. The objective of orientation is to start the new employee out right. It is only normal for

Exhibit 13.2 Sample Open-Ended Interview Questions

Education-Related Questions

1. What subjects did you enjoy the most (or the least) in high school (or college)? Why?
2. What did you learn from your high school (or college) experience that is important today?
3. How did you feel about the importance of grades in high school (or college)?
4. Did you have any part-time jobs while attending high school (or college)? Which jobs were the most interesting? Why?
5. What extracurricular activities did you participate in during high school (or college)?

Employment-Related Questions

1. What job pressures did you experience in previous jobs? Why?
2. What kind of people do you like (or dislike) working with? Why?
3. What were the main advantages (or disadvantages) of your last job?
4. Why are you considering changing jobs?
5. Do you prefer working alone or in groups? Why?

Goal-Related Questions

1. What are your career goals in the next two years? The next ten years?
2. What are your salary goals and objectives?
3. How do you evaluate this establishment as a place to help you achieve your career goals?
4. Who (what) influenced you the most in regard to your career goals?
5. What are your expectations regarding a new job?

Self-Awareness-Related Questions

1. Which of your good qualities are most outstanding? Which of your qualities need the most improvement?
2. What qualities do you have that would help you be a success in this establishment?
3. Are you a self-motivated individual? Explain why.
4. How do you react to constructive criticism from an employer?
5. Give an example of your interest in self-improvement.

a new employee to have a number of unanswered questions. The orientation step is designed to answer those questions and to reduce the new employee's anxiety. The immediate supervisor of the new employee is responsible for orientation. A written **orientation checklist** makes orientation more thorough and objective. A sample orientation checklist is presented in Exhibit 13.3. This checklist should be modified to fit the specific position, the needs of the new employee, and the individual business.

While all of the points on the orientation checklist are important, in most cases, presenting all of the information orally would overwhelm the new employee. Several successful operations have developed **employee manuals** that make the job of orientation much easier. The supervisor can point out information the employee needs to know. Then the employee can study this information later in a more relaxed frame of mind. The establishment's history, its mission, and its policies appear in the

Exhibit 13.3 Sample Employee Orientation Checklist

1. Outline the new employee's job responsibilities and duties.
2. Explain the relationship of the job to the employee's department and to the establishment as a whole.
3. Review the employee's schedule, workdays, work hours, check-in and check-out procedures, and how to use the time clock.
4. Describe acceptable procedures for reporting absences, tardiness, and sick days.
5. Point out employee break areas, eating areas, restrooms, and first aid facilities.
6. Describe acceptable methods for requisitioning and receiving supplies needed to perform the employee's job.
7. Explain the operation's standards of production and service in detail.
8. Emphasize the operation's rules for personal hygiene and its sanitation standards.
9. Explain safety rules and accident procedures.
10. Review the use of employee badges and name tags.
11. Indicate areas which are off-limits to employees.
12. Point out acceptable employee parking areas.
13. Indicate areas to be used for storage of employee personal belongings, street clothes, and personal property.
14. Show the new employee where notices are posted on bulletin boards.
15. Review the acceptable reasons for using the establishment's telephones for personal and emergency calls.
16. Tell when the employee gets paid and where the check can be obtained.
17. Explain check-cashing procedures.
18. Introduce the new employee to co-workers in the department.
19. Introduce the new employee to other personnel important in the successful completion of the job.
20. Answer any questions the new employee asks.

employee manual. It also covers both the employee's and the operation's responsibilities to reinforce the feeling of partnership between management and staff. Additionally, the fact that the new employee can easily refer back to the manual when questions arise builds self-confidence. Providing an employee manual is one way of showing that management cares about the orientation of new employees.

After the hiring process is completed, the new employee is taught how to do the job correctly. (The next section covers the topic of training.) Today's employee does not want to be told simply what to do; the "why's" are also important to the worker. Employees want to know the reasons for following the establishment's policies, procedures, and recommended work methods. The U.S. Army's food service facility at Fort Lee, Virginia, uses a unique motivational tool to explain, in part, why food production workers need to follow the organization's standards to the letter. A sign posted in its food preparation area reads, "You're only as good as the last meal you served."

Furthermore, many employees want to participate in making decisions that affect their job responsibilities. An employee who participates in decision-making feels more committed to the goals of the organization. Participative decisions become "our" decisions rather than "their" (management's) decisions. Managers usually observe an increase in employee productivity when they become more receptive to worker values and input. Managers and employees are partners in the business. The success of the business is directly related to the willingness of both groups to cooperate. This cooperation enhances the operation's profitability and contributes to its long-term survival.

As the employee settles into the new position, periodic appraisals are needed. **Employee performance reviews** are more fair and objective when they are based on the employee's job description and job performance standards. These spell out exactly what is expected of the employee in a particular position. Thus, they are standards against which the employee's work can be measured. Performance reviews should be conducted at least every six months to permit the employee to know how he or she is progressing. While reviews should be positive rather than threatening to the employee, areas for improvement should be emphasized in the performance review.[1]

Naturally, the employee's performance should improve with additional job training. Personnel training is critical to the success of the operation's sanitation program. When this activity is given low priority, the sanitation program and the operation's survival are jeopardized.

Training—The Key to a Successful Sanitation Program

It is management's responsibility to train employees. Employee training is essential because trained employees make more money for the business and for themselves. Untrained employees (knowingly or unknowingly) work against the goals and objectives of the operation. Not understanding the "why's," they are more likely to undermine management plans and short-circuit the operation's sanitation program. Training should be designed to alert all employees to the importance of performing their jobs so as to maintain the establishment's sanitation standards.

No training program can succeed without the support of the top management of the organization. Top management must provide the resources, time, and money for training. Although training drains these resources initially, the payback is more than worth the investment. The staff will only hold positive attitudes toward sanitation training if top management believes in the program and conveys its positive attitudes to others in the organization. When communicated and demonstrated to other members of the organization, these attitudes result in a highly motivated team, dedicated to doing the job right. In the final analysis, the commitment of top management to training and to a sanitary environment will be reflected in the level of sanitation achieved by the opera-

---

[1]For a detailed discussion of performance reviews and a sample performance review form, see John P. Daschler and Jack D. Ninemeier, *Supervision in the Hospitality Industry* (East Lansing, Mich.: Educational Institute of the American Hotel & Motel Association, 1984), pp. 157-174.

tion's staff. Top management must be sanitation-conscious and convey this same sanitation awareness to all members of the operation. Training should be directed toward two groups of people: management and employees.

Management Training

Trained managers can have a positive effect on the operation's sanitation management program. Information obtained during management training can be used to train employees. Thus, managers can create a climate in which employees understand and are reminded of the importance of proper food handling, correct personal hygiene, and the cleaning and maintenance of equipment and facilities.

Management training results in better control over the establishment and its resources. Employees realize that trained managers are more competent; therefore, management training increases the supervisor's credibility among employees. Trained managers experience fewer crisis situations during the course of their day. They do not fear emergencies because they have been trained to be proactive, not reactive—to anticipate instead of react to crises. Because they have planned and prepared for events before they occur, trained managers are not constantly interrupted by unusual or unplanned events. They experience fewer delays and bottlenecks. Trained supervisors have more time available to deal with important management responsibilities and, as a result, are more effective in their positions. Consequently, they feel more satisfied in their present job and in their career. They feel confident that they are in control, and this confidence is noticed by customers and employees alike.

Employee Training

A properly trained manager or supervisor is able to teach employees correct procedures. The teaching should be done by the employee's immediate supervisor or by an individual specifically designated as a trainer. In this way, employees are more likely to build close professional relationships with supervisors during the training process. Properly trained workers are more satisfied because management has given them the resources necessary to carry out their responsibilities more effectively and efficiently. Trained employees feel that the business has made an investment in their future. They realize that their performance is important to the operation and that they are being prepared for possible advancement within their present organization or within the hospitality industry. Thus, employee turnover is reduced and employee morale is raised in operations with an organized approach to training.

Trained employees commit fewer errors and are more likely to operate with a feeling of certainty that they are doing their jobs properly. Like trained managers, trained employees are more confident, and this feeling of self-assurance is projected to the establishment's customers.

Management training and employee training offer several advantages to the operation. Trained personnel maintain and constantly improve the establishment's standards of production and service. They take a genuine interest in the success of the operation and its long-term survival. Properly trained staff members can effectively reduce the cost of operations without compromising quality, cost, or sanitation standards.

The Training Cycle

Training can best be depicted as a cycle.[2] Proper training begins with planning. **Planning** identifies the goals and objectives of training. For example, the employee's job description is a good place to find objectives for the training of a new employee. It is important at this point to put in writing how the effectiveness of the training will be evaluated. In other words, when the training program is over, what should the trainee be able to do? The trainee's readiness and ability to attain the goals and objectives must be taken into consideration during planning.

Preparing can begin once the specific subject matter for the training program has been identified. Preparing involves organizing the information to be presented. At this stage, training techniques and training aids are selected. It is better if training concepts, whenever possible, are presented in writing so that the employee can refer back to the materials for refreshing and retraining. Also, any equipment or supplies necessary for training are assembled during this stage. The care with which the trainer prepares has a direct impact on the effectiveness of the training program.

Presenting a training session can be a challenge, due to the limitations of the average person's attention span. Training sessions are more interesting to the employee if creativity is used. Training can be a boring "turn-off" for employees if information is presented in a monotonous or tedious fashion. A variety of audio and visual training aids can provide a change of pace, breaking up the straight lecture format. Slides, films, plates of microbial colonies, demonstrations, role plays, case studies, and other training tools are possible alternatives. If the training takes place at the trainee's work station, all required materials should be assembled in advance so the presentation flows smoothly. Actual illustrations and stories help to reinforce training points worth remembering.

Applying involves supervising the employee while the employee performs the job. This phase of training permits the trainer to determine whether the employee can correctly carry out the training objectives. The employee's performance during the applying step demonstrates what he or she has learned during training.

Evaluating is the assessment of the trainee's level of achievement. Ideally, the employee should be allowed to participate in the assessment. Feedback from the trainee is necessary to a balanced evaluation. During the evaluation phase, the trainer appraises the trainee's progress and determines his or her level of achievement. This evaluation of trainees should result in the compilation of information on training effectiveness that can be used in planning future training programs.

Thus, training is a cycle; it should be ongoing and continuous. New recruits obviously require training before they can become assets to their operation and realize their full potential. Veteran employees and managers also require training to remind them of basic procedures and techniques and to introduce them to new ideas and programs. By scheduling educational programs for the staff on a quarterly basis, new employees are reinforced and seasoned employees are refreshed.

---

[2] For an in-depth study of the training process, read Lewis C. Forrest, Jr., *Training for the Hospitality Industry* (East Lansing, Mich.: Educational Institute of the American Hotel & Motel Association, 1983).

On-the-Job Training

Most training in the food service and lodging industries takes place on the job. For example, new food servers are usually trained by an experienced server. There is nothing wrong with **on-the-job training (OJT)** when the trainer is qualified and recognizes the importance of the establishment's standards of operation. OJT is more than a new employee tagging along behind a senior employee and observing his or her work methods. Proper on-the-job training is a four-step process:

1.   Explain the task to the employee.

2.   Demonstrate the task to the employee.

3.   Allow the employee to do the task.

4.   Follow up to correct mistakes and reinforce the positive behaviors.

Employee participation is an essential component of on-the-job training. The explanation presents the relevant parts of the task to be learned. The demonstration step shows the trainee proper form and technique. When the employee does the task, repetition builds confidence and speed. The old adage "practice makes perfect" holds true in employee training. The follow-up step gives the employee feedback on how he or she is doing. By praising the employee's correct performance of the task, the trainer can stimulate the employee to improve and do the best job possible. On-the-job training is far more successful when the supervisor conducting the training is knowledgeable and enthusiastic about the subject matter.

Other Training Tips

Training is properly designed when the needs of the learner are the primary concern. Motivated learners are preferred to those who are not motivated. The fear of punishment or other negative reinforcement dampens the training effort. An ideal training environment utilizes positive reinforcement such as rewards and constructive suggestions. The continuity of training is enhanced by scheduling a number of sessions at regular intervals. The session length should be no more than one hour if the trainee's interest is to be held.

The trainer should start with a complete overview of what is to be taught. After this overview is presented, the trainer can concentrate on the components of the task. In initial training, technique is more important than speed. Speed comes with repetition and practice, which build the trainee's self-confidence. Active participation in learning is preferable to passive training. Overreliance on lectures, films, and slides makes the trainee a mere spectator. It is important to use as many of the trainee's senses (sight, hearing, touch) as possible in the learning process. By allowing trainees to experience discovery during training instead of subjecting them to endless lectures, the desire to learn will be stimulated.

Exhibit 13.4   The Ten Rules of Safe Food Service

1. Refrigerate food properly.

2. Cook food or heat-process it thoroughly.

3. Relieve infected employees of food-handling duties.

4. Require strict standards for personal hygiene.

5. Use extreme care in storing and handling food prepared in advance.

6. Give special attention to preparation of raw ingredients (liable to contamination), which will be added to food that gets little or no further cooking.

7. Keep food above or below bacteria-incubating temperatures (above 140° F $[60°C]$ or below 45°F $[7°C]$).

8. Heat leftovers to a temperature lethal to bacteria (above 165°F $[74°C]$), or cool quickly for storage (below 45° F $[7°C]$).

9. Avoid carrying contamination from raw to cooked and ready-to-serve foods via hands, equipment, and utensils.

10. Disinfect storage areas without contaminating the stored food. Clean and sanitize food preparation and service equipment.

Source: Adapted from P. Berlinski, "Special Report on Sanitation and Safety," Restaurant Business, December 1975, p. 36.

Sanitation and safety training does not have to be dull or boring. For large groups of employees, formal lecture-style training may be necessary. However, a variety of presentation methods and audiovisual aids can be successfully used to enhance employee learning during formal sessions. Films, slides, product demonstrations, handouts, posters, role plays, discussions, guest speakers, tests, and other training aids are alternatives to the straight lecture format. Hospitality educational institutions, colleges and universities, health departments, chemical companies, and equipment dealers are readily available sources of employee training materials.

The trainer should realize that not everyone learns at the same rate. When most trainees are informed of mistakes and how to correct them they will improve, if given the chance. Trainee participation in the learning process permits newly acquired skills and knowledge to be firmly implanted and to become a part of the trainee's regular work routine.

If employee training is to be effective, concepts must be communicated to employees in a language that they can understand. To illustrate, a list of **ten rules of safe food service** is presented in Exhibit 13.4. While these rules can be used to train English-speaking workers, they would not be very helpful to employees who only speak Spanish, for example. Thus, the same rules may be translated into Spanish and used to train Spanish-speaking employees. It is also a good idea to post sanitation reminders, such as personal hygiene tips, in employee work areas.

What a Sanitation Training Program Should Cover

What should be included in a sanitation training program? This question often perplexes top management. Using the FDA's *Food Service Sanitation Manual* as a guide, a basic training program for hospitality operations can be organized into four general topics: facilities, food, food handling, and management. A general outline of topics to be covered under each of these headings is presented in Exhibit 13.5.

Exhibit 13.5 The Basic Sanitation Training Program for Hospitality Operations

---

FACILITIES

— **Cleaning/Sanitizing:** Warewashing Procedures (Manual and Mechanical), Storage of Cleaned and Sanitized Equipment and Utensils, Housekeeping Practices, Cleaning and Sanitizing Schedules

— **Nonfood Supplies:** Use and Storage of Toxic Materials, Storage of Clean and Used Linens, Storage and Use of Single-Service Items

— **Physical:** Facilities Construction, Lighting, Ventilation, Insect and Rodent Control, Maintenance of a Safe Environment

— **Personal Hygiene:** Acceptable Employee Uniforms and Appearance, Techniques for Handwashing, Acceptable Employee Habits, Elimination of Food Handlers Who Are Ill

FOOD

— **Foodborne Disease:** Fundamentals of Food Microbiology, Incidence of Foodborne Outbreaks, Causes of Foodborne Outbreaks (Including Biological, Chemical, and Physical Hazards), Prevention of Foodborne Outbreaks

— **Food Protection:** Basic Sanitation Procedures as They Relate to the Control Points (Menu Planning, Purchasing, Receiving, Storing, Issuing, Preparing, Cooking, Holding, Serving) of a Food Service Establishment

— **Food Spoilage:** Reduction of Food Waste in Each of the Control Points

FOOD HANDLING

— **Food-Handling Practices:** Techniques to Minimize Excessive Food Handling, Proper Use of Utensils

— **Operational Problems:** Identification of Commonly Occurring Deficiencies and Recommended Correction Methods

— **Sanitary:** Handwashing Methods, Plumbing, Solid and Liquid Waste Disposal

MANAGEMENT

— **Motivation:** Planning and Organizing the Operation's Sanitation Program, Economic Effects of Safe Food Handling, Safety Considerations

— **Personnel Training:** Management's Responsibilities, Employees' Responsibilities, Resources and Training Aids, Training Methods, Training Outcomes

— **Self-Inspection:** Techniques for Management and Employee Self-Inspection, Checklists for Self-Inspection, Health Regulations and Legal Requirements, Legal Liability

---

The FDA has recommended a minimum of 15 hours of training for management and employee certification. Many state, county, and local jurisdictions across the United States require that one or more managers or employees in each food service establishment be certified.

Measuring Results

How do you know if your operation's sanitation training program is effective? Basically, the answer lies in how well employees use the principles of sanitation they were taught. The effectiveness of sanitation training is indicated by the degree to which employees uphold the operation's sanitation standards. Several outcomes which should result from sanitation training are presented in Exhibit 13.6. If management observes unsanitary practices among employees, it is probably time to conduct

Exhibit 13.6 Training Outcomes for Food Service Employees

Cleaning Personnel Should Be Able To:

1. List the rules of personal hygiene and correct work habits.
2. Describe how to clean and sanitize equipment, utensils, and work surfaces.
3. Tell how to properly measure concentrations of cleaners and sanitizers.
4. Evaluate equipment and utensils to determine if they have been properly cleaned.
5. Tell how to adequately clean and sanitize facilities such as storage areas.
6. Explain how to control insects and rodents using basic environmental sanitation.
7. Describe ways to prevent cross-contamination.
8. Explain how to properly use chemicals so as to prevent food from becoming contaminated with toxic chemicals.
9. Demonstrate how to dispose of garbage and refuse correctly.
10. Summarize the causes of foodborne illnesses and how to prevent them.

Food Handling Personnel Should Be Able To:

1. Describe proper food production techniques including rules of personal hygiene.
2. Describe safe and acceptable techniques for inspecting deliveries of food products for contamination and spoilage.
3. Tell how to measure product and storage area temperatures and state acceptable time-temperature combinations.
4. Describe storage procedures for raw ingredients, cooked food products, utensils, and equipment.
5. Explain the importance of using standard recipes and procedures.
6. Explain the reasons for control point standards related to food handling.
7. List ways to hold hot food and cold food before and during service.
8. Tell what to do when a utility has failed and an emergency situation arises.
9. Describe acceptable procedures for chilling and storing leftover foods.
10. Demonstrate how to look for insects and rodents, and suggest corrective actions to be taken if they are found.

Service Personnel Should Be Able To:

1. Describe proper food service techniques including rules of personal hygiene.
2. List the operation's standard service procedures.
3. Describe physical symptoms that require employees to be eliminated from food handling and serving.
4. Summarize health regulations as they pertain to the service of food.
5. Demonstrate how to measure food temperatures during display and service.
6. Tell how to properly operate, clean, and sanitize equipment used for service.
7. Describe safe storage techniques for food in the service area.
8. Explain the reasons for control point standards related to the service of food.
9. Tell what to do when a utility has failed and an emergency situation arises.
10. Describe the procedure for treating a choking victim, including the Heimlich maneuver.

another sanitation training program. It is virtually impossible to motivate service employees to maintain sanitation standards if production employees neglect their areas. The sanitation management program must be a coordinated and integrated approach that embraces all areas and departments.

Implementation of a Cleaning Program

To be successful, the operation's cleaning program must be formalized by management. It is important to set targets and assign responsibility so that follow-up checks can be made by management. Targets should include personnel, temperature, equipment, time, and chemical requirements. Once the operation's cleaning needs have been identified and formalized in writing, a cleaning schedule can be established. A sample **cleaning schedule** is presented in Exhibit 13.7.

Written cleaning procedures are the key to a cleaning program. For each area to be cleaned (including equipment), there should be a written cleaning procedure consisting of a brief description of the cleaning task, the steps to follow to complete the job, and the correct type of cleaning materials and tools to be used. (For an example, see the recommended procedure for cleaning a meat slicer presented on page 335.) A variety of written cleaning procedures are available from distributors of cleaning and sanitizing chemicals.

It is a good idea to post the written cleaning procedures next to the equipment in a waterproof covering. Written cleaning procedures can be used for on-the-job training sessions. Posted cleaning procedures provide a reminder of correct methods for both new and experienced workers. They are also useful for management follow-up checks to determine if the operation's cleaning program is viable. A series of straightforward checklists can be developed from written cleaning procedures for management use.

Each area manager should monitor and follow up on cleaning procedures in his or her department. The business is paying employees to clean equipment and facilities. Therefore, the manager must check periodically to determine that cleaning is being done correctly. Management follow-up shows the employees who are doing the cleaning that management cares about maintaining a clean environment.

Self-Inspection

In addition to depending on training, the success of a sanitation program depends, to a great extent, on enforcement of the operation's standards. Routine self-inspections allow the staff to monitor the general sanitation levels throughout the organization. Any deficiencies which are discovered can be corrected. Thus, the result of the self-inspection should be a higher level of sanitation in the facility.

A number of sanitation self-inspection forms have been developed for use in food service establishments. The best form is one that highlights the same inspection items that are checked by the state and/or local health inspectors. At the very least, the points covered on the Food Service Establishment Inspection Report (Form 2420) and presented on page 140 should be covered by self-inspections. Use of this form for self-inspections permits the operator to anticipate the items the health inspector is likely to check during regularly scheduled inspections. State and

Exhibit 13.7   Sample Cleaning Schedule

Equipment or Area to be Cleaned	Person Responsible	Cleaning Frequency	Cleaning Manual Page Reference*
Can Opener	Dishwasher	Daily	
Ceilings	Maintenance Staff	Monthly	
Char-Broiler	Station Cook	Daily Weekly	
Coffee Urn	Server	After Each Brew Daily	
Compartment Steamer	Station Cook Dishwasher	Daily Weekly	
Convection Oven	Station Cook	Daily Weekly	
Conventional Oven	Station Cook	Daily Weekly	
Cutting Boards	Station Cook Pot and Pan Washer	After Each Use Daily	
Dishwashing Machine	Dishwasher	After Each Shift Daily	
Floors	Dishwasher Pot and Pan Washer	As Needed Daily	
Fryer	Station Cook	Daily Weekly	
Griddle	Station Cook	As Needed Daily Weekly	
Grinder	Station Cook Pot and Pan Washer	After Each Use Daily	
Hood/Filters	Pot and Pan Washer Dishwasher	Weekly	
Hot Top Range	Station Cook Pot and Pan Washer	Daily Weekly	
Ice Machine Interior Deliming	Pot and Pan Washer Maintenance Staff	Daily Weekly Per Manufacturer's Recommendations	
Microwave Oven	Station Cook	Daily Weekly	
Mixer	Station Cook	After Each Use Daily	
Mobile Food Warmer	Pot and Pan Washer	After Each Use Weekly	
Mobile Refrigeration Unit	Pot and Pan Washer	After Each Use Weekly	
Open Top Range	Station Cook Pot and Pan Washer	Daily Weekly	

Equipment or Area to be Cleaned	Person Responsible	Cleaning Frequency	Cleaning Manual Page Reference*
Overhead-Fired Broiler	Station Cook	Daily Weekly	
Plate Warmer	Dishwasher	Daily Weekly	
Pot and Pan Sink	Pot and Pan Washer	After Each Shift Daily	
Reach-in Freezer	Station Cook Sous Chef Maintenance Staff	Daily Weekly Monthly	
Reach-in Refrigerator	Station Cook Sous Chef Maintenance Staff	Daily Weekly Monthly	
Refrigerated Drawer	Station Cook Sous Chef Maintenance Staff	Daily Weekly Monthly	
Salamander	Station Cook	Daily Weekly Monthly	
Slicer	Station Cook Pot and Pan Washer	After Each Use Weekly	
Steam-Jacketed Kettle	Station Cook Pot and Pan Washer	Daily Weekly	
Steam Table	Station Cook	After Each Shift Daily	
Tilting Braising Pan	Station Cook	As Needed Daily	
Toaster	Server	Daily	
Walk-In Freezer	Sous Chef Maintenance Staff	Daily Weekly Monthly	
Walk-In Refrigerator	Sous Chef Maintenance Staff	Daily Weekly Monthly	
Walls	Dishwasher Pot and Pan Washer Maintenance Staff	Daily Weekly Monthly	
Work Tables	Station Cook	As Needed Daily	

*References are intended to be page numbers in the operation's cleaning manual.

local health departments and professional organizations also provide sanitation self-inspection forms.

When combined with routine surveillance by public health officials, in-house self-inspections can significantly upgrade the operation's sanitation levels. As Chapter 5 emphasized, it is important to work together with public health officials.

A regular program of in-house inspections contributes to the overall positive image of the business. Fundamentally, both the dedication of employees and the integrity of management contribute to the overall level of sanitation in the operation. Ideally, self-inspections should not be performed exclusively by management. Employee involvement is highly desirable. When employees are intimately involved with the sanitation program, they think of workable ideas for improvement. They become committed to the operation's program as if it were their own. Employee involvement can be achieved through the team approach.

The **team approach** to sanitation self-inspection has the potential to improve the establishment's level of sanitation. Using the team approach, inspection teams of three to five people are formed. Each team is made up of both managers and employees. They work together to identify deficiencies, take corrective action, and increase the awareness of the operation's personnel. A four-team system is probably sufficient to meet the inspection needs of most food service and lodging operations. The inspection duties should be divided evenly among the four teams.

Team One is responsible for facilities inspection. This group monitors housekeeping and maintenance of facilities including floors, walls, ceilings, lighting, storage areas, ventilation, garbage and refuse disposal, dressing rooms, plumbing, water supply, sewage disposal, handwashing and toilet facilities, and insect and rodent control.

Team Two is charged with food and food handling inspection. This group monitors raw and cooked products as they flow through each of the operation's control points from receiving through serving. Team Two closely checks product time and temperature combinations along with quality standards.

Team Three is held accountable for personnel sanitation training and performance. This group establishes and audits employee training programs covering elementary bacteriology, foodborne diseases, food infection, food intoxication, personal hygiene, employee health habits, safety, and standards for production and service.

Team Four is responsible for equipment and utensil sanitation and safety. This team regularly inspects food-contact surfaces and nonfood-contact surfaces in regard to design, construction, maintenance, installation, and location. Team Four audits warewashing equipment and procedures and the use of cleaners and sanitizers.

All teams must make routine sanitation and safety inspections and file written reports with top management. These written reports are prepared, reviewed, discussed, and acted upon. Later, the teams conduct follow-up inspections to ensure the effectiveness of the corrective action. This team concept provides a rational and objective way of implementing and monitoring a sanitation management program. Also, it intensifies the operation's commitment to high sanitation standards by means of group involvement.

To prevent boredom, employees and managers may be periodically rotated from team to team. This cross-training builds sensitivity to and an appreciation for the responsibilities of others by giving the employee or supervisor an opportunity to carry out new tasks.

The Most Crucial Inspections

In addition to the establishment's self-inspection, it has been pointed out that regulatory agencies at various levels of government provide periodic inspections for food service businesses. However, there is one other group that performs its inspections even more regularly—the operation's customers.

On any given day, a hospitality operation may serve hundreds of customers for breakfast, lunch, dinner, special functions, banquets, and/or room service. Each of these individuals performs an informal, silent inspection of the facilities, food quality, and level of service. You may wonder, "What does the customer evaluate when he or she patronizes my hospitality operation?" To answer this question, let us join a "typical" customer as he or she is about to dine in a "typical" restaurant. To simplify the allegory, the typical customer will be called "T.C."

When T.C. approaches the facility from the parking lot, T.C. looks at the windows and sidewalks to see if they are clean. T.C. also checks the condition of the parking lot and visible refuse or garbage storage areas. Upon entering the establishment, T.C. unconsciously checks for the smell of grease. T.C. notices if the lighting is adequate. When using the restrooms, T.C. is quick to judge whether they are clean in appearance and odor and brightly lit.

After being seated in the dining room, T.C. pays close attention to the servers as they handle food and nonfood products. T.C. is watching when one server picks up ice with his fingers. T.C. is disappointed. The cracked cup and scratched dish on the table reduce T.C.'s satisfaction level even further. Then T.C.'s food order is delivered by a server who has stacked plates of food on other food instead of using a tray. T.C. is disappointed again.

T.C. examines the smudged glasses that were not washed and sanitized, but merely rinsed. The entree T.C. has ordered is chicken Florentine. The unnaturally green color of the vegetables tells T.C. that the food was not prepared properly. Limp and watery salads do not meet (let alone exceed) T.C.'s expectations. By this time, the meal experience has become unpleasant and unenjoyable. However, T.C. doesn't complain or say anything critical. T.C. simply resolves never to eat here again.

Then (to add insult to injury) as T.C. leaves, neither the server nor the manager thanks T.C. for patronizing the restaurant. On the way out the door, T.C. is thinking of telling others to avoid that place.

Is this the way it has to be? Of course not. You, as a manager or employee in a hospitality operation, have the opportunity to meet or exceed T.C.'s expectations. A well-designed and executed sanitation program assists in the operation's mission of customer satisfaction. Other professional standards can help also. In 1923, the National Restaurant Association established standards of business practices for restaurateurs (see Exhibit 13.8). These standards, adopted over 60 years ago, still make sense today.

The NRA has also issued several position statements over the years

Exhibit 13.8   Standards of Business Practices of the National Restaurant Association

As a member of the National Restaurant Association, and in keeping with the spirit of the highest standards of public service and business responsibility, we pledge to:	
Food:	Provide the optimal value of wholesome food to our customers.
Service:	Maintain courteous, attentive, and efficient service in a pleasant atmosphere.
Health:	Protect everyone's health by operating clean, safe, and sanitary premises.
Employment Standards:	Establish performance standards for personnel based on education, training, and provide equitable wages and attractive working conditions.
Citizenship:	Contribute to community life by participation in civic and business development through association and cooperation with responsible authorities.
Fair Competition:	Engage in fair and open competition based on truthful representation of products and services offered.
Competitive Purchasing:	Purchase goods and services only from reputable purveyors on a competitive basis.
Industry Development:	Contribute through dedication of service to the public toward the growth and development of the food service industry.
Reasonable Profit:	Maintain the ability to earn a reasonable profit for services rendered.

Source: Public Health and Safety Department, National Restaurant Association, Sanitation Operations Manual, *1979, p. 459, L-15.*

Exhibit 13.9   NRA Position Statement—Sanitation in Restaurants

1. The National Restaurant Association believes in clean restaurants.
2. We support inspections by competent, qualified health inspectors.
3. We respect and appreciate our right to have our deficiencies called to our attention and our right to take corrective action or defend alleged violations at a formal hearing.
4. We are unalterably opposed to adverse and unfair criticism based on the opinions of individuals who are not qualified in the areas of food service sanitation as it affects the public health.
5. We object to any unauthorized entry into our premises.

We are firm in our belief that the combined efforts of the proper authorities and knowledgeable restaurateurs result in clean establishments meriting the confidence of the American dining public.

The National Restaurant Association pledges to continue its program of education in the areas of public health and safety thereby continuing to recognize and fulfill its very real responsibility to protect the public.

Source: National Restaurant Association, Sanitation Operations Manual, *1979, p. 459, L-5.*

covering a variety of issues affecting the food service industry. The NRA position statement on sanitation in restaurants, issued in March 1975, is presented in Exhibit 13.9. Exhibit 13.10 presents the NRA position statement issued in May 1977 in support of the FDA's Model Food Service Sanitation Ordinance (1976).

Exhibit 13.10   NRA Position Statement—FDA Model Food Service Sanitation Ordinance

The National Restaurant Association has long recognized the importance of sound and uniform sanitation regulations, having supported the development and implementation of the Food and Drug Administration's (FDA) 1962 Model Ordinance.

The FDA, recognizing the need of state and municipal jurisdictions for an updated tool in preparing their regulations, has now published a revised Model Ordinance.

The NRA endorses the 1976 FDA Model Ordinance, and will actively seek its adoption by all jurisdictions. In this endeavor, it will encourage and support the Ordinance implementation activities of state and local restaurant associations.

The adoption of the 1976 Ordinance by local public health authorities will benefit the consumer and the food service operator by assuring effective, equitable, and uniform regulations regardless of the geographic location. Uniformity of FDA Ordinance requirements will especially enhance the efficiency and effectiveness of sanitation and food protection programs of the growing number of enterprises operating in several public health jurisdictions.

Source: National Restaurant Association, Sanitation Operations Manual, *1979, p. 460, L-13.*

Success—The Bottom Line

This book has emphasized that, in successful operations, the operation's sanitation management program is integrated with the cost and quality control systems. Good sanitation practices must be seen as an established part of the daily routine of doing business. The four resources which must be addressed by any sanitation management program—personnel, equipment, inventory, and facilities—are all interrelated. However, success in one component does not necessarily guarantee success in the others. (If you build the most expensive facility with the most modern equipment but do not train your personnel, you cannot expect to succeed.) The objectives of the operation's sanitation management program are fundamentally to reduce microbiological contamination and spoilage risks while protecting employees and raising customer satisfaction levels, thus permitting the business to survive and financially prosper in the future. A well-organized sanitation program does not cost; it pays in increased customer satisfaction levels and reduced risks.

A successful sanitation program starts with an analysis of the establishment's basic operating activities or control points. Several essential guidelines and helpful tips were presented for each control point. Integrating the resources with these control points maximizes the overall results achieved by the business. The systematic approach promotes success in excellent food service and lodging operations. Success is achieved only through consistent adherence to standards of quality, cost, and sanitation.

Summary

Hospitality operations can be programmed to achieve success. It is management's responsibility to set up and monitor the sanitation management program. The hiring process consists of three steps: recruitment, selection, and orientation. When a vacancy exists, recruitment provides applicants. The selection phase utilizes an employee application form and a number of open-ended interviewing questions. Employee orientation is consistently thorough when a checklist and employee manual are used to acquaint the new employee with the operation. Job analyses, job specifications, job descriptions, and job performance standards are management tools used in hiring, training, and evaluating employees.

The training of employees is an important part of doing business. Top management must be committed to employee training. The training cycle involves planning, preparing, presenting, applying, evaluating, and planning again. On-the-job training and classroom-style training are options in a hospitality operation.

A basic sanitation training program for a hospitality operation covers facilities, food, food handling, and management. The effectiveness of the sanitation training program is measured by the extent to which supervisors and employees abide by the principles of sanitation. Training outcomes for food service employees help management evaluate the operation's sanitation training program. Personal hygiene tips should be posted to remind employees of their responsibilities. A management sanitation checklist can be used to help managers and supervisors recognize when it is time to hold another series of training sessions.

Self-inspection permits the establishment to identify and correct deficiencies before public health authorities perform their routine inspections. Self-inspection forms can be obtained from federal, state, and local regulatory and professional organizations. The NRA has issued some important position statements regarding sanitation management in a food service business. In the end, the positive or negative image projected to customers has a major effect on the operation's long-term survival. If the operation has been programmed for success, it will be more likely to prosper.

References

Berlinski, P. "Special Report on Sanitation and Safety." *Restaurant Business*, December 1975. 74(12):34.

——."Update: Sanitation and Safety." *Restaurant Business,* December 1976. 75(12):98.

Buchanan, R. D. "Sanitation — Is Your Training Program Effective?" *Food Service Marketing*, June 1975. 37(6):32.

——."What Makes An Effective Employee Training Program?" *Food Service Marketing,* July 1975. 37(7):42.

"Checklist for Sanitation." *Cooking for Profit*, March 1977. (315):19.

Cichy, Ronald F. "Motivated Employees Double Productivity Rate." *Restaurants and Institutions*, 1 August 1982. 91(3):20.

——."Productivity Pointers to Promote a Profitable Performance." *The Consultant,* Winter 1983. 16(1):35-36.

Daschler, John P., and Ninemeier, Jack D. *Supervision in the Hospitality Industry*. East Lansing, Mich.: Educational Institute of the American Hotel & Motel Association, 1984.

Division of Housing and Food Services, Michigan State University. *Student Employee Handbook*. East Lansing, Mich.: MSU, 1981.

Faulkner, E. "Training: Changing the Rules to Fit the Game." *Restaurants and Institutions*, 1 June 1982. 90(11):73.

Finn, M. "Good Housekeeping: Training Is the Key." *Hospitality*, November 1976. 60(11):L50.

Forrest, Lewis C., Jr. *Training for the Hospitality Industry*. East Lansing, Mich.: Educational Institute of the American Hotel & Motel Association, 1983.

Gindin, R. L. "An Educated Staff is the Best Defense." *Restaurant Business*, 1 December 1982. 81(15):156.

Green, H. "Sanitation—Can Food Service Come Clean?" *Institutions/Volume Feeding*, 1 June 1976. 78(11):44.

Holland, G. C. "Education is the Key to Solving Sanitation Problems." *Journal of Food Protection*, May 1980. 43(5):401-403.

"The Sanitation Gap." *Restaurants and Institutions*, 1 January 1983. 23(1):104-105.

Sanitation Operations Manual. Chicago, Ill.: Public Health and Safety Department, National Restaurant Association, 1979.

Wehe, H. M. and Avens, J. S. *Food Service Safety Training Program*. Cooperative Extension Service Bulletin, 505A. Fort Collins, Colo.: Colorado State University, 1980.

Strategies for Success at the Aspen Hotel

At 10:00 a.m., the GM and his staff were assembled in the lobby of the hotel for the grand reopening festivities. The mayor, who had agreed to officiate at the ribbon-cutting ceremony, was speaking to the large group of corporate executives, local citizens, and the press attending the celebration. The mayor was telling the crowd that the Aspen Hotel had been reborn and would make the community proud.

Paul James thought about his responsibilities as the general manager of the Aspen Hotel. "People want to be associated with a winner. It's up to me and every member of my staff to convey that winning attitude. The progressive steps we have made together by far outnumber the occasional setbacks we have faced, and the satisfaction of doing the job right certainly outweighs the disappointments.

"Being a leader is more than filling the top position. Leadership is action. It is my responsibility to keep the goals and objectives of this hotel clearly in view, and then to translate that vision into action."

Paul knew that success is a journey, not a destination. The general manager's personal and professional philosophy could be summarized in one statement: "No matter what I do in life, I must do it with enthusiasm, a positive attitude, and to the best of my ability." Isn't that success?

The following case studies are designed to enhance your understanding of the material in this chapter. If you are a Home Study student, use these case studies to stimulate questions about this chapter. If you are a Group or Institutional Study student, you may be asked to discuss these case studies as part of a regular classroom assignment.

CASE STUDY 13.1

Diane Davis is the new food and beverage manager at the Regency Hotel. The Regency's food and beverage department has experienced a rapid turnover of servers in the main dining room during the last six months. The general manager of the hotel has told Diane that her primary responsibility is to achieve a reduction in employee turnover and a strengthening of employee morale.

Test Your Understanding

1. Should Diane Davis examine the hotel's hiring process? Why?

2. Should Ms. Davis examine the operation's training program? Why?

3. What are your recommendations to Diane Davis?

CASE STUDY 13.2

Diane Davis recently discovered a copy of the Regency Hotel's employee orientation manual dating back to 1978. Prior to Diane's discovery, her food and beverage department was using a number of job descriptions that were written in the early 1980s. Diane has decided that it is time to revise the outdated orientation manual and job descriptions for her department.

Test Your Understanding

1. List 20 points for consideration in the revised orientation manual.

2. What information should be contained in a job description?

3. What are your recommendations to Diane Davis?

CASE STUDY 13.3

T.J. Shepard is the manager of the Balcony Restaurant on Florida's Gulf Coast. T.J. has just accompanied the health inspector on his inspection of the Balcony Restaurant. The rating was only fair, and the inspector recommended that T.J. institute an employee training program covering the topic of sanitation. Although T.J. was certified in sanitation management five years ago by the National Institute for the Foodservice Industry, he has had no refresher course since then.

Test Your Understanding

1. What should be included in T.J.'s sanitation training program?

2. How will T.J. be able to tell if the program is successful?

3. What are your recommendations to T.J. Shepard?

CASE STUDY 13.4

T.J. has decided to concentrate his initial training efforts on front-of-the-house services. Now he is in the process of planning and preparing for a training session to be presented to a group of 17 servers. He wants the session to cover the operation's standards of service as well as serving methods and techniques. However, T.J. is puzzled about how to present the session. Rather than teaching the servers himself, T.J. is considering asking one of the servers who has been with the restaurant for over 15 years to instruct the others. Even though she does a few things her own way, most of her procedures follow the restaurant's standards.

Test Your Understanding

1. Is T.J. going about training properly?

2. Are there any disadvantages to using the seasoned server as the trainer? What are the advantages?

3. What are your recommendations to T.J. Shepard?

CASE STUDY 13.5

T.J. realizes that the personal hygiene of employees is essential to the success of any sanitation program. He is planning a refresher session on the topic of personal hygiene for production and service employees.

Once the meeting is completed, T.J. wants to develop sanitation checklists for food handling and personnel practices. He will use the checklists each day as he makes his inspections of the Balcony Restaurant. The checklists must be detailed enough, but not so detailed that they require a great deal of time to fill out.

Test Your Understanding

1. What should be included in the personal hygiene checklist for the Balcony Restaurant's employees?

2. What questions should be asked in T.J.'s food handling checklist?

3. What are your recommendations to T.J. Shepard?

CASE STUDY 13.6

The Waterfront Hotel has just hired Sonny James as the new food and beverage director. The hotel has a snack- and quick-food restaurant, a formal dining room, an informal dining room, and banquet/meeting rooms for 800 people. Sonny is on his way to the kitchen to meet with the executive chef.

Upon entering the kitchen, Sonny is shocked by the evidence of poor sanitation management. When he confronts the chef on the issue of sanitation, the chef says, "You can't find hard workers now like you could in the old days. Today, people don't want to work and are lazy. They aren't interested in keeping themselves or the kitchen clean. You just can't get good help anymore."

Test Your Understanding

1. Is the Waterfront Hotel's sanitation program organized and successful?

2. Could the team approach help raise the level of sanitation?

3. What are your recommendations to Sonny James and his chef?

CASE STUDY 13.7

Sonny James has discovered that neither the production nor service employees at the Waterfront Hotel have received a formal orientation or sanitation training program. Sonny suspects that this is why some basic sanitation procedures are overlooked. For example, none of the employees take the time to wash their hands before beginning the work shift. Also, the kitchen employees do not like to wear disposable plastic gloves when dishing food, so they don't wear them. During preparation and cooking, production employees wash their hands in food preparation sinks. On a couple of occasions, Sonny has observed the cooks and servers "sampling" food when they think no supervisors are present.

Test Your Understanding

1. What are the sanitation violations at the Waterfront Hotel?

2. What are the benefits of a formal sanitation program?

3. What are your recommendations to Sonny James?

CASE STUDY 13.8

The Waterfront Hotel's executive chef has never had a formal sanitation training program, and it shows. He cools food to room temperature uncovered on a stainless steel table near the storeroom. All leftovers are saved, because the chef doesn't want to increase his food cost by throwing food out.

The chef assumes that employees know how to correctly clean and sanitize their equipment and utensils. It is true that when they are in a hurry, they don't always sanitize cutting boards between changed uses, but the chef understands. Having had over 30 years of experience in quantity food production, he knows how intense preparation rushes can be. Cleaning supplies are stored directly under preparation tables so they are easy to find and use, but everyone forgets to use them now and again.

Test Your Understanding

1. What sanitation hazards are evident at the Waterfront Hotel?

2. Design a self-inspection program to cover the hazards in Cases 13.6, 13.7, and 13.8.

3. What are your recommendations to the executive chef of the Waterfront Hotel?

CASE STUDY 13.9

Lee Franklin is the food production supervisor at The Prairie Kitchen. Each day the restaurant has an all-you-can-eat buffet featuring American country cuisine. Once food is prepared, it is transferred to holding carts operating at temperatures of 130°-132°F (54°-56°C). The carts are designed to function at 140°F (60°C) or above, but frequent openings of the door result in lower inside temperatures. The temperature of the food products is only checked once when the carts are initially loaded at the start of the meal period.

Test Your Understanding

1. Is The Prairie Kitchen's sanitation management of the holding control point viable?

2. How could product temperatures be improved at The Prairie Kitchen?

3. What are your recommendations to Lee Franklin?

CASE STUDY 13.10

The Prairie Kitchen uses three large portable steam tables to keep its food warm in the dining room. Lee Franklin has assigned one server to periodically check product temperatures of the food on the buffet line. Today's temperature readings of hot food items in the steam tables were 150°F (66°C) at 10:30 a.m., 143°F (62°C) at noon, 131°F (55°C) at 1:30 p.m., and 140°F (60°C) at 3:00 p.m.

When the temperature was checked at noon, the server noticed that the steam tables were low on water. Half an hour later, the server filled the steam tables with cold water from a water pitcher.

Test Your Understanding

1. Are there any problems with hot food holding at The Prairie Kitchen?

2. Is The Prairie Kitchen's sanitation management program under control?

3. What are your recommendations to Lee Franklin?

Appendixes

Appendix A:
A Summary of Pathogenic Microorganisms

Name of Microorganism	Environmental and Food Sources	Incubation Time
Bacillus cereus (Bah-sill-us sēr-ē-us)	Soil, dust, grains, vegetables, cereal products, puddings, custards, sauces, soups, meatloaf, meat products, boiled or fried rice	15 minutes to 16 hours[a] (1 to 5 hours)[b]
Clostridium botulinum (Claws-trid-ē-um botch-you-line-um)	Soil, contaminated water, dust, fruits, vegetables, animal feed and manure, honey, sewage, inadequately processed or heated low-acid canned foods, inadequately processed fermented foods, and smoked fish	2 hours to 14 days[a] (12 to 36 hours)[b]
Clostridium perfringens (Claws-trid-ē-um per-frin-jens)	Soil, dust, animal manure, human feces, cooked meat and poultry, meat pies, gravies, stews, soil-grown vegetables, food cooked and cooled slowly in large quantities at room temperatures	6 to 24 hours[a] (8 to 12 hours)[b]
Escherichia coli (Es-cher-ē-chēē-ah coal-eye)	Feces of infected humans; air; sewage-contaminated water; cheese; shellfish; watercress	8 to 24 hours[a] (11 hours)[b]
Salmonella spp. (Sell-mon-ell-ah species)	Intestinal tract of humans and animals; turkeys, chickens, hogs, cattle, dogs, cats, frogs, turtles, and birds; meat products; egg and poultry products; coconut; yeast; chocolate candy; smoked fish; raw salads; fish; shellfish	5 to 72 hours[a] (12 to 48 hours)[b]
Shigella spp. (Shig-ell-ah species)	Feces of infected humans; direct contact with carriers; contaminated water; uncooked food that is diced, cut, chopped, and mixed; moist and mixed foods (tuna, shrimp, turkey, macaroni and potato salads); milk; beans; apple cider; contaminated produce	1 to 7 days[a] (less than 4 days)[b]
Staphylococcus aureus (Staff-low-cock-us or-ē-us)	In and on human nose and throat discharges, hands and skin, infected wounds and burns, pimples and acne, hair, feces; cooked ham; poultry and poultry dressing; meat products; gravies and sauces; cream-filled pastries; milk; cheese; hollandaise sauce; bread pudding; fish, potato, ham, poultry, and egg salads; high-protein leftover foods	1 to 8 hours[a] (2 to 4 hours)[b]
Trichinella spiralis (Trick-in-ell-ah spur-el-is)	Infected hogs, flesh of bear and walrus	4 to 28 days[a] (9 days)[b]
Vibrio parahaemolyticus (Vib-rē-oh para-hēmo-lit-ick-us)	Marine life, sea water, raw foods of marine origin, saltwater fish, shellfish, fish products	2 to 48 hours[a] (10 to 20 hours)[b]
virus of infectious hepatitis (in-feck-shus hep-a-tie-tis)	Blood, urine, and feces of human and animal carriers; water; rodents; insects; shellfish; milk; potato salad; cold cuts; frozen strawberries; orange juice; whipped cream cakes; glazed doughnuts, sandwiches	10 to 50 days[a] (30 days)[b]

[a]Range of reported incubation times.
[b]Usual, average, or most frequently reported incubation time.

Symptoms	Controls
Nausea, abdominal pain, vomiting, diarrhea	1. Hold foods out of the TDZ. 2. Chill leftover hot foods rapidly. 3. Reheat all leftovers to a minimum of 160°F (71°C) prior to service. 4. Serve and eat foods immediately after cooking.
High fever, dizziness, dry mouth, respiratory difficulties including paralysis, loss of reflexes	1. Destroy the toxin with correct time-temperature combinations. 2. Add acids. 3. Store foods under refrigeration. 4. Add salts during curing. 5. Destroy all bulging cans and their contents. 6. Refuse to serve home-canned foods.
Acute abdominal cramps, diarrhea, dehydration, and prostration (occasionally)	1. Thoroughly clean, cook, and chill food products. 2. Reheat all leftovers to a minimum of 160°F (71°C) prior to service. 3. Hold foods out of the TDZ. 4. Enforce rules of good personal hygiene.
Abdominal pain, diarrhea, fever, chills, headache, blood in the feces, nausea, dehydration, prostration	1. Heat and chill food products rapidly. 2. Enforce rules of good personal hygiene. 3. Control flies. 4. Prepare all food products in a sanitary manner.
Abdominal pain, diarrhea, fever, chills, vomiting, dehydration, headache, prostration	1. Cook food products thoroughly. 2. Rapidly chill all hot foods. 3. Guard against cross-contamination. 4. Enforce rules of good personal hygiene.
Abdominal pain, diarrhea, fever, chills, headache, blood in the feces, nausea, dehydration, prostration	1. Chill and heat food products rapidly. 2. Enforce rules of good personal hygiene. 3. Control flies. 4. Prepare all food products in a sanitary manner.
Vomiting, abdominal cramps, diarrhea, nausea, dehydration, sweating, weakness, prostration	1. Eliminate ill humans from food production and handling activities. 2. Enforce rules of good personal hygiene. 3. Handle food products with the utmost care. 4. Thoroughly cook and reheat foods. 5. Rapidly chill and properly refrigerate food products.
Muscle invasion and soreness, weakness, swelling of muscles	1. Heat pork to an internal temperature of 150°F (66°C) or above. 2. Freezing pork will destroy the parasite.
Abdominal cramps, diarrhea, nausea, vomiting, mild fever, chills, headache, prostration	1. Cook and chill food products properly. 2. Separate raw and cooked foods. 3. Do not rinse food products with sea water.
Fever, nausea, abdominal pain, tired feeling, jaundice	1. Purchase all food products from approved sources. 2. Enforce rules of good personal hygiene. 3. Cook foods thoroughly.

Appendix B:
Agencies and Organizations

American Hotel & Motel Association (AH&MA)
888 Seventh Avenue
New York, NY 10019
(212) 265-4506

American Public Health Association (APHA)
1015 Eighteenth Street N.W.
Washington, DC 20036
(202) 467-5000

Centers for Disease Control (CDC)
Atlanta, GA 30333
(404) 329-3311

The Educational Institute of the American Hotel & Motel Association
Stephen S. Nisbet Building
1407 South Harrison Road, Suite 310
East Lansing, MI 48823
(517) 353-5500

Environmental Protection Agency (EPA)
Office of Public Affairs (A-107)
401 M Street S.W.
Washington, DC 20460
(202) 755-0700

Food and Drug Administration (FDA)
Division of Retail Food Protection (HFF 220)
200 C Street S.W.
Washington, DC 20204
(202) 245-1508

**International Association of Milk, Food and Environmental
  Sanitarians (IAMFES)**
P.O. Box 701
Ames, IA 50010
(515) 232-6699

International Food Service Executives Association (IFSEA)
International Headquarters
111 East Wacker Drive
Chicago, IL 60601
(312) 644-6610

National Environmental Health Association (NEHA)
1200 Lincoln Street, Suite 704
Denver, CO 80203
(303) 861-9090

National Institute for the Foodservice Industry (NIFI)
20 North Wacker Drive
Chicago, IL 60606
(312) 782-1703

National Restaurant Association (NRA)
One IBM Plaza, Suite 2600
Chicago, IL 60611
(312) 787-2525

or

311 First Street N.W.
Washington, DC 20001
(202) 296-0350

National Sanitation Foundation (NSF)
NSF Building
Ann Arbor, MI 48105
(313) 769-8010

United States Department of Agriculture (USDA)
Agricultural Marketing Service (AMS)
Information Division, Room 3086
14th and Independence Avenue S.W.
Washington, DC 20250
(202) 447-6766

Index